A HISTORY OF
THE THAI-CHINESE

The creation of this publication was made possible thanks to
the support of the following organizations:

PLATINUM SPONSORS

SILVER SPONSOR

มูลนิธิทองพูล หวั่งหลี
Thongpoon Wanglee Foundation

EDITIONS DIDIER MILLET

PUBLISHER
Didier Millet

GENERAL MANAGER
Charles Orwin

PROJECT DIRECTOR
Yvan Van Outrive

EDITORIAL DIRECTOR
Martin Cross

MANAGING EDITOR
Nicholas Grossman

EDITORS
Grissarin Chungsiriwat
Nina Wegner

WRITERS
Pimpraphai Bisalputra
Jeffery Sng

RESEARCH ASSISTANT
Kankanit Potikit

DESIGNER
Theerawat Pojvibulsiri

STUDIO MANAGER
Annie Teo

PRODUCTION MANAGER
Sin Kam Cheong

First published in 2015 by
Editions Didier Millet

Singapore office
121 Telok Ayer Street, #03-01
Singapore 068590
Tel: 65-6324 9260 Fax: 65-6324 926

Bangkok office
11B Vanissa Building,
29 Soi Chidlom,
Ploenchit Road, Lumphini,
Pathumwan,
Bangkok 10330
Tel: 66-2-252 2699
Fax: 66-2-252 2728

Email: edm@edmbooks.com.sg

www.edmbooks.com

Color separation by
Pica Digital, Singapore

Printed by
Craft Print International Ltd., Singapore

ISBN 978-981-4385-77-0

A HISTORY OF
THE THAI-CHINESE

JEFFERY SNG
AND
PIMPRAPHAI BISALPUTRA

for our parents

CONTENTS

Opposite page: 19th-century Chinese junks on the Chao Phraya River.

PREFACE

Because Thailand hosts the largest overseas-Chinese community in the region, a book on the story of the Thai-Chinese is necessarily an ambitious project. There are numerous Thai-Chinese who have lived significant lives, made an important impact on the kingdom, left behind significant legacies, made it big in this country and established named families here. Then there are the nameless multitudes. There are so many of them it would be impossible to mention them all, let alone address their interesting lives, achievements and contributions. Naturally, only a small number have been singled out for description in the book. We regret that many important personages, individuals and families have been left out. If told in its entirety, the history of the Thai-Chinese would be a never-ending story.

As it is impossible to include every important Thai-Chinese in these pages, we have tried instead to focus on the changing historical context encountered by successive waves of Chinese immigrants to Siam since the time of Ayudhya up till the present. We hope that conveying an impression of the changing times helps make up for our failure to tell all the stories of individual Chinese.

The ancestors of the Chinese in Thailand mostly come from the ranks of merchants, peasants, adventurers and coolies with very few members of the literati class among them. The absence of a literati tradition in the local Chinese community is reflected in the dearth of Chinese clan records. Indeed, today it is commonplace to find Thai-Chinese who do not know or care to know which village in China their ancestors came from.

The fact that Chinese family records are almost non-existent in this country has made the subject of this book a murky area not easily dealt with by students and scholars. The difficulty is compounded by the fact that the authors are descended from Peranakan and Thai-Chinese forbears, whose mother tongues are Indonesian-Malay and Thai rather than Chinese. Neither authors are literate in Chinese and we are Thailand, not China, scholars. However, we are descended from *huaqiao* ancestry and we share in the experience of being overseas Chinese. Our food, dress, social customs, folklore, bedtime stories, upbringing and toilet training are *huaqiao*. In this sense we are part of the story that we are writing.

Although we did not examine Chinese language sources we did enjoy privileged access to many family stories that have been passed down from generation to generation in the local Chinese community in Thailand. When Pimpraphai embarked on her research on Chinese exportware to Siam some 30 years ago she also began collecting personal histories, biographies and funeral books of the Thai-Chinese community. One fascinating tale led to another until she built up a large inventory of Thai-Chinese family stories. Some of these stories that we have shared in the book are revealed for the first time to the public.

In addition to information from local family sources we have relied on the pioneering works on the subject by Wang Gungwu, G.W. Skinner, Kenneth Perry Landon, Victor Purcell, C.P. Fitzgerald, Paul A. Van Dyke, Sarasin Viraphol, Subsaeng Promboon, Phannee Bualek, Li Tana, Puangthong Rungswadisab, Choi Chi-cheung, Odd Arne Westad, Lynn Pan, Jean Chesneaux, Marie-Claire Bergere, G. Coedes, Martin Stuart-Fox, Geoff Wade, Jennifer Cushman, Suehiro Akira, Yumio Sakurai, Wasana Wongsurawat and Eiji Murashima among others.

Besides the aforementioned great China scholars we are also deeply indebted to B.J. Terwiel, David Wyatt, Dhiravat Na Pombejra, Eric Hobsbawm, Victor Lieberman, Chris Baker, Pasuk Pongphaichit, Charnvit Kasetsiri, William Case, Theda Skocpol, Chaiyan Rachagool, Fred Riggs, Edward Van Roy, David Steinberg, David A. Wilson and Benedict R.O.G. Anderson. Ben Anderson's lectures and writings, including his papers *Studies on the Thai State* and *Imagined Communities*, have inspired our narrative on monopoly tax farms and the development of nationalism.

We also wish to express our special thanks to the readers of the manuscript – including Sulak Sivaraksa, Dhiravat Na Pombejra, Wasana Wongsurawat, Edward Van Roy, Choi Chi-cheung, Eiji Murashima, Julian Harding and Disphol Chansiri – for their corrections, comments and suggestions to improve the book. In addition, we are very grateful to our editor Nicholas Grossman and his team, including Grissarin Chungsiriwat, Nina Wegner and Theerawat Pojvibulsiri, for their creative ideas, elegant layout, generous support in finding illustrations as well as their indefatigable patience in going over the manuscript with a fine-tooth comb, to make improvements and polish the text. Very special thanks also go to the venerable Wang Gungwu, Wasana Wongsurawat and Kishore Mahbubani for their generous and encouraging comments included in the blurbs on the back of this book.

Lastly we have not been able to adopt a consistent system for presenting Chinese names which appear in the book. The Sino-Thai names in this book are those actually used in Siam, which may be Thai, Teochew, Hokkien, Hakka, Hainanese, Cantonese or Vietnamese. We are very grateful to Nirandorn Narksuriyan, Srethapongs Chongsanguan and Kankanit Potikit, for their invaluable help in translating the names into Chinese characters and incorporating them in a list for reference in the appendix.

We hope our collective efforts have led to a book that honors and pays tribute to the millions of Chinese and their descendants who over many centuries embraced their destinies in Thailand.

Jeffery Sng and Pimpraphai Bisalputra

CHRONOLOGY OF
CHINESE DYNASTIES SINCE 1127

Southern Song Dynasty (1127–1279)

Yuan Dynasty (1279–1368)

Ming Dynasty (1368–1644)

Hongwu	1368–1398
Yongle	1403–1424
Hongzhi	1488–1505
Jiajing	1522–1566
Wanli	1573–1620
Chongzhen	1628–1644

Qing Dynasty (1644–1911)

Shunzhi	1644–1661
Kangxi	1662–1722
Yongzheng	1723–1735
Qianlong	1736–1795
Jiaqing	1796–1820
Daoguang	1821–1850
Xianfeng	1851–1861
Tongzhih	1862–1874
Guangxu	1875–1908
Xuantong	1909–1911

Republic of China (1912–1949)

Sun Yatsen	1912
Yuan Shikai	1912–1916
Chiang Kaishek	1928–1931
	1943–1949

People's Republic of China (1949–present)

CHRONOLOGY OF
THAI KINGDOMS

Sukhothai Kingdom (1238–1438)

Ayudhya Kingdom (1351–1767)
King Ramathibodi (U Tong)	1351–1369
King Naresuan	1590–1605
King Ekathotsarot	1605–1610
King Songtham	1611–1628
King Prasattong	1629–1656
King Narai	1656–1688
King Phetracha	1688–1703
King Süa	1703–1709
King Thaisa	1709–1733
King Borommakot	1733–1758
King Uthumporn	1758
King Ekathat	1758–1767

Thonburi Kingdom (1767–1782)
King Taksin	1767–1782

Bangkok Kingdom
Chakri Dynasty (1782–present)
King Buddha Yod Fa Chulalok Maharaj (Rama I)	1782–1809
King Buddha Lert La Nabhalai (Rama II)	1809–1824
King Pra Nang Klao (Rama III)	1824–1851
King Mongkut (Rama IV)	1851–1868
King Chulalongkorn (Rama V)	1868–1910
King Vajiravudh (Rama VI)	1910–1925
King Prajadhipok (Rama VII)	1925–1933
King Ananda Mahidol (Rama VIII)	1935–1946
King Bhumibol Adulyadej (Rama IX)	1946–present

Source: Ann Håbu and Dawn F. Rooney, *Royal Porcelain from Siam: Unpacking the Ring Collection* (2013) Oslo: Hermes Publishing.

ORIGINS OF CHINESE EMIGRANTS TO THAILAND

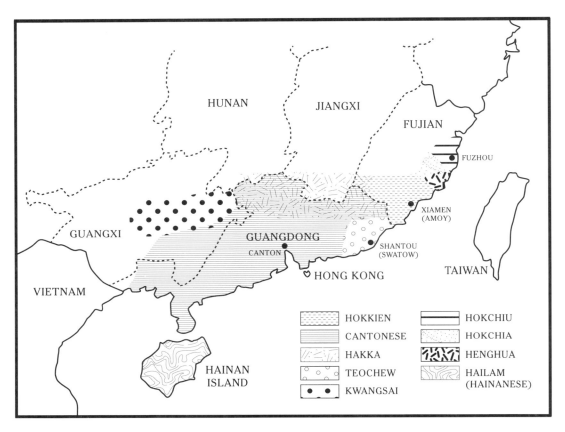

Source: Leon Comber, *Chinese Secret Societies in Malaya: A Survey of the Triad Society from 1800 to 1900* (1959), New York: J.J. Augustin.

CHINA – SOUTHEAST ASIA TRADE ROUTES

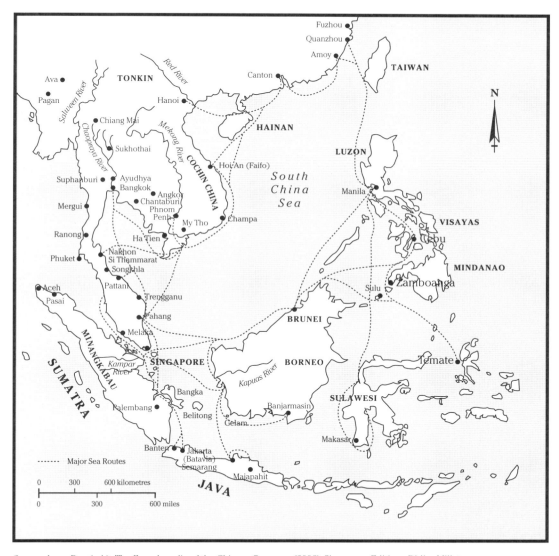

Source: Lynn Pan (ed.), *The Encyclopedia of the Chinese Overseas* (2006), Singapore: Editions Didier Millet.

AYUDHYAN CHINESE

(1351–1767)

China's geographical proximity to Mainland Southeast Asia ensured that both Chinese goods and people moved south–both overland and by sea–to the capital and ports of the Thai kingdoms. Both Sukhothai (1238–1438) and Ayudhya (1351–1767) maintained a tributary relation with China and occasional turmoil would trigger emigration from the Middle Kingdom, further spreading the Chinese Diaspora up and down the coast of what is modern-day Thailand. Prosperous private trade fueled the ascendance of powerful Chinese communities in these coastal towns. Some of the Chinese traders married local women; many became titled nobles, and a few ultimately attained high positions within the intrigue-filled Ayudhya court. In general, with its language skills, family connections and trading acumen, the Chinese community was by far the most successful and influential of all the foreign communities resident at Ayudhya, and China itself was the kingdom's most important trading partner and the engine driving Ayudhya's economic prosperity.

"Siam is the only country where a Chinese can become king. It is also the only country where he loses his identity."
—Sulak Sivaraksa, Thai social critic

The man who inspired Sulak's remark was the Chinese descendant Phraya Tak. Born of a Chinese father and a Siamese mother, he rose to become King Taksin in 1767. The saga of Phraya Tak coincided with the "Chinese Century" in Southeast Asia, a time during the 18th century when Chinese influence and involvement in the political affairs of Southeast Asian states reached an unprecedented height. As an ethnic Chinese king of Siam, Phraya Tak was the embodiment of the deep-seated Chinese presence within the body politic of a Southeast Asian state.

The case of Phraya Tak, or King Taksin as he is popularly known, was the most remarkable and important. But it was not the first time that Chinese lineage had emerged at the highest level of political power in Siam. A history of the kings of Siam compiled by the Dutch trader Jeremias van Vliet in 1640 suggests that Thao U-Thong, the founder of the Kingdom of Ayudhya (1351–1767), had come from China.[1] Subsequently, in Thailand's modern history it is commonplace to find Thai-Chinese holding high political positions as well as being prominent in industry, finance and commerce.

The position of the Chinese in Thailand is certainly unique. How could people of émigré stock wield so much power and influence in a host country with a dominant, native ethnic majority? In today's ethnic-based nation-states it is uncommon for minority groups to enjoy such power and influence. How did this happen?

To understand the Chinese phenomenon in Thailand it is important to appreciate a few basic political characteristics of the two nations, their geopolitical proximity to each other, China's political relationships with the region and the origins of Chinese penetration into Southeast Asia.

Where China Meets Southeast Asia

Today, China's southern frontier abuts Mainland Southeast Asia. Chinese transportation infrastructure is connected to Mainland Southeast Asia by a land bridge spanning from Yunnan to Myanmar, as well as through Laos and Vietnam. However, the border that the People's Republic of China shares with the polities of Mainland Southeast Asia is a product of fairly recent history, although ancient China has shared a cultural border with Southeast Asia for several thousand years.

Originally, Chinese civilization developed in the North China Plain around the

Yellow River and its tributaries in 1700 BC. The early Shang dynasty (1700–1027 BC) was an inward-looking land-based power that was geographically and politically far from any other center of civilization. China's early isolation, as well as the Chinese view at the time that their civilization was surrounded by less civilized peoples, helped to shape the Chinese sense of a cultural border.

This cultural border has for centuries been colored by a Sino-centric view of the world, dividing China from non-China, and "civilized" China from "non-civilized" societies. The cosmological view that China stood at the center of the universe, surrounded in all "four directions" by less civilized "barbarian peoples," led the early Chinese to call their country "The Middle Kingdom." This sense of cultural superiority was to govern China's subsequent interactions with Southeast Asian kingdoms, including Siam. China's refusal to interact with other societies on the basis of equality became the basis of the Chinese Tributary System under which China's relations with Southeast Asian kingdoms were subsumed.[2]

The end of the Shang dynasty marked the start of Chinese civilization's long march south. During this early period, the area encompassing the Yangtze River Basin and the current provinces of South China, including Yunnan, Fujian and Guangdong, were populated by non-Chinese peoples akin to many of today's ethnic Mainland Southeast Asian groups. By the late Shang period, Chinese influence and culture had begun to penetrate the alien peoples of the Yangtze Valley through a process of creeping infiltration and migration.

With time, the borders of the Chinese body politic gradually expanded southwards through military conquest to encompass Sichuan, Hubei, Hunan, Zhejiang, Fujian, Guangdong and the Red River Delta. To support the pacification and consolidation of newly acquired territory, Chinese settlers were sent into conquered areas as part of a long-term policy to Sinicize local cultures and incorporate the non-Chinese populace into the Chinese body politic.

After the Tang dynasty's (618–906) pacification of the south, the Red River Delta was reconstituted as the province of Annam.[3] For 250 years, Tang rule in Annam was unchallenged, ushering in a period of internal peace, social tranquility, good governance, prosperity and a cultural renaissance that made a deep impression on the Vietnamese psyche. Although it did not induce the Vietnamese to forgo their aspiration for independence, Tang rule helped to permanently recast Vietnamese culture in the Chinese mold, in which it has since remained in contrast to the rest of Mainland Southeast Asia.

On the southwestern front, when the Song dynasty (960–1279) crumbled under the Mongol onslaught, Yunnan was invaded and annexed by Mongol armies, and the Yuan dynasty (1279–1368) was established. Thus, the conquest of Yunnan was not an enterprise of the Chinese empire under Chinese rulers but rather a by-product of the Mongol conquest of China. Subsequently, after the

Wooden Guanyin from the Tang dynasty, a period of cultural renaissance, enshrined at Tian Fah Hospital in Bangkok.

Chapter opening picture: Mural painting at Wat Pradu Songtham in Ayudhya depicting (at bottom of mural) a Chinese opera performance at a festival in Ayudhya.

15

Mongols were driven out of China, the Ming emperor Hongwu invaded Yunnan in 1382 to reclaim it for the Chinese empire.

After the consolidation of the southwestern border at Yunnan, China's southward expansion seemed to have ended. China's strategic orientation shifted towards its vulnerable northern frontier.[4] Although China eventually developed naval capabilities, the state remained strategically preoccupied with the threat posed by land invasion from the north. China's northern frontier bordered the steppes peopled by warlike "barbarian" tribes who posed a constant military threat. The lessons of recent history and the Yuan dynasty were too close for comfort.

Geopolitical Proximity, Connectivity and Trade

In sharp contrast to the hostile northern frontier, China's southern frontier comprised a relatively underpopulated region inhabited by smaller, decentralized, Hinduized, mandala-style kingdoms (characterized by a focus on local power), which posed no serious security threat. Despite border skirmishes and punitive expeditions against Angkor, Java and Burma, China has never attempted to conquer and annex any Southeast Asian kingdom except Vietnam.[5] With minor exceptions, trade and diplomacy tended to dominate China's relationship with the relatively sparsely populated Southeast Asian

A 1740 map of Southeast Asia. Collection of the Siam Society.

states throughout dynastic cycles, political change and the vicissitudes of regime change.

With no real security threat in the south, China's geopolitical proximity to Southeast Asia proved to be a blessing. Overland connections to Southeast Asia through Yunnan, Burma and Vietnam, as well as coastal connections via the Nanyang Sea, represented a perfect recipe for trade between the two regions. Geopolitical proximity coupled with a large population meant that China offered a significant market for the products of Southeast Asia. Archaeological evidence and shipwreck excavations show that China's contact with the area that is now Thailand dates back almost two thousand years. Chinese earthenware from the Western Han dynasty (1st to 2nd centuries) has been found in Surat Thani in Southern Thailand.[6]

There is little evidence that explains how Chinese artifacts ended up in Southeast Asia. Historians speculate that early trade was conducted largely by land or via foreign vessels manned by Persians, Arabs, Indians, Javanese, Malays and other traders of coastal Southeast Asia. China only developed its own high seas merchant fleet after the 10th to 11th centuries, during the Song dynasty.[7]

Tributary Versus Private Trade

Trade with China was coveted by foreign traders and Southeast Asian rulers, who desired to sell tin, spices and a variety of forest products. They also sought to import Chinese luxury goods such as ceramics, tea and silk, which represented status symbols, as well as other useful products and metals such as iron and copper. Keenly aware that withholding market access or restricting supply of coveted Chinese luxury products could provide valuable leverage in foreign relations, Chinese rulers occasionally introduced sanctions regulating or limiting trade to achieve foreign policy objectives.

Asian rulers sent missions to the Chinese capital seeking imperial investiture, or official recognitions of title and rank, in order to trade with the Middle Kingdom. All official missions—even those solely concerned with trade—were regarded as "tributary."[8] The Chinese viewed the purpose of these missions as political acknowledgement of Chinese hegemony rather than commerce. For the Chinese, tribute denoted not the transfer of economic resources but, rather, symbolic submission.[9] The emperor would graciously accept the "tribute" offered but gave more expensive presents in return. In addition to tributary gifts, foreign missions could also bring goods for trade at their commercial value in Chinese markets. Thus, smaller kingdoms saw only gain from paying tribute to the Chinese emperor unless the latter sought to impose onerous exactions on the tributary relationship as China's later Mongol rulers did.

Asian rulers, however, preferred to interpret "tribute" simply as a peculiar Chinese diplomatic formality accompanying mutually beneficial trade, symbolized by the polite exchange of gifts between rulers.[10] For them, tribute missions represented a lucrative trading opportunity while imperial investiture enhanced the prestige of local rulers. Tribute missions provided privileged access to the huge Chinese market at favorable prices, with expensive gifts from the Chinese emperor thrown in to sweeten the deal.

Trade with China tended to assume two forms: tribute trade and private trade. While tribute trade coexisted side by side with private trade during the Tang and Northern Song dynasties (approximately the 7th to 12th centuries AD), private trade fluctuated depending on political conditions and government policy in both China and Southeast Asia.[11] During the early Tang and Northern Song periods, limitations on private trade were stricter. However, at the end of the 12th century, the Southern Song dynasty abolished the tributary system due to financial burdens, and integrated all foreign trade into the "maritime control (customs) system," in which trading states had to deal through customs officers at the major ports of China.[12] Consequently, all of the small states of the Nanyang were "thrown" into the ocean of the free market.

Although the Yuan government inherited the "maritime control system," Yuan leaders re-introduced the tributary trade system with a vengeance. The benign system that had prevailed under the Tang and Northern Song periods was replaced by a stricter interpretation of tributary obligations. However, the Song legacy of private trade was allowed to continue relatively freely. The Yuan dynasty's new Mongol emperor, Kublai Khan, attempted to enforce the submission of tributary states—including Angkor, Pagan and Dai Viet—by imposing heavier exactions on the previously benign, voluntary tributary relationship.

Perhaps the most irksome condition was the emperor's requirement that the rulers of vassal or tributary states travel to Beijing to present tribute in person to the "Son of Heaven." Failure to comply led to punitive expeditions against the recalcitrant rulers. Despite the Mongol armies' efforts to enforce these tributary obligations, many Southeast Asian rulers refused to comply with this condition, although they were more than willing to send envoys with presents to the Chinese court as per precedent.

Shard of a Chinese stem cup found in Siam.

In spite of these irritants in China's foreign relations, the Southern Song and Yuan periods saw a remarkable expansion of trade. The stimuli underlying the expansion of Chinese trading networks were manifold. From the 10th to 13th century, the Greater Asian region including Southern China, India and Southeast Asia enjoyed a sustained favorable climate that contributed to agricultural and demographic growth.[13] Population growth and commercial innovations during this period led to a vast expansion of maritime trade in the South China Sea.[14] The Southern Song dynasty had embarked upon an unprecedented program of boatbuilding that transformed China from an exclusively land-based power into a formidable sea power as well. This expansion of Chinese seafaring in turn promoted more trade with Southeast Asia, and the impetus that shipbuilding gave to Chinese maritime trade impacted Southeast Asia not least through the rise of a Chinese diaspora led by the growth of Chinese merchant communities in the region.

Merchants, Refugees and Emigrants

Kublai Khan, Mongol emperor (reigned 1260–94).

The eminent historian G. William Skinner wrote that Chinese merchant networks were already established in the markets and ports of the Gulf of Siam when Tai tribes penetrated the Angkorian-dominated Chao Phraya Basin.[15] Several small Tai principalities had emerged by the first half of the 13th century, including Chiang Saen and Sukhothai.[16] To the north of Sukhothai, King Mangrai conquered the Mon kingdom of Haripunjaya (1281) to form Lanna and establish his capital at Chiang Mai.[17]

These nascent Tai principalities opportunistically exploited Chinese political and military pressure on Angkor to weld together larger kingdoms at the expense of the Mon and Khmer in the Chao Phraya River Basin.[18] The king of Sukhothai sent nine tribute missions while the king of Suphan sent as many as five missions to the imperial capital in the late 13th and early 14th centuries.[19] They welcomed Chinese traders to Tai ports in an effort to woo Chinese support in the Tai struggle against the Mon and Khmer. Goaded by Mongol punitive expeditions, Angkor also reluctantly sent tribute missions and encouraged trade with China to deflect Chinese military pressure. Thus, through a mix of trade and imperialism, a large Chinese diaspora emerged in Mainland Southeast Asia. The Chinese diplomat Zhou Daguan reported the existence of a large Chinese merchant community in Angkor Thom at the end of the 13th century.

While trade and flag naturally followed each other, trade routes also spawned merchant communities. Chinese junks often visited the east side of the Siamese/ Malay peninsula ostensibly to take advantage of overland transshipment routes. The old trade routes did not go around the Straits of Malacca due to their pirate-infested waters and the long waiting time for the necessary wind to navigate the Straits.[20] Instead, Chinese junks would sail from China to the east coast of Siam and unload their goods for overland transshipment to the Andaman coast before being reshipped to India and the West.[21]

In times of political weakness, unrest and internal disorder, dynastic control over coastal provinces became less effective and often led to increased lawlessness and piracy. Foreign vessels would become invariably reluctant to call

Emperor Hongwu
(Zhu Yuanzhang;
reigned 1368–98),
Ming dynasty.

at Chinese ports while risk-averse Chinese merchants cut back on sea voyages. This was the case when the Yuan dynasty went into decline and collapsed in 1368; trade was disrupted for several decades.[22]

After the Ming dynasty (1368–1644) was founded, the first Ming emperor, Hongwu, prohibited the passage of private trading ships and brought overseas traffic strictly under government control. Thus, contrary to Mongol policy, control of private trade became stricter, although the Ming interpretation of tributary obligations was less humiliating. Consequently, when the Ming dynasty successfully re-imposed central authority at the end of the 14th century, many Southeast Asian kingdoms quickly responded and resumed official tribute missions.[23]

The nascent Siamese kingdom of Ayudhya (1351–1767) was no exception. Barely 20 years before the Yuan dynasty collapsed in 1368, Ayudhya had subjugated Sukhothai to become the dominant Tai polity in the Chao Phraya River Basin. Coming at the tail end of the long recession in world trade, as well as the disruption in Chinese trade following the collapse of Mongol power, the Ming invitation to renew tributary trade in 1370 was enthusiastically received by the kingdom of Ayudhya.

Several reasons account for the Siamese king's positive response. Although Indian Ocean trade was beginning to pick up again, the China trade had been severely curbed due to the outbreak of lawlessness and piracy. Participating in tributary relations with China was a kind of security insurance for early Ayudhya.

In any event, the Ming Prohibition Policy of 1371 provided no other way to trade with China. Emperor Hongwu issued an edict prohibiting Chinese merchants from venturing out to sea on pain of death. Prices of Southeast Asian products escalated, which in turn brought about a considerable increase in the smuggling trade. Hongwu punished Fujian officials who continued to abet private trade. His grandson and successor, Emperor Jianwen (1399–1402), continued Hongwu's attempt to force economic and political contacts into the exclusive framework of official tributary relations.[24] In 1402 the emperor passed a law threatening the use of a naval fleet to arrest and execute overseas-Chinese merchants who refused to return to China.

During the first few decades of the Ming dynasty, few private Chinese junks visited Siam.[25] This has been corroborated by archaeological evidence: Roxanna Brown, who studied salvages of 15 shipwrecks in the South China Sea, identified a general shortage of Chinese ceramics during 1325–80 and a severe shortage of blue-and-white porcelain during 1352–1487, which she called the Ming Gap.

However, Southeast Asian kingdoms seem to have had no misgivings about the Ming policy, which in effect offered foreign rulers an exclusive opportunity to trade with China. The policy also offered a boon to royal traders: once private competitors were eliminated, then the royal fleets could monopolize the China trade and enjoy monopoly profits.

Diplomatic politesse aside, the Chinese understood that there was no use in creating a policy unless it could be enforced. To do that, the early Ming had to show naval muscle. Thus, the Ming emperors continued the Mongol policy of ramping up naval development. In the reign of Yongle (1403–23), China built a huge navy and used it to project the state's influence beyond her shores into the Nanyang Sea. This gave rise to the great voyages of Admiral Zheng He, the legendary explorer.

Once Zheng He's navy demonstrated that it could effectively police the South China Sea and enforce the Ming trade policy on illicit traders, many more rulers seized the exclusive opportunity to participate in a lucrative, monopoly-trading system under imperial protection. Hence the early Ming period became the pinnacle of tributary trade.

Private Chinese traders prevented from participating in the China trade either operated tribute ships on behalf of tributary rulers, such as the Siamese king, or redirected their activities to the Indian Ocean, Ryukyu and Southeast Asian islands. Zheng He's navy ruthlessly put down Chinese pirates and persuaded overseas Chinese merchants to return to China. Those unwilling or unable to return to China became fugitives in foreign lands. Although the South China Sea became quieter, the peace did not last for long. Illicit trade and smuggling continued because local officials could always be bribed, and private trade would later return with a vengeance.

Although there is no proof that Zheng He visited Ayudhya, there is evidence that several important commanders of his naval fleet, including Ma Huan and Fei Xin, sojourned in Ayudhya.[26] The writings of Ma Huan and Fei Xin greatly commended the land of the Siamese. They took particular note of the Siamese women who impressed them deeply: "It is their custom that all affairs are managed by their wives ... all trading transactions great and small they all follow the decisions of their wives ... If a married woman is very intimate with one of our Chinese men, wine and food are provided, and they drink and sit and sleep together...."

Chinese firearm recovered from the Tha Chin River, Ratchaburi.

Ma added that husbands were usually not perturbed but flattered that their wives should be beautiful enough to please Chinese men.[27]

The fabulous stories told by Zheng He's sailors upon their return to China must have further stimulated Chinese fantasies of the opulence, trading opportunities and amorous delights lying in wait in the faraway,

A world map believed to have been compiled by Zheng He.

exotic land of Siam. Just as Western Orientalism had stimulated European travel to "experience" the decadent pleasures of the East, this Ming version of Chinese Orientalism probably stimulated trade and emigration to Nanyang.

Perhaps attesting to the cordial relations between the early Ming court and Ayudhya, Chinese annals recorded the earliest precedent of a Chinese becoming an official in the Siamese government. In 1412, a Chinese named Qie Jiamei was appointed Siam's ambassador to China.[28] Later, Xie Wenbin, a Chinese salt merchant, drifted to Siam around 1480 and became an official with the rank of *okkhun*.[29]

Trade was not the only vehicle driving the growth of the Chinese diaspora in the South Seas. Just as dynastic cycles impacted trade, they also contributed to the exodus of Chinese refugees fleeing the banditry, piracy and breakdown of social order caused by invading armies. The exodus of Chinese refugees to the South Seas was by no means a rare occurrence. Since the Qin and Han periods onward, similar events had repeatedly taken place on a greater or lesser scale whenever disturbances caused by a change of ruling dynasties ravaged the maritime districts of Southern China.[30]

Chinese political refugees were also amongst the early immigrants to Siam. Chinese annals record that Chen Yizhong, the chancellor of the Chinese empire during the final years of the Song dynasty, fled to Champa when the Mongols defeated the Song army. Unfortunately, the Mongols subsequently invaded and sacked the Cham capital in 1283, causing Chen Yizhong to flee once more—this time to Siam during the reign of King Ramkhamhaeng of Sukhothai.[31]

After the fall of the Mongols, enemies of the new Ming dynasty such as He Bahuan fled to Ayudhya in the early 1400s.[32] However, Ayudhya had already received a Ming envoy in 1370 bearing an edict from the new Chinese emperor, Hongwu, recognizing Ayudhya as the legitimate successor of earlier states and endorsing Ayudhya's subjugation of Sukothai. The Chinese court in Nanjing also acceded to King U-thong's request for investiture as the King of Xianluo. Thus, He Bahuan could not have arrived in Ayudhya at a more unpropitious time. When emperor Yongle requested the extradition of He Bahuan, the Siamese readily assented and sent He Bahuan back to China for execution.

When Portuguese traders first arrived in Southeast Asian waters, they were surprised to find that wherever they went the Chinese were always one step ahead. However, despite their frustration and envy of the wide reach of Chinese traders, the pragmatic Portuguese were more than willing to make a virtue of a necessity. When explorer Afonso de Alberquerque decided to send an envoy from Malacca to Ayudhya in 1512, he enlisted the services of several Chinese junks that were about to leave for the port of Ayudhya.[33] The Alberquerque initiative was probably not the first or last time Chinese junk merchants were used to carry diplomatic envoys. More than 200 years later, King Taksin was to resort to this expedient when he needed to send an envoy to the Qing court.

Further recorded evidence of Chinese migration comes from the early 17th century, when a Chinese source reported that the Chinese had already been settled in Ayudhya for several generations.[34] The report adds, "in this country, people have no surnames. The Chinese (residents) at first retain their own surnames, but give them up after a few generations." In view of the fact that Chinese women never emigrated in those days, the above description implies widespread Chinese intermarriage with Siamese women and rapid assimilation of mixed-ethnicity offspring. A child born of a Chinese father and Siamese mother is called *lukchin* in Thai. Since the report attested that a large Chinatown already existed in Ayudhya in the 17th century, the implication was that a new social formation of *lukchin* must have emerged in Siam as a by-product of trade and emigration.

According to 17th and 18th century maps, Chinese communities were located on and outside the city of Ayudhya to the east. Chinese communities lined both sides of the Pasak River near the main port, where Chinese junks came to anchor. Chinese settlement also penetrated into the network of *klong* (canals) to the east of the Pasak River, which joined the main river by Klong Pak Kao San, Klong Tanon Tan and Klong Suan Plu. As a result this whole area became the center of production and trade for Chinese merchants.

The Chinese community in Ayudhya was placed under the authority of

Numerous Ming shards have been unearthed in Siam.

the Choduk-Rachasretthi—the *khunnang* in the Phraklang ministry responsible for the king's trade with all kingdoms in the Pacific. Chinese who engaged in royal maritime service were given official ranks as provided in the Three Seals Code, which was the law of the land in Ayudhya.

The Choduk-Rachasretthi was head of the Port Department of the Left, or Krom Tha Sai, while the Port Department of the Right was headed by a Muslim, the Chula-Rachamontri. Besides the capital city of Ayudhya, Chinese also inhabited other port cities in the Gulf of Siam including Ligor and Patani. In 1616 the Dutch Resident at Patani observed that the Chinese far outnumbered the native population there.[35] A Chinese source in 1617 noted about business conditions in Patani, "Chinese residents are numerous, their toes following one another's heels."[36] An intriguing legend that warrants frequent retelling explains the remarkable demographic preponderance of Chinese in Patani.

According to the legend, during the reign of Wanli (the Chinese emperor from 1573–1620), a notorious pirate named Lim Tohkiam terrorized merchant shipping off the coast of Fujian and Guangdong. After narrowly escaping death more than once, Lim Tohkiam and his 2,000-strong band of pirates fled Chinese waters to seek refuge in Nanyang. Around 1578–80, following a sojourn in Pulo Condore, he went to Ta-nien (Patani), a town in the southern part of Siam.[37] After successfully laying siege to Patani with his pirate war junks, he conquered and occupied the Malay kingdom. The Malay ruler gave his daughter to Lim Tohkiam in marriage and made him heir to the throne.[37]

After a prolonged absence, Lim Tohkiam's younger sister Lim Goniao followed

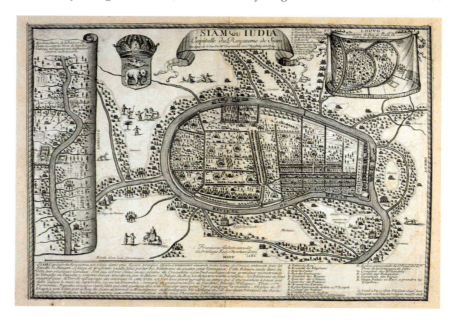

Map of the city of Ayudhya by Jean de Courtaulin de Maguellon, published in 1686. Collection of the Siam Society.

and tried in vain to persuade him to return to China. She had come on behalf of her distressed mother to impress upon her errant brother his filial obligation to return to his ancestral homeland. Her long, arduous journey in search of her brother is not only touching but is also one of the rare recorded instances of a woman traveling overseas. (Until the 19th century, women almost never traveled overseas.) Heartbroken at her failure to move her brother's filial feelings, she committed suicide near Krue Se Mosque in Patani. Lim Goniao was deified by the local Chinese inhabitants and continues to be worshipped there today. Lim Tohkiam himself ruled in Patani until he died in a cannon accident.

Lim Goniao is enshrined as a god in Patani.

To this day, many Malays at Krue Se say that they are descended from Lim Tohkiam. Although such sexual fecundity seems implausible, it is likely that Lim's Chinese comrades also fathered numerous Malay *lukchin* descendants who claim lineage to Lim Tohkiam.[38]

Not every Chinese freebooter who came to Patani to seek his fortune managed to rise to kingship like Lim Tohkiam. Chinese annals record that in 1540 the notorious Xu brothers carried out pirate operations from Patani and enlisted Portuguese freebooters to raid the Fujian coast. In 1554 two other fearsome pirates, He Yaba and Zheng Zongxing also used Patani port as a base to stage raiding expeditions on the China coast.[39] These characters were well-known pirate leaders who achieved historical notoriety, but there were certainly many other Chinese pirates who plied a more modest trade in the Gulf of Siam. Their exploits went unrecorded in the Chinese annals.

Illicit Trade Versus Tributary Trade

The prevalence of pirates in Patani suggests two interconnected situations occurring in Ayudhya and China respectively. Lim Tohkiam's life overlapped with the Chinese Wanli Reign (1573–1620), which coincided with the period of the Burmese wars. Ayudhya was invaded by King Bayinnaung of Pegu twice, in 1564 and 1569. Jeremias van Vliet, head merchant in Ayudhya of the Dutch East India Company (also known as the United East India Company, or VOC), described the dire situation prevailing in Ayudhya in the aftermath of the Burmese conquest, saying, "the country was bare of inhabitants and many places were destroyed."[40] Because the weakened Siamese state was in no condition to police the seas, pirates were able to roam the Gulf of Siam with impunity. Subsequently, King Naresuan (1590–1605), one of Siam's most revered warrior kings, who was raised as a captive prince in Bayinnaung's court at the Burmese capital of Pegu, declared war and fought several campaigns with the Burmese and the Khmer to regain control of Ayudhya's former domains. Peace and prosperity finally returned to Ayudhya by the time Ekathotsarot, Naresuan's brother, ascended the throne in 1605.

The prevalence of piracy in the Gulf of Siam and the South China Sea during the 16th century also suggests that something had gone wrong with Ming maritime policy. The "Prohibition" had caused severe hardship for people in the coastal provinces. In Fujian, of which almost two-thirds is covered by mountainous terrain, many livelihoods were intertwined with coastal activities and maritime trade. To enforce such a regressive welfare policy upon widespread Southern Chinese interests proved a costly, Herculean undertaking. Coastal people in Fujian and Guangdong provinces whose livelihoods traditionally depended on trade were emboldened by the lax policing of the seas to break the "Prohibition"—they turned to smuggling and piracy.

Through bribery of corrupt officials, illicit trade thrived. Gentry-merchant syndicates operating out of Fujian Province often controlled these illegal maritime activities. The Fujian port of Yuegang achieved notoriety as a favorite port for smugglers and pirates, and served as the conduit to the outside world for Jingdezhen porcelain as well as Fujian trade ceramics commonly known as Zhangzhou wares.

Eventually acknowledging the futility of imposing the ban on overseas private trade, the Ming authorities officially rescinded the ban in 1567 and reluctantly recognized Yuegang as a port of call in 1573. Private trade greatly proliferated after official restrictions were lifted, and, coupled with the increased global circulation of silver bullion, the demand for Chinese products boomed. Chinese merchant communities flooded the Nanyang ports and Siamese ports in particular once

Foreign tributaries en route to China during the 15th century, by Shang Xi, Chinese mural and scroll painter.

peace and social tranquility returned after the Burmese wars. During 1580–1619 Siamese tributary trade fell to its lowest level since 1370.[41]

Under King Ekathotsarot (1605–11), Ayudhya made a rapid commercial recovery by initially exploiting the boom in the China trade. The lifting of the Ming ban on private trade allowed Chinese junks to supply porcelain and raw and finished silk to Ayudhya's entrepôt trade freely. Chinese from Fujian brought "pretty large cargoes of all kinds of Chinese goods to Siam and returned with big loads of sappanwood, lead, and other merchandise."[42] However, as Ayudhya tried to recover its old position as chief regional entrepôt, it faced stiff competition from Manila, a revived Cambodia, Batavia, Patani and Hoi Anh, which had prospered while Ayudhya was embattled by Burmese invasions.[43] Despite the competition, Ayudhya recovered to become one of the most active ports in the South China Sea, attracting Chinese, Malay, Muslim, Japanese and, belatedly, Western traders.[44]

A tombstone of a Chinese lady in Patani dated 1592.

By the time Westerners arrived in Ayudhya, they found that Chinese trading networks were already well established in major towns including Paknam Pho (modern-day Nakhon Sawan), Bang Pla Soi (Chanthaburi), Paed Riw (Chachoengsao), Tha Chin (Samut Sakhon), Ban Don (Surat Thani), Ligor (Nakhon Si Thammarat), Songkhla, Phuket and Patani.[45] English merchants who sought trade in southern Siam in 1620 found that they had to deal through the Chinese merchant community there.

In fact, the Chinese population in the provinces far exceeded that in the capital city of Ayudhya. The Chinese were involved in practically every conceivable activity including shipbuilding, mining, artisan work, pig breeding, vegetable gardening, and tax farming on liquor, royal agricultural estates, gambling and peddling.[46] During the late Ayudhya period (roughly the 17th to 18th centuries), the Chinese population in Siam had reached 30,000.[47]

Europeans who came to trade in Siam barely disguised their frustration and envy of the competitive position that the Chinese merchants in Siam enjoyed. The Dutch East India Company (VOC) official van Nyenrode who came to Ligor in 1612 noted with some disappointment, "Chinese pay only ordinary tolls and duties, nobody being allowed to do them harm or cause them any trouble."[48] In Ayudhya, Chinese residents were exempted from corvée (unpaid labor for a local official or lord) and given considerable privileges and protection.[49] Ethnic Thai, Mon, Khmer, Malay, Lao and Burmese in Ayudhya were rarely discharged from their corvée obligations.

King Ekathotsarot's reign seemed especially favorable to the Chinese; as one Chinese national living during that time put it, "the inhabitants (of Siam) accept the Chinese very cordially, much better than do the natives of any other country: therefore Siam is a country that is really friendly to the Chinese."[50]

The China Trade: Fall and Revival

Chinese privilege in Siam, however, would not last forever. For those who knew where to look, signs of trouble were already apparent. King Ekathotsarot had sent embassies to Europe and Japan to promote trade. Not long after, the Japanese, Dutch, French and English would aggressively appear on the scene to challenge the Ayudhyan Chinese.

Piracy, economic troubles and peasant revolts, along with Manchu attacks, reduced the volume and increased the transaction costs of the China trade. The dwindling supply and high costs of Chinese porcelain products coupled with rising European demand led the Dutch VOC to turn to Japan to make up for the scarcity of Chinese porcelain. It was during this same period that the fortunes of the Dutch and the Japanese began to rise.

Yamada Nagamasa, an influential Japanese figure in the court of Ayudhya.

The establishment of Japanese trading colonies in Ayudhya and other Siamese ports heralded a swiftly growing Japanese influence. The situation of the Ayudhyan Chinese began to deteriorate further under the brief reign of the weak, partially blind King Sisaowaphak as Siamese *khunnang* began to harass, squeeze and exploit Chinese traders. The VOC's manager in Ayudhya, Jeremias van Vliet, wrote, "Chinese merchants from Amoy were detained by the deceit of Siamese mandarins with the knowledge of the king."

The situation worsened when Sisaowaphak was assassinated by a supporter of Songtham, his half-brother, who was a monk at the time. After usurping the throne, King Songtham (1611–28) exchanged several embassies with the shogun and maintained a personal Japanese bodyguard, reflecting his sense of insecurity after ousting the legitimate heir of Ekathotsarot.

By the late 1620s, the trade between Siam and Japan had become more important than the trade between Siam and the other foreign countries combined.[51] Chinese-type substitute imports now came from Japan, although Chinese traders were not entirely excluded from operating the Japan-Siam trade. During the reign of Songtham, Japanese influence in the Siamese court reached its height, which was reflected in the rise of Yamada Nagamasa in Siamese politics. According to Skinner, 1620 to 1632 were the precise years during which Chinese traders suffered the worst setback during the entire Ayudhya period.[52]

However, contrary to the impression given by van Vliet and Skinner, it would be wrong to conclude that the Siamese drove away the China trade by imprudent handling of Chinese traders. The nadir in the fortunes of the Ayudhyan Chinese also overlapped with the period of political turmoil accompanying the rapidly disintegrating Ming dynasty. It would make no sense for an Ayudhya struggling to recover commercially to crack down on the China trade, which had served it so well, unless the situation had changed radically.

In China, crumbling Ming authority led to lawlessness, banditry, and piracy on the seas. After 1620, pirate networks including those led by Li Dan—the godfather of an extensive trade network based in Fujian as well as in Japan[53]—and Zheng Zhilong competed with the VOC to control the lucrative China-Japan and Southeast Asia maritime sea routes. Zheng Zhilong, whose son Koxinga would later become a Ming loyalist, started out under the tutelage of the Dutch, who secretly backed him to undermine Li Dan's power. However, the brilliant and ambitious Zheng Zhilong quickly turned the tables against the Dutch. In 1628 he defeated the Ming navy's southern fleet at sea. In a bizarre deal he managed to force the helpless Ming authorities to acknowledge his control of Chinese coastal waters and even secured an official appointment as the admiral of coastal seas.

Upon King Songtham's death another succession crisis reared its head. This time the minister of war, who was the first cousin of King Songtham, killed Songtham's son, took over the throne and crowned himself as King Prasartthong in 1629. Upon ascending the throne he enacted the Royal Trade Monopoly and began to squeeze profit from Chinese, Indian, Arab and Persian traders more heavily, whereas previously Chinese traders paid very little tax.[54] Furthermore, Chinese and other private traders transacting with the ports in the southern part of Siam had to obtain permits from the king, while tin and lead now had to be delivered to the royal warehouse in Ayudhya before being exported. Van Vliet alleged in 1638, "these restrictions caused many foreign merchants to leave the country leaving only two or three rich Moors and a few rich Chinese."

Under the Royal Trading Monopoly, King Prasartthong and his brother sent ships to Canton and other Chinese ports, including a regular ship to the Coromandel Coast and occasional junks to other Southeast Asian ports. King Prasartthong's revival of the Royal Trading Monopoly interestingly came during a time when political turmoil, economic troubles and piracy plagued China.

Essentially, two developments worked to the advantage of the Ayudhyan Chinese merchant community. First, the Ayudhyan Chinese did not oppose Prasartthong's "vexatious" reforms; instead they accepted and quickly adapted to the Royal Trading Monopoly. The Chinese worked well within the system and demonstrated that they were the only experienced seamen who could access Chinese ports.

The king also realized the potential for great profits by using Chinese as ship captains, navigators, helmsmen, sailors, factors, warehousemen, accountants and clerks. Consequently, Chinese were appointed to high offices and enjoyed the favor of the king, who

Chinese junks at sea.

once again opened the doors of royal trading enterprises to provide lucrative employment for the Ayudhyan Chinese.

Second, Prasartthong moved to change his predecessor's pro-Japan policy. Prasartthong had usurped power against the desires of the influential Japanese faction at court. In 1632, fearing a plot against him, Prasartthong massacred the Japanese colony and drove out most of Ayudhya's Japanese inhabitants. Consequently, Siamese ships were banned from landing in Japan, and even the king's merchandise had to be exported to Japan on Chinese junks.

In 1634, King Prasartthong granted the Dutch exclusive rights to buy and export Siamese animal skins.[55] Moreover, after 1636, Japan's Tokugawa rulers closed the country to all foreigners except the Chinese and the Dutch. According to the historian Dhiravat na Pombejra, "these *sakoku* edicts were the reason why the Japanese in Siam and in Japan ceased to play an active part in maritime commerce between the two countries." The Japanese merchants were replaced by the Chinese, who saw great potential in exporting deer and ray skins to Japan. In 1654 the Dutch tried to protest the export of hides by the Chinese and their attempt almost led to a fight with the Chinese in Ayudhya.[56]

During Prasartthong's reign only the Dutch provided any real competition for the Chinese. Thus, after Japanese competition was eliminated, the position of Chinese traders steadily improved. Moreover, the "vexations" of the Royal Trading Monopoly were gradually relaxed as the Chinese were absorbed into the state trading system. By the late 1630s, Chinese private traders also returned more frequently to trade in Siam: "every year two or three junks came to Ayudhya from southern Fukien [Fujian] and one to three Chinese-owned junks were sent from Ayudhya to Cochin-China."[57]

Even as Chinese private trade began to return to the region, the nature of the trade was transformed by events in China. After 1630, Chinese private trade was increasingly hijacked by powerful pirate syndicates. On 22 October 1633, the aforementioned Zheng Zhilong defeated the VOC fleet at sea. Everybody, including the Dutch, English, Portuguese and Siamese who wanted to trade with China and Japan, had to deal with the Zheng clan, who could provide safe shipping routes between Zheng's two strongholds, Amoy and Nagasaki.[58] According to C.J.A. Jörg, an expert on porcelain, "Without Zheng's permission no substantial amounts of porcelain could be transported to the VOC in Taiwan or Japan."[59]

The downfall of the Ming dynasty was imminent. In Ayudhya, the Chinese merchant community played an indispensable role in providing intelligence and interpreting news and events as they unfolded on the China front. Siamese tribute missions correspondingly decreased during this period. Barely 15 years after King Prasartthong founded a new dynasty in Siam, the Ming dynasty collapsed in 1644, ending yet another dynastic cycle in China.

While dynastic change in Ayudhya was limited to factional struggles at court, in China the transition was accompanied by great political turmoil involving peasant rebellions, external invasions and the resultant exodus of Southern Chinese to Nanyang. Although history had repeated itself, the scale, duration and intensity of Chinese emigration was unprecedented.

Several factors account for this difference. Although the Manchus had conquered Beijing in 1644 it took them another 40 years before the Qing dynasty (1644–1911) finally established firm control over Southern China and its coastal seas. After losing Beijing, remnants of the Ming fled to the south and re-established themselves as the Southern Ming dynasty. Southern Ming loyalists regrouped and continued to offer resistance to the Manchu invaders. Opposition to the Manchus was especially strong in Fujian and Guangdong. At sea the Zheng clan continued to oppose the Manchus as well.

King Prasartthong had no choice but to deal with the Ming loyalists and the pirates who continued to control the seas even as Qing armies were victorious on the mainland. However, after Zheng Zhilong betrayed the Ming to the Manchus, leading to the capture of Fuzhou in 1646, Prasartthong decided to hedge his bets by sending a tribute mission, which arrived in Beijing in 1652, following which both countries came to recognize each other and Siamese ships were allowed to trade in Canton. However, Zheng Chenggong, the half-Japanese son of Zheng Zhilong, known to Europeans as Koxinga, began his own resistance against the

Reception of Foreign Envoys by the Emperor of China, c. 1660, drawn by John Nieuhoff and engraved by Franz Xaver Habermann.

King Narai
(reigned 1656–88).

Emperor Kangxi
(reigned 1662–1722).

Manchus. In search of a safe rear base in 1661, Koxinga led his forces to capture Fort Zeelandia from the Dutch.[60]

King Prasartthong dealt with both sides to keep trade channels open and to reap the benefits of the China and Japan trade. The reign of his son, King Narai (1656–88), overlapped with the reign of the great Manchu emperor Kangxi (1662–1722). Narai continued his father's dual policy of dealing with both Koxinga and the Qing dynasty. Ming loyalists continued to maintain a base in Ayudhya. In 1665 Zheng Jing, the son of Koxinga, sent a fleet of 20 ships to trade in Southeast Asia, 10 of which came to trade in Siam during the reign of King Narai.[61] Meanwhile, Emperor Kangxi escalated the war against the Southern rebels after the revolt of the Three Feudatories (1673–77).

The ensuing war to pacify Southern China was hard fought, brutal, prolonged, bloody and treacherous. To crush the stubborn southern resistance the determined Manchus launched a scorched-earth policy of devastation to deny trade revenue, ships and manpower resources to the rebels. Southern towns and coastal villages were burned and destroyed, including Jingdezhen, China's porcelain capital, in 1675.[62] Between 1662 and 1681, populations were forcibly relocated 30–50 *li* (11–18 miles) from the coast of Fujian and Guangdong, creating a belt of uninhabited land along the coastal seas.[63] Private trade was banned and Chinese were prohibited from traveling abroad.

Making the most of the situation, King Narai stepped up tribute missions to the Qing court. During his reign of 32 years, King Narai sent a record-breaking 12 tribute missions to Beijing. Narai's initiative to seize the opportunity to maximize royal profits without competition from Chinese merchants paid handsome dividends. The Royal Trading Monopoly thrived and produced fabulous revenue for the king's coffers.

Meanwhile, on the China front, Emperor Kangxi's pacification campaign wrecked the economy and social fabric of Southern China, resulting in a mass exodus of political refugees from Southern China to Southeast Asia and Siam.

Southern Chinese refugees (mostly Ming supporters, Ming officials, and those with connections to pirate networks) spilled over into Taiwan, Vietnam, Malaka and Siam, as well as faraway places in the Malay Archipelago and Borneo. Most of them were Hokkiens. The Hokkien exodus to Siam mostly settled in southern Thailand, especially in Ligor and Songkhla, while the Teochew people went to Trat and Chantabun. In Ayudhya the new arrivals established settlements outside the city moat at Klong Tanon Tan on the eastern side of the Pasak River. One Thai-Chinese family who could trace their ancestry to this community included Chaokrua Ngen (Tan Ngeng),[64] the maternal grandfather of King Mongkut (Rama IV), who was one of Siam's most beloved kings.

Under King Narai, the benefits and contradictions of the dual policy intensified. During the early part of his reign the dual policy allowed the Royal Trading Monopoly to keep the sea lanes, which were controlled by Koxinga, open. However, it also obliged King Narai to allow Ming loyalists and the pirate network to trade in Ayudhya. Besides the rights of passage through pirate-controlled waters, the dual policy enabled tribute missions to access Chinese ports and markets in Qing-controlled territory, including Canton. This gave Ayudhya an advantage over the VOC because it enabled the former to source scarce Chinese goods directly from China. While Dutch relations with Koxinga deteriorated, the Zheng clan still retained power at sea. Thus, it became increasingly difficult for the Dutch to sail safely or to obtain substantial quantities of Chinese products.[65] Meanwhile, the Siamese Royal Trading Monopoly continued to use official diplomatic channels to send tribute missions to Canton to acquire scarce Chinese products for distribution to ports and markets all over Asia. Thus, the dual policy enabled the Siamese Royal Trading Monopoly to fare well during the Transition Period.

But playing both sides can be a risky policy, and Narai incurred the displeasure of both the Ming and Qing. The dual policy also provoked the displeasure of a third party—the Dutch. Under the aegis of the VOC, the Dutch had arrived in Ayudhya in 1604 during the reign of King Naresuan, and a Dutch settlement was established to tap an abundant supply of deer skins and ray skins in Ayudhya. Because Japan held the most demand for these items, the Dutch began to use Ayudhya as a forward platform to trade with Japan. During the reign of King Prasartthong, the Dutch had become the only traders who could effectively compete with the Chinese. By the time King Narai ascended the throne the VOC

Dutch ships at Fort Zeelandia in Tainan, Formosa (Taiwan).

had become the largest single foreign trading organization at Ayudhya, buying deer skin, tin, lac and rare woods to sell in China, Japan and India as well as providing 20 percent of Siam's imports from 1633–94.[66]

It was only natural that a successful Siamese Royal Trading Monopoly would clash with Dutch interests. With an experienced Chinese crew, well-connected Chinese advisors with kinship links to Chinese officials, greater access to Chinese ports, formal diplomatic relations with the Qing court, tacit support for the Zheng trading network and Narai's own hands-on trade direction, the Royal Trading Monopoly had become more competitive than the Dutch had bargained for. To add insult to injury, the presence of Ming loyalist refugees and pirate ships in Ayudhya harbor, coupled with the heavy presence of Chinese seamen and crew in the Royal Junk Fleet, tended to create the impression that the Siamese Royal Trading Monopoly was aligned with the Zheng trading network. When Koxinga attacked and evicted the Dutch colony from Fort Zeelandia in Taiwan in 1662, Dutch forces worldwide began to clash with the Zheng trading network.

Soon, a full-blown crisis erupted at Ayudhya. Several factors played into this: the ill will between the Dutch and Chinese that arose from the humiliating defeat at the hands of Koxinga in Taiwan; King Narai's aggressive attempts to take a share of the VOC's Japan trade; and the Phraklang's efforts to monopolize trade in Siam. The tension was precipitated by the Dutch seizure of a Siamese crown junk with a Chinese crew flying under Portuguese colors off of Hainan.[67] In 1663, armed Chinese—followers of Zheng—besieged the Dutch Factory at Ayudhya.[68] The Dutch suspected the king's Persian *khunnang*, Okya Pieschijt, otherwise known as Abdu'r-Razzaq, who had recently canceled VOC trade privileges and forbidden other traders from trading with the Dutch, of instigating the incident.[69]

Constantine Phaulkon became influential in King Narai's court.

The siege of the Dutch Factory colored Dutch perceptions of their friction with Siam and blew the situation out of proportion. The VOC quickly retaliated with a naval blockade at the mouth of the Chao Phraya River, which lasted from September 1663 to February 1664.[70] The conflict was finally settled with the signing of the first Dutch-Siamese Treaty in 1664, which was gravely inimical to Chinese interests and included a blanket demand that King Narai remove all Chinese crew from serving aboard Siamese crown junks.[71]

The treaty was a bold attempt on the part of the Dutch to settle old scores with the Siamese as well as secure for the VOC the whole of Siam's trade with China and Japan. The demand to remove Chinese crew from crown junks would severely curtail Siamese and Chinese trade because the majority of that trade was carried by ships with Chinese crew. The Siamese and other rival trading interests vigorously resisted Dutch pressure. Fearing that such a blatant anti-Chinese policy would ultimately backfire on the VOC's larger interests in China, and realizing they lacked

King Louis XIV of France receives delegates from Siam in 1684.

the resources to enforce such a treaty, the Dutch eventually backed down. The king's mercantile operations continued to be managed by Chinese, both in Siam and abroad.[72]

Meanwhile, growing tensions with the Dutch arising from Siam's dual policy caused King Narai to turn to other European powers. Narai sought to woo the English and the French to counterbalance the Dutch. In 1662 Narai welcomed French Catholic missionaries fleeing persecution in Vietnam to Ayudhya. Responding to Narai's hospitality, the French quickly built a church and a seminary, making Ayudhya their headquarters in Southeast Asia.[73]

Narai also frantically sought to enlist English support, but the English, whose situation was complicated by their own entanglement with the Dutch over Ambon, refused to help.[74] Instead, Narai continued to court the French through the good offices of Constantine Phaulkon.

Constantine Phaulkon was a Greek adventurer who had taken employment at the court of King Narai and risen to become superintendent of Siam's foreign trade. Narai's distress at the Dutch threat played into Phaulkon's hands. His hatred of the English and his recent conversion to Catholicism predisposed him to favor the French over the English. Phaulkon skillfully played on the fears of the Siamese and the optimism of the French to gain influence in the Siamese court. At Phaulkon's insistence, a diplomatic mission was sent to the court of the Sun King, Louis XIV.

Phaulkon used his role as intermediary between the Siamese and the French to increase his own power and influence. To woo the French, Phaulkon proposed to the French court a secret plan to convert the Siamese king and take over the

Siamese court. Under Phaulkon's plan, French agents would take up important assignments in Ayudhya. At a propitious moment, Phaulkon's loyal followers would make a show of force; at the same time the French priests would play their role in the conversion of the king and the Siamese people.

To the Siamese, Phaulkon pledged that the French would send warships to the southern port of Songkhla to oust the Dutch. After eliciting agreement from King Narai, Phaulkon went back to the French with offers of trading concessions, missionary privileges, cessation of some islands off Mergui and rights to extraterritoriality.[75] With the support of Constantine Phaulkon, French influence at court achieved a level reminiscent of the Japanese under the Yamada era. However, the French still lacked the trading clout of the VOC and did not seriously challenge the commercial position of the Chinese.

The Ayudhyan Chinese in the Narai period comprised many capable merchants. Among the king's Chinese merchants, the most powerful and capable was Okphra Siviphot. Furthermore, royal overseas trading enterprises employed Chinese at all levels without precluding Chinese private trade. For example, the position of the Choduk-Rachasretthi, which oversaw the Krom Tha Sai, was traditionally always filled by a Chinese, not least because Chinese was the *lingua franca* of East Asian trade. During the Ayudhya period, the Krom Tha Sai oversaw relations with the Cochin-Chinese, Tonkinese, Japanese, Chinese, Ryukyu, Batavia and, last but not least, the Dutch.

Despite their dominance in the private trade sector, the Ayudhyan Chinese during the Narai period did not control the nerve center of the Royal Trading Monopoly—the Phraklang. The Chinese did not manage to control the Phraklang ministry until 1700, during the reign of King Phetracha. Nevertheless, the time of Chinese control was imminent, as the Phaulkon-French era in Siamese history would prove to be short-lived.

Phaulkon had managed to boost his power at court by arranging the arrival of six French warships carrying 636 soldiers commanded by General de Fargues. Phaulkon had maneuvered to garrison these French forces at Bangkok and Mergui instead of far-off Songkhla as initially agreed, thereby effectively blocking trade routes both by sea and land.[76] Thus, Phaulkon's pro-French forces were already strategically in place by 1688.

What Phaulkon failed to anticipate was the awesome reaction of the Siamese nobility to his meteoric rise to power and the untimely death of King Narai, his benefactor and protector. As King Narai lay dying in the palace at Lopburi, the *khunnang*, resentful of Phaulkon's monopoly of power, mounted a coup d'état. In the ensuing political turmoil, Okphra Phetracha—commander of the military's Elephant Corps, the son of King Narai's wet nurse, and effectively Narai's foster brother—shunted aside Narai's adopted son and crowned himself king.

As a usurper king, Phetracha was acutely aware of his lack of legitimacy. Not only had he seized power from Narai's legitimate heir, but his rank even before taking the throne was also in question. Although he commanded the military's Elephant Corps, his ranking was only that of an *okphra*—a *khunnang* of the second rank. Therefore, by rank he was inferior to one of his supporters, Kosa Pan, who was an *okya*, or *khunnang* of the first rank. This fact would continue to haunt Phetracha and, ultimately, it would lead to a bloody turn of events.

Desperate to legitimize his power, Phetracha's first act as king was to remove the most dangerous leaders of the pro-French faction headed by the powerful Constantine Phaulkon. After executing Phaulkon, he took immediate steps to address the issue of legitimacy by marrying King Narai's only daughter, Kromluang Yothathep. After forging marital ties into the old royalty, King Phetracha demonstrated his magnanimity by sparing the life of Phaulkon's half-Japanese wife to quickly restore peace and tranquility at court.

The death of King Narai, the rise of King Phetracha, and the prevalent anti-Western sentiment in 1688 spelled the end of French and British trade in Siam. Following the coup, English and French trading companies withdrew from Siam and cultural intercourse with Europe diminished. Only the Dutch VOC and a few British "country traders" continued to trade in Siamese ports including Ayudhya through 1767.[77]

The departure of all European-state trading companies except the VOC corresponded with a decline in entrepôt trade, which had been vigorous throughout King Narai's reign, especially trade with the Indian Ocean ports. However, if European and Indian Ocean trade had lost some luster, then Siamese-Chinese trade enjoyed a period of expansion as events in Siam and ongoing developments on the China front generated a new dynamic of Chinese-assisted

A painting shows Chinese emperor Kangxi (reigned 1662–1722 as the second Chinese emperor of the Manchu dynasty) entering Beijing.

economic vitality, which affected the whole Nanyang region in general and the Ayudhyan Chinese in particular. In China, Emperor Kangxi's harsh military pacification campaign proved successful. In 1680 Amoy was conquered by the Manchus, and in 1683 the Zheng clan was defeated.

The impact of these developments on trade was almost instantaneous. After the incorporation of Taiwan into the Chinese Empire and the stabilization of Manchu authority in Southern China, trade with Nanyang was freed.[78] In 1684, Emperor Kangxi rescinded the 28-year *hai-jin* maritime ban (1656–84) on travel, leading to an enormous increase in Chinese overseas trade. Henceforth, every year Chinese merchants brought 15–20 ships laden with all the finest goods from China and Japan to Ayudhya.[79]

The consequence of the 1688 political upheaval was that the European share of Siam's trade with East Asia fell to the Chinese.[80] By this time, too, Portugal had lost all commercial and political clout in Siam. Only the Dutch among the Europeans emerged from the disorders of 1688 with their monopoly intact. However, by 1705, the Dutch had run into severe trouble and Dutch participation in Siamese trade remained sporadic at best thereafter.[81] Thus, after the Portuguese, Japanese, English, French and Dutch fell by the wayside, the whole of Ayudhya's trade was practically served up on a plate for the Ayudhyan Chinese.

From this period forward China not only dominated Siam's external trade but also outclassed other foreign communities at court as King Phetracha (1688–1703) replaced Western specialists with other qualified foreigners, including Chinese.[82] Engelbert Kaempfer, a German naturalist who visited Siam in 1690, mentioned there was a learned Chinese, Phraya Yomarat, who became chief justice and was in charge of supervision over the royal capital.[83]

Remnant of Kangxi-period porcelain mosaic at Wat Phudthaisawan, Ayudhya. Reprinted from *Bencharong and Chinaware in the Court of Siam: The Surat Osathanugrah Collection.*

The boom in Chinese private trade continued throughout King Phetracha's reign. The new king was able to ride the upturn in the China trade, which compensated for the loss of the European trade and diminished Indian Ocean trade. With the abundance of Chinese goods in the market there was no need for Siam to send tribute missions to China. After the lifting of the Chinese maritime ban in 1684, King Narai had ceased to send tribute missions, and there is no record of King Phetracha ever sending a single tribute mission to China throughout his 15-year reign. Moreover, records show that during the 24 years between 1684 to 1708, Siam sent no tribute missions at all.[84]

It has been suggested that the real reason King Phetracha did not send any tribute missions to China was because the Qing court was unlikely to recognize a usurper king. Later, in the late 18th century, Emperor Qianlong refused to grant King Taksin's requests for investiture for 14 years on the grounds of lack of legitimacy. However, unlike Taksin, King Phetracha did not seek official recognition—with the favorable conditions of Siamese-Chinese private trade, he did not need to.

The king of Siam could now acquire goods without having to risk his ships at sea. Thus, King Phetracha redirected the Royal Trading Monopoly to other ports on the Coromandel Coast, Japan and Batavia. His was an enviable situation: declining risk was accompanied by higher profit margins derived from duties levied on the growing number of Chinese junks calling at the Ayudhya port. Burgeoning royal revenues and an enlarged war chest helped to bolster Phetracha's political position.

The Dutch in Batavia faced the same situation as King Phetracha in Ayudhya. Chinese private trade brought everything Batavia needed. Moreover, Chinese merchants were satisfied with smaller profits and Chinese junks could carry goods more cheaply than VOC vessels. The Dutch observed that the Chinese junks took all the risks at sea and even paid tolls and taxes, adding to the bargain. The *Hoge Regering* found that they could acquire Chinese products in Batavia at comparable prices to those in China, but without the cost of outfitting their own ships and incurring the risk of shipwreck. So in 1689 the directors abandoned their own direct trade between Batavia and China. Instead they encouraged Chinese merchants to increase trade to Batavia.[85] Thus the VOC policy mirrored the Siamese Royal Trading Monopoly policy regarding trade with China.

The royal revenues gained through the Chinese-assisted economic boom bought time for King Phetracha to consolidate his political position against potential rivals at court. However, this did not cure Phetracha of his insecurity about legitimacy, and he maintained an uneasy relationship with his senior officials, who had supported his usurpation of the crown. Like Prasartthong before him, Phetracha instinctively distrusted his former peers while simultaneously having to rely upon them for the administration of the kingdom. This unstable balance of power at court turned violent in 1699 when a rebellion broke out at Khorat in Nakhon Ratchasima, the gateway to the northeastern provinces of Siam.

The origins and details of the Khorat Rebellion remains shrouded in mystery. According to distant reports by foreign observers at Ayudhya, the rebellion sprang from a court conspiracy to put Phetracha's young son by Kromluang Yothathep, Phra Khwan, on the throne. Among the alleged leaders of the conspiracy was the Phraklang minister, Kosa Pan, who was formerly King Narai's ambassador to the court of Louis XIV, but who became a staunch supporter of Phetracha in the coup of 1688. Wary of the prestige,

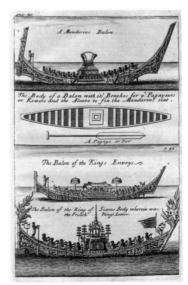

Royal barges at Ayudhya, Franz Xavier Habermann, 1710.

seniority and influence of Kosa Pan in court circles, Phetracha was predisposed to suspect the Phraklang's motives and loyalty. Besides Kosa Pan, the king suspected many other *khunnang* of being behind the plot to replace him with a more malleable boy king. The political troubles provided Phetracha with a pretext to launch a witch hunt and complete the unfinished political cleansing of 1688 through another wholesale purge of *khunnang* and court officials.

French records hinted that several waves of executions swept through the court. According to Gabriel Braud, the first series of executions resulted in the deaths of 48 *khunnang* and the confiscation of their assets.[86] The executed officials belonged to the most eminent and distinguished families in Ayudhya. Among the grandees and military commanders executed were *khunnang* of the highest ranks, including Kosa Pan, as well as several Malay officials and two chiefs of the Japanese community. Consequently, a generation of *khunnang* comprising those who had served King Narai and then sided with Okphra Phetracha in 1688 was almost wiped out in 1699.

But for the intercession of Buddhist monks, whole families of "guilty" *khunnang* would have been executed. As it happened, most of the women and children narrowly escaped death and were demoted to the status of "slave"—a standard punishment in Ayudhya.[87]

The purge of 1699 exacted such a heavy toll on talent and leadership in

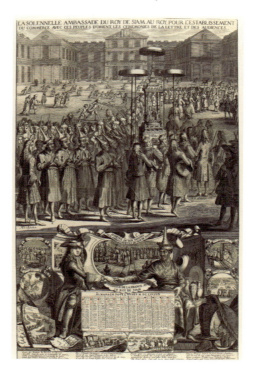

Kosa Pan (bottom right) in the almanac for the year 1687: The King of Siam's Ambassadors Arriving at Versailles in 1686. Musee National des Chateaux de Versailles et de Trianon.

the state's administrative apparatus that foreign ships calling at Ayudhya Port complained about the emergence of new, young officials with no experience in dealing with the VOC and other foreign trading organizations. [88]

The Chinese Ascendancy at Court

The fall of Kosa Pan paved the way for Chinese control of the Phraklang ministry. One Chinese *khunnang* who came to prominence in 1700–01 was promoted by King Phetracha to become Okya Sombatthiban, the supervisor of the Royal Treasury, although his true function was to replace the disgraced Kosa Pan as acting Phraklang, responsible for the king's trading enterprises and foreign affairs.

His sudden catapult to power stemmed from his rendering an invaluable service to King Phetracha—he had intercepted a treasonous letter, which played a part in leading to the bloody purge of 1699. Thus, he gained royal favor to become the most powerful *khunnang* at court while most of his colleagues lost their positions or lives. As a subordinate of Phaulkon during the reign of King Narai, he would have languished in obscurity had it not been for the Khorat Rebellion. He was, in fact, arrested in 1688 but was not executed. By a twist of fate the king who almost took his life in 1688 bestowed the greatest royal favor upon him in 1700. Indeed his appointment opened the door to a remarkable, uninterrupted Chinese ascendancy at court lasting more than 30 years—an ascendancy that was more robust and all-encompassing than that of the French under Phaulkon during the 1680s.[89]

But the career of Okya Sombatthiban proved to be short lived. Soon after his rapid rise, his royal benefactor, King Phetracha, fell gravely ill and died in 1703. Another political crisis was set in motion. Even before King Phetracha's death, two contending factions had formed around two possible heirs: the *wang-na*, Prince Sorasak, and his young half-brother, Phra Khwan—the prince whose name had been dragged into the conspiracy behind the Khorat Rebellion in 1699. The same Chinese *khunnang* who had betrayed the conspirators supporting Phra Khwan in 1699 became a conspirator to support Phra Khwan in 1703.

Behind Okya Sombatthiban, the prime mover supporting Phra Khwan's bid to succeed King Phetracha was the young prince's mother, Kromluang Yothathep. The party of *wang-na* (or "Front Palace") led by the opposing warrior prince, Sorasak, easily triumphed over the much younger Phra Khwan. Prince Sorasak initially pledged to honor his half-brother by offering to rule in his stead until Phra Khwan came of age, but the unlucky prince was soon executed, leaving Prince Sorasak's accession to the throne undisputed by other factions within the court. Following hallowed court precedent, the victorious candidate, who took the regal name King Süa, launched a political witch hunt to purge the court of "disloyal" officials. Thus, Okya Sombatthiban was duly executed in a purge of *khunnang* loyal to Phra Khwan. All his wealth and assets were confiscated by the king and subsequently bestowed upon his successor.

The tale of Okya Sombatthiban reflects a dramatic shift from fortune to misfortune. In 1699 he had decisively backed the victorious faction, yet in 1703 he ended up paying dearly for supporting the losing side. Gratitude to his royal benefactor must have motivated Okya Sombatthiban to support Phetracha's younger son by the queen rather than his elder son, the *wang-na* prince, who came from an earlier marriage that predated Phetracha's ascension to the throne. However, the difference in Chinese and Siamese views on legitimacy may also have been at play. According to Dutch diplomat Joost Schouten, Ayudhyan succession practice followed this rule: "when the king dies, it is not his son but his Brother who is heir to the crown."[90] This law is embodied in the institution of the *wang-na*, the Prince of the Front Palace—normally the king's brother if he had one. Jeremias van Vliet, writing in 1638, confirms, "there is a fundamental law ... which calls the brother of the deceased king to the throne and excludes the son."[91] Interestingly, history was to repeat itself during the succession crisis following the death of King Thaisa (1708–32), when another Chinese Phraklang supported Thaisa's son against the king's brother, Borommakot, the prince of the *wang-na*. This Phraklang also paid for his political allegiance with his life.

Unfortunately, in Siamese history the prescription of the ascension of the brother is often observed in the breach. Nevertheless, such a view appears to be alien to the Chinese concept of kingship, where the rightful heir to succeed must always be the son by the rightful queen. The fact that two Chinese *khunnang* ended up supporting the king's son, by the queen, as opposed to the *wang-na* prince, is consistent with Chinese conceptions of legitimate royal succession.[92]

Despite the fact that Okya Sombatthiban had supported Phra Khwan, the Ayudhyan Chinese continued to maintain control of the Phraklang. Okya Sombatthiban was simply replaced by "another Chinese" in 1703,[93] leaving the Phraklang under Chinese influence. It was probably not just King Süa's personal whim that dictated the appointment of another Chinese to operate the Phraklang—the Ayudhyan Chinese had come to play an indispensable role in the Siamese Royal Trading Monopoly and Sino-Siamese junk trade. Meanwhile, after the Portuguese, Japanese, French and English had left Ayudhya one after the other, the Dutch also faced difficulties in their tin, sappanwood and textile trades. Exasperated with the vexations imposed by officials, the VOC also signaled their intention to close down their factory in Ayudhya. For better or worse, the Chinese were the last men standing in Ayudhya's forsaken trade ring. Moreover, contacts between Siam and China at the turn of the century were not only regular but also more intense than previous periods. For King Süa, there were worse choices than having another Chinese *okya* Sombatthiban.

The new Okya Sombatthiban was probably a Hokkien since he had relatives in the Amoy provincial government[94] who served him well in his newfound position as head of the Royal Trading Monopoly. Although China was fast becoming Siam's most important trading partner, there were still many difficulties in the relationship that required informed and astute diplomacy to address and resolve. The Chinese government continued to regulate the number of ships, as well as the materials and seafarers aboard merchant ships, and foreign ships were still forbidden to transport Chinese passengers. Chinese participation in Siamese trade and emigration to Siam continued to be hindered by restrictive and punitive edicts emanating out of Beijing. However, the new Phraklang proved more than able to meet the challenge.

Center-periphery relations since the Manchu conquest of China in 1644 influenced Manchu policy towards Southern China and overseas Chinese communities. The Southern Chinese had offered the strongest and most prolonged resistance to the Manchu invasion. Southern China, which fell victim to the scorched-earth policy during the pacification campaign, bore the greatest hardship at the hands of the Manchu conquerors. Moreover, overseas Chinese communities in Annam, Batavia, Luzon and Siam remained hotbeds of anti-Manchu activities organized by refugees and secret societies whose aim was to restore the Ming dynasty. Their stout resistance to the southern campaign elicited fear, suspicion and distrust from the Manchus, as well as a grudging respect for their Southern Chinese counterparts. Emperor Kangxi had openly acknowledged that "the Hokkiens were a restless people and maritime Fujian was the most troublesome area of the nation."

At the end of a harsh and bloody pacification campaign, Kangxi showed considerable magnanimity and restraint by refusing to punish the coastal Hokkien. On the contrary, the Manchus strove to normalize the situation in the southern provinces as quickly as possible so that people could resume their livelihoods, fearing that festering discontent could breed another rebellion. Thus, after Kangxi had established his authority over the southern provinces, he speedily lifted the maritime ban so that the Hokkiens could resume their trade.

Although the lifting of the maritime trade ban in 1684 and the benevolent policy to restore normalcy to the southern provinces had led to a rapid expansion of Sino-Siamese trade, Manchu policy towards

Ayudhya Bencharong, Chinese export wares made to order for Siam.

overseas trade and emigration continued to be fraught with suspicion. Although Kangxi was willing to tolerate overseas trade, the Manchu court did not wish to see the proliferation of Chinese settlements abroad. An imperial edict in 1690 decreed, "Whenever people of the interior have strayed to foreign countries and wish to return by ship to their native place, they may be permitted to come back to their former territory." Despite the polite wording it was clear that the Manchus did not want to permit Chinese emigration for security reasons.

It was in this context that the Phraklang ministry sent a tribute mission to Beijing in 1708. This tribute mission, which took place during the reign of King Süa, represented the only tribute mission to occur between 1684 and 1718—a space of 34 years. The resumption of tribute trade represented a shift to a more active diplomacy to engage the Chinese again after a long interval.[95]

King Süa had a relatively short reign, and he died unchallenged in 1709. Surprisingly, his death produced no political turmoil at court. His eldest son, Chaofa Phet, became King Thaisa and his younger son, Chaofa Phon, became the *wang-na* prince, or prince of the Front Palace. Under the politically stable reign of King Thaisa, the Chinese officials in the Phraklang ministry appointed by King Sua continued to exercise great influence. The Okya Sombatthiban was known in this reign as the Chinese Phraklang.

Described by the French missionary Louis de Cice as "a decent man," the Chinese Phraklang was much liked and esteemed by King Thaisa, just as he had been by Thaisa's father, King Süa. Under King Thaisa the Phraklang rose to new heights at court. The new, young and pleasure-loving king tended to discharge the greater part of the burden of government on the shoulders of his Phraklang. Politically astute and knowing the ways of the court, the Chinese Phraklang lost no opportunity to take all possible measures to strengthen his political position and render himself formidable to his enemies. Soon he found ways to introduce Chinese girls into the palace to be continually near the queen and princesses. In addition, he appointed able Chinese to the most prominent posts—especially those connected with trade. Consequently, the Chinese were able to corner the most lucrative and important trading activities in the kingdom. Although the Siamese, Mon, Malay and Moor courtiers impatiently suffered this preference given to the Chinese, no one dared to challenge them—the sway that the Chinese Phraklang held over the king was well known.[96]

In addition to his mastery of the arts of the courtier, the Chinese Phraklang was also able to deliver on the trade front. His ability to negotiate the twists and turns in China's volatile trade policy protected and advanced Siamese interests. One astute maneuver came directly after Kangxi re-imposed the maritime trade ban in 1717. By 1718, the junk traffic to Batavia and other ports in Southeast Asia had ground to a halt.

Made-to-order Chinese porcelain tea bowl with a Siamese motif painted both in the interior as well as the exterior. The size of the tea bowl used in Ayudhya was as large as those used in the early Qing dynasty.

The Phraklang then moved to restore active tributary trade with China and fitted out a large fleet of junks owned by the king and Ayudhyan Chinese to serve as tributary vessels. Thus, when the curtain fell on private trade yet again, Siamese royal junks seized the opportunity to become active at sea. From 1720–66 Siam sent out a total of 13 tribute missions to China—roughly one every three-and-a-half years.[97]

In this way, Siam was cushioned against the vagaries of Chinese trade policy in 1718. The activation of tributary relations also opened up opportunities to ameliorate and resolve the irritations in Sino-Siamese relations arising from China's self-contradictory and erratic trade policy.

Many factors contributed to China's inconsistent trade policy. Administration of a far-away, troublesome province presented many logistical difficulties, including obtaining timely intelligence of illegal or subversive activities. The Southerners' perception of Canton was summed up in the dictum "Heaven is high, the emperor far away."

Difficulties of enforcement contributed to rampant illegal activities, including smuggling, corruption, undesirable foreign influence and illegal emigration paid for through bribes to Guangdong and Fujian officials. Many of these illegal activities posed political and security threats. Foreign demand led to the smuggling of strategic materials and commodities, which created shortages in China. Many ocean-going vessels built in Soochow were smuggled out for sale overseas, and Hokkien ships smuggled shipbuilding materials (such as ships' masts) to sell abroad, resulting in supply shortages within China's shipbuilding industry. Beijing suspected foreign involvement behind the rampant smuggling and mass exodus of Chinese to Nanyang. Fearing leaks of strategic materials and defense secrets, the government sought to discourage locals' contact with foreigners.

Besides strategic materials, the government was particularly concerned about the smuggling of rice from China's famine-prone coastal regions to sell in overseas markets. The Qing court regarded rice as an important factor in maintaining social stability in the southern coastal provinces. Whenever there was a rice shortage in Fujian, Emperor Kangxi became concerned and cautioned local authorities against possible turmoil. These concerns motivated the government to issue a series of edicts—some offering incentives, some punitive—in 1690, 1712 and 1717 to restrict trade and emigration to Nanyang. Nevertheless, the government's sensitivity to the issue of maritime security was tempered by the desire to encourage commerce. Kangxi warned custom officials nationwide that restricting merchants would damage the national economy. "Let hundreds of commodities circulate freely and the livelihoods of the people become prosperous," he said.[98] Thus, the aims of the government—to expand trade with Nanyang but not with overseas Chinese settlements—were self-contradictory.

A Chinese shopkeeper and his wife in the back room, selling porcelain and silk. Mural painting at Wat Pradu Songtham, Ayudhya.

Among all of China's trading partners, Ayudhya, with its Chinese-controlled Phraklang ministry, appeared to best understand the dilemmas informing Beijing's management of trade policy. The Siamese recognized Chinese security concerns that were couched in various contradictory, restrictive imperial edicts. At the same time, the Chinese Phraklang appeared to sense that trade prohibition would not be consistently implemented because both Kangxi and his successor, Yongzheng, tended to encourage commerce.

When news of a rice shortage in Fujian Province reached Ayudhya, the Chinese Phraklang identified another loophole to avoid the Qing court's restrictive trade regulations. Rice-abundant Ayudhya could ensure sufficient supplies of rice for China's southeastern provinces through trade. In 1722 Siam dispatched a tribute mission to China with a carefully worded letter to the emperor informing him of the plentiful supply of cheap rice in the country. Emperor Kangxi was intrigued by Siam's offer, and, in view of the famine in Fujian, gave permission for the Siamese to transport 300,000 piculs of rice to Canton, Amoy and Ningpo—a shipment that would not be subject to duties of any kind.[99]

In 1724 Emperor Yongzheng issued a decree to Chinese port authorities lifting taxes on Siamese ships bringing rice and spices on tribute missions and ensuring fair prices for their cargo. Chinese trade received a further boost when severe famine swept through Fujian's two prefectures in 1726–27, leaving many dead from starvation. The price of rice in Canton doubled. King Thaisa welcomed this new market and encouraged rice exports to China. Consequently, throughout the 10-year maritime trade ban (1718–28), trade with Siam was not only allowed but also encouraged by the Chinese, and rice was shipped from Siam to Fujian under special duty dispensation decreed by the imperial court from time to time.

Recognizing China's need for rice, the Phraklang did not hesitate to exploit China's apparent weakness in food security to leverage better terms, including the removal of further conflicts in the Sino-Siamese trade relationship. One of the irritants that affected the Chinese seamen serving King Thaisa was a punitive edict promising the execution of Chinese who illegally went to sea. The regulation represented a particular thorn in Siam's side because almost all of the king's seamen were Chinese. As long as the edict prevailed, the lives of the Chinese crew aboard royal Siamese junks remained vulnerable.

The Phraklang took the opportunity to ease matters by sending another well-written letter on behalf of the Siamese court requesting special imperial dispensation for all Chinese crew aboard royal Siamese junks. The petition proved to be effective. Emperor Yongzheng responded by decreeing that the names of 97 Chinese sailors of the royal junk fleet be withdrawn from the Chinese registry on grounds that they had permanently resided in Siam for some generations and so should not be punished for seafaring.[100]

Thus, for the first time, a strong leader had arisen from the ranks of the Ayudhyan Chinese who was not only well conversant on trade and Chinese affairs but also capable of protecting his dependents—even from the whims of the imperial court.

A loyal and talented courtier in the administration of trade affairs with a proven track record since the reign of King Sua was bound to be highly prized at court. The Chinese Phraklang almost instantaneously became the indispensable right-hand man of King Thaisa. The extent of the king's confidence in him was demonstrated when the king bestowed the command of the Cambodian campaign upon the Phraklang, who was altogether unacquainted with war. According to Captain Alexander Hamilton who sailed with the East India Company, the Phraklang reluctantly accepted command over the army of 50,000 and the naval fleet comprising 20,000 men. Not surprisingly, the Phraklang was defeated by Cambodian forces. However, he was so entrenched at court that despite his defeat he did not lose his position, and his only punishment was to pay a fine in guns, bullets and gunpowder.[101]

Besides the Cambodian fiasco, the Phraklang survived other mistakes that occurred under his watch. In 1717 and 1721, the Chinese crew in charge of King Thaisa's Japan-bound junks stole the court's only two copies of the permit *(trapai)* issued by the Japanese government, leaving the Siamese with no credentials to show. Later, in 1726–27, the Chinese merchant in charge of the *wang-na* prince's junk in Batavia tried to abscond with the royal Siamese ship and cargo, although he was arrested by the Chinese at Batavia.[102] Although these two incidents must have done much to harm the credibility and reputation of the Chinese Phraklang, the king's confidence and trust in him remained unshaken.

Emperor Yongzheng (reigned 1722–35).

The Chinese ascendancy at the court of King Thaisa, presided over by a Chinese Phraklang, was perhaps deeper and more complete than the influence of the Persian and French during the time of King Narai. In 1718, the Spanish (Manila) embassy to King Thaisa's court declared, "the Chinese held the greatest share of the trade in Ayudhya."[103] In addition, the Dutch complained bitterly about Chinese influence in the provincial government and hinterland trade—especially in the Ligor tin trade.

Unlike the Dutch who confined themselves to trade and fastidiously avoided being dragged into Siamese court politics, the French (who paid dearly for meddling in Siamese statecraft in 1688) probably had more empathy for the Chinese approach. In 1716, Imel Christiaen Cock, the VOC employee in Ligor, summed up the rise of Chinese influence succinctly: " . . . the Chinese . . . have done their utmost to further their policy with a liberal hand and insinuated themselves into this kingdom so that at present [they] have in their control the best and most prominent positions at court as well as in the provinces. This began in the year 1700 when Phra Thong Tan [King Phetracha], the grandfather of the present king, installed for the first time a Chinese as Phraklang."[104]

While Western observations about Chinese ascendancy during this period were largely correct, they also tended to reflect various biases. Western reports often exaggerated the importance of Chinese political intrigue and gave the misleading impression that the Chinese had hijacked the Siamese court. But, in fact, the upturn in Sino-Siamese trade was due to something much more mundane: it stemmed largely from Siam's successful initiation of the rice trade with Southeastern China in the 1720s.

The library of Wat Saket in Bangkok is noted for the Chinese-style paintings and the lacquered windows with figures of Western merchants.

Trade and emigration tended to follow one another. Expansion of trade brought Chinese immigrants to Siam in ever-greater numbers, despite official restrictions imposed on emigration overseas. However, Chinese emigration still tended to be male dominated, as Chinese women generally didn't emigrate until after the 19th century. Meanwhile, an interesting transformation was taking place in Ayudhyan society. As increasing numbers of Chinese and *lukchin* entered court life and took bureaucratic positions, Ayudhyan society began to witness more and more intermarriages among Chinese and Siamese *khunnang* families during the Thaisa period. This contributed to the rise of a genuinely Ayudhyan Chinese community.

Among the prominent and wealthy Chinese *khunnang* at King Thaisa's court was Phya Lauja, described by VOC member Wijbrand Blom as a man "with obliging nature and the most eminent private merchant in this country." Blom added that his wealth and commercial expertise were obviously of great use to King Thaisa.[105] The rise of a new class of Chinese *khunnang* facilitated social mobility in Ayudhyan society as Chinese merchants exchanged wealth for rank and social status. Among them were Chen Zhaokua and Ong Hengchuan. Both were Hokkiens who settled in Siam and eventually rose to become *khunnang*. Chen Zhaokua was bestowed a *khunnang* rank and title of Luang Chine-Chulee-Samutpakdi,[106] while Ong Hengchuan received the title Luang Sri-Sombat.[107] Another Chinese, who was in charge of producing the king's tin tribute in the Dinlemo district of Ligor, was given the title of Okluang Chai-Phakdi.

The Ayudhyan Chinese Crisis

Chinese ascendancy benefited the king, enriched royal coffers and helped to maintain prosperity in Siam despite the loss of European trade. But it also generated discontent and resentment among rival commercial groups including the Dutch, Indians and Moors, who lost their market shares to aggressive Chinese competition.

As long as King Thaisa was alive the Chinese position at court was unassailable. But the Siamese state was prone to succession crises. During King Thaisa's last days battle lines began to form between the king's cabinet and the *wang-na* prince. On his deathbed King Thaisa designated his son Prince Aphai to succeed him with the support of the Phraklang, although tradition dictated the right of succession to his brother, Borommakot.

Upon the death of Thaisa, the two contending parties began to confront each other at court. Prince Aphai was based in the late king's palace and backed by a faction led by the powerful Chinese Phraklang and comprising most of the highest court officials. A short distance away to the east in the Front Palace, Borommakot, uncle to Prince Aphai, could muster only about 4,000 troops against the 20,000–30,000 troops stationed at the royal palace. Court skirmishes gave way to battle, and the Front Palace forces were soon overwhelmed by superior numbers. They were on the verge of defeat when suddenly Borommakot's loyal supporter, Khun Chamnan Borirak, a descendant of an Indian Brahman, managed to rally the retreating troops and mount a swift counterattack that overpowered the leaders of the royal troops and secured the royal palace for his master, who then ascended the throne.

The new king, Borommakot, immediately launched a purge of his opponents at court. The Phraklang tried to escape by entering a temple to be ordained as a monk. According to hallowed Siamese Buddhist tradition, it was sacrilege to harm those who sought sanctuary in a temple. However, the ploy did not work because the new king cunningly sent a team of Malay assassins to seize him. Being Muslim, they had no compunctions about slaying a Buddhist monk. So great was Borommakot's hatred for his brother's Chinese Phraklang that he gave instructions to the Malay assassins to mete out a slow death. The assassins struck the Phraklang monk with a sword but did not kill him immediately—death would be administered in a cruel and painful manner in due course. The Dutchman Willem de Ghij recounted in late 1734 that immediately after King Thaisa's cremation, two "Malay officials" had been pardoned by the new king for killing the Chinese Phraklang.[108] Along with the Phraklang many other *khunnang* were executed.

King Borommakot (1733–58) immediately rewarded those who had supported him. Khun Chamnan Borirak, the hero of the palace battle, was raised to the title of *chaophraya*, putting him in charge of the Phraklang ministry. Not only had the resident Chinese community lost its chief patron and spokesman at the highest level of government, but his replacement by a Thai of Brahman descent also signaled the end of the long Chinese monopoly over the Phraklang ministry.

Despite the loss of its main benefactor, the Chinese did not disappear from the administration or the royal court of Ayudhya. In 1733 a new Okphra Choduk was appointed to handle VOC affairs.[109] Some provincial administrators, such as the governor and *krommakan* at Ligor, were also replaced by Borommakot. Otherwise, it was business as usual. The Chinese continued to trade and behave as the virtual "owners" of Ligor,[110] and Chinese expertise continued to be retained whenever possible. The Sino-Siamese junk trade was far too important to give up.

The ascension of Borommakot to the throne and the political changes attendant on the purge of 1733 had threatened the interests of the demonstrably large Ayudhyan Chinese constituency. Adding insult to injury, the beloved benefactor and protector of the Nai Kai Chinese had been

Chinese blue-and-white shards were often used as architectural decoration in Ayudhyan temples.

INSIDE AYUDHYA'S CHINATOWN

The long period of Chinese ascendency at court combined with a large influx of Chinese immigrants during the Thaisa period created a powerful Chinese constituency in Ayudhya. The base of this constituency was centered at Ayudhya's sprawling Chinatown, known as the Nai Kai Market.[111] This neighborhood was located inside the city wall along the main brick road designated on Western maps of the period as the "China Road." The main commercial district was off of the first street upon entering the city through its main gate, near Pombejra. The street runs westward along the turning of the city wall. According to Kaempfer, the China Road beyond Pratu Chine (or the China Gate) housed "the best accommodation that formerly belonged to the English, Dutch and French; as also that in which Faulcon [Constantine Phaulkon] resided."[112]

At the market itself, Chinese shop houses lined the main street and sold all manner of items, including porcelain, silk, herbs, medicine, tea, fresh and preserved fruits, Chinese sweets, spices, brass wares, iron implements and woks. There was also a large fresh market. Nai Kai Market was busy all day, especially during the junk trading season around Chinese New Year. Next to the main market was a smaller market called Talad Noi at Sam Mah, which sold furniture, carpentry products, wooden poles and woks, and housed metal workshops operated by Chinese shop hands. Talad Noi at Sam Mah was so densely populated it held a fresh market both in the morning and in the evening. Moreover, to the east of the Pasak River, there was another large Chinese settlement called Klong Suan Plu. Thus, the Nai Kai Chinatown dominated the port and Ayudhya's commercial district, stretching inside the city wall from Pombejra to Pratu Chine, whereas outside the city wall the Chinese enclaves occupied both banks of the Pasak River and Klong Suan Plu near the port.

murdered in a cruel, unscrupulous and religiously reprehensible manner. After recuperating from the purge of *khunnang* associated with the old Chinese Phraklang, the Ayudhyan Chinese community erupted in a show of discontent in the Nai Kai Rebellion of 1734. The rebellion broke out while King Borommakot was on a pilgrimage outside the capital. A group of Chinese from Nai Kai and their Siamese associates attempted to occupy the palace and enthrone a more favorable prince. However, the uprising failed. Borommakot rushed back to the capital and brutally put down the rebellion.

The rebellion ultimately failed not only because of Borommakot's swift and decisive action, but also because the Chinese failed to close ranks behind the rebel leadership. After the attack was launched, Ong Hengchuan [Wang Xingquan], a prominent Chinese who was elevated to *khunnang* under the watch of the late Chinese Phraklang, mobilized followers to suppress the uprising. The infighting among the Chinese made it much easier for Borommakot's forces to quell the uprising with considerable loss of life to the rebels. After restoring order, Borommakot executed the leaders of the rebellion and imprisoned hundreds more. Another report stated that 700 Chinese were demoted to corvée labor, condemned to a chain gang and forced to do hard public works.[113] Meanwhile, several thousand Siamese fled to the hills and some Chinese escaped the king's wrath by fleeing to neighboring Cambodia and Vietnam.[114]

The failure of the Nai Kai Rebellion reflected the competitive character of the Ayudhyan Chinese community. The Chinese bloc has been likened to a vessel of boiling water—as soon as one bubble disappeared, another rose to take its place. Thus, it was not difficult for Borommakot to divide and conquer the Chinese. As a reward for breaking ranks with the old Chinese Phraklang loyalists, Ong Hengchuan (Wang Xingquan) was later appointed Okphra Choduk,[115] the king's merchant responsible for the China trade. Thus, despite a purge of the court there was no real purge of the Chinese. Other bubbles rose to fill the places of their disgraced peers. There was, however, a thorough overhaul of the Ayudhyan Chinese at court and at all levels of the administrative apparatus in the capital and outlying provincial government.

The suppression of the Chinese in 1734 naturally affected Sino-Siamese relations, especially since the China trade had always been operated by Chinese. However, the Sino-Siamese junk trade was too lucrative and important to lose. To reduce the repercussions of the Nai Kai Rebellion, the king quickly dispatched a tribute mission to Beijing with letters addressed to the emperor explaining what had happened in Ayudhya.[116] The outcome of the tribute mission reflected the Qing court's sentiments. A Dutch document of 1737 relates that of the two junks sent to China only one returned, and the one that returned came back empty. Its cargo had been detained in Canton,[117] and the king's envoy had received a very humiliating reception, indicating that the Qing court strongly disapproved of the massacre of Chinese in Ayudhya.

A Quiet Restoration

Beijing's rebuffs did not last long. Sustained peace and political tranquility under the reigns of Emperor Kangxi and Yongzheng had led to economic recovery, prosperity and population growth in China. Consequently, China needed more rice to adequately feed its citizens. Export markets were also necessary for Chinese manufactures, including porcelain, silk and tea, and imported forest products and raw materials were needed for a rapidly expanding production sector. By 1736, Sino-Siamese trade relations had returned to normalcy and exports to China under the reign of King Borommakot resumed.

Trade restrictions were further relaxed to encourage the rice trade with Siam. In 1747 the Chinese government allowed Chinese merchants traveling to Siam to buy rice, engage in shipbuilding, and import Siamese lumber. In 1751 Beijing issued another decree stating that merchants who brought back over 2,000 piculs

Chinese porcelain
manufacturer and
store.

of rice from Siam would be honored with an imperial button. [118]

Trade with other cities and ports in Siam expanded. A Chinese report in 1747 noted that a continuous trade relationship between Fujian Province and Patani and Songkhla had developed since the trade embargo was relaxed in 1729. Riding upon the mutually beneficial economic relations between the two countries, as well as the excellent relations between the Siamese and Qing courts, the Ayudhyan Chinese began to recover some of the influence they had lost in 1734.

Upon the death of Chaophraya Chamnan Borirak in 1753, King Borommakot returned control of the Phraklang ministry to an Ayudhyan Chinese *khunnang*, phraya Phraklang (Chim), who was Chaophraya Chamnan Borirak's son-in-law. [119] Throughout the Baan Phlu Luang dynasty, China remained Siam's most important trading partner, as well as the engine driving Ayudhya's economic prosperity.

THE KING OF THONBURI

(1767–1782)

The story of how a lukchin *(half-Thai, half-Chinese) native of Ayudhya rose to become king of Siam is a sensational tale of individual skill, court intrigue and military conquest. King Taksin, who would found the Thonburi kingdom after Ayudhya was sacked by the Burmese, led military campaigns that resurrected Siam's sovereignty from the ashes. As a king desperately seeking legitimacy, he would forge the origins of what would become a new nation-state. As his personal story became intertwined with the shifting balances of power on the Southeast Asia Mainland, however, he would end up like many of the kings of the time, only able to hold on to power for so long before fate dealt a final blow. The exceptional story of King Taksin reflects the unique circumstances and opportunities that were available to the Chinese in Siam and also the challenges that threatened their remarkable success.*

King Taksin of Thonburi was born of no renowned lineage during troubled times in Ayudhya, in the year of the Nai Kai Rebellion in 1734. His father, Tae Yong (鄭鏞), was a Teochew immigrant from Hua-fu Village, Chenghai County, Shantou, Guangdong Province.[1]

Yong probably came from a merchant family because he had the reputation of being a generous young man of some means, although he had other character failings. Apparently, he was not an exemplarily filial Chinese son, being overly fond of travel and gambling.[2] This passion for taking calculated risks was also amply reflected in the character of his son, whose predatory instinct would be demonstrated again and again in the battlefields of Siam. However, Yong's virtue of generosity combined with his vice of gambling reduced him to penury, causing him to seek his fortune overseas.

Yong was not alone in his efforts to make a living abroad. The exodus of Chinese refugees to the Nanyang was by no means a rare occurrence in the 17th and 18th centuries—it was in fact a diaspora. A few decades before Yong, another Cantonese from Guangdong Province named Mac Cuu (鄭玖) also left China in 1671, just before the Three Feudatories' uprising against the Manchu, to seek his fortune in Cambodia where he was appointed to an official rank of okna.[3] In 1700, Mac Cuu and his followers founded Ha Tien, a Chinese-style town with gambling dens,[4] and its destiny was to become intertwined with King Taksin, who eventually conquered the city state. In addition to Cambodia, Cantonese refugees tended to settle in Vietnam.

Meanwhile, the Hokkiens tended to gravitate to Ayudhya and the southern part of the Siamese kingdom. Besides the Hokkiens, the Teochews—fewer in number but growing in importance and population—mostly settled on the eastern periphery of the Siamese kingdom, at Chonburi and Chantabun, adjacent to Mac Cuu's Ha Tien. The Teochew enclave at Ayudhya was located in the vicinity of Klong Suan Plu behind Wat Pananchoeng where Taksin's father, Yong, also reportedly settled. Apparently, the Chinese in Siam in those days came from different regions in China and formed distinct dialect groups without a sense of overarching Chinese identity.

Qing attitudes toward contact with overseas Chinese changed for the better following the defeat of the Ming loyalists and the Koxinga pirate network. However, the movement of Chinese émigrés to the Nanyang during the early Qing period was also different from the time of the Ming for another reason: the tendency for overseas Chinese to become aggressively involved in the political life of Southeast Asian countries was unprecedented. The late 17th century onwards witnessed a robust movement of Southern Chinese coming to help native rulers reclaim virgin lands, serving native overlords as local governors, founding overseas autonomous Chinese settlements and even running an independent port polity. Such was the character of the times when Yong left the shores of his native Teochew homeland.

There is scarcely any information about how Yong spent his life in his new adopted land. Consequently, there is much uncertainty in the historical record about the early life of King Taksin. Born as a *lukchin* of Chinese parentage during the political turmoil surrounding the Nai Kai Chinese Rebellion and subsequent anti-Chinese backlash of 1734, his family must have felt acutely vulnerable. Although more writers have written about King Taksin than any other king in Thai history and more monuments have been erected to commemorate his rule, his life before he became king remains shrouded in mystery. Differing accounts proliferate about his lineage, early childhood, youthful education and training, domestic circumstances, personal abilities, the years he spent in the town of Tak, his character traits and his role in the critical events preceding the fall of Ayudhya.[5]

An artist's impression of King Taksin of Thonburi.

Chapter opening picture: A statue of King Taksin on the Thonburi side of Bangkok.

A Tale of Two Childhoods

Among the conflicting stories about Taksin's childhood, the most-often quoted source can be found in the *Aphinihan Banphabhurut*—an anonymous Thai document dating back to the reign of King Mongkut (1851–68) and popularized by the famous K.S.R. Kularb. Another account exists in the work of renowned contemporary historian Professor Nidhi Eoseewong, titled *Kanmuang Thai Samai Phrachao Krung Thonburi* (Thai politics in the reign of King Taksin), published in 1993.

Modern-day biographers influenced by Nidhi posit that Yong settled in the Chinese community at Klong Suan Plu, across the river from Ayudhya's predominantly Hokkien Nai Kai Market, where he married a Siamese woman and had a son named Sin. The boy grew up in the nascent Teochew enclave outside the city wall, which was part of a large Chinese community located on the banks of numerous *klong* draining into the Pasak River, including Klong Baan Baht, Klong Pak Kaosan, Klong Thanontan and Klong Suan Plu.

During the late Ayudhya period, the area around Pasak River and its network of canals was densely populated. It was where the inland merchants from the north and northeast docked their barges laden with forest products—including tobacco, coconut, salt, rice, sticklac, benzoin, bagasse and animal hides—to sell in the capital. Merchants from Raheng (Tak), Petchabun and Nayom would dock their barges in Klong Pak Kaosan (well known for its liquor distillery), which was linked to Klong Thanontan and Klong Suan Plu (also well known for its distillery, as well as its pig farms).[6]

A corollary of this version of Taksin's childhood was that his relationship with Rama I, who was to become Taksin's successor, may have dated back to this

Nai Kai Market is at Rue Chinoise (G) in Jacques Nicolas Bellin's (1703–72) map, published in Paris in 1764. The Chinese community of Ayudhya is located around the port where the Pasak River flows southwards to join the Chao Phraya River flowing in from the west. Klong Suan Plu is on the opposite bank of the city wall of Ayudhya, to the east of the Pasak River. Collection of the Siam Society.

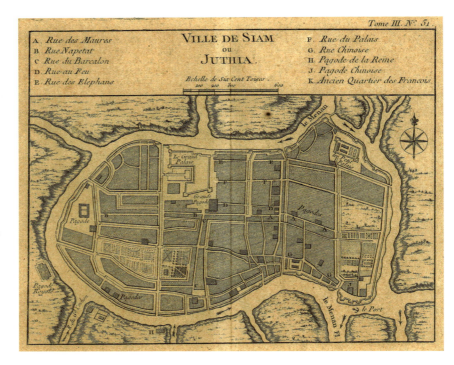

period. After all, Rama I spent his childhood in the aristocratic enclave around Wat Suwandararam, inside the city wall behind Pombejra Fort, not far from Nai Kai Market. Many other tales also assert that King Taksin and Rama I knew each other when they were young, which might explain the lifelong relationship that existed between them throughout the vicissitudes of fortune reflected in the Thonburi Kingdom's many wars.

Unlike Rama I, who traced his ancestry to Kosa Pan—King Narai's ambassador to the court of King Louis XIV—King Taksin's lineage was entirely undistinguished. Not only was his upbringing rough and unrefined, King Taksin is believed to have been acculturated in a Chinese cultural milieu, setting him apart from other Siamese rulers. According to the Bunnag family, he sported a queue when he was a boy. His fluent command of several Chinese dialects may be traced back to his childhood spent among local traders. Even after he became king, his family life reflected his Chinese upbringing, including keeping his Chinese family lineage name, Tae (Zheng).[7] Upon his death, members of his family kept the Chinese tradition of sending his garments back to China to be buried in his tomb at the Tae ancestral village of Hua-fu in Chenghai County, Shantou.

Sin did not owe his success to influential or generous parents. In fact, his father may have died when he was very young. Consequently, Sin's mother must have been instrumental in his mastery of the Thai language and acquisition of Buddhist learning. Beyond that, Sin was entirely a self-made man. Growing up among the traders of Klong Suan Plu, he was naturally inducted into the inland trade. Sin's formative years were spent working the tortuous trade routes crisscrossing the Chao Phraya Basin. Long years spent trudging up and down rivers, jungles and mountain passes must have contributed to his uncanny firsthand knowledge of terrain, which subsequently served him well in military campaigns.

Another aspect of military skill, besides knowledge of terrain, is battle experience. Because trade caravans were prey to bandits, they often doubled as private armies. Depending on the exigencies of the situation, the caravan trader could serve as a merchant or a soldier. Constant exposure to skirmishes with bandits since an early age probably conditioned Sin into becoming the astute, battle-hardened general feared by Burmese, Khmer, Vietnamese and Siamese foes alike.

Sin's Chinese background, connections and experience in working the upcountry trading networks as a caravan master helped him develop the perception that the large Chinese presence in Siam could be a potential bulwark against Burmese invasion. Thus, when he made the fateful decision to abandon the sinking ship of Ayudhya during the final days of the Burmese invasion, it was to the Teochew diaspora on Siam's eastern seaboard that he headed.

Besides exposure to foreign influence, Sin's commercial activities also led him to engage various ethnic enclaves along the overland transshipment routes linking the Bay of Bengal to the South China Sea. His remarkable polyglot skill of speaking Hokkien, Teochew, Thai, Lao, Vietnamese, Khmer and probably Burmese was yet another collateral benefit from his caravan experience.

During his time as a caravan master, Sin traded in forest products with Tak, a large market town on the Ping River where products from Burma and Lanna were brought to exchange for goods from Ayudhya. The governor of Tak became his patron and Taksin operated gambling dens for the *phraya* of Tak. When the *phraya* of Tak died, Taksin reportedly bought his way into the position and succeeded his late patron as *phraya* of Tak—hence the name Taksin, by which he became known to posterity.[8]

The *Aphinihan Banphabhurut* offers a different version of King Taksin's childhood. It claims that Sin's father, Yong, actually became quite successful in his new adopted land, going by the formal title of *khun phat*.[9] He had a son by a Siamese woman named Nok-iang, whom King Taksin later honoured with the title Somdet Krom Phra Phitak-Thepamat. According to a popular legend, when Sin was three days old he was found with a python coiled around his cot. Although the snake did not harm the baby, Yong read it as a bad omen and wanted to ostracize the child. However, Nok-iang vehemently rejected her husband's interpretation of the incident. The family quarrel reached the ears of Chaophraya Chakri, who

The center of worship for the Ayudhyan Chinese was Sam Poh Kong Temple, called Wat Pananchoeng in Thai. The temple was built in 1324. Behind the temple compound was the Klong Suan Plu Chinese community.

decided to help resolve the issue by adopting the boy.[10]

Thus, contrary to the view that Sin grew up among the socially disadvantaged community outside the walled city, the conventional version holds that through his adoption by Chaophraya Chakri, he was inducted into the ranks of Ayudhya's noble *khunnang* class almost since the day that he was born. A further embellishment of the story added that upon adopting the Chinese baby, Chaophraya Chakri suddenly found better financial success, so he named the baby Sin, meaning "wealth" in Thai.

According to this version of Taksin's origin story, when Sin came of age, he was ordained, studying and learning Buddhist texts for three years at Wat Kosawas (now Wat Choeng Tha), by the Lopburi River in the northwest section of the city of Ayudhya. Upon reaching adulthood he filled a series of posts at court. After King Ekathat (the son of King Borommakot) ascended the throne, Sin was sent on an inspection tour of the northern provinces. When he returned from the trip, Sin was appointed Luang Yokrabat of Tak and later, when the governor of Tak passed away, he was appointed the *phraya* of Tak. Thus, two diametrically opposed narratives of King Taksin's childhood both, in the end, converge at Tak.

The Alaungpaya Campaign

The year 1760, when Taksin became deputy governor of Tak, coincided with the beginning of the Burmese wars that led to the sack of Ayudhya seven years later. The Burmese campaign opened in early 1760 with the invasion of Tenasserim,[11] traditionally an outpost of Ayudhya and part of the Siamese empire's defense system. At the best of times, due to its remoteness from the center of the kingdom, Tenasserim's allegiance to Ayudhya tended to be fitful and compromised by attachment to Burma, with whom it shares a common border.

Since the 15th century, the Ayudhyan court had exercised direct control of inner core towns by sending nobles from the capital to govern. Encircling the inner towns was another tier of outer towns controlled by their own ruling families with strong allegiances to the court of Ayudhya. These included old northern cities, such as Sukhothai and Phitsanulok; port towns around the Gulf of Siam, such as Chantabun and Nakhon Si Thammarat; outposts along the porterage routes across the Andaman coast, such as Mergui[12] and Tavoy; as well as border posts commanding the approach to the east—Khorat, and west—Kanchanaburi.[13] Thus, a Burmese invading army would have to breach several tiers of Siamese defenses of increasing levels of difficulty before it could arrive within striking distance of the capital city of Ayudhya. In spite of its many faults and with the exception of the Burmese invasion of 1569, this basic strategic defense system managed to protect Ayudhya's political integrity and sovereignty for over 400 years.

However, by 1760 the Siamese defense system was not working very well. After 150 years of relative external peace Ayudhya had lost its martial élan and found few occasions to exercise the defense system, which had rusted from disuse. When King Alaungpaya of Burma, the founder of the Konbaung dynasty, invaded Tenasserim, the latter capitulated without resistance. Meanwhile, no reinforcements were sent to support the outer layers of the defence system, or to intercept and stop the Burmese from advancing deeper into the Siamese heartland.

Consequently, the outposts of Tavoy and Mergui also capitulated and fell like dominoes. Encouraged by the total lack of resistance, Alaungpaya crossed the peninsula from the south to advance on Kuiburi, Petchaburi and Ratchaburi—the inner towns that comprised the second line of defense. The collapse of both the outer and inner towns gave the Burmese invaders such momentum that they were able to rapidly enter the heartland and begin a siege of the capital by April 1760.[14] The Siamese forces, which had retreated into the walled city, were severely embattled and the royal palace was damaged by gunfire. Ayudhya would have fallen but for an accident that the Siamese could only attribute to celestial intervention.

As King Alaungpaya oversaw the artillery barrage on the enemy fortifications, the cannon positioned next to him exploded, fatally wounding him.[15] The siege stopped as the Burmese priority switched from taking Ayudhya to saving the life of their king. The Burmese army retreated hastily to take the wounded king to safety. King Alaungpaya died along the march back to Burma in 1760.[16]

Since there were no records kept, it is not certain whether Taksin was involved in any military action during the Alaungpaya campaign. However, given his temperament and martial inclinations, Taksin must have avidly followed the progress of Alaungpaya's spectacular military campaign through reports and eyewitness accounts. The question of why the great Siamese empire had succumbed so easily to King Alaungpaya's attack must have caused Taksin to rethink everything he had learned about warfare. Also, not participating in the war may have bought him time to ponder deeply the near fall of Ayudhya.

Causes of Military Weakness

What factors had brought on Ayudhya's stunning military defeat? Perhaps the most important lesson to be drawn from the spectacular success of the Alaungpaya campaign was the importance of military leadership. The Burmese had plenty; the Siamese demonstrated none. A magnetic personality and a brave warrior, Alaungpaya provided initiative and personally led his troops to engage the Siamese in battle. At each critical milestone along the invasion to Ayudhya, Alaungpaya demonstrated decisiveness.

Meanwhile, Ayudhya had responded with inaction. The leadership did not act quickly to send reinforcements to beleaguered outposts and utterly failed to decide where to make a stand against the advancing Burmese army. Consequently, Ayudhya lost control of the momentum of the war to the Burmese, who were able to use that momentum to their advantage, right up to the gates of the capital. Reminiscent of Alaungpaya, Taksin would later build up an efficient, fast-moving, hard-hitting army and personally lead thousands of men into battle.

In addition to this failure of generalship, Ayudhya had also failed to protect and militarily support its tributary states on the outer rim of the defense perimeter. Meanwhile, King Alaungpaya had done the opposite. After defeating the Mon Rebellion and restoring the Kingdom of Ava, Alaungpaya quickly recaptured the south and conquered Pegu in 1757. Having reunited the Irrawaddy Basin under Burmese rule, he wasted no time in establishing a ring of vassal states all around Burma proper, including the Shan states, Chiang Mai, and other northern Tai and Lao principalities. Once he had secured Burma's perimeter, Alaungpaya energetically swung his attention to the outermost tier of satellite principalities that traditionally fell under Ayudhya's sphere of influence—Mergui and Tavoy.

By failing to deny the Burmese control over Siam's satellite principalities and allowing them to circle the Central Plain, Ayudhya opened up the possibility for Alaungpaya to broaden the military front to his advantage. Having to defend an extended battlefront caused Siamese forces to be thinly distributed. When King Taksin later established the Kingdom of Thonburi, his military campaigns to secure the allegiance of former Ayudhyan tributary states and deny the Burmese control suggests that he had drawn valuable lessons from Alaungpaya's encirclement strategy.

Although apt strategy is important, it is not enough. Admittedly, securing the allegiance of satellite principalities surrounding the Siamese heartland would have made it more difficult for Alaungpaya to defeat Ayudhya. However, the fact remains that the Siamese military was no match for the Burmese. The Burmese had invented a new form of warfare more deadly than the traditional form adhered to by the Siamese.

During the reign of King Borommakot (1733–58), Ayudhya enjoyed a long period of peace. As a result, the Siamese military had not fought a war in over a generation. During peacetime there was no professional standing army; in times of war *phrai-luang* were mobilized and used as soldiers, together with foreign mercenaries. In addition to guard duty during peacetime, *phrai-luang* also cared for the large numbers of elephants, which formed an integral part of the traditional mode of warfare.[17]

The traditional Siamese concept of warfare—akin to the warfare conducted in other Southeast Asian theaters—was relatively non-violent in nature. The objective was not to annihilate the enemy's military force but to make a show of force to intimidate the opposing army. If the show of force were judged to be sufficiently impressive, the enemy would normally acknowledge defeat or withdraw from the field.

This conception of warfare essentially relied on the latent force of population. State power in Southeast Asia was measured by the size of the population under its control rather than on the Western notion of borders. Wars were often reduced to body-snatching affairs in which one state would raid another to steal villages and communities wholesale and relocate them within the attacker's domain. According to the pecking order, states with larger populations were regarded as stronger than states with smaller populations.

Consonant with this traditional world view, wars involved making a show of

A 19th-century copy of a 17th-century Thai manuscript depicting a military parade.

force with a massive body of men, accompanied by large elephants, drums and an impressive array of guns and cannons. If one vassal *muang* became disloyal, the king would summon a massive army with additional troops supplied by other vassals to march upon the *muang* and subdue it. However, the order of the day was not to attack but to barricade the army behind bamboo fences within sight of the enemy. Both parties would then continuously spy on each other regarding the strength and condition of their troops. Occasionally, one side would send a raiding party to create a skirmish to either test the resolve of the enemy or press an advantage.

Speed was not considered an asset; mass was considered more important. Thus, the Siamese army moved slowly. It was impossible to move quickly with heavily laden elephants and heavy artillery. Rather, the slow, coordinated rolling of the body of troops was part of the concept of battle intended to force the enemy to give in or to withdraw and avoid fighting. The loud sound of drums and cannons, the spectacular parade of decorated elephants and the stunning sight of colorful troops pressing forward with pennants held aloft were used at the right moment to unnerve the enemy.[18] Thus, the traditional Siamese system of warfare seldom involved a direct, large-scale attack. Even though cannons were used, they were not intended to blow up enemy troops as in a Western theater of war. Neither did Siamese troops shoot to kill. Instead, they tended to shoot away from the enemy to impress upon them the enormous firepower that could be brought to bear if necessary.[19]

The Burmese answer to the Siamese dance of numbers—with its brightly clad troops and elephants bearing glistening weapons rolling in slow, thunderous rhythm—was the lightning frontal attack in which troops rushed enemy lines, killing indiscriminately to gain victory. Alaungpaya showed utter disregard for the conventions of warfare that the Siamese respected. While the Siamese battle formation was passive, intended more for sparing troop lives through avoidance of battle, the Burmese relied on an attacking strategy to engage and kill enemy forces with fast-moving units. Instead of mass, the Burmese emphasized speed, mobility and surprise, marching long distances very quickly to appear suddenly before the enemy was ready to engage.

While the Burmese military had been honed to perfection by constant warfare with the Mons since the 1740s, the Siamese army went unused and unexercised. In 1760 Siamese commanders lacked the effective leadership and the measure of control over troops required to withstand the aggressive Burmese battle tactic of all-out attack. The Siamese found themselves forced to retreat behind the city walls of Ayudhya.[20] Later, during the military campaigns of the Thonburi Kingdom against the Burmese, Taksin was to use these very innovations introduced to mainland Southeast Asia by the Burmese, much in the same way that the Roman general Scipio used the military methods of Hannibal to defeat the master himself at his own game during the Punic Wars.

To make matters worse, military incompetence was compounded by political folly. While King Alaungpaya was at the height of his power, disunity over the question of succession prevailed at the court of Ayudhya. Saddled with unimpressive sons, King Borommakot hesitated to indicate his preference of heir until the end of his reign. On his deathbed the king selected Prince Utumphon to succeed him, and the prince was duly crowned in 1758.

However, immediately after Borommakot's death, another dispute arose. King Utumphon's elder brother, Prince Ekathat, challenged the succession. A deadly confrontation that would have led to one party annihilating the other was avoided by a surprising compromise reached between the siblings. Utumphon voluntarily ceded the throne to Ekathat and retired from the palace to become a Buddhist monk. Ekathat then succeeded him as the new king.

However, one appointment coming almost immediately after the other created serious consequences for the court. Ekathat's usurpation of the throne could not have come at a more dangerous juncture, for unrest and succession troubles in Ayudhya encouraged Alaungpaya to invade in 1760. Posterity has come to blame Siam's near-defeat on Ekathat's ambitious disregard for the country's political unity. It certainly prevented Ayudhya from responding effectively to Burmese military pressure on Ayudhyan vassal states and to the subsequent invasion of the Siamese heartland.

Besides disunity and princely rivalries at court, there was evidence of other, more deep-seated causes of military weakness. Out of his experience as *uparat* and contender for the throne, Borommakot had drawn lessons from the dangerous situation he faced in 1733. These lessons were embodied in a number of changes he made in the political arrangements of the state.

One of the first steps Borommakot took upon becoming king was to purge the Phraklang ministry and install his trusted right-hand man, Phraya Chamnan-Borirak, as Phraklang.[21] King Borommakot's next step was to reward Phraya Ratchasongkhram, the Kalahom who had remained neutral in the struggle for succession. While Ratchasongkhram's neutrality had to at least be grudgingly rewarded, Borommakot also did not want him to become too strong. The state administrative machinery derived its influence from the control of manpower. Therefore, the heads of key ministries were potentially very powerful because they had ready access to large numbers of armed men, particularly the Mahatthai and Kalahom.[22] Thus, Borommakot readjusted the relative power of the three most powerful ministries by changing the system of provincial control. The vital manpower of the southern provinces was shifted from the control of the Kalahom to the Phraklang ministry, which was already safely under the control of the trusted Phraya Chamnan-Borirak. The diminished Kalahom ministry also reflected how defense against external invasion was a low priority when compared to economic production for the Royal Trading Monopoly.

After reorganizing the key ministries, King Borommakot turned to the next level of state power embodied in the princely departments, or *krom*. During the Prasartthong dynasty the Kalahom was the single most powerful ministry in the state of Ayudhya. After usurping the throne, King Petracha established independent *krom* to countervail the power of the Kalahom. The *krom* sought to give a few royal princes in the line of succession their own access to manpower outside the central administration. Borommakot varied this practice even further. Whereas there were only about three *krom*—each with control over several thousand men—during the reign of King Thaisa, Borommakot created 13 smaller *krom* so that no single prince could seize the throne by himself, while several princes together could counterbalance the key ministries and their associated bodies under the control of *khunnang*.[23] However, the creation of these smaller princely *krom* backfired as the princes squabbled among themselves; infighting increased rather than decreased. Moreover, it further fragmented state control over limited and dispersed manpower, leading to disastrous results during the Burmese invasion.[24]

Peace and prosperity during the late Ayudhya period inspired the emergence of great households that managed to accumulate manpower and wealth across generations. Among the great households were old *khunnang* families, as well as new elites who originated from Brahmans, refugee Mon generals, Persians and Chinese merchants.[25] The latter in particular comprised a new social formation based on commerce and wealth as opposed to ascriptive status. As demographic growth led to the absorption of more Chinese into the lower levels of the Siamese elite and displaced older members of the court, the whole *phrai* system of hereditary obligations became destabilized.

In Ayudhya, state power was derived from the operation of the *phrai* system through control of corvée labor. Corvée labor comprised two forms: *phrai-luang* (royal retainers) and *phrai-som* (private retainers). Royal power depended on a ready supply of *phrai-luang* for royal service, public works and military conscription to fight Ayudhya's wars. *Phrai-som*, on the other hand, rendered labor service to lords, *khunnang* and wealthy landowners.

Under the traditional system, *phrai-luang* were required to render service to the king for six months of the year. This six-month service underpinned the Ayudhyan military system until the reign of King Thaisa. During the relative peace and prosperity of the Thaisa era, the king reduced *phrai-luang* service from the traditional six months to only four months of the year.[26] This had the effect of shrinking the state's command over potential manpower by 30 percent.

However, the proper functioning of the state required a stable balance between *phrai-luang* and *phrai-som*. Underlying King Borommakot's reforms was the need to balance kingly and princely power against the power of the nobles and central administration through the proper allocation of *phrai-luang* and *phrai-som*. Borommakot apparently considered it judicious to extend the new shortened term of *phrai-luang* service introduced by Thaisa because it was welcomed by the people, akin to a tax break. Structural tensions between royal and private work routines and between loyalty to the king and to factional leaders tended to make the system unstable. By eroding ascriptive status, prosperity and the growing importance of money and commerce rendered the tensions within the *phrai* system more acute. First, wider money use and market activity led to more opportunities for ministerial or princely usury and peasant borrowing, which in turn increased the incidence of *phrai-luang* becoming debt slaves. Debt bondage coupled with the asymmetric distribution of obligations between *phrai-luang* and *phrai-som* encouraged a steady flow from royal to private service.[27]

Moreover, commercial opportunities induced officials, princes and local lords to accumulate lands and to recruit *phrai* labor for cash crop cultivation. Ministers, princes and governors often instigated transfers from *phrai-luang* to *phrai-som* to augment their supply of laborers. These transfers were further aggravated by princely and factional rivalries, which caused contending parties to raid *phrai-luang* manpower stocks for their private armies. Consequently, the Burmese invasion found that the Siamese state had exhausted its supply of royal retainers to fight the invaders.[28]

The Hsinbyushin Campaign

The causes of military weakness remained uncorrected when King Hsinbyushin, the second son of the late Alaungpaya, attacked Ayudhya again four years later. Burmese military encirclement of the Siamese heartland still prevailed as in Alaungpaya's time. In 1763, Hsinbyushin reconsolidated Burmese military control over the northern Shan states and Lanna. To the west and south, Hsinbyushin reasserted control over the peripheral states that had succumbed to Alaungpaya, including Tenasserim, Mergui and Tavoy. This enabled Hsinbyushin to improve upon Alaungpaya's strategy by launching a three-pronged attack on Ayudhya.

The North Army led by General Naymyo Thihapatei comprised the first prong of the Burmese invasion force. In addition to its core Burmese force, the North Army swelled with troop levees from Lanna, Lan Chang and the Shan states. In July 1765, the North Army advanced on Kampaengphet, Sukhothai, Phitsanulok, Phichai, Nakhon Sawan and Ang Thong.[29] The second prong of the attacking force was the South Army, commanded by General Mahanawratha. The South

Army set out from Tavoy in late September 1765 and advanced on Chumphon and Petchaburi. General Mahanawratha's army was joined by a third prong, comprising a smaller contingent that crossed into the Chao Phraya Basin from the west through the Three Pagoda Pass to take Ratchaburi and Suphanburi.[30] As a result the Siamese were outflanked, cut off from potential assistance from the north and forced to fight on multiple fronts simultaneously.[31]

After the invasion had started, King Ekathat sent a massive army of 60,000 men south to stop Mahanawratha's army.[32] The Burmese attacked so fiercely that the Siamese force[33] was routed, losing many men, elephants, food and supplies to the enemy. Meeting no further resistance, the South Army took stronghold after stronghold and lived off the land and local resources until the whole of western Siam fell into Burmese hands.

Similarly, General Naymyo Thihapatei's North Army was able to take all the towns and cities in its path without much resistance until they entered the Central Plain. At Bang Rachan, General Thihapatei's troops met with stubborn resistance from the local inhabitants, which stalled the North Army for a while. Again, no thanks to Ayudhya: when the local villagers requested assistance and guns to fight the Burmese, King Ekathat refused, fearing that the guns would fall into enemy hands.[34] Abandoned and outnumbered, Bang Rachan defenses were overrun and its inhabitants massacred, leaving the road wide open to Ayudhya. By February 1766, the two main prongs of the Burmese invading force had joined on the outskirts of Ayudhya.[35]

The Siege of Ayudhya

The Siamese attempted a desperate, last-ditch effort to push back the enemy. In February 1766 a force of 50,000 men, including Taksin's regiment under the command of Phraya Phraklang, marched out of the walled city to attack the Burmese position at Wat Pha Fai. General Mahanawratha's army was on the west side of the pagoda while Thihapatei's North Army was on the east. The Siamese launched a massive attack on the west wing of the Burmese battle line. The momentum of the Siamese push forced Mahanawratha's South Army to fall back. While the western front gave way to the Siamese assault, Thihapatei's army circled to outflank the Siamese thrust from the east and cut the Siamese army into two. The Siamese vanguard that attacked Mahanawratha found itself surrounded by a closing wall of Burmese troops and was routed. The ensuing battle decimated the Siamese ranks. The Siamese death toll mounted to several thousand, with thousands more wounded and captured. The remainder of the beleaguered Siamese forces hastily retreated to the safety of their stockades and the walled city.[36]

The city of Ayudhya made preparations for defense by strengthening

A map shows how the city of Ayudhaya was surrounded by the Chao Phraya, Pasak and Lopburi rivers, which served as moats for the city.

fortifications, reinforcing the ring of stockades around the perimeter of the city, broadening the moat and mounting numerous guns and cannons on top of the walls to prevent the enemy from assaulting the city wall. The embattled Siamese had one last trump card: the approach of the rainy season. It had more than once saved the city of Ayudhya from invasion in the past. The defenders believed that if they could just hold out until the onset of the monsoon rains and the flooding of the Great Central Plain, the Burmese would be forced to retreat.

Realizing they had less than four months to go before the onset of the rainy season, the Burmese launched a series of assaults on the walled city but failed to breach Siamese defenses. Advancing Burmese troops were repeatedly cut down by heavy musket and cannon fire from atop the stockades and high brick walls of the city. Rebuffed by Siamese defenses, the Burmese drew a line of entrenchment comprising three large camps interspersed by a ring of stockades around the Siamese positions and settled down for a siege of the city.

As the Burmese prepared to reduce the city by famine, the Siamese sent out skirmishing teams to breach various points of the Burmese blockade. But even the most intrepid forays were unable to break the enemy's stranglehold on the city. Running out of options, the Siamese sent out Phraya Kalahom to negotiate but the negotiation failed.[37] The face-off continued until the rainy season.

Soon the whole Central Plain was flooded. King Ekathat hoped as his predecessors had done that the onset of the floods would force the Burmese to retreat.[38] Initially, the rains played havoc on the Burmese siege arrangements as the line of entrenchments around the city was swallowed up in the rising floodwaters. The tight cordon of Burmese troops was broken up into several corps, clinging on to artificial islands in the flooded plain. But the Burmese commanders did not retreat. They fortified high ground and commandeered boats to keep their military forces in action.[39]

Seeing that their trump card, the rains, had failed to force the Burmese to retreat, the Siamese tried again to engage the enemy, this time with water-borne expeditions. As the floodwaters scattered the Burmese forces into isolated camps on high ground, the Siamese attacked them in boats. However, the Burmese had managed to commandeer plenty of boats and met the Siamese in kind. The siege of Ayudhya continued, denying the Siamese replacements of dwindling manpower and food supplies.

Glimpses of Taksin

Looking for Taksin's early years in the Siamese military is like peering through the smoke and mist of a darkened battlefield for a glimpse of him. The view is distant, often clouded and unclear. Still, the Siamese annals offer some distant sightings of Taksin in battle. From these brief glimpses, it is possible to conclude that shortly before King Hsinbyushin attacked Ayudhya, Taksin had been promoted to governor of Tak in 1764. He was 30 years old.[40]

Hot upon the heels of his appointment as *phraya* of Tak, the Burmese North Army invaded Ayudhya. Rather than face the invasion with only 500 men, Taksin led his men down to Ayudhya to join the defense of the capital.[41] Among the 500-odd men who followed him from Tak to Ayudhya were many Thais, Mons and Chinese. Many of them presumably played prominent roles later in the critical battles of the Kingdom of Thonburi. However, due to the dearth of historical records, their individual identities remain obscured.

Nevertheless, tales of subsequent events compel us to infer that among the faceless 500 men under Taksin, there must have been at least one important fighter who later distinguished himself in many subsequent battles. Legend has it that this man was "Thong Dee the White Teeth," a commoner. Members of the nobility preferred to have their teeth blackened by coconut ash. Thong Dee the White Teeth was reportedly a famous boxer during the time that Taksin was operating gambling dens in Tak. Thong Dee attracted Taksin's attention when he defeated two of Taksin's prize fighters.

A fan of brave fighters, Taksin took Thong Dee into his employ where he became famous as the boxing champion of Taksin's gambling establishment. Although Thong Dee was not identified in the sighting of the column of 500 men accompanying Taksin on his march to Ayudhya, his reappearance at subsequent landmark battles of the Thonburi period suggest that he must have been among Taksin's original followers from Tak.

The historical mist clouding the sightings of Taksin and his cohort of the best and bravest finally lifts after their encampment at Wat Phichai during the siege of Ayudhya. Until then, however, we have to be content with shadowy glimpses and poor sightings of Taksin and his activities through the lens of historical records. Taksin apparently spent the year 1765 as an officer of the Ayudhyan army. His regiment was listed among the 60,000 troops led by Phraya Phipatkosa in the campaign to stop Mahanawratha's South Army.[42] They were defeated and retreated back to Ratchaburi.

In early 1766, Taksin also reportedly distinguished himself in action in the battle at Wat Pah Fai. As Burmese soldiers hotly pursued the retreating Siamese troops, Taksin and his men fought an admirable rearguard action to delay the Burmese, allowing Siamese troops to cross the river to safety at Pho Sam Ton, himself and his men crossing only after the Siamese contingent had gotten across.[43] Taksin's bravery attracted the notice of his superiors. King Ekathat promoted him to be the *phraya* of Kamphaeng Phet,[44] an important town listed as *muang tho*, or second-tier town of Ayudhya.[45]

Some descriptions of embattled Siam are provided in foreign eyewitness accounts. Monsignor Brigot, a French missionary in Ayudhya, remarked in 1766, "the Siamese do not know how to fight; sending out a brigade is like sending out weapons to the Burmese."[46] Fighting on the losing side and seeing many good men wasted due to military incompetence, battle indecisiveness, soldiers' hesitation to press an advantage and fear of attacking the Burmese must have disgusted Taksin.

A warrior whose combat predilections were so much at variance from his Siamese peers and superiors was bound to get himself into trouble. On one occasion during the Burmese siege, an order was issued that no cannon could be fired before permission had been obtained from the palace. Taksin disobeyed and ordered a large cannon be fired at an inviting enemy target. Consequently, he faced a court-martial and was severely reprimanded for breach of discipline.[47] The cannon incident as well as his intrepid conduct in battle reflected the hallmarks of his fighting style: decisive, flexible, quick to adapt to changing conditions and always alert to press an advantage. However, the Siamese army would soon lose this unique figure from among their ranks. Sometime after the canon incident, Taksin deserted Ayudhya.

Taksin's desertion decision must have been

A mural depicts the Siamese being attacked by the Burmese (from the Thai History Pavilion at the Jeath War Museum, Kanchanaburi Province).

based on the growing realization that Ayudhya was incapable of withstanding a prolonged Burmese siege. Prince Damrong alleged that the insubordination incident had caused Taksin to think about abandoning Ayudhya.[48] But perhaps Taksin was too much of a strategist to allow such an incident to override rational considerations. Whatever his real motivations were, Taksin must have started to carefully weigh his odds and work out his options.

Hindsight suggests that Taksin's desertion was premeditated. It is preposterous to think that he simply ran out of Ayudhya. After all, his roadmap to power reflected a rational pattern of sequential moves. He must have estimated that the starving city probably could not last out the siege and thus he planned the most viable escape route for himself and his men. If Taksin had entertained the idea of escaping from Ayudhya, it made more sense for him to reposition his men outside the city wall where it would be easier for him to withdraw his followers without being challenged by Siamese guards.

Taksin's opportunity presented itself in late 1766, when Burmese forces laying siege to the city became discomfited by rising floodwaters. The onset of hunger due to dwindling food stocks inside the city fanned a desperate urge among the embattled Siamese to replenish their food supply. They decided to send out a fleet of boats to raid the Burmese supply boats in the flooded plain. Taksin used the opportunity to move his followers to Wat Yai stockade outside the city wall.

On the day of the raid, Taksin and two other Siamese commanders, including Luang Sorasaeni and the governor of Petchaburi, rowed out from the line of Siamese stockades to intercept Burmese military supply boats. The governor of Petchaburi led the attack and moved his troops to join battle with the Burmese. He quickly became outnumbered as Burmese reinforcements arrived from nearby stockades. Taksin and Sarasaeni held back and did not reinforce Phraya Petchaburi. The governor fell during the battle and his forces were defeated. After the death of Phraya Petchaburi, Taksin and Sarasaeni did not return to the city, but Taksin established a fortified outpost at Wat Phichai just outside the city wall.

Starvation Hangs over Ayudhya

The Siamese suffered considerable military attrition. Between 1765 and 1767 the Siamese lost many battles, tens of thousands of lives, wealth and resources. Besides loss of life, the war devastated the Siamese economy and ecology and transformed the Kingdom of Ayudhya from a food-surplus to a food-deficit country. The Burmese army laid waste in the wake of its invasion path. It plundered, pillaged and lived off the land, leaving behind a desolate, depopulated and devastated Central Plain. Starvation and famine was not a collateral damage—it was a Burmese military strategy intended to break Siamese political will and bring Ayudhya to its knees.

While Ayudhya succumbed to famine under the military siege, Burmese troops grew their own rice behind the front lines and used their war boats to block supplies from entering the city. By the end of the monsoon season, the Siamese population in the city was facing starvation. Repeated Siamese attempts to attack Burmese supply boats were not only intended to test Burmese military prowess on water but to raid Burmese supply lines for food. Thus, military attrition joined with starvation to sap the will of Siamese resistance.

Escape from Ayudhya

Interspersed around the city wall was a ring of Siamese camps and stockades.[49] The camps were mostly located on temple grounds, with wooden or bamboo fences built up for defense and brick buildings of *ubosot* and *vihara* used as shelters against gunfire. Other edifices standing close to the city wall were Christian churches, mosques and the vacant Dutch Factory. Foreign communities located outside the city wall took refuge inside their respective communal and religious buildings.

The Christians walled up their church compounds and the Muslims their mosques. A Chinese volunteer force set up stockades at Wat Chaiwattanaram, a grand temple not far from the Church of Saint Joseph, and the Chinese sought the king's permission to set up camp at the Dutch Factory, as the well-built brick building was eminently suited to barricading against enemy attacks. The Chinese camp at the Dutch Factory was known in Thai and Chinese sources as the Suan Plu Chinese stockade under the command of Luang Aphai-Phipat. A third Chinese camp was located nearby on high ground at Wat Khok, located inside today's Wat Pananchoeng compound, not far from the Dutch Factory. A French missionary in Ayudhya, Monsignor Brigot, estimated that there were about 6,000 Chinese manning the last two stockades.[50] As the camp stood in the vicinity of the large Hokkien and Teochew settlements at Nai Kai Market and Klong Suan Plu, there must have been many Hokkien and Teochew fighters defending the Dutch Factory.

To help the foreign volunteers, King Ekathat distributed cannons, guns and ammunition to the camps outside the city. Apart from firearms the court gave 5,000 francs to the Christians and 20,000 francs to the Chinese to be used for food, supplies, erecting wooden barricades, and purchasing weapons and necessities.[51] Arms and food supply varied from camp to camp depending on the leaders of each respective fortified outpost.

After the defeat of the Siamese flotilla following the death of the governor of Petchaburi, Taksin and his men retreated to set up a fortified post at Wat Phichai,

Chao Mae Soi Dok Mak is the most celebrated Chinese deity in Ayudhya. Legend has it that she was a Chinese princess. The Chinese stockade at Wat Khok was located near this shrine.

nearly two kilometers upriver from the Dutch Factory. There he waited out the Burmese siege while he carefully planned his escape route.

From the time of Wat Phichai onward, historical records begin to offer a clearer view of Taksin and his cohort. The historical mask hiding the individual identities among Taksin's entourage begins to lift. Thonburi chronicles compiled after Taksin became king assert the presence of Phra Chiang-Ngen,[52] Luang Phrom-Sena, Luang Phichai,[53] Luang Phiphit,[54] Luang Rachasena, Khun Aphai-Phakdi and Mhun Racha-Seneha at Wat Phichai. Many of these men played prominent roles in subsequent events, fought side by side with Taksin in famous battles, distinguished themselves by valourous deeds and attained high office in the Thonburi Kingdom.

At Wat Phichai one can imagine Taksin holding frequent war councils with his key commanders, squatting on the sandy ground surrounding the temple, drawing a map of the larger military theater around Ayudhya in the sand and planning out his escape route through Burmese lines. The questions that must have crossed his mind are not difficult to guess. Should they leave Ayudhya or stay? Suppose they left, where would they go? What were the chances of cutting their way out of the Burmese military cordon? What would be the best escape route? If they succeeded in getting through Burmese lines, where could they get food? These were the same questions that anyone in his place would have to address.

Over the past months, the population of Ayudhya had dwindled substantially despite government efforts to stem the flow of desertions. In fact, the outflow of refugees from Ayudhya had already been in evidence since June 1765 when French missionaries and students began departing by boat for Chantabun.[55] The Dutch also began evacuating their company officials in late 1765. Many *phrai* and soldiers deserted and fled into the forest or left for upcountry destinations where they had relatives.

What were the situational imperatives that framed the dialogue of ends and means between Taksin and his followers? The most immediate and pressing problem they faced was hunger. If they left, they needed to go where there was food. The Central Plain had already been depopulated and destroyed by the Burmese military's scorched-earth policy. There was also no food in the south. General Mahanawratha's army had taken care of that. Outside Siam there was food in Cambodia and Vietnam. But that would be a long journey. Moreover, Taksin's small band was not in a position to take on the Cambodians or the Vietnamese.

Aside from Cambodia or Vietnam, another place where there was food was in the southeastern coastal region. The abundant rice fields to the east were still untouched by the Burmese war. Also, many of Taksin's followers were Teochew Chinese who had friends, relatives and contacts in the Teochew diaspora on Siam's eastern seaboard. If they went east, they could find food and get help from their Teochew brethren. Taksin himself was a Teochew *lukchin*. He spoke their language. He knew the terrain and the way there.

His ultimate destination of Chantabun was a port city. As a former trader, Taksin appreciated the importance of securing a wealthy port city. Ports also had ships, which could be converted into a military asset. Moreover, a port represents a window to obtain supplies and weapons independently of the domestic economy. To build his army, Taksin needed food, manpower, money, ships, weapons and supplies for his logistical pipeline to support his military in the field. Chantabun offered what he needed many times over. Taksin decided to head for Chantabun. Meanwhile, he waited for an opportune moment to break out of Wat Phichai.

Taksin's moment came in January 1767 when a fire broke out inside the walled city,[56] raging through the night and burning down 10,000 homes. Taksin chose that moment of confusion and commotion to evade the Siamese watch as well as the Burmese patrols, leading his men across no-man's-land and slipping through the enemy lines. Taksin and his followers were now outcasts, pursued by the Burmese and liable to be attacked by the Siamese as well. They headed east towards the coast. Their destination was the rice granaries in the southeast.

The Fall of Ayudhya

When the floodwaters receded, the Burmese reconstructed entrenchments and earthworks around the walled city and gained more complete command over the battle terrain than before. Some of the earthworks were even higher than the city wall, such that the Burmese could mount canons to shoot down on the city and the palace. After mid-November the Burmese were ready to intensify their siege operations and prepared to attack Siamese positions outside the city wall.[57] The Chinese camp at Wat Chaiwattanaram, near the Church of Saint Joseph, was overrun on 13 November 1766.[58]

Chinese documents state, "During this time the prices of daily necessities went on rising and those who starved to death were countless."[59] The situation was no better in the stockades outside the city wall. Four hundred Chinese from the Suan Plu stockade at the Dutch Factory looted the Footprint of the Holy Buddha in Saraburi, removing all the silver floor lining and other gold artifacts presumably to exchange for food. Furious at the sacrilege perpetrated by the Chinese militia, King Ekathat denounced them to their leader, Luang Aphai-Pipat, and retrieved part of the loot.

On 30 March, King Ekathat again offered to surrender and become a vassal of

Burma but the latter would agree to nothing less than unconditional surrender.[60] Somewhere along the line King Hsinbyushin appeared to have shifted his position on Ayudhya. Initially, Burma sought to compete with Ayudhya for control over the neck of the Malay Peninsula. However, as Burmese prospects of victory improved, King Hsinbyushin began to entertain grandiose ambitions of spreading Burmese power eastwards by eliminating Ayudhya as a rival economic and power center on the mainland.[61] Thus, his aim was no longer to force Ayudhya into a tributary status but to obliterate it once and for all by razing the once-glorious city to the ground. The stakes had changed.

In March the Burmese moved to attack all Siamese positions outside the city wall, including stockades, temples, churches and fortified outposts. They destroyed them one by one. On 17 February the Chinese camp at Wat Khok was overrun and more than a thousand Chinese defenders were killed.[62] By 7 March 1767, the outer wall of the Church of Saint Joseph was compromised. Also in March the Chinese camp near the Portuguese settlement was seized and many of its defenders killed.

Meanwhile, the Suan Plu Chinese stockade at the Dutch Factory continued to hold out despite heavy bombardment and repeated assaults by Burmese troops. Around 3,000 enemy soldiers were killed by the Chinese.[63] According to Mgr. Brigot, who was in Ayudhya, the Suan Plu stockade fell after a Burmese spy infiltrated the camp and shot the leader Hien Su in the head, following which Chinese resistance crumbled.[64] On 26 March the invaders overran the camp, burned down the Dutch Factory and killed the Chinese defenders. The year 1767 was "the Alamo" of the Ayudhyan Chinese. The fact that almost no remaining Thai-Chinese families can trace their ancestry back to the Ayudhyan Chinese community testifies to the scale of the Chinese massacre that took place during the last days of Ayudhya.

Ayudhya-period *naga* guarding the entrance to the Buddha Footprint at Wat Phrabutthabat in Saraburi, a popular pilgrimage destination during King Borommakot's reign.

Following the takeover of Chinese strongholds, the intervening ring of stockades, temples and fortified posts that had denied the invaders access to the city wall now became a liability to the Siamese. The Burmese now commandeered a ring of earthworks, stockades and fortified posts that allowed them to shoot upon the walled city.

Finally, on 7 April 1767, the Burmese military breached the walls and captured the city. Ayudhya had fallen, and the impact was calamitous. Numerous Siamese lives were lost in the battle for the city and the ensuing mayhem. Corpses floated in the rivers and canals, and the water of the Chao Phraya River remained undrinkable for weeks. King Ekathat fled for his life in a small boat and starved to death 10 days later.[65] Prince Utumphon, members of the royal family and the *khunnang*—including the *phraya* of the Phraklang ministry—were led away to captivity in Burma.[66] Ayudhya's political, administrative, legal, social, religious and cultural institutions had lost an entire generation of leaders.

What happened was tantamount to a social revolution effected through external invasion instead of internal class struggle. The end result was the same: the decapitation of the Ayudhyan administrative structure through the wholesale removal of its ruling class. The fall of Ayudhya lifted the political barrier that had prevented commoners from rising to elevated positions in Siamese society; this would later be embodied in the rise of Taksin and his Thonburi elite.

In addition to the death toll and social dislocation brought upon the country, the Burmese went out of their way to loot and destroy everything they could lay their hands on to permanently erase Ayudhya as a potential competing polity on the Southeast Asian peninsula. Ayudhya's temples and religious artifacts were desecrated. Gold and cultural treasures including gilded Buddha images were melted down and hauled away to Burma. The finest porcelain and jewelry in the palace were stolen, broken or lost. After this, the city was put to the torch and left in a heap of ruins. Consequently, the country's physical, ideological and intellectual resources—including the accumulated written records embodying an entire civilization of the Central Plain—were lost to posterity. Thus, 1767 was not only the year Ayudhya was militarily defeated; it was the year when Siamese civilization was—metaphorically speaking—cast back to the Stone Age.[67]

The Man of the Hour

Upon escaping the encirclement of Wat Phichai, Taksin split his cohort into small brigades to make it easier to elude Burmese patrols and subsequently rendezvous behind enemy lines. Taksin led the main brigade. Those who marched with Taksin were Thong Dee and Luang Racha, among others. The other brigades were led by Phra Chiang-Ngen, Luang Phrom-Sena, Luang Phichai, Luang Racha-Seneha and Khun Aphai-Pakdi.[68]

Phra Chiang-Ngen, who had been with Taksin from the very beginning, was effectively second-in-command, enjoying a senior rank in the cohort's pecking order. Among the prominent personalities in Chiang-Ngen's brigade were Luang Phiphit and Nak Ong-Ram, a Cambodian royal who had sought asylum in Ayudhya.

Outside the safety of Siamese stockades, Burmese patrols kept watch around every corner, and Taksin's brigade soon ran into a Burmese unit. In the ensuing skirmish the Burmese force was routed and Taksin's men captured large quantities of enemy weapons. Once alerted, the enemy sent 2,000 Burmese reinforcements in pursuit. Taksin gave battle and demonstrated his flair for tactical formation. He arranged his forces into three columns. Taksin commanded the central column and charged the advancing Burmese army with four horsemen. Meanwhile, he organized his main force into two large columns on his left and his right. While he led a frontal attack, his left wing and right wing made a flanking movement and effected a pincer attack on the main body of the Burmese army.[69]

The Burmese met Taksin's cavalry charge with 30 horsemen but Taksin's skillful charge overpowered them. The Burmese cavalry was routed and tried to retreat to the main body only to find that Taksin's pincer attack had smashed their battle order and caused mayhem among the Burmese forces. Taksin's victorious troops chanted over the cries of the fleeing enemy soldiers, "Our master possesses great merit, our master will become king. He will regain and re-establish the realm."[70]

Taksin had emerged as a hero, someone who could lead the army against the Burmese and win. This situation had upped the stakes and would prove to hold massive meaning for Taksin and the future of Siam. When Taksin and his men had left Wat Phichai, their objective was to find food and survive. The goal now was no longer survival: he and his men had their sights on the throne. His followers vowed to support his bid for kingship.

Building an Army

Taksin's stunning victories over the invincible Burmese had marked him as an extraordinary leader. The decisions he made and the commands he issued, as well as his intuition for combat, distinguished him among the best and the bravest of his peers. He won the hearts of his soldiers by showing that he could live as they did and share all the dangers and hardships they faced. Often, the commanders whom soldiers admire are not so much those who distribute honors and riches as those who help shoulder their burdens.

Taksin's commanding personality and military genius was spreading his reputation as the only man of transcendental merit who could defeat the Burmese. Taksin realized that fortune was presenting him with the perfect arena in which to exhibit his ability: a great military theater. If he could drive out the Burmese, he would demonstrate his transcendental mission and his success would bring the throne within his grasp. To realize his destiny he needed an effective army—a fighting machine that was better than King Hsinbyushin's—and he was well on his way.

Taksin's army was growing. His victories over Burmese forces encouraged men from villages and towns that had been plundered and depopulated by the Burmese invasion to join his cohort. The day after Taksin defeated the Burmese cavalry-led brigade, the master of the elephant brigade of Nakhon Nayok came to present six elephants to Taksin and asked to join his army.[71] According to the royal chronicles, "All the Thai and Chinese who were masters of secret societies and master of the sects in the villages and in the forest ... led their followers in great numbers to submit to Him as His servants."[72] As *phraya* of Kampaengpetch, Taksin rewarded them with noble titles of *mhun*, *khun*, *luang* and *phra* as befitting the number of men each had brought with him.

In addition to separating official ranks and titles from class background, Taksin also simplified the criteria for military enrollment, basing acceptance on strength, bravery and fighting skills. Contrary to law and custom, he enrolled in his army poor men with no property or status—men who had been disqualified from bearing arms.[73] Under the old, aristocratic order, the right to bear arms was the exclusive prerogative of the landed class based on the assumption that ownership of property or status guaranteed a man's loyalty to the state. Taksin revolutionized the military by throwing open the doors of the army to all who were willing and able to fight; brave *phrai* were promoted, given titles and ennobled.

The statue of King Taksin in Bangkok cast in 1953 by the Phibun Songkram government.

However, with the new privileges and opportunities also came increased obligations. Whereas Thaisa and Borommakot had reduced *phrai-luang* service from six months to four months of the year, Taksin now made it compulsory for *phrai-luang* to render service to the state throughout the year.[74] Typically, his policy made full use of the carrot and the stick. The lure of symbolic honors, rank, status and ennoblement was combined with the threat of dreadful punitive measures for those who failed to comply. Taksin tightened discipline and restored the old Ayudhyan practice of tattooing *phrai* to prevent desertions of *phrai-luang* into other occupations.

In Taksin's army, military rank was based on merit and not on social status or connection. The result of Taksin's military innovation was reflected in his being able to field a more effective and deadly fighting force than his rivals who continued to rely on the traditional Ayudhyan military system.

As Taksin passed villages and towns on his march he would request food, supplies and men. Many volunteered to join Taksin's army because they would be fed; otherwise they would have to scavenge for food in the forests. Villages that refused to provide men, food or supplies would be attacked, plundered and looted.

Taksin's practice with these villages was to make an offer that could not be refused. The bailiff of Baan Bang Dong, a large fortified village in Nakorn Nayok, refused to join Taksin. After three failed rounds of negotiations, Taksin's troops took the village by storm, scaling the walls of the stockade and cutting down the defenders who ran away, panic stricken, leaving behind elephants, silver, gold, weapons and large quantities of food. As Taksin continued his march behind enemy lines, his army became bigger, stronger and better armed.

In all these ways Taksin was the soldiers' general—a stern disciplinarian who demanded no less from himself than from his men. They feared him more than they feared the enemy. But they trusted him and were willing to put their lives in his hands, following him into the jaws of battle. One of the earliest demonstrations of his uncompromising discipline occurred in Prachinburi.

During the march, the brigade of Phra Chiang-Ngen lagged behind.[75] Taksin rode back to look for the brigade, and failing to find them, he halted the main brigade and ordered the men to set up camp to wait. Chiang-Ngen arrived three days late, accompanied by Khun Phiphit (Watee) and Nak Ong-Ram, the Cambodian prince.[76] Taksin was furious and caned Chiang-Ngen, his second-in-command, 30 strokes for being late. Taksin charged Chiang-Ngen of endangering the army and being dilatory, and ordered that he be beheaded. Only after his commanders pleaded in concert for sparing Chiang-Ngen's life did Taksin relent.[77] Stern discipline and harsh punishment were the hallmarks of Taksin's inimitable leadership style, which initially inspired awe and fear among his followers but eventually brought about his downfall 15 years later.

In Prachinburi, his cohort ran into the Burmese eastern regiment. Exploiting his knowledge of the terrain, Taksin set up an ambush with barricades and concealed entrenchments arranged in tiers and mounted with hidden guns. He positioned his main force to wait for the Burmese to walk into their trap. Taksin led 100 men on horseback to meet and lure the large Burmese army into the ambush. Once in range, Taksin's men from the trenches flanking the Burmese column opened fire with volleys of large and small guns, felling Burmese troops in large numbers.[78] When the Burmese reinforced and attacked again, Taksin discharged additional rounds from hidden, tiered guns, killing many enemy troops until the diminished Burmese regiment turned and fled. Taksin soon became the focal point of the growing resistance against the Burmese invaders on the eastern front.

After the failure of the third attempt, the Burmese, now preoccupied with preparations for the final assault on Ayudhya, sent no further troops in pursuit of Taksin. The road to the east lay wide open. Taksin arrived safely at Bangplasoi, a port in the Teochew diaspora at present-day Chonburi. There he obtained help, food and supplies.

From Bangplasoi he marched through the salt fields and spent the night along the way at his mistress Tien's village, a day's march from Na Klue. Then Taksin headed for Rayong where the governor of the port city extended his hospitality and offered food but secretly invited troops from Chantabun to attack Taksin.[79] The plot failed and Taksin attacked Rayong.

The description in the chronicles of the assault on Rayong reveals almost the full panoply of Taksin's top generals who were subsequently to play key roles in the most important battles of the Thonburi period. There were as many

Siamese as Chinese among Taksin's cohort. Among the Siamese were Phra Chiang-Ngen, Luang Chamnan-Phraison, Luang Phrom-Sena, Boonmee, Saeng, You-Srisongkhram, Nak, and Thamarong Imp. Taksin's Chinese chiefs carrying pikes included Luang Phiphit, Luang Phichai, Khun Charmuang the Robber, Mhun Thong and Luang Phrom. The Cambodian prince Nak Ong-Ram was also one of the party, and Taksin would later install him as king of Cambodia through the agency of Siamese arms.

The defenders of Rayong were no match for Taksin's little army. Taksin overran the port city and secured food, supplies, weapons and men. Soon after the capitulation of Rayong, Taksin went back to secure a string of fishing villages and towns on the eastern seaboard including Chonburi. Consequently, only Chantabun stood in the way of his control over the whole of eastern Siam.

At Rayong we get another glimpse of Taksin's politico-military approach. Taksin dispatched Phra Phichai to Ha Tien to propose an alliance with Mac Thientu, the son of Mac Cuu, who ruled that port city, to fight the Burmese.[80] At the same time he continued negotiations with recalcitrant Chantabun. Taksin's style was to always negotiate. Only when negotiations failed would he then resort to military means. If the ruler or head of a town supported him with food, supplies and men, Taksin would extend his protection. If negotiations failed, Taksin would attack and replace him with another that he could trust.

Rayong was also an encouraging milestone on Taksin's roadmap to kingship. At Rayong he reportedly gathered his men and declared that he would create an army to fight and drive out the Burmese from Siam.

The army that Taksin addressed exhibited entirely different attributes from the Ayudhyan army from which they had evolved. For one thing, the soldiers gathered

Illustration of Chantabun, an important port of call for Chinese junks.

around Taksin were a mixed group comprising as many Chinese as Siamese. The composition of Taksin's army was determined partly by the heavy toll the Burmese had taken among the skilled military men of the old order and partly by the same handicap under which Taksin labored: that of being half Chinese and without a clear, legitimate social status.

Like their leader, most of Taksin's army were men from obscure origins who had earned their positions through deeds in battle. Furthermore, many were young men of his own generation who had attained commanding positions perhaps a generation earlier than otherwise possible under the old *khunnang*-dominated traditional Siamese military system, if at all.[81]

Taksin had created a new kind of fighting machine that had proved its mettle against the Burmese and had not been found wanting. However, it was still premature for Taksin to march back and attack the Burmese—his army was still too small to take on the formidable invading force. He would need more men, supplies and weapons from Chantabun.

Taksin hoped to win over the governor of Chantabun without fighting. By this time, Taksin already controlled the greater part of eastern Siam, but he controlled mere villages compared to Chantabun—it was itself only a small town but also the main port of call in eastern Siam. Chantabun was populous and wealthy, with a sizable Chinese merchant community. The port could provide him with adequate logistical support for his military campaign to retake Ayudhya from the Burmese. Chantabun remained the prize that continued to elude him.

The governor of Chantabun had been duplicitous in his dealings with Taksin, offering nothing beyond sweet words. The former had used delaying tactics while conspiring to set Taksin up for an ambush at Rayong. After months had passed with no progress in the negotiations, Taksin prepared to attack. Chantabun would be the real test of the army he had built up.

Unbeknownst to Taksin, the governor's obfuscated responses to his overtures stemmed from the shifting political sands of eastern Siam's politics. The prospect of Ayudhya's impending military defeat had fanned Mac Thientu's regional ambitions. The situation was further complicated by Cantonese-Teochew rivalries between Ha Tien and Chantabun. During the 1760s, armed Teochew-Siamese communal groups centered in Chantabun opposed Cantonese Ha Tien's Vietnamese-backed expansion into the former's domains in the Gulf of Siam.[82] In response to the Cantonese-Vietnamese incursion into Teochew-controlled waters in the Gulf, Teochew pirates took to harassing Ha Tien's Cantonese junk trade.[83]

However, the prospect of Ayudhya's impending military defeat had caused the governor of Chantabun to mend fences with Mac Thientu.[84] As regional Siamese governors began to declare their independence from Ayudhya after 1767, the *phraya* of Chantabun harbored ambitions to claim Southeast Siam as his own fiefdom.[85] Consequently, Taksin's proposal to form an anti-Burmese alliance not only fell on deaf ears but also prompted the eastern powers to conspire to dispose of Taksin and keep eastern Siam within their orbit.

By June 1767, Taksin had advanced on Chantabun and encamped outside the city. After his ultimatum was rebuffed, Taksin returned to his camp and made his famous battle address to his troops: "We are going to attack Chantabun tonight. Smash all your cooking pots for we will have our next meal in town tomorrow or starve!"

Taksin attacked the city at night and captured it on 15 June, two months after the fall of Ayudhya. After securing Chantabun, Taksin sent Phra (Ram) Phichai[86] and Luang Racharin by sea to capture a fleet of junks harboring at Tung Yai, while he marched his troops to Trad from the landward side.[87] Phichai's fleet fought a naval battle with the junk merchants for half a day, after which the junk master Chin Chiem gave in and joined forces with Taksin, giving his daughter as well as committing 50 ships to Taksin's military operation against the Burmese.

Meanwhile, the governor of Chantabun fled to Ha Tien.[88] Taksin had captured Chantabun but the eastern problem remained unresolved. The problem would return to haunt Taksin in Thonburi.

A Chinese Who Would Be King

After the fall of Ayudhya, the political system, formerly held together by the central authority located in the capital city, disintegrated. King Ekathat was dead, the palace destroyed and the upper class decapitated; Prince Uthumphon and the entire Siamese nobility had been dragged off, as prisoners of war, to Burma. The defeated Siamese polity was forced to fall back upon what was left of their provincial administrative system to avoid anarchy. Suddenly, the town governors and village heads could no longer expect directives from the king's central bureaucracy; for the time being, many were responsible to no one but themselves.

Of course, the Burmese appointed governors in the regions they had conquered,

The ruins of the Grand Palace grounds in Ayudhya as seen today.

but they lacked the manpower to rule these regions effectively. Bandits, warlords and self-appointed heirs to the throne began to move in and carve out their own niches in the power vacuum left behind after the fall of Ayudhya.

To the northeast of Ayudhya, the rulers of Phimai and Khorat, Prince (*krommamun*) Theppiphit and Luang Peng respectively, vied with each other for control of the Khorat Plateau. To the north the governor of Phitsanulok declared his independence. In Suwankhaburi, a Buddhist monk named Fang established his personal fiefdom, and in the south the governor of Nakhon Si Thammarat declared his independence. All the while, on the eastern seaboard a daring half-Chinese general named Taksin drew on Chinese coastal communities, mercantile capital, and strategic maritime resources including ports, ships and Western weapons to build the most powerful army to reclaim the old domains of Ayudhya.

The once-unitary state of Ayudhya had fragmented into a kaleidoscopic tapestry of local centers and epicenters of petty administrative authorities. The task facing Taksin of unifying these competing and conflicting epicenters of power appeared to be more than daunting. Still, he rose to the challenge without a moment's hesitation.

After conquering Chantabun, Taksin wasted no time in making preparations to retake the fallen city of Ayudhya from the occupying Burmese forces. Taksin's military mobilization drew heavily on the coastal communities comprising the Teochew diaspora in eastern Siam. His army was now swollen with levies from Chantabun, Rayong, Trad, Bangplasoi and Pattaya. Besides rank and file troops, his stunning triumph at Chantabun also drew talented fighters from the old order to his cause, including Chaophraya Chakri–Mood, a Muslim nobleman. Among the warriors who joined Taksin in eastern Siam was Boonma, who later achieved legendary fame as Chaophraya Surasi of Phitsanulok. Not long after Boonma joined Taksin's forces, his elder brother, Thong Duang, escorted Taksin's mother from Petchaburi to be reunited with her son, and he stayed on to join Taksin's campaign to retake Ayudhya from the Burmese.

In addition to manpower, Taksin had elephants, horses, transport caravans, rice and ships coordinated in an unbroken logistical pipeline extending from the coastal port of Chantabun to his military forces at the front. Taksin's control of nearby ports made it easier for him to obtain supplies than the landlocked forces stationed deeper in the hinterland.

Moreover, he had built and borrowed over 100 ships to transport his troops and supplies to the front. Taksin's superb generalship, battle experience and uncanny talent for strategy and logistics gave him an advantage over his opponents. When he advanced on the Burmese stronghold in the Central Plain, his army and logistical support was unmatched by the remaining Burmese garrison or any other rival pretender to the throne.

First, Taksin attacked the Burmese stronghold at Thonburi. However, the great battle with the fearsome Burmese army that was anticipated proved to be an anti-climax. The Burmese defenders at Thonburi were a shadow of the strength of the Burmese invasion force that had defeated Ayudhya in April 1767. The main Burmese army had been pulled back after the fall of Ayudhya to defend Ava against a Chinese attack, leaving only small garrisons stationed at Pho Sam Ton to the north of Ayudhya.[89]

The bloody assault on the Burmese stockade at Pho Sam Ton was undertaken by Taksin's Chinese vanguard troops led by Phraya Phichai and Phraya Phiphit. The royal chronicles describe them during the battle at Pho Sam Ton in Ayudhya, which brought the final victory for Taksin, as follows:

> Pho Sam Ton Camp, the Chinese vanguard regiments of Phraya Phiphit and Phraya Phichai set up camp at Wat Klang. The next morning Taksin ordered the Chinese regiments to attack Phra Nai Khong's camp.[90] Phra Nai Khong sent his men to fight till noon. The Burmese then retreated back into the stockade. But the Chinese pursued and massacred them in the camp where Phra Nai Khong was killed.[91]

Thus, seven months after he joined his shrewd generalship and force of personality with efficient logistical support, Taksin had retaken Ayudhya back from the Burmese.

As Ayudhya was no more, Taksin decided to establish his capital at Thonburi. Afterwards, Taksin's accession to the throne was *fait accompli*. After all, he had liberated Siam from the Burmese. He was presented with the title "King" by acclamation in February 1768. However, Taksin contented himself with the modest title *Console du Royaume* (Guardian of the Kingdom), although for all intents and purposes he acted as king and was regarded as such. As befitting a king, he organized the ceremonial cremation of King Ekathat's corpse and treated with consideration the remaining members of the royal family and palace staff who could be found in Ayudhya.[92] He also left no doubt who was lord and master by taking as his consorts four members of the Ayudhyan royal family, including the daughter of his rival pretender to the throne, Prince Theppiphit.

Weeding Out Rival Pretenders

Although Taksin was triumphant in Ayudhya, rival pretenders still controlled Khorat, Phimai, Phitsanulok and Nakhon Si Thammarat. Moreover, besides Prince Theppiphit,[93] two Ayudhyan princes, Chao Chui[94] and Chao Sri-sang[95] were still at large in Ha Tien and Cambodia respectively. Furthermore, Burmese forces still remained within striking distance at Chiang Mai and Tavoy. Although none had the military resources to pose a credible challenge, their continued existence posed a constant reminder of Taksin's lack of legitimacy and gave his enemies the excuse to denounce him as a *lukchin* with no rightful claim to the throne, and consequently, unsuitable to be king.

Taksin's best defense was that he had kept his promise of successfully driving the Burmese out of the Central Plain, whereas none of the others had done as much to liberate the country from foreign occupation. However, despite Taksin's triumph over his rivals following the battle of Pho Sam Ton, the threat of a renewed Burmese invasion remained an ever-present danger.

Indeed, Taksin had barely proclaimed Thonburi his new capital when 2,000 Burmese troops from Tavoy attacked a Chinese settlement at Bang Khung in early 1768. Taksin reacted swiftly, in tune with his intrepid character. He led a naval fleet of 20 ships to block the mouth of the Mae Klong River and laid siege to the Burmese camp. Simultaneously, he sent Boonma, now Phra Mahamontri, with a large force, marching overland, to attack from another direction. The Burmese forces were outflanked and put to flight and Taksin succeeded in extending the territory under his control at the expense of the Burmese, capturing much-needed ships and weapons to boot.

Meanwhile, the Central Plain had been turned into a theater of robberies, which wrecked the country's economy and food production and resulted in widespread famine. The king faced the daunting task of reconstituting social order, alleviating starvation and rehabilitating the economy to enable people to resume their livelihoods.

At the same time, he had to re-establish central authority by subduing all rival pretenders. In May 1768 he led an expedition against Phitsanulok. The ensuing battle turned out badly for Taksin, who was wounded in the leg and had to abandon the campaign and return to Thonburi.

Leaving aside Phitsanulok for the moment, Taksin regrouped his forces and redirected them to attack Phimai. By the end of 1768 Phimai had fallen and Prince Theppiphit was killed. The following year, 1769, Taksin shifted his attention to Nakhon Si Thammarat.

The military campaign against Nakhon Si Thammarat was not led by Taksin himself but by two able generals, Chaophraya Chakri-Mood and Phraya Phichairacha. However, they were unable to subjugate the enemy and Taksin had to reinforce them with a fleet of warships. The fleeing governor and his family were later captured by Phraya Phichairacha. After the victory, Taksin feted his army and liberally distributed the spoils of battle among his troops. At the same time, he quickly restored law and order and enforced strict rules upon his soldiers, forbidding them to kill farmers' cattle or rob the populace.

The conquest of Nakhon Si Thammarat brought further benefits to Taksin. The ports on the east coast of the Malay Peninsula, which included Patani Songkhla and Nakhon Si Thammarat, also known as Ligor, had maintained maritime and commercial relations with South China since ancient times. In 1750 a Chinese from Zhangzhou named Hao Yiang (Wu Rang [吳讓]) had sailed to Songkhla and settled in Khao Daeng. In 1769, after Taksin conquered the south, Hao Yiang pledged allegiance to the new king by bringing him a gift of 50 cases of tobacco.[96]

Taksin rewarded him with the noble title of *luang* and a swallows' nest concession of the nearby islands. Subsequently, Hao Yiang brought Songkhla into the orbit of the Thonburi Kingdom and was later appointed the governor of Songkhla in 1775. Thus, through Taksin's southern campaign, the principalities of the Malay Peninsula and the tributary Malay Sultanates further south came to be more closely tied to the Siamese court at Thonburi.[97]

Meanwhile, events in the Lower North unfolded in Taksin's favor. The governor of Phitsanulok suddenly fell ill and died before he could consolidate the fruits of his victory. Upon hearing the news of his rival's death, Phra Fang, the warlord of Sawangkhaburi, attacked Phitsanulok and overran the town. Consequently, Phra Fang now controlled the whole of the Lower North, which was not directly under the control of the Burmese.

In 1770, Taksin ordered Boonma, now Phraya Yommarat and Phraya Phichairacha, the veteran of the southern campaign, to attack Fang's stronghold at Sawangkhaburi. Fang was defeated. Thus, by the end of 1770, Taksin had succeeded in eliminating all rival pretenders to the throne within the country. In a frenzy of military activity he had subdued each contender and brought most of the region that was once governed by the kings of Ayudhya under his control.

Old photograph of Hao Yiang's Na Songkhla family mansion in Songkhla.

Breaking the Burmese Stranglehold

The successful Burmese invasion of Ayudhya in the 1760s had been facilitated by Burmese control of the satellite states encircling the Siamese Central Plain. To prevent history from repeating itself Taksin sought to secure the satellite states and deny the Burmese the ability to mount an invasion of the Siamese heartland on a broad front, thus narrowing down the front along which subsequent battles with the Burmese would be fought. [98]

Taksin's military initiatives against the Burmese benefited from Emperor Qianlong's invasion of Burma in 1766. [99] The withdrawal of the bulk of the Burmese invading force after the fall of the Siamese capital enabled Taksin to retake the Central Plain and establish hegemony over Nakhon Si Thammarat in the south, Phimai in the northeast, and Phitsanulok and Fang in the Lower North. These initial victories encouraged the Malay and Lao principalities to seek Taksin's aid against Burma. In 1769, Lom Sak, Kedah and Patani sent tribute to Thonburi. In 1771 King Siribunyasan of Vientiane requested Taksin's support against Luang Prabang, which sided with the Burmese. [100]

After the successful northern campaign, Taksin positioned four of his best generals as the governors of strategic towns in the Lower North. He elevated Boonma to Chaophraya Surasi, the governor of Phitsanulok. Phraya Phichairacha was rewarded the title *chaophraya* of Sawankhalok. [101] Two other outstanding fighters were also liberally rewarded. Thong Dee the White Teeth was made *phraya* of Phichai, the town where he was born. [102] Additionally, Phraya Tai-Nham, apparently the same person as Chiang-Ngen, was awarded the title of *phraya* of Sukothai. [103] In this way Taksin sought to build up a northern army capable of fortifying the northern front against future Burmese attacks.

Beyond the Lower North lay the Burmese occupied zone. A large Burmese garrison was stationed at Chiang Mai. As long as the Burmese controlled Chiang Mai, the Lower North would be subject to their constant incursions. The prerequisite for lasting peace in the north consisted in the expulsion of the Burmese from the northern city. In 1770 Taksin led a force of 15,000 men to attack Chiang Mai. But he found that the city was too heavily fortified. Unable to find a weak spot in the city's defenses Taksin realized that the undertaking was perhaps too much for his current military resources and ordered a retreat. [104]

Encouraged by their easy victory over Siamese forces, the Burmese general in Chiang Mai made a renewed attempt to capture Phichai in 1772 and again in 1773. However, the Burmese army that threatened Phichai was drawn into an ambush and routed. In the 1773 battle, the *phraya* of Phichai, Thong Dee the White Teeth—Taksin's stalwart general—engaged the enemy at close quarters in his characteristic style: wielding two swords, one tied to each hand, and slaying the enemy until both swords snapped in half. Thong Dee did not give up but fought on until the enemy was forced to retreat, winning the immortal accolade Phraya Phichai Dab Huk (Phraya Phichai of the Broken Sword).[105]

In 1774 King Hsinbyushin successfully concluded a peace negotiation with China. That act had serious implications for the fledgling Kingdom of Thonburi. Taksin had been able to retake the former domains of Ayudhya because the Burmese army was too preoccupied fending off the Chinese invasion. The king of Thonburi knew that soon he would have to face a Burmese army that was more formidable than any he had encountered since 1767.

Fortunately, the Burmese were prevented from mounting a full-scale attack by the outbreak of a rebellion in the Mon areas of Burma. Taksin seized the opportunity to attack Chiang Mai in late 1774, while the Burmese were still distracted by their internal problem.[106] The infantry was led by Boonma, now Chaophraya Surasi, his brother Thong Duang, now Chaophraya Chakri, and Chaophraya Phichairacha, joined by Phraya Chabaan and Phraya Kawila—two chiefs who had defected from the Burmese camp and brought their men to join Taksin's Chiang Mai campaign.[107] Taksin arrived later to rendezvous with his forces at Lampang and marched on to Chiang Mai. By 1775 he had encircled and laid siege to the town, which fell easily. Taksin captured a large quantity of cannons and guns from the Burmese arsenal.

Although the siege was successful and Chiang Mai fell to Taksin's forces, the Burmese general managed to cut his way out of the Siamese encirclement at Changpuek Gate under the watch of Phichairacha. Taksin was furious at Phichairacha for his carelessness, for he had been under strict orders to not let the Burmese general escape. Taksin's reaction to the slightest weakness of his men was characteristic. Phichairacha was caned 50 strokes. In his fury, Taksin wanted to sentence all 500 men under Phichairacha to death by immolation on suspicion of conspiracy with the Burmese. Only a unanimous plea for clemency by his generals stayed his hand, and the guilty soldiers were demoted to cut grass for the elephants.[108]

Before departing for Thonburi, Taksin commemorated his victory by liberally distributing the spoils of battle among his army and rewarding those who had distinguished themselves in battle with honors and positions. Chaophraya Chakri-Thong Duang was left to oversee the pacification of the north while Taksin returned to Thonburi.

While the Thonburi forces were engaged in Chiang Mai, King Hsinbyushin sent an infantry of 5,000 to attack Ratchaburi. As the news reached Taksin, he ordered his son and Phraya Thibethbodhi to set up fortifications at Ratchaburi. Concurrently, he activated a general mobilization and recalled his commanders to Thonburi. Due to the exigency of the situation, he commanded them to report to him without delay; they were expressly forbidden to rest or even visit

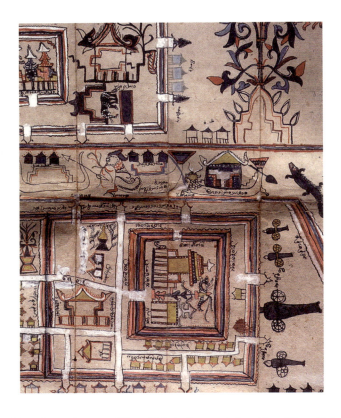

King Taksin's palace depicted in a Burmese spy map dating back to the Thonburi era. The royal pier is located to the left of the crocodile.

their families along the way. When Taksin learned that Phra Thep-Yotha, one of his commanders, had gone home before reporting to the king at court, Taksin personally beheaded him and put his head on a pike just outside the palace.[109] It seemed that during this time, when the fledgling state faced the most dangerous threat since the establishment of the Thonburi Kingdom, Taksin would not brook even the slightest disobedience of his orders, enforcing the strictest discipline and pushing himself and his soldiers to the utmost of their capacity.

King Taksin issued strict orders to his other generals to hasten to Ratchaburi while he called up reserve troops from the north. Thonburi's elite Chinese troops under the command of the Chinese Phraya Rachasretthi-Chin were sent to Ratchaburi to set up fortifications and organize the defense of the town. The king left shortly after, arriving at Ratchaburi in February and calling a council of war.

It was in this disciplined fatalistic mood that the Siamese forces faced the Burmese. Taksin's leadership in battle stood out among the best instances of generalship in war no less than the best military commanders extolled in the Chinese classic manual on warfare, Sun Tzu's *Art of War*. The Siamese convincingly won the ensuing battles. When the Burmese set up camp at Ban Bang Keo, the Thonburi forces, under Taksin's hands-on direction, surrounded and laid a tight siege of the camp.[110] Repeated Burmese efforts to break the encirclement failed until eventually starvation compelled the Burmese to surrender.

Undaunted by his defeats at Ban Bang Keo and Chiang Mai, Hsinbyushin fielded the largest Burmese invasion force against Siam in 1775, after he had ruthlessly put down the Mon rebellion. The invasion force of 35,000 was led by General Maha Thiha Thura,[111] the Burmese general who had repelled the Chinese invasion and quelled the Mon rebellion. Taksin had barely returned to Thonburi when reports of Burmese military movements reached him. They related that Maha Thiha Thura had advanced on the Lower North and besieged Phitsanulok. Chaophraya Surasi, the governor of Phitsanulok, and his brother Chaophraya Chakri had put up a stubborn resistance, stalling the Burmese force for four months.

Legend has it that Maha Thiha Thura so admired the bravery and martial prowess of Chakri that he sought a meeting with him. The Burmese general ungrudgingly extolled the generalship of Chakri, and upon looking at him, prophesied that he would one day become king. Chaophraya Chakri later became Rama I, who founded the Chakri dynasty.

Although King Taksin hastened to reinforce Chaophraya Chakri, he could not effect a junction with the Siamese forces in Phitsanulok. With dwindling supplies, food and provisions, the two brothers could not hold the town against Maha Thiha Thura's siege any longer. However, the embattled Siamese army managed to fight their way out of the Burmese encirclement and fall back to Petchabun.

Maha Thiha Thura led his army into the deserted town of Phitsanulok in June 1776 and gained control of large tracts of territory in the Lower North. At this juncture, news arrived that Hsinbyushin had died. Maha Thiha Thura decided to call off the invasion and rushed back with his main force to support the bid of his son-in-law, Singu, to ascend the throne in Ava. Although the Burmese main force had left, remnants of Burmese military units continued to fight on. Taksin's army advanced in the wake of the retreating Burmese and began defeating the leftover Burmese garrisons with characteristic ferocity.

To complete the pacification of the north and deny the Burmese use of peripheral states to mount a future invasion of the Central Plain, Taksin sent Chakri and Surasi on a mission with 30,000 men in 1777–78. They were to establish Siamese hegemony over Laos and pressure the rulers of smaller principalities on the west bank of the Mekong to transfer allegiance to Thonburi. The campaign was successful, and the Siamese forces returned home after placing vassal rulers on the throne at Vientiane and Champassak.[112]

Taksin had projected Siamese power north and gained additional resources of manpower from these conquests

King Taksin's bed as kept at Wat Intharam in Bangkok. His mother, who died while he was on campaign in Ratchaburi, was cremated there.

in the form of large numbers of Laotian captives who were forcibly re-settled in Saraburi and Thonburi.

Geopolitics, China-Trade and Imperial Investiture

The geopolitical territories on the Southeast Asian Mainland had undergone a seismic shift in the late 18th century. The growing military power of Burma in the west had disastrous consequences for the neighboring Kingdom of Ayudhya. Similarly, Quang Nam's[113] expansion into the Mekong Delta in the east inevitably made in-roads into Cambodia. Subsequently, a newly reconstituted, resurgent Siamese state emerging from the post-1767 interregnum began to check Burma's eastward expansion and posed a challenge to Vietnamese ambitions in Cambodia.

The unfolding conflicts between the three large political states on the mainland, including Cambodia, Siam and Vietnam, was further complicated by intra-Chinese ethnic rivalries between Cantonese and Teochew merchant networks and their supporters. In the geopolitics of the eastern mainland following the collapse of the Kingdom of Ayudhya in 1767, the small Cantonese port polity of Ha Tien became the fulcrum of contention between Thonburi, Cambodia and Vietnam.

The fall of Ayudhya sparked considerable interest among nearby rulers, especially in Cambodia, Ha Tien and Chantabun. The destruction of Ayudhya had upset Cambodia's delicate balancing act between Ayudhya and Quang Nam. In fact, the shift in the regional balance of power caused political turmoil in Cambodia as King Ang Ton shifted his allegiance to Quang Nam and repudiated Cambodia's vassal relationship to Siam. King Ang Ton's rival, Prince Nak Ong-Ram (known in Siam as Ang Non), who had sought refuge in Thonburi, challenged his brother on the platform of restoring Cambodia's tributary obligations to Siam.

The politico-military entanglements between Siam, Cambodia and Vietnam suggest that the economies of the coastal regions along the South China Sea and the Gulf of Siam together with the adjacent trans-Mekong hinterland were more closely linked than most observers have supposed. Trade routes link the production centers, market exchanges and ports across these three countries into a large regional political economy. In Siam the trade routes and trading networks included Bangplasoi, Rayong, Chantabun and Trat. Outside the Chao Phraya Basin, Cambodia was the alternative route by which forest products from Laos and the Middle Mekong Basin went down to the sea. The trade routes in Cambodia included Kompong Som, Kampot and Ha Tien. Some of the Cambodian trade was also re-routed into Siam via Prachinburi, while products from West Cambodia were sent to Trat and Chantabun, which were important collection centers for forest products from Cambodia. The rest found their way to Vietnam through Rach Gia, Ca Mau and Bien Hoa.[114]

During the 1760s, the ports along the coastal stretch adjoining the Mekong Delta and Cambodia became the locus of the Canton junk trade. Of the 37 junks sailing annually between Canton and Southeast Asia, about 85–90 percent traded at ports along this stretch of coast.[115] Siamese junks also visited these coastal ports for forest products to sell to China and brought Chinese, Western and Siamese goods for Cambodian and Vietnamese markets. The ability of these ports to corner the Canton junk trade must be attributed to the considerable integration of sub-regional markets, due to well-connected internal land trade routes and market exchanges.[116]

Thus, forest products from the trans-Mekong hinterland had access to several different ports along both Siamese and Vietnamese sectors of this coastal stretch. A major factor deciding which trade routes became dominant at any particular time depended upon the security situation.[117] Consequently, when trade routes passing through Siam became impassable during the 1760s due to Burmese attacks, tin and sappanwood were exported from Vietnamese ports around Cochin-China, an area that produced neither commodity, while only a trickle was exported from Ayudhya—a key supplier of both.[118]

A major factor of contention between Vietnam and Thonburi revolved around the control of this regional trade. Vietnam wanted to direct this traffic in forest products to Ha Tien and other ports in the Vietnamese orbit. Thonburi, eyeing this traffic, wanted to pull it into Chantabun and Trat.[119]

Meanwhile, at Ha Tien, the regional power vacuum caused by the disintegration of Ayudhya fanned the Cantonese ruler Mac Thientu's expansionary ambitions in the Gulf of Siam.[120] The eclipse of Ayudhya created the setting for Ha Tien, which already controlled Kampot and Rach Gia, to assert its power along the eastern shores of the Gulf towards Chantabun and Trat. Shortly after the demise of Ayudhya, Ha Tien's navy made in-roads into Teochew-controlled waters, including the islands of Koh Kong and Koh Khram, sparking an inter-communal war between Teochews and Cantonese in the Gulf of Siam.[121]

In the mid-18th century Ha Tien was in the administrative orbit of Cambodia but enjoyed strong links to Quang Nam. Under Mac Thientu's rule, Ha Tien had gravitated towards Vietnam and became to all intents and purposes an autonomous state. Since Ayudhya was no more, the former kingdom's share of the lucrative China trade appeared to be up for grabs. Mac Thientu aspired to take over the late Ayudhya's Hokkien-dominated China trade and redirect the lucrative trade routes of the eastern seaboard (which had serviced Ayudhya's booming entrepôt trade) towards the Cantonese emporium of Ha Tien.

Ha Tien was also in a similar position as Cambodia in regard to its vassal relationship to Ayudhya. Like King Ang Ton, Mac Thientu supposed that the fall of Ayudhya meant that Ha Tien was freed from its tributary obligations to Siam. Consequently, Mac Thientu exercised his special relationship with the Cambodian court of Oudong to enjoin King Ang Ton to refuse demands for Cambodia and Ha Tien to return to Siamese vassalage on grounds that Taksin was not a legitimate heir of the royal family of Ayudhya. Instead, Mac Thientu gave sanctuary to the royal Ayudhyan fugitives Chao Srisang and Chao Chui at Ha Tien to legitimize his challenge to Taksin's enthronement in 1767. By ingratiating himself with Ayudhyan royalty Mac Thientu sought to advance Ha Tien's bid to inherit Ayudhya's royal trading privileges with China.[122] Coincidentally, after a short sojourn in Ha Tien, Chao Srisang suddenly appeared in Cambodia almost as if by design.[123] Abetted by Mac Thientu, King Ang Ton refused to extradite Srisang, nor send tribute to Thonburi, to King Taksin's dismay.[124]

Thus, from the very beginning Ha Tien had no interest in supporting Taksin's proposal of a union to fight the Burmese. The pleas made by Phraya Phichai, Taksin's envoy to Ha Tien in 1767, fell on deaf ears. Taksin's attempt to re-unite the Siamese and reclaim the former domains of Ayudhya threatened Mac Thientu's regional ambitions. Therefore, Ha Tien conspired to obstruct Taksin from the outset. After Taksin conquered Chantabun, the fugitive governor fled and was given asylum at Ha Tien, confirming Taksin's worst suspicions of Mac Thientu's duplicity.[125]

After taking over Chantabun, Taksin appeared to have received considerable support from the Teochew diaspora in the Gulf of Siam. Taksin's arrival on the scene had become a rallying point in the long-standing feud between the Teochews of Chantabun and the Cantonese of Ha Tien. Mac Thientu's enmity towards Taksin gained the latter many Teochew followers, especially the Teochew merchant network, which supported Taksin's war effort with money, ships, rice, arms, cannons and other supplies. Teochew recruits also began to swell the ranks of Taksin's invasion force to retake Ayudhya from the Burmese.[126]

Thus, uniting the Teochew settlements in the eastern seaboard and the Gulf of Siam behind his leadership became a cornerstone of Taksin's politico-military strategy. Consequently, the Chinese of Chantabun played a big role in facilitating his accession to the throne. Equally important was the fact that the port of Chantabun remained open, when the rest of Ayudhya was shut down by the Burmese invasion, enabling Taksin to secure essential goods and weapons for his supply line.

Despite his failure to stop Taksin at Chantabun, Mac Thientu remained determined to bring down the King of Thonburi. While Taksin was preoccupied with driving out the Burmese, subduing rival pretenders to the throne and reclaiming the former domains of Ayudhya, Mac Thientu continued to oppose Taksin militarily, diplomatically and economically.

Following the collapse of the Kingdom of Ayudhya, the population of the Central Plain was depleted. Law and order had broken down and bandits and pirates roamed the forests and waterways. Above all, there was no food and the threat of famine hung over the region. Food shortages worsened during 1768. In 1769 outbreak of famine and disease wasted the population of the emergent Siamese state of Thonburi. French missionary reports claim that more Siamese died from starvation in 1769 than during the Burmese invasion.[127]

The statue of Mac Cuu (1655–1735), Mac Thientu's father, in Ha Tien.

King Taksin's immediate priorities were to find food for the populace, curb banditry and piracy, and restore law and order so that there was basic human security for people to resume their livelihoods. To distribute food to the people to stave off starvation, Taksin used treasury funds to import large amounts of rice, which he distributed free to the people.[128]

In his desperation, King Taksin began to call in vassal obligations for assistance. Taksin sent envoys to Cambodia requesting King Ang Ton to pay tribute to Siam in her hour of need. Taksin's plea for tribute from Cambodia was rebuffed on the ground that Phraya Taksin was not of Siamese royal birth.[129]

King Ang Ton had touched a highly sensitive issue concerning Taksin's parvenu status. Upon learning that Chao Chui was a refugee in Ha Tien, Taksin sent Tan Liang, known in the Thai chronicles as Phraya Phiphit, to Ha Tien. The envoy brought many precious gifts, including two European-made cannons, and requested the repatriation of Chao Chui to Thonburi. Taksin even promised to cede some territories to Ha Tien if his request was granted.[130]

Mac Thientu's response was characteristically duplicitous. He had no intention of extraditing Chao Chui to Thonburi as he already harbored the intention to escort Chao Chui back to Siam with the purpose of restoring the Ban Plu Luang dynasty of Ayudhya.[131] However, unlike King Ang Ton, he did not reject Taksin's request outright. Instead he sent envoys to Thonburi bearing promises to comply, although the real purpose was to spy and obtain intelligence on Taksin's military strength.[132] His spies must have witnessed an impoverished, embattled state beset with political, economic, social and military problems, barely struggling to survive.

Subsequently, when Taksin requested rice supplies from Ha Tien to stave off famine in the capital, Mac Thientu seized the opportunity to devise a plot to kidnap Taksin. He graciously acceded to King Taksin's request for food aid and promptly sent multiple shiploads of rice as evidence of his goodwill. However, Mac Thientu's real intention was to use the ships laden with rice as bait to capture Taksin. The rice convoy was escorted by his son-in-law Tu-dung with a flotilla of junks carrying heavily armed troops.[133] A trap was set up in advance. As soon as Taksin stepped on board to receive the ceremonial handover of the rice shipment, Ha Tien soldiers concealed in the ship's hold would spring out and apprehend him.[134]

Unfortunately for Mac Thientu, spies planted by Taksin at Ha Tien discovered the plot. Taksin intercepted the rice convoy at sea. Tu-dung's troop ships were prevented from entering the Chao Phraya River and the rice cargo was confiscated. Tu-dung, the commander of the flotilla, fled but died after his ships ran into a storm.[135] After this incident, Taksin and Mac Thientu were on terms of open hostility. Raging for revenge, Mac Thientu imposed trade sanctions on Siam and barred all junk traffic between Ha Tien and Thonburi, which at that time relied on rice imported from Ha Tien and other regional markets.[136] Ha Tien's trade sanctions damaged the Teochew-dominated commerce of Chanthabun and Trat, which were closely connected with the adjoining trans-Mekong hinterland and coastal ports.

Thonburi was not in a position to redress the injury to its commerce by Ha Tien. Other pressing internal and military problems commanded Taksin's attention, and for the time being he settled for a cost-effective way of handling Ha Tien. Ha Tien's weakness was its vulnerability to the recurrent threat of Teochew piracy in the Gulf of Siam. Ha Tien's attempts to encroach on Teochew-controlled waters in the Gulf aggravated intra-Chinese communal tensions in the Gulf, and Teochew pirates retaliated by harassing Cantonese shipping operating out of Ha Tien. According to Vietnamese records, just before the fall of Ayudhya, Mac Thientu sent his men to destroy the Teochew pirate base at Koh Kong, killing Huo Jan, the unassailable pirate leader.[137] Although Huo Jan was dead, tensions ran high and the potential threat of Teochew piracy remained unresolved.

Taksin decided to exploit the ethnic tensions between Teochews and Cantonese in the Gulf to his advantage. Vietnamese records allege that in July 1769, a Teochew adventurer named Tran Thai planned to seize Ha Tien with the help of bandits in a conspiracy with several members of the ruling Mac family. The plot was uncovered by Mac Thientu and the conspirators were ambushed at a Buddhist temple.[138] Tran Thai, who was suspected of being a Siamese agent, escaped and sought asylum in Chantabun. Tran Thai was subsequently sighted among the vanguard Siamese army in the attack on Ha Tien in 1771.[139]

Taksin's indirect warfare against Mac Thientu through the cost-effective use of Teochew pirates and adventurers had bought him time to address the more important problems of state survival. After distributing rice to alleviate famine in Thonburi, Taksin had to establish the economic foundations of his fledgling state. In a war-torn economy there was little room to impose a heavy tax burden on an impoverished populace to defray state expenditures. That would generate discontent and further jeopardize the security and legitimacy of his fledgling kingdom. Therefore, King Taksin's strategy was to revive the economy by promoting export-oriented trade.

In fact, traders had continued to do business in Ayudhya even while the country was under attack and intense fighting was taking place in 1767. Surprisingly, Ayudhya had continued to send tribute missions to China in 1761, 1762 and 1766, during the reign of King Ekathat, when the city was already embattled by Burmese invasion. The fact that Ayudhya still managed to send tribute to China during those troubled years suggests that the network of Chinese traders plying between the Gulf of Siam and Canton had not been severed.[140]

Although Siam's trade with China was disrupted by the fall of Ayudhya, China trade remained robust elsewhere in the region. Chinese and Vietnamese records show that customs revenues between 1724 and 1750 increased threefold in Fujian and fivefold in Guangdong, while the number of Chinese junks visiting Cochin-China increased fourfold between 1750 and 1820.[141] By contrast, commercial relations with Europe were all but dissolved due to local wars and piracy, as well as the Napoleonic Wars. Therefore, King Taksin naturally sought to restore Siam's disrupted trade with China.[142] The resumption of the China trade would allow many commodities to be imported in exchange for Siamese forest products. Taksin wasted no time to send an envoy to Canton to seek imperial investiture as the new ruler of Siam in 1768.

Mac Thientu sabotaged King Taksin's tributary mission to Canton by sending a report to the Qing court discrediting Taksin's claim to the throne and making a strong case for the rival pretender Chao Chui, who was a royal guest at Ha Tien. As a result of Mac Thientu's machinations, King Taksin's request for imperial investiture was rebuffed.[143] Emperor Qianlong suspected Taksin of being a pretender, who had usurped the rightful authority of the old ruling house of Ayudhya. According to Chinese records the Qing court praised Mac Thientu for his valiant protection of the Siamese prince who had sought refuge in Ha Tien.[144]

Despite Qianlong's rejection of his request for investiture, Taksin continued to make strenuous diplomatic efforts to gain recognition from China. But the Qing court continued to refuse Thonburi's overtures. Failing to re-establish official trading relations with China, King Taksin resorted to trade with China through private merchants.

With or without the official blessing of the Qing court, Thonburi needed to revive the China trade to rehabilitate its economy and generate government revenue in addition to taxation. With the country's agricultural lands destroyed and its skilled population wasted by war, Thonburi had no surplus rice for export, unlike its predecessor, Ayudhya. While others might have bemoaned Thonburi's lack of rice to offer the China trade, King Taksin saw a golden opportunity for the country to specialize in forest products.[145] Moreover, after subjugating Nakhon Si Thammarat, Thonburi enjoyed a monopoly over Siamese tin exports. Tin and forest products were sufficiently in demand to serve as Thonburi's export products.

Backed by a strong army, Thonburi would make an offer "that could not be refused" to Ayudhya's former tributary vassals, including the northeastern principalities, Laotian states and Cambodia, to send annual tribute and local tax in the form of forest products. These would then become Thonburi's export commodities for the China trade. In addition, King Taksin decided to launch a punitive expedition against Cambodia because King Ang Ton had refused to transfer tributary obligations to Thonburi when Taksin was calling in favors from Ayudhya's former vassal states to support Siam's economic reconstruction.

King Ang Ton was in fact part of a complicated political triangle that had developed in the Greater Trans-Mekong Delta on the Eastern Mainland. King Ang Ton was an ally of Mac Thientu because he had once sought asylum in Ha Tien when Quang Nam invaded Cambodia in 1757.[146] A fugitive prince in Ha Tien at the time, Ang Ton plotted his return to Phnom Penh with the support of Vietnamese arms. To achieve this, he sought the good offices of Mac Thientu, as well as Ha Tien's unique relations with Quang Nam, to patch his relations with Vietnam. In exchange, he offered Mac Thientu two provinces, Bassac and Tra-vinh. Mac Thientu took the opportunity and brokered relations with Quang Nam for Ang Ton. Consequently, Prince Ang Ton was escorted by Vietnamese and Ha Tien arms to Cambodia and installed as the new king, replacing his elder brother, Ang Non, who was in exile in Ayudhya. As a reward for its successful intercession, Ha Tien obtained five provinces from Cambodia, following which Ha Tien's territory stretched from west of the Bassac River to the Gulf of Siam, effectively sealing Cambodia's access to the sea and making Ha Tien the back door to Cambodia.[147]

Meanwhile, after the fall of Ayudhya, Ang Ton's elder brother, Ang Non, joined Taksin in Thonburi and sought Siamese support for his claim to the throne against his younger brother. When the latter spurned Taksin's request for tribute and refused to extradite Chao Srisang to Thonburi, the stage was set for a triangular enmity between Cambodia, Ha Tien and Thonburi.

Canton waterfront seven years before the fall of Ayudhya, painted in 1760.

Ha Tien was the perfect intermediary for Ang Ton to patch up Cambodia's relations with Quang Nam. In the 18th century, Quang Nam's economy became closely intertwined with the interests of Cantonese traders, and the Cantonese port polity of Ha Tien was a cornerstone of the regional trading network. Moreover, Mac Thientu himself was a *min-huong*—a person of mixed Cantonese and Vietnamese parentage.[148] Mac Thientu's mother was a Vietnamese woman from Bien Hoa. Thus, Ha Tien represented the interests of Cantonese settlers whose economic orientation was deeply intertwined with the fortunes of Quang Nam. Consequently, in 1708 Ha Tien became a tributary state of Quang Nam.[149] With backing from Quang Nam, Ha Tien began to assert its sovereignty vis-à-vis Cambodia and in 1739 was strong enough to beat off an invasion from Cambodia.[150]

Being a tributary state of Quang Nam did not prevent Ha Tien from making concessions to Ayudhya as well. Mac Thientu also professed to be a vassal of Ayudhya and accepted the royal Siamese title of Phraya Rachasretthi, the governor of Phutthaimas, as Ha Tien was known to the Siamese.[151] However, maintaining a middle ground between Quang Nam and Ayudhya was not easy, and in 1766 Ha Tien faced a threat of Siamese invasion. Vietnamese records state that Quang Nam sent a naval force to defend Ha Tien against an impending Siamese attack; however, the Burmese invasion of Ayudhya in 1766 probably saved Ha Tien.[152]

The conspiracy between Mac Thientu and King Ang Ton also reflected the following coincidence. Both held a royal Siamese prince in their respective courts as insurance. Both refused to recognize Taksin as the legitimate ruler of Siam. These coincidences were played out among the three kings in a remarkable game of thrones. Mac Thientu wanted to escort Chao Chui to Siam and install him as king, replacing Taksin. King Ang Ton also held a trump card up his sleeve in the form of the royal Ayudhyan Chao Srisang, which could be converted, when the time was right, into royal dividends. King Taksin, in turn, held a royal Cambodian prince, Ang Non, who was a refugee in Siam. In the wake of King Ang Ton's rebuff in 1768, Taksin entertained the prospect of escorting Ang Non to Cambodia and installing him as king, replacing Ang Ton. For Thonburi, desperate to secure sources of forest products in order to rehabilitate Siam's disrupted trade, the right time was sooner rather than later. King Taksin moved first.

In March 1769 King Taksin, who was on campaign at Nakhon Si Thammarat, dispatched Thong Duang and Boonma, then known as Phraya Aphai-Ronnarit and Phrya Anuchit-Racha, to escort Prince Ang Non to Cambodia via Siem Reap and install him on the throne at Oudong.[153] Concurrently, Taksin ordered his senior Chinese general Phraya Phichai—the Kosathibodi (another name for the Phraklang)—to attack Battambang.[154] Thonburi's two-prong invasion of Cambodia shocked Mac Thientu, and Ha Tien accelerated preparations for war.

THE CHINESE PHRAYA PHICHAI

In 1767, when Taksin left Wat Phichai, one of the commanders of his cohort was Luang Phichai. The Thonburi chronicles offer another sighting of him at Rayong: "the Chinese officers, namely Luang Phiphit, Luang Phichai . . . all carried pikes when accompanying Taksin on his inspection of troops." After Rayong, the chronicles referred to him as a *phra* and sometimes as "the Chinese Phra Phichai." He must have been one of the more senior members of Taksin's cohort who was fluent in Chinese because he was sent to rally Mac Thientu's support to fight the Burmese. Ha Tien's response was non-committal.[155]

Before the battle of Pho Sam Ton, he had already been promoted to Phraya Phichai, the General of the Chinese Vanguard Regiment. Pichai was probably the first Phraklang of the Thonburi era. In February 1769, when Chantabun sent a message that Ha Tien was preparing to invade Thonburi, the king ordered the Chinese Phraya Phichai, who was the Kosathibodi (Phraklang), to build fortifications at Phrapadaeng, Samut Sakhon and Samut Songkhram.[156] From this point onwards the chronicles refer to Phraya Phichai according to his new official position as Phraya Kosa. According to Chinese sources, the Kosathibodi's (Phraklang's) personal name was Na Lai (Lan Lai).[157] In 1769 Phraya (Phichai) Kosa was sent to attack Battambang. The unsuccessful campaign was a prelude to the 1771 war in which King Taksin led troops to Cambodia himself.

When King Taksin embarked on his Cambodian expedition in 1771, Phraya (Phichai) Kosa had probably retired from the Phraklang post[158] but remained in active military service. During the Ha Tien campaign, he led a fleet of 24 junks and 10 warships with 1,705 men to attack Kampong Som.[159] In the naval inventory of Taksin's fleet, there were only two admirals who commanded Chinese junks, namely the Kosa (Phichai) and Phraya Phiphit, while Taksin's other generals commanded Siamese warships.

After conquering Kampong Som, the Kosa (Phichai) subdued Kampot where the Cham governor, Phraya Panglima, submitted and accompanied him to pledge loyalty to Taksin in Phnom Penh. Curiously, the Cambodian campaign was the last time Phraya (Phichai) Kosa was mentioned. He probably passed away soon after.

The story of Phraya Phichai is often confusing because there were at least four distinguished generals known as Phraya Phichai during the Thonburi era. The most celebrated was the governor of Phichai (Thong Dee "White Teeth"), a boxer who had served Taksin since his days in Tak. Thong Dee was commended for his fabled loyalty because he preferred to die than serve the new king after Taksin was overthrown. The two other Phraya Phichai were Phraya Phichai Isawan and the Chinese Phraya Phichai (Na Lai), the Kosathibodi. The last Phraya Phichai was Phraya Phichai-Racha, another warrior son of Phraya Petchaburi, who became *chaophraya* of Sawankhalok.[160]

Chaophraya Phichai-Racha fell afoul of Taksin in 1776 when he asked to marry the daughter of the ruler of Nakhon Si Thammarat. He did not know that the girl was pregnant by the king while living in the palace with her elder sister, Chim, who was Taksin's consort. When Taksin learned that Phichai-Racha had asked the girl's father for his daughter in marriage, he flew into a jealous rage and accused Chaophraya Phichai-Racha of political maneuvering to become the king's brother-in-law. He had Chaophraya Phichai-Racha beheaded and placed his decapitated head on a pike by the gate of the river raft in the palace compound.

Taksin's impulsive execution of his senior general shocked the ranks of the military. This was the turning point of Taksin's prestige in the eyes of many of his trusted generals. The execution fomented a sense of betrayal among Taksin's men and sowed the seeds of disaffection, eventually leading to the king's downfall.

Quang Nam, whose economy had become increasingly dependent on the export of forest products from the Mekong Delta, found its economic lifeline threatened by Thonburi's invasion of Cambodia. King Taksin's attempt to establish suzerainty over Cambodia with Siamese arms was immediately challenged by Quang Nam.[161] Vietnamese arms came to the defense of King Ang Ton. In Cambodia, King Taksin's impulsive expedition ran into trouble. According to Vietnamese records, the Siamese army was defeated at Lok-khu (Angkor) by King Ang Ton's army, supported by Vietnamese arms. The Siamese had to withdraw.[162]

Phraya Anuchit-Racha (Boonma)'s decision to withdraw instead of attempting to recover his military reverses at Lok-khu was also precipitated by a false report from Nakhon Si Thammarat that King Taksin had been killed in battle.[163] The withdrawal compromised the military campaign in Cambodia, forcing the Kosathibodi also to draw back to Prachinburi. Outraged at being abandoned mid-campaign, the Kosathibodi sent a report to Taksin charging that Boonma and Thong Duang, his brother, withdrew their forces without permission. Thus, the first attempt to replace King Ang Ton by Prince Ang Non with Siamese arms had proved abortive.

However, the Siamese expedition into Cambodia had collateral benefits. Thonburi's forces withdrew from Cambodia with a considerable number of Khmer captives, who were resettled in Thonburi to augment the kingdom's depleted population.[164] In fact, whenever Taksin attacked a place it was his standing policy to move the population and relocate them to Thonburi to increase the kingdom's manpower and reserves of skilled labor.[165]

Therefore, if the expedition was conceived as having a minimum as well as maximum objective then the outcome was not necessarily a failure. Taksin might have failed to achieve his maximum objective to install Prince Ang Non on the throne of Cambodia. But he succeeded in his minimum objective of punishing King Ang Ton for failing to honor Cambodia's tributary obligations to Siam. The Siamese expedition underscored the message to other vassal states that reneging on one's tributary obligations ran the risk of suffering costly reprisals. However, Mac Thientu probably interpreted Thonburi's ignominious withdrawal from Cambodia as a defeat for King Taksin.

The defeat inflicted on Siamese forces by Ang Ton's Vietnamese-backed Cambodian army, coupled with the firm rebuff that Taksin received from the Qing court, emboldened Mac Thientu to launch an attack on Chantabun.[166] In September 1769, while King Taksin was still engaged in a distant campaign at Nakhon Si Thammarat, a 50,000-strong invasion force advanced on Chantabun.[167] Chao Chui was put at the head of the Ha Tien army, as a figurehead, to recast the invasion of Siam as an Ayudhyan restoration.[168]

Although King Taksin was unable to prevent Ha Tien's invasion of Chantabun, he was not completely taken by surprise. Through a spy named Ah-ma planted inside Mac Thientu's sister's residence, Taksin was kept informed of Mac Thientu's intentions and Ha Tien's military movements.[169] Taksin had been receiving intelligence since early 1769 that Mac Thientu was preparing an imminent attack, with a massive invasion force, on Thonburi via Chanthabun. The king quickly took preventive measures by sending his Chinese general Phraya Phichai the Kosathibodi (Na Lai) to organize Thonburi's defense by building fortifications at Phrapadaeng, Samut Sakhon and Samut Songkhram. However, the anticipated attack by Ha Tien did not materialize. Meanwhile, the invasion scare was overtaken by other events, including the punitive expedition against Cambodia in March 1769 and the military campaign in Nakhon Si Thammarat later in the year. When Ha Tien actually invaded Chantabun, King Taksin was in the south.

Thus, Taksin was caught in a dilemma: should he sail back and stop Ha Tien's invasion, or complete the military pacification of the South? Nakhon Si Thammarat was the source of Ayudhya's most lucrative export commodities for China—tin and birds' nests—and was very important if Taksin wished to restore Siam's trade with China. Hence, Taksin needed to conquer Nakhon Si Thammarat and Songkhla, which were the two main ports of call on the commercial route between South China and the Gulf of Siam.

Only limited military resources could be spared for Chantabun until Nakhon Si Thammarat and the southern ports were brought under Thonburi's control. Consequently, Taksin could only send 3,000 troops under the command of a Chinese general, Tan Liang,[170] to reinforce the governor of Chantabun's forces defending the city.[171] Greatly outnumbered, Tan Liang's troops could not repulse Ha Tien's numerically superior invasion force. The Cantonese-led invading army from Ha Tien overran Chantabun and captured Governor Lim Gongseng.[172] Tan Liang ordered remnants of his routed forces to withdraw while Ha Tien's army occupied the town.[173]

For Quang Nam and her satellite state Ha Tien, the capture of Chantabun was an important milestone in their expansionist ambitions in the Gulf of Siam. For the Teochew, the fall of Chantabun was a blow to their power in the Gulf. With the annexation of Chantabun, Quang Nam would be able to shift the locus of the China trade away from the control of the Teochew merchant network of Thonburi towards the Cantonese trading network centered on the coastal ports within the Vietnamese orbit.

However, soon after celebrating her triumph over Siamese forces, Ha Tien's invasion of Chantabun met with difficulties. After regrouping, Tan Liang's forces counterattacked and laid siege to Chantabun. Ha Tien's occupying forces held the city, confident that the meager Siamese forces would not be able to recapture the city. Meanwhile, inside Chantabun, Chao Chui (who was brought forward as a figurehead to legitimize the Cantonese occupation of the city) failed to arouse any sympathy among the predominantly Teochew diaspora.[174]

Unluckily for Ha Tien, an epidemic then broke out in Chantabun, which decimated the ranks of the occupying force. With a mounting death toll, Ha Tien's invasion force was reduced from 50,000 to only about 1,000 after two months. Ha Tien's considerably whittled-down forces were obliged to withdraw and the town returned to Teochew control.[175] Mac Thientu's ambitious dream of conquering Thonburi and replacing Taksin with Chao Chui terminated at Chantabun. The invasion marked the watershed of Ha Tien's expansionary efforts in the Gulf.[176] Ha Tien's failure at Chantabun was the beginning of the road to ruin.

Concurrently, with Thonburi's frenetic military activities, King Taksin's efforts to rebuild the kingdom's shattered economy proceeded apace. While warfare had wasted the country's economy, war could also be exploited to rehabilitate the economy. Perhaps the greatest structural economic problem faced by the fledgling state of Thonburi was underpopulation. War competed with the economy for manpower, and underpopulation became an obstacle to King Taksin's policy to expand trade with China and to use trade to raise government revenue to relieve the burden of taxation on the kingdom's impoverished and war-torn society.

Making the most of a necessity, King Taksin used war to snatch adversarial populations for resettlement in Siam to augment the kingdom's manpower reserves. Taksin also used war to win markets, control trade routes and gain access to supplies of suitable goods for export in the China trade. The war with Cambodia and Ha Tien had not only been about the politics of succession but also about the control of trade routes, markets, ports and access to resources from the Khorat Plateau, Cambodia and the trans-Mekong hinterland, which was coveted by Vietnam as well.

The City Pillar of Chantabun, now called Chanthaburi, where a Chinese diety is being worshipped alongside the city's protective Thai spirit.

King Taksin also needed people with expertise in trade to operate the new kingdom's commerce. To service the China trade, King Taksin turned to the merchant network that had supported him. Taksin employed Chinese merchants as privileged agents of the new kingdom's Royal Trading Monopoly.[177] Chinese were encouraged openly and tacitly by King Taksin to come to Thonburi where they were given priority and various facilities, including royal concessions, to assist their enterprise.[178]

Besides trading expertise, Chinese migrants also provided much-needed manpower as junk masters, navigators, crew, helmsmen, craftsmen, cash croppers, accountants, clerks, factors, port officials, merchandisers and miners for the

trade-driven economic strategy of King Taksin.[179] Moreover, being Chinese, many of these junk masters enjoyed familial and social networks with Chinese officials. Taksin used trusted junk merchants as his envoys to sustain his diplomacy with the Qing court and allay Chinese suspicions of his legitimacy.

Under King Taksin a new Chinese market enclave rapidly developed on the Bangkok side, across the Chao Phraya River from the king's palace in Thonburi. Unlike Ayudhya, whose commerce was dominated by Hokkiens centered in the Nai Kai Market, Thonburi's Chinatown was dominated by the Teochew merchant community.[180] French missionaries reported evidence of thriving commerce by 1770 and attributed it to the extraordinary encouragement given by King Taksin to the Chinese.[181]

In addition to generating state revenue through promoting mercantile activities, Taksin also sold consessionaire rights to the treasure that lay concealed among the ruins of Ayudhya. The Chinese bidder for Wat Phutthai Sawan compound, for example, found three shiploads of gold, while another treasure hunter at Wat Pradu found four buried caches of silver.[182] The newfound wealth generated by the interplay of immigration, opportunism, the China trade and imperialistic mercantilism on Siam's eastern frontier in turn helped Taksin to finance Thonburi's many wars. Serving the economic interests of the merchant class in turn provided the underpinnings for the economic recovery of the resurgent Siamese state.

By 1770, the fledgling state of Thonburi had become bigger and stronger than what it was in 1768. If Mac Thientu's spies had returned to Thonburi in 1770, they would no longer have witnessed an impoverished, embattled state beset with political, economic and military problems. After Ha Tien withdrew from Chanthabun, the Kingdom of Thonburi became undisputed master of all the key ports along the entire eastern coastline stretching from Trat in the east to Nakhon Si Thammarat and Songkhla in the south.

Taksin's new capital was also more accessible from the sea than Ayudhya. Consequently, in 1770 the mercantile state of Thonburi was in a better competitive position to make a bid for control of the trans-Mekong regional trade. When Taksin returned from his successful campaign in Nakhon Si Thammarat, he made military preparations to retaliate against Mac Thientu and attack Ha Tien.

After the rainy season of 1771, a large expeditionary force departed from Thonburi amidst the usual pomp and ceremony.[183] With ambitious objectives, the Eastern Campaign had begun. King Taksin had conceived the strategy of the Eastern Campaign in terms of a two-pronged attack. The first prong comprised a naval attack on Ha Tien to pay back Mac Thientu for his attack on Chantabun and to eradicate the Cantonese, anti-Teochew regime in the Gulf of Siam.

The naval expedition would be spearheaded by the Royal Fleet, commanded by the king himself and supported by several naval cohorts. King Taksin's Royal Fleet had 84 Siamese warships, and 2,242 troops. Another naval fleet comprising 34 Chinese junks, 12 royal Siamese warships and 4 private ships carrying 1,431 troops was commanded by Phraya Phiphit, or Tan Liang (the Teochew pronunciation of Chen Lai in Chinese records), who was an old hand on the eastern front. Phraya Phichai Na Lai (or Lan Lai in Chinese records) the Kosathibodi, now retired from the Phraklang post, headed another fleet comprising 24 Chinese junks in addition to 10 Siamese warships with 1,705 men. The vanguard was commanded by Phraya Phichai Aisawan with 72 warships and 1,686 men. Other lesser commanders also had their own ships and men.[184] The large naval armada sailing for Ha Tien, headed by King Taksin, embodied an invasion force of more than 10,000 men.[185]

The second prong of the Eastern Campaign comprised a land invasion force led by Thong Duang, now Phraya Yommarat.[186] The land invasion force, accompanied by Prince Ang Non, had the ambitious objective of restoring Siamese suzerainty over Cambodia by installing the pro-Siam Prince Ang Non on the throne in Phnom Penh.[187] The land invasion force via Battambang and the seaborne invasion via Ha Tien would come together near Phnom Penh for a final assault on the Cambodian capital.

In early November 1771, King Taksin's armada reached Ha Tien while Phichai the Kosathibodi's forces landed and established a beachhead at Kompong Som and captured the town. After seizing Kompong Som, he attacked Kampot. The Cham governor of Kampot, Phraya Panglima, surrendered and pledged loyalty to King Taksin. Concurrently, Siamese forces surrounded and laid siege to Ha Tien. The invasion force encountered little resistance and Ha Tien fell to Taksin on 19 November 1771, after a siege of 10 days.[188] Mac Thientu fled to Quang Nam.

Before entering the city, King Taksin issued strict orders that Mac Thientu and his family be captured but not harmed. In addition he ordered Siamese troops stationed there not to "capture or kill Chinese and Vietnamese traveling to trade in Ha Tien, but should seek to persuade people to settle and continue working. Those who violated the order would be put to death."[189] These instructions underscored the importance Taksin always given to the annexation and control of ports. Unlike other rival pretenders in 1767, Taksin alone based his politico-military strategy on the control of coastal resources and port cities.

Moreover, at Ha Tien, Taksin broke with his usual practice of removing the conquered population for resettlement in Thonburi. In fact, he expressly forbade his commanders from attempting to evacuate or resettle the trading community of the port.[190] Instead, his priority was to restore law and order so that there was minimal disruption to the town's business. Ha Tien was a valuable asset, not be despoiled but to be added to Thonburi's growing capability to dominate the region's trade. Thus, his efforts to rapidly restore normalcy to the town's commercial operations further underscored the fact that Siamese mercantile interests motivated the control of Ha Tien.

However, during the pacification of the city, Taksin found that the daughter of Mac Thientu, who was brought in by Phraya Phiphit's servant, had been raped.[191] Furious that his order had been disobeyed, Taksin personally investigated the incident. Failing to find the culprit, King Taksin ordered the caning of the servant who had brought her in, and jailed Phraya Phiphit. The king then threatened to execute Phraya Phiphit if the culprit was not found. Fortunately, the *phraya* of Chantabun managed to arrest the soldier who had abused the lady. The guilty one was immediately beheaded and Phraya Phiphit and his servant were released. King Taksin's dreadful and humiliating punishments demoralized Thonburi's Chinese soldiers and generated bitter resentment against him on the part of his trusted generals.

Before departing from Ha Tien, however, the king appointed Phraya Phiphit as Phraya Rachasretthi-Chin, the governor of Ha Tien. The appointment of Phraya Phiphit killed two birds with one stone: Phraya Phiphit Tan Liang[192] was a Teochew leader, as well as a Phraklang official well versed in the commerce of the Eastern Region. The annexation of Ha Tien and appointment of Tan Liang as Phraya Rachasretthi-Chin reflected Thonburi's commercial motivations and symbolized the displacement of Cantonese mercantile interests from southeastern Cambodia, as well as the expansion of the Teochew mercantile orbit in the Gulf of Siam. Leaving Tan Liang to garrison the newly seized port city, King Taksin departed with the main body of the expeditionary force to rendezvous with Phraya Yommarat Thong Duang at Phnom Penh for a joint attack on the capital.[193]

Phnom Penh fell easily to King Taksin's forces. Having occupied Phnom Penh and Oudong, King Taksin installed his protégé, Prince Ang Non, on the throne at Phnom Penh and another pro-Siamese Khmer, Okya Talaha Baen, was put in charge of Battambang and Pursat.[194] Ousted, King Ang Ton fled to Gia Dinh.[195] The old tributary obligations were re-imposed on Cambodia and the latter had to resume delivering tribute to supply Thonburi with exportable forest products. Consequently, it may be argued that if the war of political succession to establish Taksin's political supremacy was fought in the Chao Phraya Basin, then the war to establish the economic foundations of the Kingdom of Thonburi was fought in Ha Tien, Cambodia and the Trans-Mekong Region.

However, Thonburi's hegemony over Cambodia lasted only briefly. The eastern theater soon became an accursed stage, embodying a tragic plot in which all the royal actors suffered a cruel fate. In early 1772, Ang Ton counterattacked with a large Vietnamese army, commanded by General Cuu-dam, and defeated the Siamese force. Phnom Penh and Lovek were recaptured and Ang Ton was reinstated as king.[196]

PHRAYA PHIPHIT (TAN LIANG [陳聯], LATER PHRAYA RACHASRETTHI-CHIN)

Phraya Phiphit was a wealthy *lukchin* named Tan Liang (Chen Lian [陳聯]).[197] In 1767 Tan Liang (or Khun Phiphit in the chronicles) left Ayudhya with Taksin. Shortly before the battle for Rayong, Tan Liang was promoted to Luang Phiphit, and he was elevated to Phraya Phiphit after the battle of Chantabun. In November 1767, Phraya Phiphit led the Chinese infantry to attack Pho Sam Ton and successfully retook Ayudhya from Burmese control.

After the establishment of the Kingdom of Thonburi, Tan Liang worked in the Phraklang ministry with his senior comrade-in-arms Phraya Phichai. To raise military funds to defray wartime expenses, the Phraklang ministry operated the trade monopoly on behalf of Taksin. In 1768, when Siam needed to buy rice to stave off famine in the capital, Tan Liang was sent to Ha Tien for the supply. Taksin also charged him with the negotiation with Mac Thientu for the extradiction of an Ayudhyan royal, Chao Chui, but the negotiation failed.[198]

In 1770, Ha Tien attacked Chantabun. Taksin was in Nakhon Si Thammarat and Phraya Phichai, the Phraklang minister, was on the Battambang campaign. It fell to Phraya Phiphit Tan Liang to reinforce the defense of Chantabun.[199] Although Chantabun fell under the onslaught of Ha Tien's numerically superior forces, Phraya Phiphit organized many counterattacks that, together with the epidemic that claimed the lives of many Ha Tien soldiers, allowed the Siamese to eventually succeed in forcing the invaders to withdraw.

In Taksin's 1771 campaign against Ha Tien, Phraya Phiphit commanded a fleet of 34 junks, while the Phraklang only commanded 24 junks.[200] However, during the pacification of Ha Tien, Phraya Phiphit was severely disciplined by King Taksin for failing to ensure the safety of the family of the fugitive ruler Mac Thientu.[201] But before the king left Ha Tien in 1772, he appointed Phraya Phiphit the governor of Ha Tien with the title Phraya Rachasretthi-Chin.[202] Tan Liang was called by this title until the end of his days.

Throughout the 15 years of the Thonburi Kingdom, Tan Liang kept reappearing. When the Burmese attacked in 1774, the army of Rachasretthi-Chin was involved in setting up fortifications at Ratchaburi. Next year, when the Burmese attacked again from the north, he was in charge of the supply line of the Siamese army.[203]

A Burmese spy's map indicated that Phraya Rachasretthi-Chin lived in a Teochew enclave just across the river from the king's palace. After the death of King Taksin, Tan Liang (who must have been close to Rama I) was responsible for effecting a smooth and peaceful relocation of the Teochew community to make way for the Grand Palace of the Chakri dynasty. Interestingly, Tan Liang—the man who peacefully moved the Chinese out of the city wall down to present-day Chinatown—was completely forgotten. No lineage can be traced back to him. Shortly after his coronation, Rama I reappointed Tan Liang as the governor of Ha Tien, the town he and his followers had bravely defended. Upon Tan Liang's death in 1787, Mac Thientu's son succeeded him as Phraya Rachasretthi.[204]

There was no evidence that privileges were given to Phraya Phiphit or Phraya Phichai Kosa, the two Chinese generals of the Thonburi Kingdom, other than the merit they earned by fighting alongside their king. Despite the support of the Teochew people, there was no overwhelming evidence that King Taksin gave special privileges to the Teochew above the facilities he extended to the Chinese merchant community as a whole. The term *chin luang*, meaning "royal Chinese," popularized by many foreign observers of the Thonburi period, may suggest an undeserved connotation because in the end the Chinese betrayed Taksin. Used by different writers for different political objectives, the term has become so politicized that it has retained little descriptive meaning.

However, Battambang, Siem Reap and Kampot remained in Siamese hands. King Ang Non fell back to Kampot and established his base there supported by Siamese arms. Consequently, Cambodia became split into several zones. Western Cambodia including Battambang and Pursat was still held by the Siamese army, and south Cambodia including Kampot and Kompong Som came under King Ang Non's pro-Siamese military command. The southeastern coastal reach was in the hands of Phraya Rachasretthi-Chin, or Tan Liang, centered at Ha Tien, while eastern Cambodia, along the Mekong River and encompassing Prey Veng was under King Ang Ton and Vietnamese military command.[205]

Meanwhile, Taksin stopped at Ha Tien on the way back to Thonburi from Phnom Penh. During his stopover, Taksin sent envoys to open peace talks with Mac Thientu but the latter rejected the proposal. King Taksin's desire for peace talks was probably driven by Thonburi's inability to impose a speedy military solution to its conflict with Quang Nam. Taksin wished for a quick resolution of the Cambodian issue so that he could address the bigger threat of Burmese invasion. At that time, Burma's continued occupation of Chiang Mai represented a dagger pointed at Thonburi's back, and Taksin could ill afford having to deal with two vulnerable fronts at the same time.

Mac Thientu, on the other hand, was encouraged by King Ang Ton's successful counterattack using Vietnamese forces. Consequently, he turned down Taksin's proposal because he felt confident of recovering Ha Tien with Vietnamese arms.[206] After Mac Thientu rejected his offer of peace, Taksin departed Ha Tien for Thonburi with Mac Thientu's concubines and children, as well as Chao Chui, who was captured during the battle for Ha Tien in November 1771.[207] At Thonburi, Mac Thientu's concubines and family were held in custody. Chao Chui was executed, becoming the first royal casualty in the unfolding eastern tragedy.

After King Taksin had returned to Thonburi, Mac Thientu used Vietnamese forces to counterattack the Siamese occupation of Ha Tien. He successfully defeated the Siamese garrison defending the city. Rachasretthi-Chin, the new governor, withdrew his forces to Kampot where he regrouped his forces, and joining with reinforcements from Panglima (the Cham governor of Kampot), the Siamese launched a counterattack on Ha Tien. Rachasretthi-Chin managed to expel Mac Thientu's Vietnamese and Cantonese forces and retook Ha Tien after fierce fighting, which left the town in ruins. Thus, the Cantonese ruler had gambled and lost his last chance to recover his kingdom, his concubines and his children with dignity. Once again, Mac Thientu was obliged to flee to Vietnam.

Although King Taksin's Cambodian expedition ended as a misadventure, Quang Nam's triumph in Cambodia soon proved to be a pyrrhic victory. Quang Nam's battle in 1771 and 1772 with the Siamese precipitated internal social upheaval, which fueled the Tay Son Rebellion (1772–1802). The Tay Son Rebellion began in Central Vietnam in 1772 and soon undermined the authority of the Nguyen rulers in Southern Vietnam.

Militarily embattled by the spread of the Tay Son Rebellion, the Nguyen court and its royal Cantonese and Cambodian clients were forced to reach an accommodation with Thonburi. In March 1773, after the fall of Qui-nhon to the Tay Son rebels, an envoy arrived in Thonburi from Quang Nam bearing gifts for King Taksin and offering to return some land that the Vietnamese controlled in Cambodia as a peace gesture.[208] The envoy, who was a relative of Mac Thientu, presented an official letter to King Taksin offering to negotiate the return of Ha Tien.[209]

King Taksin, who had initially proposed peace talks in 1772, responded favorably. Mac Thientu's wives and children were released and allowed to return home. King Taksin ordered his governor of Ha Tien, Phraya Rachasretthi-Chin to return to Thonburi and hand over the devastated city of Ha Tien to Mac Thientu's eldest son, Mac Tu Hoang. As a quid pro quo, Mac Thientu arranged for the extradition of Chao Srisang, whom King Ang Ton had previously refused to hand over to King Taksin. Chao Srisang was immediately put to death upon arriving in Thonburi, becoming the second royal casualty of the eastern tragedy.

Both Ha Tien and Kampot ports, which were bones of contention between Thonburi and Quang Nam, passed from the Siamese-Teochew orbit back into the Vietnamese-Cantonese sphere of influence. Tan Liang returned to Thonburi after his position as governor of Ha Tien was revoked to assist in the defense of Ratchaburi against an imminent Burmese attack. However he retained the title of Phraya Rachasretthi-Chin throughout his lifetime.

Not long after, the Tay Son Rebellion engulfed Southern Vietnam. Tay Son armies captured Quang Nam in 1775, sending the last Nguyen king, Dinh Vuong, fleeing for his life to the Mekong Delta. The most prominent Tay Son general, Nguyen Hue, pursued the fugitive king relentlessly and sacked Saigon before catching up and killing the last Nguyen ruler at Ca Mau in 1776, ending 200 years of Nguyen rule over Southern Vietnam.[210] After the collapse of Quang Nam, Tay Son rebels captured Ha Tien and Mac Thientu was again obliged to seek asylum—this time to Thonburi.[211] After enjoying King Taksin's hospitality, the ageing Cantonese ruler became the unwitting target of a successful Tay Son–inspired intrigue to frame him and was executed together with two Nguyen Vietnamese envoys and 50 suspects in November 1780 by King Taksin, becoming the fourth royal casualty after the last Nguyen king in the eastern tragedy.[212]

Meanwhile, in Cambodia the collapse of Quang Nam in 1775 deprived King Ang Ton of his main source of support.[213] Unable to maintain himself without the protection of Vietnamese arms, and being severely disliked by his own people for his unremitting political conflicts and famines, King Ang Ton abdicated in favor

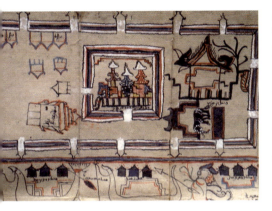

The Burmese spy map indicated that Phraya Rachasretthi-Chin (Tan Liang), the leader of the Chinese community, lived next to the palace of King Taksin's son on the Bangkok side of the river.

of his pro-Siamese rival, Ang Non. He made his brother Ang Than "Third King" and took for himself the title "Retired King."[214] Ang Non returned to Oudong to become "First King" and ruled Cambodia jointly with his two brothers. However, the shaky compromise among the Cambodian royals did not last long. Political turmoil continued at court and in 1777, King Ang Non killed his brother, Ang Than, the "Third King."[215] Grieved by the incident, "Retired King" Ang Ton died shortly after, becoming the sixth royal casualty, after King Ang Than, in the unfolding eastern tragedy.

Outraged by the cold-blooded fratricide at court and blaming "First King" Non for the deaths of both his brothers, prominent officials under the leadership of Talaha (Mu), the governor of Bassac, revolted in 1779 with military support from the remnants of Nguyen loyalists who continued to resist the Tay Sons. King Non's forces were routed at Kompong Chhnang on the Tonle Sap. King Non was captured and killed, becoming the seventh royal casualty in the eastern tragedy.[216]

Paradoxically, in this losing game of royal musical chairs, Thonburi came out as the winner in the eastern theater's military tangle. Thonburi had invaded Ha Tien and Cambodia to control the trans-Mekong hinterland and monopolize the lucrative trade in forest products. Defeated by Quang Nam, Thonburi had to cede control of eastern Cambodia, Ha Tien and Kampot in the settlement of 1773. Ironically, by failing to monopolize the regional trade in forest products through military means in 1772, King Taksin was in the end able to gain what he wanted by an unexpected method.

As it turned out, ceding eastern Cambodia, Ha Tien and Kampot to Quang Nam did not amount to a great loss. The outbreak of the Tay Son Rebellion in 1772 soon eliminated Thonburi's main competitor for this regional trade, without King Taksin having to outfit an army to do the job for him. Furthermore, the economic utility of Cambodia, Ha Tien and Kampot to Quang Nam was discounted by the fact that the Tay Son Rebellion had compromised the security of overland trade routes and disrupted commerce between the trans-Mekong hinterland and Vietnam. In fact, as the security situation worsened across the Cambodian-Vietnamese frontier, the locus of trans-Mekong regional trade shifted westward, toward the Chao Phraya Basin encompassing Siam and Laos.[217] Consequently, the repercussions of the Tay Son Rebellion benefited Thonburi, as forest products from the Cambodian and Laotian hinterland was redirected away from Quang Nam and Cochin-China. Thus, social upheaval and economic dislocation—which came as a result of unremitting warfare in Quang Nam's former domain—provided Thonburi with the opportunity to establish and maintain a near-monopoly on forest products from the Trans-Mekong Region.[218]

Moreover, the Tay Son Rebellion did for King Taksin what he could not achieve with Siamese arms—to install his protégé King Ang Non on the throne of Cambodia. When Ang Non ascended the throne in 1775 upon the abdication of King Ang Ton, Ang Non openly broke off tributary relations with Quang Nam, which was embattled by Tay Son rebels.[219] Under "First King" Ang Non, Cambodia resumed its tributary obligations to Thonburi, much to the delight of King Taksin. Consequently, control over Cambodian forest products slipped to Thonburi's merchant syndicates.

Thonburi's campaigns on the Burma front also yielded collateral benefits. During the China-Burma War (1766–74), Chinese soldiers and officials were taken prisoner by Burmese forces. When King Taksin attacked Burmese military strongholds, he liberated Chinese prisoners of war from Burmese captivity. Repatriating liberated Chinese prisoners became a key point in King Taksin's diplomacy with the Qing court.

King Taksin's diplomacy sought to change Chinese perceptions of the new Thonburi Kingdom by emphasizing the fact that they shared a common foe— Burma. Time also worked in King Taksin's favor. After 10 years, the legitimacy of the post-Ayudhya, Siamese political succession had become secure. King Taksin's resolute diplomatic efforts to win recognition from Emperor Qianlong gradually began to pay dividends.

According to the Chinese annals, Emperor Qianlong began to change his view after Taksin repatriated Chinese officials and mercenaries freed from Burmese custody between 1771 and 1776. The emperor's perception of King Taksin improved further when Thonburi followed up her diplomacy by sending a tribute mission to the imperial court in 1781. Led by Phraya Sunthorn-Abhai, Thonburi's tribute mission brought gifts of elephants, ivory and rare forest products. Moved by the king of Thonburi's goodwill, Qianlong finally responded positively to Taksin's request for imperial investiture. The tribute mission departed from Beijing in 1781 with the coveted imperial gifts, but it arrived in Thonburi too late. Taksin was dead.

Before his death, King Taksin's military campaigns to consolidate the Northern Territories and deny the Burmese control of satellite states had also yielded collateral benefits. Among the satellite states that were brought under Thonburi's vassalage during 1778–80 were the Middle Mekong kingdoms of Vientiane, Champassak and Luang Prabang. The remarkable convergence of King Taksin's Northern and Eastern Campaigns enabled Thonburi to consolidate its mercantile domination throughout the Trans-Mekong Region, including the major commercial centers of Vientiane, Champassak, Battambang and Phnom Penh.

The Cambodian revolt of 1779 caught the resurgent Siamese state of Thonburi at the height of its power. King Taksin's protégé, King Ang Non, was killed. The

Mother-of-pearl container of King Taksin's golden letter, which was engraved on a gold sheet and sent to the Chinese emperor.

rebel leader Prince Talaha (Mu) was backed by Nguyen loyalist forces. The six-year-old son of the late King Ang Ton was put on the throne with Talaha (Mu) as regent.[220] The new government repudiated Siamese suzerainty over Cambodia. This development was a direct affront to King Taksin's prestige.

To rectify the insult, King Taksin ordered a punitive military expedition led by Thong Duang (now Somdet Chaophraya Maha Kasatseuk) and his brother Boonma (Chaophraya Surasi), with 20,000 men to invade Cambodia and put Taksin's own son, Prince Intarapitak, on the throne. After the Siamese army crossed into Cambodia, a murky political crisis occurred in Thonburi. Before any fighting took place in Cambodia, Thong Duang hastily returned to Thonburi, leaving the command of the campaign to his brother.

In Thonburi a minor provincial revolt had erupted near Ayudhya and had begun to build momentum. Security forces were sent out under Phraya San from the capital, but instead of putting down the rebellion, the forces joined the rebels and called for the overthrow of King Taksin. Encountering little resistance, the rebel army marched on Thonburi and seized the king.

In the ensuing mayhem, Taksin's generals, namely Phraya Thibethbodi, Phraya Raman and Phraya Ammart, fought for their king. However, King Taksin bade them not to resist, declaring, "My merit is used up [my time has come]; do not waste more lives, stop fighting."[221]

King Taksin's reaction to the palace coup appeared to be the decision of a calm and courageous man who asked to spare needless bloodshed in his defence, rather than the inaction of an insane man afflicted by mental disease, as has been potrayed by later accounts. Judging by his last remark, King Taksin appeared to be almost eager to abdicate, as if he were glad to be rid of the burden of kingship and welcomed the opportunity to withdraw from a regal world dominated by power, greed, opulence, sycophants and insincere courtiers.

Taksin's resigned demeanor seemed to stem from an intuitive acceptance that his character and style of rule perhaps did not conform to the ideal attributes of a Siamese monarch. During the last years of his reign, he was apparently unhappy, restless and irascible—traits that combined with absolute power to make him intolerable to those around him at court.

As this story has amply demonstrated, Taksin was always—in mind, body and spirit—a martial leader. Even after he became king, he was more a general than a king and continued to run his court as if it were a military barrack. His treatment of disobedient Catholic missionaries, offending Buddhist monks, corrupt officials and courtiers who contradicted him was uncannily similar to his treatment of deserters, officers who did not promptly follow orders and those who tried to obstruct his attempt to reunify the country during his rise to power.

Taksin was an impulsive and decisive leader who often demonstrated unerring judgment. These personal attributes have made him Siam's most celebrated military leader, as well as one of the greatest generals in Asian military history. But the very qualities that made him so successful as a general on campaign hampered him when the campaigns ended, especially after he laid down his sword and took up the scepter during the last five years of his reign. The historian B.J. Terwiel observed, "The qualities that were virtues in a general who had to win battles became liabilities to a sedentary monarch. As an army commander he could give short shrift to officers who lacked courage or to men he disliked for being sycophants or hypocrites, but not so a peacetime king."[222]

Taksin did not lack the ability to be a good king. At times his edicts and actions represented the best of kingly qualities. On many critical occasions, he was just; he lifted the kingdom's moral standards; he protected the populace from predators and looters; on campaign he ordered his soldiers to respect farmers' property and refrain from molesting women and children. Although he was willful, volatile, determined and uncompromising, he could also be sincere, compassionate and benevolent, as when he used treasury funds to purchase rice and distribute it for free to the people during the famine of 1768.

Taksin was at his best when he was fighting Thonburi's enemies, pacifying the country from rebels and bandits, establishing order out of chaos and improvising solutions to alleviate crises. However, after he had reunified the country and established the new order embodied in the Kingdom of Thonburi, his restless character conflicted with the need to act slowly, patiently and win friends among courtiers and nobility. It was in meeting the needs of sedentary kingship as opposed to empire building that his character failed him.

Thus, it is not surprising that his strict, uncompromising character was unpopular. While he excelled at unifying the country, he failed to unify the nobles and courtiers, and resentment seethed against his dictatorial style. Preferring to surround himself with Spartan simplicity as opposed to ceremony, pageantry, ritual and opulence, he was looked down upon by the nobles at court as an uncouth

Toward the end of his reign, Taksin became obsessed with meditation. This famous statue at Wat Intharam depicts Taksin in transcendental meditation.

King Taksin's stupa at Wat Intharam, Thonburi, where his ashes are buried.

Chinese. His supporters alienated, he became isolated at court and stood at the mercy of conspirators who sought to topple him. During his last days, he must have realized that his rule had disappointed many people. It must have dawned on him that he could not change peoples' convictions by sheer force or deter corruption by meting out harsh punishments. At last overcome by a sense of futility to change his court in the way he knew how, he began to feel hopeless and weary. His time had come. He would not fight. He would go.

Meanwhile, Thong Duang had barely just departed on a military expedition to Cambodia, when he surprisingly reappeared again at Thonburi with a large force. His return was timely. Under his instructions, his nephew Phraya Suriya Aphai, the governor of Nakhon Rachasima, had already laid siege to the capital city with Siamese and Laotian troops brought down from Khorat. The defenders of the city were quickly overwhelmed by the forces of Phraya Suriya Aphai.

When Thong Duang arrived at the city gates, he found the capital waiting for him and nobody challenged his claim to be Siam's new king. He was invited to ascend the throne and was crowned Rama I on 6 April 1782. King Taksin was executed on 7 April 1782. He was 47 years old.[223]

Taksin's death signaled the beginning of a bloody purge at court, which claimed scores of lives, including Krommakhun Anuraksongkhram and more than 40 of his followers, as well as Phraya San's supporters and numerous Taksin loyalists. Among those who were personally attached to Taksin was Thong Dee the White Teeth, the late king's stalwart general. Thong Dee refused to pledge allegiance to the new king and was executed together with Taksin's other loyal followers. Taksin's whole family would have been exterminated by the ferocious Boonma but for the intervention of Thong Duang to spare the women and children. Prince Intharapithak, who had been in Boonma's custody since the fateful Cambodian expedition, was executed—the ninth royal casualty in the eastern tragedy after King Taksin.

BRIEF FAMILY PROFILES OF THONBURI CHINESE

The descendants of the king of Thonburi are quite numerous. Families who trace their lineage to King Taksin include the Sinsuk, Indrayothin, Pongsin, Rungpairoj, Silanond, Indrakamhaeng and a branch of the Na Nakorn family. Those who descended from King Taksin's daughters include the Issarasena, Dharmasaroja, Noppavong, Supradit, Srithawat, Watanavong, Ratanakot, Panumas and Kanchanavichai families. Besides these, in our research of over 10 years, we have found that very few Chinese families apart from the king's descendants can trace their ancestry back to the Thonburi era. Some of them are:

The Banomyong

The Banomyong family believes their clan is descended from Tan Heng, a Teochew who migrated to Siam during the reign of King Ekathat of Ayudhya. Tan Heng's mother was a sister of Tae Yong, King Taksin's father. Driven by poverty, Tan Heng decided to join his maternal uncle, leaving behind a wife and a son named Tan Seng in China. Tan Heng joined his cousin's regiment and died in the service of the half-Chinese king of Siam. When Tan Heng's mother wrote to enquire about her son, King Taksin informed her of her son's demise and compensated the family.

In 1814, Tan Heng's grandson, Tan Seng-U, known in Thai as Nai Kok, emigrated to Siam and made his living selling Chinese and Thai sweets in Ayudhya. Nai Kok was the great grandfather of Pridi Banomyong (pictured), the seventh Prime Minister of Thailand (1946) and founder of Thammasat University (1934). Pridi's parents adopted the surname Banomyong in 1866, after a temple in Ayudhya where his father was cremated.[224]

The Chatikavanij

During the reign of King Taksin, So Siang (蘇祥), a native of Zhangzhou, came to Thonburi, where his son was born in 1776. His grandson made a success of himself and was appointed Luang Aphai Vanich (Chak) during the reign of Rama III. The Su clan (called So in Thai) later settled at Bangkok's Talad Noi district, which was a Hokkien enclave with a shrine of the Hokkien deity Jo Sue Gong (Qing Shui Zu Shi). Talad Noi has been the symbolic center of Hokkien culture in Bangkok since its early days. The Jo Sue Gong shrine is the fulcrum of Talad Noi's cultural activities. The Hokkien Association stands within the shrine's grounds.

Members of the Su clan lived in adjoining houses clustered near the Jo Sue Gong shrine. So Siang was the forefather of Korn Chatikavanij (pictured), Thailand's finance minister from 2009 to 2011, as well as Anand Panyarachun, Thailand's twice-former prime minister (1991–92).[225]

The Krairiksh

According to the Krairiksh family history, Lim Riksh (林良), a Hokkien, was the linguist[226] in the tribute mission to Canton dispatched in May 1781, in which King Taksin sent 11 ships. The official envoy to Beijing was headed by Phraya Sunthorn Aphai,[227] while the trade mission headed by Chaophraya Srithammathirat stayed behind in Canton.[228] When the mission returned to Thonburi, the Chakri dynasty was already established. Lim Riksh later worked for Somdet Phra Bawornrajchao Maha Sura Singhanat (Boonma), Rama I's younger brother, as Phraya Kraikosa, the Phraklang of the Front Palace. During the reign of Rama II, Lim Riksh's son Thong Chin was appointed Phraya Choduk-Rachasretthi, master of the Chinese community in Bangkok. Poonphoem Krairiksh served as the Lord Chamberlain of King Bhumibol Adulyadej from 1978 to 1987. The Krairiksh continue to serve the kings of Siam with distinction through the present day.

The Na Songkhla and Suwankiri

The patriarch of the Na Songkhla clan, Hao Yiang (Wu Rang, 吳讓), a native of Zhangzhou, arrived in Songkhla in 1750 at the age of 34. He was engaged in farming and fisheries, and by the time of King Taksin's Nakhon Si Thammarat campaign in 1769, he was already a prosperous man, locally known in the vicinity of Songkhla as the Great Elder. Hao Yiang visited King Taksin to pay his respects and brought him a gift of 50 boxes of tobacco. The meeting went well and he was appointed Luang Inthakirisombat, the bird's nest concessionaire for two islands off the coast of Songkhla. His sons were sent to Thonburi for their education and Hao Yiang visited the king to pay his dues in person every year. As the leader of the local community and commanding substantial manpower, he was appointed Luang Suwankirisombat, the governor of Songkhla, in 1775.

Seven successive members of the Na Songkhla clan succeeded Hao Yiang as the governor of Songkhla until the death of Phraya Vichienkhiri (Chom Na Songkhla) in 1901. Many prominent members of the Na Songkhla family had served in the Thai government with distinction throughout the 19th and 20th centuries, including Chaophraya Srithammathibeth (Chitr Na Songkhla), the last *chaophraya* of Siam and a former president of the National Assembly.

The Ratanakul

Although Chin Gun, the patriarch of the Ratanakul family, gained prominence during the reign of Rama I, he was a military commander in the service of the king of Thonburi with the title of Phra Rachprasith. Chin Gun's father was a junk master who lived in Baan Prok along the Mae Klong River, south of Amphawa where Rama I used to live. Rama I later appointed Chin Gun the Phraklang, and during the reign of his son, Rama II, Chin Gun was elevated to Chaophraya Ratanathibeth, the Samuhanayok.

The Sombatsiri

The Sombatsiri clan descended from Tan Teckngeng (陳德銀, 1733–1804), a Teochew from a village in Shantou who came to Siam during the late Ayudhya/early-Thonburi period. Tan was a successful merchant and was awarded royal titles by both the Siamese and the Qing courts. In Siam both he and his son were awarded the rank of *phraya*, namely Phraya Sri Racha Arkorn and Phraya Sombat Vanich (Boonsri), respectively. Phraya Sri Racha Arkorn died at the age of 71 during the reign of Rama II and Phraya Sombat Vanich died in 1837 during the reign of Rama III. The family continued their trade as important sugar tax farmers in Siam.

The Swasdibutra

According to K.S.R. Kularb, Phraya Sawasdiwari Chim (林蔭), a prominent junk merchant during the reign of Rama III, descended from an important Thonburi junk master who came from the same village as King Taksin's mother. The village was in Petchaburi and was called Baan Laem. According to the spirit tablet at the Swasdibutra's home, Phraya Sawasdiwari's ancestral name was Lim Boonbing (林文炳、希憲), and he held the position of Luang Phibulvanich in the Thonburi/early-Bangkok era.

The Sundaravej

Samak Sundaravej, who became Thailand's 25th prime minister in 2008 and served as the governor of Bangkok between 2000 and 2004, is perhaps the most unlikely candidate to qualify as a *lukchin*. However, his ancestral tombstone in a remote corner of the Chanthaburi Royal Thai Navy Base confirmed that Samak's forefather was a Chinese living in Chanthabun during King Taksin's reign. According to the Sundaravej family, there used to be over 400 Chinese tombs on the hill before the navy excavated the graveyard and cleared away the area in the 1930s. Fortunately for the Sundaravej family, Samak's uncle, Phraya Bhetpongsa (Sund Sundaravej) was physician to both King Rama VI and King Rama VII, so he appealed to the king for special permission to retain the burial site of his ancestor. His wish was granted.

Nirandorn Narksuriyan, a Chinese linguist who studied the inscriptions on the tombstone, dated the burial site to the year 1770. Although Samak has always claimed that his Chinese surname is Li, according to Nirandorn, the Sundaravej clan name is Tan (Chen), not Li. The inscription on the tombstone clearly indicated that the deceased, a lady from the Li (李) family, was the wife of a man with the surname of Tan (Chen, 陳). Since the Sundaravej family is certain that the grave belonged to the family, the woman referred to in the tombstone must be a maternal ancestor. The translator who transcribed the inscriptions on the tombstone for Samak may have failed to note that it was the grave of a woman, causing Samak to believe that his Chinese family name is Li and not Tan. If the graveyard truly belonged to the Sundaravej family, then Samak's real lineage name must be Tan because he must take his name from the male line according to Chinese custom.

According to Samak Sundaravej's funeral book, the Sundaravej family's Chinese ancestors were Hokkien merchants who used to trade between Fujian and Vietnam. They settled at Mỹ Tho, a town on the Mekong Delta founded in the 1680s by the troops of Chinese refugee Long Mol, who fled the persecution of the Qing dynasty. The family later emigrated to Chantabun and the two sons of the deceased lady reburied their mother at the current site on an auspicious date in 1770.

Samak Sundaravej's ancestral tomb at the Royal Thai Navy Base in Chanthaburi dates from 1770.

The family then moved to Bangkok. It's interesting to note that the Sundaravejs used to live in the Sampeng area, where Phraya Rachasretthi-Chin relocated the Chinese from Chantabun. Although the Chinese from Chanthabun were predominantly Teochew, there must have been many Hokkiens there, as well as Cantonese, due to its proximity to Ha Tien and Cochin-China.

ALL THE KING'S MEN

(1782–1855)

Soon after Ayudhya was sacked, a French missionary wrote of the Chinese in Siam that "it is to their industry that one owes the prompt recovery of this kingdom." After the Chakri dynasty was formed, their skilled labor and business instincts continued to be essential, helping to boost the state coffers and earning them the respect of the early Chakri kings. The wealthiest merchants, known as chaosua, *as well as the powerful Chinese rajahs of the south such as the Na Songkhla and Na Ranong, became increasingly entangled with the traditional Siamese patronage system, intermarrying with royalty, accepting noble titles and high posts at court, and in return, building temples to glorify the kings. Booming trade and labor shortages encouraged ever more Chinese to immigrate to Siam. By the middle of the 19th century, however, the Free Trade Movement, technological advances and colonial ambitions of the West threatened the lucrative junk trade and Britain, not China, had become the most powerful force in the region.*

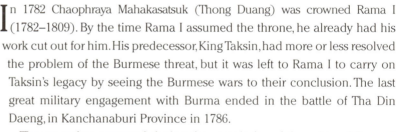

Rama I, the founder of the Chakri dynasty (reigned 1782–1809).

Chapter opening picture: Busy traffic on the Chao Phraya River as depicted in Sir John Crawfurd's *Journal of an Embassy from the Governor-General of India to the Courts of Siam and Cochin-China: Exhibiting a View of the Actual State of Those Kingdoms* (1828).

In 1782 Chaophraya Mahakasatsuk (Thong Duang) was crowned Rama I (1782–1809). By the time Rama I assumed the throne, he already had his work cut out for him. His predecessor, King Taksin, had more or less resolved the problem of the Burmese threat, but it was left to Rama I to carry on Taksin's legacy by seeing the Burmese wars to their conclusion. The last great military engagement with Burma ended in the battle of Tha Din Daeng, in Kanchanaburi Province in 1786.

The wars that occurred during the remainder of the reign of Rama I, as well as those that occurred during the reigns of Rama II and Rama III, were mostly fought outside the Siamese heartland. The only exception was the Laotian interlude during the reign of Rama III (1824–51), when Laotian forces under Chao Anou advanced to within a three-day march of the Siamese capital before Siamese military forces managed to repulse the invading army from Vientiane.

Consequently, peace and internal tranquility descended upon the country, providing a welcome respite from years of incessant fighting. This enabled Rama I to re-channel the energies of his reign to address important and belated non-military problems that had been put on the back burner while the issue of state survival had taken top priority.

The major peacetime challenge to Rama I was to rebuild a capital city that would rival the glory of Ayudhya and repair the war-torn Siamese economy. If the achievements of the Taksin era were chiefly military, then the achievements of the reign of Rama I were political, economic, social, architectural and cultural.

One of the first things Rama I did upon becoming king was to move the seat of government from Thonburi, on the west bank of the Chao Phraya River, to Bangkok on the east bank. As a military commander, Rama I's decision to move the capital was based on strategic considerations. He wanted to make the capital of the new Chakri dynasty less accessible to future Burmese attacks and the large Chao Phraya River served as a natural moat against any invasion from the west.

During Taksin's reign, the east bank of the Chao Phraya River had been a Teochew enclave where the Chinese regiment of the king resided, including the Chinese general Phraya Rachasretthi-Chin (also known as Tan Liang). As the general of the Chinese *lukchin* regiment, Tan Liang was charged with the delicate task of relocating Thonburi's Chinatown to the marshes of Sampeng to make way for the construction of Bangkok's Grand Palace.

Perhaps the move was to test the loyalty of the Chinese community to the new dynasty. In response, Tan Liang threw his support behind Rama I and was instrumental in quelling rebellious sentiments among the Teochew Chinese, some of whom were still fiercely loyal to Taksin. As a reward for the smooth relocation of the Chinese, Tan Liang was sent back to Ha Tien to serve as its governor, befitting his title of Phraya Rachasretthi-Chin.

Thus, based on the location's strategic assets, Rama I made Bangkok the capital of the new Chakri kingdom in 1782. By 1783, he had dug canals to drain the swamp and carved out a fortifiable island of approximately 9 kilometers in circumference. When Monsignor Jean-Baptiste Pallegoix arrived in Bangkok in the early 1830s, the old swamp on the east bank was gone. Instead, he saw an island fortified by crenellated walls with 80 mounted cannons running along the perimeter and flanked by intervening bastions. Part of the fortifications built by Rama I still exist today, including Fort Sumeru in Bang Lamphu and Fort Mahakarn in front of Wat Ratchanadda.

Pallegoix waxed lyrical in singing the praises of the great, beautiful and unassailable city of *Krung Thep Maha Nakhon* (City of the Emerald Buddha), known today as Bangkok. He wrote:

> *Situated in the middle of vast gardens adorned with luxurious and perpetual greenery it displays a very picturesque appearance. Ships decked with flags are lined up along the two banks. Gilded spires, domes and high, admirably shaped pyramids adorned with drawings made of many-hued porcelain can be seen rising up. The stacked roofs of pagodas are adorned with beautiful gilding and covered with varnished tiles reflecting the sun's rays. Two rows of several thousand shops float on rafts ... crisscrossed in all directions by thousands of boats.*

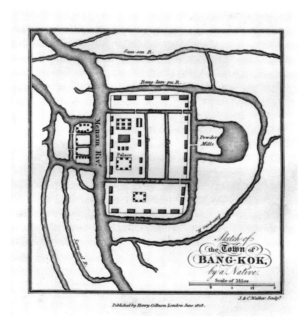

A native-drawn plan of Bangkok published in Sir John Crawfurd's *Journal of an Embassy from the Governor-General of India to the Courts of Siam and Cochin-China: Exhibiting a View of the Actual State of those Kingdoms* (1828).

The seal of the king of Siam.

This new Siamese capital at Bangkok, so ardently admired by Pallegoix, was destined to be the largest and most prosperous capital in the history of Siam.

The Royal Trading Monopoly

The historical turning point that ushered in the chain of events leading to the growth of prosperity during the Chakri dynasty was the restoration of peace to the war-torn Siamese economy. This era of stability provided the basis for an unprecedented expansion of trade.

Perhaps an important event in the early development of Bangkok was the restoration of the official tribute trade with China, which had been suspended since the fall of Ayudhya. The diplomatic initiatives of King Taksin had moved Emperor Qianlong to recognize the new ruler of Siam and grant an audience to the tribute mission of 1781. Rama I took full advantage of the resumption of official trade relations to request imperial investiture in 1782.[1] In 1786, the Chinese emperor acknowledged Rama I and gave the new Siamese king the coveted investiture in the name of Tae Hua, the son of Tae Jiao,[2] the official Chinese name of the former King Taksin. John Crawfurd, an associate of Stamford Raffles, the founder of Singapore, visited Siam in the early 1820s and gave an apt summary of the tribute mission sent annually to Canton:

> *The King of Siam acknowledged himself a tributary of the Emperor of China. His doing so does not arise from any particular necessity or consideration, or out of any actual dependence of Siam upon China, but altogether from this mercenary motive, that the vessels which carry the ambassadors may, under pretext of doing so, be exempted from the payment of all imposts. In this view two of the largest descriptions of junks, amounting to nearly one thousand tons each, sail annually from Bangkok to Canton loaded with merchandizes [sic].[3]*

Rama I was no stranger to foreign trade as he traced his ancestry back to Kosa Pan, the Phraklang official handling foreign trade during the reign of King Phetracha (1688–1703). Excellent pedigree credentials aside, Rama I proved to be skillful in economic matters. The crown earned substantial revenue from taxes in fishery, plantation, liquor distillery, gambling, agriculture, market, abattoir, as well as fees and duties levied along transportation routes on foreign ships and on shipbuilding. However, revenue from taxation was not sufficient for a state with a large standing army. When his brother the Maha Uparat (Boonma) requested a larger budget for the Front Palace in 1796, the king turned down his request, arguing that if it were not for the profits from the Royal Junk Fleet, the government would be in deficit.[4]

The benefits from foreign trade included entry fees that were charged according to the size of the visiting ships, a tax of between 3 to 8 percent on imports depending on how regularly the ship visited Bangkok, a tax on exports at various rates based on the goods being exported, and profits from the royally commissioned junk trade and the royal monopoly warehouse. Royalty and *khunnang* were also encouraged to trade. As rice was in demand in China and hardwood for shipbuilding was in abundance in Siam, junks laden with rice could be sold at very high margins in Canton. Permits for rice exports were only granted if the rice surplus exceeded a three-year supply of grain for Bangkok.

Not only was Rama I conversant in trade matters, but he also had the uncanny ability to attract capable assistants. Counting among his trusted advisors on Chinese affairs were Chaophraya Phraklang (Hon), Chin Kun[5] and Kromluang Narinronret (Thong Chin). Chaophraya Phraklang Hon, the most colorful amongst Rama I's trusted advisors, was a brilliant man. Hon has been credited with running an efficient state enterprise that minted profits from overseas trade to help finance a strong army to fight the wars of the resurgent Siamese empire. Besides being an outstanding administrator, he was also an intellectual and scholar who oversaw the translation of the great Chinese literary classic *The Romance of the Three Kingdoms* into Thai.

Chin Kun, a prominent merchant from the Mae Klong River delta, was an old trusted friend of Thong Duang before he rose to become Rama I. The king let Chin Kun manage the royal warehouse, and after Chaophraya Phraklang Hon died in 1805, he was appointed the Phraklang. Later on, Chin Kun was promoted to the premier minister post of Samuhanayok by Rama II (1809–24). Another trusted advisor was Rama I's nephew, Kromluang Narinronret (Thong Chin), who had served under Taksin as an emissary to the Middle Kingdom in 1781. His experiences in Canton must have served Rama I in more ways than one.

Rama I's skillful trade lieutenants efficiently matched the goods that Siam had to offer with the demand in the Chinese market. Many highly sought-after forest products in overseas markets were declared royal monopolies. Prince Damrong defined the royal monopoly goods during the reign of Rama II, as tin, lead, timber, pepper, ivory, sappanwood, cardamom, gamboge and elephants.[6] Once a royal monopoly had been established, local traders had to sell these products to the royal warehouse and were not permitted to sell them directly to foreign merchants. Often *phrai-luang* labor was used to gather the products for the royal warehouse. Chaophraya Phraklang was responsible for the selling of these products through royally commissioned junks. After the royal junks had loaded the goods, left over stocks were allowed to be sold to other merchants in Bangkok.

Thus, export trade became the main driver of economic recovery for the war-torn, devastated Siamese economy in the post-Ayudhya period.

The eldest son of Rama I, Prince Issara-Sunthorn, participated enthusiastically in overseas trade by using cargo space in his father's royal junks to export goods to China and import Chinese luxury products such as beautiful porcelains and Yixing teapots. Prince Issara-Sunthorn subsequently succeeded his father as Rama II (1809–24). Unlike his father, who was remembered by posterity as a warrior statesman, Rama II tended to withdraw into a ritual role while he indulged his passion for the arts, poetry and overseas trading, which brought in artistic and luxurious items.

Indeed, in trade matters his meticulous attention to profit would put many Chinese merchants to shame. Rama II took pains to know exactly what kinds of cargo should be aboard the royal junks, sending directives to his provincial governors to deliver only those that would earn high profits in overseas markets for the Royal Junk Fleet. In 1819 he instructed the governor of Nakhon Si Thammarat to buy local pepper and deliver it to Bangkok within a month, using local tax revenue. The note also urged a prompt delivery so that the royal junk would not miss the monsoon wind.

His younger brother, Prince Senanurak, also shared his passion for trading. When Prince Issara-Sunthorn became king he appointed his younger brother and youthful trading companion as the *uparat* of the Front Palace, and he became a very wealthy merchant who sometimes loaned money to his brother, the king.

During the first two reigns of the Chakri dynasty, no less than seven princes from the royal household had their own private junks that competed with the royal junks. Royal proclivity for overseas trade continued into the reign of Rama III when members of the royal household and kin, nobles, and Chinese associated with the Phraklang also engaged in overseas trade and became very rich. Prince Chetsadabodin, Rama I's grandson who was later crowned Rama III (1824–51), made such large profits from the junk trade that his father called him *chaosua*, meaning "wealthy tycoon."

Like the king, the nobles who operated the Phraklang ministry also traded a great deal on their own account and became very wealthy. During the early years of the reign of Rama III, the position of the Phraklang was undoubtedly the most important in Siam next to that of the king. This office was headed by Dit Bunnag (1788–1855), who was closely allied to the king before his enthronement. During the reign of Rama III, the Phraklang operated a very large and profitable junk trade, which he maintained throughout his life. Dit had once declined a promotion to the head of the Kalahom, probably because the Phraklang, though not as high in status as the Kalahom, offered many lucrative trading opportunities. Later,

Dit Bunnag, the Phraklang.

in 1830, Rama III repeated the offer and this time, Dit was appointed the head of the Kalahom as well as the Phraklang, a combination of offices unprecedented in Siamese history.[7]

Siamese junks carried rice, pepper, sugar, cotton, tin, cardamom, hides, feathers, ivory, various woods for furniture making, sappanwood, mangrove bark, sticklac, swallows' nests and sea cucumbers for the Chinese market.[8] On the return journey the ships carried massive amounts of porcelain, including cups, dishes and bowls, as well as tea, brassware, copperware, silk, sugar candy, playing cards, dice, paper and dried vegetables. Often the goods exported to China were much more valuable than those brought from China to Bangkok, and the Chinese had to make up the difference in silver. In addition to these goods, Siamese junks also carried large numbers of passengers.[9]

The Royal Trading Monopoly made the Chakri kings immensely wealthy. Evidence of the new prosperity among Siam's royalty and upper classes could be seen in the fine-quality porcelain imports from China during this period. Compared to Ayudhya court porcelain, the porcelain ordered by the Bangkok elite was finely potted and more expensively decorated. Gold was used extensively in porcelain decorations, especially during the reign of Rama II and Rama III, so much so that a new type of porcelain culture called *Lai Nam Thong* came into vogue. The bigger the profits from the Royal Trading Monopoly, the better the quality of Siamese court porcelain became. Aside from royalty and nobility, many Chinese residents in Siam also ventured their fortune on the China trade. Indeed, without the participation of the overseas Chinese community, the Chakri dynasty's efforts to revive the lucrative China trade might have been stillborn.

Gilded *Lai Nam Thong* porcelain stem plate imported from China during the early Bangkok period. Bequest of HRH Prince Damrong Rajanubhab's (1862–1943) Trustee to the National Museum Bangkok.

The Merchants of Bangkok

The significance of the Chinese contribution to the development of post-Ayudhya commerce was not lost upon Western observers. A letter written in 1769 by Monsignor Corre, a French Catholic missionary residing in Siam during the reign of King Taksin, to his colleague in Malacca, remarked, "The Chinese have put gold and silver into circulation in Siam; it is to their industry that one owes the prompt recovery of this kingdom. If the Chinese were not so eager for gain, there would today be neither silver nor money in Siam."

Similarly, when the Chakri kings were developing the Royal Junk Fleet in the first half of the 19th century, the Chinese played an indispensable role in expanding the royal export monopoly. Much of that trade was borne in Chinese junks, often built by Chinese shipwrights in Siam, manned and captained by

Chinese, with Chinese serving as factors, warehousemen and royal advisors for the kingdom's China trade.

Rama I owned many junks painted in various colors, including red (signifying Teochew operators) and green (signifying Hokkien operators).[10] The largest royal junk was built in Chantabun, the town that built junks for King Taksin's fleet in 1767. However, by the 1820s, Bangkok was manufacturing between six to eight junks of the largest size every year.[11] In 1833, when the Earl of Plymouth arrived before dawn at Bangkok port, he found vast numbers of Chinese blacksmiths forging iron, presumably for the junks that were being built on the banks of the river. He also said that the Chinese in Siam "possess all the mechanical employments" for engaging in junk-building and making *quallies* (iron pans), which were exported in large quantities all over Asia.[12]

William Ruschenberger, a medical officer in an American envoy in 1836, reported sighting a line of Chinese junks of 200–600 tons stretching over three kilometers in mid-stream anchorage along the Chao Phraya River.[13] According to Pallegoix who resided in Bangkok during the reign of Rama III, "Nine or 10 Arab ships come every year from Madras or Surat. At the time of the Chinese New Year, one can see arrive from Hainan, Canton, Fo Kien and other ports of China 50–60 large cargo-ships or junks loaded with merchandise and several thousands of immigrants seeking their fortune in Siam." Besides inbound ships, Pallegoix also provided information on Siam's outbound trade: "Every year, the king sends 15–20 ships to Singapore, Java and China. The high-ranking mandarins each also send two or three junks. Certain Chinese moneybags possess up to five or six."

Available records indicate that the range of export products became more numerous during the reign of Rama III. Pallegoix furnished an exhaustive list of 53 export products, which is too cumbersome to reproduce here. It may be sufficient for our purpose to note that Siamese products in the mid-19th century also comprised items that required processing through systematic labor inputs, such as sugar and coconut oil.

A mural painting shows a Chinese man with queue, a distinct hairstyle.

Economic expansion through the Royal Trading Monopoly stimulated more Chinese immigration. According to Western observers, Chinese immigrants to Siam in the 19th century were mostly males. The majority were small traders, sailors, fishermen, farmers and peasants. Upon marrying Siamese women, their children were brought up as Siamese. Karl Gützlaff, the first Protestant missionary in Siam, observed in many cases where Chinese married Siamese, "they even throw away their jackets and trousers" and became Siamese in every respect.

However, other eyewitness accounts gave conflicting views on how the Chinese dressed. Crawfurd observed, "Indeed it is commonly computed that half the population of the capital [Bangkok] is composed of Chinese . . . they invariably dress in the costume of their own country." Ruschenberger described the Chinese as easily distinguishable by their queue. "But," he added, "they have generally docked the end tail to their heads, and dress à la Siamese, with a circle of hair on the roof. But few of the long tails, the distinguishing appanage to a Chinaman's head, are to be seen." Sandals were worn by the Chinese only.[14]

Children of Sino-Siamese marriages were called *lukchin* and were initially proud of their Chinese descent. However, a few generations later they would feel insulted to be called *jek* (Chinese), presumably because the Chinese began looking up to the Thai ruling class and became self-conscious of their own status as social inferiors.[15] Ruschenberger made an interesting observation in the late 1830s that "Two

So Heng Tai, home of So Jat, ancestor of the Chatikavanich and Posayachinda families, in Talad Noi.

or three schools have begun here for Chinese children . . . but there is much difficulty in organizing and sustaining them, for the reason that Chinamen here have Siamese, Burman, Laos, and even other country women for mothers, whose prejudices are even stronger than that of the Chinese themselves." Gützlaff stated with some humor, "Within two or three generations, all the distinguishing marks of the Chinese dwindle entirely away; and a nation which adheres to its national customs so obstinately becomes wholly changed to Siamese."

The powerful influence of women in shaping the domestic culture of Sino-Siamese households often led to the erosion of traditional Chinese patriarchal values. The depth of the Siamization of the Chinese in the early Bangkok period was evidenced in the adoption of local matrilineal inheritance practices instigated by Siamese women, often against the proclivities of their Chinese husbands. When Yoo, the widow of So Jat (蘇蟹, 蘇溶哲, 1813–49),[16] a well-known Bangkok merchant who was appointed Luang Aphai-Vanich by Rama III, drew up her will, she bequeathed So Heng Tai, the ancestral house of the So family, to her two daughters despite having five sons. In doing this, she ignored the time-honored patriarchal Chinese practice of male inheritance.[17] The powerful influence of Siamese women in the family often stemmed from their role as the local partner in commercial activities. Siamese women played an indispensable role in building business contacts with the aristocratic Bangkok establishment for their Chinese merchant husbands.

Chinese merchants gained direct access to and influence at court reminiscent

Rama II (top) and his three sons, Rama III, King Mongkut and Somdet Phra Pin Klao, the second king during King Mongkut's reign.

of the Age of Ayudhya under King Thaisa. The merchants of Bangkok whose fortunes were intertwined with the Royal Trading Monopoly were showered with noble titles and became fabulously wealthy. These wealthy merchants were commonly referred to as *chaosua*. The fabled Chotikapukkana—one of early Bangkok's wealthiest *chaosua*—built a large mansion on a 100-*rai* park (roughly 15 square kilometers) on Bangkok's waterfront.

Having made their fortune through the royally sponsored junk trade, Bangkok's *chaosua* enthusiastically embraced Siamese culture. Most took a Siamese wife, often several, though they may have had other households in China.

Marriage offered a means of leveraging oneself up the social ladder through connections at court. It was common for wealthy Chinese to present daughters to the king as ladies-in-waiting and prospective royal concubines. Several daughters of *chaosua* were among the ladies-in-waiting and consorts of Rama II and Rama III. The tradition continued under King Mongkut (Rama IV), who took one of the daughters of an ennobled *chaosua* as a concubine and later elevated her to the rank of royal consort. She gave birth to Princess Saowapha, who was to become one of Rama V's queens and mother of both Rama VI and Rama VII. King Mongkut's son, Chulalongkorn, who became Rama V, was reportedly so taken by the beauty of a daughter from the Phisolyabutr clan (a Hokkien family), that he took her into the royal household. Their son was Prince Kitiyakorn of Chantabun, great-grandfather of the present queen (Sirikit). Other *chaosua* families made comparatively splendid alliances as well.

The biographies of various royal branches of the Chakri dynasty—comprising 27 royal families descended from King Mongkut and 19 royal houses descended from his brother Somdet Phra Pin Klao, as well as royal houses such as the Pramoj, Sanitwong, Kunchorn and Prawit—all reported that they had Chinese ancestors. In fact, from the very beginning there was significant Chinese lineage in the Chakri royal family. King Mongkut stated that the father of Rama I had married the beautiful daughter of a rich Chinese merchant during the Ayudhya period. The founder of the Chakri dynasty and the Bangkok Kingdom, Rama I himself, undoubtedly had more than one consort of Chinese ancestry. Rama I's own sister also married a wealthy Ayudhyan Chinese merchant and had a daughter who became Queen Suriyen, the wife of Rama II. King Mongkut was the son of Rama II and Queen Suriyen. Thus, there was not only a strong Chinese family strain within the Chakri dynasty, but also one that through reinforcement remained strong into the 20th century.

Inspired by the spectacular marriage alliances between royalty and the Chinese merchant class, many *chaosua* were lured by noble titles and high positions at court and in the government to renounce their Chinese heritage and become Siamese. All the great *chaosua* families invariably sought a patronage bond with senior members of the royal family. They propitiated their patrons with precious gifts and were rewarded with titles and higher gradations of noble rank.[18] Consequently, most of Bangkok's elite Chinese families grew closer to their Siamese benefactors among whom they lived until they ceased to remember their Chinese origins. Furthermore, Bangkok's *chaosua* patronized the Hinayana temple, rather than practicing the Chinese Mahayana version of Buddhism, and appropriated all the traditional marks of Siamese high status.

The court in turn encouraged their *chaosua* to fund the refurbishing and construction of Buddhist temples and Chinese shrines in the capital city. There are at least 17 temples in Bangkok that trace their founding patrons to Chinese *khunnang* families. Wat Prasert Suthawas in Thonburi is a good example of a temple built by a Chinese merchant. Tae Poh, the donor, was a Fujian native of Hai Teng Village in Zhangzhou, who accompanied his father Tae Tienbi (1738–1813) to Siam during the reign of Rama I. One characteristic of *lukchin* to note was the tendency to drop the generation name. Traditionally, Chinese names comprise a clan name, a generation name and, lastly, a personal name. In the case of Tae Tienbi, Tien is the generation name. However, as the majority of the Siamese names have a one-word personal name, ethnic Chinese living in Siam tended to follow suit, dropping their few-syllable names. This was so in the case of Tae Tienbi's son, Tae Poh. Tan Liang (Phraya Rachasretthi-Chin), So Jat (Luang Aphai-Vanich), Chin Kun (the Samuhanayok under Rama II) and Gao Chun (Phraya Bhisansupaphol, the author's forefather) also all dropped the Chinese generation name. Hence, in the olden days, the name of the *lukchin* in Siam had only two syllables—namely the clan and the personal name.

Tae Poh (1785–1840) was a wealthy merchant who owned several junks. He was appointed Phra Prasert-Vanich by Rama III. In 1838, when Southern Muslim discontent erupted into a revolt encompassing Kedah, Trang and Songkhla, Rama III sent a large army from Bangkok under the command of Phraya Sriphipat (Tad Bunnag) to help the governors of Nakhon Si Thammarat and Songkhla put down the rebellion. Tae Poh's junk, capable of transporting 400 men, was enlisted by the government to transport the troops to the south. Just before Tae Poh passed away in 1840 at the age of 55, he donated a large sum of money to build a new *ubosot* for Wat Klang along Rachaburana Canal and renamed it Wat Prasert Suthawas after his royal bestowed title. After he passed away, two of his five sons succeeded him to the *khunnang* title of Prasert-Vanich and were among the *lukchin* who, according to Gützlaff at the time, "becomes wholly changed to Siamese."

Tae Poh's sons did not fare as well as their father. They were engaged as tax farmers in the mid-19th century. The bids for tax concessions in Siam were very competitive at that time. Tae Poh's second son, Phra Visootvari (Mali)'s was dispossessed of his house in Sampeng because of his debt to the crown, while Tae

Scenes from *Romance of the Three Kingdoms* painted in the Zhangzhou style decorate the *ubosot* of Wat Prasert-Suthawas and testify that Tae Poh was a Hokkien.

Tiangseng, Tae Poh's youngest son who was also appointed Phra Prasert-Vanich, went bankrupt three times in Bangkok due to overbidding on tax concessions. In his old age, the unfortunate man retired to Chantabun, and this time fate was kinder and blessed him with a new, young wife and a prosperous business.

Perhaps attesting to China's Confucian tradition of venerating education, Sino-Siamese families never failed to provide a good education for their children, despite their ups and downs in business and vicissitudes of fortune. The Tae family tended to reflect this practice across several generations. Due to the high quality of education within the family, the descendants of Tae Poh have managed to remain competitive among Bangkok's social elite. When Rama VI (1910–25) introduced the use of surnames in Siam in 1913, he bestowed a formal Thai surname of Sreshthaputra to Tae Poh's great-grandsons. Today, the very successful Sreshthaputra, Bhirombhakdi, Pohsayachinda, Pranich and Sethaputra families all trace their ancestry to Tae Poh.

Perhaps the most illustrious individual among them was Phraya Pakdi-Norasreth (Lert Sreshthaputra) who founded Siam's first bus company. Phraya Bhirom-Bhakdi (Boonrawd Sreshthaputra), another great grandson of Tae Poh, also became an industry leader, founding Boon Rawd Brewery, which produces Singha Beer and is one of Thailand's most successful and wealthiest corporations. Last but not least, So Sethaputra achieved legendary fame and became a household name through his authorship of the famous Thai-English and English-Thai dictionaries.

The Early Hokkien Rajahs

The alliance between *chaosua* and the Siamese court was also reproduced in other parts of the kingdom outside Bangkok, although not in exactly the same way. When the British made inroads into the Malay states from their colonial foothold in Penang, they found that Kedah, Perlis, Satul, Kelantan, Trengannu, Nakhon Si Thammarat, Songkhla, Phuket and Ranong were "ruled" by rajahs, or *chao muang* in Thai. These rajahs answered to a viceroy, who was also the minister of war and a scion of the Bunnag family at court in Bangkok. Many of these rajahs were Hokkiens who were affiliated to Chinese secret-society fraternities, and who ran their fiefdoms as armed, Chinese, defensive strongholds, including Songkhla and Ranong.[19] Although the economic base of these Hokkien *chao muang* was not in the royal junk trade but in tin mining, birds' nests and other local products, they enjoyed similar status, influence and relationships to the court as the *chaosua* of Bangkok. While the *chaosua* might have operated the Krom Tha Sai in Bangkok, the Hokkien rajahs were charged with the task of pacifying the south and keeping the peace in the Malay states. Like the fabulously wealthy and powerful *chaosua* families of Bangkok, the *chao muang* of the south also had their share of fabled families and luminaries. The Bangkok *chaosua* families of Kalayanamitr, Chotikkapukkana, Phisolyabutr, Bisalputra, etc., had their counterparts in the Na Ranong, Na Nakhon, Na Songkhla and Na Talang families—the *chao muang* who ruled in the south, though not all of them were ethnic Chinese.

Perhaps the oldest of the southern Chinese families is the Na Songkhla. The Na Songkhla family traces its ancestry to a nascent Hokkien merchant community that thrived in Songkhla during the reign of King Borommakot. Hao Yiang (Wu Rang, 吳讓), the patriarch of the Hao (Wu, 吳) clan, arrived in Songkhla from Zhangzhou in 1750 at the age of 34. There, he married a local woman and settled down in the Chinese community that had sprouted in the southern province.

When King Taksin subdued Nakhon Si Thammarat in 1769, Hao Yiang was already an influential figure among the Hokkien settlers in Songkhla. Sensing that Taksin was a rising leader who could unite the Siamese against the Burmese invaders, Hao Yiang sought out King Taksin to pledge his allegiance. Moved by Hao Yiang's expression of loyalty, King Taksin rewarded him with a birds' nest concession in 1769. His loyalty was further rewarded six years later in 1775, when he was appointed governor of Songkhla. Following his appointment, the city was administratively upgraded, whereupon the new governor was allowed the privilege of reporting directly to the capital instead of via Nakhon Si Thammarat.[20]

The Hao clan retained its control over Songkhla for 126 years till 1901. Perhaps this was due to the family's shrewd practice of sending their young offspring to serve as *mahadlek*, or royal pages in the royal palace. Growing up in the capital, the younger generation of the Na Songkhla family became well connected and enjoyed strong social ties and close working relations with the Siamese power elite.

In 1784, during the witch hunt that took place after the fall of King Taksin, the patriarchs of the ruling families of Nakhon Si Thammarat and Songkhla were sacked by Rama I. As appointees of the late King Taksin, their loyalties were suspect. However, Rama I was acquainted with the generation of the southern ruling families who had grown up at court. He thought it expedient to appoint this younger generation of the ruling houses of Nakhon Si Thammarat and Songkhla to replace their old patriarchs respectively. A wholesale replacement of the southern ruling families might have proven disruptive to the new Chakri rulers' control over the two important southern cities.

Since the Thonburi period, the ruling houses of Songkhla and Nakhon Si Thammarat had been used to contain the restive Malay states including Patani, Kedah, Kelantan and Trengganu. Moreover, the rulers of Nakhon Si Thammarat and Songkhla had control over a vast pool of manpower that could be made available for the kingdom's military campaigns against Burma, Cambodia, Laos and Vietnam. Without the support of the southern warlords, Bangkok would have to send a large army into a distant and unfamiliar terrain to pacify the rebellious Malay states. Removing the authority of the southern warlords would clearly upset the balance of power in the deep south with unpredictable consequences for Bangkok. After weighing the odds, Rama I decided not to dispossess the power of the southern warlord families. Consequently, Boon Hui, son of Hao Yiang, was allowed to succeed his father as the governor of Songkhla, while Phat, the son-in-law of the old Chaophraya Nakhon (Noo), was appointed the governor of Nakhon Si Thammarat.[21]

In 1791 an Indian Muslim instigated the sultan of Patani to attack Songkhla. However, the newly appointed scion of the Hao family, Boon Hui, resourcefully regrouped his forces and organized a counterattack. Supported by troops sent from Bangkok and Nakhon Si Thammarat, Boon Hui succeeded in repulsing the invaders. After routing the rebels he followed up by invading Patani, where he managed to capture the sultan and repatriate him to Bangkok for execution. His remarkable military campaign against Patani won Rama I's admiration and vindicated him in the eyes of the Siamese court. Once his confidence and trust in Boon Hui's loyalty was established, Rama I quickly promoted him to the rank *chaophraya* and subsumed the principalities of Patani, Trengganu and Kedah under the administrative jurisdiction of Songkhla.

To sweeten the deal, Rama I bestowed on Chaophraya Songkhla (Boon Hui) a large, landed estate comprising the area known today as Had Yai. Under the management of the Hao clan, Songkhla became an important commercial port rivaling Nakhon Si Thammarat. Astute merchants, the Na Songkhla managed to create income for Bangkok from local industry, trade and taxes on tin, liquor distillation, gambling and birds' nests concessions.

Bangkok's strategy at the time for managing the south is best expressed by the dictum "divide and conquer." The new dynasty's policy towards the southern warlord families respectively alternated between wielding the carrot and the stick. Besides rewarding them with gifts, landed estates and honorific titles, Bangkok subtly fostered rivalry between the rulers of Nakhon Si Thammarat and Songkhla. During the reign of Rama I the pendulum swung in favor of Songkhla's ruler. In 1785, when the Burmese attacked Nakhon Si Thammarat, Phraya Nakhon (Phat) fled from the city without a fight. Consequently, he lost considerable prestige in the eyes of the king. Declaiming the cowardice of Phat, Rama I found an opportunity to remove Nakhon Si Thammarat's traditional jurisdiction over Kedah, Patani and Trengganu and subsumed the administration of the Malay states under the authority of Songkhla after Boon Hui defeated Patani in the war of 1791 and captured the sultan. Bangkok's unilateral adjustment of regional power and responsibility in the southern provinces caused bitter resentment between the two rulers. Rivalry between Nakhon Si Thammarat and Songkhla continued even after Boon Hui passed away in 1812.

However, with the advent of the reign of Rama II, the pendulum swung back in favor of the Na Nakhon family. Rama II tended to favor Nakhon Si Thammarat because the next Phraya Nakhon (Noi) proved to be intelligent, capable and competent.[22] Moreover, the daughter of the old Chaophraya Nakhon (Phat) was the consort of Rama I, and her son Prince Arunotai[23] was later appointed *uparat* by Rama III. By contrast, after Boon Hui passed away, his successors proved comparatively incompetent and inexperienced. Under these circumstances, it appears that it did not take much to persuade the king to restore the lost privileges and authority back to Nakhon Si Thammarat. Consequently, after Boon Hui passed away in 1812, Rama II reassigned Kedah, Kelantan and Perak to Nakhon Si Thammarat.

In the meantime, the rulers of Songkhla redoubled their competitive efforts to transform the city into a prosperous port. However, Songkhla's policy of promoting commerce involved encouraging large-scale Chinese immigration. This brought in its wake the vice of opium dens, which explicitly ran counter to the anti-opium policy promulgated by the central government in Bangkok. Songkhla found itself at loggerheads with Bangkok due to the rampant spread of opium addicts in the southern province.

The second issue that became a source of friction between Songkhla and Bangkok stemmed from the former's failure to satisfy Bangkok's demand for *phrai* manpower levies to meet the central government's military needs. Nakhon Si Thammarat's track record in supplying *phrai* recruits to Bangkok was consistently better than Songkhla, causing Hao Tienjong, the new Songkhla ruler, to accuse

Phraya Vichienkjiri
(Chom Na Songkhla).

Nakhon Si Thammarat of raiding villages under Songkhla's jurisdiction to forcibly move young men to Nakhon Si Thammarat for *phrai* service.

The misfortune of the Na Songkhla family reached its nadir in the later part of the reign of Rama II. Rama II's displeasure with the Na Songkhla house led to Tienjong, the governor, being recalled to Bangkok. Tienjong was severely reprimanded for disgracefully abetting opium trafficking and failing to deliver on the central government's manpower levees.

Following the death of Tienjong, his younger brother Tienseng succeeded him as governor of Songkhla. Although he was intelligent and capable, he was inexperienced, and he failed to correct Songkhla's relations with the court in Bangkok. Tienseng was also initially reprimanded and recalled to Bangkok where he was placed under temporary house arrest for his involvement in opium trafficking.

However, as Hao Tienseng matured, the pendulum of royal favor swung back to the side of Songkhla during the reign of Rama III. The critical turning point in the fortunes of the Hao clan came in 1827 when Bangkok's survival was threatened by the Laotian king, Chao Anou. The neighboring king maneuvered a surprise occupation of the Khorat Plateau, placing the enemy within striking distance of Bangkok. Hao Tienseng demonstrated his loyalty by immediately sending 1,000 troops and junks to support Rama III's general mobilization. The contingent from Songkhla became actively involved in building fortifications in Samut Prakarn. Phraya Songkhla's prompt response at Bangkok's hour of need vindicated the Na Songkhla family's loyalty to the Chakri dynasty and earned Phraya Songkhla the trust of Rama III.

After Hao Tienseng's death, successive scions of the Na Songkhla family continued to rule Songkhla until the advent of the 20th century. The last Phraya Vichienkhiri (Chom Na Songkhla) died in 1901, ending 126 years of the Na Songkhla's official rule over the province.

A New Tiger of the South

During the reign of the Daoguang emperor (1820–50), China's conflict with the West led to a series of wars with the European powers. Meanwhile, in Siam, Rama II passed away. Rama III (1824–51), who ascended the throne in Bangkok, shared Daoguang's dilemmas emanating from Western aggrandizement. Responding to Western muscle-flexing policies, Rama III increased Siam's flexibility based on a more realistic assessment of Siam's strength vis-à-vis British military and naval power. In March 1824 Britain formally declared war against the Burmese, and in December 1825 Captain Henry Burney, a British envoy, arrived in Bangkok. Rama III made tolerable concessions to the British; after the implementation of the

Burney Treaty, the British threat receded for several decades until the reign of King Mongkut.

Provisions in the treaty defined the boundaries between Siam and British Burma for general conduct of trade, and for the settlement of disputes. The commercial aspect of the treaty on the other hand entailed considerable sacrifices for Siam, including the easing of the royal monopoly on various commodities.[24] Tin, which had been controlled by the Royal Trading Monopoly since the reign of King Prasartthong of Ayudhya, was allowed to be sold in the open market under the new system of tax farming. Provincial governors who sometimes doubled as tin concessionaires were responsible for managing the proceeds from the sale of tin at source and sending the tax revenue to Bangkok. The treaty also allowed free trade between the British ports of Penang, Malacca and Singapore and the Siamese ports of Nakhon Si Thammarat, Pattalung, Patani, Phuket and Kedah.

In 1810, Kaw Sujiang (Xu Sizhang, 許泗璋), a native of Zhangzhou in Fujian, arrived at the new British East India Company trading outpost in Penang. He was a poor, young peasant who came with nothing except his clothes and a carrying pole over his shoulder. At the time, the government was distributing virgin land. After saving a small sum from his wages, Kaw Sujiang applied for a plot to farm. Because Kaw was too poor to own a bullock cart, he walked the 29 kilometers round trip to Georgetown weekly, carrying his produce in two large baskets slung across his shoulders on the very carrying pole he had brought from China. Yet, despite his hard work and frugality, prosperity still eluded him. Thus, after six hard years in Penang, he immigrated to Siam.[25]

Kaw Sujiang set up a small sundry-goods shop in Takuapa. There he received financial aid from Thao Thep-Sunthorn,[26] a wealthy local lady. Later, he expanded into coastal trading that spanned the Andaman coast from Penang to Ranong and moved his business to Phang-nga.

At Ranong, which was thinly populated because it was not suitable for agriculture, Kaw Sujiang discovered tin deposits. He applied and became a tax farmer for tin in the district. Appointed as Luang Ratanasetthi by Rama III, Kaw was given the sole right to operate the tin mines in Ranong. In 1854, three years after King Mongkut (1851–68) ascended the throne, he was appointed the governor of Ranong. As governor he was responsible for, among other duties, the defense and peace keeping of Ranong, which at that time was under the governorship of Chumphon.[27] King Mongkut was pleased with Kaw's performance and elevated Kaw to *phraya* of the same name in 1864. The province of Ranong was also upgraded by making the governor directly responsible to the central government in Bangkok.

Like all self-made men, Kaw Sujiang was hard and ruthless and ruled the Chinese mining community he founded with an iron fist. There was even a couplet made in Hokkien about Kaw's Ranong. In substance, the verse ran, "The Ranong pit is easy to get into, but it is impossible to get out." As his business continued to expand, Kaw faced labor shortage problems and had to import indentured Chinese laborers from Penang to work his tin mines. Pirates from south Burma also raided Ranong and stole his tin ore. He counterattacked and ran the Burmese pirates out of Ranong. To prevent further raids by the Burmese, he built a brick stockade where he lived and where he stored his tin ore, as well as erecting outlook posts at strategic points.[28]

By the mid-19th century tin was very much in demand by European traders for industrial use. Kaw Sujiang's Koh Guan Company was the sole representative of Siamese tin in the Penang market while the Gim Jeng Company of Tan Gimjeng, known in Siam as Phraya Anukul-Siamkit, was the sole representative in Singapore. Due to competitive bidding, in 1872 the price for tin concessions in Phuket went up 18-fold from 17,360 to 320,000 baht, while the concession price for Ranong increased 5.5-fold. Concessionaires had to squeeze wages, which resulted in labor riots and Triad problems in the south in the mid-1870s.[29]

In 1876, impoverished Chinese laborers in Ranong and Phuket staged an uprising demanding better wages and working conditions. About 2,000 Chinese laborers revolted in Ranong. The uprising became so serious that the Siamese government nearly lost control of the province. Despite his old age, Kaw Sujiang responded to the threat to his position by putting down the revolt with a firm hand and restoring the authority of the Siamese government in Ranong. Rama V (1868–1910), a grateful young monarch, showed his appreciation by making Kaw Sujiang rajah of Ranong and bestowed on him 3,000 *rai* of land as well as other honorific gifts.[30]

Conforming to the culture of the Siamese aristocracy, Kaw Sujiang was polygamous. He had a Chinese wife and a Thai wife who bore him six sons and five daughters. After the death of his first wife, he traveled to China and brought back an 18-year-old bride. Kaw observed that the ethnic Chinese in Siam tended to drop their generation name, hence losing their lineage link with their ancestral homeland as well as their connection to clan identity. Kaw carefully followed the Chinese tradition and chose the generation names of his male descendants for the next five generations. He ensured that his descendants remembered him, and also made it possible for them to easily recognize one another. Kaw Sujiang lived to be a grand old man of his day. Inducted into the nobility, he became a strong pillar of the throne in the Siamese court.

After he passed away, his youngest son, Kaw Simbee, who was appointed rajah of Trang, lived to be the most illustrious and colorful among all the Hokkien rajahs of the south. When Prince Damrong created the office of the High Commissioner of the Western Provinces on the Indian Ocean, which oversaw Satul, Trang, Phuket,

Ranong and Takuapa, he elevated Kaw Simbee to the post. Bearing the noble title Phraya Ratsda, he was without question the most brilliant administrator that the southern region has ever known. Phraya Ratsda ruled the southern territories like a sub-potentate, permitted to do much as he pleased until he died. Because his loyalty was unquestionable, he enjoyed the full confidence and trust of the court. Although the court technically held the reins, it handled them so lightly that Phraya Ratsda was never conscious of any imposition. Indeed, Bangkok never attempted to cramp his style. Arrogant, choleric and ambitious, he was so feared by the southern people that they prostrated themselves whenever he passed.

Kaw Simbee was as much a pedigree Siamese aristocrat as the best and the noblest *chaosua* of Bangkok. However, despite speaking Thai fluently, he never learned to read Thai. For many years, Kaw Sujiang's descendants in the kingdom have formed an important and integral part of Thai national life, but his descendants in Penang continue to see themselves as Chinese. His Thai descendants have adopted the surname Na Ranong and now identify with their adopted country, Thailand. Like their *chaosua* counterparts in Bangkok, the third generation of the southern named families do not speak Chinese, have Thai names and have forgotten their Chinese origins.

The *chaosua* comprised a small, glittering elite. Their trading successes reflected the heyday of the China trade, when it served as the lifeline of regional economies. It was an age dominated by tributary relationships subsumed under a Chinese world order embodied by Royal Trading Monopolies, which doubled as diplomatic missions as well as trading enterprises. In the context of a Chinese-dominated world order, the *chaosua* became the perfect interface between China and Siam. Representing the kingdom's dominant economic group, their fabulous worldly success and social adjustments in negotiating between two worlds became objects of emulation, which were reproduced in more modest ways by tens of thousands of Chinese who settled in Bangkok and its surroundings. In the same way, by long residence, marriage, royal recognition and cultural adjustments, the *lukchin* or descendants of Chinese emigrants also sought to replicate Thai ways in a more modest fashion.

Top: Kaw Sujiang, the founder of the Na Ranong family.

Bottom: Kaw Simbee, Kaw Sujiang's most-famous son.

Capitalism

Unknown to the *chaosua*, their brave new world was about to be turned upside down by forces of change emanating from Europe. While Siam was being ravaged by the Burmese wars, revolution was sweeping across Europe from 1789 to 1848, leading to the overthrow of monarchies and old regimes. Beneath the revolutionary political developments, the economic foundations of the European continent were being transformed. The result was the emergence of a totally new economic system that the world had never encountered before. Reflecting the novel political-economic incarnation developing in Europe, a new word entered the vocabulary of the world in 1860s: "capitalism." Karl Marx's monumental book *Das Kapital* was published in 1867.

The political embodiment of the new capitalist system consisted in the creation of a territorially defined nation-state with a constitution guaranteeing property and civil rights, with elected assemblies and governments that were responsible to them.[31] Energizing this great transformation lay the phenomenon of the European Industrial Revolution, which empowered the maritime powers of northwest Europe and North America. The new industrialized societies that emerged in the West were no longer the self-sufficient entities of yore but specialized communities dependent upon overseas raw materials and markets for their survival.

However, the explosion of production power was not initially matched by demand for industrial products, and existing markets in Europe remained limited. Unless these problems were resolved, the industrial revolution would only result in excess capacity and financial collapse. Industrialization in a growing population of poverty-stricken masses with no purchasing power created a crisis. The European political crises of the 1830s and 1840s were marked by the contrast between the enormous and rapidly growing productive potential of capitalist industrialization on one hand, and on the other, its inability to expand the markets for its products, let alone the capacity to generate employment at a comparable rate. During the first half of the 19th century it seemed that no conceivable industrialization could provide employment for the vast and growing surplus population of the poor, raising the specter of an impending proletarian social revolution, as well as Malthus's doomsday prophesy that world population growth would outstrip world food production, leading to mass starvation.

This 19th-century wood engraving shows an operator receiving a message in Morse code on a printing telegraph. In a box under the table are the wet cells (batteries) supplying electricity.

The above fears eventually proved groundless. The solution to Europe's industrial dilemma occurred at two levels, technological and ideological. Technologically, the breakthrough came with the invention of the railway, the steamship and the telegraph, all of which led to an explosion of connectivity capable of matching industrial productivity by multiplying the geographical size of the capitalist economy and increasing the intensity of economic transactions. The implications of this technologically generated connectivity were profound and far-reaching. Suddenly, the whole world became a part of this capitalist economy. The creation of a single, expanded world market was the most significant development of the decade 1847–57.[32] Capitalism now had the entire world potentially at its disposal. The problem was actualizing it.

The ideological counterpart of the connectivity revolution was the triumph of economic liberalism in Europe. Economic liberalism provided the justification, rationale and political will to make the potential created by the industrial and connectivity revolution operational, and to achieve an integrated, global, capitalist economy. Liberal economists and intellectuals touted forceful economic arguments equating the liberalization of private enterprise with human progress. Inspired by the philosophy of economic liberalism, British capitalists and political leaders lobbied for the establishment of a free trade system in Europe. The result was the emergence of an international movement, led by Britain, towards total freedom of trade. The mantra, underscored by an overwhelming consensus among economists, intellectuals and politicians, that free trade was the recipe for economic progress and prosperity began to have almost the force of a natural law.

Forming the vanguard of the Free Trade Movement, Britain led the way by abandoning protectionism completely after 1846. As the home country of the Industrial Revolution, the British economy had become the most competitive in Europe. For the British, free trade meant firstly that they were allowed to undersell everybody in all the markets of the world. Secondly, they could get non-industrialized countries to sell them primary products (including foodstuffs and raw materials for British factories) cheaply and in large quantities, thereby earning incomes with which to buy British manufactures. Thus, Britain stood to gain the most from free trade.

Although less-competitive European economies continued to retain varying degrees of protectionism, free trade progressively made inroads within Europe through "free trade treaties" entered into by most European powers. Gradually, the remaining institutional barriers to free trade—from the factors of production to private enterprise, and finally to anything that could conceivably hamper its profitable operation—fell before the onslaught of the Free Trade Movement.

Although free trade mostly served British interests, other European powers discovered that free trade also allowed them to gain access to superior British technology, equipment, resources and knowledge that was useful to their own industrial development. For example, booming British exports—especially railroad iron and machinery—did not inhibit the industrialization of other European countries but facilitated it. Moreover, the initial effects of removing trade barriers appeared to stimulate expansion of world commerce, which began to lift Europe out of its economic slump after 1840. Where economic stimulation failed to elicit results, gunboat diplomacy backed by superior naval power was used to force open the doors of foreign markets.

Armed with the conviction that economic liberalization represented human progress, Western capitalism presumed that the entire world was at its disposal. Anything saleable was sold, including goods that met with distinct resistance from the receiving countries, such as opium. Despite the resistance, the export of opium from British India to China more than doubled in quantity and trebled in value by the 1840s. The British answer to China's refusal to allow the sale of opium in China was the Opium War and the subsequent forcing of the unequal Treaty of Nanjing (1842) upon the defeated Chinese government. Gunboat diplomacy was again used to elicit another unequal commercial treaty signed at Tientsin in 1858. In the same year, Japan was forced to open its doors to Western trade, this time not by the British but by the gunboats of the US Commodore Matthew Perry.

Between 1850 and 1870, world trade increased by 260 percent.[33] The feverish expansion of both international trade and international investment measures the zest with which Western capitalism proceeded to conquer foreign markets. This expansion of world commerce benefited all countries in Europe, even if it benefited the British disproportionately. Thus, Europe did not begrudge Britain's economic advantage and largely supported the Free Trade Movement. The outcome was an enlarged free market across Europe. Among the major Western powers, only the United States, whose industry relied on a protected home market and little on exports, remained an unassailable bastion of protectionism—although the US was not averse to forcing Japan to open its markets to Western trade.

While the Industrial Revolution was beginning to spread from England to other countries in Europe, Southeast Asia remained beyond the ideological influence of Western economic liberalism. Nevertheless, reverberations of the West's great capitalist transformation were being felt far beyond the shores of Europe. Changing modes of production driven by the engine of the West's industrializing economies inevitably promoted the spread of international economic specialization. Accompanying this economic specialization, capitalism also gradually brought in its wake a series of scientific discoveries and technological advances that helped install a totally new economic order based on factory production to every traditional society based on agriculture that it managed to touch. The process was ultimately destined to be repeated in various forms as capitalism began to spread out of Europe to encompass the far-flung corners of the world touched by Europe, including Southeast Asia and Siam.

Siam soon felt the impact of the forces unleashed by Europe's capitalist revolution, and after 1820, the Siamese economy began to change. Raw forest products, which had been the staple of the China trade under King Taksin, began to give way in the 1820s to products that had to be grown or required human processing, such as rice, sugar, dried fish, tin utensils, coconut oil,

An 1858 engraving illustrates the European factories in Canton.

and dyes. The process reflected the transformation that the Chao Phraya River delta had undergone in the early 19th century as Chinese immigrants brought expertise in growing vegetables, pepper, sugar and commercial crops. As economic specialization in commercial crops and tin mining intensified, Chinese immigrants found themselves participating in developing a market economy rather than toiling in the old structure of indentured labor and royal service. This led to the rise of new social roles in the Chinese community; agricultural cultivators and mine owners stepped up beside the ranks of the *chaosua*. By the mid-19th century, the combination of the Bangkok Kingdom's military conquests to incorporate the domains of the Kingdom of Lanna and Lan Chang into an expanded Siamese body politic coupled with the emergence of a market economy had changed the demography of the core kingdom in ways that began to undermine the traditional political order based on patronage ties. According to Professor Nidhi Eoseewong, society was becoming bourgeois, as in Europe.

While the ideological, technological, social and economic forces emanating from Europe's great capitalist transformation changed the international trading environment and traditional societies around the world, the Siamese state remained firmly integrated in the system of intra-Asian trade, where China symbolized the commercial and political center of the regional tributary trading system. On the other hand, the Revolutionary and Napoleonic Wars coupled with the rise of the Industrial Revolution in England resulted in the resurgence of British power in Asia, reflected in the acquisition of Singapore (1819), followed by the occupation of Malacca (1824), Lower Burma (1826), the Straits Settlements (1826), the Opium War (1842), and the annexations of Hong Kong (1842), Upper

Burma (1852) and India (1858). Hot upon the heels of the British, the French began to make inroads into Vietnam, Laos and Cambodia, and the United States took over the Philippines. Evidently, capitalism was not just an economic process, replacing traditional methods of production and distribution. It was also a political movement to establish a world economic order based on Western political hegemony and industrial domination.

When the British returned to Bangkok in the 1820s, they found the river leading up to the port of Bangkok crammed with Chinese junks. Western observers estimated that the Chinese formed the majority of the capital city's population. In fact, throughout the first half of the 19th century, the enormous role and influence of the Chinese in the capital was reflected in the flowering of Chinese fashion and style among Bangkok's high society and aristocratic circles. The glittering wealth and opulence of the Siamese capital was evidently based on the lucrative China trade, which was monopolized by the Siamese court. The British were evidently envious for a share of this Sino-Siamese trade. After its founding, British Singapore tried to attract substantial Siamese trade. Despite its strategic location in the direct ocean route between Europe and China, Singapore was too far out of the mainstream China trade route, which favored the port cities in the Gulf of Siam. During the 1820s the volume of Bangkok's China trade greatly exceeded that of Singapore.

Moreover, the English industrialist lobby in Singapore in alliance with the British government was also eyeing Siam as a potentially rich market for British and Indian manufactured goods, especially textiles and cottons. From the standpoint of the British government and the East India Company (which was making a bid to substantially control Asian trade in the early 19th century), the Siamese royal monopoly over commerce was a major obstacle for British trade expansion. In 1822, the British East India Company dispatched John Crawfurd to conclude a commercial treaty with Siam and raise British concerns about the expansion of Siamese power in the Malay states and Siam's northwestern frontier with Burma. The Siamese refused to sign any treaty guaranteeing free trade because it directly threatened the treasury's source of revenue.

Although the Crawfurd mission had been rebuffed, the Siamese had no illusions that their world was changing and the old ways would perhaps not measure up to the new realities. The kingdom now had a large and growing Chinese presence. By 1822 the annual immigration of Chinese to Bangkok numbered at least 7,000.[34] Chinese immigrant labor was sucked into the expanding, trade-driven service sector as coolies, accountants, junk masters, junk crew, brokers, construction workers, merchants and entertainers. Chinese opera performances were very popular in Siamese towns with large numbers of Chinese residents.

New, modern products had appeared in the kingdom, the most significant of which to appear in early Bangkok was perhaps white sugar, which was enjoying a brisk trade. The American trader Morgan who visited Bangkok in 1818 observed that there were "700 ships of various types and sizes on the Chao Phraya River, including two American sloops loading a large quantity of sugar."[35] Crawfurd, who visited Bangkok towards the end of the reign of Rama II, remarked that Siam could produce "the whitest and best (sugar) in India, to the extent of 60,000 piculs." In 1836 Pallegoix wrote that "the great sugarcane plantations ... and sugar mills succeeded each other without interruption" in Nakhon Chaisri.

Sugarcane cultivation shared an important characteristic with tin mining, pepper growing and other cash crops in that these economic activities tended to involve Chinese wage labor. Crawfurd counted "more than 30 sugar mills, each employing 200–300 Chinese workers." The mills were fed by extensive sugar cane plantations in Nakhon Chaisri, Sakornburi and Chachoengsao, which were operated by immigrant Chinese labor.

In contrast, the traditional occupations of rice growing, fishery, and the collection of timber, ivory and forest products tended to involve *phrai-luang* and *phrai-som*, indentured manpower rather than Chinese wage labor. Tax concessionaires for these traditional products, such as *arkorn-nam* (fishery) and timber, as well as tax collection in local markets, were normally given to well-connected Siamese. In fact, as the production sector expanded, opportunities to extract government revenue from production through the sale of tax concessions began to increase. Upon ascending the throne, Rama III bestowed upon his mother the concessionaire right on teakwood. Edmund Roberts gave an estimate that 127,000 teak trees were felled and processed in Siam in 1835. However, as Chinese began to dominate the production sector, their involvement in the operation of royal tax concessions rapidly overtook the Thai. With the advent of the reign of Rama III, farming out tax concessions to the kingdom's *chaosua* became the trend, leading to the rise of another new social formation within the Chinese community: Chinese tax farmers.

In sharp contrast to Siam's rapidly growing production sector, the future of the Royal Trading Monopoly appeared bleak. The rise of European maritime hegemony had rendered the junk trade less and less competitive. European ships were more efficient, bigger, faster, and charged lower rates for bulk cargo than Chinese junks. In addition to the economics of shipping, the royal junk trade was also threatened with extinction by the European free trade ideology backed by superior European naval firepower. The problem of the royal junk trade was that it operated as a form of royal monopoly. Under the feudal system, royal monopolies could be declared to exclude foreign merchants from direct trading in certain profitable commodities. This type of trade relied on political power to create commercial profit and did not depend upon the pricing

Chinese figurine at the entrance to the *ubosot* of Wat Kalyanamitra, Thonburi. The temple was built in honor of Rama III by Chaophraya Nikornbodin (Ng Taotoh, 1784–1864).

mechanism. As Siam began to suffer a deficit of firepower relative to the Western powers, it became imprudent to resist the pressure for trade liberalization.

Moreover, European trading nations had started to apply diplomatic pressure and threatened military action to force Asian rulers to abolish trading monopolies and liberalize trade. Having received many European envoys on behalf of his father during the previous reign, Rama III had had many opportunities to study Siam's new foe, as well as develop a better understanding of European demands for free trade. Perhaps his tongue-in-cheek remark to Crawfurd of his distaste for trading was a hint that in good time the Siamese court would accede to the Western demand for trade liberalization. In stark contrast to his words, his reputation as a good trader was legendary at court, and he had made immense profits for his own account through junk trading when he was the prince in control of the Phraklang. His diplomacy with the Western powers reflected a shrewdness and prudence in assessing British power and intentions.

Rama III had seen the writing on the wall. Realizing that the junk trade would soon become obsolete, he built a life-size monument dedicated to the junk in brick and mortar at Wat Yannawa as a tribute to the Royal Junk Fleet. However, he needed more time to set his kingdom in order before acceding to Western demands for the abolition of the Royal Trading Monopoly. To compensate for the expected decline in profit from the royal monopoly, Rama III sought to accrue additional income by switching to tax farming. The first new tax proclaimed upon his accession to the throne in 1824 was the tax on salt. Subsequently in 1829, the Huey Ko Kho, a very popular state lottery was created. In 1829 he also ordered a nationwide survey of all taxable fruit trees, undoubtedly intended to boost state revenue.[36] In total, 38 new taxes were introduced during Rama III's 27-year reign.

Rama III's success in increasing revenue enabled the state to finance several large and expensive infrastructure projects, as well as build numerous temples. A new fortress was erected at the mouth of the Tha Chin under the supervision of Phraya Choduk (Thong Chin), using Chinese bricklayers. The new fortress was an extension of the defense perimeter of Bangkok, because the mouth of the Tha Chin was directly linked to the capital by Mahachai Canal. Concurrently, a large number of Chinese workers were hired to dig approximately 30 kilometers of canal to the mouth of the Mae Klong River, thereby making it possible to travel by boat from Bangkok to Ratchaburi without having to cross stretches of open sea.[37]

As the threat from Western powers loomed, Rama III tried to promote classical

Portrait of Chaophraya Nikornbodin.

Buddhist education. Temples, which were the cornerstone of public education in Siam, mushroomed all over Bangkok. The king built and renovated 38 temples while his wealthy *khunnang* and *chaosua* helped build another 40, most of which were named by the king himself. Chinese contractors and artists were hired to build and decorate many temples in Bangkok. Due to the durability of porcelain, the king preferred the use of Chinese porcelain for external mural and gable decoration instead of the traditional Thai woodwork. Beautiful Chinese workmanship dating back to the reign of Rama III still exist today, including at Wat Pho, Wat Raj Orotsa and on the spectacular stupa at Wat Arun.

Meanwhile, the failure of the Crawfurd mission coupled with the accession of Rama III to the throne in Bangkok prompted the British to make another attempt to press free trade on the Siamese. In 1825, Captain Henry Burney was sent to Bangkok to demand trade liberalization, Siamese support for the Anglo-Burmese War and cooperation to address the political and territorial problems relating to the border with Burma in the north and Kedah in the south. More than his predecessor Rama II, Rama III was psychologically prepared to address the demands of the British for free trade. Moreover, the formidable demonstration of British arms over Siam's feared traditional enemy, Burma, must have also made a strong impression on the new king. This time, the Siamese gave in to British pressure. The Burney Treaty was signed in June 1826.

However, the Burney Treaty did not result in free trade. Although Rama III signed the treaty, he was not yet ready to abolish the royal monopoly over trade. On the contrary, he toughened trade restrictions with Europe after 1830. Consequently, the expected free trade system did not materialize and British trade with Siam did not show any significant increase after the Burney Treaty, causing no small irritation to Britain and her counterparts in Singapore, who

Portrait of King Phra Nang Klao (Rama III) at Wat Raj Orotsa, Thonburi.

held a direct interest in Siam's trade.

Perhaps the war with Laos in 1826 made it imperative for the Siamese government to maximize all sources of government revenue. Abolishing royal trading monopolies at that time would have led to a reduction of government revenue when military expenditures needed to be increased. However, Rama III's attempt to establish new sources of revenue by increasing production and then taxing it created its own problems. To encourage the expansion of the production sector, Rama III had to draw more Chinese immigration to Siam. The estimated number of Chinese in Siam rose substantially from 440,000 in 1822 just before Rama III's reign began to 1,110,000 in 1849.[38] The rapid expansion of Siam's Chinese population exacerbated intra-communal frictions.

The Chinese *Kongsi*

On arrival in Siam, each new immigrant found himself locked into the regional allegiances of the respective dialect groups that constituted the overseas Chinese community. These allegiances were established either by the traditional self-help fraternity or *kongsi* that he worked for,[39] or by membership at communal shrines. Usually, these shrines were centrally located in the dialect-based communities in which their adherents lived, as well as in enclaves where the dialect was spoken and the related ethnic food was served. As the affinities of the Chinese were to their hometowns and fellow provincials, each dialect-based overseas settlement tended to be distinctive. Gim Lohchae, the patriarch of the Posayanonda family, professed that when he and his Teochew friends first arrived in Siam during the reign of Rama II, they headed for Bangplasoi in Chonburi because of their Teochew connections.

The linguistic and temperamental differences between Hakka and Hailam, for instance, might seem insignificant to Thais, but they were fiercely important to the local Chinese. Even marriage to a Chinese outside one's own dialect group was looked down upon. Loyalties were intensely local; strong comradeship bound together the speakers of a common dialect, blunting the edge of their homesickness and their feelings of alienation. Clashes between Hokkien and Teochew, the two largest dialect groups in Siam, continued to erupt throughout the 19th century, causing concern in the government. The opposing spirits of different dialect groups struck the Earl of Plymouth, who was in Bangkok during the reign of Rama III, to remark, "it was as if they belong to rival nations." It seemed that the Chinese diaspora in 19th century Siam had no overarching Chinese identity.

In Chantabun the animosities were so strong that the king had to replace Chin Toh, the Chinese governor of the port city, because of resentment created by his treatment of various dialect groups. In his place, Phraya Choduk-Chim, the minister of Chinese affairs, who was a *lukchin* of some social standing, was sent from Bangkok as the *phraya* of Chantabun to mediate in the conflict.

Yet, in August 1824 at the Hungry Ghost Festival, another brawl erupted between the Teochew and the Hokkien of Chantabun. To revenge the injury suffered by his men, Chin Chuang—the foreman or *lungcho* of a Teochew peanut oil factory—gathered 700–800 men and attacked a Hokkien *kongsi* at Bangkacha and the house of Phraya Sunthorn-Sretthi, the head of the Hokkien community. Chim, the new governor of Chantabun, sided with the Hokkien and Chin Chuang was captured and sent to jail in Bangkok.

Appreciative of the way Chim handled the Chinese unrest, Rama III later elevated him to Phraya Pholathep, head of Krom Na, the Ministry of Cultivation, where he was responsible for the collection of the government's share of the rice crop and the settlement of land boundary disputes. He remained an important minister there until his death.

In addition to communal violence, Chinese immigration also contributed to the proliferation of Chinese secret societies and Triad organizations in Siam. Without the protection of their home government, which discouraged and proscribed emigration, Chinese immigrants had to rely on their traditional *kongsi*. Sometimes, *kongsi* became very large through the takeover of rival *kongsi* or through amalgamation, and they often came under the influence and control of secret societies.[40]

To their credit, *kongsi* provided invaluable support to their members by giving loans and donations for accidents, funerals, etc. However, they also served as front organizations for criminal activities, including piracy, loan sharking and opium smuggling. In 1842 the Chinese in Nakhon Chaisri and Sakornburi were divided into three gangs led by Chin Eia, Chin Kim and Chin Piew, each with about 1,000 men. Members of these gangs robbed villages and junks in the Tha Chin River delta area.

To quell the uprising the government had to turn to leaders of the Chinese community who carried clout with the Chinese *kongsi* to help negotiate a peaceful solution. The man who played an instrumental role in assisting the Siamese authorities suppress the revolt was Phra Sombat-wanit, whose presence alongside the police force helped to break down the resistance.

The involvement of a *chaosua khunnang* with a Sombat-wanit title seems to have become a legend among the Chinese sugar plantation workers—several years later in 1848, during another Chinese uprising in the central province of Chachoengsao, the

Top: Guanyin at Kudee Chin, a revered worship site in Thonburi, not far from the old palace of King Taksin. Kudee Chin has been a Hokkien village since the early days of Bangkok.

Bottom: Delicate wood carvings at Kien Ann Keng Shrine, a shrine built by the Hokkien community during Rama III's reign. It has been managed and maintained by the Simasathien family until the present day.

longchu of the sugar mills sought out Thanpuying Hoon, the widow of Phraya Sri Raj-arkorn,[41] and requested her to negotiate with Chaophraya Phraklang for a peaceful resolution to the conflict.

Labor unrest that manifested itself in intra-communal violence was also related to Rama III's efforts to generate more sources of government revenue. When Rama III imposed more indirect taxes on the population, the burden fell heavily on Chinese merchants and wage laborers, who were the main consumers of alcohol and often enjoyed gambling. Chinese were also the operators of tax concessions in sugar and tin mining, which were minting huge profits for the crown.

It was hardly surprising that the locus of labor unrest tended to occur in the main sugar and peanut oil production areas of Chachoengsao, Sakornburi and Chanthabun. The hardships of the poor plantation workers were aggravated by the actions of rapacious, corrupt officials. In 1848, a street fight between Thai and Chinese workers in Chachoengsao, northeast of Bangkok, snowballed into a Chinese revolt when the governor, Phraya Wiset-Ruchai, used the opportunity to extort money from the Chinese workers. Evidence from official interrogations indicated that the governor had abused his power and jailed more than 100 Chinese—some of whom were not involved in the incident—to force them to buy their release from prison. Enraged by the governor's corruption, the Chinese *kongsi* led a mob comprising 1,200 sugar plantation workers and seized several sugar refineries and a local town hall.[42] Phraya Wiset-Ruchai tried to subdue the angry mob to no avail. He was decapitated and killed in the mayhem.

Rama III sent Chaophraya Phraklang (Dit) and Chaophraya Bodindecha (Singh), his most senior general, with several thousand soldiers to put down the revolt. The military pacification employing ethnic Siamese troops took on racial overtones as thousands of Chinese were massacred. In the aftermath of the suppression, many *longchu* were rounded up and imprisoned and a large number of sugar plantations were destroyed during the hostilities. While Siamese chronicles reported the Chachoengsao uprising as a Triad revolt, the incident may have been caused by worsening economic conditions in the sugar plantations resulting from the imposition of new taxes. A subsequent foreign report alleged that "the insurrection which took place had its origin in the imposition of a new or an augmented tax to be levied on the sugar boilers."[43]

Opium

In addition to war and labor disturbances, the country began to encounter a new social problem: opium addiction. This new social malady was directly related to the new market-oriented economy, Chinese immigration and Western free trade activities.

The British East India Company was becoming increasingly involved in the opium trade. The Western political pressure on China and other Asian countries to accept free trade went hand-in-glove with the East India Company's attempt to sell opium in Asian markets. When receiving countries resisted the British, traders resorted to illicit trade and promoted opium smuggling on a large scale. The Chinese government's attempt to clamp down on opium smuggling sparked the infamous Opium War (1842–45), which resulted in a humiliating defeat for China. In Siam, as in China, opium smuggling and pervasive opium addiction had become a major problem that commanded the attention of the Siamese court and government.

The Bangkok government had prohibited the use of opium since the reign of Rama I. Although discreet use of opium continued through the reigns of Rama II and Rama III, the habit was confined to the Chinese community and opium smoking continued to be proscribed. However, with the British directly abetting the illicit opium trade, the problem was becoming harder to contain.

In 1839 a conflict between Chinese and Siamese opium smugglers erupted into violence, which led to the loss of many lives.[44] Rama III charged Prince Rakronaret, Chaophraya Bodindecha (Singh) and Chaophraya Phraklang (Dit) with the task of ridding the kingdom of the scourge of opium. The printing press of the American missionaries was used to print 10,000 copies of the royal edict against the sale and use of opium. Phraya Choduk, the minister of Chinese affairs,

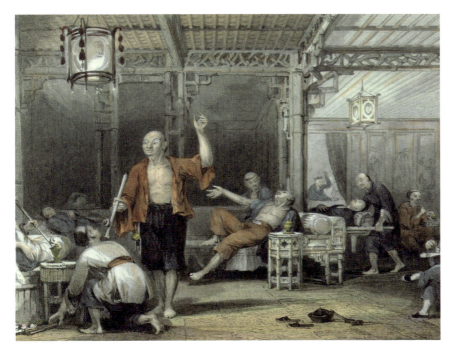

Thomas Allom's painting from the mid-19th century depicts Chinese opium smokers.

was tasked with publicizing the royal edict to all the Chinese communities in Siam. In one celebrated case, Chaophraya Bodindecha even caned his son, Saeng, 100 strokes in front of many senior *khunnang* for his involvement in the opium trade.[45]

Opium arrests during the reign of Rama III were mentioned in detail in the royal chronicles authored by Chaophraya Tipakornwongse (Kham).[46] Kham was the chief of police for opium suppression, known then as Chamhun Rachamat. In 1845 he made sweeping arrests of several Chinese Triad leaders in the south, from Prachub Kirikhan down to Surat Thani, catching several *tuahia* gang leaders and their cohorts from various dialect groups including four Cantonese, three Hailams, three Hokkiens, one Teochew, one Hakka and two *lukchin*.

One opium trader, Chin Piew, was arrested several times but each time he bribed his way out of jail through Phraya Mahathep, the chief of police. As Chin Piew prospered, the extortion amount became larger and larger until one day in 1848 he refused to pay. Instead, he conspired with the *longchu* in Sakornburi whose livelihoods were affected by the sugar boiler tax to rise against the government. When Mahathep requested troops to put down the uprising, Kham bluntly refused to send troops, informing his father, Chaophraya Phraklang (Dit), that he had already arrested Chin Piew several times, and that this time perhaps Mahathep should make the arrest himself.

Phraya Mahathep, accompanied by Phraya Sawadiwaree, made his way to Sakornburi to arrest Chin Piew and the 300-strong Triad gang supporting him. Similar to Phra and Phraya Sombat-wanit, Phraya Sawadiwaree was a very powerful and influential Chinese shipping tycoon. It was Sawadiwaree's ships that carried the bulk of Chinese indentured laborers from China to Siam. Consequently, he wielded a great deal of influence with the Chinese *kongsi* and *longchu* that operated the affairs of the overseas Chinese community. However, upon approaching the rebels, Mahathep was felled by a bullet. Fatally wounded, he ordered his troops to retreat back to Bangkok where he died. The authorities sent a punitive expedition led by Chaophraya Phraklang (Dit), who crushed the rebels as they were trying to escape to Burma.

End of Tributary Trade

When the British sent Raja James Brooke to Siam in 1850 to protest the infringements of the Burney Treaty, it was hardly a surprise that his efforts proved to be in vain. It was left to King Mongkut (1851–68) to carry on the tax farming reforms initiated by Rama III and bring them to a logical conclusion. Rama III had already bought time by making conciliatory gestures to the British by signing the Burney Treaty. But simply paying lip service to free trade would not work for much longer in the face of mounting British pressure.

Moreover, Mongkut's accession to the throne was greeted by foreboding developments in and around China. Time-honored protocol since the Ayudhya period dictated that upon ascending the throne, Mongkut should send a tribute mission to Canton to request imperial investiture. King Mongkut immediately dispatched a tribute mission to Canton but the mission was not allowed to proceed to Beijing because the Qing court was still mourning the death of the Daoguang emperor. A year later, the king again sent two tribute ships. This time the Siamese envoy traveled to Beijing where they met five other envoys, including from Korea and Ryukyu. On the way back to Canton in 1853, the Siamese mission was attacked and robbed by bandits near Shangqiu City in Henan Province. The Siamese translator accompanying the envoy went missing and was presumed dead. All the valuable gifts bestowed by the Chinese emperor upon the Siamese king were stolen.

This incident precipitated a break in the tradition of paying tribute to the imperial Qing court. When China was perceived as the most powerful country and the largest market in the world, tribute symbolized acknowledgement of Siam's inclusion within the constellation of states comprising the Middle Kingdom's sphere of influence. However, the British victory over China in the Opium War of 1842 shattered Siamese perceptions of China's invincibility. The war ended with the Treaty of Nanjing in which the Chinese government suffered the humiliation of having to open up the country to foreign trade, permit missionaries to proselytize Christianity on Chinese soil, accept foreign extraterritorial rights and cede Hong Kong to the British. The relative might of European weaponry and the British command of new technologies became solidly established in the eyes of the Siamese, and for Siam, Britain had beyond a doubt displaced China from its preeminent position as the most powerful country in the world.

Like his predecessor, Rama III, Mongkut knew that the good old days were gone. He began adjusting Siam's position on a broad range of issues in accordance with the realities of a new world order where France and Britain rather than China ruled supreme.

The lessons of the devastating Opium War were not lost upon the Siamese. Because opium was promoted and sold by the British, King Mongkut recognized the futility and impracticality of banning the substance. Instead, Mongkut opted for regulating opium use by subsuming it under the institution of a Chinese opium farm in 1851. Thus, opium was allowed to be sold

Treaty of Nanjing under which China ceded the island of Hong Kong to the British in 1842.

151

through a Chinese contractor, which allowed the authorities to regulate its operation. Opium could only be sold to the Chinese but not to the native Thai, Mon, Lao, Burmese, Khmer, Brahman and native Portuguese who comprised the corvée labor of the Siamese state. These laborers represented the bulwark of the military system of the Siamese state, so the authorities were very protective of them. If the government allowed the *phrai* of the state to become infected by the "Chinese vice," it ran the risk of eroding the integrity of the entire Siamese military system.

By and large the system seemed to work because it was in the interest of the tax concessionaire to respect the regulation rather than be shut down or replaced. However, loopholes continued to exist. Non-Chinese addicts and other local natives continued to buy opium by wearing a queue to pass as Chinese. While the system was not perfect, it was manageable, and the opium problem was largely contained within the Chinese community.

Meanwhile, the robbing of the Siamese tribute mission by Chinese bandits in 1853 provided King Mongkut with an excuse to put Siam's relations with China on a new footing. After 1853, King Mongkut suspended the tradition of sending tribute to China. In response to Chinese messages and protestations received 10 years later, Phraya Choduk, head of the Bureau of Chinese affairs, sent a brief acknowledgement to the governor-general in Canton. But in another letter sent to the manager of Hang Punkang,[47] the Siamese offered a detailed explanation of its position on sending an envoy:[48]

> *Siam and Peking have long been friendly, and each time tribute was due, Siam always remembered to send it, so as to not harm the friendship that had so long been maintained. However in [1853] . . . [the envoy of] Siam. . . was attacked by bandits who forcefully took away all of the emperor's gifts given in return to the court of Siam. . . . When it came to the monsoon season of the year of the Hare [1856] . . . which was when the tribute to China was due, it was learned that the rebels were causing even more trouble than before, and therefore the tribute was waived. Then [in 1860] . . . it was again time to send tribute to China. This time it was learnt that the city of Canton was at war with England, and that the Governor-General himself was not residing there.[49] If Siam were to send envoys, no one would receive them. Then [in 1862] . . . it was learnt that England and France were penetrating as far as Beijing and that Beijing was in the midst of a great war.*

The Siamese policy of sending tribute to China was formally terminated in 1882 during the reign of King Chulalongkorn (1868–1910).

An *Illustrated London News* sketch showing boats of the British ship HMS *Medea* attacking armed pirate junks in a harbor on the southwestern coast of China, 1849.

Meanwhile, the unfinished business of free trade, which had been left hanging after Rama III signed the Burney Treaty, came back to haunt King Mongkut. In 1855, the British sent the governor and commander-in-chief of Hong Kong and plenipotentiary of China, Sir John Bowring, to negotiate a new commercial treaty with Siam. Unlike the previous envoys who came under the authority of the government of India, Bowring was a direct representative of the British Crown. Moreover, his rank and position carried all the connotations of Britain's military might, which had defeated China in the Opium War and forced the opening of five treaty ports under the Treaty of Nanjing in 1842. True to form, Bowring arrived in Siam with two British warships—the *Raffles* and the *Grecian*—which entered Bangkok's waters with a booming 21-gun salute. Under such military pressure, the Siamese court under King Mongkut capitulated. To the full satisfaction of the British, the Bowring Treaty was successfully concluded with the Siamese government on 18 April 1855.

THE PHRAYA CHODUK-RACHASRETTHI OF THE EARLY 19TH CENTURY

From the days of Ayudhya, Siamese kings conducted foreign affairs through the Phraya Phraklang, who was head of the royal treasury and cross-border trade. It was an apt duty in those days because all trade with foreigners was the exclusive right of the monarch under the Royal Trading Monopoly. In fact, up to the early Bangkok period, foreign travelers were sometimes called *luk kha phanich*, or commercial clients.

The Phraklang was responsible for the royal junk trade, the royal warehouse, foreign relations and foreign affairs, including the collection of import/export taxes and the Chinese poll tax. The Phraklang also oversaw the foreign communities in Siam and the administration of several provinces in the Central Plain with large Chinese settlements. All foreign affairs were supervised by Krom Tha, the Harbor Department, a part of the Phraklang. The Krom Tha Sai, headed by Choduk-Rachasretthi, looked after all affairs of the South China Sea, and the Krom Tha Khwa, under Chula-Rajmonti, was responsible for foreign affairs of the Indian Ocean and beyond.

Following his accession to the throne in 1782, Rama I revised and amended the old Laws of Ayudhya and reorganized the Siamese bureaucracy, including provincial administration. The Phraklang was responsible for nine central and eastern *muang*, while the administration of the southern provinces—which had been within the jurisdiction of the Phraklang since the days of King Borommakot—was given back to the Kalahom.

Thus, all Chinese affairs, both internal and external, were under the care of Choduk-Rachasretthi, whose rank could be a *luang*, *phra* or *phraya* depending on the seniority of the individual occupying the position. However, from the reign of Rama III through Rama VI, heads of the Krom Tha Sai were given the rank of *phraya*, and were commonly called *phraya choduk* in Thai. Due to a lack of primary documents, few details on the earlier *phraya choduk* survive except from the early 19th century onwards until 1932.

Phraya Choduk Chim

The Phraya Choduk during the reign of Rama II was Chim, probably a *lukchin* of some social standing in the Siamese court. He was sent by Rama II to govern Chantabun and manage the recurring problems between the Teochew and Hokkien communities there. Later, during the reign of Rama III, he was appointed the head of Krom Na, the minister in charge of land and rice cultivation. His daughter was a well-known dancer in Rama III's court who restored Wat Apsornsawan.

Phraya Choduk Thong Chin Krairiksh

Thong Chin was a son of Lim Riksh (林良), an interpreter in the last tribute mission sent to China by the king of Thonburi, who later worked for the first *uparat* of the Bangkok Kingdom. Lim Riksh's daughter also worked in the inner court, but it was his niece, Ampha, who became Rama II's favorite concubine, bearing him six children including Prince Pramoj—forefather of Seni and Kukrit Pramoj, the famous Thai prime ministers.

To implement Rama III's extensive development plan, Thong Chin was made directly responsible for finding Chinese contractors and workers to build forts and dig canals. Despite being a *lukchin* who was very conversant on the China trade, he found himself beleaguered when he operated the Krom Tha Sai. Rama III was an experienced trader who had supervised the Phraklang before he ascended the throne. Consequently, he could be a very demanding task master. In June 1836, the missionary Dan Beach Bradley reported that two senior *phraya* including Phraya Choduk (Thong Chin) and Phraya Piphat Kosa had been arrested and imprisoned. Their crime, apparently, had been to allow Chinese junks to export large amounts of rice to China. Although rice exports brought in considerable revenue for the treasury, Rama III was displeased. The king believed that more income could have been made if the Chinese had been coaxed to buy sandalwood instead of rice because of its higher profit margins. Thong Chin was punished and replaced by another of the king's trading partners, Boonma. Later, after Boonma passed away, Rama IV reinstated Thong Chin as head of the Krom Tha Sai. As was customary among senior officials of Rama III, Phraya Choduk Thong Chin restored Wat Thong Nopphakhun in Thonburi.

Phraya Choduk Boonma

Boonma was another wealthy junk merchant friend of Rama III who was promoted to the title *phra wiset-wari* upon the king's accession to the throne. Except for the mention of his name in the Thai chronicles as the *choduk* replacement of Thong Dee, everything about this man seems to have disappeared from existing historical records, leaving no family to trace. Even a grand Theravada temple named Wat Chodtanaram (also known as Wat Phraya Krai) that he had built for the king vanished. By 1907 it fell into decay and became a deserted temple next to the East Asiatic's sawmill. Subsequently, Queen Saowapha sold the property to the East Asiatic Company. After the roof of the *vihara* collapsed, the plaster image of Buddha was moved to a temporary shelter at Wat Traimit in 1935. An accident 20 years later chipped off the plaster coating of the statue and the solid gold underneath the plastered surface was revealed. The five-and-a-half ton Buddha image was tested for gold content. Among the various parts tested, 40 percent of the body consisted of gold, the face 80 percent and the hair and topknot, weighing 45 kilograms, consisted of 99 percent pure gold.

Phraya Choduk Tienjong

After Thong Chin was reinstated by King Mongkut, he served the king for only two years before his death. In fact, his death occurred at the critical moment when the Siamese tribute mission was robbed and its interpreter killed. Thong Chin's successor, Ng Tienjong, was a merchant from the Ng (Huang) clan sharing the same clan name as Chaophraya Nikornbodin, one of the most senior ministers of Rama III.[50] Later, he was appointed Samuhanayok by King Mongkut. Having spent 27 years as a Buddhist monk, the new king knew very little about trade, and the appointment of Phraya Choduk was probably recommended by the king's senior ministers.

After Siam signed the Bowring Treaty with Great Britain, which institutionalized extraterritorial rights, the responsibility of the Phraya Choduk shifted from the China trade to the administration of the growing Chinese population in Siam. Many Chinese in Siam became British or French subjects to qualify for legal protections. Unless Chinese perceived that they could obtain adequate legal protection under the Siamese legal system, they opted to become colonial subjects of Western powers. To satisfy the Chinese community, a Chinese court of law was set up, which was headed by the Phraya Choduk and based on Chinese legal codes and practices.

Ng Tienjong was appointed the first head of the Chinese tribunal. In his old age, Phraya Choduk Ng Tienjong was promoted to Phraya Rachanuchit. He donated a large sum of money to the renovation of an old Theravada temple on Klong Dan called Wat Nang Chi during the reign of Rama III. The Srivikorn, who are descendants of Khunying Wad Srivikornmatit, and the Ingkanonda family have traced their ancestry to Ng Tienjong.

THE AGE OF EMIGRANTS

(1855–1900)

The second half of the 19th century saw a flood of Chinese emigrate to Siam. The largest group were Teochew, followed by the Hokkien, and to a lesser extent, the Hailam, Hakka, Cantonese and Straits-born Chinese also arrived by steamship and junk. Each group tended to gravitate toward their own, forming ever more influential business networks and social communities. The seafaring Hokkien, for example, settled in the ports, and dominated the south. The Teochew were specialists in agriculture, and thrived by helping in the export of the new commodity of sugar. Some Chinese came as coolies to build railroads and clear forests, while others were well-educated English-speakers who worked in Western firms. Together, they formed an enormous non-native population in Siam. The monarchy prospered from their labor, taxes and the selling of concessions, and also from their vices: gambling, drinking and smoking opium. But the massive influx of Chinese, often attached to and protected by secret societies or foreign governments, also presented challenges to law and order that increasingly alarmed the Siamese government.

"Of raw import to Siam the Chinaman certainly heads the list."
— H. Warington Smyth, a British national working for
the Siamese government from 1891 to 1901.

Sir John Bowring, the British governor of Hong Kong and the minister plenipotentiary to the courts of China, Japan, Korea, Siam and Vietnam, arrived in Bangkok in early April 1855. The outcome of his mission, the Bowring Treaty, set the pattern for similar treaties concluded between the Siamese government and various Western nations in the following two decades. The Bowring Treaty replaced the traditional, Siamese royal-monopoly trading system with a system of free trade. Bowring's personal account of his mission gave a vivid account of Siam in 1855:

> *It is estimated that in the kingdom of Siam there are more than a million and a half of Chinese settlers; in the city of Bangkok alone there are supposed to be two hundred thousand. In fact, all the active business appears to be in their hands. Nine out of ten of the floating bazaars which cover for miles the two banks of the Meinam are occupied by Chinamen; very many of them are married to Siamese women, for a Chinawoman scarcely ever leaves her country; but the children are invariably educated to the Chinese type: the tail is cultivated if it be a boy, and the father alone seems to model the child's nature and education … With rare exceptions, the Siamese women are well treated by their Chinese husbands … The Chinese not only occupied the busiest and the largest bazaars, but their trading habits descend to the very lowest articles of barter; and hundreds of Chinese boats are vibrating up and down the river, calling at every house, penetrating every creek, supplying all articles of food, raiment, and whatever ministers to the daily wants of life. They penetrate to and traffic with the interior wherever profits are to be realized. As a community they are nearly isolated from the Siamese, though professing, for the most part, the same religion. They have their own temples, and carry on their worship of Buddha, not according to the usages of the priests of Siam … The signs over their warehouses, shops, and houses are all written in Chinese, in the Chinese language they carry on all their correspondence; nor do I remember an example of a Chinaman being able to write, though they almost all speak, the Siamese language.*[1]

Sir John Bowring also recorded in his personal journal a firsthand observation of the Siamese ruling class in April 1855:

Soon after ten o'clock, we went to the first Somdet's palace. It was the first formal and official meeting. We were received, as usual, by a guard presenting arms; and within the gates were several pages clad in yellow with pikes. We passed through a crowd of people, and entered the great hall, gorgeously ornamented with richly-gilded buffets, services, and other decorations. In the centre, the most elevated spot, sat the senior Somdet;[2] at his left, the King's brother;[3] at his right, the second Somdet;[4] and on the same elevation with myself, and opposite, sat the Phra Kalahom,[5] obviously the master-mind of the assembly, and who carried on most of the conversation. The discussion lasted more than six hours, and every article of the treaty was talked about; and as we reached a result, a record was made on a succession of black tablets by a scribe who knelt at the foot of the Kalahom . . . A great number of ministers also attended the council, and we soon observed a bulky Chinese—the great monopolist, who farms no less than ninety articles of produce, and who, when the treaty proposal to abolish the existing monopolies was read, was called forward, and looked like ten thunderstorms on hearing what, if effectually carried out, destroys "Othello's occupation."[6]

Top: Sir John Bowring.

Bottom: Somdet Chaophraya Si Suriyawongse (Chuang Bunnag) was the Phra Kalahom at the time of Bowring's visit.

Chapter opening picture: The entrance of Sampeng, a Chinese enclave in Bangkok.

According to existing records, there is no instance in Siamese history in which ninety tax farms were awarded to one man. As this bulky Chinese merchant, Koh Chun, solemnly dressed in mandarin attire as required by the Siamese court for its official function, was a forefather of Pimpraphai Bisalputra, the co-author of this book, perhaps a qualifying note must be added to clarify that Bowring may have been misinformed.

Koh Chun (1815–62) was a locally trained junk tycoon, a *lukchin* born in Bangkok during the reign of Rama II. His mother, according to K.S.R. Kularb, traced her descent to King Taksin's junk master, and Koh Chun's maternal uncle Phraya Sawasdiwari (Chim, 林蔭) was a junk master whose fleet had served the Siamese king with distinction during the reign of Rama III. Koh Chun himself was granted a noble position in the Krom Tha Sai[7] with the title of Phraya Phisan-Supaphol.[8]

An obituary of Phraya Phisan (Koh Chun), who died in 1862, described him as "a Chinese of extraordinary powers, standing at the head of all his countrymen here, as well as the Siamese, in commercial affairs, the sole owner of a large portion of Siamese shipping by which he had accumulated a fortune of six or seven millions of dollars."[9] He probably attended the meeting with Bowring as the representative of the Chinese merchants and tax farmers. Having grown up in the Chinese community in Bangkok that had served the junk fleet of the king of Siam for several generations, Koh Chun's gloom was probably due to the realization that the heyday of the junk trade was ending.

Othello's Occupation Gone

Koh Chun was aware of the obvious advantages of the Chinese junk trade that had enabled it to compete successfully with Western ships prior to this time. Because of the exclusive access to Chinese ports other than Canton enjoyed by Chinese private junks, the Siamese court commissioned Chinese sailors and Chinese vessels. Early 19th century Western observers noted that Sino-Siamese junks called at ports scattered along the entire coast of China from Hainan to Tianjin. A partial list of the Siamese junks sailing to China in 1813 reveals that two-thirds called at ports other than Canton.[10]

From the Chinese officials' point of view, the commodities obtained from Siam and Southeast Asia complemented the needs of the local economy of Southern China. In fact, China's reliance on the importation of goods from the Nanyang over several centuries implied that China was not entirely self-sufficient economically. Moreover, the imports from Southeast Asia during the Qing period were largely primary staples. Official reservations about Western trade may well have arisen from the recognition that the manufactures and opium imported by Western ships were not necessary to China's economy. In contrast, many Chinese officials appreciated the contributions of the junk trade to the provincial economies on China's maritime border.[11] Arguments in its support emphasized the employment it provided Chinese coastal dwellers, its stimulating effect on local handicrafts, and the provincial revenue it engendered. Consequently, the junk trade was allowed to continue relatively freely during the 18th and 19th centuries.

Koh Chin Sóó, Koh Chun's son, in Chinese attire similar to what his father would have worn during the meeting with Sir John Bowring.

When King Mongkut abolished the Royal Trading Monopoly, the junks that had been used for this purpose were no longer needed. Siam changed its policy partly as a result of the enlarged role assumed by Western powers in Asia after the Opium War and partly from the willingness of Siam's leaders to seek accommodation with Western nations.[12] The impact of the decline of the Sino-Siamese junk trade and Siam's departure from the Chinese tributary orbit cumulatively exerted a negative impact on Koh Chun's empire. However, the negative repercussions on Chinese merchants in Siam reflected an even more serious misfortune affecting the Qing court.

China Proper showing the individual provinces, with the names of ports open to foreign trade underlined, circa 1880.

China in the Early 19th Century

The traditional Siamese view of China was that of a powerful and wealthy country whose trade was much coveted. The China trade was the mainstay of Siam's economic prosperity during the 18th century. After Ayudhya was destroyed by the Burmese invasion of 1767, it was the China trade that continued to provide the underpinnings of economic prosperity during the early Bangkok period.

Thus, in the traditional Siamese world view, China had always occupied the center of the Asian region as a powerful country that drew foreigners from all over the world and served as the standard bearer in philosophy, politics, diplomacy, taste and style.[13] Consequently, it was fitting in Siamese eyes that the Chinese empire was surrounded by states that acknowledged Chinese suzerainty—especially those to the south and east along Asia's coastline.

Siamese tributary missions to China in the 18th century observed a country that was secure against external invaders and had a robust economy on par with Europe. Domestically, irrigation and transportation were well developed, and diverse markets—dealing not only in Chinese classical products like silk, tea and porcelain but encompassing almost everything from tools to candlesticks for the after-life—had begun to emerge.[14]

However, after the death of the Qianlong emperor, China went into decline. The

161

gradual disintegration of China was not as much social or economic as it was the product of dynastic decline, weak emperors, misrule, foreign invasions, wars and peasant rebellions. Qianlong's son and grandson, the Jiaqing (r. 1796–1820) and Daoguang (r. 1820–50) emperors, were poor leaders who had none of the ability of the early Qing emperors including Kangxi, Yongzheng and Qianlong. Jiaqing's ineffectual military campaign to suppress a Buddhist millenarian revolt led by the White Lotus Society drained the treasury, imperial prestige and his personal power. In 1803 he suffered the indignity of being mobbed in the street. To add insult to injury, a band of conspirators was emboldened to attempt to storm the Forbidden City in 1813, reflecting the contempt in which the emperor was held. When Jiaqing was struck by lightning on his way to the summer palace in 1820, one of his advisors remarked that his departure from life was the most exciting initiative the emperor had ever undertaken.[15]

Following the death of Jiaqing, the weakness of the imperial office haunted his son and successor, Daoguang, during his 30-year reign. The Daoguang emperor was a sickly, weak-willed and indecisive man given to sudden reversals of policy depending on the most recent report or recommendation to reach him. Consequently, he became hostage to powerful factions at court. The emperor himself tried to imitate the practice of his great forbears—his grandfather Qianlong and his great-great-grandfather Kangxi. But while the Qing founders demonstrated admirable leadership, decisiveness and innovativeness, Daoguang labored helplessly to restore China's glorious past, which he did not understand, while watching his empire slide into disarray and subjugation.[16]

The weakened Qing state could no longer effectively contain Western influence. Moreover, the Western powers in the 19th century had become more powerful than a century ago. Perceiving the growing weakness of the Qing court, the Western powers became more strident in their demands for reduction of trade restrictions and access to more ports in addition to Canton, which Qianlong had set up in 1757 as the only harbor open to trade with Western ships to contain the activities of Western merchants.

The item that sparked off war between China and Britain was opium. The Daoguang emperor believed strongly in opium prohibition. By his second decade in power, the emperor's war on drugs was becoming central to his other ineffectual policies against administrative inefficiency, corruption and disloyalty. Daoguang's decision to crack down on opium smuggling by free traders occurred just as the opium trade had become central to Britain's China strategy.

The Qing court's failure to develop a foreign service to deal with the growing Western presence in China handicapped the court when it needed

Top: Emperor Jiaqing (reigned 1796–1820).

Bottom: Emperor Daoguang (reigned 1821–50).

Emperor Daoguang reviews forces in Peking in preparation for the first Opium War.

accurate intelligence on the intentions and military strength of foreign powers. The situation was further aggravated by rival factions at court, which competed with one another in advocating a tough line on all things foreign as a way of currying favor with the emperor.

Consequently, the Chinese government mishandled the enforcement of the campaign against opium smuggling and misjudged the response of the foreign powers. In 1839, Chinese troops moved into the Western enclave and seized 1,200 tons of opium from foreign warehouses. The Chinese then demanded that foreigners who had injured or killed Chinese officers during the crackdown be handed over and that all foreigners sign an oath to desist from smuggling opium into China. Led by the British, the foreigners responded by imposing a trade embargo on Canton.

War broke out not because of Chinese attacks on foreign ships, but because the Chinese government tried to protect foreign vessels breaking the British embargo. In November 1839, British warships attempted to stop one of their own barques, the *Royal Saxon*, which tried to enter Canton. The Chinese navy responded by moving in to protect the *Royal Saxon*. The British fleet opened fire, sinking four Chinese vessels. The Opium War had begun.

From the very beginning, the technological superiority of the British fleet was obvious. With naval bases in Aden, Singapore, India and Sri Lanka, the British could send their warships into East Asia and have them supplied and re-equipped on the way. While uncertain of winning military engagements on land, the British had no doubt about the superiority of their navy even when fighting in foreign territory without support from shore.

By early 1840, no progress had been made in negotiations between Britain and China. The British laid siege to Canton and occupied key cities in the coastal provinces of Fujian and Zhejiang. Within a year, foreign ships controlled the mouth of the Yangtze River and the southern entrance to the Grand Canal, as well as towns in the delta, among them what was to become Shanghai. Manchu troops fought bravely in Central China but could not prevent the British from using their navy to take control of the country's economic lifelines. The war devastated the economic fabric of the southern provinces and left chaos and anarchy in its wake. In 1842, the emperor sued for peace, dreading the potential domestic consequences of prolonged war and its impact on the dynasty's own survival.

The Chinese government was forced to accept harsh terms in exchange for peace. Under the Treaty of Nanjing signed in 1842, the Chinese government suffered the humiliation of having to open more ports to foreign trade, permit missionaries to proselytize on Chinese soil, accept foreign extraterritorial rights and cede Hong Kong to the British. Consequently, the curtain fell on the Canton system, which had been used to regulate all foreign maritime trade with China since the reign of Qianlong.

Sino-Siamese Trade After the Opium War

China's defeat in the Opium War and the subsequent abandoning of the Canton system had a far-reaching impact on Sino-Siamese trade. The Treaty of Nanjing provided for the opening of Amoy, Fuzhou, Ningbo and Shanghai to international shipping. As long as the Canton system was in place the Siamese Royal Trading Monopoly, which employed Chinese vessels and crews, could maintain a competitive edge over Western trading. Once Western ships could access other ports, Siam lost its advantage.

Consequently, many Chinese traders who settled in Southeast Asia could now lade their cargoes on Western ships between Europe and China without fear of discrimination at the newly opened ports. Others built their own square-rigged sailing vessels or purchased Western-made steamships, as the Siamese did, to carry their trade to the new treaty ports. In fact, Siam had been constructing square-rigged vessels for the Siam-Singapore trade since the 1830s. Although Siam's share of the shipping at the treaty ports was small compared to that of Western merchants, the arrival and departure of Siamese vessels was regularly reported during the 1850s and 1860s.[17] The new cost-efficient steamships soon dominated long-distance ocean transport as traditional junks became marginalized.

Jennifer W. Cushman aptly summarized the end of the Sino-Siamese junk trade in her book *Fields from the Sea: Chinese Junk Trade with Siam During the Late Eighteenth and Early Nineteenth Centuries* as follows:

Unlike China, which was forcibly drawn into relations with the West, Siam's leaders purposely chose a more conciliatory approach in meeting Britain's demands. Although the Chinese experience must have served as an object lesson to the Siamese, they were, nonetheless, already adept in the use of diplomacy, and demonstrated considerable flexibility when confronted by powers possessing obviously greater military might. Their recognition of China's failure in this respect may explain the growing disenchantment with Siam's position in the Chinese tributary system. Dissatisfaction was expressed that China did not treat Siam as an equal, and that for Siam to maintain her status as a vassal state was to court the ridicule and disdain of the West. Implicit in this attitude was the fear that Siam, as a tributary to China, would appear weak, thereby increasing the likelihood of her being made a pawn in Western power politics in Southeast Asia. From an economic standpoint, it was also felt that close ties with the West and concessions to Western trading interests would yield greater economic benefits in the long run than those derived from state and tributary trade with China. The Siamese perception of Siam's place in the Asian world changed as the traditional economic and diplomatic structure was altered by the Western intrusion. Siam's vigorous response to British overtures hastened the process by removing the final advantages enjoyed by the Chinese native trade at Bangkok. As Siam moved closer to the West, her disengagement from the Chinese tributary system became inevitable …

The international trading environment that had prevailed in the South China Sea was being replaced by new trading conditions and patterns after the mid-19th century. In Siam, King Mongkut stopped sending tribute to China after

An illustration of Amoy in the mid-19th century.

A Bo Ju Lee Gee tea caddy decorated with a scene from the *Ramayana*, a popular epic poem well read in Thailand.

his 1853 mission was robbed on its way back from the imperial palace in Beijing.[18] According to the history of Chinese porcelain imports to Siam written by Prince Damrong,[19] after the suspension of tributary junks, orders for Chinese porcelain were no longer handled by the royal trading enterprise, but rather were primarily placed through Bangkok-based Chinese merchants. Prominent among importers of porcelain were Phraya Choduk-Rachasretthi (Pook), under the trademark of Gim Tung Hok Kee (Jin Tang Fu Ji), and Phraya Phisan-Supaphol (Koh Chun) under the trademark of Bo Ju Lee Gee (Bao Zhu Li Ji). Thus, ironically, Koh Chun—the Chinese merchant whom Bowring had caricatured in 1855 as looking like "ten thunderstorms on hearing what, if effectually carried out, destroys 'Othello's occupation,'"—in fact had benefited from these changes.

Perhaps unknown to Bowring, in 1843 Koh Chun had already established a trading foothold in Hong Kong called Koh Nguan Seng (高元盛), located in the Nan Bei Hang area.[20] The intelligence obtained from the Chinese trading network in the British colony had prepared him for the future world of open markets. Moreover, Siamese merchants were quite adept in shipping as they had financial backing from the crown and from Siamese noblemen, especially from the Bunnag family. Once they were convinced that the future lay in steamships, they acted swiftly and decisively in upgrading their fleets. The first steamer to be built in Siam was completed in 1855 and by the early 1860s, Siam had 23 steamships in addition to 76 square-rigged sailing vessels.[21] Koh Chun became the proud owner of the first Siamese steamship servicing Bangkok and Hong Kong as well as Huay Chung Long—the Steamship Terminal—a large commercial property comprising several two-storied buildings interconnected and subdivided into small offices for rent. The terminal's prime waterfront location opposite Sampeng, Bangkok's Chinatown, ensured that it was fully occupied all year round. Perhaps copying the concept of Nan Bei Hang in Hong Kong, where merchants from Canton, Chaozhou, Fujian, Shandong and Shanghai opened shops in 1851, Huay Chung Long in Bangkok had its own merchants' guild as well.

The Taiping Rebellion (1850–64)

After the Qing court accepted the conditions of the Treaty of Nanjing, the Western threat temporarily abated. However, a new, domestic problem was developing. The humiliating defeat of the Manchu armies combined with a series of natural disasters and economic problems precipitated the outbreak of the Taiping Rebellion (1850–64), a millenarian movement led by Hong Xiuquan, a religious visionary who believed he was the brother of Jesus Christ.

The Hakka-led Taiping Rebellion inflicted even more damage than the Western invasion across large parts of southeastern China, in which over 10 million people lost their lives. The rebellion engulfed the emigrant areas of Guangdong and Fujian, leaving famine and disease in its wake. In many areas anarchy and disorder continued for years after the demise of the Taiping movement. Conflicts between the Hakka and the Cantonese in Guangdong during the years 1864 to 1866 resulted in 150,000 deaths.[22] Banditry, petty uprisings and fighting among various dialect groups continued to occur in the emigrant areas in Guangdong, Fujian and even Hainan through the period leading up to the revolution of 1911 and also through its immediate aftermath. Moreover, the methods of pacifying the rebel areas were so ruthless and brutal as to encourage people to flee the area. After the collapse of the Taiping Rebellion, thousands of its adherents emigrated to seek refuge abroad in the wake of Manchu reprisals against the Hakka.

Statue of Hong Xiuquan, leader of the Taiping Rebellion.

In the meantime, Western powers also seized the opportunity to squeeze more concessions from the embattled Chinese government. When the Qing court resisted, the Anglo-French expedition to China known as the Arrow War started, lasting from 1856 to 1860. Manchu forces put up a fierce resistance but were smashed by European artillery. With considerable casualties on both sides, Western forces finally occupied, ransacked and torched the summer palace Yuan Ming Yuan after looting the accumulated cultural treasures of Chinese civilization. The 1860 looting of the summer palace was the greatest act of plunder of the 19th century, yielding treasures that still command pride of place in many prestigious Western museums.

Overpopulation

The damage inflicted by the wars with the Western powers and peasant rebellions caught China at the height of its population expansion. Peace and economic prosperity during the 18th century led to rapid population increases in Fujian and Guangdong, which continued up to the early 19th century. Faced with an inhospitable mountainous interior and scarcity of arable land, the southern provinces of Fujian and Guangdong had become dangerously overpopulated by the mid-19th century. Under these circumstances, the recurring floods and droughts in the area resulted in famine and death. Thus, the convergence of demographic pressure, natural disasters, wars, peasant rebellions and the breakdown of social order resulted in a population exodus from Fujian and Guangdong. Chinese left in droves to escape a world that was crumbling around them.

Growth of Treaty Ports

The abolition of the Canton system and the opening up of treaty ports including Canton and Amoy in 1842 and Shantou in 1858 led to the emergence of a dual society and economy consisting of two parts: a vast countryside where foreign presence was negligible, and an archipelago of islets where a new, urbanized society was developing. Colonial enclaves like Shanghai and Hong Kong grew rapidly, attracting immigrants from all over the country, especially Fujian and Guangdong. Between the mid-19th and early 20th century, many Chinese coastal cities doubled in size as Qing restrictions on travel and urban residence faded, and economic opportunities were created. Just before World War I, there were 48 so-called treaty ports controlled by foreigners.

It was in these foreign enclaves that China began to re-invent itself through a process of social transformation and metamorphoses driven by its exposure to Western ideas, contacts, opportunities and practices. As the weakened Chinese state could no longer contain Western influence, Western armies, companies, missionaries, ideas and products inserted themselves into the country. It was a time when people who viewed themselves as Chinese transformed their lives and ways to become players in a global form of modernity. In the process, the opportunities for families and individuals to engage in employment, trade, studies and religious pursuits that took them abroad expanded. In spite of official disapproval, Chinese traveled, sojourned and settled abroad in unprecedented numbers at the end of the Qing era.

View of the Port of Shantou (Swatow).

Consequently, China's new cities became a powerful engine churning out Chinese emigration as far away as the steamers would take them. The process of migration was greatly facilitated by the availability of more ports for embarkation and availability of cheap steamer tickets. During the second half of the 19th century, unscheduled steamers plied with increasing frequency between Bangkok and Hong Kong and, to a lesser extent, directly between Bangkok and the South China treaty ports such as Amoy

Chinese people read the Treaty of Peking of 1861 as posted on a city wall.

and Shantou. By 1876, it was possible for Chinese emigrants from major emigrant areas to travel by scheduled steamers to Bangkok via Hong Kong. Eventually, the Manchu government's ban on emigration was withdrawn by degrees. The first step was the legalization of emigration under European auspices provided by the Treaty of Peking in 1860. The last step consisted in the promulgation of the new Qing code in 1910. These factors combined to produce the tsunami of Chinese emigration that swamped Southeast Asia.

The flood of emigrants from South China to Siam during the period 1850–1949 made the Chinese emigration of the 18th century seem like a trickle. Of some 20 million who left China before the Communist Revolution of 1949, over half went to Southeast Asia. The majority that arrived in Siam came from the southern coastline provinces of Guangdong and Fujian. These emigrants formed a heterogeneous lot that could be differentiated into the five major speech groups of Teochew, Hakka, Hailam, Hokkien and Cantonese.

The Teochew

The Teochews, by far the largest group of Chinese in Siam, migrated from the northern area of Guangdong near Shantou. Teochews were renowned as enterprising and excellent sailors long before the rise of Shantou as a treaty port in 1858. In the old days, Zhanglin was the main inland port of embarkation for the "red junks" (red indicated a junk operated by the Teochew). William Ruschenberger, who visited Bangkok in 1835, noted that the crews of most of the junks arriving in Bangkok were Teochew. According to Jennifer Cushman, the Teochew areas that carried on trade with Siam during the first half of the 19th

Top: An old man sits by the Old Pun Tao Kong Shrine in Songwad, the heartland of the Teochew in Bangkok.

Bottom: Siangkong Shrine, a small Teochew shrine behind Wat Pathum Khongkha on Songwad Road in Bangkok.

century were Haiyang, Chenghai, Raoping, Jieyang, Nan-ao and Donglonggang.

The Teochew exodus to Siam due to rice shortages in both Fujian and Guangdong provinces dated back to the 18th century. Later, the accession of King Taksin, a Teochew *lukchin,* to the throne of Siam in 1767 attracted another big wave. Contemporary reports in the 1830s alleged that Teochews were the largest of the Chinese dialect groups in Bangkok. One writer called them "much the most numerous," while another stated that the "Chinese residents [of Bangkok] are chiefly from Teochew."

Back in their homeland, the Teochew specialization was in cash crop agriculture, which probably explained the huge number of Teochew laborers involved in Siam's cash crops such as pepper and market vegetables. Moreover, the Teochew emigration areas were famous for their production of sugar for export. In fact, sugar cane was introduced to Siam by Chinese settlers in 1810.[23] Within a few years sugar became the leading export of Siam until about the 1880s. Reports from other parts of Southeast Asia also noted that the Teochew were agriculturalists and plantation workers par excellence.[24]

The most rapid plantation development existed in the valleys of the Chantabun, Bang Pakong, lower Chao Phraya, Tha Chin and Mae Klong rivers. When missionary Dan Beach Bradley made a trip to Chantabun in 1836, he was "thronged with the wondering multitudes … [of] Tachu and Hokian Chinese" in town, while upriver in a rural area, he found the land "almost wholly occupied by Tachu-Chinese [who] … raised chiefly sugar-cane, pepper and tobacco."[25]

By the mid-19th century the Teochew workforce dominated the cultivation areas in the Central Plain but they seemed to refrain from venturing into the dense forests of the hinterland. The exception to this was Tak and Chiang Mai, where Chinese merchants had already established settlements since the late Ayudhya period because of the comparative commercial importance of both towns, which served as crossroads in the caravan trade connecting Lanna and lower Siam by river to Paknampho. As such, these towns attracted Teochew and Hokkien merchants from lower Siam and lower Burma who traded in foreign goods imported via Bangkok and Rangoon and in the products of southwest China.[26] The Teochew *lukchin* King Taksin had been trading along the Ping River in the 1760s before he became the king of Thonburi. Subsequent tales of other Teochew families confirmed their familiarity with the Ping River route. The story of Mae Kamthieng[27] told of her forefather, Tae Hor, a member of Taksin's Tae (Zheng) clan, using the Ping River route in the north when he had to escape the second purge of Taksin's kin in 1809. The descendants of Tae Hor can be found among the prominent families of Chiang Mai, namely the Chutima and the Nimmanahaeminda.[28]

The prominence of Teochew traders in the Ping River valley was also confirmed by another source. Acclaimed China scholar Skinner cited the story of Akon Tia U-Teng (Teng Sophanodon, 1842–1919), the owner of Gim Seng Lee, as an example.[29] A poor Teochew boy from Chao'an, Tia U-Teng was in debt 18 baht for his passage to Siam. Once in Siam, he worked as a cook, a "coolie," and an oarsman taking people across the Chao Phraya, earning three baht a month. He then moved on and worked as a hired hand in vegetable farming for 10 baht a month.

Soon, he had enough savings to lend money to those even poorer than him and established a small trading business of his own in Tak in 1882. He then had the good fortune of marrying into an influential family of the north. After moving to Chiang Mai, his mother-in-law landed him with an excellent teak concession. He also became a sub-tax farmer for three gambling houses and a spirit (alcohol) farm operator. Together with two other Chinese merchants, Akon Teng was appointed as a tax farmer to collect transit fees from boats plying the Ping River. Gim Seng Lee was established in Bangkok in 1893 to handle the teak and rice trading business. At the same time, Akon Teng continued to fulfill his responsibilities as a monopolistic tax farmer in northern Thailand for opium, spirits, gambling and lotteries. His success in Siam was such that even King Rama V declared, "No tax farmers could compete with Gim Seng Lee."[30]

Meanwhile, transportation between Guangdong and Bangkok became easier with the opening of Shantou as a treaty port. This occurred just as Siam's fleet of merchant steamers was being built in 1858. Siamese-flag shipping with China peaked in 1868. Thus the serious entry of the new Thai fleet into the China trade came just in time to catch the huge tide of Teochew and Hakka emigration from the port of Shantou, although most of the emigrants from Shantou still went by junks or square-rigged vessels up to 1872, when only 22 percent of emigrants traveled by steamer.[31]

In 1882, the Bangkok Passenger Steamer Company began a regular steamer service between Bangkok and Shantou. This venture was a spectacular success story as the number of emigrants from Shantou to Siam exploded. Skinner's study indicated that "before 1882 only about 15 percent of all Shantou emigration went to Siam. In the decade between 1882 and 1892 the figures rose to about 20 percent, 1893 to 1905 about 33 percent and from 1906–17 about 50 percent. The preference of Teochew and Hakka emigrants for Siam grew steadily more marked until approximately half of all Shantou emigrants were going to Siam."[32] The average departures from Shantou to Bangkok rose from 8,381 per annum in the 1880s to 48,538 per annum in the decade after 1905.[33]

The Hakka

The forebears of the Hakka formerly occupied the lands bordering the Yellow River or Henan, Hubei and Shaanxi provinces in Central China. During periods of war and civil unrest, they migrated to the southeast and brought with them their Hakka language. The Chinese characters for Hakka (客家) literally mean "guest families." Although small numbers of Hakkas had started to travel to the Nanyang earlier, mass Hakka migration did not occur until the 19th century. Hakkas from Guangdong Province formed the nucleus of the Taiping Rebellion (1850–64) in the 19th century, and it was among them that the Hakka exodus started.

The struggle for "living room" in Guangdong between the native Cantonese ("Puntei") and the numerous Hakka immigrants erupted into another small-scale war known in history as the Hakka-Puntei War (1864–66). It was from this war-torn area of Guangdong that the Hakkas left for Southeast Asia, which partly explained why a great majority of overseas Hakkas worldwide came from the inland part of Guangdong—particularly the Xingning and Meixian areas.

During this time, several Hakkas came to prominence in the Nanyang world, namely Chung Kengquee (1821–1901), the "Capitan China" of Perak and Penang, and Yap Ah Loy (1837–85), the "Capitan China" who was regarded as the founding father of modern Kuala Lumpur.[34] Both were leaders of the Hai San Secret Society in their areas of influence. In Siam, King Chulalongkorn appointed Liu Kianhin (Liu Qianxing 1826–94), also of Hakka descent, to the position of Phraya Choduk-Rachasretthi (Thian), the governor of the Chinese in Siam. Although these cases were unrelated, perhaps the rise of Hakkas to prominent positions in the traditional Hokkien and Teochew spheres of influence in the late 19th century deserves further study.

The Hakka migration caused by civil unrest in Guangdong in the 1860s came after the opening of Shantou, the nearest port of departure for most Hakka

A Hakka sawmill belonging to Ng Miaongian Lamsam.

migrants, as a treaty port.[35] As prospective Hakka emigrants poured into Shantou, their choice of destination in the Nanyang was naturally conditioned by available transport to various Southeast Asian ports, including Bangkok, which had a good passenger-line service from Shantou. Successful Hakka in Siam include Ng Miaongian Lamsam, a prominent teak concessionaire in the lower North and Jia Geesee, the founder of the town of Hadyai in the South.

The Hailam

Hailam junks began to appear in Siam during the 18th century, and by the early 19th century considerable junk traffic had developed between Hainan and Bangkok. Foreign observers in the capital of Siam reported that annually some 40–50 junks from Hainan came to trade.[36] Hailam junks picked up timber, rice, raw cotton and bone for fertilizer from Siam.

In fact, Hainan Island's southerly position and the direction of trade winds made Bangkok a natural destination for Hailam shipping. Hailam junks could depart from Haikou and other ports on the island with the northeast monsoon and reach Bangkok every year before junks from any other part of China. According to Crawfurd (1830), it was usually the first Hailam junk arriving in January from which the Siamese court astronomers obtained the Chinese almanac each year.

Geographical proximity and favorable monsoon winds spurred on maritime links between Hainan and Siam. Unlike the large and seaworthy Hokkien and Teochew junks, Hailam junks were small vessels that rarely risked a trip across open sea to the Philippines or the Indonesian archipelago. Hainan's major trade was with the coastal ports of Guangdong, Vietnam, Cambodia and Siam, which could easily be reached by small junks without losing sight of land. Hainan's closure to foreign shipping during the first three-quarters of the 19th century also restricted maritime activity to small junks. Thus, the characteristics of Hailam shipping and geography coupled with the history of Western expansion in China conspired to strengthen the ties that Hailam sailors and traders had with Bangkok and established Siam as the chief destination for Hailam emigrants prior to 1876.

As the home markets in Hainan were limited, Hailam merchants found it difficult to compete with the sophisticated mainland merchants from Fujian and Guangdong in establishing a strong foothold in Bangkok. Since the port cities and urban commercial centers around the Gulf of Siam were already dominated by Hokkiens and Teochews by the early 19th century, the Hailam, who were relative newcomers, were forced to the periphery of the kingdom's economy. Consequently, the Hailam became the real pioneers in opening up the hinterland of Siam for commercial development.

Coming from the most tropical latitudes in China, the Hailam proved to be better suited to the physically demanding work of clearing virgin forests and swamps for cultivation, pig farming and commercial exploitation. Moreover, the Hailam had a special advantage in their innate resistance to malaria and other tropical fevers. They could survive in fever-ridden areas where Teochews and Hokkiens would die in vast numbers. Also, as hardy tropical islanders, the Hailam manifested a special skill in fishing and boat building, which allowed them to venture up the rivers into the interior. Opportunities for timber trade made them successful timber merchants in northern towns like Lampang, as well as operators of shipbuilding yards at Tha-Lo and Paknampho.[37]

The Hailam set up small markets in all the villages and towns of the river valleys of the north and lower northeast. The major area of Hailam settlement was near the Yom and Nan Rivers, the shorter tributaries of the Chao Phraya River above Paknampho. Many towns along the Nan River from Phichit up to Nan and on the Yom River from Sukhothai up to Phrae—such as Srisamrong in Sukhothai and Tha-Lo in Phichit—were settled by Hailam. Consequently, in the northeast as well as in the Nan, Yom and Wang river valleys are found numerous Chinese shrines dedicated to the deity Jui Buay Niao, the Hailam deity par excellence.[38]

As the interior of Siam began to open up and the demand for manual labor and domestic service increased, regular emigration junk traffic began to develop between Hainan and Bangkok. The major ports in Hainan for the Siamese trade and emigration in the 1870s was Puqian, Haikou and Qinglan. In 1886, a British steamship company inaugurated a direct service between Bangkok and Haikou, which created a sharp rise in Hailam emigration to Bangkok in the last two decades of the 19th century. Due to the direct steamer service between Bangkok and Haikou, the Hailam junk trade with Siam died a slow death, although the Chinese trading junks remained a prominent feature of Bangkok harbor until World War I. Nevertheless, from all accounts, after the turn of the century, Chinese immigration by junk was negligible for all but the Hailam traffic.[39]

The Cantonese

Among the five major speech groups in Siam, the Cantonese were much smaller in number despite the fact that Canton had been the principal port of call for foreign trade for over a century. According to the missionary Bradley's patient records for 1835–36, of the 934 Chinese treated in Bangkok, 713 were Teochews, 150 Hokkiens, 51 Hailams, 15 Cantonese and 5 Hakkas.[40]

When mass emigration took place in the 19th century, both Canton and Hong Kong channeled Cantonese into the most distant emigration traffic—namely to the Western hemisphere, Australia and New Zealand, thus affecting the number of Cantonese immigrants in Siam.[41]

Skinner also observed that Amoy and Canton were treaty ports open to foreign shipping from 1842 to 1858 while Shantou and Hailam ports were not. This meant that patterns of emigration from the Hokkien and Cantonese areas to European colonies in Southeast Asia were well established before the pool of labor from Teochew, Hakka and Hailam emigrants became available for exploitation in areas of European control. The demise of the royal tribute missions between Bangkok and Canton also entailed a further decrease in Cantonese immigration to Siam. The convenience of direct ship routes tended to enhance the predominance of Cantonese in other Southeast Asian destinations, which were subsequently continued and intensified everywhere except Siam and Cambodia.[42]

Moreover, Cantonese seldom settled outside major towns because of their occupational specialization in artisan and mechanical trades. The records of the Cantonese Association in Bangkok placed the total number of Cantonese in the city and environs at only 2,000 in 1877.[43]

Top: Beautiful wood carving at Kian An Keng, a Hokkien shrine at Kudee Chin in Thonburi.

Bottom: Jo Sue Kong, a Hokkien shrine at the center of the Hokkien community in Talad Noi, Bangkok.

The Hokkien

The predominance of the Hokkien community in the capital of Siam seemed to have ended with the destruction of Ayudhya. Descendants of old Hokkien families in Siam recount that their ancestors emigrated from the coastal areas including Zhangzhou, Tong'an and Quanzhou. Being predominantly sailors and merchants, as Gutzlaff reported in the 1830s, the Hokkiens almost never moved out of the major trading towns (except to pursue tin mining), while Teochews were found in both towns and the rural hinterland.[44] According to Skinner, the Hokkiens were prominent among merchants and dominated the important tea business in particular. As urban dwellers, a large number of Hokkien *lukchin* entered the government services, and through their connections in town many Hokkiens were involved in bidding for concessions and tax farms, a preferred occupation by the wealthy few.[45]

As the Hokkiens were seafarers involved in the junk trade, they settled in various ports in the Gulf of Siam, from Trad on the east coast all the way down to Patani in the south. Hokkiens were also actively involved in the tin mining industry, which had been one of the main export items of the junk trade since the Ayudhya period. By tracing the locations and prevalence of Hokkien shrines in Siam—most of which were dedicated to Tianhou Siaboh, revered by Nanyang seafarers—Skinner concluded that there were no Hokkien communities north of Ayudhya.

When King Taksin conquered Nakhon Si Thammarat, he found large Hokkien settlements in the southern part of the country. These settlements originated from trading communities that subsequently expanded into tin mining towns. In many areas the Chinese outnumbered the native population. Besides possessing numerical strength, they were also organized into defensive communities under traditional fraternity organizations. The leader of a powerful Chinese group, Hao Yiang (Wu Rang), known as the First Elder, paid tribute to King Taksin with boxes of tobacco in 1769 and was appointed the *phraya* of Songkhla in 1775.

As Chinese communities expanded with the growth of tin mining in the south, the rulers in Bangkok extended the precedent established by King Taksin of using local powers to strengthen Bangkok's political authority over the south. By the reign of Rama III, the policy of using local rajahs and Chinese *capitan* to control the south and its tin mining towns had become well established.

During the early Bangkok period, many Hokkiens were absorbed into the Siamese bureaucracy. As they assimilated into the social circles of Siamese nobility, they seemed to lose not only their ethnic Hokkien identity but their contact with China as well. However, in south Siam where the Hokkien *chao muang*—such as the Na Ranong and the Na Songkhla—actively promoted Hokkien labor immigration, the Hokkien identity was better maintained.

These powerful Hokkien *chao muang* and Chinese *capitan* played an indispensable role in the pacification of the south and the expansion of the Buddhist domains of the Bangkok Kingdom in the Muslim-dominated areas. One

A fortified Chinese village in Patani.

of the legendary Hokkien fighters well known in the southern peninsula was Tan Bui, whose exploits bear retelling. Tan Bui[46] was born in Hai Teng, a small village in the Zhangzhou area of Fujian, in 1809. His grandfather, Tan Guangliang, a legendary swordsman, was a local leader of a Chinese secret society known as the Heaven and Earth Society. However, internal feuds within the organization forced him to flee into exile. Tan Guangliang's parting instructions to his only son was, "Be hard working, do not take advantage of others, nor enter the government service, renounce politics and teach your children not to take up arms; do not serve the Manchus; live a simple life as a farmer or a trader; if our land degenerates send our children to other towns to find fertile ground." With these parting remarks, Tan Guangliang departed on a junk never to return.[47]

Tan Julai Tantanawat was ennobled as Phra Chinkananurak.

Several decades later, when life in Zhangzhou became difficult, Tan Bui—Tan Guangliang's youngest grandson—left home at 18 with a group of friends to seek his fortune abroad. He sold all his pigs to pay for the transportation cost. Joined by 25 men, Tan Bui embarked on a long journey that took them to Hainan, Hanoi, Trad and Chantabun, with Songkhla as their destination.

The young men were lured to Songkhla because of the good reputation of the Hokkien rajah of Songkhla, also a native of Zhangzhou. Reports of his benevolent patronage of emigrants from his native land had spread far and wide. Tan Bui and his friends were inspired by the success story of this son of Zhangzhou and longed to follow his footsteps.

Out of 25 who departed with Tan Bui, only eight determined young men managed to arrive in Songkhla. The others had succumbed to distractions or fallen by the wayside. When they arrived in Songkhla, war had erupted with the Malay Kingdom of Patani, and Phraya Vichienkhiri (Hao Tienseng Na Songkhla), the governor of Songkhla, was busy organizing the defense of the city. Tan Bui and his men were among those recruited and sent to attack Patani in 1839. The first battle was lost due to ill-prepared provisions of food for the soldiers. In the second attack, the Chinese prepared for a prolonged battle by hanging short bamboo casks filled with cooked rice around each soldier's body. The second attack was successful.

After the victory, Tan Bui was recommended by Vichienkhiri to be the Chinese *capitan* of Patani with the noble title of Luang Samretkitkorn. Tan Bui settled down in Patani and became part of the colorful story of the town. His son Tan Julai, known in Thai as Phra Chinkananurak, succeeded him as the Chinese *capitan* while another son, Tan Jubeng, expanded the family's mining business and was nicknamed "the Datoh of the mines" (the word *datoh* denotes Malay titled nobility). The family lived in Patani and played host to Prince Panuphand's visit in 1884, when Patani was a town of 3,000 households with a population of 20,000, of which 600 were Chinese, 200 were Thai and the rest Malay.[48]

According to Skinner, "Prior to the establishment of good overland communication between Bangkok and the south, Chinese immigrants to the lower peninsula came either directly by junks to such southern ports as Songkhla or indirectly via Singapore and Penang."[49] After the opening of Amoy in 1842 as the treaty port for foreign shipping, emigration from the Hokkien areas to European colonies in Southeast Asia became well established.[50] Regular and direct passenger traffic by steamer from Amoy to Singapore and Manila, which began in 1870, also meant that Hokkien emigrants were again disproportionately directed to the Philippines and the areas served by Singapore. Hence, in the late 19th century, there was a decline in the number of Hokkien emigrants to Siam.[51]

The Straits-born Chinese

Chinese from China were not the only emigrants Siam had played host to. Since the time of Ayudhya, Siam had been the hub of the overseas-Chinese trading network that linked the Chinese diaspora scattered throughout Southeast Asia, including Malacca, Palembang and Batavia. With the arrival of British naval power in the region, new maritime outposts were established at Hong Kong and the Straits Settlements on the Malay Peninsula, including Penang, Malacca and Singapore, to service Britain's mercantile interests.

By the mid-19th century, a lively commercial traffic had developed between Bangkok and the British Straits Settlements, especially Penang and Singapore.

European expatriates with their Chinese compradors in 1908.

The Straits-born Chinese graveyard on Silom Road in Bangkok testifies to the existence of a prominent Straits Settlements Chinese community in Bangkok dating back to the 19th century. Straits Chinese who branched out to Siam include Tan Kimcheng (Tansakul, Verangkul), Seow Kenghee, the grandfather of Seow Hoodseng (Sribunruang) and Cheong Sweeleong (Cheongvisut) of the Cheong clan in Malacca.[52] Chinese of the Straits Settlements, being well educated in English, often worked as compradors in Siam.

In the Canton system (1700–1845), provision purveyors or compradors were officially licensed by the Chinese authority to sell provisions to visiting foreign ships. They wore a wooden license around their waist so as to be easily seen from a distance.[53] The word "comprador" is a Portuguese word meaning "buyer." The English and Americans called both the person who supplied provisions to the ships in Whampoa and their chief clerks in the Canton factory comprador.[54] In late 19th-century Bangkok, the Chinese chief clerks of Western firms were also called comprador. Western firms and employers often preferred to work with Straits Chinese for their English-language skills.

King Mongkut (Rama IV) with a Buddhist text written on palm leaves.

The life and times of the legendary Singapore Chinese comprador-cum-tycoon, Tan Kimcheng (1829–92), embodied the remarkably influential role of the Straits Chinese as a go-between for Siam and the British Empire, which was represented by Singapore during the reign of King Mongkut and King Chulalongkorn. Siam's counsel in Singapore, Tan Kimcheng, known in Siam as Phraya Anukulsiamkit, was a famous Hokkien lobbyist whose life did not follow the fabled overseas-Chinese success story of "rags to riches."

Tan Kimcheng was born into a wealthy Hokkien merchant family in Singapore. He was the eldest of the three sons of renowned merchant and philanthropist Tan Tockseng (1798–1850), the founder and financier of today's Tan Tock Seng Hospital in Singapore. Tan Tockseng's interest in trade took him to Bangkok and it was there that he chanced to meet Vajirayano Bhikkhu, a monk who several years later saved him from business ruin.

The venerable monk was Prince Mongkut, who was later crowned Rama IV. Tan Tockseng, Esq., a British subject, became an agent (or comprador) for Vajirayano Bhikkhu in Singapore in his purchase of tea, paper and other items, including a printing machine from the United States for publishing Buddhist texts. According to the instructions given to his American friend (a Mr. Eddie), the prince preferred that the printing machine be sent via Singapore instead of the usual missionary route via Chinese ports because he had no agent in China and the Chinese route was notorious for piracy.[55]

Tan Kimcheng had spent his younger days in Bangkok and Vajirayano Bhikkhu

Tan Kimcheng.

knew him quite well. It was in Bangkok that he learned Thai, a language that served him well throughout his career. [56] Later, after Vajirayano Bhikkhu became king, the firm Tan Tockseng, Esq., in Singapore ran into financial difficulties and Tan Kimcheng sought the king's assistance. King Mongkut awarded him a sappanwood concession at Kho Luc to help him out.[57]

Tan Kimcheng inherited his father's successful trading business located at Boat Quay in Singapore. Besides family backing and good luck, Tan also inherited his father's exceptional intelligence and an uncanny ability to deal with the powers that be. When King Mongkut had to procure gunpowder from Singapore, it was to Tan Kimcheng that the king turned. Tan was made the Siamese consul to Singapore and bestowed the official title of Phra Phitetpanit on 21 November 1863 at the age of 34.

In Singapore, Tan Kimcheng was also prominent in Straits Settlements politics. Many observers believed he was a leading member of the Triads in Malaya, for the simple reason that during those days no *capitan* China could effectively run the affairs of the overseas-Chinese community without the backing of the Triads and Chinese secret societies. In 1871, when the British inspector-general of police found that all registered Chinese secret society leaders' names in Singapore were aliases, he had to seek the assistance of Tan Kimcheng and Ho Ahkay (Whampoa) before he succeeded in getting the real headmen on the record.[58]

Tan Kimcheng's prestige and polyglot skills put him in a perfect position to mediate between the local Chinese and the British. As a multicultural businessman, Tan could switch effortlessly between the world of politics and the world of business. Consequently, he played an important role in fostering relations between the local Malay rulers and the colonial government. Tan Kimcheng and W.H. Read,[59] his colleague, helped Raja Muda Abdullah by approaching

A view of Singapore from the roads, with a merchant barque, a merchant brig, junks and other shipping.

Governor Sir Andrew Clarke on his behalf, which resulted in the British supporting Raja Muda Abdullah as the Sultan of Perak. This helped to secure the Treaty of Pangkor that ended the Chinese Triad involvement in the Larut Wars in 1874.[60] British intervention in Perak represented the first step in a series of moves that eventually resulted in direct rule over the Malay States.

In Siam, King Mongkut seemed a bit wary of Read and Tan Kimcheng's concession hunting. The king turned down several schemes submitted by Tan Kimcheng, including a proposal to make Read (an active member of the Freemasons) Siam's political lobbyist in Europe based in London. Read's proposal to build railroads and telegraph lines were also shot down. King Mongkut also declined to take Tan Kimcheng's suggestion to appoint Delphen Henri de Vallande as Siam's consul to Paris.[61]

King Chulalongkorn in Chinese attire.

However, Mongkut agreed to Tan Kimcheng's request for the tin concession in Kraburi and even appointed Tan the governor of Kraburi. The hidden issues on both sides involved the French interest in digging the Kra Canal to link the Andaman Sea and the Gulf of Siam. The Kra Canal,[62] if implemented, would shorten the distance to French Indochina and the Far East considerably and bypass both Singapore and Penang. While the Kra Canal would benefit French Indochina at the expense of Singapore, King Mongkut was afraid that the Kra Canal could turn into a dangerous and explicit line of demarcation between Siamese and British interests over the Malay States.[63]

Unwilling to capitulate to French pressure on Siam to dig the Kra Canal, Mongkut used Tan Kimcheng to deflect French requests. According to Prince Damrong, King Mongkut had appointed Tan Kimcheng as governor of Kraburi to play off the French against the British to protect Siam's interest in the Malay States. Because Tan was a British subject, it seemed that Kraburi was now in the British zone of influence.

After King Mongkut passed away in 1868, his son Prince Chulalongkorn succeeded him as Rama V. King Chulalongkorn became the first Chakri king to travel abroad when he embarked on his steamship tour of Singapore and Batavia on 9 March 1870. The young king was impressed with both Singapore and Tan Kimcheng, with whom he formed a lasting friendship. They corresponded regularly on various issues, including news of the Malay States, until Tan's death in 1892.

Tan Kimcheng soon gave up the Kraburi tin concession after subcontracting to unsuccessful operators. Perhaps the tin deposits had been small, but others had strong opinions on the matter. The Kalahom, Chaophraya Surawongse-Waiyawat (Von Bunnag), observed, "Tan only wants to enrich himself . . . but does not know how to operate or maintain [the mining industry]."[64] However, in 1872, when the price of tin ore skyrocketed in the world market, Tan submitted a proposal to operate the Phuket concession by increasing the bid price of 17,360 baht per annum submitted by Phraya Wichitsongkhram, the governor of Phuket, to 320,000 baht. Somdet Chaophraya Si Suriyawongse (Chuang Bunnag) had to recall the governor to Bangkok for a private talk and asked him to resubmit the bid. Finally, the concession was awarded to the old concessionaire at 336,000 baht and Tan was given a commission of 16,000 baht for raising the bidding price of tin to the world market price. However, the price of tin continued to escalate, so in 1874, upon receiving the news that the governor of Phuket had gone blind, Tan resubmitted another bid of 640,000 baht per annum for the concession. This time, even the Siamese government hesitated, as a high tax concession price could create discontent in the local community. In considering the proposal, the Kalahom voiced the opinion that Tan Kimcheng was a British subject while the governor of Phuket was a Siamese citizen. King Rama V finally awarded the concession to the governor at the total sum of 480,000 baht, explaining that according to tradition the tax was partly for the development and administrative expenses of local communities, which were the responsibility of the governor.

As the rice business boomed after 1869, Tan Kimcheng expanded his trading business into rice milling in Bangkok as well as in Saigon. The Kimcheng Mill had the distinction of being the first to produce No. 1 white rice in Bangkok. Tan's control of rice mills in Siam and Vietnam made him a dominant player in the international rice trade, and in 1888 he established a branch office in Hong Kong. Besides developing his business in rice and tin from Siam, Vietnam and the Straits Settlements, Tan Kimcheng also leveraged himself into the shipping industry, for which he had already prepared by setting up the Tanjong Pagar Dock Company— the forerunner of today's Port of Singapore Authority (currently known as PSA International)—in 1863.

Perhaps Tan Kimcheng's case was unique; nonetheless, several Straits-born Chinese had moved to Bangkok and were active in serving as compradors or go-betweens for the European and American firms and the local Chinese community in Siam, as well as linking Siam to the world market in Singapore and Hong Kong.

The Trader Pattern

The latter half of the 19th century was the high point of Chinese migration to Southeast Asia. Wang Gungwu, a distinguished Chinese scholar, reflected on the changing patterns of Chinese migration over the years by classifying them into several distinct categories, including the *huashang* or the trader pattern; the *huagong* or the coolie pattern; and the *huaqiao* or the sojourner pattern. We shall examine some of these different patterns with regard to Chinese in Siam during the reigns of King Mongkut and King Chulalongkorn.

According to Wang Gungwu, the *huashang* or trader pattern of migration

Koh Chin Sóó, Phraya Phisan-Pholpanich.

> *refers to merchants, artisans and other skilled workers who went abroad, or sent their colleagues, agents or members of their extended families or clans abroad to work for them and set up bases at ports, mines or trading cities. When this proved successful, the business abroad, or the mining business, could expand and require more agents or young family members to join it; or new business and mines were established into a network, also requiring more agents or family members to be sent out to help the new ventures. Over a generation or two, the migrants, mostly male, would settle down and bring up local families. But even as they themselves did not settle down their local families did and, more often than not, remained as recognizably Chinese families to keep the business going. The more successful the business, the more likely their families kept up their Chinese characteristics, if not all their connection with China. But, where there was sufficient inducement or political pressure to do so, some of these families abandoned their Chineseness and became local notables. For the most part, the requirement of their business ensured that not all members of these families could depart too far from the Chinese connections necessary for their continuing success.*

The *huashang* pattern was the dominant pattern from early times in various parts of Southeast Asia. The story of Phraya Phisan-Supaphol (Koh Chun) was a classic case of a successful overseas-Chinese family who gradually abandoned their "Chineseness" after settling in Siam for several generations. Phisan-Supaphol had become, to all intents and purposes, a Siamese notable facing the dilemma of losing his "Chinese connections."

Ten years ago when we, the authors, started to collect information on the Chinese in Siam, we found to our surprise that neither the Bisalputras' legend nor the spirit tablet of the Koh Gao family kept at the local temple in Klongsan mentioned the hometown of Phraya Phisan-Supaphol, or Koh Chun. All traces of his Chinese genealogy had been lost. Many of his great-grandsons could not speak, read or write Chinese. Koh Chun's connections in Siam seemed by far more exalted compared to the connections he had had with his Chinese homeland.

From Siamese historical records we learned that Koh Chun was appointed

Koh Mahwah & Co. Ltd. was established by Koh Mahwah under his head office, Yuan Fat Hong, in Hong Kong.

a tax farmer for salt in Petchaburi Province during 1857–58, for sappanwood and fish during 1859–60, and for the 3 percent export taxes during 1866–68.[65] The Petchaburi tax farm connection seemed to support K.S.R. Kularb's account, which asserts that the Chinese forebears of Koh Chun's mother came from the same town in Petchaburi Province as King Taksin's mother.

In 1855, the year of Bowring's arrival in Siam, Koh Chun won the bid for opium tax farming for the period 1855 to 1856. Subsequently, he lost it and regained it in 1860 with the annual contracted revenue of 404,400 baht.[66] Koh Chun was indeed an influential man of his day. When the tax farmer responsible for the collection of the market tax in both Bangkok and Nonthaburi failed to deliver, the government turned to Koh Chun for advice. As the opium monopolist, Koh Chun had eyes and ears in all local markets where the Chinese had been actively involved. It was through the good offices of Koh Chun that King Mongkut appointed Kian as the *kamnun talad* responsible for market-tax collection in Bangkok and Nonthaburi in 1858.[67]

The above records seemed to confirm the reputation of Koh Chun as a "Chinese of extraordinary powers, standing at the head of all his countrymen here as well as the Siamese, in commercial affairs." Thus many promising young Chinese emigrants had passed through his hands as apprentices. Two of them, Koh Mahwah (Gao Chuxiang) and Tan Suang-E (Chen Xuanyi), were hardworking and gifted traders who had gone on to establish their own rice trading companies at the Nan Bei Hang area in Hong Kong in the 1850s.

Although the Koh family had become an influential Siamese family integrated into the Siamese social hierarchy through serving the government, their very Siameseness began to pose a problem. In fact, the stronger their Siamese connections were, the weaker their Chinese connections became. By departing too far from their Chinese connections, the Koh merchant house had become less competitive.

To renew the Chinese connections necessary for his firm's continuing success, Koh Chun turned his attention to his promising apprentice Koh Mahwah, a Chenghai man from the same Koh clan, though he was not a blood relation. On the pretext that he had no competent successor to manage the Hong Kong operation, Koh Chun sold his Hong Kong business to Koh Mahwah,[68] his trusted manager, in the early 1850s, and thus forged a long-term bond with one of the most capable rice merchants on the China front. Koh Chun's shrewd judgment of character was to prove useful for the survival of his family firm after he passed away.

In 1862, the news of Koh Chun's sudden demise caused the authorities great concern, as the crown had been the major financier of Koh Chun's mercantile empire. Somdet Chaophraya Si Suriyawongse ordered the immediate arrest of Koh Chun's eldest son, the 22-year-old Koh Chin Sóó (Sóó Bisalputra, Gao Jinshi, 1839–91) to make sure that the family did not abscond. The Phraklang (Thuam Bunnag) negotiated with his brother, Si Suriyawongse, on Chin Sóó's behalf, and a loan restructuring plan with a 10-year payback term was agreed upon.[69] Upon his release, Chin Sóó decided to make partial early repayment by transferring one of his steamships, the *Alligator*,[70] to the Siamese government. It was then renamed *Sri Ayutthayadet*.[71]

After the financial restructuring, Koh Chin Sóó managed to keep both his stately mansion opposite Rajawongse Pier and Huay Chung Long, the steamship terminal, with its handsome rental income intact. His father's contacts both at home and abroad had also proven useful. It enabled him to continue the lucrative rice-trading business, meet the loan obligation and help return him to a position of respectability in the Siamese capital. Koh Chin Sóó was appointed Luang Phisan-Polpanich in 1863, then promoted to a *phra* in 1880, and finally a *phraya* of the same name in 1887.

In the meantime, Koh Mahwah (Gao Chuxiang)[72] changed the name of the Hong Kong company to Yuan Fat Hong and made it one of the major Chinese import-export trading companies in Hong Kong. After the 1870s, he expanded Yuan Fat Hong's operations from trading and shipping to rice milling, real estate and finance, with associate companies in Bangkok, Singapore, Malaysia and

Funeral of Koh Chun's grandson, with his three great-grandsons in Chinese attire receiving guests.

Japan.[73] In his early days in Bangkok, Koh Mahwah married an able Siamese wife named Piam, who was a *lukchin* from a well-to-do family. She had a prosperous business of her own dealing in gold, a commodity closely linked to the paddy trade.[74] The relationship between gold and rice is reflected in the old saying, "When the paddy (price) is expensive, gold is cheap; when paddy is cheap, gold is expensive."

The story of Tan Suang-E (Chen Xuanyi), who worked aboard one of Koh Chun's ships in the 1840s, is another classic success story of "rags to riches." Suang-E came from the Tan (Chen) lineage of Qianxi Village in the Chaozhou area. He was a fisherman who earned himself the nickname "water ghost buddha" for his skill in diving. Soon, Suang-E and his relatives saved enough to buy a junk to carry cargo between Hong Kong, Shantou, Shanghai and other Chinese coastal ports.

In 1851 he and his fellow clansmen together rented an office in Bonham Strand West in Hong Kong and started their own import-export business called Kin Tye Lung.[75] It was a rice import-export company as well as a remittance and shipping agent. The company flourished partly due to the demand for local Chinese products and remittance services for the Chinese laborers in Southeast Asia, and partly due to the demand for rice in South China. In 1865 Suang-E's eldest son, Tan Tsuhuang (Chen Cihong), arrived in Bangkok and rented an office at Huay Chung Long from Phisan-Pholpanich (Koh Chin Sóó) to incorporate an associate company called Wanglee. Fourteen years later, nine members of the Tan lineage in Quanxi Village founded yet another associate company called Tan Seng Lee (later renamed Tan Guan Lee) in Singapore, managed by Tsuhuang's cousin Chen Cizong.

The Tan lineage of Qianxi demonstrated that when business abroad was successful, the clan could expand by enlisting young family members to establish and incorporate new business areas into the network. In Bangkok, Tan Tsuhuang married a niece of a prominent Teochew merchant named Kim Lohchae[76] who lived up the river not far from Huay Chung Long. The couple bought the land next to Huay Chung Long and built the Wanglee House, a stately mansion that has become a landmark of Klongsan.

Tan Tsuhuang Wanglee.

Koh Chun's rival, Phra Phasisombat (Lau Poh Yim, or Chaosua Yim),[77] who outbid him for the opium monopoly in 1857, was a man with formidable connections. Yim's father, a Hokkien tea merchant, was the favorite supplier of tea to King Mongkut. Yim inherited a bird's nest tax farm from his father in 1854 and gained his entry into the predominantly Teochew sugar industry when he married Prang, daughter of Phraya Sombatwanich (Bunsri Sombatsiri), an influential Teochew sugar tycoon.

In the 1860s Yim expanded on his father-in-law's business networks in Nakhon Chaisi by setting up one of the first modernized sugar refineries in Siam.[78] In 1857, Yim and his associates outbid Koh Chun for the opium monopoly in Bangkok by doubling the price to 320,000 baht per annum. Koh Chun then won it back during 1860–62, just before he died, by offering a sum of 404,400 baht per year.[79] The year after, Yim again won the bid and was allowed to operate the opium monopoly for 573,200 baht per annum until the end of the reign of King Mongkut.

According to historian Suehiro Akira, "Yim planned opening a new canal in order to directly carry sugar from Nakhon Chaisi to the port at Bangkok. The construction of this canal later known as the 'Klong Phasicharcon' began in 1866 and was completed in 1872 … Since Yim by himself could not cover this cost, he asked the king [King Mongkut] to appropriate royal funds provided by the opium taxes that he collected on behalf of the king. Finally his proposal was approved, and a great amount of royal money was invested into a canal which had originally been designed to serve Yim's private business interest."[80]

Top: Prince Kitiyakara.

Bottom: Phraya Boriboon-Kosakorn (Li Huad).

Yim's son, Luang Sathorn-Rachayut (Yom), was the developer of Klong Sathorn, the famous estate situated along a beautiful canal with mahogany-tree-lined roads. The name of the newly dug canal called Klong Poh Yom was later changed to Klong Sathorn in honor of the developer. Yom was also one of the four promoters of Siamese Canal Land and Irrigation Co., Ltd., which was established in 1888 to develop irrigated paddy fields covering over 128,000 hectares.[81] In the meantime, Yim's influence was strengthened when his daughters Uam (Chao Chom Manda Uam) and Aim entered the inner court. Chao Chom Manda Uam's son, Prince Kitiyakara, the patriarch of the royal house of Kitiyakara, was later appointed finance minister.[82] Yim had another daughter married to Phra Boriboon-Kosakorn (Li Huad), son of Phraya Choduk (Pook), the governor of the Chinese in Siam appointed by Si Suriyawongse. In 1868, Li Huad outbid his father-in-law, Yim, and became the new opium tax farmer for Bangkok.

Although Yim had not been appointed the Choduk-Rachasretthi, the official head of the Chinese community in Siam, he was closely linked with three subsequent *choduk*. First, Phraya Choduk (Li Huad) was Yim's son-in-law; second, Phraya Choduk (Lau Chongmin)'s father was kin from the same clan village and worked for Yim's *kongsi* when he first arrived in Siam, and lastly, Phraya Choduk (Phong) was Yim's grandson.

The careers of these Chinese groups followed the *huashang* pattern of migration, which continued to flourish in the latter half of the 19th century due to the expansion of the Siamese economy, especially in the rice industry. Up to the early 19th century, China was the chief market for Thai rice. The preferred rice for this market was rough or cargo rice because of its long storage life. Upon arrival in China the Chinese treated it in their pounding mills.[83] In the latter half of the century, however, the development of colonial industries in Southeast Asia using immigrant Indian and Chinese coolies changed the market demand for rice. Siam became an important supplier of the staple for the "rice-eating wage laborer" of

Bangkok during the reign of King Chulalongkorn.

Southeast Asia, as well as its traditional South China market. Demand for white rice escalated resulting in a boom in rice milling as well as rice exporting. Koh Chin Sóó responded well to the growing demand by building three modern mills, known as the Koh Hong Lee Rice Mills, using Scotch-making machinery, while his younger brother, Koh Kim, owned another mill in Samsen called Guan Tit Lee. Both Koh Mahwah and Tan Tsuhuang also set up their own modern rice mills, as well as their own marketing firms in Singapore. [84]

During this time the three major commodities that constituted more than 85 percent of Siam's export was rice, tin from the south and teakwood from the north. The Chinese *huashang* traders were actively involved in the first two industries but not the last. The export of teak from Siam was mostly confined to Europe, Bombay and Hong Kong. Consequently, the teak trade was said to have been a "British trade, carried on by British capital and British management."[85]

The Coolies

Wang Gungwu defined the *huagong* or the Chinese coolie pattern as "the immigration of large numbers of coolie labor, normally men of peasant origin, landless laborers and the urban poor. This was not significant before 1850 . . . On the whole this pattern of migration may be described as transitional. It was transitional in that a large proportion of the contract laborers returned to China after their contract came to an end. But it was also transitional in that it was put to an end very quickly in the Americas by the end of the 19th century, and not long afterwards in Southeast Asia by the 1920s."[86]

Among the most common push factors cited ad nauseam to explain the outpouring of these coolies from Southern China during the late 19th century to the early 20th century were natural disasters, wars and poverty. The aims and motivations of the *huagong* emigrants differed from the *huashang* in that their intention was not to establish a network of Chinese colonies abroad; their roots were in China, and they left wives and families behind. Their aim was to acquire money with which they could return and raise the status of their families.[87]

In Siam, the preference of indigenous Siamese for rice farming and village life led to a scarcity of labor for commercial cultivation, industry, mining, construction and urban services, resulting in relatively high wages for Chinese labor. Other local habits also gave rise to lucrative occupations; for example, Siamese declined to breed and slaughter animals because of their Theravada Buddhist beliefs. Traditionally, slaughterhouses were run by Muslims with the exception of pig farming. This lucrative sector was left to the Chinese.

The development of nascent capitalism in Siam after 1870 generated a huge demand for Chinese labor. The expansion of urban Bangkok required increasing numbers of workers in the construction and building trades. Bangkok's busy port absorbed more and more dockworkers and lighter crews. Mushrooming rice mills and sawmills needed both skilled and unskilled labor in ever-greater numbers. Between 1890 and 1910 Bangkok changed from a city of canals to one based on roads. New roads were constructed in the capital as well as thousands of shop-houses, Western-style residences and government buildings. Hundreds of Chinese construction firms sprouted up to do the job, each with dozens of apprentice-laborers. The construction business was dominated by Cantonese and Hakka.

In addition to roads, Siam began to develop a railway system. In the construction of the main lines of the Siamese railway system, which began in 1892, most coolies employed were newly immigrated Teochews and Hakkas, while most of the skilled laborers were Cantonese. When construction began in jungle terrain, the mortality from malaria and other fevers rose to frightening proportions, leading to an acute labor shortage. It became, therefore, "a matter of difficulty to the contractor to engage the necessary coolies, and of even greater difficulty, and one requiring infinite tact

Hon Wong, a Hakka shrine in Talad Noi, was built in part by a large donation from Liu Kian, an influential Hakka.

The perilous life of the common man depicted in a mural from the Early Bangkok period at Wat Bhawanapirataram.

on the part of the sectional engineers . . . to persuade them to remain." In fact, thousands of Chinese lost their lives prior to 1910 on railway construction in Siam. It was reported that 300 Chinese laborers were buried in the Phrayafai forest after falling victim to jungle fever while constructing the stretch from Saraburi to Khorat. Consequently, the turnover rate was high due to desertions in the face of what seemed to be imminent death. Chinese coolies who worked on the railways, earthworks, bridges and rails during the first 20 years of railway construction must have numbered in the tens of thousands.[88] Both King Mongkut and King Chulalongkorn admitted that their preference for using Chinese wage labor in public works instead of Siamese *phrai* was an act of mercy to their native Siamese subjects.[89]

The number of Chinese immigrants in Siam failed to keep up with the demand, and laborers were in short supply from 1880 up to 1903. Consequently, Chinese labor commanded premium prices and coolie wages had to be increased. According to Skinner, "[in the 1880s] it was recorded that the Chinese laborer in Siam could earn wages double those prevailing in south China ports and live both better and cheaper than in his own country."[90] By profession, the Teochews constituted a large portion of dockworkers and labor on canal and railway construction, as well as peddlers and vegetable farmers. The Hokkiens mostly worked as tin miners in southern Siam. Hakkas worked as petty tradesmen, silversmiths, leather workers, tailors, hawkers and barbers. Hailam were fishermen, market gardeners, miners, peddlers, waiters and cooks, while Cantonese laborers were predominant in the construction industry.

Skinner's estimate of arrivals and departures of ethnic Chinese in Siam between 1882 and 1917 seem to confirm the growth of the *huagong* type of migration. The rate of departure back to China increased from 56 percent of arrivals during the 1880s to 82 percent during the first five years of King Vajiravudh's reign (King Rama VI, r. 1910–25). However, the arrival of Chinese in Siam had also substantially increased over the same period. The average annual arrival of 12,550 in the 1880s increased to 26,860 in the 1890s, and then doubled to 52,520 in the 1900s before gradually dropping down to 48,630 between 1910 and 1916.[91]

The Chinese Secret Societies

The explosion of Chinese immigration to Siam after the mid-19th century created tensions within Siamese society. The administrative system of the kingdom was ill prepared to cope with the emergence of an unprecedentedly large community of alien Chinese. Part of the problem was that the Chinese community fell outside the traditional Siamese social system.

Since the time of the Ayudhya Kingdom, the Chinese in Siam had been free men exempt from corvée, unlike native Siamese who were subject to corvée obligations to the king or the lord who provided them with protection. Instead of providing corvée labor, the Chinese paid a triennial poll tax of 2 baht per person. The poor who could not afford to pay the tax were rounded up and sent to do public works for one month. The Chinese poll tax was raised to 4 baht by Rama III (r. 1824–51) and was fixed at this rate until 1909.[92]

Because of the special status of Chinese immigrants, the Siamese have always provided for the Chinese community to be run by their own leaders. The time-honored precedent since the Ayudhya period was to allow Chinese leaders to govern the Chinese community, and they in turn reported to the Choduk-Rachasretthi of the Phraklang ministry.

Being exempt from the corvée system, the Chinese were free to travel and settle anywhere in the kingdom without restriction. However, it also meant that Chinese immigrants had no patron or government official to protect them in times of need. The disadvantage of not having a master with political clout meant that the Chinese had to fall back on their own resourcefulness to create the missing social and political safety net that could protect them in times of crisis.

Instinctively the Chinese turned to their traditional secret societies, which had protected them from rapacious government officials and predatory bandits in their homeland. Chinese immigrants transplanted their native secret societies that had served them in China to their new adopted land in Siam. According to Leon Comber, "Secret Societies are mainly significant because they are associated with frontier conditions or with shortcomings in the social and political structure of government." The overseas-Chinese secret societies with chapters in Siam included Ghee Hin (known in Siam as Ghee Heng in the Teochew dialect), Ghee Hok, Toh Peh Gong (Thai documents call it Pun Tao Gong), Hai San and numerous smaller ones.

In the early 19th century, Thai sources called secret societies *tua hia*, meaning "big brother" in the Teochew dialect. Later, during the reign of King Rama V (r. 1868–1910), the official word used was *angyi* (Hóng Zi) or the "Hóng League," which in fact was one of the more militant groups among the secret societies. The "Hóng League" was also the term used in Malaya and took its name from the slogan "Overthrow the Qing and restore the Ming," with "Hóng" representing the name of the first Ming emperor, Hóngwu.

Meanwhile, as the Chinese population in Siam exploded, the government found that the vulnerability of the new Chinese immigrants played into the hands of the Western powers, who were carving up colonial domains on Siam's western, southern and eastern frontiers. Christian missionaries encroaching into the Mae Klong, Tha Chin and Bang Pakong river basins also preyed on the vulnerabilities of the Chinese to gain converts. Missionaries not only offered charity, donations and education to poor Chinese but also sided with Chinese Christians in social conflicts. The priests often lodged complaints to the European consuls in Bangkok on behalf of their Chinese Christian parishioners.

During this period, in addition to the divided loyalties of Christians, Chinese traders also saw that becoming colonial subjects awarded them legal privilege under the protection of European powers. Consequently, many Chinese merchants bribed Western consuls to list them as colonial subjects. The Siamese government was understandably concerned about European consuls extending their influence to give protection to Chinese working in Siam.

This legal loophole opened up by unequal treaties had been abused by many who wanted to flout and evade Siamese regulations with impunity. Even before the end of King Mongkut's reign, the American and Portuguese consulates in particular made an open business of selling certificates to all comers. American certificates issued in 1867 stated, "Know ye that I ... have granted the protection of this Consulate to [so and so], a subject of the Chinese empire ... [who has] made known to the undersigned that he had no Consul resident of his own nation to assist him in case of need." These certificates led to the hasty recall of J.M. Hood, the American consul who had issued these documents. However, the practice of issuing certificates to Chinese who were not bona fide European subjects was continued by the Portuguese, the French, and, to a lesser extent, the British and the Dutch off and on for the rest of the century.[93]

The Siamese authorities grew alarmed at the rising number of both Chinese

Christian converts and Chinese subjects of European states, leading to the emergence of an alien privileged class in the midst of Siamese society. The large Chinese community could become an internal fifth column in the event of a conflict with the Western powers, as had occurred in Indonesia and the Philippines. Under Si Suriyawongse, the regent ruling on behalf of King Chulalongkorn, the government opted for the traditional way of dealing with the Chinese. After all, in Siam, a tried and tested precedent of pacifying the Chinese through their local leaders already existed. More explicitly, Si Suriyawongse reasoned that an effective way to counter the Western influence of the Christian community and the growing class of Chinese colonial subjects from undermining Siamese sovereignty was to promote and empower Chinese self-governing bodies, including Chinese secret societies, their associated *kongsi* and other benefit societies. Since the Triads were the natural enemies of Christians, missionaries and Westerners in general, Si Suriyawongse sought to use the Triads as a counterpoise to the inroads of Western influence.

Si Suriyawongse perceived that hostility between the Chinese Catholics and the Triads could be traced back to their animosity back home in China. The Triads—which were originally a quasi-religious fraternity that worshipped Guan Yu, the Taoist god of war—hated the missionaries with a vengeance. Even after their migration to Southeast Asia, the Chinese secret societies remained implacable enemies of Christianity and did all in their power to prevent their associates from being converted.

Si Suriyawongse wielded immense power. King Chulalongkorn, who was a minor when he ascended the throne in 1868, still needed time to mature, and Si Suriyawongse ruled in the interim as regent. Throughout the regent years, 1868–71, he was the de facto ruler of the kingdom, and under his watch priority was given to redressing Chinese grievances.

One of the major grievances of the Chinese community was in the local juristic system, which was foreign to them. For example, the law of inheritance in Siam allowed daughters an equal right to the estate as their male siblings. In 1868, Si Suriyawongse established the Chinese tribunal court headed by Phraya Choduk-Rachasretthi (Jong or Tienjong). This court of law aimed to make the Chinese feel at home by using Chinese customs and legal practices in solving conflicts between two Chinese parties.[94]

In addition to encouraging the use of Chinese customs and practices for resolving conflicts within the Chinese community, the regent adopted a hospitable policy towards Chinese fraternity organizations for self-protection. Many of these self-help and benefit associations were ostensible fronts for Chinese secret societies. The regent himself knew many Chinese Triad leaders well. Much gossip in town accused him of nurturing *angyi*, which was not far from the truth. During

The *angyi* chart, a coded document used by Siamese secret societies.

the regent's rule, Chinese secret society leaders in the provinces were given official recognition. Among them were Luang Prachimnakorn (Jia Bek-E), who was the master of Pun Tao Gong, a secret society in Krabi; Luang Aramsakornket (Tan Tam),[95] who was the Pun Tao Gong–appointed *palad chin* of Phuket in 1870; Luang Amnartsingkhorn (Oh Keechuan), the master of Ghee Hin, who was also appointed *palad chin* of Phuket; and Luang Kitchachinsiam, who was the Triad leader in control of Ratchaburi Province. [96]

Besides coopting Triad leaders to help the Siamese authorities resolve conflicts, keep the peace, and maintain order within the Chinese community, the regent also continued the precedent established by Rama III in the early 19th century of appointing Chinese sheriffs or *nai amphur chin*[97] and *palad chin*[98] to every district and town with Chinese settlements. These appointees oversaw Chinese affairs, including settlement of conflicts among Chinese, preventing illicit opium trading, registering Chinese residents, and collecting the Chinese poll tax. As the Chinese largely governed themselves, many of the *nai amphur chin* and *palad chin* appointed by the government were local leaders from the Chinese community, with appointed names such as Khun Kamchad-Chinpan, which literally translates as the "Terminator of Chinese Thugs."

Although this system enjoyed its heyday during the period of 1851–71 when Si Suriyawongse wielded great power at court, it continued to survive until 1889 when King Chulalongkorn took back almost all of the Bunnag family's power and influence. A letter dating back to 1889 not only confirms that the regent's Chinese policy was still in place but also sheds an interesting light on how the system was working in the outlying province of Trad. The letter, dated 20 November

1889, appoints Tae Tienjin, grandson of Tae Poh, a Hokkien patriarch of the Sreshthaputra clan, to the position of Phra Pranee-Chinpracha, the *palad chin* of Trad, one of the eastern provinces along the coast of Siam near Batambang. The letter informs us that apart from being prominent in the Bangkok community, Tae Tienjin was also the son-in-law of the late *palad chin* of Trad. It instructs Pranee-Chinpracha to report to the governor of Trad and the town council, and tells him to assume the responsibility of solving conflicts among Chinese. However, the letter states that conflicts between Siamese and Chinese must be considered in consultation with the governor. It enlists the responsibilities of the *palad chin* in the enforcement of the law, monitoring and reporting on various Chinese activities, including prevention of violence and *tua hia* gangster rackets that may be harmful to the community. In doing so, he may employ Chinese assistants. The *palad chin*, dressed in Chinese robes, must represent the Chinese community in all official functions including the ceremony to "pledge loyalty" to the king of Siam.

The regent's policy of thrusting the responsibility of peacekeeping among the Chinese on the leading members of the local Chinese community, which sometimes included Triad leaders, was somewhat successful. For example, Triad disturbances caused by petty theft in Ratchaburi were brought to a peaceful end when instructions were given to the Triad leader, Luang Kitchachinsiam, to deliver the culprits and four guilty members to the authorities.[99] Appointments of prominent *lukchin* in the Chinese community to the position of *palad chin* also ensured proper communication between the authorities and the Chinese community. The Siamese government seemed to understand their local Chinese in a more intimate way than the British in the Straits Settlements, where there were no European government officials in Malaya who understood the Chinese or their language and customs until 1871.[100]

As a result of the Siamese government's Chinese policy, the second half of the 19th century saw a reduction in the number of violent incidents in the Mae Klong, Tha Chin and Bang Pakong river valleys, although the collapse of the Siamese sugar industry in 1870 and the migration of many Chinese away from the area were also contributing factors. To the extent that the regent's policy was also intended to promote anti-Christian sentiment within the Chinese community, the policy proved successful. After Si Suriyawongse's death, in Ratchaburi Province alone there were 283 cases of complaints launched against Christian Chinese by Siamese, Chinese, Laos and Khmers. [101]

However, the strategy of using the Triads as a counterpoise to Western influence in Siam was a controversial

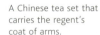

A Chinese tea set that carries the regent's coat of arms.

approach laced with moral ambiguities. At worst, it was a Machiavellian policy to out-devil the devil. Although the Triads in China have traditionally been anti-Western, the *modus operandi* of the organization is shrouded in secrecy, symbolism, blood ritual and black sorcery. Even though the Triads may have shared the Siamese's antipathy towards Christian proselytizing and Western aggrandizement, the former tended to operate in the shadows. Consequently, in the final analysis, the Triads were accountable to no other authority but themselves. The fact that some of the most eminent leaders of the Chinese community who were acquaintances of the regent had Triad affiliations did not detract from the organization's sheltering of unsavory characters and bestial elements.

In fact, the propensity for Chinese fraternity self-protection organizations to become fronts for criminal rings and rackets in Siam concerned Rama III, who had sought to establish some form of official control and supervision over their activities. The policy of abetting the Triad's anti-Western and anti-Christian agenda was fraught with the risk of backfiring onto the government. For the regent, it was a calculated risk to check the Western powers' growing influence in Siam without having to be in open conflict with the latter. To his credit, the Chinese were well governed under his watch throughout 1851–73. The policy ran into trouble after the second coronation of King Chulalongkorn in 1873, when power within the kingdom became fragmented between the king and the ex-regent.

After his second coronation, anxious to assert his formal powers, King Chulalongkorn began to unilaterally introduce institutional changes, including the creation of a state council in May 1874. In addition to this, the young king also created another body called the privy council in August 1874, comprising carefully selected members who were to be personal advisors to the king. These two bodies were effectively used by the king as a vehicle to push through his reform initiatives. Although many reforms were commendable in principle, they were too hastily implemented and alienated the ex-regent as well as many segments of the government. Among some of the king's reforms were measures that affected the kingdom's tin mining operations in the south.

There had been a growing feeling among the king's close advisors that the ex-regent and his followers had mismanaged the collection of royal revenues. In 1874, the head of the Krom Na, Phraya Ahanborirak, a nephew of the ex-regent, was charged with misappropriation following his refusal to disclose details regarding the land collection tax. Since the tin mining areas in the south including Nakhon Si Thammarat, Ranong and Phuket fell under the jurisdiction of the Krom Kalahom, controlled by Von Bunnag, Si Suriyawongse's son, a suspicion arose that the assessment and collection of tin revenue from the south was grossly undervalued.

The main instigator was a prominent Straits Chinese merchant with Triad secret society affiliations, Tan Kimcheng, who had rendered good offices to the late King

Mongkut. Tan, who had won the confidence of the inexperienced young king was more than eager to avail his knowledge of the price movements of the world tin market to assist his royal patron. As previously discussed, with the approval from the new king, Tan Kimcheng repeatedly submitted bids to wrest the Phuket concession from the current concessionaire Phraya Vichitsongkram, the Governor of Phuket, by offering to pay exceedingly more than the old contracted price. The offers came in the wake of the bull market in commodities, especially tin, which attracted many investors, particularly the Chinese, into the tin mining industry on the western peninsular of Siam. The embattled Bunnag faction in the government countered by arguing that a high tin-concession price would drive the Chinese operators out of business and disrupt the production of a militarily strategic commodity because tin ore was used as materials for bullets in the kingdom. In addition, a high price would force mine operators to squeeze labor costs leading to dangerous discontent which could erupt in riots as had happened in the neighboring Malay States. Consequently, a chagrined King Chulalongkorn was prevailed upon on more than one occasion to reject the exorbitantly high bid price offered by Tan Kimcheng. Nevertheless the concession prices were adjusted substantially upward.

As it turned out the self-serving arguments of the Bunnag faction proved to be prophetic. In 1871 the populations of Ranong, Takuapah, Phangnga and Phuket were more Chinese than Siamese.[102] The fluctuation in the price of tin had caused severe competition and conflict in the mining districts which in turn strengthened the power of the Secret Societies. The southern Triad kongsi in the mining areas took on a different form from the rest of the country. First, there were only two

The town of Phuket.

main *kongsi*, namely the Ghee Hin and the Pun Tao Gong. Second, each *kongsi* included members from several dialect groups. For example, the Ghee Hin in Nakorn Si Thammarat had members from all five dialect groups while the Ghee Hin in Takuapah had Hainanese, Hokkien and Cantonnese members.[103]

Each *kongsi* worked with their own affiliates in Penang to handle their output of tin, and conflicts between the two *kongsi* were caused by competition for resources and marketing. In the great Penang riots of 1867, which lasted more than 10 days, both the Ghee Hin and the Pun Tao Gong sent reinforcements from their branches in Phuket.[104]

Competitive bidding for tin concessions in the South wreaked havoc in the tin mining industry when the price of tin in world market dropped in 1876. Many mines closed down; those still in operation suffered severe losses. In Ranong, one owner of the Pun Tao Gong mine suffered a heavy loss and could only afford to pay his workers half wages. The angry miners killed him and 300 miners went on rampage. The jobless coolies and other Pun Tao Gong members joined in. A day later about 600 Triad members robbed and burned down the town. Phraya Ratanasretthi (Kaw Simgong Na Ranong), the governor, had to request military back up from Chumphon and Langsuan. The Siamese troops captured 105 Triads while some 300 Pun Tao Gong managed to escape and join their colleagues in the Phuket riots, which were also taking place. The Ghee Hins managed to remain uninvolved in the chaos at Ranong.[105]

In Phuket, operators of tin mines suffered from Phraya Vichitsongkram (Tad Ratanadilok)'s panic cut-backs on the usual government loans to tin mines for fear of losing the principal. Lack of working capital coupled with a crash in the tin price put several Pun Tao Gong mines out of business. Just as Chinese discontent with unemployment and the high cost of living reached a boiling point, Vichitsongkram announced that he would increase Phuket's Chinese poll tax from 40 cents to 2 dollars and 60 cents. The Pun Tao Gong were up in arms accusing the governor of corruption, unjust rule and abuse of power. On 4 November 1876, 2000 Pun Tao Gong men raided and burned down more than 100 houses in Phuket, as well as, other small towns in the vicinity. Chamun Sameochairaj (Chun Bunnag), the representative sent by the king to oversee the governor, called in the leaders of the Pun Tao Gong and promised to hear their grievances and

Chinese mining in Phuket.

give them fair trials. He also sent for Siamese troops from six nearby towns to march into Phuket. The riots continued for several days, until the arrival of the Siamese troops from nearby towns after which the ring-leaders fled. The remaining rioters were rounded up and incarcerated by the newly arrived troops. However, after the incident Chamun Sameochairaj kept his promise and pardons were granted after the leaders had signed parole agreements with the authorities.[106]

Although the locus of Triad activities tended to be in the tin-mining areas in southern Siam, there were other conflicts between competing groups of Chinese abetted by secret societies in other provinces, including Chantabun. The pattern of Triad disturbances in Chantabun revealed that the former regent's attempt to harness the strong anti-Western sentiments among the Triads sometimes backfired.

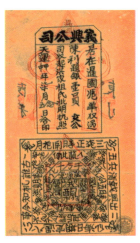

A receipt for a membership fee paid to the *angyi*.

Chantabun was a major town with a large Chinese settlement and a history of hostility between the Teochews and Hokkiens since the early 19th century. In 1895, the leader of the local branch of the Hokkien's Ghee Hok *kongsi* was Chin Amphon, son of Phra Phrasitponraks. Although Chin Amphon was a Siamese citizen, all three of his subordinate gang leaders were French subjects. On the other hand, the local branch of the Ghee Heng *kongsi,* which consisted mainly of Teochews, was headed by Choi, the widow of the late Chin Chaw, and her son Akon Nguanseng. They shared their power with another gang leader who was a Dutch subject. Complications arose when the French navy moved in to occupy Chantabun in 1893. During the French occupation (1893–1904), many Christian Chinese as well as members of the Chinese secret societies in Chantabun applied for and were accepted as French subjects despite the governor's objections that they were emigrants from China and some were local-born *lukchin*.

During the French occupation, the Siamese governor's power was undermined and the racketeers were allowed to extort merchants and residents alike. The rivalry of the two *kongsi* erupted into a street fight on 1 March 1895. After the riot, both *kongsi* built up their martial strength, hiring trained fighters and stockpiling weapons to prepare for a Triad war. Phraya Vidchayathibodi (Vard Bunnag), the governor, was faced with a dilemma because he did not have enough manpower to suppress the Triads. He had to ask the French for permission to move in Siamese troops from nearby towns. To the surprise of the Siamese government, permission from the French authority was speedily granted. A week later, seven Siamese brigades arrived to make arrests and confiscate weapons in the various strongholds of both the Ghee Heng and Ghee Hok. The captured leaders were sent to Bangkok for trial and punishment.[107]

The usual punishments for the ringleaders of the Triad incidents in the south consisted of executions of one or two culprits, canings of 30–60 strokes and jail terms. However, ordinary followers were mostly released on parole so as not to disrupt the labor supply of the mining industry. Mass executions of Triad members only occurred when they killed Siamese governors, as in the Chacheongsao sugar riots in 1848 when 3,000 Chinese were massacred (see Chapter 3). During the Krabi incident in 1878, when the Triads murdered Phra Issarathichai, the governor of Krabi, all 35 members of the Pun Tao Gong involved in attacking his residence were executed. [108]

Over time, many Chinese secret societies degenerated due to poor management, corruption, illegal racketeering and abuse of power among their leaders. The number of new members started to decline as the benefits of joining a *kongsi* became unclear while the risk of being arrested due to illegal activities of fellow members tended to increase. In the meantime, the Siamese government was quite efficient in proving to resident Chinese that it could rule justly. In comparison to their hometowns in China, Bangkok and the major Siamese towns were relatively peaceful; hence there was less need to join secret societies. Over the years, the two major *kongsi*, the Ghee Heng and the Pun Tao Gong, disintegrated into smaller groups. In Bangkok, according to Phra Artikorn-Prakas's report, [109] in 1906 there were at least 30 Chinese secret societies including 13 Teochew, 8 Cantonese, 7 Hailam and 2 Hakka. [110]

Major incidents that finally convinced King Rama V to outlaw all Chinese secret societies occurred in the capital. First, repeated street fights at Talad Plu between the Ghee Hok and Ghee Heng Triads in 1882 reignited in 1895 involving about 200 gangsters. Second, in 1889, Triad wars between the Teochews in the middle of Charoen Krung, the main commercial street, involved over a thousand Chinese taking to the streets to fight for two days. The clash started when two brothers walking to the market to send 12 dollars of their salary home to China were attacked by a rival gang. The elder brother was wounded and thrown into the river where he drowned. This war between the Ghee Heng and the Siew Li Gue resulted in over a hundred casualties and 20 killed. [111] As there were too few police to solve the conflict, both the army and the navy were sent in to make arrests and end the riot. The Secret Society Act took years to amalgamate and was finally decreed on 1 October 1897.

Chinese and the Siamese Government Revenues

Despite the havoc wreaked by the Triads, the Chinese continued to enjoy a remarkable economic ascendency during the early Bangkok period. Through the part they played in expanding the Royal Trading Monopoly under the early Chakri kings, the Chinese had achieved an almost unassailable privileged position in Siam. It was this privileged position that gave the Chinese their greatest leverage and ensured their economic predominance. The rising fortunes of the Chinese had been inextricably tied up with the successful establishment of the Royal Trading Monopoly. However, in the second half of the 19th century, the dominance of the royal monopoly as well as the Chinese-controlled, lucrative junk trade with China was challenged by the rise of Western naval hegemony and the advent of the steamship. Facing Western aggrandizement, Rama III responded with greater flexibility than his Chinese counterpart, the Daoguang emperor. Unlike Daoguang who adopted a confrontational policy towards the Western powers, Rama III made tolerable concessions to the British envoy in 1826. After the Burney Treaty, the British threat receded for two decades until the reign of King Mongkut.

In 1855, when Sir John Bowring arrived to push for trade liberalization and a complete abolition of the Royal Trading Monopoly, Siam was already prepared. By that time the Siamese court had shifted the state's financial dependence on the Royal Trading Monopoly to other sources of revenue based on new taxes, sale of concession rights and tax farms, which were introduced to counteract the effects of trade liberalization. The government's Chinese allies were compensated for their loss of trading privileges with lucrative concessions and tax farms. The most lucrative of these were opium, gambling and alcohol.

The opium tax farm was established by King Mongkut in 1852. The spirits, lottery, and gambling farms were allowed to expand to the limits that the traffic could bear. Thus, the Chinese revenue farmers gained innumerable benefits as the operators of tax farms on behalf of the government.

Four of the most lucrative farms—including opium, liquor, lottery, and gambling—which together provided between 40–50 percent of the total state revenues during most of the second half of the 19th century were based essentially on Chinese consumption.[112] Somewhat paradoxically, it seemed that while the country depended on Chinese virtues for the expansion of

Opium smokers depicted in a book by James B. Lawrence, *China and Japan, and a Voyage Thither: An Account of a Cruise in the Water of the East Indies, China, and Japan* (1870).

commerce and industry, the government also relied on Chinese vices for the expansion of public revenue.

While legalizing vices, the government also attempted to regulate them. King Mongkut introduced measures to restrict opium smoking to the Chinese community. He decreed that any Siamese who smoked opium must wear a queue and pay the Chinese triennial poll tax, on the grounds that by adopting the Chinese vice he forfeited all claims to good standing as a Siamese. W.A. Graham's handbook on Siam published in 1912 stated that "every other man encountered in the streets of the capital wears a pigtail." By the 1880s, the opium farm had become such a huge operation that only syndicates of the richest Chinese could make successful bids. By 1905/06, the annual revenue from the farm was more than 10 million baht, amounting to between 15–20 percent of government income.[113] The government, however, eventually took control of the opium traffic and abolished the tax farm during 1907–9. Nevertheless, revenue from opium remained high for many decades thereafter.

In the case of gambling, Chinese gamblers provided the majority of customers throughout the existence of the farm. Under the law, people could gamble freely for three days each at the Chinese and Siamese New Year, but at all other times gambling was permitted only at houses licensed under farms. Revenue from gambling farms amounted to 5,700,000 baht in 1903/04.[114]

After opium and gambling, the liquor monopoly was the next largest source of revenue for the government. The liquor monopoly, which carried sole rights to distill and sell rice liquor, was also farmed out to the Chinese; by the mid-19th century there were liquor farmers for every part of the country. The Bowring Treaty and subsequent treaties with Western powers were disastrous for the Chinese operators of the alcohol tax farms. The kingdom became flooded by cheap rice spirits from Hong Kong, Macao, Batavia and Singapore because importers only had to pay the 3 percent customs duty rather than the various excise fees and taxes that were levied on local spirits.[115] Consequently, imported alcohol could be sold more cheaply and demand for imported liquor soared. The value of spirits imported into Siam tripled between 1865/66 and 1867/68, from 26,505 Mexican dollars to 79,065. In 1879/80, spirits imported reached a value of 467,609 Mexican dollars, or about 17 times that of 1865/66.[116]

To cash in on the bonanza, many importers, wholesalers and retailers sought to become protégés of the foreign treaty powers in order to gain immunity from legal action brought by the liquor tax farmers, whose monopoly they threatened. When unlicensed liquor operators who were foreign subjects were arrested by the tax farmer, the relevant consul would launch a protest and the

Late 19th century opium lamp.

Siamese government, all too aware of how imperial powers used little incidents like these to justify their intervention in a country, would invariably acquiesce to the release of the foreign subject and the return of the confiscated goods. The situation reached the point where some consuls even issued their own liquor licenses and retailers would flout the Siamese authorities by flying the flag of their adopted country outside their liquor stores. A female American missionary observed with horror and disgust:[117]

Prince Prisadang
(1851–1935).

> *Some years ago an American so dishonored our flag that now we dare not unfurl the stars and stripes above our homes, even on our national holidays, without the natives considering it the sign of a liquor establishment. It is charged that this American issued papers to vendors of spirits who were thus enabled to sell imported goods, free of duty, under the protection of our dear old flag. The stars and stripes went up and down the rivers and canals on little whiskey boats, and fluttered from doors in the principal streets in Bangkok and other cities of Siam, where the "water of sin," as my old native teacher aptly calls it, was sold.*

In March 1882, King Chulalongkorn appointed his cousin Prince Prisadang as the first Thai Resident Envoy Extraordinary and Minister Plenipotentiary in London. He was tasked with negotiating a revision of the unequal treaties, specifically in regards to the spirits trade. Prince Prisadang managed to conclude a treaty with Great Britain in April 1883 with the proviso that all other treaty powers must agree on the same terms before it could be ratified, which ultimately took more than two years of negotiation to achieve. The last to agree to the ratification of the spirits treaty was France, in August 1885. It was a major coup for the Siamese government, marking its first step in revising the unequal treaties and regaining its fiscal and judicial sovereignty.[118] The revenue from liquor farms reached 4,200,000 baht in 1903/04, or over 9 percent of all national revenue, and in 1909 the government started direct collection of excise duty on locally distilled spirits.[119]

Besides profiting from the legalization of Chinese vices, the government also levied a direct tax on the Chinese in the form of the poll tax payable every three years. During the reign of Rama II, the tax was apparently set first at 1.50 baht payable annually. From 1828 until 1909, the tax was triennial and fixed at 4.25 baht. The tax remained constant throughout the reigns of King Mongkut and King Chulalongkorn, testifying to the government's lenient tax policy to encourage Chinese immigration and to keep Chinese in the country.

At the same time, this "Chinese-immigration friendly" policy of the Siamese government concealed an exploitative motivation. The legalization of Chinese

A parlor in the house of wealthy Chinese in Siam as depicted in Mary Buckus' book, *Siam and Laos: As Seen by Our American Missionaries* (1884).

vices was cynically intended to depress remittances to China. The Chinese poll tax, income from the monopolies and the amount of remittances were largely interdependent variables. Many observers note that the savings of the Chinese immigrants were continually being depleted by enticements to gamble, drink, and smoke opium, often causing immigrants to stay in Siam longer than they intended. As it turned out, the balance of these forces resulted in exactly what the government desired: an increasing supply of the Chinese commercial skill and labor necessary for the expansion of the Siamese economy, high revenues indirectly garnered from the Chinese, and low remittances to China.

For righteous young men who did not fall into the vice trap, Siam opened up vast arrays of real opportunities. Skinner, a leading researcher of Chinese society in Siam, boldly stated in his book that "The rags-to-riches story was if anything more common among the Chinese in Siam than among the European immigrants in the United States during the same period and arose from a similar expansion of the national economy." The roadmap for success was simple: hard work, thrift and dependable, good kin. However, despite a fair chance of success, the rate of successful return back to the Chinese hometowns of able young men were still very low—only about half of those who left ever returned. Thus, in China, before each young man's departure, the mother would whisper into her son's ears one last parting instruction well known in every Teochew village: "Do not get married in Siam!"

THE PHRAYA CHODUK-RACHASRETTHI OF THE LATE 19TH CENTURY

After King Mongkut (1851–68) terminated the Royal Trading Monopoly, the role of Phraya Choduk-Rachasretthi, head of the king's Chinese communities and the royal tribute trade, narrowed to the governing of the Chinese in Siam, which in itself was a difficult undertaking given the large influx of migrant Chinese into Siam during the reign of King Chulalongkorn (1868–1910).

Phraya Choduk (Pook)

During the early days of King Chulalongkorn's reign before the king came of age, the most powerful man in Siam was Si Suriyawongse, the regent. According to historian B.J. Terwiel, the regent "commanded most of Siam's army, supervised much of the government's income and expenditure and he and members of his family occupied many key positions in the administration."

The regent appointed a Teochew merchant named Pook (Li Hok, 李福) as *choduk* succeeding Phraya Choduk (Ng Tienjong), who was promoted to another honorary title in his retirement. Unlike previous *choduk* who were local *lukchin* of some social standing in the Siamese court, Pook was a Teochew merchant and owner of Lee Tit Guan (李得源), a shipping company with a trading network in Siam as well as the neighboring Straits Settlements and a trading branch in Hong Kong called Man Fat Cheung (萬發昌).

Prince Damrong, who wrote about the history of Chinese porcelain in Siam, alleged that both Pook and the regent were keen porcelain collectors and the regent relied on the opinion of Pook for authenticating Chinese antiques. The qualifications that recommended the appointment of Pook as head of the Chinese community were first, that he was a Teochew from Shantou (the new, booming port of call in Guangdong); second, that in the eyes of local Chinese in Bangkok, the majority of which were Teochew, an appointment of a Teochew as the head of the community was appreciated and considered more appropriate than his Hokkien predecessors; and third, his father was a respected scholar. Pook was not an unfamiliar figure in Bangkok; his wife was a direct descendant of Phraya Aphai-Phipit (Soon), a well-respected Siamese junk master from the family that had sailed the seas on behalf of the Siamese court since the reign of Rama I.

When Si Suriyawongse appointed Pook to succeed Ng Tienjong as *choduk*, he automatically became the head of the Chinese tribunal court, an institution set up by the regent to judge civil cases between Chinese living in Siam based on the same legal code and practice as in China. In an interview with the co-author, Pook's great-grandson, Police General Pan Chotikapookana, described his residence situated on the bank of the Chao Phraya River as a large, Chinese-garden compound opposite Wat Yannawa. It was here that Choduk Pook conducted his business as well as the hearing of civil cases among Chinese. Deep inside the garden, a long way from his mansions, there were jails for Chinese criminals awaiting deportation.

Choduk Pook's eldest son, Huad, was appointed his assistant under the name Phra Boriboon-Kosakorn. In 1868, the young Boriboon-Kosakorn outbid his own father-in-law, Chaosua Yim, for the opium monopoly and won the contract for 633,200 baht. It was a losing venture—Huad gave up and returned the contract to the Kalahom before the term ended.

Unlike previous *choduk* who raised funds to build a Theravada wat, Pook was assigned the responsibility of restoring Wat Uphai Rachabumrung, a Mahayana Buddhist temple in Talad Noi, perhaps to service the rapid expansion of the Chinese community in Bangkok. In those days, Mahayana ceremonies were performed by monks of the Annamese sect, and all Mahayana temples in Siam were Annamese.

Phraya Choduk (Thian)

The patriarch of the Jotikasthiras, Liu Kian Hin (or Thian or Liu Kian) was a *lukchin* son of Chin Cheu, a Hakka junk merchant who lived near Wat Bophitpimuk in Sampeng. According to the tablet kept at Wat Mangkorn, his mother, Sim Keungpok, was a respected *lukchin* who had been conferred a noble rank by the Siamese inner court. The Jotikasthiras traced Liu Kian's forefather to Klong Suan Plu in Ayudhya. In 1851, Liu Kian was appointed as the *lata*, or the supercargo of the tribute ship named *Vidhayakom* sent by King Mongkut to Canton in late 1851 to inform the Chinese emperor of his coronation and to pay respects to the late Daoguang emperor. He also served in the same position on the next tribute voyage the year after.

The Jotikasthira family tale informed us that Liu Kian's wife, Khunying Sun, had been the trusted lady-in-waiting of Queen Debsirindra from her maiden days, as well as Prince Chulalongkorn's wet-nurse. Hence, Liu Kian's family had been in the inner circle of courtiers surrounding the prince even before he was crowned King Rama V. In 1871, Liu Kian was known as Phra Bhibunpattanakorn and was among the entourage accompanying the 18-year-old monarch on his visit to Singapore, Malacca, Penang, Moulmein, Rangoon, Calcutta, Delhi, Agra, Lucknow, Kanpur, Bombay and Benares.

In 1872, after the overseas trip, the king submitted a formal program for reform to the regent proposing to abolish the corvée system, slavery and gambling, to reform the legal courts, and to develop a salaried bureaucracy, police force and a regular army. These plans were rejected as impracticable by the council of ministers headed by the regent. Less than a year later the king was formally re-anointed and the period of regency came to an end.

The most important reform at the early stage of Chulalongkorn's reign was the restructuring of state revenue. King Chulalongkorn established the position of Hor Rasadakornpiphat inside the Grand Palace to consolidate tax collections, audit tax farmers in arrears and urge them to repay the state. He also attempted to improve the bidding system and instituted more direct control by the central officers. Liu Kian was personally assigned by the king to work for Hor Rasadakornpiphat under Prince Mahamala. During this period, Liu Kian was known as Phraya Noranartpakdi-Sri-Rasadakorn, the chief accountant. The state revenue quickly increased from 3.5 million baht in 1868 to 5.9 million baht in 1874, and much later, in 1895, just after Lao Kian passed away, the state revenue reached 18.1 million baht.

In 1879, after Choduk Pook passed away, the king appointed Liu Kian, whom he personally knew and trusted, as the governor of the Chinese community in Siam. This was a big surprise to the Chinese because Liu Kian was a Hakka. The Hakkas were very much a minority group in those days, constituting only about

10 percent of the total Chinese population in Siam.

As a salaried bureaucrat, Liu Kian continued his work at Hor Rasadakornpiphat overseeing the bids for concessions and tax farms. In order to repay Liu Kian for his support, King Chulalongkorn once assigned him the bidding of the crown monopoly privilege in teak and salt for which Liu Kian earned 5 percent commission. Phraya Choduk (Thian or Liu Kian) was promoted to the director of the customs department in 1893 just before he passed away.

Liu Kian was very proud of his Hakka ancestry and made a large contribution for the building of a Hakka shrine, Hon Wong Gong, known among local residents as "the Shoe Factory Shrine," in Talad Noi. According to the list of contributors, his name is listed as Khunban Kian, a position that indicated he operated a lottery concession as well.

Another important landmark in Bangkok that linked Liu Kian to his Hakka heritage was Wat Mangkorn Kamalawat, the most prominent Chinese Mahayana temple in Siam. The temple was conceived in the early 1870s by the Venerable Sok Heng, a Hakka Chinese Mahayana monk, together with Liu Kian and a few other prominent Hakka such as Chi Yi Gun, the father-in-law of Chin Lamsam (Ng Miaongian). Chi Yi Gun, who was the owner of a Chinese medicine shop, was probably a secret society leader respectfully known as Chi Yi Gun, or "the Second Elder Xi," by the local community.

Through Liu Kian's court connections, King Chulalongkorn ordered that some 6,500 square meters of land along the north side of Charoen Krung Road be vacated to make way for construction of the temple in 1873. The temple was consecrated as Wat Leng Nei Yi and King Chulalongkorn accorded it the Siamese royal name of Wat Mangkorn Kalayawat, meaning "the dragon and lotus temple" (equivalent to Leng Nei Yi in Chinese).

While Liu Kian was preoccupied with the king's assignment on Siam's financial reform, he was supported by two of the most-respected members of the Chinese community in his role as the governor of the Chinese and head of the Chinese tribunal court. First, the Venerable Sok Heng was a loyal ally and had been known to help Liu Kian mediate cases of conflict, especially among the Hakka community. Another was his friend and relative by marriage, a Hokkien named Lim Fak who succeeded him as the next Phraya Choduk.

Phraya Choduk (Fak)

After Liu Kian passed away, his colleague who was also the father-in-law of Liu Kian's son, Phraya Sawasdiwamdit (Lim Fak), was appointed to the *choduk* by King Chulalongkorn. The relationship between Liu Kian and Lim Fak dated back more than 40 years, back to when both were *lata*, or supercargoes, of different ships in the same tribute mission to Canton. Lim Fak was a learned man fluent in both Thai and Chinese. He had translated *Kai Tian Ti Di*, a literal tale about mythological rulers and cultural heroes from ancient China, into Thai.

Unlike Liu Kian, who was assigned multiple jobs by the king, Lim Fak had always worked for Krom Tha Sai. Because he was an educated man, Lim Fak had been one of the jury in the Chinese tribunal court since the day it was founded. He had been sent to the south several times to clear up Chinese conflicts on opium as well as tin concessions. Being of Hokkien descent, perhaps he felt at home in the south, as most of his personal businesses (such as birds' nests, coconut oil and spirit concessions) were also in the south. As the official of Krom Tha Sai, Lim Fak was also assigned to deliver official correspondence to the sultanates of Kedah, Perlis and Satun. Lim Fak chaired the construction of Weahart Chamrunt, the Palace of Heavenly Light, a beautiful Chinese palace set in the garden of Bang Pa-In, which was built for King Chulalongkorn by the Chinese community in Siam.

Phraya Choduk (Huad)

Meanwhile, after Choduk Pook had passed away in 1879, his son Li Guat Chew (李發洲) or Huad in Thai, succeeded his father at Li Tit Guan and expanded the business into rice milling. The mill located on valuable waterfront property near the Li residence specialized in high-quality rice for the European market as well as lower-quality rice for direct sale to Hong Kong, Singapore and Shantou.

Huad also continued his father's successful business of importing porcelain utensils to Bangkok under the house brand of Jin Tang Fu Ji, but he slightly adjusted the hallmark of the porcelain to Jin Tang Fa Ji, known in Bangkok as Gim Tung Huad Kee, to accommodate his name. King Chulalongkorn, who was himself an avid collector of Chinese porcelain, affectionately called Huad "Chao Khun Gim Tung," meaning "Lord Gim Tung," while his noble name was Boriboon-Kosakorn. Huad had maintained a close relationship with the inner court partly through his work as a sale agent providing various supplies and materials such as porcelain utensils, and partly because his wife was the sister of Chao Chom Manda Uam, a royal concubine. In 1888, the king commissioned Boriboon-Kosakorn to be his agent in acquiring beautiful tea sets decorated with Rama V's monogram, Chor Por Ror, from Jingdezhen. These tea services remain the most sought-after porcelain by collectors to this day.

Despite his success in overseeing a thriving empire, Huad seemed to have a weakness for bidding on the opium monopoly. After losing money on the contract in 1868, Boriboon-Kosakorn again bid for and won the monopolistic right of opium for the year 1891. This time he lost another hefty amount of 144,000 baht, a major loss in those days. Huad preferred spending his time in business, and apart from servicing the royal court with its supplies, he was not called upon to the administrative service until late in his career when the old Hokkien Choduk (Lim Fak) passed away. King Rama V selected Boriboon-Kosakorn as his successor, making him the second member of the Li clan to be appointed as the *choduk*. This was an unprecedented appointment—in the history of the selection of *choduk*, the court had always refrained from selecting someone from the same family more than once.

By the first decade of the 20th century, the government had attempted to take more direct control of both opium and spirit taxes, and tax farmers were forced to shift their activities to other business. King Rama V described this change in 1907: "Now, however, we collect these taxes [opium and spirit] and administer these monopolies ourselves, leaving only a few unimportant ones to Chinese tax farmers. The Chinese turn increasingly to private enterprises, of which rice milling is an example, and become further separated from involvement in government administration."

The Chinese self-governing system of *palad* and *nai-amphun chin*, as well as the Chinese tribunal court conceived by Si Suriyawongse, fared no better than the Chinese tax farmers. With the centralization of the Siamese administration and the extension of the direct authority of Bangkok to the rural principalities, local Chinese leaders were stripped of all power except those of mediator and guarantor. Within a few years, the system died a natural death.

Phraya Choduk (Min)

Phraya Choduk-Rachasretthi (Min Laohasretthi, or Lau Congmin, 劉聰敏) was the liquor tax farmer in Bangkok who inherited his business and a substantial land ownership in the Sampeng area from Phra Charoen Rachaton (Theng, or Lau Mahteck), his father. Lau Mahteck left his home village near Amoy, Fujian Province, at 15 to work for Chaosua Yim, a distant relative who was one of Bangkok's leading tycoons. Through the Lau (Liu, 劉) clan connection, he managed to secure the birds' nest concession in Chaiya, Pathew, Chumpon and Bang Nangrom. However, his specialty was in spirit and sugar tax farming, and he controlled numerous areas including Bangkok.

Lau Congmin was born in Bangkok. His father followed the common practice in those days of sending his son back to his home village to be educated according to Chinese tradition. As a result, Congmin was able to communicate in Thai, Chinese and English. After he came back, he expanded his father's business by setting up Seng Joo Tye rice mill and Hang Meng Seng rice trading company with branches in Hong Kong and Singapore. In 1910, the military cracked down on the Chinese strike that paralyzed the city for days, and over 400 Chinese were arrested and jailed. It was Lau Congmin and his friend, Sophonpetcharat (Tia Kiangsam), who helped negotiate with the government for the early release of the prisoners.

Lau Congmin was one of the most-respected members of Bangkok society and was appointed as the director of the Red Cross Society in 1929. He was a devout Buddhist and an honest, refined man. He was warm-hearted and public-spirited. He was one of the founders of the Tian Fah Hospital as well as Yueyong (越永) and Yuetiesunian (越貼素薫學校) Chinese schools.

Phraya Choduk (Phong)

The last Phraya Choduk-Rachasretthi, Li Tai Phong (李泰鵬), was the son of Choduk Huad and grandson of Choduk Pook, making him the third member of the Li family to be appointed as the official head of the Chinese community in Siam. By this time, the Chinese tribunal court had been abolished and Chinese in Siam were under the jurisdiction of the modern Siamese court of law, and the title of Phraya Choduk-Rachasretthi was honorary.

METAMORPHOSIS

(1855–1925)

The transformations during this period were physical: steamships, new roads and railroads connected people and markets, both local and global; banks and a proper currency were introduced; and the rice trade boomed, while sweeping institutional reforms transformed both the economy and monarchy; and they were also psychological: a sense of nationhood and nationalism were forged, first inclusive of the Chinese and then later exclusive of them. Western modes and ideas began to usurp traditional Asian values. A tug of war between competing ideologies ensued. China, for the first time saw its overseas communities as an asset, while in Siam, they were viewed as a problem. Flourishing newspapers led to unprecedented dialogue and debate about what it meant to be "Thai" and where the funds and energies of the Chinese in Siam should be channeled. It was a period of dramatic change that would plant the seeds of a revolution.

The post–Bowring Treaty period was dominated by the frenetic attempts of the Siamese government and the controlling economic interests in the kingdom—namely, the merchant class—to adjust to the new commercial regulations that would entirely change the way trade was conducted in Siam. Gone was the old trade system dating back to early Ayudhya, which had brought wealth and power to the Siamese state and allowed it to dominate Mainland Southeast Asia.

In the name of free trade, British capitalists and European political powers had extended their global network to incorporate Siam. With the Bowring Treaty, Siam became integrated into the worldwide capitalist economy in which protectionist barriers preventing the free flow of factors of production were dismantled. This enlarged free market of which Siam had become a part already encompassed Europe, most of the Far East, India and large parts of Southeast Asia, including the British Straits Settlements, Burma and the Netherlands Indies.

However, the Bowring Treaty was quite unlike the free-trade treaties signed between Great Britain and other European powers. Rather, it was an unequal treaty that provided for extraterritorial rights for Great Britain and consular jurisdiction for British subjects. Instead of being based on the model of the free-trade agreements voluntarily entered into by the European powers during the Free Trade Movement, the Bowring Treaty was based on the model of the Treaty of Nanjing (1842), signed between Great Britain and China after the latter was defeated in the Opium War in 1842.

Like the Treaty of Nanjing, the Bowring Treaty forced the Siamese to accept extraterritoriality, the abolition of Royal Trading Monopolies and transit dues, as well as the establishment of ad valorem rates of 3 percent on imports and 5 percent on exports. In fact, the 3 percent import duty was worse than the duty imposed on China in the Treaty of Nanjing (1842) and the subsequent Anglo-Japan Treaty of Amity and Commerce (1858). In both treaties, ad valorem rates were set at 5 percent. The Bowring Treaty encumbered Siam with the lowest import duty system in Asia.[1]

Bowring was clearly elated with his achievements. From the deck of his warship returning to China, he wrote to Lord Clarendon, the secretary of foreign affairs, "I feel myself one of the happiest men ... And I am really amazed at my own success which once or twice seemed hopeless." Through the Bowring Treaty, the longtime desire of Great Britain to remove all Siamese restrictions on foreign trade was almost perfectly realized. British subjects were given the freedom to trade directly with anyone in Bangkok, while exported products were to be taxed once either as an inland tax, a transit tax or an export duty, and a most-favored nation clause was also attached.[2]

Another onerous condition imposed by the Bowring Treaty was the stipulation

on the land tax. Taxes on land held by British subjects were fixed at low rates and could not be changed; consequently, all land-tax rates remained static, as the Siamese government was not prepared to tax its own subjects higher than it did foreigners. In addition, earlier prohibitions on the export of rice were removed.

Britain had been obsessed with forcing the Siamese to abolish the Royal Trading Monopoly since the 1820s. They finally succeeded in 1855, but much had changed since 1820. Although the British may have valued what they received even more in 1855 than if they had succeeded in 1820, what the Siamese negotiators conceded to Bowring had lost some importance since 1820.

For example, the Siamese court had already set up and operated an alternative revenue base to replace the income loss from the abolition of the Royal Trading Monopoly and the phasing out of the junk trade with China. Newly created revenue farms were introduced after 1826 to cope with exactly this kind of contingency and its potential negative impact on royal revenues and trading profits. The local Chinese rushed in to bid for newly created revenue farms all over the country. This new, win-win deal between the Chinese and the Siamese court resulted in substantial income for the government, the principal amongst which were those in opium, gambling, lotteries and alcohol.

During the brief era of free trade and British hegemony in the region during the mid-19th century, the Chinese ascendency in Siam appeared unassailable. However, by the late 19th century, the profound effects of Siam's integration

Top: Painting in the throne hall of the Grand Palace in Bangkok, showing a meeting between British envoy John Bowring and King Mongkut.

Chapter opening picture: Koh Chun's daughter-in-law and her grandson. Koh Chun's family assumed the surname of Bisalputra.

213

into the capitalist world economy began to appear. These creative, dislocating, sometimes destructive and transforming effects were inextricably intertwined, and they reinforced one another across economic, political and social dimensions.

The Age of Steamships and Railroads

As Siam became integrated into the global capitalist economy, the whole course of the country's economy and social development after 1855 became increasingly determined by external factors emanating from industrial Europe. First and foremost among these was the expansion of modern communications into the region. Indeed, few changes in the economic framework of the region were more striking than the transportation revolution.

Until the last decade of the 19th century, transportation difficulties tended to set strict limits to the intensity of governance in areas remote from Bangkok, and to restrict trade by land. Movement along the coast was much easier than over land, and most local trade was conducted by coastal vessels and junks. Logistical difficulties tended to dictate a political system of vassalage embodied in the traditional Mandala state with its tributary rulers, *chao muang* and Hokkien rajahs, rather than steady administration, which later became the attribute of the reinvented Siamese state under King Chulalongkorn.[3]

Steamships, offering cheap bulk transport, led the way in Siam's transport transformation. By the 1860s, steam-powered British shipping lines had begun regular service in Southeast Asia. These steamships greatly strengthened Bangkok's

Chinese workers clearing the jungle on the north-bound route.

connections with the outside world and the port cities in the region including Singapore, Penang, Rangoon and Batavia. British steamships were joined in the following decades by increasing numbers of French, Dutch, German, American, Japanese and locally owned Siamese steamship lines. Modern steamships steadily increasing in tonnage, frequency and scope of service provided the most fundamental link between Siam and the world economy and became one of the major agents of economic change by making the region's export boom possible. During this boom, steamships carried hundreds of thousands, then millions, of tons of rice, timber, tin and rubber, and brought in manufactured goods such as textiles, canned foods and heavy machinery, including steam engines for saw mills and rice mills, trains and rail tracks.

King Chulalongkorn (Rama V).

Besides its indispensable role in supporting the expansion of Siamese trade, the most important role of steamships was in facilitating Chinese immigration to the kingdom. Between 1865 and 1886, steamships increasingly took over the bulk of passenger traffic between China and Siam. It was steamships—not junks—that carried most of the rising numbers of Chinese immigrants to Siam in the half century before 1930. However, steamships played a less revolutionary role than railways in Siam.

Compared to water-borne and coastal transportation, land transport in the kingdom had always been slow, expensive and difficult. In the 1850s, it took one-and-half months by ox cart to reach Bangkok from Nongkhai on the bank of the Mekong River. Moreover, many of the kingdom's rivers were not very navigable beyond the lowlands. Therefore, the impact of the railway was quite decisive.[4]

Political and military considerations rather than economic concerns prompted King Chulalongkorn to build the railway. The first railway line, the construction of which began in 1892 and reached Khorat in 1900, was intended to help counter the French advance through Laos. From Khorat the lines were extended to the Mekong in the 1920s and 1930s north to Udon Thani and Nong Khai, opposite Vientiane, and east to Ubon Ratchathani. Meanwhile, the construction of a second major line commenced, running north and reaching Uttaradit in 1909. After a pause, construction was resumed and the line was extended to reach Chiang Mai in 1921. Perhaps the pause was due to the commencement of a third line, in 1909, to the south reaching Penang in 1922.[5]

King Chulalongkorn, pressed between the two dangerous colonial neighbors, of France and Britain, kept political considerations foremost in mind when framing railway policy. The Siamese government gave the Germans a major role in the railway department because Germany was not a threat to Siam. In addition, the Siamese government took care to pay for all its early railway projects from current revenue rather than from foreign loans. Only after a settlement was reached with the British on the final division of the Malay States between Britain and Siam did the Siamese government accept a British loan for completing the line from Bangkok to Penang.[6]

The political and economic effects of the railway were impressive. By 1930, a national system of 3,017 kilometers centered on Bangkok greatly enhanced the primacy of the capital city and the government located there, which derived tangible benefits from the railway, especially in the north. In fact, it was only after the railway reached Chiang Mai that Bangkok was able to collect taxes in earnest throughout the north. The reinforcement of Bangkok's sovereignty over the north led to the replacement of the Indian rupee by the baht as the basic currency there. Much the same was true in the northeast; the railway proved to be particularly important in binding the country together.

Besides the central government based in Bangkok, the railway benefited the country's economic interests, especially the Chinese. Chinese crews brought over by steamships after 1870 built the approximately 3,220 kilometers of railway in Siam. As the railway grid fanned out into the interior hinterland, Chinese commercial interests followed closely; Chinese moved outward in tandem with the expansion of the railway system to each railhead, in turn reinforcing the railway network with their own commercial network. Thus, the expansion of connectivity, coming in the wake of a nationwide railway system, stimulated trade and expanded internal commerce, which was dominated by Chinese. In fact, the installation of the northern and northeastern lines permitted major rice exports from these areas for the first time.[7]

A Siamese train and its conductor.

In addition to linking the country together, the railway provided important connections to the outside world as well. As the northeast line was not counteracted by any French railway into Laos, it strongly reinforced a long-standing tendency for the Mekong Lao to orient themselves to Bangkok. However, in the south, the railway had an opposite effect. The southern line reinforced an earlier tendency for the southern part of the kingdom to orient itself economically towards Penang. As most Chinese tin miners in Phuket and surrounding areas had emigrated there via Penang during the 19th century, there already existed strong links between Phuket and Penang. Consequently, in the 20th century, the area's tin usually went to Penang for smelting. The establishment of the railway to Penang simply reinforced this trend and resulted in a reduction of Bangkok's economic sovereignty over the south, which was not effectively challenged until the 1960s.[8]

THE RAILWAY MAN: KHUN NIPATCHINNAKORN (JIA GEESEE)

Jia Geesee (1886–1972), the well-known founder of Hadyai, spent most of his lifetime building railroads in Siam. Jia was a Hakka from Meixian who arrived in Siam in 1904, when his parents decided to move with their six children to Siam. The family paid $5 per person for steerage in a crowded Japanese steamship, a journey that lasted seven days and seven nights. Once they arrived in Bangkok, the 19-year-old Jia Geesee worked in a liquor store for a year before moving on.[9]

In 1909, when King Chulalongkorn took a loan from Britain to extend the southern railroad, Jia was hired as a foreman by one of the railroad subcontractors. Thousands of laborers were employed, and Jia worked under an Italian engineer's supervision. The line was divided up into many sectors of approximately 30 kilometers each. The Hakka were assigned to clear the jungle, the Teochew built the earthen base, and the Cantonese built the railroad. Hundreds of Chinese workers lost their lives in the jungle. Jia later became a successful railroad contractor, and while supervising the construction he would also survey the site for mineral deposits such as tin, iron and wolfram.

While camping near U-Tapao station, he bought a 50-*rai* piece of land for 175 baht where he built his home and developed the nearby site into a small market town. The town continued to expand and became the present-day city of Hadyai. In 1929, while visiting the south, King Prajadhipok awarded Jia Geesee the title of Khun Nipatchinnakorn, and in 1939 Jia became a notarized Siamese citizen.[10]

Currency and Banking

Besides steamships and railways, economic frameworks of other sorts, though less dramatic and visible, were no less important. Not least among them was an improved monetary framework embodied in a standardized currency system. In the mid-19th century, traditional currency units were too small and cowrie shells were still being used. Indian rupees continued to circulate in Chiang Mai and Mexican dollars were being used in the southern Chinese tin mining areas. Minted coins introduced during King Mongkut's reign simplified matters somewhat, but it was not until foreign coins were made legal tender in 1857 at 5 baht to 3 Mexican dollars that the difficulties occasioned by foreign commerce and exchange were rendered manageable.[11]

Banking Hall of the old Siam Commercial Bank.

With the standardization of the currency system, private banks, joint stock companies, insurance firms, and legal firms began to appear. Banks centered in Bangkok stood at the center of ever more complex financial systems, and alongside them, informal Chinese networks presided over the expansion of credit systems. Subsequently, European and Chinese chambers of commerce representing export-oriented interests and their respective business communities added to the growing institutional complexity of Siam's evolving capitalist economy.

The interactive and reinforcing effects of the installation of modern transportation, monetary and financial frameworks, coupled with a liberal policy towards Chinese immigration, gradually removed the outstanding impediments to export development in Siam. Before these innovations, conditions were not conducive to export development. The country was sparsely and unevenly populated; labor was in short supply. Transportation of goods was slow and difficult. Economic transactions were conducted mainly by barter; taxes were mostly collected in kind and in the form of corvée; there was very little currency in circulation or use of credit. It was a landscape of small, local, and largely self-sufficient villages only loosely associated throughout the provinces, whose common bonds were more cultural and social than economic.

However, Siam's integration into the world capitalist economy subjected the state to rising world market demand for exportable commodities. The tug of outside markets for rice provided the impetus for Siam's rice export boom.

The Rice Export Boom

In 1825, Captain Henry Burney reported that rice was Siam's largest export. However, during the reign of Rama III, Siam remained at best a supplier to localized regional markets in China to alleviate the effects of drought, famine and natural disasters. Nevertheless, as the world entered the 19th century, the international trading environment that was to transform Siam into a major player in the world rice trade was already taking shape.

Before 1800, Western merchants only came to Southeast Asia for commodities that either had a scarcity value or commanded a high price in the Chinese market. In as much as Western merchants interfered with local production, it was primarily done with a view to restricting rather than increasing supply. A case in point was the trade in spices and forest products.

The Industrial Revolution in Europe caused a paradigm change in the world trading system—emphasis shifted away from rarity towards abundance. One consequence of this development was an explosion in shipping capacity, which made Western ships comparatively more cost efficient than Eastern junks. This revolution in Western shipping technology gradually facilitated a shift in the nature of Siamese exports from high-value, low-volume goods to low-cost, high-volume commodities. High-value, low-volume items like ivory and cardamom increasingly gave way to bulk commodities like rice and sugar. The broader ramification of this process was reflected in the decline of the spice trade, the eclipse of many traditional products, and the rise of new ones, which in turn created needs of their own.

This evolution in the characteristics of international trade was itself a reflection of a more fundamental worldwide transformation whose effects were being increasingly felt in Southeast Asia. In effect, the impact of Western industrialism was converting the region into a major source of a handful of primary raw materials and a major market for the West's industrial products. In the meantime, while island Southeast Asia was being groomed by the new industrial imperialism to concentrate on the cultivation of profitable cash crops and the exploitation of mineral resources, the great rice bowls of Mainland Southeast Asia were molded into rice granaries in line with the Western goal to make Asia the supplier of non-manufactured goods.[12] Rice was among the first of many economic opportunities that opened up after Siam's integration into the world capitalist system. In Europe, rice was used for making alcohol, starch and animal feed, while world population growth also generated a large demand for Siamese rice from overseas. Moreover, Western impact in the region had created new markets as rival Western powers carved up colonial territories and urban treaty ports sprung up across Asia and Southeast Asia. These new colonial markets also generated a demand for Siamese rice.

It did not take much for Siam to rise up to the challenge and become a major supplier to meet the growing world demand for rice. The alluvial flood plains of the Chao Phraya Basin were eminently suited for rice production. The country's rice production could be easily expanded to meet the world demand because the Chao Phraya Delta had not been heavily settled. In fact, even in the Ayudhya period the only extensive area of rice cultivation was in the narrow corridor of flood plain running south from Chainat in the center of the delta.[13] Even after the economic expansion during the Bangkok period when Siam resumed exporting rice to China in the early 19th century, rice cultivation was still largely confined to this tract. Around 1850, three quarters of the delta's land area was still unused and the total population of the Chao Phraya delta region was probably only around 500,000 people.[14]

By contrast, the Red River Delta and Java, which also produced large quantities of rice, had to support heavy populations. Consequently, these latter areas could not yield an exportable surplus whereas Siam's underpopulated Chao Phraya Delta had vast tracts of underutilized land that could be turned into rice paddies. Moreover, the strategy of increasing production by simply putting more land under cultivation obviated the need to increase agricultural productivity; nor did it require any major change of rice-growing technique. Thus, for Siam, producing rice for export was easy.

To encourage more rice production, King Mongkut initiated a land utilization policy that allowed peasant cultivators land ownership. In 1857–58, a law was passed exempting newly cultivated lands from taxation for the first year, a provision extended to three years by King Chulalongkorn in 1874–75.[15] Thus, as

A mural at Ananta Samakom Throne Hall depicts King Chulalongkorn and his mission to abolish slavery.

a result of a series of political decisions beginning in the reign of King Mongkut and continuing into the reign of King Chulalongkorn, Siamese society was characterized not by big landlords but by peasant smallholders. In fact, until the 1970s, this smallholder peasant society represented four-fifths of the population and formed the engine driving the economy, especially the rice export sector.[16]

Distributing lands and offering tax incentives were the easy part. The difficulty lay in widespread implementation: on the eve of the export boom, the peasants' economic mobility, willingness and ability to assume new economic roles were limited. Before Chulalongkorn's social reforms, the peasants had been subsumed under slavery and the *phrai* system, which attached them to their patrons and restricted their mobility. Furthermore, the Siamese peasant was influenced by Theravada Buddhist culture, which encouraged contentment with his peaceful village life surrounded by family and friends. Lack of greed also limited their upward mobility.

Unless the problem of peasant mobility was resolved, the necessary manpower required to substantially expand rice production would not be forthcoming. Slavery, forced labor and corvée stood as economic impediments to the growth of a rice cash-crop export trade.[17] It was necessary to revolutionize the regressive, traditional, Siamese social system. Complementing Mongkut's earlier reforms, Chulalongkorn initiated the process of abolishing slavery and forced labor.

Once adequate incentives were in place and the social shackles that prevented their mobility were removed, the peasant response was swift and massive. When worldwide demand increased, hundreds of thousands of peasants in or near the delta moved steadily out over the uncultivated stretches to practice a significantly more extensive agriculture, yielding a saleable surplus. This frontier movement of peasant colonization gradually engulfed the entire landscape of the Lower Chao Phraya Basin, transforming it into one of the world's main rice granaries.

The growth of cities and industries in colonial Asia, including rubber plantations and tin mining, required large numbers of immigrant workers. The late 19th century saw a rapidly growing demand for rice from the expanding colonial territories, of which the port of Singapore was the main trading center. Consequently, Siam became the most important staple supplier for the "rice-eating, colonial wage laborers" of mostly Chinese and Indian origin.[18] In fact, Siam supplied from 47–59 percent of imported rice in Singapore between 1880 and 1910, and almost all of the imported rice at the port of Hong Kong. The expansion of steamship service, the opening of the Suez Canal and the establishment of telegraphic communications linking overseas markets further fueled the world rice-export boom.

Siam's rice exports soared from an average 100,000 tons during the 1860s to 200,000 tons in the 1870s, to five times that amount by the turn of the 20th century.[19] After 1890, export taxes in rice and tin were used to finance the railway systems built in the kingdom, while railways in turn facilitated further rapid increases in rice exports.

Although availability of rice was a necessary condition underlying Siam's rice export boom, it was only half of the story. The production role of the Thai peasant was perhaps the most fundamental contribution to the development of Siam's rice export economy. But other parts of the export process including collection, milling, distribution and marketing were equally important.

Although the Thai peasant had responded enthusiastically to the growing world demand for rice, their response did not extend beyond the production dimension. Even after producing millions of tons of rice, they continued to remain comfortable villagers. Their way of life did not change substantially, although they had more disposable income. They readily opened new land, increased production, adopted kerosene lamps and made greater use of cash, but their economic mobility did not extend much further.[20] There was no need to move as they already enjoyed a better quality of life. Between 1880 and 1910, the price of rice doubled while the daily wages of unskilled laborers in the urban centers remained unchanged, thereby making smallholder rice production comparatively attractive.[21] Consequently, very few Siamese peasants were willing to leave their villages to work for wages in the city. Confined in their comfortable role as small-scale growers rooted in the pleasant world of rural villages, they were almost always content to leave it to others to get the rice to the market.[22]

The opening of Siam to the world economy and the conversion of rice from a subsistence produce to a cash crop added a new dimension to the rice industry, which from the outset grew outside the Thai peasant realm and was dominated by the Chinese. In sharp contrast to the peasant-dominated, subsistence-mode production sector, the marketing side of the rice industry controlled by Chinese entrepreneurs was modern and sophisticated, employing Western state-of-the-art rice milling technology.[23]

Chinese participation in the marketing of rice assumed two basic patterns. The first pattern was that of the small cash crop dealers and middlemen. The Chinese middleman existed at the meeting point between the peasant world and the new, international, rice-export economy centered in the port cities, namely Bangkok. The tremendous growth of rice milling and export in Siam led to the emergence of a specialized type of trader in lower and middle Siam: the itinerant Chinese paddy dealer who rowed upstream in his boat to collect paddy crops from peasant villages for transport to Bangkok rice mills.

As the government-backed colonization of frontier zones by peasants opened up new tracts of alluvial flood plain for rice cultivation, it was the Chinese crop dealers who followed peasants into barely accessible regions to collect and transport the harvested paddy for distribution. They would deliver the harvest to the rice mills in the port cities to be processed for export to overseas markets. The gradual development of an exchange economy made possible by rapid increase in economic specialization and foreign trade engendered a growth in the number and kind of middleman functions to be performed. The expansion of rice cultivation required cash to purchase at least the cost of seed rice. Loans for the operation were often advanced by the Chinese dealers in town seeking to retain continued loyalty and regular supplies of agricultural products from a good village agent.[24] By the turn of the century, Chinese middlemen were virtually ubiquitous in the interior and their roles developed considerable complexity. They bought paddy and other local produce, advanced credit and supplies, lent money, brought consumer goods to sell to the peasant and the inland trader, and transported goods in both directions.

If large Chinese rice mills using Chinese wage labor dominated in Bangkok, in rural areas the Chinese network of small capitalists-cum-middlemen became a familiar sight. Since there were few landlords and these few were native Thai and since European rice mills in Bangkok quickly gave way to Chinese competition after the 1890s, the only real partners of the peasants in the rice industry were the Chinese middlemen. Although the People's Party in Bangkok in the 1930s would be much perplexed by the dominance of the Chinese middleman over the rural economy, the peasants found the Chinese middleman indispensable and easy to deal with.[25]

The cash crop middleman in Siam was very competitive. Powerful village

CHIK IAH, "THE HONORABLE SEVENTH"

By far the most popular and respected leader of the Bangkok Chinese community was Koh Huijia (Gao Huishi, 高暉石, pictured) of the Gao family, also known as Chik Iah, or "the honorable seventh." Koh Huijia was the chairman of the Chinese Chamber of Commerce for five terms between its conception in 1910 and 1923. He was the seventh son of Koh Mahwah (Gao Chuxiang) of the Yuan Fat Hong syndicate, one of the major Chinese trading companies in Bangkok and Hong Kong. Besides trading and rice milling, Yuan Fat Hong was the Hong Kong shipping agent for the Scottish Oriental Steamship Company, the Nord-Deutscher Lloyd steamship company, and, after 1919, the Butterfield and Swire Steamship Company.[26] In this role, the company's earnings were further enhanced as these foreign shipping companies monopolized the Bangkok–Hong Kong routes at various times.

The company success earned Koh Mahwah and his descendants a respected social status among the high societies of Shantou, Hong Kong, Singapore and Bangkok. Koh Mahwah was one of the founders of an influential Chinese institution, the Tung Wah Hospital, in Hong Kong in 1872. His eldest son by his Thai wife was a Juren imperial degree holder while Koh Huijia, the seventh son, was a Gongsheng degree holder.[27]

After the death of Koh Mahwah in 1883, Yuan Fat Hong became a "common" company owned by the nine sons. Koh Huijia, who was born in Hong Kong, took over the care of its Siamese business. Sincere and warm-hearted, Huijia was well liked by fellow merchants. Koh Huijia became the chairman and major promoter of the Chinese Chamber of Commerce, the Thai Rice Millers Association, Tian Fah (Tianhua) Hospital and Peiying School.[28] He was conferred the title of Luang Phakdee-Puwanart by King Chulalongkorn.

Each of Koh Huijia's brothers held ownership in the "common" company in addition to conducting their own businesses. After the Xinhai Revolution (or the Chinese Revolution of 1911), the family invested extensively in the financial sector, including investment in several Chinese-native banks. Koh Huijia's nephew Koh Sengjue was a revolutionist and a patriotic entrepreneur who founded an electric company, a water company and a textile factory in Shantou.

However, when the world entered the depression period of the late 1920s, the Yuan Fat Hong empire began to crumble. The rice crisis bankrupted the Yuan Fat Hong associated companies in Bangkok. The economic crisis spread to rural Southern China and following the collapse of four native banks in Shantou, the Gaos of Yuan Fat Hong suffered bankruptcy in 1934.[29]

The only exception to this family catastrophe was a small branch in Bangkok led by Koh Behjiang (Kovatana), whose private rice-trading company not only survived the financial crisis but also prospered. In 1927, Koh Behjiang and his friends, Tan Jinggeng (Tantuvanich), Mah Lapkun (Bulakul), Low Tiekchuan (Bulsook; pictured) and Tan U-Seng (Payakkaporn) established Five Fortune Shipping (Ngou Hok), so that the freshest lychees in Bangkok could be served at their table.

agents, often Siamese, who built up a clientele in the village, could shop around among the town dealers, seeking the highest commission.[30] Peter Gosling in his comparative research on Chinese crop dealers in Malaysia and Thailand opened an article with the following comparison:

> *"The Chinese has no heart. He is one big stomach which eats everything I have. He is the reason I am always poor," says a Malay farmer.*

> *"The Chinese is the only person who is honest with me. He gives much more than he takes," says a Thai farmer.*

The middleman who doubled as inland upcountry trader also served as agent of the major Chinese rice miller and international commodity trader located in Bangkok. The latter represented the next basic pattern of Chinese involvement in the rice industry. In fact, it was the entry of European and Chinese capital into the rice industry coupled with the influx of Chinese immigrant coolies into Siam that generated the momentum to kick-start the rice cash-crop export economy.[31]

At the turn of the century, with the emergence of a vast free-trade area in the East encompassing the British colonial territories including India, Singapore, Hong Kong and Burma, the white-rice trade was marked by "chiseling competition and ephemeral price levels." The Asian rice trade as a whole increased from 396,358 tons in 1870 to 1,521,181 tons in 1910 with Bengal and Burma as the leading exporters.[32] Singapore and Hong Kong became the redistribution centers for the rice trade. From Hong Kong, rice was sent to the rice-deficient provinces of Southern China, Japan, Hawaii, and even California, while Singapore redistributed rice to the British colonies in Southeast Asia and elsewhere.

The market nature of the rice business was more intense in Siam, where the whole business of buying, milling and exporting paddy was interrelated. Westerners were in no position to secure paddy, for collection was in the hands of Chinese middlemen with whom Chinese millers made arrangements. When competition was intense, these millers could send Chinese agents into the interior to ensure a continuous supply. Moreover, the major foreign markets for Siamese rice were Singapore, Hong Kong and South China, where the importing firms were largely Chinese. The British consul in 1897 lamented, "It is impossible under the conditions of trade prevailing in the East for the European to compete with the astute Chinaman in (the rice) business."[33]

As the Chinese gained dominance in rice milling, many Western mills sold out to Chinese millers and those that burned down were abandoned and not replaced. By 1907, there were 49 rice mills in the

A well-known Chinese merchant in Sampeng, Tiansang Chungyampin (1866–1927).

kingdom, most of which belonged to Chinese, with only three under Western control. By 1925, only one of 84 rice mills in Siam was Western-owned.[34]

The Chinese capitalists who gained hegemony over the rice industry between 1855 and 1930 spawned several generations and did not comprise a homogenous group. As the kingdom's dominant economic group in the mid-19th century, the rich Chinese *khunnang* and tax farmers were among the first to invest in the growing rice industry, namely Phraya Boribun-Kosakorn (Li Tit Guan),[35] Phraya Phisan-Pholpanich (Koh Hong Lee and Guan Tit Lee),[36] L. Xavier,[37] Luang Sophon-Petcharat (Gim Seng Lee),[38] Phraya Choduk-Rachasretthi (Lau Beng Seng),[39] and Phra Phibun-Patanakorn (Tan Siang Gee Jang).[40]

Meanwhile, an altogether new generation of Chinese entrepreneurs emerged over the late 19th century and early 20th century. Unlike their predecessors, they had neither political patronage, royal connections nor government appointments. Rather, they were port merchants who expanded their businesses by establishing their own marketing networks and financial channels in the intra-Asian rice trade encompassing the three major port cities of Shantou, Hong Kong and Singapore.[41] Their operations were characterized by links to overseas branches or head offices outside Bangkok. Their businesses involved importing manufactured goods from and exporting rice and other local products to China and the Straits Settlements. The Koh Mahwah and Wanglee families exemplified this pattern of business development.

In 1871, Tan Tsuhuang (Wanglee), the son of Tan Suang-E who had apprenticed with Koh Chun, arrived from Hong Kong to establish his buying office in Siam.

Koh Chun's grandson, Phra Phisan-Pholpanich, the owner of Koh Hong Lee rice mills, in Chinese Mandarin and Thai *khunnang* garb.

Other members of the Tan family went to establish branches in Singapore, Muar and Saigon. In Bangkok, Tan Tsuhuang married into one of the oldest and most illustrious *chaosua* houses, the Poshyananda family. He established two rice mills with modern machinery to produce rice for the family network around the region. Subsequently, the business expanded to four rice mills, textile import, insurance, remittance bureaus, property and shipping. With its extensive regional network, the Wanglee family became one of the most successful among this new generation of Chinese entrepreneurs centered on port cities.[42]

Another success story was Mah Tongcheng, who arrived in Bangkok as a coolie in the late 19th century. He worked as an assistant to a German rice mill engineer and learned to maintain and repair modern machinery. Subsequently, he accumulated capital to invest in one of the largest rice mills in 1917.[43] To this, his son Mah Lapkun Bulakul added another rice mill, a bank, an insurance company, a shipping business and a network of companies in both Hong Kong and Singapore.

Straits-born Chinese such as Tan Kimcheng, Tan Kahkee and Na Kimseng (who was a director of Sze Hai Tong Banking Corporation of Singapore)[44] also established rice mills in Bangkok. In the last half of the 19th century, millers were earning enviable profits, and some Chinese firms had acquired large fortunes. Prominent in the rice trade were the Teochew Koh Mahwah (Kovatana),[45] his son-in-law Ngo Hiepyu (Hemachayat) of Kwang Hup Seng, Tan Tsuhuang (Wanglee), Low Banseng and Lee Taihua (Nandabhiwat). Of other dialect groups, Cantonese traders such as Leong Shaushan and Mah Lapkun were quite active in rice trade, but the Hakka and Hailam were not. The exception to the rule, briefly in the 1920s, was the Lamsam family.[46]

Typically the Chinese overseas network tended to use family, kinship, region and dialect ties to construct an inner circle of the fiduciary community, which in turn conspired to set up selective criteria for recruiting employees to achieve internal corporate harmony and smooth business relations.[47] Large profits from the rice trade enabled these families to develop other institutions required by the business, such as carriers, remittance bureaus, shipping companies or agencies, and hostels.

By the first decade of the 20th century however, the trade was anything but flourishing, despite the larger export volume. Exchange rate fluctuations and competition between the mills contributed to diminishing profit margins. The rice crop failure during the consecutive years of 1909 and 1910 escalated the domestic price of rice, and failure in finding sufficient supply caused many bankruptcies among the major rice traders, including Tom Ya, whose vision to trade in the London market had turned sour.[48] The rice crisis created a financial crisis in which four Bangkok banks failed between 1907 and 1913, namely Yu

Seng Heng Bank, Monthon Bank, Bangkok City Bank and Bank Chin Siam.[49] Soon the privy purse, who was the major financier of the rice industry in those days, became the largest owner of Bangkok rice mills as the Chinese businesses failed.

Competition and ephemeral price levels also drove the market to new grounds further away from Bangkok, while development of technology and competitive advantage allowed new entrants to the market. Soon, fierce competition from newly established upcountry rice mill operators, who had better control of the purchase price as well as lower transportation costs, overshadowed the Bangkok mills. The new Rice Trader Association was formed by merging two rice merchants' guilds in 1924. The merger was led by Tan Gimleng (Kiangsiri) and a group of rice merchants representing upcountry rice mills, their offices lining Songwad Road.[50]

Strong demand and high prices led to further expansion of rice cultivation in the Siamese Central Plain in tune with the other rice-growing regions of Burma, Cambodia and Vietnam. Simultaneously, in the early 1920s, the United States, Canada, Australia and Argentina expanded wheat cultivation. During these years, it seemed as though harvest fluctuations in the two grains were complementary: good years in wheat offset bad years in rice, and vice versa. However, from about 1926, the price of both grains began to slide.[51] Then, in 1928, there was a bumper harvest in both wheat and rice. In the following year, the ominous 1929, Canada had to put yet another good harvest into the wheat market due to lack of storage space as the 1928 crop was still in store—and suddenly, the price

Chinese rice mill in Bangkok, circa 1910.

THE DEVIL'S BUSINESS

During the first quarter of the 20th century, two very wealthy rice merchants, Tom Ya and Lee Teck-ow, were given the same *khunnang* title of Luang Jitchamnong-Vanich. Although they assumed the honorary titles at different points in time, both were bankrupted by the volatile rice market. Tom Ya, a native Thai, was appointed Luang Jitchamnong-Vanich during the last days of King Chulalongkorn's reign, while Lee Teck-ow, a Teochew merchant from the Lee (Li) family of Chenghai County near Shantou, was appointed Luang Jitchamnong-Vanich under the reign of King Vajiravudh. Although the two men came from different backgrounds and had different aspirations, they shared the same determination to face and corner the rice market; hence, their stories are worth retelling.

Tom Ya

Tom Ya's father died when he was young and his mother remarried Chaophraya Aphairaja-Yuktithamthorn (M.R. Lop Suthat). Through his stepfather's connections, Tom Ya became a royal page for the crown prince Maha Vajirunhis, who died in 1895. He then left the palace and married Chaem, the eldest daughter of Chaosua Yom, one of the richest real estate developers in Bangkok.

Yom was the third son of Phraya Phison-Sombatbul (Yim), the sugar tycoon who also owned the Chao Phraya steamship that serviced the Bangkok–Singapore route during the reign of King Mongkut. However, it was real estate development that fascinated Yom and he became the promoter for the opening of the Sathorn Canal in Bangkok. Yom was also one of the four promoters of Siam Canal, Land and Irrigation Company, established in 1888 to develop irrigated paddy fields in Rangsit. Unfortunately, Yom died young, in his 30s. The responsibility of managing the business empire, including more than 86 *rai* of land along Sathorn Road, a beautiful mansion in a large garden (which would later house the embassy of the USSR), and "several thousand *rai*" of paddy in Rangsit, passed over to Yom's eldest daughter, who was married to Tom Ya, on behalf of her younger siblings.[52]

Following his wife's inheritance of several thousand *rai* of paddy in Rangsit, Tom Ya decided to invest in two modern rice mills. Instead of selling his product through the Hong Kong and Singapore agents, which charged 2 and 3 percent selling commissions respectively, Tom Ya appointed D.M. Hon as his representative in London with a retainer fee of £100 a month. His European market strategy was very profitable, and he committed to a six-month, fixed-price contract. Unfortunately, in 1909 a flood severely damaged the local crop, and in 1910 a drought followed. The price of rice skyrocketed and Luang Jitchamnong-Vanich (Tom Ya) was sued for bankruptcy. With three entire generations of cumulative wealth from Chaosua Yim, the sugar tycoon, and Chaosua Yom, the real estate tycoon, wiped away, Tom Ya died of heartbreak soon after.[53]

Lee Teck-ow

Lee Teck-ow was born in Chenghai County near Shantou. His second uncle Lee Taihua (Nandabhiwat) had left home and become a successful rice merchant in Bangkok before establishing two rice mills in 1899. Teck-ow's third uncle Lee Tainguang, father of Lee Ben (Bencharit), oversaw the Lee (Li) trading firm at Connaught Road West in Hong Kong. When he was 10, Lee Teck-ow was sent to Hong Kong while his brother Lee Teck-koi was sent to Bangkok as an apprentice in the rice trade. In Hong Kong, Teck-ow grew up wildly and developed spendthrift habits. He was caught stealing thousands of dollars from his uncle and was jailed for several days before the uncle dropped the charges and sent him packing to Bangkok with 4,000 dollars.[54]

After surveying the market, Lee Teck-ow opened a silk shop in Sampeng. By deeply undercutting prices, his shop became very popular, helping to establish his reputation as an able trader. According to a family tale, Teck-ow was so engrossed in business that he slept with an abacus by his side.[55] Soon he established a rice-trading firm called Lee Khun Seng. As a brilliant young trader, his reputation attracted partners and financial supporters for the newly founded company, which operated by renting old defunct mills from the privy purse. His brother Lee Teck-koi, who had a special gift in mechanical matters, oversaw the reconditioning of the old mills. By the mid-1910s, Lee Teck-ow had five rice mills under control with an accumulated profit of 4 million baht.[56]

During World War I, noticing the absence of German shipping, Lee Teck-ow entered the shipping industry by renting 10 ships of approximately 2,000–3,000 tons each to service the routes between Bangkok, Haikou, Hong Kong, Shantou and Singapore. The rapid rise of Lee Teck-ow put the Chinese merchants on the mainland and Haikou in awe. His fortune was estimated to be over 10 million baht by the end of the war.[57]

However, in Bangkok his rise was complicated by several forgery lawsuits. Lee Teck-ow's strategy had always been to drive prices to the extreme. However, in 1917, a flood damaged about 20 percent of the rice paddies in Siam; then in 1919, a drought damaged approximately 43 percent. Meanwhile, the price of rice in the international market continued to rise. British and Japanese firms competed to buy rice for export, raising the price in Bangkok from 9.61 baht per *hap* to 19.27 baht. While other traders stalled, Lee continued to buy. At the end of the season, he had accumulated about 70 percent of the total rice stock in Siam. The price and shortage of rice created a political crisis. To push down the price, the government prohibited further rice exports, a measure used from time to time to keep the cost of living stable. Lee Teck-ow sought ways to make several "secret sale contracts" with international buyers, one of which was D.M. Hon. Meanwhile, claiming that the rice was Lee's old stock, Lee recevied special permission from the court to export, allowing him to meet his international obligations.[58] Thus, he not only avoided bankruptcy but ended up making huge profits as well.

That same year, when Queen Saovabha, Vajiravudh's mother, passed away, Lee Teck-ow arranged an elaborate Chinese funeral rite to honor the late Queen Mother. Lee became a committee member of the Chinese Chamber of Commerce in 1917 and 1919, and the vice chairman in 1923. By 1920, Lee Teck-ow's business included 10 rice mills, shipping firms, and huge investments in real estate. He took over Hua Heng Bee from his uncle Lee Taihua, whose business had failed, as well as numerous assets of other failed rice merchants. Among his charitable works, Lee Teck-ow was the first manager of Peiying Chinese School for Teochew children in Bangkok. In 1922 King Vajiravudh conferred upon him the title of Luang Jitchamnong-Vanich.

In the local market, Lee Teck-ow's habit of price manipulation coupled with hard-driven undercutting had earned him the nickname *sieow chik* or "the crazy seventh," mimicking the honorific name of *chik sia* or "the seventh master," a common moniker for the seventh son of a well-to-do family.

Problems arose towards the end of the reign of King Vajiravudh. Lee Teck-ow was sued by D.M. Hon in 1924 and was jailed for another offence in 1925.[59] While his risky style of price manipulation rapidly raised him to great wealth, in the end it finally bankrupted him during the depression years of 1929–30. Lee left for Shantou in exile, where he died a mysterious death. His family suspected that he was poisoned.[60]

of wheat collapsed. The combined effect of enormous grain surpluses in the temperate west and the tropical east brought the price of all grains down to pitiful levels. The price of grains remained low until 1933, underpinning the depression experienced by the world during those years.[61]

The impact of the depression in the East was swift and devastating. The tax farming sector disappeared entirely from the rice business. Several rice trading companies in Bangkok failed, including very well-established firms, such as Gim Seng Lee, Lau Beng Seng, Tan Siang Gee Jang, Kwang Hup Seng (in 1931), Koh Mah Wah (in 1931) and Lee Khun Seng (in 1931). The last belonged to Luang Jitchamnong-Vanich (Lee Teck-ow) of the Lee (Li) family, who was at the time the leading Teochew miller handling over 60 percent of Bangkok's exports.[62]

The City

During the great economic transformation that swept across the country and spurred Siam's rice-export boom, Bangkok served as the most important point of contact with the new capitalist world economy. The city was the bridge between the new Westernized capitalist world and the old traditional world of the Siamese. The greatest impact from the forces of change was demonstrated first in the city itself, then continued to reshape the traditional state, economy and society. Although the city had always existed in Siam—Ayudhya had been a great city during the previous era—it became fundamentally changed.

The old city of the mandala state was laid out in concentric circles. In the innermost circle, temples and the king's palaces dominated. The next ring of settlements comprised the homes of the princes, government officials, retainers and families.[63] The mercantile quarters made up the outer ring, which was usually located outside the city wall, surrounding the inner core, and spreading into the countryside. Siam's integration into the world economy began to turn the traditional urban arrangement inside out. Increasingly, the center of gravity of the city shifted from the palace grounds to the commercial quarter. From Sampeng, Bangkok's Chinatown, the city extended down Charoen Krung to form a new commercial heart around Siphraya, Silom and Sathorn. Thus, the citadel gave way to the market as mammon became king and economic gain became the *raison d'être* of the city, as well as the driving force of most who came to live there whether peasant, Chinese emigrant or Western profiteer.

Bangkok and the new towns that sprouted up expanded rapidly to become the epicenters of new, intensified economic energies. A case in point is Phuket, which was transformed from a sleepy fishing village into a modern, Westernized town, becoming the first provincial city in the kingdom to have paved roads and automobiles after 1910. Led by Bangkok, the other port cities and urban locations that developed or expanded during Siam's economic boom became conduits for funneling rice, tin, timber and other local products into the world and regional colonial markets. The main function of the cities and towns was to serve trade and commerce by draining the country of its primary products and pumping in consumer goods.

In the process of fulfilling their economic roles, cities and towns were also reinvented as important communications and administrative centers for the surrounding countryside. Inland towns became junctions for networks of rail and roads, which transported not merely rice, tin, kerosene, powdered milk and textiles but also people and ideas. At the same time, improved communications facilitated the buildup of increasingly elaborate administrative systems ranging from health outreach networks to police outposts and educational centers. The interactions between town networks and administrative systems further reinforced each other.

Various Chinese herbal drinks in Yaowarat, Bangkok's Chinatown.

From the towns moved carriers of modern values, Westernized urban culture, and Chinese emigrants seeking job opportunities and livelihoods in Siam's newly opened and expanding frontier hinterlands. In the city it became common for people, especially Chinese emigrants, of one ethnic or dialect group to live in the same quarter, which created ethnic enclaves dominated by people of a certain speech group. The center of Bangkok's Talad Noi was a Hokkien colony where the Hokkien Association was located. The Teochew concentrated around the waterfront of Songwad, Talad Plu, Tanon Tok and in the heartland of Sampeng. The Hailam built their shrines in their villages at Klong Padung-Krung-Kasem, between Hua Lampong and Talad Noi, as well as Samsen. The Hakkas were spread in small niches on Charoen Krung Road near Plubplachai, Tha Din Daeng in Thonburi, Talad Plu and Yaowarat.

Increasingly, ethnic, class, and social diversity created opportunities for specialization, skill development and creating relationships with others of differing backgrounds and experiences, affording new points of common interest and expanding liberty of thought and action. The cultural melting pot of the city became the platform that engendered an overarching, inclusive sense of ethnic identity—regardless of regional differences—necessary for the emergence of both Chinese and Siamese nationalism and their fateful clash after the turn of the century.

The city also tended to increase proximity among strangers, leading to a sense of insecurity. Seeking new forms of social security or self-improvement, urbanites created voluntary associations. Professional and commercial guilds, recreational clubs, study groups and religious societies, among others, blossomed in the city of Bangkok. Merchants comprised the best-organized Chinese social group. They established professional guilds organized according to a common service, craft or product, as well as *huikuan*, which were organized according to a common place of origin. Each of these associations or clubs set out to create and advance common interests, embodying the desire of city dwellers for improvement. The activities of voluntary associations trained members in organizing groups, running meetings, keeping accounts, transmitting information and other organizational skills.

This aspiration for improvement was also made manifest in the emergence of a modern school system whose locus was in the capital city. Siam's integration into the world economy did not only result in the growth of an export economy, improved maritime communications with the world, and the installation of a railway and road system, it also brought modern education. In addition to the Western consumer goods that entered the country, a Western model of education was introduced as well.

Western colonialism and Western aggrandizement came armed not only with gunboats but also with a powerful discourse on civilization and enlightenment that justified conquest and domination.[64] Under the threat of Western colonization, which claimed the mission of bringing enlightenment through the liberation of Asians from ignorance and godlessness, Siamese rulers found it necessary to demonstrate that it was already doing as much as neighboring colonial governments to spread knowledge and civilization among the kingdom's populace. In fact, the Siamese government outdid the neighboring colonial administrations with the exception of the Philippines in spreading education in the kingdom.

Pu-Yi (Xuantong), last Emperor of China (reigned 1908–12).

By the mid-1930s, 45,000 Siamese students out of a population of 14 million were enrolled in secondary schools. In addition, considerable numbers of students were studying at universities overseas at a higher rate than any other country in the region except the Philippines. Soon after came the rise of the newspaper, with public education spreading basic literacy and voluntary associations clamoring to propound their views on social improvement. With Siam's increased literacy, the press became a vitally important tool in the dissemination and discussion of new ideas.

By the 1890s, most of the principal cities in the region already had at least one local newspaper publishing fairly regularly, as well as a host of smaller, less regular weeklies and monthlies—often published by voluntary associations. Few coffee shops or tea houses, even in the rural villages, did not offer a newspaper from time to time, which could be read aloud to the illiterate and argued over by budding politicians.[65] In the realm of literacy and robust dialogue, Siam in this era was not out of touch; in fact it was a pace setter.

The first newspaper, the *Bangkok Recorder*, which was published monthly in Thai and English, appeared in Bangkok as early as 1844. It was founded by a famous and influential American Protestant missionary, Dr. Dan Beach Bradley (1804–73). In 1903, the first Chinese newspaper, the *Hanjing Ribao*, pioneered by Cantonese emigrants, was established in Bangkok. Subsequently, other Chinese-language newspapers, such as the *Tongqiaobao* and *Meinan Ribao*, appeared in Bangkok, largely initiated by Cantonese.

The editors of the Chinese newspapers in Siam during these times were split into several political factions reflecting the major contending groups in Chinese politics. The reformist pro-monarchy newspaper at the time was the *Qinan Xinbao*, while the anti-Manchu Chinese newspaper was the *Huaxian Xinbao*. The announcement of a capitation tax on Chinese immigrants in 1909, for example, was one of the issues that engaged the kingdom's nascent local and foreign-language press in a robust debate as opposing political camps publicized their views through newspapers. This led to the Chinese general strike of 1910, which was to have reverberating effects on the entire populace of Siam.

After the turn of the century, Chinese nationalism and political conflicts between reformists and revolutionists in the Chinese mainland became projected overseas and was re-enacted in the politics of the Chinese diaspora throughout Southeast Asia, including Siam. The majority of Chinese in Siam lived in urban areas, especially in the capital; hence, it was characteristically in the cities that modern Chinese politics and cultural activity found its liveliest expression.

The Chinese Xinhai Revolution of 1911 was largely financed by overseas-Chinese capital; many of Bangkok's wealthy Chinese merchants were among the prominent donors to the Chinese revolutionary cause. The abdication of the Manchu emperor in 1912 was greeted with euphoria in the Chinese-dominated cities of Singapore, Manila, Saigon and Bangkok, fueling an explosion of Chinese nationalism and leading to the expansion of Chinese schools all over Southeast Asia. The boom in Chinese education was reflected in the proliferation of study and reading clubs with political overtones and a flourishing, Chinese popular press in Bangkok.

The outpouring of Chinese patriotic sentiment through the Chinese educational movement fed into a highly polarized split more than a decade later, this time between the Nationalist Guomindang (abbreviated as GMD or KMT) and the Chinese Communist Party (CCP) in 1927. The intensity of overseas-Chinese identification with the political developments in the Chinese mainland greatly fostered internal Chinese cohesion and awareness of Chinese distinctness. With

Koh Gueyin, Koh Chun's great grandson, undergoing a Thai-Brahmanic top-knot cutting ceremony upon coming of age.

a newly strengthened sense of overarching Chinese identity that transcended dialect and provincial backgrounds, overseas Chinese faced an obstacle to assimilation in host societies. Suspicious of where Chinese loyalties lay, the Siamese responded with an unprecedented growth of anti-Chinese sentiment.

If education and the popular press was the vehicle of new ideas, the city was its cradle. Bangkok eventually became the stage where the recipients and producers of new ideas—the urban intelligentsia—clashed. At the turn of the 20th century, the city, like her nascent intelligentsia, was small by contemporary standards. But its importance lay outside the realm of numbers. Its importance lay in the city's ability to give birth to a new, intellectual elite whose aims and ideas owed much to the West and its organizational forms. This new elite was influenced not only by the phenomena of urbanization and Western education, but also by the presence in its midst of a powerful, alien, Chinese mercantile community in the throes of ideological ferment in an Asian region on the threshold of revolutionary change.

Assimilation

Since the Ayudhya period, the Siamese court had always encouraged Chinese assimilation, which had continued through the early Bangkok period. Economic and cultural intercourse with the Chinese created a remarkable royal precedent whereby prominent Chinese merchants who rendered services to the Siamese court were ennobled and absorbed into the Siamese ruling elite through marital ties, leading to the emergence of a new, wealthy, noble middle class. This was in sharp contrast to the Chinese experience in neighboring colonial territories, such as British Malaya, the Philippines and the Netherlands Indies, where Chinese were persistently distinguished as Chinese. Unlike the hospitable attitude of the Siamese royalty, European racial prejudice made marriage into the white ruling class a social taboo.

In all the colonial territories, the white ruling class took steps to prevent Chinese from mixing with the native populace by requiring that they be segregated into their own quarters under their Chinese *capitan*. In the Netherlands Indies, the Dutch passed a number of measures that tended to differentiate the Chinese from the native Indonesian populace. Since the 17th century, Chinese had been separated from the native population and confined to special ethnic settlements. In these settlements, the Chinese were organized under their own leaders, customs and languages. After the rebellion of 1734, segregation was tightened and a special permit was required for a Chinese to live outside the Chinese quarters.[66]

This was quite different from the Siamese case where the Chinese immigrant, after paying the standard poll tax, was permitted complete freedom of movement within the kingdom. The colonial system was not much different in British Malaya, where the Chinese Protectorate System was institutionalized to prevent the Chinese from assimilating into the Malay population as well as segregating them sharply from the white ruling class. Colonial citizenship was not easily granted.[67] Consequently, there were many second- and third-generation Chinese in British Malaya to whom no other citizenship was available to them other than Chinese.

The strong consciousness of race that the British brought with them had been responsible for the terms of their treaties with the Malays as well as their attitude towards Chinese and Indian immigrants in the colonies. None of the latter who suffered British racial discrimination held a national perspective or identity until they learned the painful lesson from their British masters. As a result of these clearly defined racist policies, the Chinese subjects in all the colonial territories tended to "remain Chinese." By contrast, the Siamese government regarded all Chinese immigrants who were not European subjects as Siamese subjects.

The Siamese experience proved that in the absence of policy obstacles, Chinese immigrants demonstrated a natural tendency to assimilate into the native populace. The pull of Siamese civilization had always been strong, although little effort was ever exerted by the Siamese government beyond their well-known position that Chinese descendants in the kingdom were considered Siamese subjects and were treated as such. Under an Asian ruling class with whom the Chinese could identify, the process of assimilation continued naturally, and the descendants of early Chinese immigrants have long since been absorbed into the present-day Thai race. Moreover, the primary interests of second- and third-generation Chinese in the kingdom—epitomized by the conspicuous conversion of the merchant class into Siamese Buddhists—quite certainly lay in the land of their adoption. In the eyes of the Siamese ruling elite, second- and third-generation Chinese immigrants were not considered Chinese at all. Nowhere was this more conspicuous than at the apex of the Siamese social hierarchy, where the royal household traditionally took the daughters of wealthy, ennobled Chinese merchants as royal consorts.

The same pattern of assimilation existed among the Chinese occupying the lower rungs of the social hierarchy. In fact, many hardheaded, money-minded, Chinese petty traders married clever, tactful, politically minded Siamese women. Their union produced a new generation who considered themselves Siamese and took insult if they were ever called "Chinese." These assimilated Chinese differentiated themselves from the wave of newly arrived Chinese immigrants who were considered their social inferiors.

Kenneth Landon, writing in 1941, described a touching personal encounter:

Many Thai-Chinese grew their hair and fashioned it back to the traditional Manchu-style queue. This picture of Koh Gueyin was taken on his wedding day.

*A prominent Chinese merchant whose face was unmistakably Chinese
and whose father was Chinese although his mother was Thai, took
immediate offence when he was playfully called a "Chek"—this was in
spite of the fact that his shop signs were in Chinese, that he spoke two
Chinese dialects, that he kept his accounts in Chinese, sent his children
to a Chinese school. He himself spoke Thai perfectly, regarded himself
as Thai and particularly supported the modern nationalist movement
with large donations to the armed forces.*

The man described by Landon was typical of many Thai-Chinese. It was
common knowledge that most of the well-to-do commoner families who
formed the bureaucratic official class in the reign of King Chulalongkorn had
Chinese blood in their veins. Paradoxically, it was this official class, born of King
Chulalongkorn's bureaucratic reforms, that formed the main constituency of the
Siamese nationalist People's Party whose policies had a decidedly anti-Chinese
character in the 1930s.

Local Chinese Leaderships

H.S. Hallet, an Englishman who visited the kingdom in 1884, declared, "the
Chinamen in Siam seem to be ubiquitous. Half the population of the Menam
delta—the Bangkok area—is Chinese and very few of the people are without
some trace of Chinese blood in them."[68] The Chinese population in the
kingdom had become so large that they no longer formed a "community" with
established leaders who could be coopted by the court, such as the Choduk-

Kosol Hoontrakul
(left), leader of the
Hailam community,
and his two
younger brothers.

Rachasretthi or *capitan* China.[69] The Chinese now were simply
too many, too varied, too mobile and too scattered for the old
technique to work. Moreover, many were scattered in the newly
opened frontier tracts and railheads all over the country, far
from Bangkok. New patterns of concentration and dispersion
made the authorities' attempts to control the Chinese much
more difficult.

The turn of the 20th century saw a changing of the guards
of the Chinese leadership in Siam. New elites usurped the
leadership of local Chinese. After the Angyi Act of 1898 banned
Chinese secret societies, the professional guilds and *huikuan*
were no longer able to inhabit the shadowy zone straddling the
self-defense civil society and the criminal underworld.

The official registers of the Chinese guilds and their *huikuan* offer a glimpse into the emerging new elites and their social networks within the Chinese community at the time. The Hailam *huikuan* was registered in 1905 by Wun Tokkeng (Hoontrakul) and the Hakka Association followed suit in September 1908. The Bangkok Chinese Club, a front for the underground Tongmenghui, which was founded by Seow Hoodseng (Sribunruang), was registered in 1907. In August 1909, a group of prominent merchants who were mostly reformists, including Koh Huijia, Sophon-Petchrat (Tia Giangsam of Gim Seng Lee),[70] Tan Tengbo (Vadthanakul),[71] Liao Chiangsoon (Sethbhakdi),[72] Ng Miaongian (Lamsam)[73] and Tan Lipbuay (Wanglee) banded together to establish the Chinese Chamber of Commerce (CCC) in Siam.

Tan Lipbuay (Wanglee).

Among the new elites were the council of the CCC and the leaders of the professional guilds and voluntary associations. The next most influential group was the Chinese newspapermen, like Seow Hoodseng, who were affiliated with the mushrooming voluntary associations spawned by the city.

Finally, the philanthropists, whose generous donations supported the construction of schools, hospitals and other charitable organizations that provided for poor immigrants, made up a significant number of new elites. Their generous contributions were not limited to Siam but extended to cover the cause of modernization, reform or revolution in China, which bought them history's immortal accolades. Although these new elites and their affiliated organizations differed in their political stances and often conflicted during the first half of the 20th century, they shared a common objective—to help the Chinese ancestral homeland in its hour of need.

An Overseas-Chinese Policy

Siamese history has been pockmarked with incidents of Chinese unrest. Several times in the 1840s and 1870s, troops had to be mobilized to quell riots and restore order. The southern town of Ranong was "almost lost to the government" during a miners' riot in the 1870s. When a gunboat was sent to put down the miners' rebellion, the Chinese mob reacted by rioting in Phuket, burning and looting the town. In 1889, rival Chinese gangs fought pitched battles in the center of the capital for several days. When King Chulalongkorn attempted to increase the Chinese poll tax in 1910, the Chinese rioted and called a general strike, which shut down the city of Bangkok for three days until troops arrived to enforce order.

The capability of the organized urban Chinese community to shut down Bangkok for several days gave the Siamese rulers grave concerns about the implications of a complete Chinese ascendency over the country's economy, commerce, ports, transport, utilities and urban services. Repeated incidents of Chinese rebelliousness fed a growing sense of insecurity among the Siamese ruling

The landing of Japanese troops and the advance of the senior command of the 2nd Army to Yung-Ching in Shantung during the Sino-Japanese War on 25 January 1895.

elite concerning the loyalty of the kingdom's powerful economic minority—a loyalty that until lately had always been taken for granted.

At a time when relations between the Siamese government and the Chinese minority was becoming increasingly strained, changes in Chinese government policy on emigration introduced a further complication. While Siam had always maintained a positive attitude towards Chinese immigration and encouraged it, China had traditionally never encouraged its people to leave its shores. Since the Ming dynasty, China had regarded emigrants as unpatriotic or as criminals and rebels deserving execution.

However, China's humiliation at the hands of the Western powers had necessitated a change of attitude. During the military confrontations with the Western industrial powers, China's hard power was found wanting. Consequently, China was belatedly forced to revalue other potential sources of soft power at its disposal, in particular its overseas-Chinese resources. In fact, until lately, China had shown no interest in its overseas Chinese; almost no effort was expended to study or gather information about them. Western colonial officials had a better understanding than the Chinese government of the overseas Chinese, many of whom had become colonial subjects.[74]

After China's military defeat in the Sino-Japanese War of 1895, a growing awareness emerged within the reform-minded Chinese intelligentsia that overseas Chinese had been exposed to many aspects of Western modernity by living in regions colonized by the European industrial powers. Thus, overseas Chinese had successfully acquired wealth, modern techniques and entrepreneurial skills. With this awareness came the recognition of the potential advantages of allying with overseas Chinese whose wealth and skills could be harnessed for the great task of strengthening and modernizing China. Moreover, large numbers of overseas Chinese were still recognizably Chinese and felt discriminated against by the policies of the colonial governments.[75]

Meanwhile, outside China at the turn of the century, the expanding Chinese diaspora throughout the Nanyang, including Siam, felt growing shame that the Manchu government did so little to help the victims of the extensive coolie trade and to prevent discrimination against Chinese.[76] Overseas Chinese had no protection other than that offered by traditional secret societies and self-help or self-defense organizations. When the new commercial treaties offered consular protection to colonial subjects during the late 19th century, some overseas Chinese availed themselves of this new insurance against the risks and uncertainties of the overseas-Chinese world. Nanyang Chinese from the Straits Settlements preferred to travel to China as British subjects because they enjoyed the benefits of British consular protection against the extortionate demands of menacing, corrupt Manchu officials.[77]

However, this protection was available only to a privileged minority among the overseas Chinese. The most disadvantaged and uneducated Chinese emigrants were condemned under the exploitative system of Chinese contract labor within the colonial territories where they received little or no protection from the Chinese government.[78] The situation of the Nanyang Chinese differed somewhat in Penang, Singapore and Siam, where the Chinese were actively welcomed and where they eventually achieved social and economic dominance.

It was only near the turn of the century (1895–1912) that the overseas Chinese acquired a distinct and coherent identity transcending the division of the Chinese community into dialect groups. After centuries of neglect by the Manchu government, the overseas Chinese had finally come into their own as an influential social formation wielding substantial economic clout. The growing awareness both within and outside China of the phenomenon of the overseas Chinese was reflected in the increased use of the term *huaqiao*, meaning "Chinese person or community, residing abroad," to refer to overseas Chinese.[79]

One of the earliest Chinese leaders to draw attention to the importance of this overseas population was the loyalist reformer Kang Youwei. Ousted from power by the empress dowager's palace coup, which abruptly ended his One-Hundred-Day Reform in September 1898, Kang Youwei was forced into exile.[80] In 1900, during his exile, Kang Youwei toured the extensive Chinese diaspora of the Nanyang region. After the Manchu court had turned its back on his reform program, Kang's only hope of getting China on the track of

Kang Youwei
(1858–1927).

Empress dowager Tzu Hsi of China.

modernization was to gain the support of the overseas Chinese.

However, when he arrived in the Nanyang, Kang was dismayed to find that no prevailing consciousness of being part of the Chinese nation existed among the overseas Chinese. Worse, he was shocked and appalled by the rate at which the overseas Chinese were assimilating into their host cultures and communities.[81] Kang Youwei realized that it was not enough for China to launch a modernization campaign at home. To succeed, it was imperative for China to convince her own people of the superiority of the culture of their fatherland. Enlisting the overseas Chinese for the daunting task of modernizing China would prove impossible unless they identified wholeheartedly with their ancestral land.

Consequently, Kang felt it was first necessary to remind the Chinese people—especially the overseas Chinese who had fled poverty and political turmoil in their native land—of the glorious past of Chinese civilization. Kang Youwei traveled throughout the Nanyang preaching to overseas Chinese the importance of racial and blood ties with their ancestral homeland. He lamented the lack of classical education in the Chinese tradition among the overseas Chinese. He was dismayed by the second-generation Chinese emigrants' inability to master the language of their ancestors. He saw Chinese education as the most important tool for ensuring that the Chinese race retained Chinese cultural values and identity.[82] Kang Youwei sought to encourage the development of a Chinese consciousness through the establishment of a Chinese educational system throughout Southeast Asia.

Kang Youwei saw himself as a loyalist reformer in the classical Confucian tradition—his loyalty was to the emperor. Despite his rejection by the Manchu court, his mission was to promote China's modernization and to reform the Chinese empire into a constitutional monarchy with the Qing emperor as the true head of state. To accomplish this, he established the Association for the Protection of the Emperor, or Baohuanghui. However, to enlist the support of the overseas Chinese, the emergence of a Chinese consciousness would be crucial. Kang's campaign to rally support for the development of overseas Chinese education was part and parcel of his reform agenda. While mobilizing support for the Baohuanghui, Kang Youwei simultaneously propagated his Three Protections Doctrine: protect the nation, protect the race and protect education.[83]

Kang Youwei advocated the development of bilingual education in Chinese schools. Although he accepted the inclusion of English as part of the curriculum, seeing it as an essential tool of modernization, he regarded the teaching of standard Mandarin Chinese as the top priority. Chinese literacy was the most important means of fostering patriotism among the younger generation. Through

Chinese literacy, cultural and ideological ties with the ancestral homeland would be strengthened and the young generation would be less likely to identify completely with the native society of their host country.[84]

After the disastrous consequences of the Boxer Uprising at the turn of the century, the empress dowager realized that swift moves towards modernization might be the only way to save the Qing dynasty from extinction.[85] Ironically, after purging Kang Youwei, the loyalist reformer, the power elite around the empress dowager had come to his point of view that the Nanyang Chinese were not only in a position to help the Qing court, but they were also an essential factor in China's salvation. Closely monitoring the progress of Kang's flirtation with the overseas Chinese, the Manchus became convinced that financial support from their own Nanyang Chinese was a safer option for China's modernization projects than taking loans from the Western imperialist powers.

Moreover, gaining the goodwill of the overseas Chinese would also undermine the support enjoyed by dissident factions in the Nanyang region. More dangerous than Kang Youwei were the new breed of revolutionaries led by Sun Yatsen, who was also fundraising and campaigning for support among the overseas Chinese. Unlike Kang's Protection of the Emperor movement, the Tongmenghui's agenda wanted nothing less than full-scale revolution. Tongmenghui cadres were rallying the overseas Chinese to assist in the overthrow of the corrupt, oppressive, ineffectual Manchu regime and remake China as a republic.

By 1912, thousands of overseas Chinese had become involved in voluntary associations and political organizations that agitated for reform or revolution in China. Overseas Chinese had even produced their first martyrs in the abortive Huang Hua Kang Uprising in Canton in 1910.[86] Through their agitation, the reformers and revolutionaries aroused an intense public concern for the future of China. Their propaganda sought to exploit the age-old, anti-Manchu ideology of the Chinese secret societies, which were still alive and well in the overseas Chinese communities in the Nanyang. The Manchu court that had neglected the overseas Chinese for centuries was, after all, their archenemy. Indeed, the fall of the Ming in 1644 was the main reason why so many of their forebears had fled the ancestral homeland in the first place.

To deny the dissidents and revolutionaries the use of the Nanyang as a platform to launch their subversive activities, the Manchus broke with their long-standing tradition of disdainful neglect of the overseas Chinese. Instead, they sent envoys to establish official contacts with the Nanyang Chinese and garner as much financial support as possible.

Tan Suang-E in Chinese Mandarin attire.

Thus, early Manchu diplomacy with the overseas Chinese was characterized by the crude tactic of selling to wealthy Nanyang merchants and capitalists what they wanted most from the Qing court—that is, acceptance and recognition in the form of official positions and ceremonial gowns that could be bought with hard cash.[87]

Despite its apparent novelty in the colonial territories, this custom of awarding honorary titles and ceremonial gowns to leading members of the Chinese community had a precedent. According to the Bisalputra's spirit tablets, three generations in the family, namely, Koh Chun (1815–62), his son Koh Chin Sóó (1839–91) and his grandson Koh Leechai (1861–96), had the honorary titles of Feng Zhi Dafu, Zhi Zheng Dafu and Feng Zhi Dafu respectively. In the Wanglee clan, Tan Tsuhuang (1844–1921)[88] and his father Tan Suang-E, who founded a Hong Kong trading firm in the 1850s, were both awarded mandarin honors. Likewise, other Chinese merchants who donated substantial sums to help the homeland received honorary recognition. However, these precursors to the fundraising effort by the empress dowager's government, coupled with the transfer of Chinese labor remittances home, resulted in a large outflow of money from the Siamese economy. The Siamese government declared its grievance when the kingdom's Chinese subjects continued to make huge donations to charities in China while failing to pay tax concession obligations to the government.

As the 19th century drew on, the donations became larger and larger as evidenced by the higher honors held by Siamese-Chinese during the last days of the Qing dynasty. Phraya Phakdi-Phattrakorn (Lao Gibing, 劉繼賓), the monopoly tax farmer for opium, was awarded the Lanling (藍翎) official hat, as well as the Zijiangsanyanhualing (紫韁三眼花翎) official hat adorned with a peacock plume. In addition, he was bestowed the position of imperial commissioner in the Navy Affairs Office (文化殿大學士).[89] Phra Anuwat-Rajaniyom (Tae Teeyong), the wealthy operator of the *huay* lottery, was awarded the Rong Lu Dafu. Nevertheless, the fabled success story of the empress dowager's "Southern Expedition" by the Manchus rapidly improved the Qing court's position in relation to the overseas Chinese. By 1903, one of the most successful overseas-Chinese capitalists, Zhang Bishi,[90] was summoned twice for an audience with the empress dowager, who appointed him to an edified official position as her personal advisor on the question of China's modernization.[91]

Breaking the ice with the overseas Chinese through superficial activities like granting symbolic honors to wealthy Nanyang capitalists was easy. The difficult part lay in establishing the Manchu government's credibility with the masses of overseas Chinese who were being courted by anti-Manchu reformers and revolutionaries. To succeed against the competition, the Qing court had to show that they were doing at least as much for the welfare of the poor and

Motor cars in front of Ananta Samakom Throne Hall, which was built by King Chulalongkorn in a Western architectural style.

disadvantaged overseas Chinese—not just for rich capitalists.

Belatedly, the Manchu government decided to address the problems facing the overseas Chinese based on the presumption that the disadvantaged among them would welcome Chinese official recognition and protection. Consequently, the Chinese government had to acknowledge those aspects of international law, immigration regulations and colonial statutes pertinent to a new policy of active support for its Chinese subjects abroad.[92] The Qing court rapidly took a number of dramatic steps to legalize the position of Chinese living overseas. The imperial prohibitions against residence abroad had been taken off the books in 1893. As a gesture of goodwill projected to overseas subjects, the Qing government passed the Qing Code or Nationality Law in 1909 to legalize the position of Chinese abroad and to define their legal status.[93]

China's new nationality policy had far-reaching implications for Siam. Under the Qing Code of 1909, all children of a Chinese parent were considered Chinese subjects irrespective of where they were born. Evidently, the Manchu government intended to use the law as a means to claim ownership of China's newfound asset, namely, the vast resources of the overseas Chinese diaspora with its accumulated capital of financial, technical, and entrepreneurial assets, as well as skilled manpower.

The Qing Code of 1909 was in direct conflict with the Siamese claim that all children born in Siam were Siamese subjects unless they were registered by their parents as foreign nationals with the legations and embassies of those powers with whom Siam had treaty relations. This fundamental conflict in legal ideology was reflected in subsequent attempts by both countries to determine the number of Chinese in Siam.[94]

The Statistical Yearbook of Thailand (1939–44) registers the number of Chinese in the kingdom in 1939 as 524,062.[95] On the other hand, the Chinese Yearbook of 1938–39 gives the number of Chinese in Siam as 3,000,000. This means that out of a population of 14,464,105 in 1937, one out of five citizens of Siam were Chinese subjects. If Siam were to accede to the Manchu government's claim, the ownership and control of almost the entire economy and labor force would officially be in foreign hands. Moreover, Chinese capital and labor were the major driving forces behind King Chulalongkorn's modernization projects, causing the Siamese government to be very possessive of their Chinese subjects.

Besides this fundamental clash in legal ideology, there was another complication. China and Siam did not have treaty relations. Consequently, there was no Chinese embassy or representative office where Chinese parents could register their children. This led to the accusation that many Chinese children had been forced to become Siamese subjects against the wishes of their parents. With the awakening of a new nationalist consciousness at the turn of the century, Siamese law provided resident Chinese no opportunity to become Chinese subjects if they had been born in Siam. To rectify the problem, the Chinese government pressed for the establishment of treaty relations.

However, the conflict between Siamese law and the Qing Code of 1909, coupled with the problem of extraterritoriality, meant that if treaty relations were established Siam would have to host a massive population of foreigners with special rights and privileges. Consequently, the Siamese continued to resist Chinese overtures to establish formal treaty relations. In fact, formal diplomatic relations between Siam and China were not established until after the Pacific War in 1945.

From Mandala to Nation-State

At the end of the 19th century, Siam was remade from a mandala state to a modern nation-state, which involved a total overhaul of three interlocking frameworks of the traditional Siamese polity, namely, the monarchy, the old administrative system, and the ancient *phrai* social system based on population control and corvée labor. This constituted a paradigm change. Under the old system, the main function of the ruler as divine Lord of Life was simply to "be," symbolizing in his person an accepted social order and a cultural ideal reflecting a state of harmony between the terrestrial world and the cosmos.[96]

When King Chulalongkorn succeeded his father in 1868 and began his 42-year reign, this conception of the king as the axis of cosmic harmony was replaced by a more modern, Westernized conception of kingship. Imported concepts of the unified nation-state, nationality, national identity and centralized governing bureaucracy were imposed from the top down. The vision of a modern, progressive, strengthened Siamese state capable of holding its own against Western imperialist aggression and colonial takeover was embraced by the Siamese absolute monarchy. By the first decade of the 20th century, the new Siamese Leviathan could boast unprecedented powers: overwhelming military superiority, new technological prowess, modern infrastructure and larger revenues. The roadmap leading to the Siamese absolute monarchy was paved with revolutionary changes to the traditional Hindu-Buddhist state.

Reinventing the Monarchy

The transformation of the Siamese monarchy from a traditional Brahmanic Buddhist institution of kingship into a Westernized model of absolute monarchy reflects the story of its encounter with capitalist modernity, how it engaged that modernity, and was shaped by that modernity. The Siamese monarchy was not alone in having to cope with the dislocating forces of capitalism that accompanied the arrival of Western maritime hegemony in Asia—other Asian monarchies, including the Qing dynasty and Meiji Japan, faced the same threat. As Siam's exposure to the West increased, the critical issue facing the successive kings of the Bangkok dynasty was how to reform the polity to cope with the social changes of the market economy and to avoid the threat of colonization.

What the Siamese monarchy did was nothing extraordinary; it did what most Asian monarchies attempted to do with varying degrees of success—that is, to adopt Western organizational forms and features of the state system that they believed had made the West strong. Meiji Japan, especially, had adopted Western

Phra Meru built for the cremation of King Mongkut.

organizational methods and military technology as part of a self-strengthening movement to parry colonial takeover. In colonial, occupied territories, the reinvention of the state had been directed by the colonial governors who had displaced native rulers. In Siam, the same process of modernization and state reorganization was instituted by the Chakri court, which implemented policies to modernize the kingdom and reinvent the traditional Siamese state as a Western-style, Buddhist nation-state. This would change the entire political landscape of the region beyond recognition.

King Mongkut had been a reformist at heart. He had started his first reform while he was a monk. Noticing what he saw as serious discrepancies between the rules given in the Buddhist Cannon and the animistic practices of Siamese monks, Mongkut set up the Thammayut sect in 1833. In 1857, a few years after ascending the throne, King Mongkut sent a Siamese delegation to Britain to collect information on Western science, modern transportation and political institutions. He hired an English governess, Anna Leonowens, to teach English and Western manners to his children. Western advisors were employed to bring progress to Siam. The king told Leonowens he would "doubtless without hesitation abolish slavery for the distinguishing of my reign."[97]

King Mongkut also introduced secular ceremonies such as the King's Birthday and the Coronation Anniversary.[98] In addition, new orders of merit or honors were announced and presented during these events. As an adjunct to the Western notion of the birthday celebration, Mongkut introduced an innovative festival to commemorate the Birth, Enlightenment and Death of the Buddha. Much of what is distinctive in the pageantry of today's cult of the monarchy has its roots in the legacy of King Mongkut.

Through these celebratory activities, today's monarchy has become the focal point of loyalty and solidarity for an ethnically diverse Thai society, helping it to become a nation in the modern sense through the embodiment of its religious, social and political values in the person of the king. Through his leanings towards Western secularism and humanism, Mongkut led the way in changing the public image of the monarch from a divine, Brahmanic Lord of Life, sanctioned by the magical and supernatural rites of Brahman priests, to a human king assuming the

A Chinese funeral for Khun Thamrongpan-Phakdi's mother in Patani.

role of paramount defender of the realm, as well as patron of Siamese Buddhism.[99]

Thus, the Hinduistic ideology of divine kingship was replaced by the ideal of the Great Man. However, this reinvention of the role of the monarch begs the question, if the king no longer rules by divine right, then by what right does a mortal human king claim to rule? The justification provided is that he represents the Buddhist ideal of the Great Man who protects the realm and rules so that the welfare of the people may be improved.[100]

The implication of this secularization of the monarchy was far reaching. It undermined the basis of legitimacy of the old regime. The progressive erosion of the old idea of divine kingship tended to deprive the rites, rituals and ceremonies (which continue to be used to legitimize the institution of the monarchy) of their metaphysical significance and reduce them to the level of picturesque customs of a bygone age. Moreover, as demographic changes led to the predominance of Chinese in the kingdom's new market towns and urban centers, there was increasingly less propensity on the part of the populace to be moved by the sacred aura that once dominated the royal ceremonies.[101] By the 1930s, the "masses" had no longer any real understanding of the rites of tonsure, nor did they understand the significance of building Phra Meru, although they still retained "an innate love and respect for all forms of royal pageantry. It is the magnificence of the state procession, the splendor of the Urn enthroned upon the catafalque, or the brilliantly illuminated Phra Meru, that impress them that their king is a great king."[102]

In the end, it was this loss of understanding and respect for the rituals that had once led to the deification of the monarch as a living god that made it possible for a group of Siamese rebels, in 1932, to consider overthrowing the monarchy as a basis for the legitimacy of government. Moreover, without the divine mystique to legitimize and protect the monarchy, the king's claim to rule in the interest of the people could easily be turned against him. The Revolution of 1932 was justified on the grounds that absolute monarchy had not improved the welfare of the people. The rebels believed that under absolute monarchy, Siamese society had remained virtually unchanged, and Siam continued as a quaint backwater country where time stood still while the rest of the world rushed feverishly by.

As the old social order began to crumble under the onslaught of capitalist modernity, King Mongkut perhaps strove to restore a measure of order through the creation of a more hierarchically ordered kingdom under a more edified monarchy. Mongkut did not "rule" as such. Rather, somewhat like the Pope or the Chinese emperor, he reigned by issuing numerous decrees and royal proclamations that were not administrative orders but statements of principle or precepts that were intended to guide the actions of officials and subjects. Chris Baker interprets these orders as attempts to refine the specialness of the monarchy and to distance it from the rest of society:

> *"He laid down rules on the use of* rachasap, *the heavily Khmer-derived language for use in addressing the king ... forbade personal descriptions of the king ... ordered the use of regnal years for the calendar. He laid down a very precise hierarchy within the royal family based on age, the status of the mother and genealogical distance from the reigning king ... He changed inheritance laws to limit the extent to which polygamy might disperse family wealth, especially in the royal family. He laid down forms of address for every level of the social hierarchy from king to slave ... "*[103]

Building on the secular foundations of the monarchy established by his father, King Chulalongkorn took the reform of the monarchy a step further and in a new direction. While Mongkut's initiatives largely centered on the innovative use of ritual to reinvent the monarchy as the focal point of loyalty and solidarity for the Siamese people, Chulalongkorn changed it from a ritual to a decision-making institution. However, it would be misleading to argue that both Mongkut and Chulalongkorn deliberately intended to transform the role of the monarchy. Their main concern was to create a viable basis for legitimizing the Siamese polity at a time of secularism, humanism, populism and imperialism to avoid colonization. To that end, both kings saw that it was expedient to appease Western world opinion—to change the popular image of the Siamese monarchy from that of a god king ruling by supernatural right over a subject population, into the image of the Great Man serving his people by promoting true religion and morality.

Thus, the Chakri policy was primarily directed towards strengthening the Siamese polity against the threat of Western imperialism by making swift moves towards modernization. Indeed, Siam, a mandala state, was able to empower the monarchy and increase the effectiveness of its control over its own people through borrowing from the West.[104] However, in the process, the Chakri dynasty also changed the character and public image of the monarchy itself. In fact, the monarchy was so central to the traditional Siamese polity that any innovative actions on the part of the king had a retroactive impact upon the role of the monarchy.

Moreover, absolutism traditionally rested on sacred, ritually defined premises, which a modern role contradicted. Therefore, the kings had to simultaneously transform the monarchy as they modernized the country—a process that necessarily undermined the foundations of the traditional concept of kingship. In other words, King Chulalongkorn did not reform the government in his role as absolute monarch. Rather, he transformed and thereby subverted the traditional role of the monarchy itself. In so doing, he created a new role for the monarchy as "Head of Government" in contrast to "Head of State"—a role that King Mongkut had approximated as reigning monarch.

However, this function as Head of Government was also one that could not be monopolized by a hereditary ruling family indefinitely. The seizure of power by a commoner oligarchy in 1932 was in many ways a protest against the aggrandizement of power by the absolute monarchy and its attempt to monopolize all political power exclusively in the hands of the immediate royal family. Thus, the new function of Head of Government created by Chulalongkorn proved in the end to be ephemeral to the monarchy itself, although it was to become a permanent addition to the Siamese polity.[105] Hence, King Chulalongkorn had undermined the power of the monarchy even as he was trying to enhance it.

So momentous were the changes stemming from the transformation of the monarchy concurrent with the reform of the political, economic and social structures of the Siamese state that David Wyatt pronounced the course of Siamese history from 1910–41 as "essentially the political working out of the social consequences of the reforms of Chulalongkorn's reign." In fact, the real revolution was not the change of ruling oligarchies in 1932, but, rather, those changes initiated by King Mongkut and King Chulalongkorn in the second half of the 19th century that affected all aspects of political, social and economic life in the kingdom, as well as the nature of the monarchy itself.[106]

However, the changes in the role of the monarchy instituted by Mongkut and Chulalongkorn did not become fully apparent until the time of their successors. The problems of the reigns of King Vajiravudh and King Prajadhipok, culminating in the overthrow of the absolute monarchy in 1932, were in large part the natural consequences of the forces set in motion by the previous reign.[107] However, in retrospect, Siam could hardly have avoided the impact of Western imperialism. Even to the most superficial observer it was quite obvious that had Mongkut and Chulalongkorn not responded adequately to this challenge, they would have forfeited their rule and Siam would have been annexed as a colony—the fate that befell Burma.[108]

Reinventing the Bureaucracy

The primary result of the secularization of the monarchic role was the creation of a new, Westernized bureaucracy. The expansion of a comprehensive bureaucratic framework both built upon and hastened the pervasive economic transformation of the kingdom during the reign of Chulalongkorn. Government policy sought to reinforce the growing interconnectedness of bureaucratic and economic frameworks, which encompassed contract laws, railway development, tax collection, banking, immigration, education, the army, the navy, national integration, countrywide bureaucratic centralization, and the creation of new institutions.

Early Siamese post office.

In the economic sphere, the government encouraged the development of banks to facilitate the integration of Siam's rice-export economy into the world market. Initially most of the banks were British, including the Chartered Bank of India, Australia and China, and the Hong Kong Shanghai Banking Corporation. These were followed by US, French, Japanese and, shortly before World War II, nationalist Chinese banks. Together with local Chinese capitalists, overseas Chinese also founded a number of banks that confined their operations within the country. Chambers of commerce representing export-oriented interests in the kingdom's expanding commercial sector also became part of the evolving bureaucratic-economic framework.

Increasingly, officials extracting revenue from the expanding market economy, as well as entrepreneurs extracting profits, desired new methods to discipline people, mobilize resources and protect wealth. The growing population called for increasingly complex administrative methods that reliance on personal ties alone could not deliver. More and more people were rejecting the traditional political structure in favor of a modern conception of an effective state, which was already rapidly taking shape in neighboring colonial territories.

Thus, the kingdom's bureaucratic expansion occurred because of rapid economic growth, and this bureaucracy in turn served to further economic growth. Export taxes and revenue farms did much to finance the installation of bureaucracies and railways; railways in turn facilitated the expanding geographical reach of administration and enabled the government to collect taxes from outlying areas. King Chulalongkorn's bureaucratic modernization

SUNSET ON THE GAMBLING TAX FARMS

When the government began its gradual abolition of revenue farming, the last tax farms to be abolished were the vice taxes on opium, gambling and alcohol, which were based primarily on Chinese consumption. These tax farms had provided the Siamese state with a stable income to create a strong, centralized bureaucracy. Between 1888 and 1892, the number of gambling houses in Bangkok was reduced from over 400 to 16. The drop in gambling revenue was covered by income from the capitation tax and the revised land tax. By 1906–7, all the provincial dens were closed.

Faced with threats of closure, many gambling tax-farming clans began to diversify into other commercial activities. The second generation in particular began to use their accumulated wealth to invest in the new, capitalistic opportunities made possible by the expanded economy. Competition with the West was the goal of second-generation Chinese tycoons, among them Phra Sophon-Petcharat (Tia Giangsum) of Gim Seng Lee, the major concessionaire controlling spirits, opium and gambling, as well as several forest concessions in the north. Phra Swamipak-Bhuwanart (Tae Taichin), son of Khunphat Hoi (Tae Hoi), who operated several gambling dens in Sampeng and Talad Plu was another of these investors.

Tia Giangsam, known to the local Chinese as Po Gee Sia, was the only child of Luang Udonphanpanich, commonly called Arkon Tia U-Teng,[109] a self-made Teochew millionaire and managing partner of Gim Seng Lee. The list of tax monopolies awarded to Gim Seng Lee in Chiang Mai in 1894 was extensive; it included paddy, tobacco, coconut, betel nut, swine, cattle and opium. The major revenue of Gim Seng Lee, however, came from opium, alcohol and gambling dens in several northern towns.[110] By 1908, Gim Seng Lee had diversified into rice and other businesses. He owned five rice mills, three saw mills and one shipyard in Bangkok, as well as a rice mill in Paknam Pho (Nakhon Sawan). The name Gim Seng Lee also appeared among the founding shareholders of the Siam Commercial Bank in 1906.

As dictated by Chinese custom, Arkon Tia U-Teng returned to China in his old age and became a prominent member of the Shantou Chamber of Commerce. In Chao'an he purchased land for his burial site and helped out poor relatives in his home village. But the cold winds of Southern China no longer suited the old man, and soon Arkon Tia U-Teng returned to Bangkok where he died peacefully at Gim Seng Lee in Samsen in 1919.[111] His son, Tia Giangsam, Luang Sophon-Petcharat (pictured), succeeded him as one of the richest men in Siam.

An amusing tale of Sophon-Petcharat's wealth, often told to generations of Chinese in Sampeng, described a scene when he casually dropped by a luxury-item store. A charming crystal set caught his eye, so Sophon-Petcharat asked to see the crystal glasses, one after another. The shopkeeper, who was accustomed to serving well-dressed royalty and Westerners, behaved rudely, taking in her client's attire from head to toe. When he requested to see yet another beautiful glass, the girl frankly questioned his ability to afford the crystal. Tia grasped his cane and smashed the entire counter and asked the manager who rushed in to send the bill to Gim Seng Lee.[112]

The casual dress style of Bangkok's Chinese community not only attracted

the attention of Westerners but also the overseas Chinese themselves. In 1930, Wu Jiyue, a Hakka journalist who arrived by train from Java, noted in his memoir that "[Bangkok] is lively, full of Chinese like Singapore, and some parts reminds me of Shantou." What he found strange was the shabby attire of the Chinese. Nobody wore Western suits. Most people in the street walked around with a singlet over black Chinese trousers. Some wore only shabby shorts and walked the streets with bare feet. This sort of image of the Chinese would never be found in Java, Wu Jiyue wrote. He added, "In Singapore one seldom found a Chinese walking the streets bare chested, or bare foot, but here in Bangkok the streets are full of them. I must admit that it is an unsightly view of our compatriots. No wonder people at the inns in Shantou and Hong Kong called Siam the city of bare feet."[113]

Despite his appearance, Sophon-Petcharat was a learned man and a leading member of the Chinese community in Siam. He had returned to China to sit for the imperial examination, and in Siam, he was one of the founding members of Tian Fah Hospital, which was established for the poor in 1903. When Sun Yatsen came to Siam in 1908 advocating revolution against the Manchu dynasty, Sophon-Petcharat welcomed him at an event held at the Bangkok Chinese Club and organized by the Tongmenghui Bangkok branch under the leadership of Seow Hoodseng. Sophon-Petcharat's name also appeared amongst the 11 prominent Chinese merchants who petitioned for the registration of the Chinese Chamber of Commerce on 17 August 1909.

As the government closed down gambling tax farms, Sophon-Petcharat knew he had to restructure his business empire. The rice crisis of 1909–1910 also affected his rice milling operation. In an effort to stay ahead of the competition, he dove into modern industry by investing in the Chino-Siam Bank and the Chino-Siam Steam Navigation Company in 1909–1910. The latter aimed to break the existing monopoly of the German shipping line Nord-Deutscher Lloyd between several South China ports and Siam. Moreover, while the fever of saving China from imperialist aggression spread wide among the Chinese in Siam, Sophon-Petcharat also invested extensively in the Chinese market, such as railroad projects between Chaozhou-Shantou, Canton-Hankou and Tianjin-Pukou. He also held shares in the Imperial Bank of China and other major businesses, such as mining and land reclamation.

Tae Taiching was also a second-generation tycoon who inherited a large fortune from his father, Chaosua Hoi.[114] Hoi was a poor farmer who left his wife and three young children in Chenghai in 1864. Epitomizing the hard-working peasant, Hoi managed to save some money and set up his own business in Sampeng where he had another 13 children by his Siamese wife. In those days, the poor sanitation in Chinatown claimed many lives, and all of his children but three—a daughter and two sons—died. After his Siamese marriage, his fortune improved and he won bids to operate gambling dens. His wife had placed the family under the patronage of Prince Devavongse Varoprakarn, the foreign minister of Siam between 1881 and 1923. It was the prince who arranged the marriage between Hoi's beautiful daughter and the prince's own cousin, Pluem Sucharitkul. Praphai Sucharitkul, Hoi's granddaughter from this marriage, later became Queen Indrasaksajee, the consort to King Vajiravudh. Tae Taiching, Hoi's eldest son and the queen's maternal uncle, was appointed Phra Swamipak-Bhuwanart.[115]

Apart from being the major operator of gambling dens and the *huay* lottery in Chinatown, Tae Taiching and his brother Taihao helped their father expand the family business into related fields, establishing a courier and money-forwarding agency, a pawn shop, and an exchange service. The family also founded Sung Hok Seng Bank in Sampeng, Hong Kong, Shantou and Singapore, as well as Seng Sung Lee, a famous gold shop on Yaowarat Road. When several influential local Chinese leaders called a meeting to set up the Chino-Siam Steam Navigation Company based on Chinese nationalist sentiment at the time, Taiching was asked to invest.

The Chino-Siam Steam Navigation Company was formed on the novel idea of breaking up the Western monopoly on shipping. During the first decade of the 20th century, the Nord-Deutscher Lloyd shipping agency held a monopoly on the Shantou-Bangkok passenger traffic after its purchase of steamers from the Scottish Oriental Steamship Company. Its monopoly was challenged briefly in 1903 by another German company from Bremen, which brought the fare down greatly and sent the number of Chinese emigrants to Siam skyrocketing. Four months after the arrival of this competition, Nord-Deutscher Lloyd incorporated the rival fleet and raised fares, causing Chinese passenger arrivals to fall sharply in 1904. Another challenge came from Nippon Yusen in 1906, but the competition lasted only two years. Another price war began in 1909, when the Chino-Siam Navigation Company entered the market.

The establishment of the Chino-Siam Navigation Company could be seen in the light of Eastern businessmen trying to best their Western rivals as the years of foreign imperialism in China generated tales about the humiliation of the Chinese. Prejudices against the Chinese spilled over to the Nanyang. In 1895, when the Chinese consul in Singapore, Thio Thiausiat (Zhang Bishi), sent an agent to purchase a first-class steamship ticket, the German shipping company he approached refused to issue the ticket on the grounds that non-Europeans were not permitted to travel first-class.[116] Similarly, in Bangkok, the German shipping company often gave the German trading house of Windsor & Company priority to load their rice cargoes.

Sophon-Petcharat, famous for smashing shelf-loads of European crystal, chaired the Chino-Siam Steam Navigation Company with its registered capital of 3 million baht. The names of its board of directors read like a "who's who" of the Bangkok business community, including Lau Chongmin (later Phraya Choduk); Luang Jitchamnong-Vanich (Tom Ya); Phra Swamipak-Bhuwanart (Tae Taiching); Phra Anuwat-Rajaniyom (Tae Teeyong, commonly known as "Second Brother Hong"); Ng Miaongian (Lamsam) of the Hakka community; Wun Tokkeng, leader of the Hailam, and Chin Sum, a Cantonese. The Chino-Siam Steam Navigation Company dropped the standard fare of 20–25 baht charged by Nord-Deutscher Lloyd to 10 baht. The Germans counterattacked by dropping the fare further to 5 baht.

Despite the persuasive power of its shareholders, the company suffered a heavy loss for four years, and in 1912 the company was sold to the Chinese government. Many of its major shareholders were left in financial ruin, including Sophon-Petcharat, Tom Ya and "Second Brother Hong."[117] In 1914, Nord-Deutscher Lloyd and other German shipping companies withdrew their operations after the outbreak of World War I.

A rare portrait of King Vajiravudh relaxing with Queen Indrasaksajee.

program replacing the old, patronage style of administration with a countrywide, Westernized network linking far-flung corners of the kingdom was in tune with the needs of the time.

What stands out in the administrative and economic reorganization of Chulalongkorn's reign was the unprecedented role played by the government. Nowhere was this more evident than in the area of tax collection. The traditional Siamese state farmed out monopoly rights on natural resources, essential foodstuffs, opium, gambling and liquor to the highest bidder. All of these were gradually replaced by centralized, bureaucratic tax collection.

Chulalongkorn's centralization of tax collection fatally undermined the economic dominance of the Chinese monopoly tax farmers. As the government began to take back or refused to renew tax farming concessions, Chinese tax farmers engaged in intense bidding wars to secure the remaining tax farms. Competition for the few opium, gambling and liquor concessions increased to the point where margins became thin and Chinese bankruptcies common.[118] Many among the richest Chinese tax farmers went bankrupt during the late 19th century, among them the legendary Gim Seng Lee business empire (see "Sunset on the Gambling Tax Farms"). Subsequently, none of the noble Chinese dynastic families of the 19th century with tax farming backgrounds survived as leading entrepreneurs in the 20th century.

In 1906, the government closed tax farms altogether.[119] Ironically, it was largely tax farm revenues that had initially helped Chulalongkorn finance the installation of a modern bureaucracy. Subsequently, that same bureaucracy that tax farms had helped finance gave the government a vehicle to collect taxes directly, bypassing the Chinese tax farmers, resulting in the phasing out of tax farms and forcing the Chinese to diversify into other forms of businesses.

Concurrently, the fall of tax farmers extended administrative centralization into the hinterland, changing age-old relations between Bangkok and the traditional elites, especially with the Hokkien and Malay rajahs in the peninsular south. Under Chulalongkorn, the Hokkien and Malay rajahs were gradually replaced by senior bureaucratic officials posted as governors. By 1910, the old *khunnang* elite in the central region, as well as the *chao muang* or rajahs in the outlying regions, had been pensioned off. Consequently, from Bangkok to the district level in the outer regions, Siam was henceforth governed by a new bureaucratic power elite of civil servants.[120]

Siam was not alone in its bureaucratic revolution. The early years of the 20th century were a watershed in the administrative history of Southeast Asia. The last corners of the region were being incorporated into six large states—Siam, French Indochina, British Malaya, Burma, the Netherlands Indies and the Philippines—in which basic administrative grids were established. The advent of the 20th century found the European and Siamese bureaucracies in full running order, with graded hierarchies, regular recruitment and promotion procedures, and paperwork up to international standards.

These new bureaucratic Leviathans were quite different from the traditional administrative systems that they replaced. The old administrators operated on the basis of precedent and personal ties, and they strove to maintain the existing order, not to change it, because their *modus operandi* depended on that order. By contrast, the new Siamese bureaucracy existed primarily to "do," providing themselves with a crowded agenda of specific tasks to accomplish. They felt a compulsive need to tidy up casual and irregular old customs and bring uniformity to numerous small, local societies in their jurisdictions.

Initially, when communications were poor and geographical reach was limited to field officers living far apart in separate districts, the new system made allowances for local cultural practices and style of rule. However, after the new administration gained greater revenues, better communications and more staff, the accommodation to indirect rule began to give way. While the bureaucrats consolidated their control, they kept a watchful eye on the still-indirectly ruled outlying areas and closely supervised the general affairs of the populace.

Having taken its place in the emerging, largely European-dominated community of states in Southeast Asia, the reinvented Siamese state had come of age. The absolute monarchy had acquired almost all the trappings of a Western nation-state, with functioning bureaucratic, economic and communications frameworks, ruled by a Great King over an increasingly literate Siamese populace freed from slavery.

Reinventing the Siamese Social System

The new bureaucracy not only impacted but also reshaped the traditional Siamese social system, especially the *phrai* system, generating contradictions that pushed back against the absolute monarchy. As the market economy made inroads into the kingdom, money became more important to the ruling elite than exactions of direct labor service and appropriation of surplus produce from the tillers of the soil.

In addition, the world demand for rice put tremendous pressure on Siam to use more land for rice cultivation. Siam's transition from a subsistence barter economy into one based on commodity production necessitated loosening control over the *phrai* and encouraging them to colonize frontier lands to produce surplus rice for export. The "free" *phrai* could open up uncultivated lands not only for their own benefit but also for the state.

In 1873, in his newfound legislative role, King Chulalongkorn formally promulgated the gradual abolition of slavery in Siam. He decreed that no child born in his reign was to become a slave, and children who were already born into slavery were to be freed when they became 21 years old. This ensured that slavery would die a natural death.

In 1897, he issued another decree prohibiting all traffic in slaves, including the right of the individual to sell him or herself into slavery. Finally, in 1905, slavery as an institution was abolished altogether.[121] The *phrai* system was concurrently phased out. By the end of the century, a series of acts replaced all forced labor and other forms of personal obligations to the state with a capitation tax with provisions for various exemptions.

The peasantry felt the liberating effects of the abolition of slavery, and it was to be remembered as one of the greatest achievements of the Chakri dynasty. This substitution of forced labor by hired labor not only ensured the country's smooth transition from a subsistence rice-producing economy into a rice cash-crop export economy, but it also neutralized the revolutionary potential of the peasantry and guaranteed that the next revolution would not be a peasant revolution.

Equally important was the fact that the reforms promoted an explosion of commercial agriculture in the kingdom. By the 1930s, the spread of commercial agriculture and the high value of land had drawn the Siamese workforce towards agricultural pursuits. The Siamese preference for working the land coupled with the boom in the rice trade, which caused a tenfold increase in the price of rice during the second half of the 19th century, tended to make agricultural labor in the countryside almost wholly Siamese, leading to a scarcity of wage laborers in Siam. The lack of wage laborers drove up labor costs higher than anywhere else in Asia. The higher pay also neutralized the potential of a workers' revolt despite poor working conditions.[122]

Chinese miners in the south of Siam.

Thus, the Chakri reforms benefited the Chinese, who responded to the high wages and filled the new jobs created by the building, transportation, railway construction and processing industries. The Chinese were also willing to work long hours under conditions intolerable to the Siamese peasant. Moreover, Chinese skill and insularity ensured that the wage labor market remained a virtual Chinese monopoly.[123] Consequently, in the emerging new social system, labor became divided along ethnic lines, with agriculturalists remaining mostly Siamese and urban labor—in the docks, rice mills, railway crews and service industries—dominated by Chinese.

The longstanding partnership between royalty and Siam's Chinese community was deeply appreciated by King Chulalongkorn, who expressed his high valuation of the role and contribution of the Chinese thus: "It has always been my policy that the Chinese in Siam have the same opportunities for labor and for profit as are possessed by my own countrymen. I regard them not as foreigners but as one of the component parts of the kingdom and sharing in its prosperity and advancement."[124]

This salutary view of the Chinese held by King Chulalongkorn in 1907 perhaps represented the Indian summer of relations between Siamese royalty and its Chinese subjects. By 1910, the tax farming system that had flourished in the second half of the 19th century was already being replaced by bureaucratic tax collection. The longstanding alliance between the royalty and the Chinese was no longer sustained by strong mutual interests and finally came to an end. Symbolizing the end of the era of partnership was the gradual abandonment of the practice of ennobling Chinese. With the phasing out of this practice, an important mechanism for assimilating Chinese into Siamese society was removed. Unable to gain status and recognition in Siamese society, many ambitious and talented Chinese turned to find fame, power and status in Chinese nationalist politics after the turn of the century. Moreover, Chinese capital and investments were increasingly directed into new opportunities opened up by capitalism. Consequently, Chinese ascendency over the economy came to be seen in a new light.

Nationalism

By the turn of the century, the attempt to mold a national community out of a diverse ethnic and cultural landscape had created explosive tensions throughout an enlarged polity remade into a nation-state, which encompassed an ethnically stratified society with royalty and new bureaucratic elites on top and the peasantry below, a centralized bureaucratic apparatus operated by new power elites and imposed upon outlying regions, and a capitalist-style export economy based on commodity production dominated and controlled by

Chinese. Concurrently, urbanization created a crucible for new tensions—abetted by innovative organizational forms, new social roles, a nascent print media, exposure to international events and imported political ideas—to foster the emergence of nationalism in Siam.

The early phase of post-Chulalongkorn Siamese nationalism that formed between 1910 and 1932 had two major components: the growth of anti-Chinese sentiment, and the emergence of an ideological commitment to an overarching Siamese identity embracing the nation-state's various indigenous groups collected within its newfound borders. The new nationalism paralleled the reinvention of the state and germinated during the early decades of the 20th century, although it did not flower as a major social movement until the 1930s.[125] The rise of a nascent nationalist consciousness threatened the new absolute monarchy and Chinese dominance in Siam.

The seeds of nationalism were sowed in the ethnically stratified social system resulting from Siam's encounter with capitalist modernity during the 19th century. This ethnic coloration within the Siamese social system served as the basis for nationalist propaganda directed against the Chinese to rally the people behind a unifying Siamese identity that simultaneously excluded the Chinese.

However, the phenomenon of nationalism in Siam cannot be explained simply by the existence of anti-Chinese prejudice among the native populace. For one thing, the eruption of anti-Chinese sentiment during the early 20th century was unprecedented. Hitherto, the Chinese emigrant community had assimilated into, cooperated and coexisted with the native populace at all levels of the Siamese social hierarchy. Deep-seated anti-Chinese racism did not appear to exist in Siamese society, in contrast to the Western colonial territories where the Chinese experienced racial discrimination by the white ruling class who forced them into segregated communities.

However, this is not to say that there was no native prejudice at all against Siam's emigrant Chinese community. Obviously, contact between ethnic groups as different in character as the Chinese and Siamese was bound to lead to some stereotyping, further sharpened by divergent occupational specializations. It was not unnatural for one ethnic or cultural group to feel slightly superior to another. The Chinese emigrant holding the traditional perspective of the Middle Kingdom tended to regard the Siamese as "barbarians," while the Siamese considered the Chinese as uncouth—especially the new wave of coolie immigrants. That was about as far as it went; until the first decade of the 20th century, neither Chinese nor Siamese had been concerned about national political loyalties. The Chinese had happily assimilated into Siamese society and the Siamese had always been hospitable to Chinese emigrants. These stereotypes and prejudices assumed political importance only as the Siamese elite became exposed to Western influence and absorbed Western notions of nationalism.[126]

After the mid-19th century, the Siamese court developed an increasingly pro-Western orientation; court taste changed in favor of Western goods and Western culture. After 1860, the court started to hire Western advisors to assist in Siam's modernization.

In the late 19th century, most Western diplomats, capitalists and colonial administrators tended to hold a strong racial prejudice against Asians in general and Jews and Chinese in particular. While they sometimes romanticized natives as "noble savages," they were also disdainful and patronizing in their attitude towards native peoples, considering them ignorant, indolent, naïve and lethargic. Edward Said has tried to explain how Western prejudices inform the West's view of Oriental culture and peoples in a coherent doctrine called Western Orientalism.[127]

The co-author's grandfather also changed his style of dress and hairstyle from the queue, which was common among the Thai-Chinese of his younger days.

Many of these prejudices were the result of the cumulative encounters of Western civilization and Oriental societies and culture. In Siam, Western interaction and competition with the overseas Chinese through trade and commercial dealings demonstrated its own specific pattern. The development of the new capitalist economy in Siam after 1855 by Western imperialist powers initially gave Chinese capital a great impetus. The expansion of the Siamese economy must in the first instance be attributed to Western initiative, innovation and enterprise. However, Chinese entrepreneurs quickly learned from the West and soon outdid the Westerners in exploiting new opportunities in Siam's market economy, to the chagrin of the latter.

Moreover, although Chinese merchants and owners of capital were dependent on foreign trade and acted as compradors for foreign capital, their sharing in these common activities and capital interests did not preclude conflicts between the Chinese and foreign powers. In 1898, the European business community formed the Bangkok Chamber of Commerce, which restricted membership to Western firms. The Chinese capitalists reacted by forming the Chinese Chamber of Commerce in 1908. Not only did the chamber represent Chinese big business, it also claimed to act on behalf of the Chinese as a whole and soon became the acknowledged leader of the Chinese community in official eyes as well.[128] Chinese economic ascendency was also reflected in the formation of other voluntary associations, such as the Insurance Business Association and the Rice Merchants' Association, founded in 1917 and 1919 respectively.

Equally important were developments in modern banking at the turn of the century. The Siam Commercial Bank, which was granted royal permission to operate as a full-fledged commercial bank by

King Chulalongkorn in January 1907, had an initial capital of 3 million baht. Two branches were established in 1920 and 1927 respectively, one in Nakhon Si Thammarat, which was short-lived, and another one in Chiang Mai.[129] Three other important banks financed largely with Chinese capital also appeared during the early part of the 20th century. In viewing the cooperation between royal capital and Chinese capital, one should not assume that there were no contradictions between the two rival capitalist interests, for cooperation was also accompanied by intense competition and conflict.

The anti-Chinese element of Siamese nationalism was underscored by the clashing interests of Western, Chinese and royal capitalists in the Siamese economy. The ambivalent relationship of competition, cooperation and conflict between these powers often annoyed Western expatriates in Siam, generating specific stereotypes of the Chinese in the Western mind. European advisors hired by the Siamese court were naturally wont to share their prejudices with their Siamese clients.

One of the early purveyors of Western anti-Chinese sentiment in Siam was Warrington Smyth, a high-level British advisor to the Siamese court. In 1898, he wrote, "Beyond the very high qualities of which he is undoubtedly possessed— qualities shared perhaps equally by the buffalo—I confess I have no great admiration for the Chinese coolie."[130]

In another passage, which tended to find a familiar echo in subsequent Siamese nationalist propaganda, he added:

> *The Chinese ... are the Jews of Siam. They have on the whole enjoyed an immunity from official interference which they have neither merited nor appreciated. Their only return has been the species of high handed rowdyism which results from the methods followed by Chinese secret societies. By judicious use of their business faculties and their powers of combination they held the Siamese in the palm of their hand. The toleration accorded them by the government is put down to fear; they bow and scrape before the authorities but laugh behind their backs; and they could sack half Bangkok in a day.[131]*

His remarks would prove prophetic. They were also echoed by J.G.D. Campbell, the education advisor to the Siamese government in 1902. Campbell also compared the Chinese to the Jews and was of the opinion that "the quiet, loving natives have virtually sold to him (the Chinese) their birthright for a mess of pottage." In another remark, he categorically expressed the European antipathy towards the Chinese: "It cannot be said that they (the Chinese) are employed by Europeans on account of any great love inspired by them, but simply because necessity knows no choice . . . they are only tolerated as a necessary evil.[132]"

Campbell's remarks reflected the anti-Chinese hysteria sweeping across the Western world. By the turn of the century, Chinese immigration had been prohibited in most Anglo-Saxon countries as the frenzy over the threat of the Yellow Peril reached feverish levels. Many Western expatriates became alarmed by the influx of the Chinese into Siam, and they did not hesitate to voice their fears. Campbell for one warned the Siamese that the Chinese "are more likely before many years to be the dominating people of Siam. . . and either to swamp the indolent and lethargic natives or transform them by fusion and intermarriage until they are past recognition."

An image from the Yellow Peril campaign, showing the Western world's hopes to defend itself from the Asiatic menace with warships.

In 1903, a Western geographer predicted, "One day will see the Siamese race no longer in existence and the Menam Valley peopled only by Chinese."[133] The entire Western expatriate community of the region had become preoccupied with the Yellow Peril. An article in the *Revue Indo Chinoise* alleged that Siam "will be completely absorbed by the Chinese element." Another article alleged that Chinese immigration into Bangkok was part of a grand Chinese imperialist design.[134]

The Western-educated Siamese elite could hardly avoid these racial prejudices, especially when their official capacity required them to work with European advisors. Exposure to the prejudices of high-ranking and influential European advisors must have greatly formed the attitudes of the new Siamese administrative elite. Many European advisors presumed their intellectual superiority over Siamese officials to whom they dispensed professional opinion and technical advice, and they were wont to impose their views on matters beyond the scope of their expertise. Smyth reportedly congratulated a Siamese special commissioner at Phuket for having adopted anti-Chinese policies. He also encouraged the official to tax the Chinese more heavily and suppress the Chinese secret societies as the British had done in Malaya.

Moreover, many Siamese officials were predisposed to accept the prejudices of these European advisors by virtue of their Western education. They had attended British, French and American schools; they associated with the Western commercial and diplomatic set in Bangkok; they read the English-language newspapers published in Bangkok and they worked under the supervision and guidance of Western advisors and consultants. Those select few among their peers who had the opportunity to study abroad in Europe became even more brainwashed by the doctrines of anti-Semitism and the Yellow Peril than locally educated officials.[135]

Indeed, the first-recorded expression of Siamese anti-Chinese sentiment came from a lawyer educated in England. Upon returning to Siam, he started a journal in the 1890s, which warned that the Chinese were becoming too numerous in Siam. The journal was closed through the personal intervention of King Chulalongkorn, who considered the subject best left alone.[136] Chulalongkorn remained unmoved by the new wave of anti-Chinese sentiment and kept the growth of the movement in check.

Anti-Sinicism remained marginalized outside mainstream Siamese public opinion for a long time, being largely contained within the European community, among the Western educated intelligentsia and the new bureaucratic elite. However, during the first decade of the 20th century onwards, a series of events occurred both within and outside the country that had important repercussions on the monarchy and the Chinese community. The events leading up to the Xinhai Revolution (1911), the appearance of the first Chinese-language newspapers, the establishment of Chinese schools, the mushrooming of Chinese associations, the abolition of tax farms and the Chinese triennial tax, and the outlawing of Chinese secret societies in Siam—the convergence of all these events marked the end of an era,[137] one that had unfolded under the long shadow of the partnership between Siamese royalty and the Chinese.

The year 1910 was a turning point; it saw the calamitous Chinese general strike in Bangkok. The strike proved to be a failure and a disastrous mistake. It was a reflection of the bankruptcy of the old, Chinese secret-society leadership and the pro-Manchu faction of the Bangkok Chinese community. The strike was opposed by the pro-revolutionary newspaper run by Seow Hoodseng. Rice millers, who were forced to close down just when the rice trade was booming, were equally

An advertising card printed in Germany illustrating the Chinese Revolution that overthrew the last imperial dynasty and established the Republic of China. It shows Dr. Sun Yatsen, the republic's founding father and first president, and a naval battle in the harbor of Hankou, circa October 1911.

unsupportive of the strike, while compradors took no part.[138]

In addition to splitting the Chinese community, the average Siamese-Thai urbanite was also badly inconvenienced by the whole episode. Siamese outrage at the general strike did much to intensify latent prejudices against the Chinese. For the educated Siamese intelligentsia, the strike bore a fateful lesson. The extent to which the Siamese populace had become dependent on Chinese trade and commerce was made glaringly apparent. The moral was obvious: if Chinese ownership and control over the economy were allowed unfettered progress, the Siamese populace would be completely at their mercy.

Furthermore, the strike served to demonstrate that the resident Chinese were in Siam only to exploit the country, that they were not willing to contribute their share to the common good and that they valued money above loyalty, obedience and justice. King Chulalongkorn's tolerance was badly shaken by the 1910 general strike and shutdown of the capital city. The whole fiasco cast the Chinese in an unfavorable light and put them in an extremely vulnerable political position.[139] Perhaps, more than anything else, the general strike caused the hitherto marginalized anti-Chinese sentiment that existed in isolated pockets to spill over into mainstream Siamese public opinion.

Jews of the Orient

The year 1910 was a turning point for the Chinese in Siam in yet another way: it saw the death of King Chulalongkorn, a friend to the Chinese. His passing away symbolized the end of the traditional royalty-Chinese partnership and also occured just before a watershed event in the history of China itself: the Xinhai Revolution, which took place the following year.

The events leading up to the Xinhai Revolution in 1911 stimulated the birth of Chinese nationalism, which had widespread repercussions among the overseas-Chinese diaspora throughout the Nanyang region, including Siam. The rise of nationalist sentiment among the overseas Chinese was naturally accompanied by the strengthening of ties with the Chinese ancestral homeland. Inspired by the Chinese education movement promoted by Kang Youwei and Sun Yatsen, Chinese schools mushroomed throughout the Nanyang. Between 1908 and 1911, the Tongmenghui, either directly or through its front organization, the Chinese Association, established several study societies and the Huayi School. The royalists countered with their own study societies and the Seng Hua School. Several other schools were established in the following years, the most important being the Bangkok Xinmin School, which was also founded under the auspices of the Tongmenghui.[140] Besides establishing Chinese schools abroad, the reformists also sought to encourage the younger generation of overseas Chinese to return

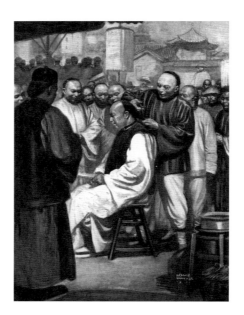

The Chinese Rebellion of 1911, also known as the Xinhai Revolution, saw the end of 2,000 years of imperial rule. After the revolution, Chinese men had their queues publicly cut off. The queue was of Manchu origin and were required to be worn by all men when the Manchus conquered China in 1644.

home where they could receive a formal education according to Chinese imperial standards.[141]

The movement to spread Chinese education among overseas Chinese was motivated by the desire to preserve overseas Chinese loyalties toward their ancestral homeland, and the Xinhai Revolution gave new impetus to the campaign. If the overseas Chinese were allowed to completely assimilate and embrace citizenship in their host countries, such as Siam, they would have no reason to continue to support the newly established Republic of China with their hard-earned resources.[142]

Whatever conflicts existed in the Chinese-Siamese communal relationship, the Siamese government was not willing to accept China's claim over the local Chinese by allowing them to completely re-Sinicize through Chinese education. The post–Xinhai Revolution period saw an intensification of the struggle between China and Siam to gain control of the education of the Chinese community in Siam, reflecting the clash of two nationalist movements striving to stake a claim on their subjects.[143]

The Xinhai Revolution also contributed to the changing pattern of Chinese emigration to Siam. With the rise of the Republic, deterrents of Chinese emigration rapidly disappeared. For the first time in Chinese history, women began to follow and even accompany their husbands to Siam.[144] The emergence of female emigration had serious implications for the Chinese community in Siam. Suddenly, the Chinese household emerged in Siam, which previously did not exist.

Before, the Chinese emigrant always joined a Siamese home. By marrying a

Siamese or a *lukchin* woman, he linked up to the local community. The presence of Chinese women meant that Chinese emigrants no longer married Siamese women, and intermarriage rapidly declined. The Chinese home had replaced the Siamese home. Furthermore, with the Chinese home came the Chinese child.[145] Consequently, the Chinese child replaced the *lukchin* of old. In contrast to the *lukchin*, the sympathies and loyalties of the Chinese child were directed by their Chinese parents towards the Chinese ancestral homeland.

With this new development, a new pattern of two-way drift steadily replaced the old, one-way traffic pattern of Chinese assimilation in Siam. On the one hand, there was the old pull that still drew many Chinese emigrants into the kingdom's national life. On the other, there was now a new, much-publicized tendency to establish Chinese homes and communities that placed emphasis on Chinese national and cultural life.[146] As a result of the increase of Chinese homes and also the great surge forward in the education of the common people in China, Chinese communities opened Chinese schools in which children were educated in Chinese literature, patriotism and social customs.

Siam's Chinese émigrés became passionately loyal to the Chinese motherland, sending money back not only to their ancestral villages but also to patriotic organizations. Their new values and aspirations were reflected in the proliferation of Chinese newspapers, educational institutions and voluntary associations in Siam. Newspapers and politically inspired Chinese associations in turn created a sharpened sense of national consciousness among many Chinese, which had never existed before in Siam.

Before the rise of political nationalism in China, assimilation was not an issue. But after the Xinhai Revolution, suddenly, the centuries-old integration into Siamese civilization—once an inexorable process—began to freeze. Consequently, many among the new, educated Siamese intelligentsia began to perceive that the Chinese were building inassimilable alien communities loyal not to Siam, but to China.

The rise of Chinese nationalism at the turn of the century and the Xinhai Revolution in 1911 was to have the most profound influence in the development of nationalism in Siam. Wasana Wongsurawat has argued that "no alternative political ideology or mode of government was introduced to the general public via Western education. Instead, this information entered into public consciousness, becoming vastly popular among the lowest roots of urban society, through the writings of Chinese revolutionaries like Sun Yatsen, whose ideas were published in numerous Chinese newspapers of the time and translated into Thai by Overseas Chinese activists and journalists."[147]

While Chinese nationalism was the most decisive formative influence in the emergence of nationalism in the Siamese kingdom, Western influence also

A Sino-Siamese family: the two daughters of Tan Tsuhuang (Wanglee), Tongyoo (Wanglee) Lamsam, seated on the left, and her sister Pook (Wanglee) Bulsook, seated on the right, grew up in Bangkok and became Thai. All the boys, however, were sent back for their Chinese education in their ancestral village in the Teochew area.

played a part, particularly through the racial bigotry that had filtered into Siam through Western educated elites. The single person who exercised the greatest influence on the development of Siamese nationalism, King Vajiravudh (Rama VI), had studied at Oxford University, where he was influenced by variants of Western Orientalism, including anti-Semitism.[148]

Vajiravudh ascended the throne against a backdrop of great anxiety within the Siamese ruling elite, provoked by revolutionary political agitation within the émigré community and the Chinese nationalist propaganda that was carried in the Bangkok Chinese newspapers.

Vajiravudh was also influenced by the Chinese general strike, which occurred just before his reign began, and by the Xinhai Revolution. Coming nearly at the same time as the death of King Chulalongkorn, these two events exercised a profound impact on the future relations between royalty and the Chinese. Almost overnight the generations of goodwill that existed between Siamese and Chinese disappeared. For the first time, the Chinese in Siam became objects of official discrimination and public antipathy, and spearheading this new anti-Chinese sentiment was none other than King Vajiravudh himself.

Both Skinner and Anderson attribute the two kings' contrasting attitudes towards the Chinese to the strike and revolution. It was apparent that the new king never forgot nor forgave the Chinese general strike, saying, "We try to conduct ourselves like men of goodwill. But we are only ordinary human beings and there is a limit to our self-control. If there should be another incident like the Chinese strike I should not care to be responsible for the outcome." The new king's reproach to his Chinese subjects barely concealed a thinly veiled threat.[149]

Vajiravudh's concerns about the Chinese were not motivated only by bigotry. Chinese nationalism tended to destabilize the Siamese government. The Chinese general strike had been instigated by the pro-Manchu political faction within the local Chinese community, and the Xinhai Revolution set an ominous precedent that threatened the future of the absolute monarchy of Siam.

Besides its threatening aspects, Chinese nationalism had other intriguing ramifications for domestic Siamese politics, which were not lost upon the unorthodox, Oxford-educated king, who already evinced a predilection for drama and literature. The paradox of nationalism is that the formation of one brand of nationalism automatically generates a counter-nationalism. The touting of Chinese nationalist sentiment in Siam had made the Siamese more conscious of the existence of "aliens" in their midst. Moreover, Chinese nationalism in Siam provided the Siamese with first-hand exposure to a community that evinced a nationalistic standpoint, and the Siamese became aware that they were not included in that standpoint. Thus, as a nascent consciousness of Siamese identity emerged, Chinese dominance over the economy and ethnic stratification within Siamese society took on a new light.

Consequently, Siamese outrage at being inconvenienced and discomfited by the Chinese general strike in 1910 quickly assumed an anti-Chinese character. Intelligent and endowed with a flair for the dramatic, King Vajiravudh saw an opportunity to use this budding anti-Chinese sentiment to rouse his people to their national destiny. When it became obvious, early in his reign, that the purveying of seditious ideas by the Chinese-language press was getting out of hand, Vajiravudh made the fateful decision to join the fray and engage the pundits in an unprecedented political exchange through the print media to advance his own political agenda.[150]

Cosmopolitan, cultured, polyglot, educated in England from boyhood on, and counting Europeans among his closest friends, King Vajiravudh appeared aptly suited to draw on his knowledge of the West to point out his peoples' shortcomings and potentialities. Vajiravudh became the philosopher par excellence of Siamese nationalism, and the first to attempt to channel the undercurrents of patriotic and anti-Chinese sentiments within Siamese society into a coherent doctrine of ideological commitment to an overarching Siamese identity.

The nephews of Tongyoo in Hong Kong.

Under the pen name "Asavabhahu," in a series of articles that included *The Jews of the Orient* and were printed in the Thai vernacular press, King Vajiravudh compared the Chinese to the Jews, and echoed both the undercurrents of anti-Chinese sentiment circulating within the Western expatriate community in Siam and the anti-Semitism of Western Orientalism.

The Jews of the Orient represents the classic statement

of the Siamese case against the Chinese in Siam. The most concise summary of Vajiravudh's lengthy diatribe against the Chinese has been made by Skinner:

> *The Chinese first of all were said to be unassimilable: because of their racial loyalty and sense of superiority, they remain always Chinese. They regard residence in Siam as temporary, their only purpose in coming being to make as much money as possible. When they marry Thai women, they force their wives to become Chinese and rear their children as Chinese. Second, they were accused of being opportunistic and two faced: the Chinese profess Buddhism and political allegiance only for the advantage they get out of it; in fact they are neither loyal nor Buddhist. Their gentle manners towards Thai are an opportunistic deception. Third, the Chinese were held to be devoid of civic virtues: they expect all the privileges, but refuse the obligations, of citizenship. Their attitude towards the state is treacherous, secretive, and rebellious. Fourth, the Chinese were said to worship Mammon as their sole god: for money they endure any privation, perform the vilest deeds, cheat, embezzle, rob and kill. In money matters they know neither morals nor mercy. Finally they were accused of being parasites on the Thai economy: the Chinese buy little that is produced in Siam for their own consumption, preferring to import clothes and food from China and they drain off the wealth of the country in the form of remittances to their homeland.* [151]

Undoubtedly, many of Asavabhahu's claims were exaggerated and based only on the recent changes in the attributes of the Chinese community under the influence of Chinese nationalism. The tremendous contribution that Chinese emigrants had made to the kingdom in the course of more than a century were totally ignored. The courageous Chinese journalist Seow Hoodseng rebutted Asavabhahu's allegations in the Thai vernacular newspaper, *Chino-Siam Warasap*, and criticized Asavabhahu for stooping to racial stereotyping to malign the Chinese. However, many influential Siamese remained convinced of the truth of Asavabhahu's accusations.

Nevertheless, the purpose at hand is not to rebut Vajiravudh's arguments, but to consider the role of anti-Chinese sentiment in Vajiravudh's political agenda. *The Jews of the Orient* was the first coherent articulation of the Siamese national standpoint. When Kenneth Landon posed the interesting question: When did the Chinese and the Siamese develop their national standpoints respectively? His answer was "whilst arbitrary dates are hard to set, approximate dates might be said to be 1910 for China and perhaps 1920 for Thailand." [152]

A portrait of a Chinese man and a local Siamese woman. The Chinese living in the southern cities often forged close relations with the Straits Settlements Chinese as reflected in the lady's attire, which differed from Bangkok *lukchin*.

When Vajiravudh ascended the throne, Chinese nationalism was already a robust political movement that many Chinese émigrés in Siam espoused. However, at that time, Siamese nationalism did not exist.

Nevertheless, the building blocks for a national community had already been laid in the form of a common Bangkok Thai "national language," a common official "national history" and a common official "national Buddhism," all of which were taught through state education. However, what a Siamese national identity consisted of beyond a common national language, history and Buddhism remained less clear. Building on the legacy of state education, Vajiravudh attempted to exploit anti-Chinese sentiment to help his people develop a national consciousness.

In the same way that Chinese national identity tended to exclude the Siamese, King Vajiravudh defined a Siamese standpoint by excluding the Chinese. But after an extensive discussion of the numerous negative attributes making up the Chinese identity, *The Jews of the Orient* failed to define what a Siamese identity was. However, it clearly affirmed what it was not—it was not Chinese. Thus, the Siamese identity was defined in opposition to Chinese, and anti-Chinese sentiment was used to create a Siamese national consciousness reflecting an imagined community, whose members share a common Siamese identity, encompassing autochthonous ethnic groups within the kingdom.

Vajiravudh's writings did much to rouse fear and distrust between the Chinese and Siamese. It symbolized a break in the relationship of confidence and trust between the crown and the Chinese community. *The Jews of the Orient* and other articles written by Asavabhahu notified the Chinese that a new era was at hand in which the Siamese were determined to be fully sovereign and supreme in their own land.[153]

However, the Chinese policies during the reign of King Vajiravudh should not be judged solely on the basis of the controversial views expressed in *The Jews of the Orient*. While the essay is a vicious, racist, ideological attack on the Chinese, the king's anti-Chinese campaign was more or less exclusively confined to the ideological level. It is to the credit of King Vajiravudh that his reign was marked by only a few comparatively minor anti-Chinese measures. One such innocuous anti-Chinese measure was the 1913 regulation requiring all rickshaw pullers to be licensed, for which they had to pay a small fee, be physically fit, conversant in the Thai language and aged between 18 and 40. Other measures related to the Chinese problem include the law calling for registration of voluntary associations (1914) and the law on private schools (1918) which require schools to teach Thai language and inculcate national values. Neither could be called repressive or legally anti-Chinese.[154] Compared with the track record of the later People's Party, which came to power in 1932, Vajiravudh's watch was characterized by a remarkable absence of substantive anti-Chinese policies.

Moreover, under Vajiravudh, the Siamese government promulgated the first Nationality Act, which like the counterpart Chinese Nationality Act of 1909 affirmed the principle of *jus sanguinis,* which stipulated that every person born to a Siamese father on Siamese or foreign territory was Siamese. The new law also claimed as Siamese every person born on Siamese territory. This law could hardly be regarded as anti-Chinese as it embraced almost all the Chinese in Siam.

Despite his public attack and condemnation of the Xinhai Revolution, Vajiravudh never really closed down any Chinese newspapers, although he found their printed views on monarchy deplorable and the pages full of revolutionary and seditious content. The relatively liberal atmosphere that prevailed under his reign was admirable, even by today's standards. The courageous Chinese editor of *Chino-Siam Warasap*, Seow Hoodseng, who bluntly rebutted the king's allegations against the Chinese community, was never charged with *lèse majesté* or incarcerated, and his newspaper was permitted to continue.

Remarkably, Vajiravudh was sporting and shrewd enough to make political use of Seow Hoodseng, the influential and talented journalist, by financially subsidizing his newspaper in exchange for useful intelligence on the Chinese émigré community. Although Vajiravudh asked Phraya Yommaraj to monitor Seow Hoodseng's activities, the government also closed one eye to Seow Hoodseng's efforts to recruit supporters and raise funds for Sun Yatsen's revolutionary cause.

The anti-Chinese character of Vajiravudh's reign was not accompanied by any attempt to nationalize Chinese companies, expropriate Chinese assets, discriminate against Chinese in employing state officials or restrict Chinese immigration. The Nationality Act embraced all Chinese within the kingdom, even sometimes against their will. Therefore, it is difficult to say that King Vajiravudh's policies were anti-Chinese *per se*.

What can be said is that King Vajiravudh deliberately exploited anti-Chinese sentiment to advance his own political agenda to create a nationalist movement under the aegis of the Siamese absolute monarchy. In sharp contrast to European anti-Semitism, nationalism was never used by Vajiravudh to evict or exterminate the Chinese, as in the case of German National Socialism. On the contrary, Siamese identity was allowed to include the Chinese in the end.

It is interesting to trace the steps in this apparently contradictory process that began with the exclusion of the Chinese and ended with their re-inclusion. Although anti-Chinese sentiment was first used to create a Siamese consciousness, once a Siamese identity could be said to exist, the door that was initially shut on the Chinese was re-opened to admit them to partake in the newfound Siamese identity. Although these two movements tended to occur concurrently, logically they can be separated.

The bridge that allowed Vajiravudh to reconcile two apparently contradictory attitudes consisted in a new premise that he introduced. This premise equated Siamese identity with loyalty to the Siamese monarchy, and *voilà*, the apparent contradiction was resolved. Even if a Siamese identity was defined by exclusion of the Chinese, the latter automatically partook in Siamese identity by pledging loyalty to the monarchy. The notion of the unity between Thai identity and belief in the Thai monarchy as well as the restructuring of the apparatus of state power through administrative centralization reflected two complementary aspects of state formation under Bangkok expansionism. While state restructuring involved the exclusion and displacement of local princes and rulers by the new power elite in Bangkok, these same displaced local elites could be readmitted into the ranks of the new national elite by pledging loyalty to serve the absolute monarchy.[155]

The essentiality of loyalty to the king is stressed again and again in Vajiravudh's writings and addresses; it is a permanent theme throughout his reign.[156] In an essay in 1915, Vajiravudh made loyalty to the king part of the definition of a "true Thai." The notions of loyalty and Thai identity were incorporated into a new doctrine of Thai nationalism expressed in the union of three components: *chart, sasana, phramahakasat*—literally meaning "nation," "religion" and "king."

What began as a project to arouse a sense of Siamese identity was co-opted by Vajiravudh and subsumed under Royalist Nationalism, which demanded of the people unquestioning loyalty to the monarchy as part of their newfound national identity, regardless of their previous regional political rulers or ethnic origins. Loyalty to the absolute monarchy of Siam and the Siamese identity were

King Vajiravudh
(centered) with the
Wild Tiger Corps.

indivisible. The Royalist Nationalism movement was embodied in the formation of the "Wild Tiger Corps," a quasi-military organization founded by Vajiravudh in 1911, whose recruits comprised royal dependents and civilian bureaucrats close to Vajiravudh's circle. Its *raison d'être* was not military but ideological: "The military training teaches you discipline and order of command; it also plants love for the king, the nation and religion and makes you ready to sacrifice your lives for them." [157] This speech was typical of Vajiravudh's many lectures to the members of the Wild Tiger Corps. The principal aim was to strengthen and enforce loyalty among royal servants and officials.

Vajiravudh's legacy can be said to be the emergence of the first Thai nationalist movement. Its doctrinal development and the symbolic power of "nation, religion and king", which remains today, owes much to him. As the originator of the kingdom's nationalist movement, he tirelessly moved all the policy levers of the Siamese absolute monarchy, including compulsory state primary education, state propaganda, official rewriting of history and evocation of militarism, amid endless affirmations of the identity of dynasty and nation.

Vajiravudh left an indelible mark on the future development of Thai nationalism. He would be remembered as its most important philosopher, and his ideological legacy was inherited by the People's Party. However, his attempt to save the absolute monarchy by putting it on a strong ideological foundation failed to prevent political power from slipping out of the monopolistic control of the royal family. Like the innovations of his father, his own innovations would also prove to be ephemeral for the monarchy though lasting for the polity.

LUKCHIN OF THE VAJIRAVUDH ERA

The Southern Tycoon: Phraya Pradinun-Bhumirat (Liao Chiangsoon) and His Son Khun Sethbhakdi (Liao Jingsong) of Surat Thani

In 1867, Liao Chiangsoon (1853–1925, pictured left) left his hometown in Chenghai District near Shantou to seek his fortune in Bangkok when he was 15. The young King Chulalongkorn had just ascended the throne a year earlier. Fortunately for Liao, in Bangkok his uncle had left him the legacy of a domestic shipping business, which gave him the opportunity to travel to southern Siam frequently. There, he became acquainted with Phraya Nakhon Si Thammarat (Noo Na Nakhon) and was taken under his patronage. Impressed by the hard-working young man who always delivered, Phraya Nakhon Si Thammarat provided him with many opportunities, and soon Liao was able to bid for several bird's nest concessions in the south.[158]

At the turn of the century, Liao Chiangsoon gained the largest monopoly of the bird's nest industry in Siam. The small market town of Ban Don, Surat Thani, was the capital of his bird's nest industry, and Liao built a sprawling market with a modern cinema, a rice mill, a saw mill and an ice-making factory.

Liao Chiangsoon was a well-known face at court due to his role as the palace's supplier of the best-quality bird's nests, and also owing to his generosity in supporting charitable projects. Liao enjoyed the privilege of being well liked by King Vadjiravudh, who appointed him Phraya Pradinan-Bhumirat, while in private the king called him "the bird's nest man." Indeed, very few Chinese were elevated to the rank of *phraya* during this reign. In 1924, a devastating typhoon hit Chaozhou. Pradinan-Bhumirat, who was elected the ninth chairman of the Chinese Chamber of Commerce, informed the king of the misfortune suffered by his countrymen and His Majesty kindly donated 5,000 baht to help the victims in China. This gesture by King Vajiravudh led to considerable contributions from the rest of the country.

Liao's second son, Liao Jingsong (1892–1980, pictured below) later expanded the business to other provinces in the south, namely, Chumphon, Nakhon Si Thammarat and Songkhla, where he invested in power stations to provide electricity to the towns. In recognition of his development efforts, Liao Jingsong was appointed Khun Sethbhakdi by King Prajadhipok. In Bangkok, the Liao family also expanded into banking, insurance, shipping and rice milling.[159]

Although Sethbhakdi was a second-generation Chinese born in Nakhon Si Thammarat, he was a cultivated man of letters. His Siamese mother died in a boat accident when he was three, and little Jingsong was sent to China for education under the care of his Chinese stepmother. Having grown up in Shantou at the turn of the century, Sethbhakdi was a patriotic entrepreneur who later promoted Chinese education in Siam. He was one of the founders of the Xinmin Chinese School in Bangkok and the Thao In Chinese School in Surat Thani.

Sethbhakdi was a staunch supporter of Seow Hoodseng's anti-Japanese movement and was a major donor in fundraising campaigns to help China's war efforts against Japan. In efforts to help the war-torn fatherland, Sethbhakdi and his compatriots, including Hia Guang-iam (Iamsuree), Tae Juebing (Techapaiboon), Tan Gengchuang (Tanthana) and U Chuliang (Uahwatanasakul), founded the Teochew Association, the *Zhongguoriibao* Chinese newspaper and a rice-exporting company to send cheap rice to Shantou to feed the poor. Sethbhakdi traveled extensively among the southern towns to raise funds for China. His motto was "National prosperity or catastrophe depends on the dutiful son."[160]

When the Japanese landed in Siam on 8 December 1941, Sethbhakdi and 13 of his compatriots were arrested by the Thai police. The officer who interrogated him tried in vain to convince Liao to cooperate. When he refused to betray his principles, he was sentenced to lifetime imprisonment and his brother Lek Sethbhakdi was sentenced to a 16-year term. Fortunately, both were released after the Pacific War ended. One fellow compatriot, Tan Gengchuang, who was also jailed in Bangkhwang prison, was not so fortunate. The anxiety of being jailed deteriorated his health and he died soon after he was released.

Sethbhakdi was blessed with longevity and lived to see the new dawn of Thai-Chinese relations. At the age of 86, he was on the welcoming committee when Deng Xiaoping visited Bangkok in 1978.[161]

Luang Siththepkan (Ngou Gimliang—Leo Wangtan) of Banpong, Ratchaburi

Charnvit Kasetsiri described Banpong, a small town in Ratchaburi, where his father happily settled, as "a new town built with the arrival of the railroad in 1895. Not many influential families, except the Vongsarote (who were distant relatives of the Chakri dynasty and successive governors of Ratchaburi during the early Bangkok period). Many of the Banpong elite were Chinese. Prominent community members included Luang Siththepkan and Kit Supyen who were elected to the municipal council repeatedly."[162] Both men were leading members of a large Catholic community with extensive family ties all over Ratchaburi and Nakhon Pathom.

Since the mid-Ayudhya period, the population of Ratchaburi had been predominantly Mon due to waves of mass migrations from Lower Burma. Added to these were the Chinese mercantile communities who traded along the Mae Klong River and a few Catholic settlements that arrived in the 19th century. Siththepkan's mother, Cecilia Petch Cheng (1863–1928, pictured, far left), was a third-generation Mon-Chinese who lived in the Catholic village of Don Krabueng in Banpong District. Her husband, a Teochew from China, died when she was 37. Cecilia Petch continued her rice, peanut and sesame trading business to support her nine children with the help of Gimliang, her eldest son, whose Christian name was Leo.[163] Both Cecilia Petch and Leo Gimliang were devoted Catholics. The family would get up very early in the morning, around 5am, to attend their daily church service.

Leo Gimliang started his career as a dealer in agricultural

Siththepkan (sitting on a chair, in white) with the Catholic community at St. Magarita Church, Bangtan.

commodities. In those days, rural tradesmen often extended loans, as there were no banking services beyond Bangkok and the big towns. Apart from money lending, Leo Gimliang also applied for and won the concession right to supply firewood for the railway at Klong Bangtan, a refueling station near Banpong. Seeing potential in the farmland near the station, Leo Gimliang branched out from his family *kongsi* in Don Krabueng to buy 500 *rai* of land in 1912, where he built a beautiful two-story brick mansion.[164] At his new home village, Leo Gimliang donated land and built a community church for the Catholic mission called Saint Margarita, as well as a small school.[165] An old lady reminisced that in those days Bangtan was full of devoted Chinese Catholics who went to church twice a day, once in the morning and again in the evening. Some prayers used in this church were also recited in Chinese.[166]

When Prince Svastivatana visited Ratchaburi in 1916, Leo Gimliang hosted the hunting party's stay at his new home in Bangtan. The prince was so impressed with his host's palatial mansion that he gave Leo Gimliang the new surname of "Wangtan," meaning "the man who owns a palace in Bangtan."[167] Leo Gimliang's reception for King Vajiravudh's visit to Banpong was equally successful. The king was pleased that Leo and his workers managed to build a spacious camp for the training of *suapah* (Wild Tiger) scouts in Banpong within a period of three weeks, well ahead of schedule. Leo Gimliang was granted an honorable title of Luang Siththepkan in 1924.

Another favorite occupation of Siththepkan was real estate. In those days clearing the jungle for cultivation to claim land deeds was still encouraged by the crown. In 1928, he embarked on an ambitious project to claim 10,000 *rai* at Preak Nhamdaeng. Here he built long walls around the land to block salt water and divided the property into several income-generating projects, such as coconut plantations, rice fields and fish ponds. It was a noble idea but the means he used was a controversial one. Siththepkan had a huge workforce divided into seven brigades.[168] Many of these workers were money borrowers who had failed to pay their debts and were thereby put to hard labor. In 1931, 300 people filed complaints to the governor of Nakhon Pathom claiming that Siththepkan had forced them into slave labor in order to settle their debts.[169]

Siththepkan's money-lending operations with its large network in Ratchaburi and Nakhon Pathom also earned him a notorious name that echoed the name Shylock, the Jewish money-lender in the *Merchant of Venice*, a Shakespeare play that had been translated into Thai by Vajiravudh.

In 1934, Siththepkan moved to Banpong, a booming town on the banks of Mae Klong River, which was

easily accessible by road and rail from Bangkok. Here he built a new headquarters, a market, a saw mill, a rice mill and an ice-making factory. In 1938, he expanded his land holding to Huay Krabork by purchasing several hundred *rai* of land at 25 *satang* per rai. Six years later, the government granted his request to settle Chinese laborers there to work on his sugar plantation. Siththepkan also built approximately 60 kilometers of roads linking Huay Krabork to other villages and towns and donated them to the government.

Despite the poor image presented of Siththepkan in public records, he was always portrayed as generous in the Catholic mission's records.[170] He donated 300 *rai* of land in Huay Krabork and built Saint Teresa Church together with the Thepwidhya School for the Catholic mission.

On 9 September 1954, the town of Banpong caught fire. The fire burned uncontrollably for six hours, and fire trucks had to be sent from Ratchaburi and Bangkok. The fire destroyed two markets and 800 families were left homeless. Over half of the properties damaged by the fire belonged to Luang Siththepkan (pictured), who owned the upper market, and another large portion destroyed by the fire belonged to Tongkam Vongsarote, the owner of the lower market.[171]

Siththepkan's wealth and extensive land holdings, as well as his controversial life, was an open invitation for enquiries. Many farmers who lost their lands when he foreclosed on unpaid loans lodged complaints against Siththepkan for squeezing his fellow townspeople for repayment—sometimes by questionable means. Many lawsuits were filed and Siththepkan was jailed for about a year. He had to give up about 10,000 *rai* of land[172] before being able to negotiate his release.

During the reign of King Prajadhipok, Siththepkan's enormous wealth and aggressive approach were reported by both the *Bangkok Daily Mail*, and later *The New York Times*. In fact, King Prajadhipok was surprised by *The New York Times* article titled "Siam's Young King Foils Unique Plot," published on 30 March 1932.[173] The king was sent the article by the Siamese ambassador in Washington, D.C. It alleged that Siththepkan made loans to youths in the region that were repayable by private military service. As Siththepkan's loyalty to both his God and his king were common knowledge in the capital, King Prajadhipok dismissed the news and instead questioned the standard of reporting of the *New York Times* journalist.[174]

Charnvit Kasetsiri's book on Banpong seems to classify Siththepkan as a royalist by mentioning a rumor circulating in Banpong in the early 1940s, which alleged that Siththepkan air-freighted trunk loads of money to the abdicated King Prajadhipok in London.[175] However, according to the Catholic mission's records, it is more likely that Luang Siththepkan was donating trunk loads of his wealth to God.

Leo's funeral was attended by long lines of mourners from Ratchaburi's Catholic community, a community that he had helped develop.

Tongyoo Bhumadhon: Chaomae of Nakhon Si Thammarat Market

Phuthorn Bhumadhon, the Thai master curator of historical sites and a prominent conservation advocate, is probably the last person you would suspect of being Chinese. But in fact, he is descended from a pedigree Chinese lineage. His grandmother had deep roots in Siam's Chinese community that date back all the way to the Ayudhya period.

Tongyoo, Phuthorn's grandmother (pictured), was born in a distinguished neighborhood in Sampeng facing Klong Ong Ang, the city moat where most of the old-named Chinese, including the Jotikasthira and the Sundaravej, lived. According to Tongyoo, her forefathers lived in Ayudhya, on the bank of Klong Suan Plu where King Taksin's father Tae Yong once lived. Her great-grandfather, a Teochew named Tae Hud, came down to Bangkok by land; those who came down by river had very little chance of making it because Burmese looters robbed and killed those who traveled by boat.

Tongyoo's grandfather, Tae Suo, was a porcelain junk master who worked the China trade, but her father preferred to stay in Bangkok and serve the nearby Burapha Palace. Tongyoo's mother was a lady-in-waiting to Princess Yingyaowalak, one of King Mongkut's elder daughters. Unfortunately, when the princess became pregnant by a Buddhist monk, the punishment according to traditional Siamese inner palace law was very severe, and Tongyoo's mother, who was the princess's confidant, also suffered caning. Traumatized by the extreme physical pain inflicted upon her, she became psychologically withdrawn and lost her capacity to speak. Subsequently, the only words that passed from her mouth were "Yai-Yingyaowaluk, Yai-Yingyaowaluk!" until she died. Tongyoo and her brother were left unattended.

One day during her childhood, Tongyoo fell asleep in her grandfather's junk. By the time her grandfather realized that his little granddaughter was aboard, the ship had already passed the delta on the way to China. Tongyoo spent a year in Shantou where she learned to speak Teochew fluently.

Back in Siam, Tongyoo's relative, who lived next door, had a *likae* theatre with a dance troupe called "Luang San's Likae Troupe." Because they lived in Sampeng, the performances had to be adapted to local Chinese tastes. The dancers performed stories from Chinese legends such as *Shou Tang Yan Yi*. Although the songs and dances were performed in Thai and accompanied by Thai music, all of the dancers were dressed in Chinese opera costumes. When Tongyoo and her husband later moved to Nakhon Si Thammarat where making a livelihood was easier than in Bangkok, they took the *likae* troupe south with them.

Like most *lukchin*, Tongyoo was a working woman. She owned a food store in the main market of Nakhon Si Thammarat. Being a strong-willed woman, she made her own rules and became respected as a local *nakleng* within the small community. Impressed by her mother's unfortunate experience, Tongyoo tended to sympathize with the underdog. In Nakhon Si Thammarat Market, she made it a rule that at 8am every morning, the store would stop business and instead serve the mentally and physically impaired, who lined up for their meals. Every beggar would be fed before the store returned to business as usual.

Based on an interview with Phuthorn Bhumadhon, July 2014

DIVIDED LOYALTIES

(1900–1945)

The first half of the 20th century was the most contentious and difficult for the Chinese in Siam. As an overarching sense of a Chinese identity began to unite the Chinese in Siam, a speech by Chinese revolutionary Sun Yatsen in Bangkok in 1908 and the Chinese General Strike of 1910 alienated King Vajiravudh and his court. Further exacerbating tensions, the local Chinese leadership threw its considerable influence behind Sun Yatsen's republican agenda for China through fundraising and newspaper editorials. The euphoria felt over the success of the Xinhai Revolution which ended the Qing dynasty would be short-lived. The ensuing decades would see competing nationalist and communist agendas divide not only China but also its overseas communities. After the 1932 revolution ended absolute monarchy in Siam, anti-Chinese sentiments began to boil over. As Siam aligned itself with the emerging Asian power of Japan, which invaded China in 1937, the local Chinese leadership instigated strikes against Japanese businesses. As the stakes rose for the new Thai leadership, an anti-Chinese campaign saw almost all Chinese schools and newspapers closed, and the exile and even assassination of many prominent Chinese leaders.

In June 1910, Bangkok woke up to a crippling general strike. All Chinese shops, gambling dens and fresh markets in Bangkok Chinatown had closed down. All rickshaw men, boatmen, coolies and porters servicing Bangkok and its port stopped working. Most Chinese workers, employees and businesses in nearly every sector went on strike, bringing Bangkok to a standstill for three days.

The general strike was a reaction to the new capitation tax introduced by the government, the last in a series of tax reforms under King Chulalongkorn's administration. Under this new tax law, all foreigners including Chinese would be taxed at the rate of 6 baht per annum, whereas before, Chinese paid a triennial tax of only 4 baht.[1]

Exploiting the workers' discontent at the increase in taxes, the general strike had been instigated by the conservative, pro-establishment leaders of the Chinese community and their mouthpiece newspaper, *Qinan Xinbao*. The Chinese secret society thugs who distributed leaflets and roamed the streets to enforce the strike demonstrated to the Siamese ruling elite that the Chinese enjoyed complete ascendency in commerce and the wage labor force. The leaders' hidden agenda was to use worker discontent as a platform to air their grievance that the Chinese government had no representative in Siam to assist its subjects in their hour of need.[2]

King Chulalongkorn did not stand down. The Siamese army was called in to break up the demonstration and restore law and order. Hundreds of striking Chinese workers and their Triad backers were arrested and imprisoned. During the strike, soldiers teamed up with Thai workers and food vendors to keep part of the capital city running.

The king had clearly demonstrated that he would not tolerate any open challenge to political authority and would not hesitate to bring the coercive power of the state upon its dissident Chinese subjects. However, the situation was not without a certain irony: modern state formation had occurred under the shadow of the alliance between the court and the kingdom's dominant Chinese economic group. The latter now became a victim of the institution that it had helped create.

In using the power of the military to end the strike, Chulalongkorn acted less in his role as king than as the head of the government. It was the power of the state that prevailed over the Chinese tax revolt. Thus, the state had unwittingly replaced the king as the center of power in the kingdom.

King Chulalongkorn's reforms to strengthen the absolute monarchy had paradoxically also weakened it; the monarchy was now dependent upon the state and the new elite of state functionaries who operated the state apparatus for the crown's protection. Meanwhile, the autonomous state functionaries were aware of the enormous power that they wielded, as well as the dependence of the absolute monarchy on that power. This introduced a new dynamic of instability into the relationship between the monarchy and the state. The coercive power of the state would be called to play again at a future juncture in Thai history, not always in support of the absolute monarchy.

For the moment, the military had demonstrated that it could be used effectively to restore law and order and uphold the legitimate political authority of the kingdom. The quick suppression of the general strike was also due to the prevailing disunity within the Chinese community. The opposing anti-strike newspaper, the *Huaxian Xinbao*, as well as the *Chino-Siam Warasup*, were the mouthpieces of Sun Yatsen's Tongmenghui revolutionary party in Siam, which was headed by Seow Hoodseng. Seow saw an opportunity to exploit the Chinese discontent to gain the goodwill of the government.

King Vajiravudh (Rama VI, reigned 1910–25).

Chapter opening picture: Primary students in the classroom of Yumin Chinese School in Thailand during the 1950s.

Seow Hoodseng strongly defended the Siamese government's position on the tax issue. His running editorial line argued persuasively that the new tax rate was fair; that as Siamese subjects the Chinese should be taxed the same rate as other foreigners in Siam; that the new tax rate was not discriminatory against the Chinese because the native Siamese were not paying any less than what the Chinese had been asked to pay. Seow Hoodseng's political gambit worked. His prudent condemnation of the Chinese tax revolt impressed upon the Siamese government that there was also a strong loyalist faction among the Chinese community. Through his skillful editorial positioning during the general strike of 1910, Seow Hoodseng emerged, in the eyes of the government, as the most important opinion leader of the Chinese community in Siam.

Seow Hoodseng had much to be pleased about. Not only had he emerged as the acknowledged leader of the Tongmenghui revolutionary movement, but he also became the most prominent Chinese in Siam at the start of the reign of King Vajiravudh. Not long ago, he had been regarded as a brash young lawyer who had dared to challenge the authority of the powerful elder Triad leader, Yi Goh Hong, or "Second Brother Hong,"[3] who was Seow's senior by 14 years. Second Brother Hong, or Tae Teeyong—elder of the Triad Brotherhood, chairman of the French Chinese Commercial Association, and a philanthropist whose illustrious name graced the boards of the Poh Teck Tung Foundation, the Tai Hong Gong Shrine and the Peiying Chinese School—was the seemingly untouchable leader of the Bangkok Chinese community. However, Second Brother Hong must have had a secret misgiving that his glory rested on unsure foundations.

The Philanthropist "Second Brother Hong"

Tae Teeyong was a self-made man who owed his power and position in the Chinese community neither to wealthy parents nor impeccable lineage. He was

Phra Anuwat-Rajniyom
(Tae Teeyong) or
"Second Brother
Hong" (Yi Goh Hong).

a *lukchin* born of a Chinese father and a Siamese mother in Bangkok in 1849. His father operated a small shophouse in Bamrungmuang. Commonplace among Chinese immigrants in the mid-19th century, his father kept two homes: a Thai home with his Siamese wife in Bangkok, and a Chinese home in his ancestral village in Chao'an, Guangdong Province. His Chinese wife ran the home he had left behind during his sojourn in the Nanyang.

Following tradition, when his son Teeyong turned seven, he was sent back to his ancestral house in Chao'an to be educated and raised as a respectful, filial son. Teeyong was not happy in his new Chinese home and missed his Siamese mother. When his Chinese stepmother remarried following the news of his father's death, Teeyong ran away from home. He found his way to the port city of Shantou and did whatever work was available to earn enough money for food and for his passage by ship back to Siam.[4]

When Teeyong set foot in Siam again he was already 16 years old. Brimming with hope and child-like expectation, he set out for his father's shophouse in Bamrungmuang to find his mother. His fantasies and longings to be reunited with his Siamese mother were dashed when he arrived at Bamrungmuang. His mother had moved to an unknown destination after his father's death.

Teeyong had realized his dream to return to his home in Siam—here he was at last. However, instead of the warm reunion he had pictured in his dreams, the reality was cold and empty. He found himself alone, with no mother, friends, family or relatives. In addition, Teeyong was penniless.

It was as if he was reliving his nightmare in Shantou all over again, alone, in a big city full of strangers. Except this time, he had the knowledge and confidence of having done it before. He would survive!

Just as he had done in Shantou, he began to look for any kind of work. At that time, the biggest countrywide opium tax farmer, Phraya Phakdi-Phattrakorn (Lao Gibing), was a Teochew from Chao'an. As a native of Chao'an, Teeyong received an introduction and was readily employed by Phraya Phakdi-Phattrakorn.

Opium and gambling tax farms comprised the dark underbelly of the Chinese-dominated economy in Siam. While the kingdom depended on Chinese virtues for the expansion of commerce and industry, the public treasury relied on Chinese vices to generate government revenue. Phraya Phakdi-Phattrakorn was the powerful godfather in the shadowy world inhabited by vice dens and their gangs of enforcers. Lao Gibing's stature and influence among the Triad secret societies was such that even the Siamese authorities had to enlist his help to quell troubles among warring Triad gangs.[5]

Young, able-bodied, strong and toughened by adversity, Teeyong demonstrated all the characteristics of a born fighter; naturally he was attracted to the martial solidarity of the secret society brotherhood, with its rituals, blood oath and code of silence. Teeyong was soon initiated into the *Sa Tiam* (Three Dots) brotherhood. His character suited the culture of the brotherhood: not highly educated, fiercely loyal and possessing the daredevil's carelessness of danger, but at the same time protective of the weak and defenseless. He embodied the *raison d'étre* of the Triad self-defense organization—to defend the poor, vulnerable, disadvantaged Chinese coolies overseas, whose own government had abandoned them. Through his Chao'an connections, Tae Teeyong clawed his way up the disciplined hierarchy of the Triad organization to become a *yi goh* or "Second Brother," signifying an important rank within the Triad secret society fraternity.

It is not clear how long he served under the powerful Phraya Phakdi-Phattrakorn. He appeared to have built up a following and established an independent base of operations in Chiang Mai, where he met his Siamese wife. Drawing on his formative experiences, connections and insider knowledge of Chinese secret society operations and tradecraft, he naturally followed in the footsteps of his powerful patron.

His opportunity to rise came during the period of administrative centralization that accompanied Bangkok expansionism into the outer regions of Siam during the last two decades of the 19th century. New tax farming concessions in opium, liquor and gambling were opened up in the north and northeast, contrary to the general policy of replacing tax farms with bureaucratic collection. In fact, during 1888–92, the number of gambling houses in Bangkok was reduced from 400 to 16, while other tax farms in the central region and the peninsular south were also gradually phased out. Teeyong seized the opportunity that opened up in the north to acquire his own lucrative liquor concession. This soon made him immensely rich.

In the process he struck up a relationship with the family of another powerful patron, Tia U-Teng, known in Siam as Akon Teng—the largest tax concessionaire in Siam. Although Akon Teng's main source of revenue was from his teak monopoly concession, he also held major opium, gambling and liquor concessions all over the north. This enduring relationship influenced Teeyong's subsequent involvement in several critical future events, including the anti-US boycott and the fateful general strike of 1910.

Teeyong had come into his own as a powerful and influential leader. By the turn of the century, he had risen to the commanding heights of the secret brotherhood in Bangkok. More power translated into more wealth, and he maneuvered his way into another big government concession—the lucrative *huay*, or lottery concession,

Porcelain chips used in Bangkok gambling dens.

in Bangkok. Befitting his financial clout and his status in the Triad fraternity, he was henceforth called Yi Goh Hong—Second Brother Hong—of the secret brotherhood. With his rapidly expanding business interests, Yi Goh Hong found it expedient to become a French subject and use the privilege of French consular protection to shield his bootlegging activities from the exactions of Siamese official regulators. His growing power and influence within the Chinese secret society, as well as his standing within the French business lobby, was reflected in his elevation to the prestigious, honorary position as chairman of the French Chinese Commercial Association founded in 1909.

When Sun Yatsen sought the good offices of the French to contact leaders of the overseas-Chinese community in Bangkok, the deputy French governor general in Hanoi, Charles Hardouin, formerly the French consul to Siam, gave Sun letters of introduction to meet three influential Chinese in Bangkok who were French subjects. They were Ng Miaongian Lamsam, a Hakka Chinese timber merchant; Akon Teng, a Teochew teak trader and rice miller; and Yi Goh Hong.[6]

Yi Goh Hong met with Sun Yatsen during his first visit to Bangkok in May to June of 1903. There is scarcely any information on what took place in that meeting, but they must have talked about serious business. Sun Yatsen had hatched a conspiracy to invade Southern China from French Indochina. He wanted French military support to overthrow the Manchu regime and establish a republic in China. It was an open secret that France harbored ambitions to extend its influence in the provinces of Southern China, including Guangdong, Guangxi and Yunnan, in order to better protect French possessions and interests in Tonking.[7] To this end, Sun Yatsen spent six months in Hanoi, from December 1902 until May 1903, to lobby French political, diplomatic and military circles for support. Sun asked the French for arms and military advisors, proposing in exchange to grant France concessions in the southern provinces.

Sun Yatsen had also lobbied the Chinese community in Hanoi but did not succeed in receiving any significant financial support from them. One must assume that his purpose in coming to Bangkok in 1903 was to get financial support for the planned invasion of Southern China, which he had failed to receive from the overseas-Chinese community in Hanoi. Moreover, Sun Yatsen knew that Yi Goh Hong was a powerful leader of the Siamese Triad fraternity.

Sun Yatsen during the 1910s.

During that period, Sun Yatsen was also deeply involved with the Triads and had close affiliations with the Triad lodges in both Hawaii and San Francisco.[8] His recent conspiracies against the Qing government could not have been undertaken without the organizational support and manpower supplied by the Triad network in Southern China. Both the failed Canton uprising in 1895 and the Huizhou uprising in 1900 were undertaken in cooperation with the Triad network.[9] The planned invasion of Guangdong from French Indochina would also depend on Triad support. Thus, Sun Yatsen was not only appealing to Yi Goh Hong's patriotic sentiments; he was also coming to ask for Hong's help as a member of the secret brotherhood.

Whatever happened in that meeting, Sun Yatsen apparently came away without the help that he had sought from Yi Goh Hong. What the other French subject recommended by Charles Hardouin, Akon Teng, told Sun Yatsen during their meeting may be helpful for understanding what might have taken place between Sun Yatsen and Yi Goh Hong. Scholar and historian Eiji Murashima summarizes what Sun Yatsen reportedly told Akon Teng:

> *If there were no revolution to change China into a republic, China would become a European colony. In (Siam) there were many Chinese residents, and as Akon Tia Teng was a wealthy man, he could assist the revolutionary cause by mobilizing some funding and helping to create nationalist sentiment among his Chinese compatriots. [Sun Yatsen] asked for help to raise money to buy arms also. In Guangxi Province there were as many as 200,000 revolutionaries, but no arms. If they had some funds to buy arms, the French could be asked to assist in transporting them into Yunnan so they could be used for the revolution in Guangxi and Guangdong where a republic could be established and gradually expanded to cover the whole country.*[10]

Akon Teng reportedly turned down Sun Yatsen's request on the grounds that the merchants in Siam were simply traders and did not understand politics. Thus, raising funds would be impossible and he could not accept responsibility for the matter.[11] Presumably, Sun Yatsen said more or less the same thing to Yi Goh Hong and received more or less the same response.

In 1903, the Chinese in Siam were psychologically unprepared to handle Sun Yatsen's revolutionary request. In fact, at the turn of the century, most Chinese, even in China, would not understand Sun Yatsen's discourse on setting up a republic in China. Moreover, the Chinese in Siam enjoyed a long-standing alliance with Siamese royalty. By bestowing official ranks, the Siamese court co-opted Chinese leaders to help administer the affairs of the Chinese community according to their own customs. Yi Goh Hong's patron was ennobled by King Chulalongkorn with the title Phraya Phakdi-Phattrakorn. The Triads in Siam did not understand the meaning of a "republic"; they supported the Thai absolute monarchy.

However, by the turn of the century, the Chinese émigré world that Yi Goh Hong thought he understood was changing rapidly in ways he could barely

Yi Goh Hong's mansion in Bangkok, his family photograph and a portrait of himself as shown in *Twentieth Century Impressions of Siam: Its History, People, Commerce, Industries, and Resources* by Arnold Wright and Oliver T. Breakspear (1914).

comprehend. The intrusions of Western armies on Chinese soil coupled with peasant rebellions had devastated large parts of the country, destroying the livelihoods of countless people. As internal turmoil caused a mass exodus from South China, the nature of Chinese emigration began to change. The new wave of immigrants who came to Siam after the second half of the 19th century were often victims who carried a sense that foreigners and outsiders had done a great wrong to their country. The impact of this new wave of Chinese emigration was to change the nature of the Chinese community in Siam.

Some of the changes were good. A new spirit was emerging among the Chinese; it came in the wake of the change occurring within the Chinese community in Siam. For the first time, cutting across social class and dialect groups, Chinese people began to evince a sense of outrage at what they believed to be a wrong done to their country. From this outrage sprang a new sentiment that infected and electrified the entire Chinese community in Siam from top to bottom. It began with small voices here and there, but they were repeated more and more frequently until they coalesced into a roar that reverberated through the entire Chinese community. From boardroom meetings to street-side tea stalls, Chinese were sharing their new sentiment:

> *Chinese, stop competing with one another*
> *to make more and more money;*
> *put the pain and agony of the people in your heart.*

In 1903, at around the time that Yi Goh Hong met with Sun Yatsen, his own revered patron, Phakdi-Phattrakorn (also known as Lao Gibing), and five other leaders of the Chinese community pledged to join together to raise funds to buy land to build a hospital for the poor. The six founders of Tian Fah Hospital symbolized the new spirit of unity that transcended regional and speech groups among the Chinese in Siam. Hong's patron, Lao Gibing, was Teochew; Ng Miaongian Lamsam was Hakka; Tia Giangsam, the son of Akon Teng, was Teochew; Wong Hangchao was Cantonese; Koh Huijia, a British subject and son of Koh Mahwah, was another Teochew; and lastly, Min Laohasetthi, later appointed Phraya Choduk-Rachasretthi, the official leader of the Chinese in Siam, was a Hokkien. Among the leaders of the Chinese mentioned above, Akon Teng and Ng Miaongian Lamsam had met Sun Yatsen.

After centuries of conflict the Chinese in Siam had finally overcome their dialectal and regional differences and achieved a more united vision and consciousness of sharing important things in common as Chinese. In 1903, the Chinese in Siam exulted in their newfound unity and common identity as a people whose country had suffered at the hands of foreigners. Suddenly, at such a time, Sun Yatsen was asking them to fight one another again. The Chinese in Siam were in no mood for that kind of message. Hence, they did not join him; instead they joined hands with their compatriots from different speech groups and localities in a common philanthropic endeavor to express their newfound overarching Chinese identity.

The Tian Fah Hospital was completed two years later. King Chulalongkorn attended the ceremonial opening on 19 September 1905. Greeting the king's approach and gracing the main entrance of the Tian Fah Hospital was the large memorial message, "Putting the pain and agony of the people in one's

Three of the six founders of the Tian Fah Hospital.

own heart," which embodied the compassion of the Chinese in Siam for their compatriots in China. The hospital, located in Bangkok's Chinatown and equipped with 250 beds, was officially opened on 20 September, the king's birthday. The total cost of the building was 160,000 baht, contributed largely by the local Chinese community. The king donated an additional 8,000 baht at the ceremonial opening.

The establishment of the Tian Fah Hospital was an important milestone in the emergence of an overarching Chinese identity. The project to build the hospital was the first-ever cooperative effort among the five dialect groups of Teochew, Hakka, Cantonese, Hailam and Hokkien.[12] The Tian Fah

THE TIAN FAH PHILANTHROPISTS

Tian Fah Hospital in Bangkok's Chinatown. The hospital's origins date back to 1903.

This period of turmoil in China changed the profile of the Chinese immigrant as more and more desperate peasants were forced to leave the fatherland and join the Chinese communities overseas. Thus, the priorities of Bangkok Chinese soon changed from making money to the sentiment embodied in such lines as "Putting the pain and agony of the people in one's heart." A sign with this message was hung at the entrance of Tian Fah Hospital in the heart of Yaowarat, demonstrating the compassion the Chinese felt for their fellow countrymen during those troublesome days of the early 20th century.

In 1903, six philanthropist leaders of the Chinese community joined together to raise funds to buy land and build a hospital for paupers. They included Koh Huijia, later the chairman of the Chinese Chamber of Commerce; Lao Chongmin, who was later appointed Phraya Choduk-Rachasretthi by King Vajiravudh; Luang Sophon-Petcharat, a respected tycoon who represented the Chinese community at King Vajiravudh's coronation; Lao Gibing, Ng Miaongian and Wong Hangchao.

Lao Gibing (劉繼賓): Phraya Phakdi-Phattrakorn (Ow Jiew Utokaparch)

Lao Gibing left Gaolongpu Village in Chao'an County, Guangdong Province, as an ambitious teenager, crossing the sea with the determination to better himself in Siam, a land with more opportunity. Over the years, his courage and fighting spirit earned him respect and he matured to become a well-known opium tax farmer as well as an influential figure among the Triad community in Bangkok.[13] He was commonly known as Ow Jiew Tao.[14] Some believed that Lao Gibing was a Triad leader, citing the complaint that was launched against him in 1895 when his men blocked the northbound waterways in search of illegal opium. The ships found with opium but without a receipt from Lao's *kongsi* were fined 50–60 baht each.[15]

At the peak of his career, Lao Gibing owned four rice mills as well as shipping and mining businesses. Lao was the patron of Yi Goh Hong (Tae Teeyong), another well-known Triad leader who came from the same

village in Chao'an. The young Hong worked as an accountant for Lao Gibing.

As a community leader, Lao Gibing was a charitable man who was both feared and admired. When poor peasants arrived in town but had no money to pay for the arrival fee, Lao Gibing would finance them without exception.[16] His philanthropist spirit to help these poor, homeless migrants was well known among the Chinese in Bangkok. In those days, the Chinese emigrant's experiences of crossing the sea to Siam were often heart-rending. Moreover, residing in an unfamiliar land in tropical heat they were unaccustomed to, there were many who could not adapt and fell ill. Many embarked on the journey by themselves with no relatives in Bangkok. Ill and penniless in an unfamiliar land, seeking medical advice proved difficult due to language barriers. Hence, Lao Gibing, together with several prominent merchants, founded the Tian Fah Hospital for paupers in 1903 to provide medical service free of charge.[17]

According to Thai sources, Lao Gibing led an extravagant and lavish lifestyle. His huge charitable contributions both in China and in Siam, as well as his involvement in many other operations, heavily drained his cash flow. By 1895, his opium concession payments were backlogged and Lao was indebted to the crown by over 2 million baht, a huge amount in those days. Then in 1908, he suffered a heavy loss in the *huay* lottery venture and soon after went bankrupt.[18] Lao Gibing passed away peacefully in 1919 and was survived by three sons and a daughter, Chao Chom Buay.

Ng Miaongian (伍淼源): The Hakka Timber Man (Lamsam)

Ng Miaongian was from the poor farming village of Songkou, Meixian, a Hakka district in the interior of Guangdong Province. Born in 1850, he became an orphan at a young age when both his parents died in the same year. The struggle for "room to live" in Guangdong between the native Cantonese ("Puntei") and the Hakka erupted into a small-scale war known as the Hakka-Puntei War (1864–66), which caused a complete breakdown of social order around the Meixian area. With no parent to care for him, Ng left his hometown and crossed the ocean to Siam where he became a low-paid kitchen hand of a spirit shop in Bangkok.[19] The master at the spirit shop was also a dealer in timber, which he accepted in exchange for spirits when his clients came to town. Despite poverty, Ng enjoyed growing up in a timber yard in this peaceful city. He had to wake up early before dawn to prepare everybody's meal before moving on to load and unload the timber, measure the wood and classify them as well. Gradually, he learned the timber trade as well as his way around Bangkok.

Within 10 years, still in his prime, Ng managed to set up his own timber shop called Kwong Nguan Long by the river in Chakkrawat. His reputation as a bright, hardworking young man preceded him and Ng was soon married to the daughter of one of the most prominent Hakka community leaders in town, Xu Meizhang, commonly called "Second Elder Xu."[20] Xu Meizhang owned a Chinese drug store in Sampeng and was a major donor to the Chinese temple Wat Mangkon Kamalawat when it was founded in 1873.

Ng Miaongian later bid and won timber concessions in Suphanburi, Uthaithani, Kampengpetch, Lukon and Phrae. In those days the logs were floated down to Kwong Kim Loong, Ng's saw mill in Samsen.[21] Being of Hakka descent, his daughter was allowed to work alongside him in a man's world. Ng trained her to ride and shoot, and taught her his secret technique of evaluating floating timber. Nei, Ng's daughter, boasted to her grandson that she could tell the value of timber by standing on each floating log.[22]

Having experienced the hardship of poverty, Ng empathized with the poor. When famine struck his hometown, Ng sent low-cost rice to help. Typical of many Sino-Siamese philanthropists, Ng Miaongian returned to his hometown of Songkou to donate money to local schools to encourage higher education, which he himself was deprived of when he was young.[23]

Ng Miaongian was also a charitable leader of the Hakka community in Bangkok. His projects included fundraising to purchase land for a Hakka cemetery in Bangkok's Silom area. At that time, he was in the north, but the purchasing of the land for the cemetery required his presence, so he returned to Bangkok. As it turned out, the government was auctioning timber concessions at the time, which he promptly bid for and won. The profit on this concession more than made up for the donation he had made for the cemetery. Hence, Ng believed that charitable virtue had its own rewards.[24]

Ng passed away at the age of 59, and his body was moved to a burial site in Songkou. In Siam, his son Ng Yuklong continued to expand the Lamsam trading business. Later generations carried on what he started. Chote Lamsam, Ng Miaongian's grandson, established Kasikornbank and was also the president of the Hakka Association. Julin Lamsam was a member of Parliament. Kasem and Banthoon Lamsam were both elected the chairmen of the Thai Bankers' Association.

Wong Hangchao (王杏洲): The Canton Comprador

The Cantonese leader who funded Tian Fah Hospital was Wong Hangchao. He was educated in Hong Kong, and after mastering both the English and Chinese languages he entered the service of the Hong Kong Banking Corporation. Later, he was transferred to Bangkok and was appointed the comprador of the bank.

When his overseas compatriots asked him to co-found Tian Fah Hospital, Wong was very helpful. Although he was only a bank officer and could not donate a large sum of money like the others, he arranged to provide a loan from the Hong Kong Banking Corporation, which allowed the hospital project to finish on schedule.

Wong was a patriot and was enthusiastic in promoting public welfare for overseas Chinese. When Sun Yatsen came to Siam to advocate revolution, Wong became a strong supporter of the movement. He joined the Tongmenghui to help organize support for the revolution. When the Republic of China was established, he received great praise and honor.[25]

Hospital not only stood for public health service, but also as a symbol of unity among the Chinese in Siam.

Building upon the successful cooperation that had created the Tian Fah Hospital, the five dialect groups again united in another unprecedented common endeavor to oppose what they saw as unjust racial discrimination against Chinese in US immigration policy. Anti-Chinese paranoia fanned by racist Western doctrines like the Yellow Peril had led the American government to pass a law barring further Chinese labor immigration into the US in 1882.

On 16 July 1905, Feng Xiawei, an overseas Chinese who was detained and maltreated by US Immigration, returned to China and set fire to himself in front of the American Consulate in Shanghai. Feng's dramatic suicide highlighted the desperate plight of Chinese laborers who suffered injustice at the hands of US immigration policies and officials. Newspapers carried articles and images of Chinese immigrants detained for months in unsightly wooden sheds, subjected to the indignity of naked medical checks and harsh interrogation by US officials, and humiliatingly deported back to China.

The dramatic self-immolation of Feng in protest of the racist anti-Chinese US immigration policy, coupled with the scandalous publicity of injustices committed by US officials, suddenly personalized the arbitrary authority of foreign powers over Chinese people and, by implication, over China. Millions of Chinese in China were moved by what they learned in newspapers, novels, speeches and songs about racial discrimination in America. Outraged Chinese public opinion began calling for a universal anti-American boycott. Boycott

A Chinese man and his three children in Chinatown, San Francisco, California in 1897.

rallies attracted thousands not only in China but across the Chinese diaspora around the world, including the Chinatowns throughout Southeast Asia, Australia and Europe.

The timely completion of the Tian Fah Hospital in mid-1905 allowed the hospital, which symbolized the unity of the Chinese in Siam, to be used as a venue for organizing a united Chinese anti-US movement both inside and outside the country.[26] The Chinese protest took the form of a strict boycott of US goods beginning in August 1905. Chinese dockworkers and coolies refused to unload US goods, including wheat flour, cigarettes and lamp oil. Chinese importers at Bangkok port sent all the boycotted goods back to Hong Kong and Singapore. Triad gangs combed the city streets confiscating American cigarettes that had evaded the boycott and were being sold in Bangkok shops, bringing the confiscated goods to Tian Fah Hospital.

The international boycott was relaxed in mid-October. The easing of the boycott beginning in Shanghai followed in Bangkok—the boycott of American wheat flour and lamp oil, two American products important in the daily life of both Siamese and Chinese, were relaxed.[27] However, the Chinese had discovered an important political tool that would be used again at a future juncture in Siamese history with telling effect. The Chinese in Siam had just discovered their potential as a powerful political force.

The exhilarating sense of empowerment that swept across the Chinese community was most keenly felt among the *huaqiao*.[28] Yi Goh Hong detected a new sense of pride among the *huaqiao*, from intellectuals down to coolies and rickshaw pullers. This pride had never existed before, but it was being reinforced by a flowering of Chinese language, culture, education, newspapers and a nascent sense of belonging to the Chinese homeland, which pervaded the Chinese community as a whole. It was an awakening that even he experienced. For the first time, Yi Goh Hong began to feel a glowing sense of pride in being a *huaqiao*, and he was filled with a sense of liberating metamorphosis as the world that once regarded Chinese émigrés as pariahs now watched their outstanding economic achievements in the Nanyang region with grudging respect.

Suddenly, through the emergence of the print media and the Chinese newspapers, he felt connected to his counterparts in China and other parts of the Nanyang; he had become a part of a larger whole. With this newfound identity came a sense of empowerment. The Manchu court was suddenly beginning to shower attention upon the overseas Chinese after centuries of neglect. Yi Goh Hong could not suppress a feeling of pride at the thought that representatives from the Qing court had come to request the support of the *huaqiao*, to whom he gave his unreserved empathy and identification.

However, there were other important changes in his world about which he felt uncertain. The phasing out of monopoly farms appeared to have an isolating effect on the Chinese community in Siam. Moreover, by 1907 all the provincial gambling dens were closed. Tax farmers had to re-invent themselves by using their accumulated wealth to invest in the new capitalistic opportunities that the expanding economy opened up.

It was the need to diversify into other commercial activities that caused him to partner with Sophon-Phetcharat in the unfortunate shipping venture that was to cost him dearly. In 1909, Yi Goh Hong and Luang Sophon-Petcharat, Akon Teng's son, co-invested in the China Siam Steamship Company, formed by a group of *huaqiao* businessmen, to break the shipping monopoly of the German Nord-Deutscher Lloyd shipping line on the Bangkok-Shantou route. However, due to a price-cutting war, the China Siam Steamship Company became a financial catastrophe for its wealthy shareholders, including Yi Goh Hong.

Perhaps the most unwelcome change of all was the Angyi Act of 1897, which outlawed secret societies in Siam. Suddenly, the shadowy, secret world that Yi Goh Hong inhabited had been blown apart and the leaders of the secret brotherhood saw their monopoly of power suddenly disappear. As they came out into the open, they had to share the leadership stage with the new generation of educated Chinese intelligentsia who had come up through the ranks of open civil society organizations and voluntary associations, including upstart journalists like Seow Hoodseng.

However, Hong bowed to the inevitable. As some of the formerly shadowy organizations were registered as associations, he took his place with the new generation of Chinese leaders whose base was in the capital city's voluntary

Tai Hong Gong Shrine and an altar for the spirit of Yi Goh Hong, who donated the land for the Poh Teck Tung to build the shrine.

associations. Hence, Yi Goh Hong adapted himself to the new situation and reinvented himself as a philanthropist.

His first philanthropic donation can be traced back to 1899, after he became very wealthy. It helped to finance the establishment of Baan Don Cemetery for burying the poor and homeless Chinese. The donation of land for building Tai Hong Gong Shrine and the headquarters of the Poh Teck Tung Foundation followed in 1909; and in 1916 he donated to the construction of Peiying Chinese School for Teochew children. Through his generous donations, he laundered his image and partook of the prestige achieved by the legendary Zhang Bishi and philanthropists of Straits Settlements fame. Perhaps more than anyone else, his compassion for the underdog made him a legend among the poor Chinese in Siam, where his name was a household word in the corridors of the Chinese working-class districts.

Although most *kongsi* had come out into the open as officially registered associations, Triad influence and control over the coolie labor force remained unchanged. Hong combined his newfound role as a respectable philanthropist with his older role as a powerful Triad godfather of the Chinese labor movement. Triads continued to remain an ineradicable force within the Chinese community, and continued to be courted by whomsoever wanted to bring power to bear on an issue, event, person or group. Lying low most of the time, they would surface during times of trouble. They were an important part of the power equation that could not be ignored.

As mentioned before, even Sun Yatsen had to resort to Triad support to organize the Canton Uprising and the Huizhou revolt. Members of the Huaxinghui, the precursor to the Tongmenghui, had to undergo a Triad-style ritualistic swearing of allegiance to the aims of the revolution "to eliminate the Qing dynasty and establish a republic."[29] Shortly after the failed uprisings, Sun Yatsen was formally initiated into the Triad lodge Hong Chen Tian Ti Hui in America. Cognizant that the age-old anti-Manchu ideology of the Triad secret societies was still alive among the overseas Chinese, he astutely couched his appeal to them with the slogan "Overthrow the Qing," garnished with a sprinkle of modern republicanism.[30]

Despite Yi Goh Hong and Sun Yatsen's shared sense of belonging to the secret brotherhood, other competing loyalties pulled at the two brothers in divergent directions. Hong's main identification was with the Tian Fah movement to which his close associate Tia Giangsam and his patron Phakdi-Phattrakorn belonged. Sun Yatsen's attempt to enlist Yi Goh Hong's support for launching a civil war in South China naturally fell on deaf ears. Hong's position was embodied in his support of the Tian Fah spirit. In 1905, he had demonstrated that support by throwing the full weight of the Triad organizations behind the anti-US boycott. Those were the good old days, reminisced Hong, when the Chinese in Siam enjoyed an unassailable united front.

Subsequently, the courtship of the Nanyang Chinese by divergent political forces, though initially flattering, began to undermine the Tian Fah spirit, causing the exhilarating though momentary unity of the Chinese in Siam to crumble. In 1906, Sun Yatsen returned to Bangkok again.[31] This time he did not meet Yi Goh Hong but stayed incognito at the Sampeng home of a Hainanese *lukchin* revolutionary named Lin Wenying. There, he met Seow Hoodseng, the man who was destined to become the most influential opinion leader of the Chinese community in Siam.

Seow Hoodseng

Seow Hoodseng (Xiao Focheng, 1863–1939), the co-founder of the *Meinan Ribao* in 1904, was a Hokkien born in Bangkok.[32] He was among the *huaqiao* intelligentsia spawned in Siam's newly emerging urban social milieu that was bubbling with new ideas inspired by international political influences and Western organizational forms which were emulated in voluntary associations, reading clubs and other recreational bodies. At the turn of the century, Seow Hoodseng embodied the emergence of a new role model in Siamese society— the revolutionary activist.

Seow's background singularly suited his activist role. His ancestors had fought on the side of the anti-Manchu resistance, and after the fall of the Ming dynasty, joined the Ming loyalist naval forces based in Taiwan. When the Manchus gained control of Taiwan, the Seow family fled to Malacca. Five generations later, Seow Hoodseng's father left the Straits Settlements for Bangkok, attracted by Siam's rice-milling boom. Seow Hoodseng grew up in Bangkok where he initially worked for the Bang Yi Khan distillery. After that, he went on to become a successful attorney.[33] During his formative years, Seow was influenced by the revolutionary ideas of Sun Yatsen, although he apparently did not meet Sun Yatsen during his trip to Bangkok in May 1903.[34] Inspired by the Chinese revolutionary cause, Seow partnered with a Cantonese intellectual, Tan Genghua, to found a Chinese newspaper called the *Meinan Ribao*, or "the Maenam daily." Because of insufficient funding, the paper soon floundered.

Sun Yatsen used his second visit to Bangkok in 1906 to establish the local chapter of the underground organization Tongmenghui. Seow Hoodseng was appointed chairman, Tan Genghua became the first secretary general, and Sam Hingsi, a Cantonese comprador in the Bangkok branch of the Banque d'Indochine, became its first treasurer. Wong Hangchao, one of the six founders of the Tian Fah Hospital, was also among the first leaders of the Tongmenghui.

In 1906, Seow Hoodseng launched a new bilingual revolutionary newspaper called *Huaxian Xinbao*, which included eight pages in Chinese, and the *Chino-*

Seow Hoodseng
Sriboonruang.

Siam Warasup, which included four pages in the Thai vernacular. The new newspapers edited by Tan Genghua and Seow Hoodseng became one of the most successful of the early publishing ventures in Bangkok. The *Huaxian Xinbao* and *Chino-Siam Warasup* served as mouthpieces of the Tongmenghui, prompting the beginning of intense confrontation between the supporters of the establishment and the revolutionaries who demanded the overthrow of the Manchu dynasty and its replacement by a republic.[35]

Anti-Manchu propaganda and promotion of the revolutionary cause went hand-in-hand with fundraising. The success of any revolutionary cause depended heavily on financial backing. During his first visit in 1903, Sun Yatsen appeared to have relied upon a strategy of directly approaching Chinese tycoons, which proved unsuccessful; the Chinese capitalists were not ready to espouse Sun Yatsen's revolutionary cause.

In 1906, Sun Yatsen went beyond direct personal contacts with wealthy Chinese to establish an organization in Siam—the local branch of the underground Tongmenghui organization. The Siamese chapter of the Tongmenghui became a vehicle for mobilizing funds for China's republican revolution. Seow Hoodseng was put in charge of the fundraising campaign. Under Seow, Sun Yatsen's previous strategy of directly approaching leading Chinese capitalists shifted to a broad-based appeal to the public for support. Personal marketing that targeted individual tycoons was supplemented by mass social marketing through the vehicle of revolutionary propaganda carried in the Tongmenghui's daily newspapers.

Seow Hoodseng's strategy of using the newspaper to build mass support for the revolutionary cause, then turning the groundswell of public sympathy into a platform for fundraising, proved to be effective. The Tongmenghui's revolutionary propaganda struck a responsive chord with the public in Bangkok's Chinatown because of their continuing family, business and cultural ties with the ancestral homeland, and because most emigrants had come to Siam specifically to escape the difficult living conditions and political turmoil they associated with the corrupt and incompetent Manchu regime.[36] Although the strategy of approaching wealthy capitalists was never abandoned, Seow's novel contribution was in opening up a new market of political financing for the underground movement in Siam. Moreover, the new fundraising strategy carried with it a built-in advantage. The Chinese in Sampeng had a well-established remittance system whereby funds were mailed to family members in China.[37] Seow Hoodseng's network of underground revolutionary cells became adept at exploiting this mechanism to smuggle considerable sums to Guangdong, as well as to other revolutionary compatriots operating within China. Seow also targeted cultural events and Chinese festivals for fundraising. Contributions were collected from the public at heavily attended Chinese operas performed at the Sri Rachawong Theater on the south side of Yaowarat Road.[38]

Meanwhile, most of the Tian Fah leaders went in another direction. The founders of the Tian Fah Hospital comprised the most prominent and wealthy elements in the Bangkok Chinese community and embodied the interests of mainstream Chinese capitalists. This group tended to be conservative, and most of them responded to the Qing's courtship of the overseas-Chinese community. The conservatives were quite happy to make donations to Chinese government-sponsored projects in return for receiving symbolic honors.

Yi Goh Hong had made large donations to the Chinese government and received the ceremonial gown and title denoting a "Mandarin of the First Class." Many other Tian Fah founding leaders had also been decorated with prestigious and honorable titles by the Qing court. Some of the highest honors held by Thai-Chinese during the last days of the Qing dynasty went to Phakdi-Phattrakorn (Lao Gibing), who was awarded the Lanling (藍翎) official hat as well as the Zijiangsanyanhualing (紫韁三眼花翎) official hat. He was also bestowed the position of Imperial Commissioner in the Navy Affairs Office (文化殿大學士).[39]

These contributions to the fundraising drive by the Chinese government coupled with the transfer of Chinese labor remittances home resulted in a large outflow of money from the Siamese economy, which became a contentious issue between the Siamese government and its Chinese subjects. The Siamese government's resentment fed into undercurrents of anti-Chinese sentiment, which contributed to the stereotyping of the Chinese as the "Jews of the Orient."

Moreover, the interests of this conservative Chinese lobby naturally overlapped with the pet project of the Qing court at that time. Qing attempts to mobilize the financial support of rich overseas Chinese were frustrated by narrow-minded local officials whose behavior tended to alienate returning wealthy Chinese merchants. The latter were often put off by the menacing attitudes and extortionate demands of corrupt local officials whom they encountered upon returning to their ancestral homeland. To address and correct the problem, and to improve relations with Chinese merchant communities, the Manchu government promoted the establishment of Chinese chambers of commerce throughout coastal China and the Nanyang. The Qing court's motivation was to use the institution of the Chinese Chamber of Commerce as a vehicle to mobilize Chinese merchant capital, both domestically as well as overseas, to invest in China's self-strengthening and modernization projects.

The Qing court's campaign to promote the spread of Chinese chambers of commerce throughout the Nanyang resonated with a long-felt need in Siam's overseas-Chinese community. In the wake of the establishment of the British Chamber of Commerce in 1898, Chinese and Japanese commercial interests would be disadvantaged unless they too established a chamber of commerce to represent and protect their common interests. Around the turn of the century, Japanese commercial interests seeking a foothold in the Siamese market often cooperated with the longer-established Chinese economic presence in Siam.

Japanese merchants who already had a consulate in Bangkok were in a position to render their good offices to their disadvantaged Chinese counterparts, who had no embassy to look after their interests. Relations between the Chinese and Japanese had not yet turned completely sour, despite the Sino-Japanese War in 1895. In the early 20th century, China's intelligentsia still looked up to Japan and sought to emulate the great strides towards modernization that Japan had successfully undertaken. China's intelligentsia, including Sun Yatsen, joined in common activities with their Japanese counterparts to learn from them.

Unlike the Japanese who were represented by their consular office, Chinese subjects in Siam often felt they were not adequately protected under Siamese law. Although Siam had tried to reform the courts, the result was incomplete, and the Chinese continued to face legal difficulties. Consequently, it was not uncommon for Chinese to hire Japanese lawyers to represent them.[40] Against this backdrop, the Japanese consul in Bangkok, Yoshifumi Toyama, registered the Oriental Chamber of Commerce on 31 October 1901 for the purpose of facilitating the activities of "Chinese and Japanese residents of Siam engaged in trade." Its charter stipulated that the association's objective was to "increase profits from trade and manufacture for the Japanese and Chinese residents in Siam."[41]

Thus, the newly opened chamber sought to attract Chinese membership by offering Japanese protection. Consequently, large numbers of Chinese joined the Japanese-sponsored Oriental Chamber of Commerce, seeking the protection of their commercial interests. The launching of the Oriental Chamber of Commerce represented the high-water mark of Chinese and Japanese cooperation in Siam. Their amicable relations were such that the first Chinese-language daily newspaper, *Meinan Ribao*, was launched by the Oriental Chamber of Commerce on 10 October 1904 and printed on the chamber's premises, with the participation of Tan Genghua, Seow Hoodseng and Sam Hingsi.[42]

With the crystallization of an overarching sense of Chinese identity came a strong sentiment within the Chinese merchant community for having its own Chinese Chamber of Commerce in Bangkok to better protect Chinese commercial interests. At the same time, under the initiative of Zhang Bishi, the campaign to promote Chinese chambers of commerce in the Nanyang became a pet project of the empress dowager. Thus, the Qing court and Chinese commercial interests in Siam cooperated to establish a Chinese Chamber of Commerce in Bangkok. Building on the earlier precedent of popular Chinese participation in the Oriental Chamber of Commerce, many luminaries of the Chinese community, including Koh Huijia, Sophon-Phetchrat (Tia Giangsam),[43] Tan Kaihor (Vadthanakul),[44]

Liao Chiangsoon (Sethabhakdi),[45] Ng Miaongian (Lamsam)[46] and Tan Lipbuay (Wanglee) congregated in 1907 to launch the Chinese Chamber of Commerce.

In late 1907, the Qing court sent a mission led by Yang Shikee, the commerce minister, to Siam. On 29 November 1907, the Chinese minister was granted an audience with King Chulalongkorn. The meeting turned out to be a dialogue of the deaf. The Chinese envoy was naturally concerned about the outstanding issue of treaty relations between the two countries, while the Siamese court had grave reservations on this topic. The Bowring Treaty signed between Siam and Great Britain in 1855 had established an undesirable precedent in the form of a clause conferring extraterritorial rights to British subjects. Subsequently, Siam had to concede the same terms to every treaty it had entered into with other Western powers.

Phraya Pradinun-Bhumirat (Liao Chiangsoon) with his wife Khunying Pradinun-Bhumirat, one of a very few Chinese *phraya* appointed by King Vajiravudh.

Moreover, the issue of extraterritoriality was often cynically abused by the French and the British to gain political leverage against the Siamese at the expense of Siam's outlying tributary domains. The issue of extraterritoriality became a major irritant in the relationship between Siamese royalty and the Chinese, which undermined the sense of long-standing partnership between them. Consequently, the Siamese government's response to the Chinese envoy was non-committal. The envoy was informed that the policy of the Siamese government on the local Chinese community had always been clear: they were subjects of Siam. The king assured the Chinese minister that his government treated the Chinese as if they were his own people with the same rights and privileges.

A year later, following Sun Yatsen's third visit to Bangkok in December 1908, the Chinese revolutionary movement gained further momentum. In the preceding days, revolutionary propaganda through the newspapers of the Tongmenghui had prepared public opinion to receive Sun Yatsen, who arrived in Bangkok with the organization's brilliant propaganda chief Hu Hanmin. The Tongmenghui's strategy of relying on a broad-based appeal to the public made it imperative for Sun Yatsen to deliver a speech to the Chinese community.

Sun Yatsen's visit coincided with the opening of the Chinese Association, Zhonghua Huikuan, which was established by Seow Hoodseng as a front organization of the underground Tongmenghui. On 18 November 1908, Chaophraya Yommarat (Pan Sukhum), the metropolitan minister, was invited by Seow to chair the grand opening of the beautiful clubhouse of the Chinese Association. King Chulalongkorn's portrait graced the high altar table in the reception hall. The special objective that differentiated this club from existing *huikuan* in town was its *huaqiao*-inspired aim to unite the Chinese across different speech groups, contrary to the traditional *huiguan* that organized itself according to a common place of origin. On 1 December 1908, during the welcome party attended by more than 100 local Chinese, the clubhouse became the venue of Sun Yatsen's controversial keynote speech attacking the institution of the monarchy.

That famous speech sent shockwaves through the kingdom's capital city. Seow Hoodseng had to apologize to an outraged Yommarat for Sun Yatsen's seditious speech. After the fiasco, several conservative members of the association withdrew their memberships fearing that the Manchu government might punish them upon their return to China.

Sun Yatsen also delivered another oration to another large gathering in Sampeng. Moved by the large crowd that came to listen to him and sensing great interest and excitement among Sampeng's Chinese populace for the revolutionary cause, he delivered another aggressive and rousing speech in support of the revolution. He called for overthrowing the Manchu dynasty and establishing a republic in China and included, as usual, an appeal for financial contributions to the cause. The speech succeeded beyond expectations in inflaming Chinese public opinion against the Manchu government. To renounce their affiliation with the Qing dynasty and identify with the revolution, many Sampeng Chinese cut off their queues—a widely detested symbol of submission to Manchu rule. Many more donated generously to the republican cause.

After the two provocative public speeches, the Siamese government ordered Sun Yatsen to leave the country. Several factors accounted for his tirade against the monarchy. During his early visits, Sun Yatsen had taken care to avoid any overt act of defiance to the monarchy. However, the stress of living in exile and his repeated failures to overthrow the Manchu dynasty had intensified his revolutionary fervor, which was reflected in his increasingly inflammatory rhetoric (for which he was also expelled from Japan in 1907 and then from Indochina in 1908).

In advocating the overthrow of an imperial dynasty and its replacement by a republican government, Sun was implicitly challenging the political status quo in Siam. His speech at Sampeng, which was the furthest he had ever stretched his welcome in Siam, not only energized the emerging spirit of Chinese nationalism among Siam's Chinese subjects, but also increased the concerns of Siam's royalty over the political reliability of its large overseas-Chinese population.

Coming at a time when outstanding extraterritorial issues with the Western powers had not been resolved, Sun Yatsen's 1908 oration must have also further reinforced Siamese reservations about establishing treaty relations with China. Although the issue of extraterritoriality was finally resolved with France and Britain by 1909 through agreements involving the ceding of substantial territories to the Western powers, the Qing Code of 1909 posed a new threat—this time not from the Western but the Eastern quarter—preventing Siam from putting the whole issue of extraterritoriality finally at rest.

Under the Qing Code of 1909, all ethnic Chinese living overseas became China's subjects. Based on its new Nationality Law, the Manchu government was putting pressure on Siam to establish treaty relations so that China could establish an embassy to better represent the interests of "their" so-called subjects in Siam. Four years later, in 1913, King Vadjiravudh, who had succeeded his father in 1910, countered the Chinese claim by declaring all those born in Siam as Siamese citizens, based on the principle of *jus soli*.

Besides, the Siamese government was naturally concerned with the implications of a growing Chinese governmental influence over its Chinese-Siamese subjects, especially when much of the country's economy was under Chinese ownership and control. Understandably, the Siamese government was not happy to see the outflow of capital from Siam to invest in China when the kingdom itself needed scarce capital for its own modernization projects. Hence, the Manchu government's intention to use the Chinese Chamber of Commerce to mobilize capital from the overseas-Chinese community was at odds with the interests of the Siamese court.

Consequently, the Siamese government was reluctant to accede to the request for official recognition of the newly formed Chinese Chamber of Commerce in 1908. The Siamese government also feared that the Chinese Chamber of Commerce could serve as a Trojan horse inimical to Siamese security interests, becoming a front to co-opt influential leaders of the Chinese community to influence domestic politics in the kingdom. Concerned that the chamber could become a vehicle for exerting Chinese governmental influence in Siam, Chulalongkorn was only prepared to acknowledge the chamber's de facto existence but refused to permit its official registration. It was only after the Manchu dynasty had been overthrown that the Chinese Chamber of Commerce in Siam was allowed to be registered, in 1914, by King Vajiravudh.

Sun Yatsen's speech has been given against the backdrop of increasing tension and intense polarization between the conservative and revolutionary factions of the Chinese community in Bangkok. In November 1908, the emperor Guangxu and the empress dowager both passed away. The conservative faction including the Chinese Chamber of Commerce and the

Front page of the French newspaper *Le Petit Journal* on 29 November 1908, depicting the funeral of Emperor Guangxu and Empress dowager Cixi at the Pavilion of Imperial Longevity in China.

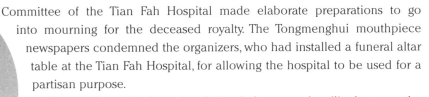

Tan Kaihor
Vadthanakul.

Committee of the Tian Fah Hospital made elaborate preparations to go into mourning for the deceased royalty. The Tongmenghui mouthpiece newspapers condemned the organizers, who had installed a funeral altar table at the Tian Fah Hospital, for allowing the hospital to be used for a partisan purpose.

The attack on the funeral activities led to open hostility between the conservatives and the revolutionaries. Seow Hoodseng reminisced that the Tongmenghui's propaganda offensive "angered the bull-headed people with power."[47] The conservative-royalists retaliated with an enforced boycott of Seow's newspapers, causing the daily sales of *Huaxian Xinbao* to fall from 300 to 100, while the conservative *Qinan Xinbao* maintained their sales at 300, prompting a defiant Seow to announce that he would continue printing "even if there was only one reader!"[48]

The conservatives had their revenge in early 1909, when Ma Xingshun, a major backer of *Huaxian Xinbao*, went on a business trip to Canton. The royalist faction tipped off the viceroy of Canton of his arrival. Ma was arrested and imprisoned as a revolutionist and Seow Hoodseng had to send Tan Genghua to Hong Kong to secure his release.[49] When Tan Kaihor, who had become the most powerful figure on the Tian Fah Hospital Committee, found out that his friends had used the name of the hospital to send a petition to the police for the release of Ma Xingshun, he furiously objected to the use of the hospital for that purpose.

The tit-for-tat between the conservatives and the revolutionaries continued through 1909. Of the two, the conservative faction was by far the stronger. Besides being the numerically larger faction, the conservatives enjoyed the support of powerful Chinese leaders like Yi Goh Hong and Tan Kaihor, a founding member of the Chinese Chamber of Commerce and, later, its chairman. It was also in a strategically stronger position through its alignment with the government in power in China.

As a member of the weaker faction, Seow Hoodseng felt it was strategically imperative for him to gain the goodwill of the Siamese government to counterbalance the preponderant power of his rivals, who enjoyed the backing of the ruling Manchu government. Moreover, the Tongmenghui's revolutionary platform represented a potential liability in Siam as demonstrated in Sun Yatsen's speech at the Chinese Association clubhouse.

Sun's 1908 oration put the Tongmenghui on the Siamese government's bad side. Alienating the Siamese government would put the revolutionists in the unenviable position of having to fight on two fronts at the same time. Unless quick steps were taken to qualify the Tongmenghui's anti-royalist position, the revolutionary faction ran the risk becoming politically isolated.

To redress the situation, Seow launched a propaganda campaign to defend the institution of the monarchy in Siam. He wrote articles belaboring the point that the monarchy had brought modernization and progress to the kingdom, and that it had proved to be good for the people, unlike in China.

Seow Hoodseng's equivocation was incredible: the Tongmenghui was anti-royalist in China, yet it was pro-royalist in Siam. He denied that he harbored any ill intentions toward the monarchy; he insisted that his republicanism was reserved exclusively for China—and for good measure, he added more praise of the king. Nevertheless, the Tongmenghui found itself in an untenable position by virtue of its revolutionary platform. The revolutionaries remained on the defensive until the eruption of Chinese-labor discontent in 1910.

Although the capitation tax was specifically aimed at the Chinese who were paying a lower tax than their native Siamese counterparts, the new rate represented a sudden, steep tax rise for the poor Chinese wage laborer. Moreover, the daily wages of unskilled workers had not increased between 1880 and 1910, while the price of rice had doubled during the same period to the benefit of native Siamese rice growers. Yi Goh Hong, the champion of the poor Chinese coolie, harbored the sense that an injustice had been done to the Chinese when the Siamese government enforced the tax hike. Discontented that the Chinese government had no representation in Siam, Qing agents instigated a protest against the tax increase. Under pressure to do something to protect the interests of poor Chinese wage laborers, the Triad fraternities posted leaflets calling for a general strike to shut down the capital city in protest against the new tax law.

Seow Hoodseng was well aware of the pro-Manchu faction's hidden agenda in supporting the general strike. The Tongmenghui had no interest in promoting the establishment of treaty relations between Siam and China under the Manchu government's watch. The opening of diplomatic relations would increase Manchu influence in Siam at the expense of the Tongmenghui's freedom of movement and allow its operatives to be extradited to China. Consequently, the 1910 general strike organized by the "bull-headed" conservatives suddenly presented him with an opportunity to kill two birds with one stone: he would show his support for the monarchy while undermining the conservative leadership's unassailable position in the local Chinese community.

The crippling general strike, lasting three days, had inconvenienced the native Siamese populace in their own land. The show of Chinese power caused great resentment among the Siamese intelligentsia and Western-educated elite. It awakened hitherto marginalized anti-Chinese sentiments in Siamese society and caused latent currents of anti-Chinese prejudice to boil over into mainstream public opinion.

The strike proved to be a disastrous miscalculation on the part of the conservative faction. It jeopardized Yi Goh Hong's standing and relationship

Phraya Yommarat.

with royalty and the Siamese government, undermined the prestige and credibility of the newly formed Chinese Chamber of Commerce, and further diminished Triad influence in the leadership of the Chinese community. Seow Hoodseng did not hesitate to exploit the situation fully to the advantage of the Tongmenghui.

Following the strike, the Tongmenghui mouthpieces criticized the newspapers in China for publishing biased reports that exaggerated the intensity of the crackdown and the number of Chinese arrested in Siam.[50] Seow Hoodseng threw the weight of the *Huaxian Xinbao* newspapers behind the Siamese government. He informed Phraya Yommarat that Shanghai news reports alleged Tae Teeyong, or Yi Goh Hong, of urging the Manchu government to send a warship up the Chao Phraya River to express the Chinese government's displeasure over the crackdown on Chinese subjects in Bangkok.[51] The report proved to be financially ruinous for Yi Goh Hong, who was subsequently blacklisted by authorities and disqualified from receiving further monopoly concessions.[52]

The local government's initial suspicions of Chinese government influence within Bangkok's newly formed Chinese Chamber of Commerce was confirmed by a report from Prince Chakkrabongse alleging that the general strike was backed by the Shantou Chamber of Commerce. It was further noted that many prominent business leaders in Siam were represented in the Shantou Chamber of Commerce, including Akon Teng, father of Sophon-Phetcharat. Furthermore, the Siamese minister in Paris reported that the Chinese minister to France had lodged a complaint against the crackdown on Chinese subjects in Bangkok.

Having warned the Chinese community not to follow "those bull-headed people with power," Seow Hoodseng must have noted with satisfaction that the repercussions of the 1910 general strike left the conservative Chinese leadership in disarray. With his credibility severely damaged, Yi Goh Hong lost his sway over the Chinese community. The Triads also largely faded from the scene; hundreds of gangsters and enforcers were arrested and deported. Triad power did not revive until military hostilities in 1927 between Chinese and Japanese forces at Jinan unleashed a violent reaction among the overseas-Chinese communities. Exposed as a front organization of the Qing government, the reputation of the Bangkok Chinese Chamber of Commerce was also tarnished.

Riding on the momentum of his political advantage, Seow Hoodseng found another occasion to emphasize his support for the monarchy when King Chulalongkorn passed away on 23 October 1910. His *Chino-Siam Warasup* joined all Chinese newspapers to grieve the death of the king. Seow's editorial ran a moving obituary for King Chulalongkorn quoting Zhong Gua Bao, the local newsprint:

We hated the Manchu ruler and cried for its destruction. Then why do we mourn the passing of the Siamese king? Please understand that ·the Qing emperor is our enemy but the Siamese king is our benefactor. That is why we love him. Should we succeed in overthrowing the Qing dynasty in China and found a Republic, should there be a Manchu prince who is as benevolent and capable as the Siamese king who passed away, we will elect him our President.[53]

China Goes Republic

A year later, the Xinhai Revolution swept the Qing dynasty from power, ending 268 years of Manchu rule in China. The revolution was greeted with euphoria throughout the Nanyang Chinese diaspora, including Bangkok. Siam's Chinese community suddenly acquired a new sense of coherence and self-respect after the overthrow of the Manchus, and the burst of heady nationalist propaganda by Sun Yatsen celebrating the birth of a republic in China was spread through the Chinese newspapers.

With his prophecy of the dawn of a new republic in China vindicated, Seow Hoodseng seemed less concerned that the 1911 revolution also brought its share of problems for the Chinese in Siam. The internal conflicts of the early republican era opened a new floodgate of Chinese emigration to Siam. Unlike the older wave of Chinese emigration to Siam, the post-Xinhai Revolution immigrants were less assimilable; with a large portion of women among them, the resultant effect was to promote the proliferation of "Chinese homes" instead of "Siamese homes." Besides women, the new emigrants also comprised large numbers of teachers and educated intelligentsia. Consequently, the Xinhai Revolution resulted in the proliferation of Chinese schools, study clubs, and more Chinese newspapers and associations with political overtones.

Coming in the wake of the disastrous Chinese General Strike of 1910, which inflamed undercurrents of anti-Chinese sentiment in the native Siamese, this sudden intensification of Chinese identity could not have come at a worse time. Through the eyes of a journalist, Seow saw that almost overnight the generations of goodwill and mutual trust between Siamese and Chinese had vanished and for the first time public opinion raised the issue of the "Chinese problem."

This new anti-Chinese spirit was led by none other than King Vajiravudh, who denounced the divided loyalties of Siam's Chinese subjects and called them the "Jews of the Orient." For the first time the Chinese in Siam became the objects of official discrimination and public antipathy. However, the Chinese community survived the King's words with remarkably little collateral damage. Seow Hoodseng, who enjoyed a certain credibility with the Siamese government for his outspoken opposition to the general strike, defended the Chinese. He publicly countered Vajiravudh's charges and reiterated the enormously positive contributions that the Chinese had made to the welfare and economic progress of the kingdom.

Seow Hoodseng realized that Vajiravudh's attitude towards the Chinese community was more ambivalent than downright anti-Chinese. Beneath Vajiravudh's posturing, Seow Hoodseng discovered that the new king was not difficult to deal with. Both of them were intellectual by temperament; although they disagreed passionately and attacked each other ideologically through their writings, they could understand each other. Vajiravudh's anti-Chinese propaganda was apparently intended to register his grievance against the divided loyalties of Siam's Chinese subjects. His objective was to wean the second- and third-generation Chinese away from Chinese nationalism towards an identification with Siam through the Siamese monarchy.

Under the reign of King Vajiravudh, substantive anti-Chinese policies were relatively few. Vajiravudh's anti-Chineseness was only ideological; it was never operationalized into immigration, economic or social measures. Under Vajiravudh the Chinese Chamber of Commerce was officially recognized, Seow's newspaper *Chino-Siam Warasup* received government financial support, and many Chinese associations and guilds were allowed to be registered.

Nevertheless, the reign of King Vajiravudh ushered in a new era—it announced the beginning of a growing estrangement between the host society and its Chinese minority. Under King Vajirvudh, the practice of ennobling Chinese died out. Once denied access into the Siamese nobility, a distinct Chinese elite began to take root. Locked out of fame and status in Siamese society, the post-Vajiravudh Chinese elite increasingly shifted their allegiance towards the Chinese nationalist movement to find substitutes for the fame, honor, and recognition that they could no longer expect from their host country. A local Chinese community with divided loyalties had emerged.[54] The divided loyalties of the Chinese in Siam were underscored by the Chinese community's preoccupation with events and political developments on the Chinese mainland, which created a ripple effect in the life of the Chinese community in Siam.

Following Sun Yatsen's victory in China, the authority of Seow Hoodseng came to be recognized by most Chinese in Siam, including the Chinese Chamber of Commerce (CCC), which increasingly came under the control of the Tongmenghui. Seow could remember that since its inception the CCC had at best been lukewarm to Sun Yatsen's Tongmenghui. In 1913, Seow endorsed Wang Hangchao, his old Tongmenghui colleague, to become deputy chairman of the CCC. That same year, Seow Hoodseng presided over the Tongmenghui's official reincarnation as the Guomindang (GMD) on 23 March 1913.

On that day, 200 out of the CCC's total membership of 700 attended the function, including Seow's old adversaries Min Laohasetthi and Lao Gibing—luminaries who had been ennobled by the late King Chulalongkorn. The CCC rapidly became a new force in the Chinese community; within a few years of its founding it had assumed broader powers than its counterparts in Western countries.[55] It became the most important Chinese organization representing the Chinese community as a whole and even overshadowed the GMD, to Seow's chagrin, when the fortunes of the republic began to wane.

Sun Yatsen's triumph and Seow Hoodseng's euphoria over the Xinhai Revolution proved to be short-lived as political disunity and its attendant centrifugal political forces pulled the new Chinese republic apart. The weakness of the central government led to the rise of warlordism as regional military commanders usurped power and created their own fiefdoms. To Seow's dismay, King Vajiravudh was quick to publicly discredit the Xinhai Revolution, arguing that republicanism could not work in Asia, and that the outcome of revolution was leading to the disintegration of China. Vajiravudh's reactionary propaganda offensive against the revolutionaries had taken the wind out of the sail of Seow Hoodseng's republican discourse.

Top: Yuan Shikai.

Bottom: Chiang Kai-shek.

The fragmentation of China was reflected in Bangkok with the Chinese Chamber of Commerce supporting the military strongman Yuan Shikai and the northern warlords while Seow Hoodseng and the Tongmenghui loyalists rallied behind Sun Yatsen's attempt to form a southern government at Canton. With the underground organizations of the Tongmenghui still under Seow Hoodseng's control, Sun Yatsen was supported by the entire Chinese press in Bangkok when he was elected president of the new Guomindang (GMD) Nationalist government at Canton in 1921.

With Chiang Kai-shek as the military commander of the newly formed Nationalist army, Sun Yatsen turned to the task of re-taking power from the northern warlords to unify China. Unable to gain support from the West, Sun Yatsen turned to the nascent Soviet Union for political and military assistance, to the dismay of Seow Hoodseng and the right-wing faction of the GMD. Soviet agents, technical experts and advisors came to assist the fledgling Nationalist government. Directed by the COMINTERN (Communist International), the Chinese Communist Party (CCP) founded in 1921 supported Sun Yatsen's Nationalist government while simultaneously strengthening its own position, thereby ushering in a period of unity between the GMD and the CCP.

This working alliance between the CCP and the GMD in China gave rise to new newspapers and Chinese political organizations in Siam. Two leftist newspapers, including the Teochew *Lianqiaobao* and the Cantonese *Qiaoshengbao*, began publication in Bangkok. Nationalists and

King Prajadhipok
(Rama VII, 1925–35).

Communists also cooperated and supported each other during the May 30th Movement in 1925, which resulted in an anti-British boycott in South China.[56]

By October 1925, the Chinese community in Siam had raised 700,000 baht for the relief of the Canton strikers. Coming in the wake of the growing strength of leftist elements, the organized movement targeting British interests alarmed King Prajadhipok, who succeeded his late brother Vajiravudh in late November. The new king was in no position to offend Great Britain, still the dominant power in Asia in the 1920s before the emergence of the Japanese challenge in the 1930s. Only the timely personal intervention of Prajadhipok reportedly preempted the declaration of a formal boycott of British goods in Bangkok.[57]

Although a formal boycott was avoided, all the Chinese newspapers in Siam vehemently condemned the British and voiced support for the May 30th Movement. On account of inflammatory statements in connection with the May 30th Movement, the Siamese government shut down Seow Hoodseng's newspaper, *Huaxian Xinbao*, and two other pro-Communist newspapers, including *Lianqiaobao* and *Qiaoshengbao*.

The first major pro-Communist organization in Bangkok, the Li Qing Shu Bao She, was also founded during this united-front period. Meanwhile, the GMD branch in Siam possessed the same status as branches in provinces of Mainland China.[58] The Chinese of Siam sent delegates to the first and second National Congress of the GMD in 1924 and 1926 respectively. The most prominent of these representatives were Lin Boqi and Seow Hoodseng. Seow was not only the head of the GMD in Bangkok, he also held a position in the GMD Central Executive Committee in China, overseeing overseas-Chinese affairs. Besides the main GMD branch, the Communist faction in the GMD also established a sub-branch in opposition to the mainstream right-wing faction under Seow. By 1925, the organization of GMD branches in Siam was already well advanced, and the extreme left wing of the party reportedly boasted 400 members.[59]

GMD flags flying in Bangkok served as a barometer reflecting the progress of the Nationalist army's campaign against the northern warlords. On the "Double Tenth," or 10 October, Chinese National Day in 1925, only about a fifth of the flags flown in Bangkok were those of the GMD. The majority, including the flag flying over the Chinese Chamber of Commerce, were the old five-barred flag of the northern warlords centered in Beijing. A year later, the proportions were reversed and by New Year's Day 1927, only a few five-barred flags were to be seen in Bangkok. When the news broke that Hankow and Shanghai had fallen to Chiang Kai-shek's armies, the GMD flag flew everywhere in Bangkok.

The gradual polarization within the Chinese Nationalist movement between the GMD and the CCP was projected abroad and re-enacted in the politics of the overseas-Chinese community in Siam.[60] In the wake of Chiang Kai-shek's anti-Communist witch-hunt in 1927, thousands of Leftists fled the country to seek refuge in the Nanyang, including Siam. In fact, the peak of Chinese immigration into Siam, which occurred during 1927–28, coincided with Chiang Kai-shek's bloody purge of the Communists in Guangdong in 1927. Among the new wave of emigrants, more than 30 high-profile Communist militants escaped to Siam between 1927 and 1929. Most of them found work teaching in Chinese schools, which had sprouted up during the 1920s in Bangkok and other big towns. Others worked in saw mills, which were predominantly owned by Hailams.

The GMD-CCP split was followed by a vigorous press war in Bangkok, with the *Liqingbao* and *Lianqiaobao* defending the Communists against the other right-wing newspapers.[61] Reflecting the split, the *Guominribao,* a new, strongly pro-GMD Bangkok newspaper, was founded in 1927 and it immediately took the Chinese Chamber of Commerce to task for its persistence in flying the old five-barred flag. As in China, the GMD propaganda prevailed. Circulation of the *Liqingbao* fell and its editor was expelled in 1928 by the Siamese government on political charges. The *Lianqiaobao* also folded shortly after it was allowed to re-open.

In addition to the newspaper propaganda war between the Nationalists and the Communists, each side tried to outdo the other in their patriotism, militancy and effectiveness. The outbreak of Sino-Japanese military hostilities at Jinan in May 1928 gave Seow Hoodseng an opportunity to show that the newly purged and re-organized GMD could outdo the embattled Communists—whose ranks had been depleted by arrests—in attacking Japanese interests in Siam.

Using the GMD branch's organizational resources and political influence over the Chinese community, Seow Hoodseng instigated a boycott of Japanese goods and formed a committee to enforce the boycott.[62] Merchants trading in Japanese goods were notified and fined. Naturally, many importers and retailers specializing in Japanese goods were reluctant to cooperate; thus, organized Triad activity, which had suffered an eclipse since the disastrous Chinese General Strike of 1910, was revived.

In June 1928, the Tie Xue Tuan, literally "Iron and Blood Corps," began terrorizing Japanese and Chinese merchants breaking the boycott. Threatening letters with the Triad symbol of a red heart pierced by two daggers were distributed and posted on the doors of shops carrying Japanese goods. Those caught breaking the boycott were mobbed, kidnapped or shot. Chinese dockworkers refused to handle goods to and from Japan.

Seow Hoodseng's anti-Japanese boycott proved to be very effective, although he publicly denied that he or the merchant class had anything to do with it. By

July, the position of ordinary Japanese shops had "become grave indeed."[63] The manager of Mitsui lamented that Triad terror was so effective that "few Chinese merchants dared to do any business with us."

Seow and 11 GMD members were summoned and investigated by the Siamese authorities, and the newspaper *Zhonghuaminbao* was closed for two weeks on the grounds that it had encouraged bad feelings between Chinese and Japanese.

The Siamese government arrested many involved in the boycott, and several Triad members were deported. A gunman involved in several sensational assassination attempts was sentenced to life imprisonment. Eventually, in August, Siamese workers were brought in to break the Chinese strike in the dockyards. The boycott was finally broken in October 1928. However, by the end of the year, the Chinese in Siam had collected a fund of 600,000 baht for the victims of the Jinan incident.

The GMD emerged as the most powerful force in the Chinese community in Siam. Its influence was pervasive, but its operations were not transparent—it wielded power through front organizations and underground cells reminiscent of the secret society style of the old Tongmenghui. The Zhonghua Association and the Hainan Association, both of which had been formed before the Revolution of 1911, were the major front organizations in Bangkok. By the beginning of 1928, regular GMD membership was estimated at about 20,000. These members were organized into 38 underground "cells" in Bangkok, with about 100 more throughout the rest of the country. Divided factions within the GMD were a major problem, however, and some were still controlled by the Communists, although they had suffered a heavy toll during Seow Hoodseng's ruthless internal purge of the party organization.

Although the GMD had emerged as the dominant Chinese political organization in Siam, the Communists were not eliminated as a political force. In fact, the reverses suffered by the Communists in China caused an influx of leftist elements

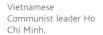

Vietnamese Communist leader Ho Chi Minh.

during 1927–1928, contributing to the growth of a Communist underground movement in Siam. Furthermore, at the behest of the COMINTERN, the Vietnamese Communist leader Ho Chi Minh came to Siam in March 1930. Before he left, he founded the Communist Party of Siam (CPS) on 20 April 1930.[64] Its original members consisted mostly of overseas Chinese and Vietnamese.

During the early 1930s, the CPS conducted an intense propaganda campaign to promote revolution in China, Indochina and Siam. Besides calling for a revolutionary Soviet-style government in Siam, the party also established a Communist Youth Group, an Anti-Imperialist League and a General Labor Union.[65] However, the mission imposed by the COMINTERN on the nascent Communist Party of Siam to liberate the three countries of Siam, China and Indochina was unrealistic, as its members were more concerned with the liberation of their homelands (China and Indochina) than Siam. The formation of an underground Communist Party alarmed the Siamese government, however, and in the same year that the CPS was formed, the government mounted an active anti-Communist campaign based on information received from the British. This resulted in 127 arrests, among which 80 Chinese and 2 Vietnamese were deported, 26 were released because of insufficient evidence, and 19 were jailed.[66]

Meanwhile, a concerted and sustained campaign was mounted by the Chinese government to secure treaty relations with Siam. Four leading officials of the CMD government were successively charged with the treaty negotiations: Cheng Yansheng in 1928, Seow Hoodseng in 1929, Dr. Wu Chaoshu in 1930 and Zhu Hexiang in 1932. All four were put off by the Siamese government through one excuse or another.

Finally, the Siamese government capitulated and reached a partial agreement. The Chinese minister to Tokyo and Siamese representatives worked out a compromise allowing for the stationing of an official Chinese commissioner of commerce in Bangkok. However, the powers of the new Chinese commissioner were strictly limited to signing consular invoices and did not include any other diplomatic functions or privileges.[67] The Chinese government appointed Tan Siewmeng, the newly elected chairman of the CCC and scion of the Wanglee family—one of the most wealthy and influential named families in the Chinese community—as China's first commissioner of commerce in Bangkok.

Tan Siewmeng

Tan Siewmeng was born on 20 October 1904 at the Wanglee home in Qianxi Village, Longdu District, Raoping County, in the Chaozhou region of Guangdong Province. Common among overseas Chinese in Siam, Siewmeng's father, Tan Lipbuay, kept two homes—a Siamese home in Bangkok and a Chinese home in Guangdong.

There is little information about Tan Siewmeng's childhood and early youth. One of the earliest recorded impressions of Tan Siewmeng came from the mayor of Thonburi in 1925. His father had just appointed Siewmeng to succeed him as head of the vast Wanglee trading empire in Bangkok, which encompassed rice trading, import-export and remittance operations. To announce the changing of the guards at the commanding heights of the Wanglee business empire, Siewmeng undertook the customary round of visits to Chinese business leaders, high-

The hearse that contained the coffin of Tan Libuay at his funeral parade.

ranking officials and important personages in Siamese society. Siewmeng paid a courtesy call on Phraya Mahaisawan (Kor Sombatsiri), the mayor of Thonburi.

Mahaisawan recalled that the meeting was a little awkward, because Siewmeng spoke as little Thai as Mahaisawan spoke Teochew. However, given the fact that Mahaisawan was a fifth-generation member of the Sombatsiri family, which was among the oldest, ennobled, Teochew tax-farming families, his command of Teochew must have been passable enough to help the young man out. That first encounter with Tan Siewmeng left Mahaisawan puzzled: Why had his friend Chaosua Tan Lipbuay selected his polite, soft-spoken second son to run the family's mainstream rice-trading empire in Bangkok? After all, Chinese custom dictated that the choice should have gone to the first-born son.

Five years later, in the depths of the Great Depression in 1930, Mahaisawan had occasion to recall his first personal encounter with Tan Siewmeng. By that time, Tan Lipbuay, the Wanglee patriarch and Siewmeng's mentor, had already passed away. In 1930 the Wanglee business empire faced the onslaught of the Great Depression with Tan Siewmeng fully in charge. The depression took a heavy toll on the commodities trade. The price of rice had collapsed through the floor, and countless large grain-merchant houses saw their accumulated wealth and assets wiped out and their trading empires reduced to rubble.

Mahaisawan marveled at the fact that while businesses all around the country were falling like flies in the ravages of the depression, the Wanglee enterprise led by Tan Siewmeng was still left standing. Amazed at the remarkable entrepreneurial resilience of the Wanglee merchants, Mahaisawan realized that his late friend Tan Lipbuay had made the right choice in betting on his second son. The well-mannered young man he had met for the first time five years ago was not only diligent, he was also a genius in business. Under Tan Siewmeng, the Wanglee business empire not only navigated safely through the rough seas of the depression but expanded and became more diversified, acquiring new interests in banking, insurance, shipping and property.

By 1932, the depression had already done its worst to the overseas-Chinese businesses in Siam. The damage control measures introduced by the outgoing chairman of the CCC, Mah Lapkun, helped to contain the dislocating effects of the depression on the Chinese community. However, Chinese businesses in Siam were severely embattled. The innovative leader of the CCC himself suffered greatly from the deflationary effects of the depression.

During the leadership elections of the CCC in 1932, the demoralized Chinese business community had almost no leaders to offer. The business community prevailed upon the young Tan Siewmeng, at 28, to accept the chairmanship of the CCC. Representing a glittering success story in the bleak economic landscape of the depression, a Wanglee leadership of the CCC would be equal to the philanthropic obligations that necessarily came with the prestige of becoming the leader of Siam's Chinese community.

Tan Siewmeng's reputation as the capitalist who had bested the depression also won him the recognition of the GMD government in China. When the Chinese government searched for a suitable candidate to fill the new post of China's first commissioner of commerce to Bangkok, Tan Siewmeng became the natural choice. Moreover, as the current head of the CCC, he was doubly qualified: the appointment also dovetailed with China's long-standing aspiration to control the CCC in Siam. With Tan Siewmeng as China's commissioner of commerce in Bangkok, the chairman of the CCC became an official of the GMD government in China. The capture of the CCC by the GMD symbolized the complete hegemony of the GMD in Siam—a hegemony the Communists never succeeded to overthrow

Tan Siewmeng Wanglee (third from left) receiving guests at the Wanglee Mansion in Thonburi.

313

throughout the dwindling fortunes of the Nationalists, until their final eviction from Mainland China to Taiwan in 1949.

The 1932 Revolution

In a modern state the actual ruler is necessarily and unavoidably the bureaucracy, since power is exercised neither through parliamentary speeches nor monarchical enunciations but through the routines of administration. This is true both of the military and civilian officialdom.
— Max Weber, *Economy and Society* (1978), vol 2, p. 1393.

On 24 June 1932, a group of middle-level officials in the military and bureaucracy launched a coup d'état toppling the government of King Prajadhipok. The problems of the reigns of King Vajiravudh and King Prajadhipok, which culminated in the overthrow of the absolute monarchy in 1932, were largely the result of forces set in motion by the reforms of King Mongkut and King Chulalongkorn.[68] The key ringleaders of the coup, who called themselves "the Promoters," included Colonel Phraya Phahon-Phonphayuhasena, Colonel Luang Phibun Songkram, Khuang Aphaiwong and Pridi Banomyong. The Promoters of the 1932 coup represented the new elite manifested in an organizationally coherent collectivity of state officials, both civil and military. As a strategically located cadre of officials, they wielded considerable power inside and throughout state organizations. Unlike the royalty it displaced, this new elite—created during Chulalongkorn's re-invention of the bureaucracy and the subsequent administrative centralization of the late

The military announces its coup d'état on 24 June 1932.

19th century—was relatively insulated from ties to the kingdom's dominant Chinese socio-economic interests.

Although the Promoters of 1932 represented a new generation, they belonged to the same state-centered elite that plotted the failed Military Officers' Rebellion of 1912. The arrest of the rebellion's leaders in 1912 had temporarily decapitated the movement, which awaited the emergence of a new generation of revolutionary torchbearers in the 1930s. This new generation of torchbearers came in the form of the Promoters of 1932. Like their predecessors—the hundred-odd plotters of the 1912 rebellion[69]—the Promoters involved both military and civilian bureaucrats. Together they made up the new cohesive elite of career bureaucratic and military officers who attended training schools that taught techniques and ideas of national economic planning along with more traditional military skills.

The Military Officers' Rebellion of 1912 occurred against the backdrop of Japan's military victory in the Russo-Japanese War in 1905, and the Xinhai Revolution, which enjoyed favorable public opinion through the robust reporting of the event in the local Chinese press. Japan's victory was attributed to its progressive constitutional reforms, which had resulted in the country's modernizing transformation into a powerful Asian state capable of defeating a Western power. In contrast to Japan's military prowess against Russian aggression, Siam was too weak to withstand French and British military aggrandizement and the latters' encroachments on its territorial integrity.

The 1912 rebellion advocated that the loyalties of the Siamese people should no longer lie with the king but "in the land, in the country and in the welfare of the people and in the nation."[70] Thus, the rebels challenged Vajiravudh's definition of the nation as bounded by loyalty to the king. They also demanded that progress be more widely shared. In so doing, they redefined the purpose of the nation-state as promoting the well-being of the people as opposed to serving the absolute monarchy.

The Promoters of 1932 shared a sense of ideological purpose with their predecessors of 1912. They both believed in the possibility and desirability of using state intervention to replace the sovereignty of the monarchy with the sovereignty of the people; strengthen the country through swift moves towards modernization; and increase the welfare of the people through economic progress. They regarded the Military Officers' Rebellion of 1912 as the precursor to their own successful attempt at using military force to take control of the state.

Pridi Banomyong and his wife, Poonsuk.

The background and career of Pridi Banomyong represented some of the salient attributes of this new elite social formation. Born in 1900, Pridi was a commoner and a *lukchin* whose father, in his own words, was a "Chinese petty bourgeois" merchant from Ayudhya. Although Pridi was partially Chinese, he did not come from the dominant Chinese economic group or ennobled class of Chinese tax farmers.

Pridi was educated in a Buddhist temple school from the age of five to 11 before he was sent to school in Bangkok. He was 14 when Siam entered World War I on the side of the Allied Powers. He completed secondary school and entered the Royal Law School at 16. He was a brilliant student and graduated with the degree Bachelor of Law First Class when he was 19, and he joined a law firm.

However, the Siamese have always regarded government service as the most desirable occupation open to young men of promise. Perhaps in every culture there is a social group that is more admired than others; in China it is the scholar, in India it is the holy man or ascetic, in England it is the gentleman and in America it is the business tycoon. In Siam it is the civil servant.

In the Siamese mindset, a civil service office represents an achievement of authority and power. In traditional Siamese society, each rank of officialdom groveled before the one above and domineered over the one below. With this civil rank and authority came social position. The bureaucracy represented select society, and those of the higher ranks were very exclusive.

Consequently, Siamese rushed to fill the steadily expanding ranks of the government bureaucracy during the period of administrative expansion under the reign of King Chulalongkorn. Many were the sons of old ruling elites who were bypassed in the late 19th century. In 1892, the total number of salaried bureaucrats in all ministries was about 12,000. At the beginning of the 20th century, the state employed more than 25,000 civil servants. The following decades saw even further expansion creating a bloated state apparatus staffed by 81,000 officials by 1920—almost 1.7 percent of the kingdom's male workforce.[71] Siam's absolute monarchy possessed an oversized bureaucracy.

This very Siamese bias in favor of government service rubbed off on the assimilated second- and third-generation *lukchin* raised in "Thai homes," unlike the China-born *huaqiao* emigrants who were China-oriented in their allegiance. These second- and third-generation Chinese, especially those of mixed parentage, were often sold on this native bias in favor of a civil service career. Large numbers of Chinese obtained jobs in semi-government occupations, such as railways, and many more successfully sought careers as government officials.[72] As the tentacles of bureaucratic organization radiated out from the central region in an ambitious attempt to cover the whole country with a Western-style administrative grid, enormous numbers of officials and clerks were recruited to meet the insatiable appetite of the growing bureaucracy for personnel.

Sons of Lanna and Lao princes, *chaosua*, and Chinese *khunnang* loosened their connections to their regional origins and affiliations as they were coopted into the national Siamese elite. Even young men from middle- and lower-level

Chinese families that were engaged in humble commercial pursuits also joined the expanding bureaucracy. Bureaucratic positions were highly sought after as they afforded a chance to mingle with nobles and royalty. Moreover, a civil service job offered the opportunity to escape from the less-esteemed Chinese preoccupation with trade to a more genteel class in society. Another aspect was the titles that were conferred according to the degree of advancement of the individual. For the Chinese who longed to become Siamese, these titles represented a badge of achievement. Through the pull of officialdom, more and more Chinese of commercial origins were absorbed into the official life of the country as government employees of all grades.[73]

After 1900, a civil service career became the dominant ambition of the new "middle sector," which included many Chinese. Like so many of his Chinese peers and predecessors, the young Pridi also felt officialdom to be his calling. After a brief stint at a legal practice, he joined the civil service. Pridi's induction into the bureaucracy occurred just before the curtain was lowered on Chinese recruitment into government service. By the 1920s, the era of bureaucratic expansion had basically ended. There was no longer a lack of educated officials—more applicants appeared yearly than could be accepted.

Lucky for Pridi, he had caught a ride on the bureaucratic train just before the rollercoaster dipped on its way down.[74] In 1920, he won a government scholarship to continue his postgraduate studies in law at Paris. While he was a student in Paris he befriended Khuang Aphaiwong and Phibun Songkram.

Phibun was also a commoner born in 1898, in a village close to Bangkok. His father was an orchard grower. Like Pridi, he had attended temple school in his village and later went to another temple school in Bangkok. A hard-working student, he gained admission to the royal military academy and graduated at the age of 20, after World War I. At the royal military academy he was among the few selected to continue his military studies in France, where he met Pridi and other Siamese students, many of whom were among the conspirators in the coup of 1932. Thus, the socialization of this elite group was informed by a background in the civil service, coupled with a common experience of higher education and prior career interests in France, where French statist and nationalist ideological influences were absorbed.

However, the most senior member of the Promoters was not one of the Paris group. Phraya Phahon was born into a military family in 1887. Although his father was a commoner as well as a *lukchin*, he had received the noble title of *phraya*. When Phahon was born, he already had the military rank of colonel.

Phahon's father must have been among the early batch of officer cadets who were recruited into the modern, Western-style military founded by Chulalongkorn in the 1870s. The year 1873–74 marked the beginning of the royal bid to centralize administration by dislodging the Bunnag nobility from its command of political power. The newly formed military played an indispensable role in the monarchy's attempt to take over political control at the expense of the nobility. The centralization of administration went hand in hand with the dissolution of the localized structures of power, embodied by powerful *chao muang* and local nobility who formed the resource base of the Bunnag nobility. The outcome of this administrative reform was the replacement of the old nobility by new, commoner elites of educated, professionally trained military and bureaucratic civil servants.

A disciplinarian, Phahon's father began his son's education early and enrolled the boy in the royal military academy at the age of 12. Phahon graduated first in his class at the age of 16. He was sent to Germany to further his military training, becoming one of the earliest non-royal students to be sent abroad. Phahon lived in Europe for nine years and studied at military academies in both Germany and Denmark, where he underwent his basic socialization as a professional soldier.

He was reportedly recalled after he enraged the Chief of Staff Prince Chakrabongse, together with other students, by asking for a higher allowance. This seemingly innocuous incident was perhaps symptomatic of the growing discontent within the ranks of the military officer corps. The Chinese General Strike in 1910, Chulalongkorn's death in the same year, the Xinhai Revolution in 1911, the failed 1912 Military Rebellion and Prince Damrong's retirement in 1915 all signaled the passing of an era, further disturbing the uppermost levels of royal power.

A member of the Wild Tiger Corps in full uniform.

Furthermore, King Vajiravudh's creation of a parallel quasi-military organization, the Wild Tiger Corps, was bitterly resented by the regular, professional military elite

and contributed to an increasingly restless state apparatus that was conscious of its own autonomous power, upon which the absolute monarchy depended for its survival. Moreover, Vajiravudh's decision to bring Siam into World War I against Germany greatly irritated the kingdom's German-trained military officers like Phahon, who did not perceive Germany as the enemy of the Siamese state.

On the contrary, the kingdom's new military elite embodied by Phraya Phahon and his German-trained peers regarded Western imperialism led by France and Britain to be Siam's real enemies. During this period of modern state formation when the bureaucratic, communications and territorial frameworks of the Siamese nation were being laid, the enemy that threatened the nascent Siamese state was the imperialism of France and Britain.

The infant military forces of Siam during Phahon's father's generation had fought to fend off French territorial encroachments on Siam's eastern frontier. In the eyes of the professional state functionaries, the fledgling Siamese state had suffered injustice at the hands of France and Britain. In the institutional memory of the Siamese state, significant parts of French Indochina, as well as British Malaya—including Kelantan, Terengganu, Kedah and Perlis—rightfully belonged to Siam.

From his return to Siam shortly before World War I until 1932, Phahon served in a variety of military posts and rose to the highest rank available to a non-royal officer. His serious engagement with the other Francophile Promoters occurred after their return to Siam in 1929. He joined their conspiracy largely because of dissatisfaction over the monopoly of top posts in the military by high princes and their favorites.[75]

Phraya Phahon-Phonphayuhasena (1887–1947) and Hia Guang-iam (right).

During Phahon's formative years, the government service had been crowded with princes who occupied high posts in the army, navy and government ministries. The Ministry of Foreign Affairs contained the highest percentage of princes closely followed by the Ministry of Finance.[76] By the beginning of the reign of King Vajiravudh, there were more princes in government service than at any other time in the Bangkok period.

State personnel recruited from commoners and those associated with the court aristocracy were potentially in conflict. While the state bureaucracy became massively large, complex and responsible for a vast geographical area, the top remained very narrow. At the apex of the hierarchy stood the crown and a small coterie of royal rulers; below them were the traditional state officials; then came the newly recruited army and civil officers and numerous clerks who were originally *phrai*.

However, an essential component of a modern bureaucracy consists in the rationalization of administration through the replacement of arbitrary decisions with established rules. As the institutionalization of the bureaucracy progressed, a built-in contradiction began to develop between officials who enjoyed a privileged position because of their aristocratic status and the commoners whose promotions were based on merit.

The contradiction that exists between modern, rational, rule-bound administration and absolute monarchy is essentially irresolvable. An absolute monarchy by definition reserves the right to assert its political will in any manner it pleases. Absolutism cannot admit any limitations without ceasing to be absolute. The sharp division between princes and commoners was reinforced as one between arbitrary privilege and merit.

Thus, from an administrative viewpoint, the system was spreading favoritism, contrary to the newborn spirit of bureaucratic rule. Instead of the "Brave New

World" based on rationality and merit that they had been taught to uphold in their education and professional training, the members of the new state apparatus found that they were treated as no more than just another category of "royal servants."

Consequently, although princes continued to enjoy great advantages under absolute monarchy, their prominence in the state hierarchy was no longer unquestioned by talented and immodest commoners who found their careers impeded or blocked by nobles. One of Phahon's main grievances was that although he was more professionally qualified in military matters, he had to serve under princes whom he felt were incompetent.

Thus, a separation developed between the roles of the court's ruling clique on the one hand and the proliferating professional bureaucrats on the other. The contradictions between the court and the bureaucracy belied the fact that it was the latter that was in actual control of the management of the state machinery. These frustrations came to a head during the Great Depression, when the government of King Prajadhipok faced a shortage of funds.

As long as the bureaucracy was expanding, the road for Siamese social mobility seemed limitless, although some moved faster and further than others. When bureaucratic expansion stopped, opportunities for social mobility among the middle sector were naturally impacted, and for the first time, significant discontent appeared within its ranks. The situation was naturally compounded when bureaucratic downsizing occurred in the wake of deteriorating government finances and the Great Depression.

Moreover, the impact of the Great Depression on Siamese society was uneven. Least affected by the economic downturn was the rural sector, for which the blow was cushioned by the absence of a significant, landless peasant class, coupled with the fact that monasteries could take in a fair number of unemployed as monks.[77] The hardest hit was the growing class of state-centered officials in the bloated government bureaucracy and military services.

To save money, the government reduced the state payroll and cut expenses from the royal court down. The result was the lay-off of 1,292 civil servants in 1929.[78] These massive lay-offs signaled the prelude to the coup d'état led by Phraya Phahon two years later, which toppled Siam's absolute monarchy.

The Promoters were united in their common opposition to the absolute monarchy. Politically, they were opposed to the monopoly of political power by the court; ideologically they rejected the doctrine of royalism promoted and used by King Vajiravudh to establish an ideological monopoly over Siamese nationalism. For Vajiravudh, royalism was not only compatible with nationalism, it was one and the same. In his eyes, loyalty to the king was an essential part of the Siamese identity.

King Vajiravudh's attempt to subsume nationalism under royalism must be seen against the backdrop of the Xinhai Revolution. The replacement in China of the Qing dynasty by a constitutional republican regime posed a challenge to the legitimacy of absolute monarchy. Under the influence of the Xinhai Revolution, the ideas of republicanism and constitutional government had acquired a veneer of respectability and were being touted in the local Chinese newspapers as the wave of the future. King Vajiravudh's related attempt to redefine Siamese nationalism was intended to shore up the deteriorating ideological foundations of the legitimacy of the absolute monarchy. Vajiravudh's philosophical prescription that nationalism is royalism implied that constitutional rule, socialism, and republicanism were all out of sync with the "Great Siamese Tradition." Consequently, these ideas and their corresponding political institutions were anti-Siamese and harmful for the country.

The theme of the harm of parliamentary democracy recurs in King Prajadhipok's memorandums. He noted that a parliament would only open the door for the Chinese to take over the country, stating, "A parliament would be entirely dominated by the Chinese party. One could exclude all Chinese from every political right; yet they will dominate the situation all the same since they hold the hard cash."[79]

The Revolution of 1932 represented a rejection of Vajiravudh's attempt to create Siamese nationalism under the banner of "Nation, religion and king." Instead, the Promoters of 1932 called for a people-centered nationalism. They argued that under absolute monarchy the country had remained backward and the welfare of the people had not improved.

Beyond their common foe of the absolute monarchy, the Promoters comprised a variety of backgrounds with different ideological persuasions, abilities and concerns. Initially, Phahon and his military colleagues comprised the most important elements. It was inconceivable to attempt to topple the absolute monarchy without the participation of the military. The direction and execution of the actual coup d'état to detach the palace leadership from the apparatus of government was in the hands Phahon, Songsuradej (another German-trained officer) and other military officers. At dawn on 24 June 1932, a group of military officers moved their troops to occupy key government installations. The absolute monarchy had lost control of the machinery of government.

However, Phahon and the military elements did not have the requisite skills to run a government. The Promoters particularly needed administrators with expert legal skills to restructure the monarchy-centered political system and create a new framework of government. The Promoters had to turn to Pridi Banomyong and his team of administrators for the necessary legal input in running a government.

The Francophile-group led by Pridi was more influenced by Marxist ideas and tried unsuccessfully to give a socialist direction to the new regime, which Pridi laid out in his *Comprehensive Economic Plan*. But this plan raised fears of Bolshevism among the right-wing military elements and the English-educated elite who also supported the 1932 Revolution.

Pridi's attempt to push the revolution in a socialist direction created a political backlash. His economic plan was rejected and his government was toppled. Hounded by charges of Communism, Pridi was forced into exile. The pendulum of power swung back to Phraya Phahon and the military faction who replaced the Francophile group with English-educated lawyers, administrative bureaucrats and their English advisors.

The fall of the Francophile group caused a shift toward a more pronounced anti-Chinese tendency in the government. Ironically, the Revolution of 1932, which was made possible largely by Sino-Siamese officials, lawyers and officers who gave the revolt its first political orientation, eventually led to an intensification of anti-Chinese policies. Out of the 57 members of the People's Senate, at least 21 were of Chinese ancestry—and far from hiding it, they were proud to announce the fact. A People's Party senator and judge who addressed the Chinese Chamber of Commerce said, "What is so curious is that in general the Siamese are of Chinese origin …I who consider myself Siamese is of Chinese origin. The Chinese, who have become Siamese, have the right to give their opinion of the political affairs of the country."[80]

By contrast, the bulk of the native Siamese population in those days had little political consciousness and seemed unlikely to cause political instability. National consciousness and anti-Chinese sentiment were, for the most part, confined to the royalty, bureaucrats, military officers and the Western-educated Siamese intelligentsia.

However, the apparently cordial relations between the People's Party and the Chinese community were perhaps misleading. Although many People's Party leaders paid lip service to their ethnic Chinese origins, and many platitudes such as "We are all the same people" were uttered, the initial niceties barely concealed an internal conflict that existed within Siam's Chinese community, mainly between the *huaqiao* Chinese emigrants, who were China-oriented, and the *lukchin* Chinese, who had assimilated into Siamese culture and identity.

The China-born *huaqiao* regarded themselves as Chinese, spoke Chinese dialects in daily life, observed Chinese customs, were completely absorbed by political events in China, were loyal to China rather than to Siam, and generally did not care about local Siamese politics. Like their China-born kin, many of the *lukchin* leaders of the 1932 Revolution were also Chinese, but they were Chinese who espoused a Siamese standpoint. They didn't identify with the China-born and the new emigrants who were oriented towards China. While they deprecated their

China-oriented kin for their divided loyalties, those sympathetic to China despised Chinese who "betrayed the call of their blood."

Moreover, after 1932 the Chinese who had assimilated into Siamese identity had joined the ranks of the ruling class, where they began to perceive things from their newfound class position. The most powerful among them were the state-centered Nationalist leaders of the 1932 Revolution—the collectivity of military-cum-civilian officials, namely Pridi, Phahon and Phibun. These leaders were not only Chinese who evinced a Siamese standpoint; their foremost identification was with the institutional interests of the state.

As managers of the ship of state, Pridi, Phahon and Phibun deplored internal disturbances that threatened political stability or damaged the Siamese state's relations with the big powers. Saddled with the responsibility of forming a government that had to deliver on economic progress and development, they viewed Siamese-Chinese remittances to support philanthropic causes in China as an undesirable drain on Siam's economy.

Moreover, the rejection of Pridi's *Comprehensive Economic Plan* deprived the People's Party of its economic agenda to address the problems of rural poverty, inequality of wealth and the country's racially stratified economic system. Consequently, the party's pledge to bring about economic progress remained largely unfulfilled, causing the government to look for convenient scapegoats to blame and deflect attention from its own failures. Who could be a better scapegoat than the alien Chinese in their midst with no political rights?

Meanwhile, Chinese divided loyalties irritated Siamese nationalist sensibilities

The cabinet of Phraya Phahon-Phonphayuhasena (first row, center) with Phibun (second row, fourth from left) and Pridi (third row, fourth from left) as members.

and fed into the growing Siamese pre-disposition to take out their frustrations on Siam's Chinese minority. The escalation of military hostilities between China and Japan on the Chinese mainland in the 1930s set the stage for a clash between Siamese and Chinese nationalism, as Sino-Japanese hostilities translated into disturbances in Siam. Following Japan's invasion of Manchuria in 1931–32, every Chinese newspaper in Siam attacked Japan vigorously.

Popular indignation with Japan exploded again, reminiscent of the anti-Japanese hysteria that swept through Bangkok in 1928. Notwithstanding the robust anti-Japanese sentiment in the Chinese community, the Great Depression had made it impossible to provide economic aid to China on the scale of 1928. In 1932, when Tan Siewmeng, the newly elected leader of the CCC, organized a committee for the relief of war refugees in Shanghai, it managed to collect only a meager sum of 21,000 baht.[81] Although some enthusiastic groups called for retaliatory measures against the Japanese, Tan Siewmeng refrained from committing the CCC to a boycott of Japanese goods.

Moreover, a Chinese community embattled by the depression was in no position to mount effective economic sanctions against any country. Consequently, an anti-Japanese boycott was only half-heartedly sustained by isolated groups until early 1933. Despite the sporadic boycotts, Japanese trade with Siam increased considerably between 1931 and 1933. The renewal of a vigorous anti-Japanese campaign had to await important leadership changes within Siam's Chinese community.

Under Tan Siewmeng, the role of commissioner of commerce and chairman of the CCC became interchangeable, and the CCC functioned as an unofficial legation of the Chinese government. It negotiated with the Siamese government

Tan Siewmeng Wanglee and his wife, Tongpoon Lamsam.

on behalf of the local Chinese and issued consular invoices acceptable all over the Far East.[82] The establishment of the office of China's first commissioner of commerce was welcomed in Nanjing as a milestone in the roadmap towards full diplomatic relations between China and Siam. Understandably, the GMD did not want to rock the boat by antagonizing the People's Party, which had come to power after 1932.

Seow Hoodseng enjoyed good relations with many of the leaders of the 1932 Revolution. Seow was related to the wife of Phraya Phahon, the leader of the coup d'état—Seow was her uncle and both Phahon and his wife called him *pae*. Although Seow was in Canton when the absolute monarchy was toppled in 1932, he immediately sent a telegram to the People's Party to congratulate them on the successful coup d'état.

The new Siamese intelligentsia shared many common

political ideals with the followers of Sun Yatsen, and many Promoters were avid readers of Seow Hoodseng's newspaper *Chino-Siam Warasup*, admiring his pro-republican political platform. Seow's daughter even married a cabinet minister of the People's Party.

As the son-in-law of the Hakka leader Ng Yuklong Lamsam, Tan Siewmeng was also close to Seow Hoodseng. Personally, Seow Hoodseng had always been close to the Hakkas and had helped Sun Yatsen found the Hakka Association in Bangkok in 1908. In addition, following the recent split within the GMD between the Chiang Kai-shek faction and the southwest faction, Seow was seeking someone he could influence. These close personal relationships at the top level during the early 1930s helped contain the potential conflicts between Chinese and Siamese interests and kept political differences within manageable bounds.

Both sides—the *huaqiao* Chinese hardliners and the *lukchin* Siamese nationalists—apparently made sincere efforts to smooth over differences through high-level personal interventions, Chinese goodwill missions and promotion of Sino-Siamese Friendship Associations in Shanghai and Bangkok. However, on the eve of the Sino-Japanese War, the Chinese community in Siam, which appeared relatively composed, was actually politically divided into two rival camps—the Teochew group of the southwest faction (Xinan) and the pro–Chiang Kai-shek *shang zhuan* faction led by Tan Siewmeng.[83]

This was all the more remarkable considering that the 1930s witnessed a relative intensification of anti-Chinese measures and policies compared to the days of King Prajadhipok.[84] The People's Party introduced tighter restrictions on the activities of the Chinese, including a new compulsory education law that imposed limits on Chinese schools and Chinese-language education. In 1933, the new government enacted anti-Communist laws to contain the influx of left-wing elements into Siam. Restricting Chinese schools and curbing Communist influence tended to inform the early policies of the People's Party towards Siam's Chinese minority.

However, despite the growing incidence of anti-Chinese measures, the government's policies were neither consistently nor efficiently implemented. Conflicting objectives of different ministries and government departments coupled with inefficiency and the prevalence of bribery meant that many loopholes existed. In fact, the attitude of the People's Party towards the Chinese during this period has often been characterized as "the policy of drift." However, the cycle of suspicion and reactionary measures leading to mounting discrimination against Siam's Chinese subjects only aggravated the growing separateness of Siam's Chinese community.[85]

The honeymoon relationship between the GMD and the People's Party during the first half of the 1930s became severely tested by the outbreak of the Sino-

OUR RICE MERCHANT: MA BULAKUL—MAH LAPKUN
(MA LIQUN, 1897–1964)

The chairman of the CCC prior to Tan Siewmeng was Ma Bulakul (Mah Lapkun). Ma Bulakul's father, Mah Tongcheng, a Cantonese, was the leading mechanical expert of rice-milling technology in Bangkok. Mah Lapkun, his son, was born in Taishan District, Guangdong Province. By the time he grew up, his father's business success had expanded into rice-milling operations. Mah Lapkun was sent to St. Stephen's College in Hong Kong before he joined his father in Bangkok in 1916.[86] In 1919, the company ranked third among leading rice exporters, second only to Lee Teck-ow and Koh Mahwah.

Mah Lapkun was the founding member of the Rice Miller Association, in which he was appointed the chairman in 1925. During the depression that started in 1929 and lasted several years, the price of rice dropped from the usual average of nine baht to only five baht per *picul*[87] in 1931. The outstanding achievement of the association was the agreement among members to scale down production. Despite the cooperation among members, many rice merchants suffered severe financial losses, including Mah Lapkun who at the time was the chairman of the CCC (1929–32) as well as the president of the Kwong Siew Association.[88]

As the leader of the Chinese community in Siam, Mah Lapkun had always been a generous philanthropist. He donated a substantial sum for the founding of the Zhonghua School. In 1921, when China suffered from the Yellow River flood, Mah was elected to chair the Siamese Overseas Chinese Aid Association. In the following year, he constructed Tangzhi Street and founded a school in his home village. During the 10-odd years between World War I and World War II, he helped transport the remains of fellow overseas Chinese to be buried in their homeland. Mah built the Kwong Siew School and Kwong Siew Hospital for the Cantonese community. In 1938, during the War of Resistance against Japan, Mah Lapkun did his utmost in promoting the sale of government bonds; however, on the business front he had not recovered from the heavy losses inflicted by the Great Depression.

Fortunately for him, in 1938 the Thai government decided to incorporate the government-owned rice-exporting firm called the Thai Rice Company in retaliation against the anti-Japanese boycott organized by the local Chinese merchants. The authorities selected Mah Lapkun, an old hand in the rice industry, as their general manager working under the government-appointed board of directors.

The company rented Mah's Chin Seng Mill and started to churn out rice for export to the Japanese market in December 1938. The venture did well, and when the Thai Rice Company expanded, Mah Lapkun applied for Thai citizenship in 1940. Phibun Songkram, the Thai prime minister at the time, was pleased and named him Ma Bulakul.

In 1944, he was awarded the Third Class Order of the White Elephant for strengthening the unity of Thai farmers and promoting rice production, stabilizing Thailand's economy and contributing to the Thai government. He represented the Thai government at rice conferences around the world, and traveled to rice-producing countries on the Thai government's goodwill trade mission. In 1964, President Chiang Kai-shek awarded Mah Lapkun an elegiac tablet and a horizontal, inscribed board meaning "public-spirited."

Nationalist soldiers
with a portrait of
Chiang Kai-shek.

Japanese War in 1937. The importance of wooing Siamese leaders to establish treaty relations gave way to the more urgent need to mobilize overseas-Chinese resources and support for China's life-or-death military struggle with Japan. GMD policy in Siam shifted from a focus on the "unofficial legation" activities in Bangkok to mobilizing support for China's war effort. The role of the chairman of the CCC became more important than the role of the commissioner of commerce.

Under Tan Siewmeng, the role of the chairman of the CCC was unofficially subsumed under the role of the commissioner of commerce, as internal GMD politics made the balance of responsibilities difficult to maintain. As the commissioner of commerce, Tan Siewmeng had to liaise with the Chinese central government in Nanjing. The "unofficial legation" in Bangkok increasingly came under the authority of the mainstream faction of the GMD under Generalissimo Chiang Kai-shek. Tan Siewmeng found himself reporting and responding to directives from Chiang Kai-shek, and his official trips took him to Nanjing, the capital of the Republic of China, rather than to Canton.

Hu Hanmin, the leader of the GMD's southwest faction based in Canton, had enjoyed a close relationship with Seow Hoodseng since 1908 when he visited Bangkok with Sun Yatsen. The politics of the GMD became polarized between the ruling faction under Chiang Kai-shek and the southwest faction under Hu Hanmin. This split within the GMD in China was inevitably mirrored in Siam. Due to the close personal relationship between Seow and Hu Hanmin, the GMD branch in Bangkok aligned itself with the southwest faction. When the split occurred in 1931, Seow Hoodseng was appointed to the central committee of the Xinan government and moved to Canton.[89]

Tan Siewmeng's leanings towards Nanjing and his establishment of the *shang zhuan* faction created tensions between the CCC and the GMD branch under the control of the southwest faction. The *shang zhuan* faction built up a large following through its promotion of philanthropic activities through the CCC and the establishment of its own newspaper, the *Huaqiaoribao*, which by 1938 had the largest daily circulation among all Chinese newspapers at 10,000 copies.[90]

Resistance

The impending war with Japan and the shifting political currents within the GMD divided the interests and goals of the GMD branch and the office of the commissioner of commerce in Bangkok. The Nanjing government focused on the "unofficial legation" office of the commissioner of commerce, and its major efforts were directed towards securing a treaty with Siam and establishing diplomatic relations. For this purpose, Nanjing could not have had a better unofficial ambassador in place than Tan Siewmeng, with his excellent business and political connections in Bangkok's high society.

But for Seow Hoodseng and the southwest faction, the most urgent priority was to build support among Siam's overseas Chinese for resisting the Japanese in the impending war between China and Japan. For this purpose, the Office of the Chairman of the CCC was more important than the Office of the Commissioner of Commerce. While Tan Siewmeng was an excellent diplomat who enjoyed good access to the corridors of power in the People's Party, he was not cut out for the rough-and-tumble job of rousing the Chinese masses to rally behind China's war effort. He also appeared to be unwilling to challenge Chiang Kai-shek's reluctance to resist the Japanese militarily. A different type of leader than Tan Siewmeng—a man of the people rather than a suave business aristocrat—was needed to incite passionate anti-Japanese sentiments and inspire the Chinese in Siam to rise to their patriotic duty of sacrificing for the ancestral homeland in its hour of need.

Moreover, anti-Japanese activities in Siam were a dangerous business that would ultimately provoke the Siamese authorities to crack down on the Chinese community. Therefore, in Tan Siewmeng's view, it was imperative that the unofficial legation be sheltered from any potential political backlash stemming from organized, illegal anti-Japanese activities. However, this view was not shared by a large number of local Chinese in Bangkok who wanted to see a more aggressive approach to help the fatherland. As the CCC commanded the leadership of the Chinese community, the southwest faction submitted new candidates to take over the chamber in 1936. The move was spearheaded by Teochew elements rallying around Tan Gengchuang, Liao Gongpow (Khun Sethabhakdi),[91] Tae Juebing, U

Chuliang and Hia Guang-iam.

This group was deeply embedded in the southwest faction: Tan Lengsue, father of Tan Gengchuang, was a close friend of Seow Hoodseng. Tae Juebing was previously inducted into the Tongmenghui by Seow Hoodseng. Moreover, at Tan Muiteng's funeral, where Seow and Lim Baegee were the hosts, almost everyone from this group and their followers, which later comprised the Teochew Association, attended, while none from Tan Siewmeng's *shang zhuan* faction showed up.[92]

Although the *shang zhuan* faction led by the incumbent chairman, Tan Siewmeng, opposed the southwest takeover, Hia Guang-iam won the popular vote to be selected as the new chairman of the CCC in an election on 1 March 1936. Hia Guang-iam received 195 votes, while Tan Siewmeng came in second with 140 votes. However, the next step—the election of the chairman of the CCC by the newly formed 15-member Executive Committee—proved to be complicated.[93] Suddenly, committee members with strong credentials—including Ng Yuklong Lamsam, Mah Lapkun[94] and B.L. Hua (Pangsriwong)—withdrew and left the chairman position vacant for two months. Finally, the issue of the chairmanship was resolved in an election on 13 May when Tan Siewmeng received two votes while Hia Guang-iam received 11. With Tan Siewmeng's defeat, the pro–Chiang Kai-shek *shang zhuan* faction was displaced by the southwest faction in the Chinese Chamber of Commerce. Under Hia Guang-iam, the policies and activities of the CCC demonstrated a remarkably different style reflecting the strong personality of the new leader.

Hia Guang-iam

Hia Guang-iam, who was Tan Siewmeng's senior by 25 years, was born in 1879 to a desperately poor family in Chenghai District, Guangdong. His parents died when he was five and he was raised as an orphan by his uncle's wife, who was a widow. His education was interrupted by poverty. Throughout his childhood, he attended school for only three months, leaving school and working when he was nine. However, his hard life made him physically strong.

At 17 he decided to seek his fortune overseas. Through clan connections, he was offered a job in a distillery at the Cambodian town of Banum, southwest of Phnom Penh. He could not afford a steamer ticket so he traveled by junk, taking 40 days to reach Saigon instead of the usual seven days by steamer. He worked as a coolie for six years, but the pay was very low and he could not save any money. Thus, Hia decided to move to Bangkok and try his luck there. He was 23 when he arrived.[95]

His first job was at a pickle factory called Siang Gee in Bangkok's Chinatown, which belonged to the Tantasrethi family. His indomitable spirit and inborn leadership qualities, which were to serve him well later in life, shone through though he was only a coolie. Laboring beside him was a skinny boy from his home village in Guangdong. The remorseless foreman would pick on the skinny boy because he could only carry two sacks of vegetables on his back instead of the usual four. Hia Guang-iam protected the boy by offering to carry six sacks per load to help the boy meet his daily quota. Hia's honesty, kindness and compassion for the weak as well as his willingness to work like an ox earned him respect among all the coolies. His reputation brought him to the attention of the management and soon Hia was appointed foreman in charge of transportation.

Ten years later, Hia Guang-iam had made a success of himself in the transportation business. Now in his 30s, Hia already owned a barge company, Guang Heng Lee, specializing in bulk transportation and plying the route between Bangkok and the deep-sea port at Sri-chang Island, where ocean-going vessels came to berth. At the beginning of 1939, he had 20 barges that moved 6,400 tons. In addition, he owned more than 10 rice mills and a wine shop.

Hia Guang-iam became involved in philanthropic activities in 1923, when his ancestral village in China was ravaged by severe floods, claiming a heavy death toll. He received news that his relative who owned the Cambodian distillery at which he had worked like a slave for six years lost all his family members but one. When the CCC organized a fundraising drive to help the flood victims, he decided to join. Being an energetic, robust, hands-on man, Hia even traveled back to his home village to help the relief effort. It was there that he adopted a flood orphan, Hia Muigao, who later grew up to become a vice president of the Chinese Overseas Association in Beijing.

Deprivation of education in his youth made Hia Guang-iam realize the value of education as a human right. He also became chairman of Xinmin Chinese School and continually supported its operation. The school grew from about 50 students at its inception to become the largest Chinese school in Bangkok with almost

Left: Hia Guang-iam's family.

Right: Hia Guang-iam (seated, fourth from the right) and the board of directors of the Poh Teck Tung Foundation in 1938.

1,000 students just before the Phibun government closed down all Chinese schools in 1939. One of his major contributions to society was his unwavering support for education, especially schools for the poor and underprivileged run by *huaqiao* intellectuals. He donated generously to Chinese schools both in Siam and China, including Assumption College in Bangkok, as well as schools that teach the Thai language to new Chinese immigrants.

After his business empire was firmly established, Hia Guang-iam left the control of business operations to his wife, Lao Yiek-eng, and devoted himself full-time to charitable and humanitarian works in support of the poor and disadvantaged in Chinese society, both in Siam and China. His devotion to the principle of corporate social responsibility, which he once summed up as "When we receive from society, it is our duty to give back," created domestic conflicts with his wife, who was naturally more concerned for her children's welfare than the welfare of people at large.[96]

His son, Amporn Iamsury, shared his reminiscences of daily life in Hia Guang-iam's household:

> *One day, my father woke me up early in the morning ... Just as our car was leaving the house a group of paupers were waiting for my father at the gate. He asked the driver to stop the car and talked to them one by one. After listening to their grievances, he instructed his assistant to give appropriate help if possible. We went to his office where he spent about an hour giving instructions to his subordinate ... When the car left his office another group of paupers awaited to air their grievances. Some were unemployed, some had gravely ill relatives. My father would talk to them one by one and gave them some money when he felt it appropriate. Then he took me to visit a sick man living in a shack by the railway. He was very thin; my father sat down and spent a while with him. I still remember the grateful look on his face when my father gave him money for hospital bills. Then we visited several others before a simple lunch. In the afternoon my father attended several association meetings before going to Zhonghua medical center for yet another meeting. I waited for a long time and dozed off. I was woken up when he finally entered the car and we headed home. I remembered my father humming his native song—happy from a good day's work.*

Although he donated generously to many public charities, he hardly spent any money on himself or his family. In his rented house, only the drawing room was decorated, in order to receive visitors. There were only three beds in the house, one for himself and his wife, one for his adopted son Hia Muigao and one for his eldest daughter. The other nine children slept on the floor. He gave his children 10 satang a day for lunch but he made them donate five satang a day to help the anti-Japanese war effort in China. He didn't buy shoes for his children— they went barefoot to school like many of their friends. Hia and his wife never bought toys for the children but preferred to give them a good education. They were sent to Canton, Singapore and Saigon to study.

His friendship and respect for Seow Hoodseng led him to become involved in the politics of the CCC in early 1936. They shared the same conviction that it was the patriotic duty of all Chinese to help protect the ancestral homeland against Japanese imperialist military aggrandizement. Hia Guang-iam felt that the leadership of the Chinese community in Siam was not living up to its patriotic calling, and taking control of the CCC was the first step in his ambitious plan to launch a strong anti-Japanese movement among the Chinese in Siam. In 1936, Hia Guang-iam succeeded in his bid to become chairman of the CCC.

However, Hu Hanmin's death on 12 May 1936 led to the collapse of the southwest faction, after which Seow Hoodseng fled to Bangkok to escape arrest by Chiang Kai-shek. Meanwhile, a war between China and Japan appeared imminent. The new Teochew leadership of the CCC led by Hia Guang-iam joined with the newly returned Seow Hoodseng to organize a strong anti-Japanese movement in Siam reminiscent of 1928.

From Bangkok, Seow Hoodseng wrote letters to Chiang Kai-shek urging him to resist the Japanese and proposing many strategies. Military hostilities escalated into full-blown war following the battle between the Chinese and Japanese in July 1937, which is now known as the Marco Polo Bridge incident, and the capture of Nanjing by Japanese forces in 1937. Hia and Tan Gengchuang decided to register the Teochew Association on 4 February 1938 as another vehicle for carrying out anti-Japanese activities.[97] The same gang of five who spearheaded the takeover of the CCC from the *shang zhuan* faction became the founders of the Teochew Association: Tan Gengchuang became the first president with[98] Sethabhakdi serving as vice president, Hia Guang-iam as treasurer, and U Chuliang as secretary. Led by Hia Guang-iam, this gang of five also set up an underground unit called the Anti-Japanese League, whose mission was to sabotage Japan's war effort.

To boost the group's organizational resources for building a strong anti-Japanese movement in Siam, Hia Guang-iam and his gang of five invested in issuing the Teochew Association's own newspaper, *Zhongguoribao*, on 1 October 1938. A relative of Sethabhakdi named Lee Keehiong became the editor. Intellectual, well educated, and holding an economics degree from Shanghai, Lee Keehiong proved to be an extremely able editor of the newspaper.

The establishment of *Zhongguoribao* sharpened the rivalry between the

The funeral of "Second Brother Hong" in 1936 at his mansion in Plabplachai before his body was taken back to a burial site in China.

Teochew faction led by Hia Guang-iam and the *shang zhuan* faction led by Tan Siewmeng. The *Zhongguoribao* and the *Huaqiaoribao* engaged in propaganda campaigns against each other to build support among the overseas-Chinese community for their respective political positions. The political split within Siam's Chinese community became apparent even to overseas observers of Siamese affairs. The Taiwan-based newspaper *Chronicle of Overseas Chinese* reported, "There are two leaders in Siam. One is Tan Siewmeng, the Chinese Commercial Councilor, under China's Ministry of Foreign Affairs. Another is Hia Guang-iam, the Chairman of the Chinese Chamber of Commerce. The two individuals were respected and always played major roles leading the Chinese community. Both have their own organizational members and newspapers."[99]

However, despite their rivalry, both Hia Guang-iam and Tan Siewmeng were operating under the GMD, which faced a common foe: Japan. The outbreak of war in China in July 1937 finally galvanized the GMD political forces in Siam. The Chinese Communist Party (CCP), on the other hand, had already changed its political strategy. Following a change of policy by the COMINTERN in 1935, Communists in Siam shifted their focus from promoting revolution to opposing Japanese imperialism.

Thus, the advent of 1938 saw growing convergence in the strategies of the Teochew faction and the *shang zhuan* faction, as well as between the GMD and the CCP, in supporting the movement called Allies of Save the Nation Anti-Japanese War. Indeed, help came from all parties within the Chinese community for the alliance.

Within the GMD camp, the faction under Hia Guang-iam was the least anti-Communist and the most open to forming a united front with the CPS. In fact, the establishment of the *Zhongguoribao* was an open invitation to cooperate with the Communists. The inaugural issue on 1 October 1938 declared the position of the Teochew Association faction as such: "The pressing mission of China at the moment is liberating the nation, and newspapers are one of the important tools to help achieve this."

The *Zhongguoribao* declared its opposition to the mainstream GMD faction's anti-Communist line:

> . . . our nation in the last 10 years has been bloody due to Anti-Communist Resistance. But now the CCP has abandoned their class struggle theory and support the Nationalist Party. They respect the Three Principles of the People and support the Anti-Japanese United Front which strengthens our national power. So China no longer has a Communist problem.

Demonstrating solidarity with the Communists, *Zhongguoribao* published Mao Zedong's report, *The New Level of Improvement of the War of Resistance and Anti-Japanese United Front*, in October 1938.[100] It also printed the CCP's bank account number in Hong Kong to enable Communist sympathizers to donate money to the Communist cause. When Zhou Enlai launched a recruitment campaign of overseas-Chinese volunteers for the CCP's Eighth Route Army and the New Fourth Army, Hia Guang-iam ran the advertisement in the pages of his newspaper.

The anti-Japanese activities of the Chinese-nationalist united front essentially took three forms: propaganda in Siam, fundraising and recruitment for China's war effort and, lastly, the local enforcement of another boycott of Japanese goods. All Chinese newspapers, especially the *Huaqiaoribao* and *Zhongguoribao*, engaged in anti-Japanese propaganda. In addition to its pro-Communist line, the *Zhongguoribao* reported extensively on the activities of overseas Chinese who were exiled to Shantou, including the work of the Association of Siamese Chinese Against Enemies, led by Xu Xia.

Also covered were the activities of left-wing teachers who taught in local Chinese schools. Following the closure of Chinese schools by the Phibun government in August 1939, Chinese teachers found themselves unemployed. Of those who had to go back to China, many returned to Shantou to help support China's war effort against Japan. Reflecting his unswerving commitment to education, Hia Guang-iam did everything he could to give moral and financial support to these returned teachers from Siam in Shantou. Tan Siewmeng also did much to support the Whampao Military Academy's recruitment campaign in Siam. Among the students that Tan Siewmeng sent to Whampao was Prasit Rakpracha (Pan Ziming), whose autobiography graphically described life in China during the war.[101]

Hia Guang-iam also sent Teochew Association representatives to participate at the Overseas Chinese Conference held in Singapore on 10 October 1938 to find ways to help victims of the war in China. Participants came from Malaya, Burma, Hong Kong, Indonesia, the Philippines and Siam. Although Siam was home to the largest overseas-Chinese community in the region, the kingdom had the fewest participants because the Phibun government had prohibited all anti-Japanese war efforts. Only Hia Guang-iam's Teochew Association faction attended the conference from Siam in defiance of the Thai government's prohibition.[102]

When war broke out, both GMD nationalists and Communists put in a great deal of effort to raise funds and donations for China's war effort, although their actions tended to be done separately rather than jointly. Nationalist fundraising activities tended to revolve around selling Chungking government bonds. Hia Guang-iam's Teochew Association faction established a branch unit in Siam called the "Government Bond Selling Campaign Committee Branch in Siam," with Seow Hoodseng serving as its president.

The gang of five of the Teochew Association, led by Hia Guang-iam, became the five vice presidents of the bond-selling committee.[103] The office-bearers of the bond-selling committee were all appointed by the Chungking government. They were relegated the responsibilities of promoting and selling bonds to the Chinese in Siam and charged with the task of sending all the bond sales revenue to the GMD party headquarters in China. Although Tan Siewmeng was one of the 24 members in the committee selling Chinese war bonds, his name did not appear in the Teochew Association documents, reflecting the ambivalent relationship between the two groups.

This reticence may also have been due to the clandestine nature of the organization's activities. Bond selling fell under the restricted activities outlined in the Fund Raising Restriction Act (1937) enacted by the People's Party government, which banned fundraising that could be injurious to the country's relations with Japan.[104]

Despite government restrictions on fundraising, the Chinese managed to send considerable sums of money to China by various means. The GMD and the Communists had a well-organized underground network of cells, study groups and secret societies that penetrated civil society organizations including the CCC, trade unions, guilds, Chinese schools, speech-group associations, charitable foundations, factories, trading companies, remittance bureaus, hospitals and temples, all of which could be used as vehicles for fundraising. The CPS also reshaped its mass organizations, and under the leadership of Liu Shushi, Qiu Ji (Khu Gip Lekawat) and Li Hua founded the "Anti-Japanese National Salvation Alliance of Siam Chinese from Differing Walks of Life" (Kang Lian). Outside the two main parties, a number of unaffiliated Patriotic Youth organizations also sprouted up.

By creating a plethora of organizations and decentralizing their activities, the Nationalists and the Communists succeeded in effectively evading government restrictions and mobilizing the Chinese community against the Japanese by collecting money and selling bonds to help finance the war in China. Organizations involved in illegal fundraising activities covered their trail by sending money through individuals and leaving no documentary evidence. Fundraising was conducted monthly as well as sporadically—whenever it was convenient. After collection at the grassroots level, the funds were passed up to bigger organizations such as the CCC. The latter would finally send all the money to the Chungking government.[105]

Between the GMD and the Communists, the former managed to raise more money because most of the Chinese in Siam were pro-GMD. Also, GMD supporters included big merchants and capitalists; therefore, the GMD received money easily without much coercion. By contrast, the Communists often had to resort to coercion to raise funds, and many pro-GMD merchants became subjected to Communist extortion. When the war became prolonged, these merchants were targeted because they had gone back to trade with the Japanese, rationalizing that they had already donated a great deal of money to the Chungking government. The Communists and their Patriotic Youth organizations kept a close eye on these merchants, some of whom even belonged to the Teochew Association faction.[106]

Historian Eiji Murashima estimated that from August 1937 to February 1938, Hia Guang-iam managed to raise 705,086, baht through the CCC.[107] However, according to Tan Siewmeng's report, from July 1937 to the end of 1938, the Chinese in Siam sent an estimated amount of 13–15 million Chinese dollars, of which 80 percent came from donations. Consequently, when Ling Chee, the representative of the Chinese government, arrived in Bangkok in February 1938 to sell government bonds, cash flow in the Chinese community had somewhat dried up. However, Tan Siewmeng, the commercial councilor, negotiated a barter deal arrangement whereby the Chinese government agreed to accept rice as payment in kind for the Chinese government bonds. A total of 101,200 *piculs* of rice were gathered to help China's war effort, of which 8,000 *piculs* were exchanged for Chinese government bonds.[108]

Fundraising activities often went in tandem with disaster relief efforts, such as sending rice, clothing and medicines to China. Hia Guang-iam launched a campaign through the Teochew Association to help impoverished inhabitants of the Teochew heartland in Guangdong who were ravaged by famine due to the effects of war and drought. Both Tan Siewmeng and Hia Guang-iam sent cheap rice from Siam to relieve the famine. Hia established a rice-trading company to sell rice at subsidized prices to China. In 1938, Hia sent 20,000 sacks of rice to the famine zone. In 1939 there was another outbreak of famine, and Hia again sent more rice. The Teochew Association newspaper, *Zhongguoribao*, reported that part of the rice was distributed to war victims and fishermen in Raoping, whose livelihood was disrupted by war-time conditions. These supplies were stopped after the Japanese army occupied Shantou in June 1939.

Although acting separately, during the war years both the GMD and the CCP formed a united front to fight the Japanese. Hia Guang-iam gave moral, financial and material support to both camps without discrimination. Even the formerly anti-Communist *shang zhuan* faction closed ranks with other Chinese groups to fight the Japanese. Tan Siewmeng's newspaper, *Huaqiaoribao*, ceased attacking the Communists. When 22 Communist leaders were arrested in Siam in February 1938, Tan Siewmeng expressed sympathy and sent representatives to visit and assist the families of those who had been captured.[109]

The president of the Japanese Chamber of Commerce in Bangkok, Hirano Gunji, alleged that Tan Siewmeng was "secretly anti-Japanese," as he was known to be involved in promoting the sale of Chungking government war bonds. In addition, Tan Siewmeng helped to establish the Huaxi Property Development Limited Company, which channeled overseas-Chinese investments in agriculture, industry, mining and trade in Yunnan to support China's war economy. He made large investments in China and was appointed to the Second National Peoples'

Tan Siewmeng (first row, fifth from left) attended one of the NPC meetings in China.

Congress (NPC) in 1940, becoming one of six overseas Chinese among the 240 members of the NPC.

However, the most militant and effective anti-Japanese groups were the Communists and the Teochew Association faction led by Hia Guang-iam. Together they staged the most daring, dramatic and damaging attacks on Japanese interests in Siam and some of their leaders, including Hia Guang-iam, paid for their activities with their lives. Perhaps the most damaging anti-Japanese united-front activity was the enforcement of another boycott of Japanese goods reminiscent of 1928. To implement the boycott, they turned to the southwest faction's veteran enforcer of the successful 1927–28 boycott, Longchu Teck.

Longchu Teck (Lim Ngekheng) was Bangkok's most prominent construction tycoon. He was a major contractor for government infrastructure projects during the reigns of King Vajiravudh and King Prajadhipok, including bridges, roads, railways, tram lines, markets, temples and theaters. He also won great fame for building Bangkok's Lumpini Park. A senior member of the southwest faction, as well as a right-hand man of Seow Hoodseng, Longchu Teck ran the Triad assassination squads that punished Chinese merchants who broke the anti-Japanese boycott in 1928.

Upon his appointment as enforcer of the Teochew Association's Anti-Japanese League charged with the task of threatening and assassinating traitors who broke the boycott, Longchu Teck reactivated his veteran Triad network and convened a countrywide assembly of Triad secret societies leading to the establishment of the Federation of 18 Teochew Angyi. As chairman of the federation, he appointed Chiang Pingchai, the boss of the Three Dots secret society, to be commander of the Triad armies of the Anti-Japanese League, which was tasked with hunting down traitors.[110]

A 1938 picture of Hia Guang-iam and Madame Xu Zonghan, widow of Huang Xing, on her tour of Thailand to solicit support for the anti-Japanese war.

Beginning in late 1937, Chinese dockworkers refused to unload shipments of Japanese goods. Chinese merchants stopped trading with Japanese companies, ceased handling Japanese merchandise and discontinued supplying Thai products to Japanese trading companies. Although the CCC and the Teochew Association fully backed the boycott, their organizational documents made no mention of their involvement in these illegal anti-Japanese activities. However, unlike the Teochew Association, the Communist Kang Lian group was more explicitly involved in anti-Japanese boycott activities.

The Kang Lian deployed factory workers to spy on their bosses and managers to see whether they traded with Japanese suppliers or companies. Chinese merchants who continued doing business with the Japanese became targets of terrorist acts carried out by the Patriotic Youth groups in league with Triad secret societies. Chinese merchants who broke the boycott were warned, threatened or fined.[111] Those who persisted in doing business with the Japanese were punished by having their shops burned, or, in some cases, they were assassinated.

The boycott movement caused severe damage to Japanese interests in the kingdom. The Thai government became very alarmed that the boycott would harm relations with Japan. On 12 February 1938, 200 police descended on Chinatown and arrested 22 leading members of the Anti-Japanese League, Longchu Teck included. Hia Guang-iam appealed to the Chinese community to help make life bearable for the prisoners. The Teochew Association sent three delicious Chinese meals a day to the prisoners in jail. Tan Ekyu Chunsue, the best Chinese lawyer in town, was appointed to represent them.

Longchu Teck's wife, who was related to the royal family, tried to persuade her husband to accept a plea bargain offered by the authorities, which would allow him to stay in the country. But he categorically refused to admit to any wrongdoing. Instead he asked his wife to convey his message to the police that "patriotism to one's fatherland is not a crime." All the prisoners except three doctors were deported on 24 March. Many Chinese came to the pier to see them off, and the CPS sent 10 security guards to accompany their heroes back to China.[110] But the worst was yet to come.[112]

The year 1939 proved to be a terribly traumatic year for the Chinese community in Bangkok. This was the year that Siam changed its name to Thailand, and the *lukchin* in military and government services were required to change their names and surnames to Thai.[113] In February, the Japanese occupied Hainan, upsetting many Hailams, the second-largest dialect group in Bangkok. Seow Hoodseng passed away in May, and in June the Japanese occupied Shantou, the heartland of the Teochews, causing great distress in Thailand's Chinese community. In 1939, the Thai government also closed down more than 200 Chinese schools, as well as every Chinese newspaper except one. The last action by the Thai authorities only worsened the relations between the government and its Chinese minority and exacerbated the growing separateness of Siam's Chinese community.

This year, 1939, would be remembered by the Chinese in Siam as "The Year of the Assassins," referring to the assassination of three high-profile Chinese leaders within a space of three months, including Ng Yuklong Lamsam, the ex-chairman of the CCC. Attackers broke into his house and assassinated him in his own home. Another sensational assassination occurred on 12 August 1939. A high-profile overseas-Chinese banker from Singapore was killed in his Bangkok office. The

THE GOOD DOCTOR: LUAN VONGVANIJ (1891–1964)

Luan Vongvanij, or Huáng Youluán (pictured), was born in 1891 to a modest family in Wenchang on Hainan Island. His mother died when he was only seven, and a year later his father also passed away. To look after Luan and his younger brother, his only sister—who was married and lived in another village—had to walk miles to cook for the boys every few days.

In 1899 the price of food in Hainan skyrocketed due to a poor crop, but the misfortune did not stop there. Not long after, in 1900, there was an outbreak of plague in areas around Shantou and Haikou, which spread far and wide. His elder sister succumbed to illness and his younger brother also died. With the entire family wiped out, Luan's brother-in-law decided to take Luan along to seek a new life in Bangkok working for a soda factory near Si Kak Phraya Sri. Luan had a thirst for learning, so his brother-in-law allowed him to attend a Catholic school, the Assumption College in Bangrak. Later, Luan would tell his children that he was so poor at the time that he had to walk 7.5 km to school every morning with no money in his pocket. On a good day, when he earned a few coins from odd jobs, he was able to buy a banana for lunch.[114]

Despite his own disadvantaged position, Luan was a spirited young man. He once stepped in and helped a friend who was being beaten by a group of bullying boys in the neighborhood. Being severely outnumbered, Luan tricked them by shouting, "The police are here!" That day Luan remarked to his friend, "Fight only when you have advantages."[115]

A few years later, Luan's brother-in-law passed away. Alone in Bangkok, Luan had to quit school. However, walking up and down New Road every day had its own merits—Luan, who was an observant young man, noticed many job opportunities. He soon found himself a job at a dispensary on New Road, which allowed him to continue his education by attending night school. Luan was intrigued by medicine, so in order to learn more, he moved to work for the British Dispensary (Snake Brand) and then the Bangkok Dispensary (Elephant Brand). Here he was fortunate enough to work as an apprentice of Dr. O. Schneider, a German lecturer at the Faculty of Medicine at Chulalongkorn University. The hard-working young man was soon offered the position of assistant manager and assistant doctor at Yaowarat Dispensary working under Dr. Gardetti, who was also a lecturer at the same medical faculty. Around this time, he volunteered to serve in the medical team under Dr. Modern Cathews, and Luan came face to face with the epidemic that had caused the premature deaths of the members of his family. The team put down the plague that was ravaging Bangkok in 1915.

At the age of 26, after passing the medical exam for pharmacist and general practitioner, Luan and his Hailam friends, including B.L. Hua, founded the Smith Pharmacy in 1923. He was appointed the general manager as well as the doctor of the store located in Chinatown.

Luan was honest and hard-working. He compared his life with a man who kept tilling the soil: there was enough water in the fertile soil for everybody to make a living. He once said, "Taking advantage of others will only create resentment and hate; however, if you allow people to benefit from you—even a little—they will love and help you in the future with no questions asked." Luan found luck five years later when a group of expatriates sold their shares in the British Dispensary. In 1928, Luan bid for and won the takeover of the largest pharmaceutical company in Siam for the total sum of 100,000 baht. He was only 37 years old.

Like most of his compatriot Hailams in Bangkok, Luan was highly patriotic with regard to Chinese affairs. In 1937 when the war with Japan escalated, Luan and his friends supported the fatherland by sending large quantities of medical supplies and teams of relief workers trained in providing first aid and medical assistance to China. However, the relief effort was frowned upon by the Thai government, who was careful to control any anti-Japanese activities in Siam that threatened to disturb diplomatic relations with Japan. Thus, Luan was arrested and exiled.

Luan set up a dispensary in Hong Kong where his wife and their four children later joined him. The dispensary soon became the locus of Thai students studying in Hong Kong, especially for the boys studying at St. Stphen's College, Phichai Rattakul and Kasem Chatikavanij included. Luan's family helped 31 Thai students return home when the Japanese troops took over Hong Kong after 18 days of fierce fighting. Barred from entering Thailand, Luan went to work with the Chinese Red Cross Hospital in Guangxi. His medical contribution in the battlefields of China was legendary and he was invited to Chungking to meet Chiang Kaishek, who honored him with the title of "Overseas Chinese Commissioner." Towards the end of the war, Luan helped Sa-nguan Tulalak, the representative of Pridi Banomyong, to inform the Chinese government of the anti-Japanese effort in Thailand. After the war the Thai government promptly pardoned Luan Vongvanij and Pridi hosted an honorable homecoming celebration for Luan, the honorable Overseas Chinese Commissioner of the Republic of China.

murdered man, Tan Hongngee, was the owner of Tan Peng Shun bank; his crime was financing Chinese merchants who traded with the Japanese.

The sensational murder of Tan Hongngee sent shockwaves through the Nanyang Chinese community. The reverberations eventually reached the doorstep of the Hia Guang-iam household in Bangkok. The late Tan Hongngee had been a personal friend of Hia, and the family members on both sides were well acquainted with one another.

In fact, when his friend was killed by the assassin in Bangkok, Hia Guang-iam had been in China. Given the family circumstances involved, it appeared quite unlikely that Hia had ordered the assassination of his friend. Tan Sialink, the son of the murdered man, wanted revenge. Tan Sialink came to Bangkok and hired a gunman to avenge his father's death. Hia Guang-iam returned to Bangkok from China in October 1939. He was gunned down on 21 November 1939.

Three days later, the police arrested a Chinese assassin named Heng Bing, who confessed that he was hired by Tan Sialink to kill Hia Guang-iam. However, Hia Guang-iam's death raised more questions than it answered. Had Tan Sialink acted on substantive evidence that Hia was responsible for his father's murder? Or had he acted on hearsay? Could Tan Sialink have been duped by Japanese military intelligence and made to believe that his father's friend Hia Guang-iam had put

A public memorial service for Hia Guang-iam at the CCC on Sathorn Road.

out a contract on Tan Hongngee's life, thereby becoming a pawn in a conspiracy by Japanese intelligence to eliminate a suspected Chinese leader of the anti-Japanese boycott? These troubling questions remain unanswered.

Following the confession of the assassin Heng Bing, Tan Sialink was arrested and convicted. Tan Sialink was incarcerated in a Thai prison until the end of the Pacific War. But he did not live to see freedom. Both Tan Sialink and Heng Bing were mysteriously murdered in prison. Meanwhile, after the death of Hia Guang-iam, the Phibun government cracked down hard on Chinese anti-Japanese political activities. Large-scale arrests were made. Several thousand Chinese accused of involvement in acts of terror against Chinese merchants were deported to China. With the death of the leader of the Teochew Association faction coupled with mass arrests and deportations, the backbone of the anti-Japanese resistance in Siam was largely broken before Japanese invasion forces established a military presence in the kingdom with the consent of the Phibun government in December 1941. Tan Siewmeng reporting to Chungking affirmed that the "campaigns to help China fight Japan in Siam had largely fizzled out after the death of Hia Guang-iam."

Feng Erhe was the caretaker chairman of the CCC after Hia Guang-iam died. On 3 April 1940, Tia Langsing (Sahas Mahakhun), the newly elected chairman of the CCC, sent a telegram to Chungking informing the leadership "that with due respect to the Thai government, from now on, overseas Chinese organizations in Thailand may not be able to follow the Chinese government's policy and instructions."[116]

Of the gang of five from the Teochew Association, Hia Guang-iam had been assassinated. Shortly before that, the leader of the southwest faction and mentor of the group, Seow Hoodseng, had also passed away in 1939. U Chuliang managed to flee to safety in Penang before the arrival of Japanese military forces. In 1942, the Thai police arrested Sethabhakdi and his brother Lek. He was asked to cooperate with the Phibun government's pro-Japanese policies, but he refused and chose to remain in prison. Tae Juebing had passed away; his son Udane Techapaiboon, who enjoyed excellent connections in high places in the Thai government, was arrested for one day and released. Tan Gengchuang was also arrested and given a term of life imprisonment. With the elimination of the Teochew Association faction, the locus of the leadership of the Chinese community in Siam gravitated to the moderate faction.

Collaboration

The upsurge of anti-Japanese activity in Siam proved to be injurious to the kingdom's foreign relations with Japan. There were many elements in the pro-Japanese lobby of the People's Party who welcomed the rise of Japanese power in the Far East. The pro-Japanese lobby tended to regard the Western imperialism of France and Britain as the historical enemy of Siam, at whose hands the Siamese kingdom had been burdened by unequal treaties and had had its former domains in Indochina and the Malay States forcibly taken away at the turn of the century.

In fact, modern state formation and the creation of Siam's modern military had occurred under the shadow of the threat of colonial takeover. Consequently, many state-centered officials, bureaucrats and military elements who dominated the People's Party leadership regarded Chinese nationalism—which opposed Japanese imperialism in Asia—as inimical to Siam's national interests. Thus, strong Chinese nationalism clashed with the attempt of the People's Party to create a strong state and foster the growth of a strong Thai nationalism.

Furthermore, the state-centered elite had not formed close personal or economic ties with the dominant Chinese economic class, unlike the traditional royalty. In response to the perceived political crisis caused by Chinese nationalist agitation, a growing chorus of voices from the Thai nationalist lobby began to call for dealing firmly with the Chinese and ending "the policy of drift," which had characterized the government's relations with the Chinese minority. Perhaps due to the party's weak links to Chinese economic interests, the former tended to demonstrate a stronger political will to dispossess the dominant Chinese economic class than the previous monarchical regime. In 1936, the government nationalized the lucrative liquor industry, which was operated by the Chinese, with encouraging results.

With the rise to power of Field Marshal Phibun in 1938, the policies of the People's Party took on a National-Socialist coloration through the use of state power to implement socio-economic reforms and industrialization programs aimed at enhancing the country's international standing in the world. Building on successful precedents like the nationalization of the liquor industry in 1936, Phibun began to make nationalization of privately owned productive assets and the development of state enterprises a cornerstone of his economic policy. In

1939, Phibun established the Thai Rice Company, with the express purpose of dismantling Chinese domination over the rice industry.

Prominent Chinese entrepreneurial talents, like Mah Lapkun, were recruited to provide the government with the necessary know-how to operate the rice business. Following the establishment of the government rice company, Chinese rice mills were nationalized. The Thai Rice Company also acquired a controlling interest in the cooperative movement. Hot upon the heels of this development came direct purchasing of rice from farmers, using state capital to procure seed for planters. In 1940, the first of a series of paddy-buying stations were set up at Rangsit, dealing a mortal blow to the Chinese middlemen.

Middlemen and money lenders, most of whom were Chinese, became scapegoats for the People's Party's failure to address the problem of rural poverty after Pridi's *Comprehensive Economic Plan* was jettisoned by the right-wing faction of the party in 1933. With no alternative economic agenda to replace Pridi's plan, lack of rural credit made the role of Chinese middlemen indispensable to the Thai rice growers. In fact, no adequate system of rural credit was ever established prior to 1941, thereby forcing the Thai farmer into the arms of the Chinese moneylender.[117] To compensate Thai rice farmers for depriving them of the convenient services of the Chinese middleman, rentals on rice lands were reduced by one fifth.

The government also created new companies in the distribution sector to "put businesses into the hands of Thais," thereby displacing Chinese merchants. Even the Guang Heng Lee company of the late Hia Guang-iam was taken over and subsumed into the barge company founded by the government, with the Iamsuree family reduced to a shareholder in the semi-state enterprise. Lastly, the government followed up these measures with legislation reserving certain categories of jobs for Thais and justified its action by citing the need to guarantee employment for native Thais.[118]

Students of Peiying School on Songwad Road.

Before Phibun became prime minister, the Chinese community had operated more than 250 schools and supported over 10 newspapers. In 1939–40, Phibun closed all Chinese schools and all but one Chinese newspaper, the *Zhongyuanbao*, which had been established by Hia Guang-iam's faction. Large numbers of Chinese teachers, reporters and journalists found themselves unemployed overnight.

As part of Phibun's ethnic cleansing of the Thai economy, in January 1939 all "alien" food sellers were ejected from the premises of various government ministries. The officials charged with carrying out the order did not bother with the niceties of checking birth certificates before evicting the hawkers. Rather, they simply evicted those who looked Chinese, since the term "alien," in the context of the times, was almost synonymous to "Chinese."[119] The only positive step during this period of increasing repression came in April 1939, when the government opened the way for Chinese subjects to obtain Thai citizenship, which had previously been denied them.[120]

Japanese Minister of War Hideki Tojo shaking hands with Prince Wan Waitayakorn of Thailand in 1940.

The euphemisms of "aliens" or "foreigners" were used whenever the targets of the policy were actually Chinese. By couching its anti-Chinese policies in terms of an overarching policy on aliens, the spin doctors of the propaganda department could avoid calling a spade a spade. It provided the Phibun government with a certain plausible deniability in the face of protests by the Chinese government over the Thai government's discriminatory policies towards the kingdom's Chinese minority. The same technique was to be used again in 1941, when Phibun declared large areas of the country off-limits to all aliens and foreign residents and gave the Chinese, who had lived in these places for most of their lives, 90 days to evacuate.

The Phibun government's anti-Chinese measures signaled to the Japanese government that Thailand could provide valuable support to Japan's imperialist ambitions in Asia. When Japanese military forces landed in Thai territory on 8 December 1941, the Phibun government offered only token resistance. Indicative of Phibun's zestful willingness to side with the Japanese, the government lost no time to reach a series of agreements with the occupying forces.

Barely three days after the invasion, the Thai and Japanese military signed a Provisional Agreement of the Treaty of Alliance between Siam and Japan. The following day, Phibun delivered a radio address to the nation to announce the new relationship with Japan. The Publicity Department of the government followed up with a confirmation that "Japan is Thailand's friend and together we shall cooperate in enhancing honor." Two days later, the Thai and Japanese military signed another agreement that stipulated guidelines for cooperation between the Thai and Japanese armies against the British and Chinese armies in Burma.[121] Then, on 21 December 1941, the two countries signed yet another agreement called the Treaty of Alliance, under which Thailand pledged to support Japan "in all political, economic and military ways," while a secret understanding attached to the treaty document stipulated that "Japan should cooperate in fulfilling Thailand's demands for the recovery of its lost territories."[122]

Following the Treaty of Alliance with Japan, Phibun declared war on Britain and the US on 25 January 1942. On 3 February, Vijit-Vadakan, the Deputy Foreign Minister, sent a telegram to Direk Jayanama, the Thai ambassador in Tokyo, telling him to sound out the Japanese about Thai participation in the Axis Alliance. This last Thai initiative to join the Axis Alliance suggests an interesting underlying pattern in the relationship between the two countries. In the courtship between Thailand and Japan, the initiative seemed to be on the side of the Thai partner rather than the other way round.

Thai perceptions of the courtship during this period serve to confirm the view that the war-time Japanese suitor was a good catch in the sense of the proverb "Marriage is a man chasing a woman until she catches him." That Phibun fully desired the partnership with Japan was underscored by a poignant remark by his confidant, Lt. Colonel Chai Prathipasen, at a government meeting on 1 January 1942: "We should give the Japanese army the things it demands. Our helping Japan does not make us slaves of Japan. It's the same as providing someone with a tool if we want to get him to do something for our benefit. If we help Japan today we'll get our repayment another day."

What that repayment consisted of was embodied in the secret attachment to the Treaty of Alliance. At the start of the war, as Japanese armies swept across Southeast Asia and the Axis Powers prevailed in Europe, Phibun intended to use Japan's growing hegemony in Asia to expand Thailand's territory and increase its influence across the region, thereby making Thailand the dominant power in Southeast Asia after Japan. When Vijit-Vadakan was negotiating a cultural treaty between Thailand and Japan in May 1942, he pressed for broadening the provisions to include the clause "to establish Thailand as the cultural center of Southeast Asia."[123]

Inspired by this vision, Phibun became an ardent advocate of the Japanese propaganda line, "Asia for the Asians," and the Asian Greater Co-prosperity Sphere. Like a religious zealot, he proselytized the new Japanese doctrine of "Asia for the Asians" to the Chinese and urged Chiang Kai-shek to make peace with Japan "for the betterment of Asians who are all brothers," adding that "the Thai people concurred in the alliance with Japan because the Japanese who were highly virtuous people had genuinely good intentions for the peoples of Asia."[124]

Within Thailand, Phibun largely acceded to Japanese demands to disseminate propaganda, supply war materials, build roads and extend railway outreach to facilitate Japanese military logistics. In a note on the construction of the infamous Thai-Burma railway, Phibun wrote, "It's alright for Japan to build it. We will follow behind the Japanese and spread our culture. That's cooperating as an ally."[125]

Meanwhile, the Phibun government's "Thai-ification" program combined with severe repressive measures against the Chinese had all but cowed the Chinese community into submission, even before the Japanese invasion of Thailand. With the arrival of Japanese forces, Chinese leaders went underground. Tia

Langsing (or Sahas Mahakhun), the chairman of the CCC, also went into hiding, although he reappeared later to offer his cooperation. U Chuliang fled to Penang. Sethabhakdi and Tan Gengchuang were arrested and imprisoned. Several other Chinese leaders and journalists were also arrested. The Youth Group for the Three Principles of the People and the "Blue Shirt Unit," comprising operatives infiltrated by Chungking to carry out anti-Japanese activities headed by General Dai Li, were put on the blacklist and marked for suppression.[126]

Thus, the Chinese community was forced by both the Phibun government and the Japanese occupying forces to cooperate. Before Sahas Mahakhun surrendered to offer his cooperation, the Japanese approached the former chairman of the CCC, Tan Siewmeng, to lead the CCC. He declined. Finally, another prominent Chinese, Chu Tiasua, agreed to become interim chairman of the CCC.

On 25 December 1941, Chu Tiasua brought the board of directors of the CCC— including Wun Tokkeng (Kosol Hoontrakul), Nai Kuitai (Luang Sitsuropakorn), Tan Jinggeng (Jittin Tantuvanit), Tan Ekyu (Ekyu Chansue), Tan Yongchiang and other leaders of the Chinese community—to call on Wanit Phananon, a minister without portfolio, who was a central figure in the pro-Japanese faction of the People's Party. Wanit led them to call on Phibun. The contingent told Phibun that the Chinese community whole-heartedly supported the alliance with Japan and reiterated that the CCC believed Thailand's alliance with Japan would benefit all Asians.[127]

Three days later, the group convened an All-Thailand Overseas Chinese Assembly at the CCC, with over 10,000 local Chinese in attendance, along with officials from the Japanese embassy and officers from the Japanese army, as well as representatives of the Indian Independence League. The chairman of the CCC, Sahas Mahakhun, came out of hiding to give an opening speech on behalf of the CCC. Wanit Phananon delivered a speech prepared by Phibun. At the ceremony, Tia Langsing and the representatives of the six Chinese Assembly Halls (Teochew, Hakka, Hailam, Cantonese, Hokkien and Shanghainese) professed support for Thailand and Japan and pledged to defend Thailand's national policy and cooperate in building a new order in East Asia. The CCC pledged to organize a fundraising drive on behalf of the Thai government.

On 2 January 1942, the day after Phibun's confidant, Lt. Colonel Chai Prathipasen, told a meeting of government leaders to accede to Japan's demands, the Thai government had the Chinese community send a shortwave-radio message to Wang Jingwei, head of the government in Nanjing, pledging support for the pro-Japanese Chinese government. Meanwhile, another message was sent to Chiang Kai-shek in Chungking asking him to make peace with Japan and join in eliminating the influence of Anglo-Saxons from East Asia. On 18 February 1942, the day the Japanese army

A portrait of a Thai-Chinese volunteer during the anti-Japanese war sent home to his parents in Bangkok in 1942.

triumphantly entered Singapore, the CCC celebrated by flying the three flags of Japan, Thailand and the Chinese flag of the Nanjing government.

Thus, the Japanese had gained the full cooperation of the Thai government and at least superficial cooperation from the leaders of the Chinese community. There was no further overt opposition to the Japanese, and the Chinese community experienced only minimal repression by the Kempetei, the Japanese military police, unlike the Chinese communities in Malaya and Singapore. By offering to cooperate, the Chinese community had spared itself the brutal treatment meted out to the Chinese in other parts of the Nanyang by the Kempetei. However, not all forms of cooperation were as benign as attending ceremonial gatherings, reciting pledges of support to Phibun or sending telegrams to Nanjing—some kinds of cooperation were very onerous and distasteful.

In 1943, the Japanese were under pressure to complete the strategic Thai-Burma railway. On 2 March 1943, the Phibun government was ordered to provide construction equipment and 13,000 coolies to work on the railway. Phibun refused to send Thai workers, and instead ordered the Ministry of Interior and Defense Ministry to carry out the forced recruitment of Chinese labor. At the same time, Thai officials pressured the CCC to organize Chinese work gangs for the railway construction.

The superintendent general of the Metropolitan Police, Phra Phinit-Chonkhadi (a Hailam whose Teochew name was Tan Yokseng), together with the governors of Bangkok and Thonburi, went to persuade Tan Siewmeng, who had now become the chairman of the CCC, to cooperate. Unable to refuse, Tan Siewmeng could only insist that Chinese workers should be voluntarily recruited and paid instead of being taken by force as Phibun had intended. On 5 April 1943, the Japanese

The "Death Railway" in Kanchanaburi Province.

embassy hosted a dinner for Tan Siewmeng, Kosol Hoontrakul, Sahas Mahakhun and other leading members of the CCC to discuss the arrangements. On 6 April, Phibun modified his earlier order to forcibly recruit Chinese labor, saying, "We will talk about doing regular hiring first, after that forced recruitment is okay!"

Sahas Mahakhun, who was in the construction business, headed an employment committee that began recruitment activities on 12 April and raised the 200,000 baht needed to cover costs by collecting donations from the Chinese community. Unlike the old days under Hia Guang-iam when the CCC raised money for China's war effort against Japan, now the chamber was required to make contributions for Japan's war effort. Responding to the CCC recruitment drive, the Chinese assembly halls supplied substantial numbers of workers, as did coolie contractors, attracted by daily wage rates that were markedly higher than the market rate.

By 26 May, the CCC had enlisted 11,577 coolies for the Japanese army, and another 1,500 coolies from outside Bangkok had been placed under the chamber's responsibility. Apparently, the recruitment was not entirely voluntary— the CCC had carried out some coercive recruiting as well. Many of the workers had been recruited against their will and quickly escaped. Even among those coolies who had not been forcibly recruited, there was a high rate of desertion due to the abysmal working conditions, poor food and disease at the work sites, which became known as the infamous "Death Railway."

On 9 June 1943, the Japanese ordered the Thai government to supply another 23,000 coolies. The Phibun government again passed the responsibility to a reluctant CCC. However, some Chinese benefited from the construction of the Thai-Burma railway. Tia Langsing, for example, profited from the opportunity to supply large quantities of gravel to the Japanese army. But in general the position of the Chinese leadership of the CCC was extremely unenviable, for they were caught in between the Phibun government and the Japanese army. Even Lt. Colonel M.C. Phisit, a Phibun confidant, observed at a government meeting on 28 July 1943, "Chinese leaders are under threat of punishment unless they deliver." The dreaded Kempetei was wont to punish Chinese leaders for being pro-Chungking if they didn't cooperate.

Consequently, in July and August of 1943, the CCC, provincial governors and Chinese merchants in the provinces recruited another 13,000 Chinese coolies for the Thai-Burma railway. However, in this second recruitment drive only 43 percent of the enlisted coolies arrived at the railway work stations while the rest fled en route. To the chagrin of the Japanese army, both recruitment exercises showed poor results.

Meanwhile, the Thai-Japanese military alliance ran into problems when Thai expectations regarding the benefits of its relationship with the Japanese were not met. After signing the Treaty of Alliance with Japan, Phibun looked forward to seeing Thai forces embark on a foreign military campaign to expand Thailand's territory as promised in the treaty's secret protocol. In anticipation of this event, on 2 March 1942, the Interior Ministry announced that the Shan, Karen and Mon peoples in Tennaserim were part of the Thai race and would be given Thai nationality should they emigrate to Thailand. In fact, this announcement was reminiscent of a precedent that had occurred during Thailand's dispute with French Indochina two years earlier. At that time, the Phibun government had made a similar announcement regarding Thai peoples living in Laotian and Khmer territory. Thus, the statement clearly signaled Thailand's interest in territory currently belonging to Burma.

However, to Phibun's great disappointment, the Japanese withheld permission for Thai forces to launch a military campaign to expand Thai territory. Phibun would not be put off easily. Following the conclusion of a supplementary agreement concerning joint Thai-Japanese military operations on 5 May 1942, Phibun suddenly sent a Thai expeditionary force into the Shan States and occupied the area after ejecting Chiang Kai-shek's forces. Again to Phibun's chagrin, the Japanese military refused to allow formal reversion of this territory to Thailand. Thus a victorious Japan carelessly disregarded Thailand's expectations that it would march alongside its ally and also benefit from the new order in East Asia. Consequently, from mid-1942 onwards, Thai-Japanese relations cooled rapidly.[128]

Other factors also played a part: aggressive profiteering and economic inroads made by Japanese companies in the Thai economy, the Japanese army's disregard for Thai laws and contempt for Thai officials and people, Japanese meddling in Thai domestic affairs, the failure of Japan to transfer enemy assets in Thailand to the Thai government, and the Japanese practice of treating Thailand like an occupied territory all contributed towards a hardening of Thai attitudes against Japan. Initially, Thai Nationalists were willing to tolerate all these disadvantages and indignities in the expectation that greater benefits would be gained from the alliance with Japan. But Japan's disregard for Thai expectations rapidly turned Thai sentiments against the Japanese.

One of the first indicators of cooling relations between the two countries was Phibun's abolishment of the Thai-Japanese Coordination Committee Office. On 5 May 1943, M.C. Phisit declared at an internal government meeting chaired by the foreign minister, "Our best policy is neutrality, not taking sides with either Japan or the other side."[129] Phibun's discontent with the Japanese grew apace, and the deteriorating alliance with Japan was reflected in a studied uncooperativeness among Phibun's closest cohorts. The Thai government procrastinated over meeting Japanese military requests for assistance.

Bangkok after being bombed by the Allies.

The change of attitude became evident to the Japanese. In May 1943, Thailand's ambassador to Tokyo, Direk Jayanama, reported to Phibun, "Some officials in the Greater East Asia Ministry and newspapers are saying if the Thai people do not cooperate resolutely with Japan for victory in the war, it is questionable whether Thailand can maintain its independence and sovereignty." Tokyo had made a thinly veiled threat to the Phibun government. The Japanese also made efforts to improve relations with Thailand. Condolence money paid by the Thais to the Japanese for the accidental deaths of Japanese soldiers at Baan Pong was returned by the Japanese in the form of condolence money for the families of Thais killed at the onset of the Japanese invasion in December 1941. In July 1943, Prime Minister Hideki Tojo visited Bangkok. The visit was underscored by Japanese recognition of the incorporation of the four Malay States and two Shan States into Thailand, and the problem of enemy assets was also resolved. The retrocession of lost territories that comprised Siam's former domains had long been Phibun's most important nationalistic goal, and Tojo's acceptance of the Thai claim pleased him. However, as a measure to draw out greater cooperation from Thailand, it had come too late. The tide of war was already turning against Japan.

On 19 December 1943, the Allied Powers carried out their first air raid on Bangkok, signaling the start of aerial bombing attacks on the Thai capital. Two days later, on 21 December 1943, a ceremony celebrating the Second Anniversary of the Thai-Japanese Alliance was held. Phibun took the bold step of conspicuously absenting himself from this important event. As the war proceeded to go badly for Japan, Phibun initiated covert efforts to betray the Japanese.

In January 1944, Phibun initiated contacts with Chiang Kai-shek's Chungking government through the Thai expeditionary force in the Shan States to request that Chiang Kai-shek broker relations with the British and the Americans on Thailand's behalf, although nothing came of this initiative.[130] In Bangkok, the Thai government's studied uncooperativeness with the Japanese grew more pronounced. Phibun was on the point of recalling his ambassador to Tokyo. However, before that could happen, Phibun was thrown out by a "no confidence" vote in Parliament and his government was toppled.

Meanwhile, deteriorating relations with Japan were also reflected in a gradual reversal of the Phibun government's anti-Chinese policies. In 1943, Phibun had suddenly issued a permit for a new Chinese newspaper, the *Taihuashangbao*. Another one of his confidants, Phairot Jayanama, who had recently been put in charge of overseeing espionage operations against Japan, installed a pro-Chungking Chinese journalist, Li Cheksing, as editor. The new newspaper sought to revive Chinese patriotic sentiments by providing a corrective to the *Zhongyuanbao*. However, for the sake of appearances it had to make a pretense of paying lip service to Japan's wartime propaganda activities.

In another conciliatory gesture to the Chinese community, Phibun revived the old royalist policy of conferring decorations on Chinese leaders. Julin Lamsam, son of Ng Yuklong, the general manager of the semi-state enterprise Thai Niyom Co., received the King's Crown Decoration Third Class on 10 December 1943. Tan Siewmeng received another one on 26 January 1944. However, Phibun's conciliatory gestures towards the Chinese were also too little, too late. There was already so much ill feeling in the Chinese community against Phibun that the latter distrusted Phibun's intentions and regarded the Chinese leaders who collaborated with him as traitors.

After the fall of Phibun, the Khuang Aphaiwong government further relaxed restrictions on the Chinese. The body of laws and measures that had epitomized the anti-Chinese policy of the Phibun government—including the law reserving certain jobs exclusively for native Thais (1941), the order expelling Chinese from

Julin Lamsam.

restricted zones and provinces (1941 and 1943), and the recruitment of exclusively Chinese labor for the Death Railway—was wholly or partially rescinded by the new Khuang government and the changes took effect on 24 November 1944, although by that time construction of the railway was already largely completed.

However, the issue of Chinese labor for the Thai-Burma railway remained unresolved because the Japanese army continued to coerce the Thai government to facilitate the recruitment of an additional 5,000 coolies for maintenance of the Thai-Burma railway. Tan Siewmeng was again prevailed upon to deliver more Chinese labor to the Japanese army. Under the shadow of punishment for being a pro-Chungking sympathizer, he had no option but to cooperate. However, he put up a hard bargain to get the daily wage rate increased from 1 to 6.5 baht per day. After protracted negotiations, a compromise was reached at 6 baht, from which the Japanese army would deduct 1.5 baht for rations.

Following this, 2,032 Chinese coolies were recruited. Although they received a 10 baht advance to cover departure arrangements, many of the recruits absconded and ran away. Only 61 of the 718 workers recruited for the third delivery reached Kanchanaburi, and 405 in the fourth delivery disappeared while still in Bangkok. As of 19 January 1945, only 170 new recruits were actually at the railway work sites. The CCC's last two efforts on behalf of the Thai government to employ workers for the Thai-Burma railway construction supplied almost no laborers at all.[131]

Although there is no concrete evidence, all appearances point to another instance of studied uncooperativeness on the part of the Thais and the CCC, charged with the unpleasant and thankless task of delivering their fellow Chinese into the jaws of the Death Railway. Udom Yenrudee, the Thai secretary of the CCC, alleged (in his interview with Khunying Chamnongsri Ratanin) that the chamber had helped Chinese workers escape by manipulating name lists and switching worker names with those of prisoners of war from Malaya.[132] By leaving many loopholes that allowed recruits to evade going to the work camps, it was no surprise that few Chinese workers actually worked at Kanchanaburi. Due to the abysmal results, the Japanese army abandoned recruitment through the CCC altogether to the relief of Tan Siewmeng and his chamber colleagues.

As Japan became increasingly embattled across the Pacific War theater in the course of 1944, the Communist party, the GMD and Allied espionage units including the Free Thai Movement stepped up underground operations against the Japanese in Thailand. Chinese underground organizations including the Youth Group and their Thai compatriots cooperated in escalating anti-Japanese activities. In Southern Thailand, the Communist Grand Siam Anti-Japanese Alliance and the counterpart Anti-Japanese Volunteer Army carried on a guerilla war against the Japanese army with the covert cooperation of the Thai army and police. Pro-Communist Chinese and Thai workers engaged in sabotage at Japanese factories.[133]

In the wake of the growing strength of anti-Japanese resistance in Thailand, both the Communists and the GMD began to pursue people they considered traitors and collaborators. The growing influence of the Communists and the Chungking underground network dampened the willingness of the local Chinese leadership to cooperate with the Japanese during the last stage of the war and helped draw funds to the anti-Japanese movement.

On 17 April 1944, the Communist underground newspaper *Zhenhuabao*, founded in July 1942, ran an editorial headline reading, "Beware of Treacherous

The funeral book of Tan Siewmeng.

Chinese Profiteers Who Help Bandits." Written by the local Communist leader Li Qixin, the editorial attacked big Chinese merchants by name. The article called on all workers and laborers to cease working for traitors and profiteering merchants.[134] On 5 September 1944, the *Zhenhuabao* carried another article on the same theme attacking the directors of the CCC. It stated, "The two traitors Tan Siewmeng and Tia Langsing have always disregarded the nation's laws and been contemptuous of their fellow Chinese, and at a recent meeting of the Japanese-puppet CCC, the two called for recruiting 5,000 workers for the Japanese."

The article added that when the Japanese requested more workers for the Thai-Burma railway, despite a 12 July warning broadcast by Chungking Central Radio Station directed at the CCC directors, Tan Siewmeng and Tia Lansing (Sahas) continued to comply with the enemy's demands.

The anti-Japanese propaganda attacks against the CCC leadership poignantly underscores the stress that the chairman of the CCC was undergoing due to the threat of dreadful punishment by the Kempetei. It also offers a glimpse of Communist infiltration into the inner halls of decision-making within the top leadership of the CCC.

In June 1945, *Zhongguoren*, the underground newspaper of the GMD, reported an attack on Lio Chiahung, a leader in a Japanese-run counter-espionage organization, whose job was to break up anti-Japanese groups. The article stated, "On 5 June 1945, at one o'clock in the afternoon at the intersection in front of Laem Thong Restaurant, a traitor was punished in a sacred attack. After fulfilling his heroic duty the noble patriot calmly left the scene."[135]

At 16:30 on 16 August 1945, one day after Japan surrendered, Tan Siewmeng left his office at the CCC. As he walked down to the Anglo-Thai pier, three men wearing sunglasses followed. Tan Siewmeng was gunned down as he headed

Tan Siewmeng's funeral rite.

towards his boat to cross the Chao Phraya River to the Wanglee mansion on the opposite bank. His Thai chauffeur, who was unarmed, ran from the car to get help but was shot nearby.[136] The assassin departed and disappeared into the twilight. Sixty years later, a Communist source confided to Henri Chen KeZhan, a celebrated Singapore artist, that a Hailam Communist assassin had done the job. Henri belongs to the Singapore branch of the Wanglee family.

HIA GUANG-IAM'S WIDOW: LAO YIEK-ENG

U Chuliang, the founder of the Teochew Association, summed up his closest friends in a terse statement: Tae Juebing had a good son (meaning Udane Techapaiboon), Tan Gengchuang had a good friend (meaning U Chuliang himself) and Hia Guang-iam had a good wife (meaning Lao Yiek-eng).

When she was 16, Lao Yiek-eng accompanied her elderly parents from Teo-an to Bangkok to live with her elder sister at a fabric shop in Bangrak. A year and a half later, a matchmaker had arranged for her to be married to Hia Guang-iam, who was 47 years old and a three-time widower with seven children. His eldest daughter was older than her.

Within a month, Hia Guang-iam realized he had a very capable wife. One morning he came to her with a big bunch of keys on a chain and told her to manage both the family and the company finances. "I want to spend more time on social causes from now on," was his statement.

Hia Guang-iam's dedication to serving the people was best recorded by Sahas Mahakhun, the next elected chairman of the CCC after Hia Guang-iam was assassinated. According to Sahas (Tia Langsing), Hia confided his simple life philosophy[137] as such:

> I came to Southeast Asia empty-handed. What I have earned I have to return to the community. Without (a good) society, there would be no wealth. With no nation, my identity would vanish. Accumulating wealth for future generations only undermines their motivation to be successful. I was successful because I came empty-handed. I have given a good education to my children. (That is enough.) Their future is in their own hands. It depends on their determination to succeed . . .

Lao Yiek-eng worked hard to nurture Hia's empire as well as his family of 14 children after Hia passed away. Apart from the Thai government's takeover of Hia's shipping operation, all went well. Lao Yiek-eng strictly followed her husband's aspiration to help society. She built the Iamsuri School in Bangpoo and donated it to the Ministry of Education. When Udane Techapaiboon enlisted her help, Lao Yiek-eng donated 10 million baht to support the development of the Huaqiao Chinese University.

Hia Guang-iam (front row, second from right) and his wife stand for a photo with Madame Xu Zonghan, widow of Huang Xing, on her tour of Thailand to solicit support for the anti-Japanese war.

TAN SIEWMENG'S WIDOW: TONGPOON WANGLEE

Tongpoon Wanglee, the co-author's grandmother, recounted that she was playing in the vegetable garden behind her house in Charoen Krung when the news reached her that she was to be married to Tan Siewmeng, her cousin who had just arrived from China. In those days, almost all marriages were arranged by the elders. Because they were cousins, the marriage had to have the special approval of the Tan clan's elders, and her candidacy passed with flying colors as she was a cousin with a different clan name. Tongpoon was the fourth child of Ng Yuklong Lamsam.

Tongpoon remembers well the prophesy she received from a mystical card reader a few days before 16 August 1945: *Spare yourself of the anxiety—what will be, will be*. The fortuneteller warned Tongpoon of a grave danger ahead.

A few nights after Tongpoon received this message, Udom Yenrudee, Tan Siewmeng's Thai secretary, came to the Wanglee residence in Thonburi. Udom brought news of disturbances in Chinatown and asked Tan Siewmeng not to go out as the situation had become too dangerous. Tongpoon agreed. She was very concerned about the safety of her husband. The fortuneteller's whispered warning rang in her ears that night.

The next morning, Tan Siewmeng, grandfather of the co-author, shrugged off his promise not to go out. Khunying Leka had sent a missive that Khuang Apaiwongse, the prime minister, wanted to see him. "There is nothing to be afraid of," were his parting words to his wife. However, his destiny had been decided, and he died later that day.

After Tan Siewmeng passed away, Tongpoon was left with the responsibility of 13 children. Her eldest child, the co-author's mother, was 18. Although Tongpoon was the executor of his estate, most of his assets were tied up in the Wanglee *kongsi*. All she had was a few thousand baht and his personal assets. That was when Tongpoon, a housewife, stepped forward to build her own business empire, which later became the Poonphol Group of companies.

Everyone helped. Her brother Julin and her brother-in-law Tan Siewting were very supportive. Tan Lipping, the comprador of Hong Kong Bank, a relative from the same clan village as the Wanglee family, granted her a loan using land in Rangsit as collateral. Money lending, warehouse rental, commodity trading, construction and real estate development were gradually added to her portfolio as her sons returned from the United Kingdom and America to help Tongpoon expand the Poonphol Group interest.

On the social front, Tongpoon built and donated land for a school called Tongpoon Utit in Rangsit. Over the years, her foundation also supported scholarships at Chulalongkorn University's Medical School.

Looking back, Tan Siewmeng must have been proud of his wife. His children were all well educated. His eldest son, Suvit Wanglee, continued his community-oriented spirit and later became the chairman of the Thai Chamber of Commerce. Sukit Wanglee is the current chairman of the Poonphol Group, and Pimpaka Wanglee, a granddaughter, is the managing director of Future Park Rangsit, a mega-mall in Bangkok's northern suburb.

THE OVERLAND CHINESE
Story by Kankanit Potikit

Apart from the overseas Chinese, overland Chinese also crossed into Thailand by land. Many of these migrants ended up residing in northern Thailand and played a major role in the industry of the Golden Triangle. They are sometimes referred to by locals as "Haw" or "Chin Haw," which they find rather derogatory. Not considered as sophisticated as their fellow *huaqiao*, the Haw are sometimes mistaken by Thais as a hill tribe.

"Haw" is a collective name used to describe Chinese settlers in the north. The term originally referred to Muslim traders from Yunnan who had been coming to Chiang Mai and Chiang Rai since the 13th century. However, after a major influx of former Nationalist Chinese troops during and after World War II, Haw began to refer to non-Muslim refugees. Eventually the term came to mean any "overland Chinese" migrant to the area.

Large waves of Chinese immigration occurred during and after World War II and the Chinese Civil War. The triumph of the CCP in the mainland in 1949 brought about the entry of the remnants of the Chinese Nationalist armies. As Chiang Kai-shek and his troops retreated to Taiwan, the remaining forces in Yunnan, known as the 93rd Division, escaped to Burma's Shan States. The Burmese government, however, considered their military activities a threat to Burma's sovereignty and national security. The government filed an appeal with the United Nations in 1953, and in 1953–54 and 1961, troops were evacuated to Taiwan. However, many soldiers and refugees were unwilling to go to Taiwan. They opted to remain in Burma or crossed to Thailand and Laos for many reasons: some preferred the similarities between the region and their hometown in Yunnan over Taiwan, some married the locals, and some wanted to continue their anti-Communist activities.

After the 1961 evacuation, General Li Wenhuan's 3rd Army and General Duan Xiwen's 5th Army intended to stay and fight Communism. These two troops escaped the Burmese purge of guerillas. The 3rd Army established their base in Tam Ngop in Chiang Mai and the 5th on Doi Mae Salong in Chiang Rai. Both areas remained home to the Haw until the present. Ties between the Taiwan government and the remaining Guomindang armies were severed. Lacking financial support, the armies depended on opium and drug trafficking to survive.

The Thai government tacitly allowed their stay due to the anti-Communist ideology of the armies, as well as the obligation to protect refugees according to international practice. The troops cooperated with the Thai government in fighting Communism among the northern border during the Cold War period. It was said that at the time the Thai "were frankly more concerned with Communist insurgency than with the logistics of drug trafficking." (Forbes: 1997) More refugees from Yunnan were permitted to enter Thailand after the refugee warriors won several battles. However, the troops finally weakened and disbanded in the 1990s.

Due to their educational value, Chinese schools were founded in the Haw villages to educate later generations. Regarding Taiwan as their fatherland, the village schools taught Chinese during off-hours. Their loyalty towards the Taiwanese government is made apparent from the photos of Chiang Kai-shek hanging next to the pictures of the king of Thailand. Taiwan, which has become prosperous, offered scholarships to Yunnan's students to study in Taiwan between 1979 and 1992. Those who finished school in Taiwan tended to settle there because of the better opportunities the society offers. However, a great number of immigrants stay in Thailand and have fairly good relations with the Thai. The settlement mainly includes agricultural activities, although there is some animal husbandry and commerce. Some later generations left to work in Bangkok.

IN AND OUT OF THE BAMBOO CURTAIN

(1945–1975)

After World War II, Thailand allied its foreign policy with the US and became staunchly anti-communist. Meanwhile, China closed its doors. Thus the stories of the Chinese in Thailand were no longer defined by nationalism, immigration and global trade but by their sincere contributions to the emerging new identity of Thailand within this new world order. In the post-war period, several Thai-Chinese were instrumental in modernizing Thailand's fiscal sector. The financial wizard, Chin Sophonpanich, established Bangkok Bank, while brilliant technocrat Puey Ungpakorn's leadership of the Bank of Thailand sparked impressive economic growth. The Srifuengfung, Osathanugrah, Phornprapha and Chokwattana families used joint ventures and international expertise to take advantage of huge domestic demand for everything from glass to modern medicines to cars to toothpaste. Lukchin not only excelled at business, they also became more philanthropic and ambassadors of culture: businessman Udane Techapaiboon led the charitable foundation Poh Teck Tung and established a university and hospital; Wu Jiyue was recognized as an eminent journalist and writer; and Zhuang Meilong reinvented Chinese opera for a modern Thai audience.

Right after the Pacific War, in January 1946, a treaty establishing formal relations between Thailand and the Republic of China was finally signed by Mom Rajawongse Seni Pramoj, the prime minister who led the American chapter of the Free Thai Movement. In 1942, Seni had been the Thai ambassador to the US, and his refusal to deliver Phibun's declaration of war to the American government had preempted the US government from declaring war on Thailand.

After Japan's defeat, Chiang Kai-shek gained tremendous influence and prestige in the international arena. By contrast, Phibun had become a war criminal. To avoid becoming an enemy country, the new Thai civilian administration under Prime Minister Seni Pramoj sought Chiang's good offices and support in the post-war negotiations with the Allied Powers.

As a condition for signing a peace treaty with Thailand, Britain demanded war reparations in the form of rice shipments to Malaya, while France demanded that the Indochinese territories annexed by Phibun Songkram be returned to France. The Soviet Union insisted on the repeal of all anti-Communist legislation enacted by the Thai government. Seni Pramoj successfully settled these issues and Thailand was spared international condemnation. Seni also changed the name of the country back to Siam, pleasing many, including British Prime Minister Winston Churchill.

Under the liberal policy of the Seni administration, Chinese schools and newspapers were again allowed to open. As China came out the victor in the Pacific War, "Chineseness" was no longer looked down upon. Many members of the ruling elite began to claim that they were of Chinese descent and touted their Chinese names: Pridi Banomyong was a Chen; Thamrong-Navasawad was a Zheng; and Vijit-Vadakan was known to have the Chinese name Tan Gimliang.

In 1946, Li Tiezheng was appointed the first Chinese ambassador to Siam. The

Chiang Kai-shek (left) and his wife, Madame Chiang Kai-shek (right) sit with US President Franklin D. Roosevelt and Britain's Prime Minister Winston Churchill, in Cairo, Egypt, on 25 November 1943. During the "Sextant Conference" the Allied leaders and Chiang Kai-shek planned their next moves against Japan.

Chapter opening picture: Chinese coolies unloading rice from the incoming boats at the rice mill in 1955.

Embassy of the Republic of China located on Petchaburi Road opened with fanfare in October of the same year.[1] Thus, for the first time on Siamese soil, the overseas Chinese could address their grievances directly to an officer of the Chinese government, no longer having to depend on the charitable efforts of secret societies and overseas-Chinese organizations.

A child and her chaperone on the first class deck of a ship at port in Hong Kong.

Siam, which had always been open to Chinese immigration, was not difficult to enter as long as one paid an entry or alien registration fee of 15 baht. The practice of charging an entry fee was instituted after King Prajadhipok visited the Dutch East Indies in 1928. Upon his return to Siam, he adopted the Dutch practice of using immigration to raise government revenue. However, there were no Chinese exclusion acts like in the Dutch East Indies, where Chinese laborers were prohibited from entering. Unlike overpopulated Java, Siam suffered from an acute shortage of wage labor. The entry fee, however, was raised incrementally until in 1936 it reached 100 baht, which was considered very expensive at the time.[2] The Japanese occupation of Guangzhou (formerly known as Canton) and Shantou put a stop to immigration for a while, but another big wave arrived directly after the war.

Post-war famine and social dislocation coupled with poor economic conditions again sent out waves of emigrants overseas. In August 1946, the *Bangkok Post* reported that "40,000 to 50,000 Chinese were waiting to embark from famine stricken southern China to Siam." Traveling conditions on board were terrible as many vessels ignored the regulations and allowed over a thousand to embark on an 800-passenger ship. According to the *Bangkok Post*, in October of the same year, "20 people died on board one boat, dubbed the 'hell ship,' in which at least 4,000 people were packed into a vessel that normally accommodated a thousand."[3]

Due to poor sanitation and overcrowding, sometimes cholera broke out aboard, and the Siamese government refused to allow the vessels entry. Sou Gungkiam and Huang Hongqiu, the presidents of the Teochew and Kwongsiew Associations respectively, were instrumental in negotiating with the authorities to allow the passengers to disembark at a temporary camp at one of the old Wanglee rice mills.[4] A government site was organized to quarantine Chinese immigrants from these overcrowded ships for medical evaluation at a hospital in Klong San. According to the Poh Teck Tung Foundation, which arranged free food and water for thousands of immigrants upon arrival in Bangkok, the number of immigrants during the first year after the war reached 86,000.[5]

In the national interest to cope with the crisis, the prime minister, Luang Thamrong-Navasawad, who was himself a *lukchin* born in Ayudhya, decided for the first time in Thai history to put a limit on the number of Chinese immigrants. In 1947, after an extended negotiation with Li Tiezheng, China's ambassador to Thailand, both governments agreed on a quota of 10,000 persons per year.[6]

Meanwhile in China, Chiang Kai-shek's triumph did not last long as he lost one stronghold after another in the civil war that followed. The rising fortunes of the Communists in the Chinese civil war affected the overseas Chinese, leading to a resurgence of Chinese patriotic sentiment that reflected the divided loyalties of the Chinese community in Siam. The capital city of Bangkok became the stage for a renewed clash between Thai and Chinese nationalism reminiscent of the pre-war period.

The resurgence of Chinese patriotism in the kingdom was visible and tangible—in March 1948, the Ministry of Education closed 14 Chinese schools in and around Bangkok because they refused to fly the Siamese flag.[7] A month later, a military faction known as the Soi Rachakru group associated with former Prime Minister Phibun, Police Chief Phao Sriyanond and another old Phibun supporter, Field Marshal Phin Choonhavan, toppled the civilian government and seized power in a coup d'état.

Phibun's return to power embodied a Thai counter-nationalism to the surge of Chinese nationalism on Siamese soil. Phibun characteristically reduced the quota for Chinese immigration from 10,000 to 200 persons per year. Siam was renamed Thailand once more, underscoring his determination to reset the country on a nationalist course.

Most drugstores in Thailand are operated by Thai-Chinese.

A year later, on 1 October 1949, Mao Zedong proclaimed the People's Republic of China (PRC) with its capital in Beijing. Chiang Kai-shek, together with approximately 2 million Nationalist Chinese, retreated from the mainland to Taiwan in December 1949. Despite having gradually lost faith in the generalissimo's military competence, the overseas-Chinese community was shocked by his defeat. Overseas-Chinese entrepreneurs witnessed their multi-millions of dollars' worth of assets in China vanish. Confusing news arrived with each new batch of refugees. Numerous families were aggrieved by the severance of ties to their ancestral homeland. Chinese immigration to Thailand, which had been restricted to an annual quota of 200 in 1948, remained low for the following two decades due to the closing up of the PRC.

In the wake of Communist unification of China in 1949, Phibun intensified Thailand's assimilationist

Chairman Mao
Zedong (1893–1976).

policies through legal, social, economic and political measures. Again, Chinese
education suffered under the government's assimilation campaign; those who
wanted to live in Thailand were required to change their names to Thai, and
suspected Communist sympathizers were deported. Phibun's harsh suppression
coupled with factional disputes between Communists and Nationalists during
1949–51 led to the demise of Chinese associations and chambers of commerce
throughout many provinces. Dozens of Chinese communities were left with
no formal organization and no leaders willing to accept responsibility for
community endeavors.[8]

Phibun's efforts to suppress the growth of a Chinese nationalist movement in
Thailand failed to entirely dampen the euphoria of some over the Communist
victory in China. Within the local Chinese community, a liberated China seemed
to be an attractive choice, and shiploads of intelligentsia and youth left for
China in the 1950s. On 12 November 1953, the Norwegian ship *SS Deviken* was
the second ship in a week to leave Bangkok for the Communist Chinese port of
Shantou carrying 1,000 mostly ethnic Chinese passengers. The majority of these
passengers returned voluntarily; only 250 were deportees.[9] Special permits to
transport Chinese with divided loyalties back to Communist China were granted
on a case-by-case basis by the Phibun government until 1957.

Phibun's Nationalist onslaught against Chinese political, social and economic
institutions succeeded in degrading Chinese dominance over the economy.[10]
Under the banner of political nationalism, state enterprises intended to promote
banking and import substitution industrialization displaced Chinese economic

Chinese banker, Lim
Pek Kee, in 1955.

control. However, bureaucratic inefficiency and a lack of expertise in operating state enterprises led the military elite to reach outside the state apparatus to re-engage Thai-Chinese entrepreneurs in a subordinate role through the granting of contracts and operating licenses to economically favored, but politically marginalized, Chinese groups. Under this new post-war crony capitalism that developed, Chinese business interests invited their patrons—the military leaders of the Soi Rachakru clique headed by Field Marshal Phin Choonhavan, Police Chief Phao Sriyanond and their representatives—onto the directorial boards of their enterprises.

The locus of this bureaucratic-Chinese patronage system tended to revolve around the new opportunities that opened up in the banking industry. The retreat of European colonial banks in the wake of the Japanese invasion provided the impetus for the development of the Thai banking industry. Although some Chinese banks were already operating during the pre-war period, they were not very competitive and were servicing a small circle of Chinese clientele in the capital. However, the Pacific War changed all that. During the war, the Thai government took over the Western banks that had monopolized international transactions. Local officials were sent in to work and collect data on international banking practices.

When the bureaucratic officials turned to the Chinese for operational assistance in the banking sector, many merchants and entrepreneurs responded enthusiastically because the government's nationalist economic policy had made it difficult for Chinese rice millers and exporters to develop their businesses from 1938 onward.[11] Consequently, commercial banking and insurance services became an attractive alternative for Chinese business people.

Between 1942 and 1945, five new Thai banks opened for service. Capital was raised among the new elite of bureaucrats, businessmen and ethnic Chinese investors, including Chin Sophonpanich of Bangkok Bank, the Kiangsiri family and Tan Siewmeng Wanglee of Bangkok Bank of Commerce, Chuan Ratanarak of the Bank of Ayudhya (known today as Krungsri Bank) and the Lamsam family of Thai Farmers Bank (known today as Kasikornbank).[12] Among these nascent Thai bankers, Chin Sophonpanich, a *lukchin* born in Thonburi, eventually emerged as a towering figure, revolutionizing the Thai banking system and opening Bangkok Bank branches overseas as well as in the provinces. Other local banks followed the example of Bangkok Bank and opened branches in the provinces.

Besides the business acumen of the Chinese, the success of local banking must be attributed to the government's effort to help the local banks by restricting the entry and operation of foreign banks. In 1938, more foreign banks than Thai banks existed in Thailand. After the war, in 1949, the situation was reversed, and 13 local banks competed with 10 foreign banks. Thirty-five years later, 16 local banks with 1,816 branches outnumbered the 14 foreign banks with a paltry 20 branches.[13]

In a parallel fashion, the Phibun government attempted to facilitate the development of an import substitution industry by setting up protectionist barriers to prevent import competition; restricting entry of competitive foreign firms; providing low-interest loans from government financial institutions; and offering other incentives to attract local capital to the nascent manufacturing sector. For foreign firms with a clear technology advantage, entry restriction often meant that they had to share technological knowledge and skills with local capital or enter into licensed production without equity participation. Examples of local Chinese capitalists who benefited from these technology-transfer arrangements with Japanese firms during the early post-war period included Kiarti Srifuengfung and Asahi Glass (see page 382), Thavorn Phornprapha and Nissan (see page 379), and Surat Osathanugrah and Lipovitan-D (see page 376).

Meanwhile, Phibun's anti-Chinese suppression elicited strong protests from both Beijing and Taipei in 1950. In the wake of international Chinese pressure, Phibun began to lean on the Americans and concluded a series of agreements with the US for educational exchange, technical assistance and military aid. Phibun's support for the American Far Eastern Policy led Thailand to support the United Nations' intervention in Korea by sending rice and a Thai expeditionary force to fight in the Korean War.

Simultaneously on the Chinese front, the image of the PRC in the eyes of its Asian neighbors began to change at the Bandung Conference in 1955. At the "first intercontinental conference of colored peoples in the history of mankind," as President Sukarno of Indonesia announced, Zhou Enlai, the premier and foreign minister representing the PRC, gave a memorable speech. China had come to Bandung "to seek unity and not quarrel ... to seek common ground and not create divergences ... [Thus the conference should] seek common ground among us while keeping our differences ... None of us is asked to give up his own views, because difference in viewpoints is an objective reality."[14]

At the Bandung Conference, Zhou Enlai entered into an agreement on dual nationality with Indonesia, marking the first time in history that China abandoned the long-held principle of *jus sanguinis*—that descent was the basis of Chinese nationality. Thus China's acceptance of *jus soli*—that anyone born in that country was entitled to become a citizen of it—was the olive branch offered to the newly independent countries of the 1950s. Many Southeast Asian countries were heartened by Zhou's willingness to drop the *jus sanguinis* principle and appreciated his admonition to the overseas Chinese to comply with the laws and

Top: Chuan Ratanarak of the Bank of Ayudhya.

Bottom: Bancha Lamsam of Thai Farmers Bank.

Zhou Enlai delivers
a speech at the First
Asia-Africa Conference
in Bandung in April
1955.

customs of their adopted country. However, none of the other countries followed the Indonesian path of negotiating a solution with China bilaterally.[15]

Despite Thailand's increasingly pro-US orientation in the 1950s, Phibun—in characteristically Thai fashion—arranged to send to China two children of Sang Phathanothai, his closest advisor, with the intention of establishing a backdoor channel for dialogue between China and Thailand. The girl, aged eight, and her brother, aged 12, were sent to be brought up under the care of Zhou Enlai as his wards. In early 1957, the Thai government also allowed Chinese films from the mainland to be shown in Yaowarat and a large batch of Thai tobacco was exported to the PRC.[16]

However, this relaxed attitude toward the PRC did not last long. That September, Phibun was overthrown by Field Marshal Sarit Thanarat. Phibun sought political asylum in Japan, where he remained until his death in 1964. The Thai government under Sarit strictly followed the anti-Communist Cold War policies of the US. The nationalist economic policy of the Phibun era was replaced by one that was more open to foreign investment, especially from the US. State enterprises, which had served as the economic base of the Soi Rachakru military elite, were scaled back. In contrast to Phibun, Sarit promoted private enterprise as the new engine of economic growth.

Meanwhile, the US government began allocating multi-millions of dollars' worth of arms and other military equipment to Thailand for use in resisting the "Communist menace." This was followed by economic and technical assistance for the improvement of Thailand's agriculture and irrigation, health, transport, harbor development and commerce. Economic conditions during the Cold War benefited the Chinese in Bangkok and generated capital accumulation for Thai-Chinese business groups.

The Cold War had this important impact: the overseas-Chinese capital that centuries of Southeast Asian rulers had sought with limited success to trap within their respective countries was suddenly voluntarily on offer as overseas Chinese became unwilling to transfer their wealth to a Communist country. During the 10 years from 1927 to 1937, China enjoyed a capital inflow of 20 million baht from Siam, which was equivalent to one-sixth of the kingdom's total exports covering that period.[17] Consequently, the Southeast Asian countries hosting overseas Chinese capital boomed. Also, after 1949, China's Communist economy offered few opportunities for capitalist investment. Hence, local Chinese capital tended to remain in Thailand, and became available for financing industrial development.

Under Sarit's watch, commercial banking registered a dramatic growth that continued into the 1970s. Reminiscent of the Soi Rachakru patronage system, the new entrepreneurs provided their military patrons with chairmanships, directorships and free stocks in return for economic privileges and security.[18] The patronage system based on the alliance between the bureaucratic power elite and Chinese commercial interests led to the rise of powerful conglomerates centered in Bangkok.

However, the political history of the Chinese during this period belies another dimension of Chinese society in Thailand that has often been overlooked. It would be wrong to conclude that all prominent and successful Chinese in Thailand were consumed by a driving ambition for wealth or power. The history of the Chinese narrated in the last chapter showed that at critical periods, idealism, self-sacrifice and support for the ancestral homeland prevailed over many Chinese capitalists' acquisitive instincts. The Tian Fah spirit—the support for the revolutionary cause of Sun Yatsen—and the courageous and generous support for China's War of Resistance against Japan testify to the occasions when Chinese have placed other values above the quest for riches.

To remind the reader that such a spirit is still alive and well among the Chinese of the modern period, we have included some examples of Thai-Chinese figures that fly in the face of the stereotype of the greedy Chinese, such as Dr. Puey Ungpakorn, or Amphan Charoensuklarp, a master of the Thai-Chinese opera, and Wu Jiyue, a veteran Chinese journalist. Although a dozen stories selected for this chapter could hardly be representative of the community, they are nevertheless representative tales worth sharing, reflecting the life and times of the ethnic Chinese and the enormous talents trapped in Thailand after the fall of the Bamboo Curtain in China in 1949.

Dr. Puey Ungpakorn, former dean and rector of Thammasat University.

"The Quality of Life of a Southeast Asian"

Dr. Puey Ungpakorn (Ng Buaykiam, 1916–99), MBE, a second-generation *lukchin*, was a brilliant technocrat who became a symbol of integrity that inspired generations of young officials in government service, especially at the Bank of Thailand where he served as governor for 12 years from June 1959.

Puey's father was a fish merchant who died young. Puey's mother had to support the family and the education of her young sons by herself after she refused her brother-in-law's suggestion to send her boys back to China. Puey attended Assumption School before winning the Thai government scholarship to study in the UK in 1938. Following the outbreak of the Pacific War, Puey joined the Free Thai Movement and the British parachuted him back into Thailand as a spy. After the war ended, Puey resumed his studies and received a Ph.D. from the London School of Economics in 1949.

Dr. Puey Ungpakorn was the principal architect of the government strategy that sparked Thailand's impressive economic growth. He strengthened the Thai financial system through three major innovations: the liberalization of the multiple exchange rate, the establishment of the budget bureau, and the introduction of national economic planning.

Later, as dean and rector of Thammasat University, Puey sought to instill in his students the "precious sense of idealism that could be kindled into an understanding and compassion for the common man, especially the farmer." [19]

"The Quality of Life of a Southeast Asian," also known as "From Womb to Tomb," is the best-known writing of Dr. Puey Ungphakorn. Written in 1973, the simple piece is reprinted in its entirety here:

> *While in my mother's womb, I want her to have good nutrition and access to maternal and child welfare care.*
>
> *I don't want to have as many brothers and sisters as my parents had before me, and I do not want my mother to have a child too soon after me.*
>
> *I don't care whether my father and mother are formally married, but I need them to live together in reasonable harmony.*
>
> *I want good nutrition for my mother and for me in my first two or three years when my capacity for future mental and physical development is determined.*
>
> *I want to go to school, together with my sister, and to learn a trade, and to have the schools impart social values to me. If I happen to be suitable for higher education, that opportunity should be available.*
>
> *When I leave school I want a job, a meaningful one in which I can feel the satisfaction of making a contribution.*

I want to live in a law-and-order society, without molestation. I want my country to relate effectively and equitably to the outside world so that I can have access to the intellectual and technical knowledge of all mankind, as well as the capital from overseas.

I would like my country to get a fair price for the products that I and my fellow citizens create.

As a farmer, I would like to have my own plot of land, with a system which gives me access to credit, to new agricultural technology and to markets, and a fair price for my produce.

As a worker, I would want to have my share, some sense of participation in the factory in which I work.

As a human being, I would like inexpensive newspapers and paperback books, plus access to radio and TV (without too much advertising).

I want to enjoy good health, and I expect the Government to provide free preventive medical service and cheap and readily available, good curative service.

I need some leisure time for myself, and to enjoy my family, and want access to some green parks, to the arts, and to traditional social or religious festivities.

I want clean air to breathe and clean water to drink.

I would like to have the security of co-operative mechanisms in which I join to help others do things that they cannot do alone and they do the same for me.

I need the opportunity to participate in the society around me, and to help shape the decisions of the economic and social as well as the political institutions that so affect my life.

I want my wife to have equal opportunities as me, and I want both of us to have access to the knowledge and means of family planning.

In my old age, it would be nice to have some form of social security to which I have contributed.

When I die, if I happen to have some money left, I would wish the Government to take some of it, leaving an adequate amount for my widow. With this money the Government should make it possible for others to enjoy life too.

These are what life is all about, and what development should seek to achieve for all.

In 1965, Dr. Puey Ungphakorn won the Magsaysay Award in recognition for his outstanding government service.

Chin Sophonpanich

The story of Chin Sophonpanich is a classic rags-to-riches tale. Chin, or Tan Biakching, who by the time of his death in 1988 ranked among the world's richest overseas Chinese, was a Teochew born on a small raft-house in a Thonburi orchard near Wat Sai in 1910. As the eldest boy, Chin was sent to live with his Chinese grandmother in his father's home village in Chaoyang around 1915. As a poor farmer, he had some schooling but missed many classes to help out in the field, which provided the family's only income. When Chin was 17, his father lost his job, and Chin was recalled back to Bangkok to support his mother and four sisters. After doing odd jobs for a few years, Chin worked as a clerk for a lumber company that later burned down. He then went back to China for a brief, unsuccessful stint before returning to Bangkok to work for a construction-materials trading company.[20]

Chin was diligent, and despite his limited education, he was a prodigy with financial figures and concepts. Trading suited him and when he was 29, Chin was able to establish his own building supplies business, Asia Company, on Charoen Krung Road in Bangkok. He also traded in the gold market from a small shop tucked behind Baan Moh. During the Pacific War, the gold price rose to 20 times the pre-war levels. The rise in metal prices during the war and the demand for construction materials for the reconstruction of Bangkok established Chin as a success. Around this time Chin also expanded into the remittance and foreign exchange services as well.[21]

During the Pacific War, all of the allied banks were closed down. In order to service the financial needs of the country, the Thai government encouraged

Chin at his mother's funeral at Wat Sai in Bangkok.

the establishment of Thai commercial banks. In 1944, Chin Sophonpanich and his friends established Bangkok Bank, one of the five Thai banks that sprung up during this period.[22] Chin's familiarity with the financial world, especially money remittance, gave him an entrée into the new ruling military clique that came to power in 1947. Soon he became the business contact for Phao Sriyanond, the director general of the national police, who was a key figure in Phibun Songkram's government.[23]

Chin Sophonpanich (seated) and Prasit Kanchanawat.

Although Chin was one of the founding shareholders of Bangkok Bank, initially he was the bank's comprador, preferring to spend more time on his own businesses. However, in 1952 the bank was in financial difficulty due to mismanagement and Chin assumed a full-time role as the general manager. Chin restructured the bank by bringing in professionals like Prasit Kanchanawat, Prayoon Vinyaratn and Boonchu Rojanasthien. His close contact with government officials also enabled Chin to increase the bank's equity through government participation.

Following his study of Western banking practices, Chin competed for funding by offering high interest rates to small depositors, which consisted mostly of shop keepers and well-to-do locals. He also courted wealthy Chinese clients by introducing personalized accounts.[24] On the lending side, Chin established a solid client base by giving credit to small merchants and medium-sized enterprises with good earning potential. Bangkok Bank also expanded aggressively in the provincial capitals after it had opened its first provincial branch in Ubon Rachathani in 1950.[25]

More importantly, Chin provided international financial services to a host of Thai-Chinese middle-class entrepreneurs. These small- and medium-sized businesses found it difficult to obtain loans from the more rigid Western banks because of their lack of assets. By the mid-1950s, Bangkok Bank had established branches overseas and was running 16 domestic branches, with declared assets approaching $50 million dollars.[26]

However, at the peak of his career, Chin's strategy of cultivating close government connections backfired when his political patron, Phao Sriyanond, was sent into exile by his rival, Sarit Thanarat in 1957. To escape the ensuing political turmoil, Chin left for Hong Kong and stayed there until Sarit died in December 1963.

Chin's stay in Hong Kong turned out to be a blessing in disguise. While his trusted professionals took care of the bank's domestic operations, Chin built up its foreign network, which strengthened the group's links with a wider pool of overseas-Chinese businesses. In the two decades after his return to Bangkok in 1964, Chin steered the bank's expansion and made it the biggest bank in the ASEAN region. During this time, Chin also adopted a more cautious political profile. Instead of relying on a single patron, the bank avoided political risks by cultivating a wide range of contacts. This shift from a system of a single patron to multiple political connections was characteristic of a general trend among Thai-Chinese conglomerates.[27]

Chin also had a gift for spotting talent, both inside and outside his own organization. Many of the most talented Bangkok Bank executives later became actively involved in politics and government; some like Boonchu Rojanasathien and Amnuay Virawan were among the most successful technocrats in the history of modern Thai government. From the 1950s, Bangkok Bank also played a major role in the expansion of the Thai economy by extending credit to a host of small entrepreneurs eager to cash in on economic opportunities. The bank lent at high interest rates, but the conditions were right, the evaluations astute, and many of the businesses succeeded. For over two decades from the 1960s on, Bangkok Bank led the way in financing over 40 percent of the country's total exports.[28]

Khunying Chodchoy Sophonpanich, Chin's daughter and an elected senator of Bangkok, attributed her father's success to his ability to be "the first banker to a large number of Southeast Asian millionaires."

Wu Jiyue (吴继岳): Thailand's Veteran Chinese Journalist

When the People's Republic of China opened up to international relations in the 1980s, a book was published in Beijing to introduce "outstanding" overseas Chinese. Among the listed were three Nobel laureates—Samuel CC Ting, Tsung-Dao Lee and Chen-Ning Franklin Yang—and Louis Cha Leungyung, a best-selling Chinese author who sold over 100 million copies of his work. He is commonly known by his pen name, Jin Yong. Only two overseas Chinese in Thailand were included. One was the Bangkok Bank founder Chin Sophonpanich, and the other was Wu Jiyue, who was at one point the oldest working journalist in Thailand. "Wu is not rich or famous. For wealth is not to be judged by his earnings but instead by the work he had produced," wrote the *Bangkok Post*'s Saowarop Panyacheewin.[29]

Wu Jiyue (1905–92) was born into an educated family in the Hakka heartland of Meixian in Guangdong. When he was 12, Wu and his widowed mother left their poverty-stricken village to work in the Dutch East Indies. They headed for Batavia where he toiled as a handy boy in a large store run by his relative. Wu returned home at 18 to consummate the marriage that had been arranged for him when he was only 7 and his wife was 4. After an extended stay at home in a village with "no future for young men," Wu returned to Indonesia to work with his father-in-law in a flour mill.

Although his family was very poor, when he was young Wu learned to read and write from an elderly relative who ran a study room in his clan village. He loved reading and poverty did not discourage Wu from educating himself. His favorite pastime while working in Java was reading the Shanghai newspapers as well as Chinese classical literature. Although his boss treated him well, he soon became discomfited by the working atmosphere at the factory. The Chinese were exploitative of the local natives, buying up products at unfairly low prices. After his wife passed away, Wu quit his job and left to pursue his dream of becoming a journalist in Bangkok.

In Siam in 1931, at age 27, Wu Jiyue started a new chapter in his life. Less than six months after beginning work as a proofreader, Wu proved to be a capable writer and was soon promoted to the rewriting desk, then to a position as a reporter for *Huaqiao Ribao*. Among his first news reports were stories on the opening of Parliament and the king ratifying the nation's constitution.[30] However, in 1939, Wu's peaceful life in Bangkok was shattered when Phibun closed down all Chinese schools and Chinese newspapers except one. Almost all of the Chinese, educated intellectuals in Bangkok lost their jobs overnight.

Wu Jiyue was more fortunate than most as his writing skill had already made a name for him overseas, and *Xingzhou Ribao* in Singapore offered him a job. Working in the same office in Singapore was Yu Dafu, a renowned poet whose works reflected a serious-minded critique of China's political plight. Wu was duly impressed by Yu, admiration that was reflected in his later works. Unfortunately for Wu, however, a year later the Japanese attacked and occupied Singapore. The Chinese in Singapore suffered traumas much worse than their peers living in Bangkok. Wu was among those who were selected to dig their own graves in the five-day massacre of ethnic Chinese. He narrowly escaped by sneaking into the line of "good citizens" just before being ushered to the truck headed for the execution ground. Wu and his family of five children survived three and a half years of wartime unemployment, tilling the hilly soil in a suburb of Singapore. Their savings had dried up and they were down to just a two-week supply of food when the war ended.

Wu returned to Bangkok in 1946 and continued his successful writing career, this time with *Zhongyuanbao* as the front page editor, as well as the sports and entertainment editor. Already a well-known sports newsman, Wu was appointed the team secretary, taking the local overseas-Chinese basketball and badminton teams to compete in Malaya, Vietnam, Hong Kong and Singapore, as well as the 1948 National Games in Shanghai. In his memoir, Wu described the city of Shanghai as "politically rotten, economically degraded. Lives of the Shanghainese did not improve after the (Pacific) War but worsened; the society chaotic and confused. As the civil war raged in the North, the morale of the city people dropped, the value of their money nose-dived while prices jumped steeply. It was a sick, suffocating atmosphere ... "[31] As a journalist who covered the progress of his motherland, Wu admitted that he was disappointed with China in 1948. He remarked that Chinese society just before the Communist takeover was "rotten, lawless and immoral. The sort of world that creates monsters out of men."[32]

Wu returned to a successful career in Bangkok. The golden age of Chinese newspapers in Thailand lasted from the 1930s until the 1950s according to Wu. He said of the newspapers of this era, "They were rich with high-quality content and had a literary flavor."[33] However, readership declined as the result of the government's assimilation policy, which tightly controlled the number of Chinese schools operating in Thailand, and Chinese literacy dropped at an alarming rate in the 1960s.

When Field Marshal Sarit Thanarat staged a second coup to consolidate his power in October 1958, Wu Jiyue was among many journalists charged with being a Communist sympathizer. Among those detained at the Police Club in Pathumwan was Saguan Tulalak, a leading member of Pridi's Free Thai Movement and the first Thai ambassador to the Republic of China in 1946. Many MPs from the northeast, such as Kleao Norapati, Tongpak Piengket and Sutee Puwaphan, were also detained there. Wu managed to avoid arrest for eight months, however, later he was captured and sent to Lardyao Prison where he met Suwat Voradilok, Tongbai Tongpao and Charoen Subsaeng.

Wu recalled later that life as a political prisoner was not too tough; he spent time playing cards and watching television. "If I had known it was so comfortable, I would have let them arrest me a long time ago," Wu jokingly told the *Bangkok Post*.

At Lardyao, Wu got to know Chit Phumisak, the author of the influential book *The Face of Thai Feudalism*. At the time, Chit was studying Chinese and sometimes dropped by to see Wu when he needed help deciphering Chinese characters. While detained, Wu wrote short stories, poems and his autobiography, *Haiwai Wushinian*. In it, Wu recorded some 50 years of his experience inside and outside of the newspaper business. He serialized his autobiography through two daily newspapers he worked for during 1972–74 and later published it in two volumes.

Wu went back to work as the domestic news editor for *Dongnan Ribao* and later, for *Xinzhongyuanbao*. He was invited by the PRC to visit China twice in 1976 and 1985, and was given a Senior Journalist Award by the Thai Prime Minister, Banharn Silpa-archa, in 1990. Forty years after its Chinese publication, *Haiwai Wushinian* was translated and published in Thai in 2014 and became a "must read" for those interested in the Bangkok Chinese community during the mid-20th century.

Udane Techapaiboon (Tae Ngoulao): The Last of the *Huaqiao* "Old Guard"

During the first half of the 20th century, the *huaqiao* community was vibrant, energetic and glued to mainland Chinese political events on a scale never seen before or after. The driving force was the synergy of five leading members of the Teochew Association, namely Hia Guang-iam, Khun Sethbhakdi (Liao Jingsong), Tan Gengchuang, U Chuliang and Tae Juebing, the father of Udane Techapaiboon.

When the imperial examination was terminated in 1905, Tae Juebing, a member of a well-educated family in Chaoyang, was truly disappointed. He had spent years studying the classics in the hope of passing the examination and getting a post in the government just like his forefathers. To find an alternative living, Tae Juebing left his ancestral village at age 18, joining the *huaqiao*'s educated stream of emigrants who preferred to seek their fortune abroad rather than stay behind in decaying Qing China. This was an unprecedented event—such a mass emigration of educated literati had never occurred in Chinese history until the last days of the Qing dynasty.

Tae Juebing decided to leave for Bangkok, then known as the "Shantou of Southeast Asia," where some of his Chaoyang peers had already settled and become prominent pawn-shop owners. Soon he established himself as a liquor manufacturer and pawn-shop operator. As an educated man, Tae Juebing was well respected and became a leading figure in the Chinese community. He was one of the founders of the Teochew Association established by his friend, Hia Guang-iam, the chairman of the Chinese Chamber of Commerce. In 1937, when the Marco Polo Bridge incident sparked off the second Sino-Japanese War, Tae Juebing and his friends were at the forefront of the anti-Japanese movement in Bangkok. A few months later, the group took over Poh Teck Tung, a charitable organization run by a Bae family from Chaoyang that provided burial services for the poor. Hia Guang-iam restructured its mission and broadened its objectives to include other services, such as nursing, and registered it as a foundation for community services. Tae Juebing helped to draft the constitution, as well as the rules and regulations. Udane Techaphaiboon, Tae Juebing's 22-year-old son, was appointed the vice chairman on his father's behalf while Hia Guang-iam was elected the chairman of the foundation.

Udane Techapaiboon.

Udane Techapaiboon, Tae Juebing's eldest son, was born in 1913. Although Tae Juebing was extremely patriotic and a teacher of Chinese classics, he sent all his sons to Assumption College, a Catholic missionary school,[34] to prepare them for the modern business arena.

Udane's entry into business started in 1950. With the help of U Chuliang, one of the five "old guards" of the Teochew Association, he became managing director of Bangkok Metropolitan Bank,[35] and he eventually became the controlling shareholder. In the late 1950s, he joined the liquor company, Sura Mahakhun, organized by Sahas Mahakhun, a former chairman of the Poh Teck Tung Foundation. Eventually, the Techapaiboons came to control this company as well and renamed it Sura Maharas. As the exclusive producer of liquor in the Bangkok metropolitan area, it was an important source of profit for the Techapaiboon family. However, Udane's former partners, who had lost the bid, obtained the license for producing liquor outside the Bangkok area and in the early 1980s began challenging the supremacy of Sura Maharas, thus starting the so-called "whisky war." Subsequently, the Techapaiboon family suffered heavy losses and Udane sold his interests in the company.[36]

Through these ups-and-downs, however, Udane remained committed to Poh Teck Tung, a *huaqiao* foundation dedicated to the welfare of underprivileged Chinese and the propagation of Chinese culture and civilization. He sought to nurture a strong *huaqiao* spirit through various community services. He established a Huaqiao Hospital and a Huaqiao University, and he supported emergency medical services for victims of road accidents and other disasters. Other *huaqiao*-inspired activities included aiding, helping, and bailing out Chinese immigrants jailed for illegal entry in the 1950s and 1960s. It was because of his philanthropic and cultural legacy that Udane Techapaiboon is recognized as one of the great pillars of Chinese society in Thailand.

Svasti (top), the father of Surat Osathanugrah (bottom).

Osotspa, a Household Name

In the last quarter of the 20th century, few large conglomerates were still using their Chinese name. One of them was Osotspa (also known by its Chinese name, Teck Heng Yoo), which continues to sport a logo of a *qilin*, a mythical Chinese creature. The chairman of Osotspa, Svasti Osathanugrah, must have been a second- or third-generation *lukchin*, as his funeral book fails to mention his clan name and the family's ancestral village in China. Other sources listed the family as belonging to the Lin clan.

Svasti's father, Nai Peh, was a man of property who owned a shop in Sampeng that sold goods to upcountry shop owners, including crockery, pots and pans, pins and needles and grocery products. Before he entered the monastic order, Buddhadasa Bhikkhu (a well-known and widely respected Thai philosopher of the 20th century) was a regular customer of Teck Heng Yoo, buying supplies for his father's grocery shop in Chaiya market. Nai Peh and Buddhadasa's father were friends who shared an interest in herbal medicine.

When Svasti was 11 years old, B Grimm & Co.—the supplier of imported products at Nai Peh's shop—placed a consignment of medicine that sold very well. It inspired Nai Peh, an amateur herbalist, to produce his own recipe of herbal medicine called *ya krisna kran* for upset stomachs. The drug was effective and became very popular. It was on the list of medicines recommended by King Vajiravudh to his Sua Pah (Wild Tiger) corps. That was how Teck Heng Yoo first made its name in pharmaceuticals and Nai Peh's family was awarded the honorary surname of Osathanugrah by the king.[37]

The logo for Teck Heng Yoo, also known as Osotspa.

Svasti entered Chulalongkorn University to study medicine, but had to leave school when his father died in 1918 and the responsibility of the family business fell to him. At the time, the store had five employees. In the 1930s, however, under the new name of Osotspa, the business began improving distribution and marketing, as well as adding more modern medicine such as Than Chai, an aspirin that also became a household name.

In the post-war period, with economic expansion and production of its own house brand of medicines, Osotspa underwent accelerated growth and became one of the top companies in pharmaceuticals in the 1960–70s before Surat, the third son of Svasti, diversified the company into other consumer products,[38] including energy drinks such as Lipovitan-D, M100 and M150, as well as cosmetics and toiletry brands such as Shisedo and Baby Mild.

As Thailand went through a period where one military regime after another attempted to govern the nation, Svasti steered clear of politics, although he had powerful connections. However, Surat joined the Democrat Party and was elected a member of Parliament. In 1975, Seni Pramoj, the Democrat prime minister, appointed him Communication Minister, but Seni's government lasted only a few weeks. Eight years later, Prem Tinsulanonda asked Surat to return to public service and appointed him the Deputy Interior Minister and later, Minister of Commerce.

However, Surat Osathanugrah's lasting legacy was in education. He founded Bangkok University and the Southeast Asian Ceramics Museum with the famous Dr. Roxanne Brown as its first curator. Svasti and Surat had both had life-long passions for antique ceramics, and the museum boasts one of the best collections of Mainland Southeast Asian ceramics in the world.

Fu Xuzhong (符續忠): The *Huaqiao* Factor

When the Communists took over Mainland China in 1949, part of Chiang Kai-shek's army retreated to Hainan. In spite of its local Communist movement, Hainan was liberated later than the mainland because it is an island. Its location created difficulties for the Communist troops, who, despite their enormous strength of over 100,000 men, had no ships with which to cross the channel. The Guomindang controlled five armies and two divisions, a naval fleet totaling more than four dozen warships, a marine regiment, and four groups of the air force with 45 aircraft of various kinds that were assigned to defend the island. By April

1950, however, the Peoples' Liberation Army had mobilized a total of 2,130 junks and over 4,000 civilian sailors. Meanwhile, the 15,000-man Communist Qiongya Column on the island mounted a campaign against the Nationalist garrison to embroil them in a separate battle, resulting in insufficient Nationalist resistance on the beachheads when the Communist landing took place. By May 1950, the Communists had succeeded in taking over the entire island.

Fu Xuzhong, who lived through the liberation of Hainan, came from a wealthy Hainan family. His ancestors owned a restaurant in Bangkok called Yan Fang Lou and later a rice-trading company located in what is now the River City at Talad Noi. Fu's father was an agent of the Thai-registered Ngo Hok (Wufu) Steamship Company in Haikou. The five steamships that traveled between Bangkok, Hong Kong and Shantou would have a stopover in Haikou every 10 days. Fu explained that Hailam were proportionately fewer in Bangkok because Hainan was sparsely populated compared to the Chaosan area. Nevertheless, the fortunate few who came to Thailand had done well for themselves. There are many famous Hailam in Thailand, including the Hoontrakul, Sarasin, Vongwanij, B.L. Hua (Pangsrivongse), Chirathivat and Piyaoui families.

Fu recollected that when he was a boy, the Japanese army invaded and occupied Hainan for about six years; hence his animosity towards the Japanese. In 1952, Fu left town to pursue higher education. While the People's Liberation Army was traveling south to Hainan from Beijing, Fu was heading in the opposite direction, north to Beijing. People from Hainan seldom went to study in the north; the furthest they went was to Guangzhou or Shanghai. Very few went all the way to Beijing—perhaps only two in a hundred years. Not only did these Hailam students have to be fearless; they also had to be able to pass the necessary exams. Fu was determined to get an education, so he sold his gold savings for 200 yuan, enough to pay for everything. Under the Communists, tuition was waived for all university students, and living expenses, learning materials and all other necessities were free.

In 1948, Mao Zedong argued that to facilitate agrarian reform "one-tenth of the peasants . . . will have to be destroyed." Ren Bishi, a member of the party's Central Committee, was more explicit in his speech given the same year, stating, "30 million landlords and rich peasants will have to be destroyed." The actual number of people killed in the name of land reform may have been lower but still ranked in the millions, following the policy to select "at least one landlord, and usually several, in virtually every village for public execution."[39]

In Hainan, arrests by local authorities were widespread—people who had money, gold or land were found guilty. Fu's father, Fu Biaowen, was among the wealthy landlords arrested and jailed by the Communists. The family was frantic; they spread the bad news to relatives, even those who lived overseas, and asked for help. Fu's father was in prison for some time. Finally, on his execution day in 1953, a telegram arrived from Beijing ordering the local authorities to spare Fu's life. Apparently Fu Zhaoguang, Fu's uncle in Bangkok, had written to Zhou Enlai pledging that his brother, Fu Biaowen, was not a landlord, nor were the Fu a family of exploitative "landlords" who had become rich by taking advantage of peasants. The letter informed the government that Biaowen was a member of a wealthy *huaqiao* family who had earned their wealth overseas and had donated money in the past to help the fatherland. This was welcome news for the PRC because after 1952, remittances from overseas Chinese had begun to dry up. Some stopped sending money altogether as news of property confiscation and execution of their relatives traveled overseas. Not only was Fu's father's life spared, but in 1956, Fu Biaowen became one of the only two Hailams invited to Beijing. His assignment was to help raise funds from the overseas-Chinese community for the development of the People's Republic of China.

Realizing the damage that land reform was causing to the government's relations with millions of overseas Chinese, the policy was reconsidered, and the status of overseas Chinese was officially changed. *Huaqiao* businessmen were no longer the enemy of the revolution. Fu's father was given a permit to travel freely to Hong Kong, Singapore, and Thailand, and he managed to raise funds from abroad for the building of the Huaqiao Dasha Hotel in Guangzhou.

In 1957, Fu Xuzhong was in his junior year at Shanxi University. He went to Hong Kong with his father in July for a family reunion. The Anti-Rightist Movement had started in the PRC that year as a reaction to the Hundred Flowers Campaign. In August or September, when the anti-rightist policy was implemented, Fu Xuzhong was still in Hong Kong. Initially, he had intended to return to Beijing to finish school and had gone to Guangzhou to prepare for the journey north. Once there, however, he received a letter from a friend warning him not to return—given his background, he would be categorized as a rightist and be arrested. Thus, Fu backtracked to Hong Kong. He later realized that he was very fortunate. His friends remaining on the mainland suffered persecution for the next two decades.

In 1986, during the Zhao Ziyang regime, Fu Xuzhong was invited back to China. By this time, he had become famous for his written works. Returning to Shanxi University where he was warmly welcomed, he received the graduation certificate he should have earned previously, and he was finally able to feel the pride of graduating after 29 years.[40]

Phornprapha: From Picker to Industrialist

Typical of many Chinese immigrants arriving in Siam, Tan Tailong, the Teochew patriarch of the Phornprapha family, was a poor farmer from Chaoyang with nine siblings. Young Tailong's job in his humble village was collecting night soil to sell as fertilizer. Poverty eventually drove the newly married man to leave his ancestral village and sojourn overseas. He arrived in Siam in his late-teens around 1909.

Charoen Krung was still a dirt road then. Typical of Chinese immigration practices, his relatives who came from the same village housed him and contributed 5–6 satang to his start-up fund. Tailong became a coolie, doing all sorts of odd jobs, such as loading and unloading goods.

He noticed many pickers roaming the streets of Bangkok, collecting and buying bottles, old newspapers and other out-of-use items. He thought it was a good job for a young man like himself, as he could carry bigger loads than older men. Tailong went out early one day and started buying up all the used bottles. He carried his load to the second-hand shops lining the streets of Siangkong, the junkyard area of Bangkok, only to find that these shops only bought certain types of glass bottles and jars, of which he had very few. The rest of his heavy load was valueless.

That evening, the tired and hungry Tailong frowned at the 2 satang left in his dirty hand. The cheapest meal would cost him 1 satang, but that would mean he would not be able to afford to buy any more bottles the next day. So he decided to walk to the nearby shrine and fill his stomach with free drinking water. The day, at least, had provided him with a valuable lesson–not all the junk is the same! Thus began the tale of a family enterprise that evolved to become one of Thailand's largest industrial groups.

Tan Tailong proved to be a talented picker; soon he and his friends were co-investing in scraps and old, defunct mills. They dismantled them and then sold the parts. Tan Tailong's third son, Thavorn Phornprapha, born in China in 1916, admitted that he hardly ever saw his father, who seemed to be working all the time. From the age of six, Thavorn accompanied his father to Bangkok, making him fluent in Thai. By that time, Tan Tailong already owned a scrap shop

Tan Tailong and his wife.

called Tan Tonghuad in Siangkong. Thavorn remembered rolling out his collapsible bed next to the scrap-metal stockpile each night, and in the summer, when it was very hot, they slept out on the front porch. Life in the crowded scrap alley next to Chinatown was lively, recalled Thavorn, who is fond of boasting that he graduated from "Siangkong University"—it taught him to be street smart.

The children of Siangkong were taught how to be dealers of second-hand goods at a young age. Thavorn started to bid for goods when he was in his teens. Luang Raksa, the government auctioneer, was particularly fond of this charming and courteous young man; he would quicken his count in order to award the contract to Thavorn. In addition to being good at his job, Thavorn's good manners and trustworthiness gave him access to

The Phornprapha family, with Tan Tailong seated in the center and Thavorn on the far left.

many old houses on Siphaya, Surawongse and Silom roads. He managed to buy and sell old automobiles on a daily basis. Khun Sethbhakdi, another patron, sold all the equipment in his old rice mills to Thavorn.

Thavorn loved traveling, and just before the Pacific War, in 1936, he visited Japan with his friends. Noticing the cheap price of mechanical spare parts in Japan, Thavorn began to rethink his business strategy. Old scraps had limited supply but new manufactured goods had unlimited potential. Thus, after his return from abroad, Tan Tonghuad started to import new spare parts and bearings from Japan as well as sheet iron from Belgium. But the businessman's old "picker" spirit never died. After World War II, Thavorn traveled to England, Germany and the Netherlands to buy old military jeeps and trucks. He sent several shiploads of these vehicles back to the East and managed to sell almost all of them in Singapore.

In 1950, Thavorn left his family business and set up his own company, the Siam Motor Company, which later became the sole dealer of Nissan. Japanese cars were hardly known then, but he was convinced that they would sell in Thailand. Thavorn initiated the deal by ordering 60 trucks. Given his excellent connections in town, orders for buses and taxis soon followed. Thavorn initially confined his activity to marketing, but as import restrictions were imposed, he started assembling and, later, ventured into parts production.[41] Other Japanese joint ventures followed, such as Hitachi elevators, Daikin air-conditioning, NSK bearings, Yamaha, etc. "Sincerity and trustworthiness," a message he had given to his first Japanese partner, Nissan, stood the test of time. Thavorn Phornprapha became the chairman of the Federation of Thai Industries during the 1980s.

Thavorn Phornprapha was a trustworthy friend who acknowledged those who helped him become a successful entrepreneur. His memoirs read like a "Who's Who" of Bangkok. Both Sarit Thanarat and Phin Choonhavan helped during Tan Tonghuad's moments of crisis. Chalerm Chiewsakul, his life-long friend, helped him with translation during the Nissan negotiation. Suriyon Raiwa convinced him to become a Thai citizen. Chote Lamsam, then the comprador of Yokohama Bank in Bangkok, helped him clear his first imported shipment. Chin Sophonpanich, U Chuliang and Lim Juemeng in Singapore had all helped finance his deals. Dr. Kawamata of Nissan Motors and Mr. G Kawakami of Yamaha Motors were good partners. Most important, perhaps, was his wife, Usa, who kept a professional eye on the company's accounting and finances.[42]

The Srifuengfung Family: The Boys from Suphanburi

Kiarti Srifuengfung was born the eldest son of Phuyai Jui of Banglee, a small market town in the province of Suphanburi. Young Kiarti did not spend much time with his parents, as his father, a tailor, was always busy, and his mother was even busier attending to her "mom and pop" shop that sold almost everything. Thus, growing up, he was generally left on his own.

Reminiscing about his happy boyhood, Kiarti related to his daughter and biographer, Arunee Srifuengfung:

> *Our house in Suphanburi was an ordinary three-storey shophouse.... I remember my hometown was just like Venice in Italy. Every year when there was a high tide, we would have to vacate the ground floor of our shophouse, which became inundated with water. The whole town and small businesses would move up another floor as well. The mode of travel changed from foot to rowboats—a lovely sight though peculiar since the street became the river! That was very nice ... Suphanburi had very good food, especially fragrant and sweet mangoes, and a variety of fresh fish. At that time there were many fish in the river. It was so easy to catch them. All I had to do was throw some cooked rice into the water and swarms of fish would come. With a net and one scoop into the water I would catch more fish than I needed.*[43]

Kiarti Srifuengfung (standing on the right) with his wife, Janie, and his three children, together with Phuyai Jui, his father.

Kiarti's grandfather from China wanted his eldest and beloved grandson to learn Chinese, so he sent for a teacher from China to come to Suphanburi to impart to Kiarti the knowledge of the great civilization of China.

Thus, Kiarti was trained to write and memorize from the Confucian Classics. When he was 14, he was sent to the famous Xinmin School in Bangkok. The school provided no boarding, so he stayed at his father's friend's rice shop in Chinatown. In a biography of Kiarti, his daughter wrote:

Kiarti slept on the shop floor where the rice sacks were stacked. "Some nights I would be sleeping near the ground, but the next night I would be way up high, depending on the loading and selling of the rice sacks. It was a different bed arrangement every night ... The mosquitos were very ferocious and plentiful ... I was heard swearing at night that I would one day own my own building!" And by golly he did![44]

Two years later, his grandfather insisted that Kiarti must go to China to learn how to be a good Chinese. He studied in Shantou for a year but the town was too small for him. Meanwhile, he met a friend who was going to Hong Kong, so Kiarti tagged along and studied English at the famous Saint Stephen's College. He thrived in the excitement and cosmopolitan scene of Hong Kong. However, his fun was short-lived, for his grandfather soon came after him: "Grandfather was a traditional Chinese man. He complained to me that he did not want me to be Thai, so why was I studying English and being a European in Hong Kong? Together with my father he brought me to Canton to stay with a relative there and study at Beichan Middle School."[45]

Kiarti continued on to a university in Canton but had completed only one year of study when war broke out. Somehow, his family did not manage to transfer the funds needed for his tuition fees, so Kiarti enrolled in the Air Force. Because he was a Thai subject, he was placed with the American Allied Forces and was sent to Luke Field, Arizona, to be trained as an Air Force pilot.

Upon his return to the East, Kiarti had become a captain and was known among his peers as Captain Tom Cheng. He was sometimes lovingly called the "Runaway Captain" due to his leadership of a "bomb-and-run" group against the Japanese. (He had to "run" because the Japanese planes were light and more mobile than the large American planes). He was fortunate enough to be sent to the 14th US Air Force Base in Kunming, led by General Chennault, the commander of the famous "Flying Tigers."

Kiarti was a pilot at the US Air Force Base in Kunming.

"Wartime is a scary time, especially when your good friends are killed. My roommates are not the same every day," confided Kiarti who was a bomber pilot, cargo pilot, land-air survey pilot and a teacher at the Chinese Cadet School. "People think that I should be the first to die because I was such a daredevil, but I did not die," Kiarti said. This constant flirtation with life and death must have steeled Kiarti to throw aside his inhibitions and to live life the way he wanted—by his own rules. He made a name for himself, not in the conventional sense of a wartime hero, but as a first-class survivor.

After the war, Kiarti was fortunate to work as a liaison officer for Dr. Sun Foo, China's Minister of Justice, and also the son of Dr. Sun

U Chuliang, a prominent member of the Teochew Association.

Yatsen before moving on to the Canton Provincial Bank. When the bank tried to obtain a license to establish a branch office in Thailand, it did not succeed. Kiarti then offered to try again on behalf of the bank. After traveling to Bangkok, he discovered that his grandfather came from the same clan village as Luang Thamrong-Navasawad's father, so he asked to be introduced to Thamrong-Navasawad, the eighth prime minister of Thailand.[46]

The meeting went well for Kiarti, and the bank's license was granted in Kiarti's name for the Canton Provincial Bank. Kiarti established the branch office, which opened its doors to Bangkok's business community in 1946. Kiarti became the manager, but only for two years. When this bank closed after the Communist Revolution in China, Kiarti found himself without a job but with a bank license in his name. He approached the old guards of the Teochew Association, namely, U Chuliang, Khun Sethbhakdi and Udane Techapaiboon. This relationship soon created new investors for what was to become Bangkok Metropolitan Bank. In August 1950 Kiarti was appointed managing director of the bank.

However, Kiarti was too energetic to be "just a salary man." Later he became associated with Major General Pramarn Adireksarn, Field Marshal Pin Choonhavan's son-in-law. They established two insurance companies and two textile factories, including the Thai Teijin Company, a joint venture with Teijin of Japan. In the early 1950s, Kiarti also started Cathay Theatre Co., which subsequently evolved into the major finance and security company Cathay Trust.

Kiarti had always loved the sea, and he enjoyed traveling to the seaside on holidays. It was one of his holiday trips that inspired him to diversify into glass production. It all started when the pro-active Kiarti Srifuengfung noticed how white the beaches of Thailand were. Thailand is abundant in silica, the active ingredient in glassware, and the presence of high-quality silica was what made the beaches gleaming. Thus, Thailand boasted a natural comparative advantage in silica-related industries like glass, yet the kingdom had no glass factories. Kiarti suddenly saw his opportunity. In the late 1950s, he started forming joint ventures with foreign companies, and today the Srifuengfung family is the Thai partner of such major joint ventures as Thai Asahi Glass, Thai Caustic Soda, Thai Diamond Shamrock, Goodyear (Thailand) and Thai Occidental Chemical. In the mid-1970s, Kiarti sold his holdings in Bangkok Metropolitan Bank and withdrew from banking.[47]

In 1987, Kiarti—the joint venture king—was instrumental in establishing China's first float glass company, the Guangdong Float Glass Company, Ltd., in Shekou, Shenzhen Special Economic Zone. The project was a joint venture between Thailand, four Chinese state enterprises and the US Pittsburgh Plate Glass Company (PPG). On its opening day, Kiarti beamed with pride. Imagine how proud his grandfather would have been that his boy from Suphanburi had made it in the international arena.[48]

The key family members of Kiarti's team included his younger brother Boonsong Srifuengfung, who was chairman of the Thai-Chinese Chamber of Commerce for over 20 years between 1987 and 2008, and Kiarti's two nephews, Sombat Panichewa and Paibul Panichewa. The extended family is engaged in a wide range of businesses, including the Don Muang Tollway, but chemical-related manufacturing is still the hub of its activities.

Tiam and Saipin Chokwattana

The story of Tiam Chokwattana (or Li Hengtiam) and his wife Saipin is one of the most widely known success stories in Thailand. Tiam, the consumer products tycoon who founded the Saha Group, shared his modest start with seven siblings. Almost all the scenarios from the tale of his rise to fame are familiar to the Thai-Chinese community. The scene of his modest father, an immigrant from Puning, running a grocery store and his mother rolling cigarettes for sale were common images in Bangkok.

When he was 15, Tiam had to leave his studies at Peiying School to help his father in the shop, where he carried heavy sacks of sugar and other grocery supplies. Two years later, his father contacted a matchmaker to find Tiam a bride. Tiam's mother had just passed away, so his father felt he needed a daughter-in-law to attend to the household chores.[49] Matchmakers were common in Bangkok in those days and their habitual gathering place was Luang Nava Market in Bangrak.

Saipin's family, on the other hand, had a gold shop in Rajdamri. Her father

Saipin Chokwattana and her mother.

came from a wealthy family in Chaoyang. Her mother was a *lukchin* who grew up in Thailand and accompanied her father home to China, where she married Saipin's father. After giving birth to Saipin and her sister, Saipin's mother found the pressure of having to bear her husband a son unsettling, so she persuaded him to come to Bangkok.

He was a talented goldsmith, and in Bangkok they established a successful gold shop. Saipin attended the Xinmin School for three years before her parents asked her to quit her studies to help take care of the family. Due to her mother's efforts to have a son, Saipin had five younger sisters to take care of by the time she left school. When she was 19, the matchmaker approached her parents on behalf of Tiam. Saipin was hesitant because he was two years her junior, but according to Chinese custom it was a suitable match—the girl was supposed to be slightly older than the boy. She only agreed after Tiam paid them a visit, and peering at him from behind the curtain, Saipin found him to be a good-looking young man. Just before Saipin left the family shop in Rajadamri, her mother gave birth to a son, Damri Darrakanonda. It was a happy occasion indeed.[50]

Tiam turned out to be a resourceful man. He observed that in those days, provisional suppliers would wait for customers to call at their shops located in well-known commercial hubs. To get ahead of the competition, Tiam started visiting his customers and offering them his products. The "visiting salesman" was a new concept before the war, and his sales improved. Around 1940–41, Tiam and his father parted with the original *kongsi* shop they shared with relatives. Tiam set up a new grocery supply store on Yaowarat Road for his father, but his heart had always been in consumer products, which offered a much higher profit margin. In support of her husband, Saipin went to see her father and borrowed 20,000 baht. In 1946, Tiam opened Hiap Seng Chiang, a consumer product store, which became the forerunner of Sahapat, Thailand's largest consumer products conglomerate.

Tiam was a workaholic who was eager to learn new things, even in his old age. His motto was "a businessman must be a man of tomorrow, modern and always abreast of global trends." But Tiam was also known to be down to earth. He knew his market very well. Thus, it was the products for "the common man of tomorrow" in which Tiam became an expert. Detergent, toothpaste, soap, instant noodles, shampoo, socks, and underwear were among the list of products that Tiam manufactured for the masses.

Paiboon Damrongchaitham, chairman of GMM Media PLC, fondly recollected his days as a trainee in Sahapat when he accompanied Tiam on his frequent upcountry trips. Paiboon was asked to check Sahapat products at the confectionary

Tiam and Saipin Chokwattana with their two eldest boys.

corner of the local cinema. According to Tiam, the shop in front of the cinema, paying high rent, would make it their concern to know local customers well. Thus, their product selection was based first, on the popular items in the local community, and second, the product that the seller preferred because of the high profit margin. Tiam was careful to have both types of products on Sahapat's lists in order to capture the market and expand his customer network.

Tiam's lunch was always simple and brief, as he preferred to take long walks in the market to check on his products. Garbage bins got special attention, for Tiam would always check for leftover packaging, which in Tiam's opinion was the most accurate report on market share.

Like several successful Bangkok tycoons, namely, Chin Sophonpanich, Thavorn Phornprapha, Kraisorn Chansiri and Charoen Sirivadhanabhakdi, Tiam did not have the opportunity to study at a university. Charting the course for the next generation however, Saipin made sure all her eight children except one were well educated. Tiam sent Boonsith Chokwattana to work in Osaka right after he graduated from Peiying and Wat Sutat schools. Boonsith is now the president of Saha Group, a business worth 100 billion baht and 100,000 employees as of 2012.

Lin Taishen (林太深): A Path Out of China

Lin Taishen was born in Chao'an in the Chaozhou region in 1939. After China was liberated in 1949, the Thai government started to curb Chinese immigration. Travel between Bangkok and Shantou came to an almost complete halt by the 1960s, and Lin Taishen could not join his father in Bangkok. However, in Lin's hometown, his family was victimized for being well-to-do. In 1955, Lin left Chao'an for Guangzhou to further his studies. Unlike universities, secondary schools collected tuition fees, which Lin's father sent from Thailand. But life in China was hard, especially when famine struck in 1958 and then again in 1961. In 1965, just before the Cultural Revolution, Lin and his three friends decided to leave China. To do that they had to get across the border to Macau.

The route from the mainland to Hong Kong via the New Territories was closely guarded by soldiers and army dogs. Lin and his three friends took a bus from Guangzhou to Shunde and then walked the hilly route south during the night for fear of being arrested. After seven days, they arrived at a tiny bay east of Zhongshan prefecture called Tang Jia Wan (唐家湾) where they swam the rest of the way to Macau. In order to float in the water, Lin tied three plastic balls together for use as a life jacket. In those days, tens of thousands of people tried to swim out, but success was not guaranteed. Approximately one third would perish at sea, drown or be shot dead. Those captured were punished. Lin's group left at nightfall, but one friend was arrested before he could reach the water.

Lin Taishen remembered that he had to swim for six hours, avoiding villages with lights, before he landed in Macau territory. He and his friends had neither relatives nor friends, so they went to the police for help. In those days, a UN organization cared for refugees escaping from China. Lin believed that altogether there were more than a hundred thousand refugees who swam to Macau.

Intending to join his father in Thailand, Lin stealthily entered Hong Kong by hiding underneath the floorboards of a boat. If captured, he would surely be deported back to China, as Hong Kong police were strict about illegal immigration and trafficking. Lin observed that the laws were somewhat strange: the police would arrest any illegal attempts to enter Hong Kong onboard a boat, but if the refugee managed to land in Hong Kong without being captured, they could walk up to the police and seek assistance. The police were helpful and even

"Nang Loi" fragrant water.

provided Lin Taishen with travel documents.

In Hong Kong, Lin's father, Akom, sent him some money to buy a plane ticket to Bangkok. People who had no money would usually be stuck in Hong Kong, as at that time labor was very much in demand. Thousands of refugees, including women, swam across the sea to the outside world. Most people who immigrated to Thailand already had family in the kingdom.

Lin Taishen's family tale in Thailand was no less intriguing than Lin's escape. The family had been the producer of "Nang Loi" fragrant water, which has been widely used in Thailand for over two generations, especially during the Songkran festival. Lin's grandmother, Hiang, a *lukchin* born in Siam, was given the recipe for the traditional fragrant water by her friend who worked in the palace. The product sold well and became an established name of Thai fragrance.

Hiang married Lim Baengnam, a Teochew from Chao'an, and became pregnant. Baengnam was jubilant at the prospect of becoming a father. Although he had a wife in China, they had no children. As a son, Baengnam had a filial duty to carry on the family line; having no children by his first marriage, he could not fulfill his moral obligation to his ancestors. He prayed to his ancestors to grant him a son so that he could fulfill his filial responsibilities and soon his prayers were answered.

His Thai wife bore him a son whom she named Akom. However, his wife was naturally attached to her first-born son and would not hear of being separated from the child. Lim Baengnam had a dilemma. Surely his old parents wanted to see their new grandson. All his friends abided by the custom of sending their sons—especially the first-born—back to China to be educated and raised in the proper Chinese way. Many Thai women who married Chinese had to bear the pain of being separated from their young children. But his wife would not hear of it.

Left with no other recourse, Baengnam kidnapped his one-year-old son, Akom, when his wife was unaware and departed on a ship to China. After having ceremoniously discharged his filial duties before his ancestral tablets and delighting all his family, Baengnam left Akom to be raised in his Chinese home and returned to Bangkok to face his wife, whose anger seemed to know no bounds. All he could do was to promise to give her many more children to make up for the loss of her first born. Ultimately, the storm passed and Baengnam continued to live with his wife until he died.

Lim Baengnam's wife in China took good care of Akom and raised him well. Akom Ta-Chiangtong was a filial son to both mothers but he finally returned to live in Bangkok and carried on his mother's legacy in turning *nam ob* "Nang Loi" into a Thai household brand.[51]

Zhuang Meilong: The Chinese Opera Master

One evening in October 2006, the stage curtain of a theater in Guangzhou opened to reveal the familiar stage props of the Chinese opera. The performance that evening was a Bao Gong story.[52] The sound of drums and gongs ushered in two characters, the dark-faced elderly Bao Gong and his nephew, Bao Mian. An elderly mother and her daughter-in-law followed. When the actors began to sing, the audience let out a cry of approbation. They could not understand a word of their favorite opera. It was all in Thai!

The composer and the director of the first Thai-Chinese opera was Zhuang Meilong, well known in Thailand as "Meng Por Pla," the actor in the 1996 award-winning energy-conservation commercial. His Thai name is Amphan Charoensuklarp. Amphan was born into a Chinese working-class community in the Samyan-Sapanleuang area. His mother was a great fan of Chinese opera and Amphan had been exposed to Chinese opera performances since he was a baby. He often snuck out to volunteer to train with the local troupes when they came to perform in his neighborhood.

After the liberation of China in October 1949, many Chinese students living overseas returned to China. Despite warnings from their parents, who had suffered hardship and destitution in China a generation earlier, these young minds believed they could create a better world and personally enjoy a better future in China. Amphan, who went to Singhfah Chinese School located at Chula Soi 15, felt the same way.

Amphan knew he needed to go away to pursue a career in song and dance, which was considered a "profession with no future" in Thailand at the time. The Chinese in Thailand, including his father, looked down upon those who made their living as performers. Moreover, Amphan had heard good things about the People's Republic of China from his teachers and friends. It was a new society where one got to eat well and live well. Education was free for everybody. Being in China meant he had the chance to study music and his favorite performing art, the Chinese opera.

Although Amphan lived comfortably in Bangkok, his curiosity got the better of him, and he decided to accompany his friends to China. His father, who was a progressive man, was the founder and committee member of the Singhfa School.[53] He subscribed to the *Quanminbao*, a left-wing newspaper, to follow the anti-Japanese news and later the civil war in China. Hence, it was not difficult for Amphan to convince his father to support his plan and pay for all his traveling expenses. His mother cried for 11 days begging him not to go. It was 1957 and he had just turned 16.

Although all regular transportation between Thailand and China had already been terminated, Amphan left on one of the last direct ships to

Zhuang (front row, second from the left), with his classmates in Shantou.

Communist Shantou that had been granted special permission by the Thai government in 1957. His friends who had instigated the trip all opted out, as they could not obtain permission and the necessary financial support from their parents. Amphan was thus alone in his quest to study Chinese music.

Back then, after the Bandung Conference, shiploads of *huaqiao*, especially those in Southeast Asia, were returning to China. Not knowing what China was like because he was born in Thailand, Amphan was personally curious. Coming from Samyan, a densely populated Chinese area in Bangkok, Amphan noticed that there were not many returnees from Yaowarat, the old Bangkok Chinatown. Amphan supposed this was because they were either too rich or too well established to leave Bangkok. However, in China, he met many Thai-Chinese teenagers coming from the northeast and the south. He was surprised how naïve he was to think that the Chinese only lived in Bangkok.

During the first few months, Amphan was homesick. Life in China was poorer and more difficult than in Bangkok. However, the education was good and free and Amphan was determined to pursue his dream of a career in music. First he went to Shanghai but stayed for only two days. Finding the language difficult to understand, Amphan moved south to Guangzhou, Xiamen (formerly known as Amoy) and Shantou. Teochew was his family's tongue. He joined a performing troupe in Guangdong and studied at the same time. It was stage acting, not Chinese opera, but he had a chance to learn about Chinese opera as well. Later he joined a Teochew Chinese Opera troupe in Shantou. Guangdong and Teochew opera are different not only in language but also in music and instruments. In China, Amphan learned script writing, song and music composition, and directing.

After eight years, Amphan decided to return to Bangkok. The Communists practiced segregation and were always suspicious of outsiders. Because they regarded him as Thai, not a local-born Chinese, a prevailing atmosphere of suspicion hampered his freedom of movement and behavior. Moreover, people were poor and often hungry. He missed the freedom and abundance he used to enjoy growing up in Thailand, and he yearned to return to Bangkok.

However, coming back was difficult. One needed permission from the government, which was quite difficult to get. Some people risked their lives and escaped China by swimming to Hong Kong because they could not get approval to leave the country. Amphan (or Zhuang Meilong) submitted his request to travel to Thailand many times. Fortunately, an acquaintance helped to process the approval.

Amphan arrived back in Bangkok in 1964, just after Field Marshal Sarit Thanarat passed away. Thailand was in the mist of the Cold War and traffic between Thailand and China had dried up. However, Chinese opera was still very popular. The majority of the operas were Teochew, with one or two Hainan operas performing at the Hainan shrines.

Chinese opera had always been the main event that drew crowds to worship at the shrines on special events and festive seasons. Every province in Thailand had a Chinese shrine, and in 1964, there were about 40–50 Chinese opera troupes working in the country. However, the number of troupes declined substantially after many shrines replaced operas with movies.

In those days, there were no Isan performers. However, starting in the 1970s, due to the scarcity of Chinese-speaking performers, trainers of Chinese opera troupes started recruiting non-Chinese singers from the northeast. Despite their language deficiency, these recruits were very talented and could perform by memorizing the lines. They all came from the same village called Noensoong in Nakhon Ratchasima.

Before Amphan left to be educated in China, there were five Chinese opera theaters in Yaowarat. However, they gradually disappeared, due to the dwindling audience numbers. By 1964, there was only one theater left: Lao Yee Lai Chun Bang. Apart from the regular performances on offer at Lao Yee Lai Chun Bang, the only remaining occasions for Chinese opera performances were on religious festival days at the shrines of Chinese deities and at local Chinese associations. In an attempt to attract larger audiences, a Thai narrator was often hired to interrupt songs to translate the Chinese lines into Thai. This was for the benefit of the new generation who could no longer understand Teochew and other Chinese dialects. However, the interruptions were often clumsy and disruptive to the momentum of the performance.

In spite of these challenges, there was still potential for Chinese opera in the contemporary period as the Chinese cultural legacy remained strong, and every time there was political upheaval,

After the liberation, many Thai-Chinese students returned to China to study, including Amphan Charoensuklarp, seated in front in this 1959 photo of overseas-Chinese students from Thailand and Cambodia.

political satire in the form of Chinese opera would be staged.

The famous Ngiu Thammasat is a good example. Ngiu Thammasat existed long before Thai-Chinese opera. Amphan used to help Seni Pramoj (the three-time prime minister of Thailand) by teaching opera gestures and conventions to the actors. However, Amphan insists that Ngiu Thammasat cannot be considered Chinese opera. It is political satire with the superficial trappings of Chinese opera. The actors are not trained in opera vocal skills; they are performers dressed in classical Chinese costumes and airing a political message in Thai. There is no singing, no melody and no music, only free-style dialogue to the accompaniment of drums and gongs. Chinese opera, on the other hand, is a performing art with a mixture of many kinds of skills, including the art of dancing, singing and talking, as well as the art of makeup, costume and musical instruments. However, the fact that Ngiu Thammasat had become a tradition in the most prestigious political university in Thailand reflected the deep-rooted Chinese cultural legacy in Thai politics.

According to Amphan, Chinese opera originated in the Han or Tang dynasty. Ngiu, a name that Thais use for Chinese opera, might be derived from *youling* in Mandarin. *Youling* were comedy actors who put on makeup and costumes to mimic officials and noblemen. Short, one-man shows were later developed and turned into full-cast performances with music, scripts and many actors. By the Ming dynasty, the shows were more complete with composers and scripts. The stories were also more complete with male and female protagonists and villains. Chinese opera in Mandarin was called *xi* or *ju*.

By the time Amphan started his career in Bangkok in 1964, Yaowarat opera houses had mostly disappeared. However, the owner of Chaloemrat Theater in Soi Plaengnam hired an opera troupe from Hong Kong to perform on a short-term contract because there was still an audience. Amphan joined forces with a Chinese opera *towkae* to set up a new troupe in Yaowarat. In 1970, they signed a contract for three or six months and hired Thai actors. Amphan was both the composer and director. He started his new opera experiment of catering to local crowds by producing Chinese opera with stories set in modern Bangkok and dialogue performed with a mixture of Teochew and Thai, but all the rhymes were sung in Teochew.

From his experience in Yaowarat, Amphan concluded that the local people liked to watch Chinese opera. The obstacle was that the new generation of Chinese in Thailand could no longer understand Chinese. Amphan pondered whether he should compose a piece in the Thai language. The opportunity to do so presented itself in 1982 when Chansamorn Wattanavekin commissioned him to write a Thai-Chinese opera for the Bangkok Bicentennial Celebration with Princess Sirindhorn as the guest of honor at the gala opening. Thus, the first

Amphan (seated in the front row, wearing a bow-tie,) with a Teochew opera troupe in Bangkok, 1965.

Chinese opera in Thai, *Bao Gong Executes His Nephew, Bao Mian* was composed. It proved to be very popular.

Thirty-two years later, the piece is still being performed by 10–20 Chinese opera troupes. It has become a piece of Chinese performance art that everyone in Thailand can enjoy. Amphan holds the copyright on the rhyme but he does not mind if it is performed by other opera casts.

Amphan went on to produce *Dayu Tames Huanghe* for the king's 72nd birthday. Dayu was the first emperor of China who built a dam on the Huanghe River to prevent floods. Dayu's son was the first emperor of the Xia dynasty. Amphan compared King Bhumibhol to Dayu, the man who loved and devoted himself to his people. He felt that the people of Thailand were lucky to have such a devoted king. Currently, there are about 30 Chinese opera stories written about life in Bangkok.

"To save this special form of performance art in Thailand, we need to establish a Chinese opera school to teach people who are interested in the art and the beauty of Chinese opera," were the master's wise words to the Thai public.[54]

KRAISORN CHANSIRI
Story by Nirandorn Narksuriyan

Kraisorn Chansiri (or Tan Hangsu) was born in 1935 in a small village named Dakeng in Chaoyang district, Guangdong, China. Due to the persecution suffered by his family for being in the landlord class, Kraisorn decided to move to Hong Kong before finally emigrating to Thailand in the early 1960s. Today Kraisorn Chansiri, chairman of Thai Union Frozen (TUF), is listed among the world's top business leaders by *Forbes*.

In a speech given at Chulalongkorn University in April 2013, Kraisorn shared his life story—a rare occurrence—and attributed a major part of his success to Thailand, the country that gave him the opportunity to succeed in life:

> *My life started here (in Thailand), with three zeroes. No education, no money and no credit.*
>
> *First Zero: Although I had some schooling in China when I was very young, I had to leave school because of poverty. I did not have the privilege of attending a school in Thailand. Not for a single day.*
>
> *Second Zero: I came empty-handed. (After working on odd jobs) I managed to accumulate 10,000 baht to start my own business.*
>
> *Third Zero: I had no credit. I was an unknown poor man. Even though I was willing to pay the exorbitantly high interest rate of 2 percent per month (24 percent per annum), nobody wanted to give me a loan.*

Kraisorn started his career in Bangkok as a tea boy, messenger, salesman and office boy. In 1965, he got 10,000 baht from a "revolving share," a traditional means of raising money among the Chinese, which he invested with two other friends in the establishment of his first company importing car wax and paint. He later co-invested with his friends in an automobile repair shop in Sapan-Kwai, which he managed. The group expanded into textile trading in 1973.

All of this, however, seems an unlikely start for a giant seafood conglomerate billionaire. In 1977, Kraisorn bought a failing tuna cannery with 150 employees and annual sales of US $1 million. Over the ensuing decades, a few financial crises occurred, each laden with opportunities for his company to grow. According to Kraisorn, when the baht devalued "in 1997 our profit doubled (with revenue earned in American dollars and costs in Thai baht). The company share price jumped from 3–4 baht to 17–18 baht. After the crisis, known to posterity as the 'Tom Yum Kung Crisis,' we took over Chicken of the Sea in the US. That was the first time I had my own international brand."

Kraisorn recalled triumphantly that this success was all because he had refused to take out loans in American dollars before the crisis: "I did not have any USD loan, even though my financial advisor pestered me every day to convert our loan to USD. But I did not agree. Although we had a one-year contract, I terminated the advisory service just after 6 months. A few months later, the Asian Financial Crisis broke out and the financial consultant's firm went bust." TUF, which has been listed in the Stock Exchange of Thailand since 1994, was seen as a hot company in 1997. Many foreign banks offered to finance the company's expansion plan. However, in early 1997, Kraisorn became concerned over the possibility of the Thai baht devaluing and canceled the plan at the last minute. He admitted that if he had taken that American dollar loan, he would not be here today. "I don't like talking to financial advisors," he says. "Listening to their plans may convince me to do something I should not have done. Deep down, my own business sense told me then, no—not to commit to an American dollar loan."

Dr. Kraisorn was the Olympic torch bearer for both Thailand and China where he was given honorary citizenship.

His son, Thiraphong Chansiri, explained TUF's conservative approach to *Asiaweek* a few years later: "We stick to what we are good at. We didn't go out and buy hotels, didn't branch out into telecommunications. We are in the seafood business . . . a few years back, we were the stupidest company in the market . . . people asked why we did not borrow and expand."[55] The family decision to remain debt-free set the company apart when the Thai government went through with the devaluation.

Again, during the US "Hamburger Crisis" in 2008, Kraisorn worried that the financial situation would get out of hand. He called meetings to implement preventive measures to minimize the damage to his corporation. Later, Kraisorn proudly announced that in 2008, the company did not suffer but in fact thrived. Its profits increased 25 percent, and then 52 percent in 2009, while the share price jumped from around 30 baht to 60 baht. Thiraphong explained, "Our tuna business generally becomes flat when the economy is in high-growth mode, as people opt for other foods. But whenever the economy is in bad shape or grows slowly, our business thrives." A year later, as the result of the financial crisis, the Chansiri family spotted a golden opportunity for a takeover of MW Brands ("MWB"), one of the European leaders in tuna and other seafood products with the iconic brands John West, Petit Navire, Hyacinthe Parmentier and Mareblu. The fair market value for the company was €800 million but Kraisorn discovered that his competitor was weak. He bid at only €680 million and won. Moreover, the exchange rate in September 2010 when the transaction took place was more favorable than the studied period. The price of the Euro fell from 50 baht to 40.3 baht. "We were very lucky . . . altogether we managed to save over 7 billion baht in this deal," Kraisorn says.

Kraisorn is very proud that his company, Thai Union Frozen Product PLC, is now the leading global seafood expert with factories all over the world. Its success was achieved through hard work, careful planning and a few miracles. Thus concluded the chairman of TUF, "It's time to give back to the community. Large and small donations make equal merit. What counts is the goodwill of the donor. We must give back to the society." In 1985, when Kraisorn went back to China to visit his relatives, he donated towards road construction in his home village. Since then, he has continued to support the building of hospitals, schools and scholarships for hundreds of poor students. The Shantou authority named Kraisorn Chansiri an honorary citizen.

In 2008, when the Olympic torch passed through Thailand on its way to China, Kraisorn was one of the torchbearers relaying the torch through Yaowarat, Bangkok's Chinatown, representing the Thai-Chinese community. Later, when the torch passed through Shantou, Kraisorn was also invited by the town council to be an honorary torchbearer as well. It was an appropriate recognition from both Thailand and China of a man who had contributed so much in helping to bring about economic prosperity to both nations.

NEW BEGINNINGS

(1975–PRESENT)

The 1970s were a historic period of transition for both Thailand and China. As the United States exited commitments across Asia, Thailand wound down its Cold War alliance with the US and renewed its friendship with China, which had re-emerged on the international stage. Symbolic of this new rapport, Thailand's Princess Sirindhorn, who is fluent in Chinese, became a very popular, unofficial ambassador to China. The economic boom that swept over both China and Thailand in the late 1980s and 1990s created new business opportunities for a large number of Thai-Chinese entrepreneurs. The first official foreign investor to come through China's newly opened door was the Thai-Chinese-run agribusiness company, CP Group. Its CEO, Dhanin Chearavanont, is frequently cited as Thailand's richest person today. Thai-Chinese businessman Charoen Sirivadhanabhakdi, whose core business is the beverage sector, emerged as another leading business tycoon and philanthropist, while telecommunications heavyweight Thaksin Shinawatra made a fateful move to focus on politics, a career change that also changed the course of Thai history.

In 1972, the historic meeting between US President Richard Nixon and China's Chairman Mao Zedong took place in Beijing. Reminiscent of Geneva in 1954, the immediate effect was an end to China's pariah status in the international community of nations.[1] Overnight, China regained international standing.

In the early 1970s China had no diplomatic relations with any of the five members of ASEAN. The breakthrough came in mid-1974, when Malaysia and China recognized each other.[2] Through the good offices of Malaysian rubber tycoon Lee Intong, Malaysian Prime Minister Tun Abdul Razak went to meet Chairman Mao, following in the footsteps of US President Nixon.[3] After the US defeat in the Second Indochina War and the fall of Saigon, Thai Prime Minister Kukrit Pramoj also visited Beijing in July 1975.[4]

Hot upon the heels of the withdrawal of US hegemonic power from Southeast Asia, Thailand had switched her support to the state that would clearly become the next regional hegemon: China. Thailand became the third ASEAN country to establish diplomatic relations with the PRC after the Philippines. Over the next decade more than 40 countries recognized China, and the PRC regained her seat as a permanent member of the UN Security Council, replacing Taiwan.

Even when the Thai military retook power in a bloody coup d'état in 1976, nothing was done to jeopardize Thailand's newfound friendship with Beijing. After the fall of Vietnam, the US withdrew from Mainland Southeast Asia to its sole remaining bases in the Philippines. In the resultant, regional power vacuum, the USSR established a strong military presence in Vietnam.[5] As Soviet influence grew, China's de facto alliance with the US against the USSR caused ASEAN states to lean on China.

Chapter opening picture: Yaowarat Road, the main street of Bangkok's Chinatown.

Prime Minister Kukrit Pramoj presents gifts to Chinese Communist leader Mao Zedong on their historic meeting on 30 June 1975.

Meanwhile, after effecting China's strategic re-positioning in the evolving Cold War world order, both Zhou Enlai and Mao Zedong passed away in 1976. Their deaths symbolized the passing of an era in Chinese history. The departure of the two Communist giants among the old guards paved the way for the fall of the Gang of Four and the return to power of the former secretary general of the CCP—Deng Xiaoping.

Deng, who had been rehabilitated in 1973 in the aftermath of the Cultural Revolution, had witnessed the shift in direction of Chinese foreign policy. More of a shrewd pragmatist than a rigid theoretical Marxist, Deng was aptly suited to continue in the new direction of foreign policy that Mao had set for China. By the time Deng had fully consolidated his succession to power in post-Mao China, relations with Vietnam had begun to cast an ominous shadow over Southeast Asia.

Containing Soviet Influence

In November 1978, Vietnam signed a Treaty of Friendship and Cooperation with the Soviet Union, which provided for consultations in the event that either was "attacked or threatened . . . with a view to eliminating the threat."[6] Emboldened by Soviet support and China's untested new leadership, Vietnam launched an invasion of Cambodia in December 1978, causing considerable panic in Thailand and other ASEAN states.

For Deng, the Vietnamese invasion represented a test of the mettle of the new China after Mao. Demonstrating tough resolve and reassuring ASEAN neighbors that China was a reliable ally, China's new leader retaliated with a punitive invasion of Vietnam in February 1979. Deng's shrewd willingness to use military means to check the expansion of Soviet and Vietnamese influence in the region helped to reinvent China's image as a champion not of revolution but of the regional status quo—an image that China was at pains to project. Although Chinese forces withdrew from Vietnam, China continued to allay Thai security concerns by pursuing a policy of containment against Vietnam.

Beijing initiated an alliance with Bangkok to supply Khmer Rouge forces fighting the Vietnamese. The Thais opportunistically extracted a price in return for allowing the transit of Chinese arms through Thai territory. China had to accede to the Thai request to end its support for the insurgency led by the Communist Party of Thailand and to close down the clandestine radio station in Yunnan, from which the exiled Thai leader Pridi Banomyong used to broadcast.[7] China also pledged to come to Thailand's aid in the event of a Vietnamese invasion. This was exactly what the Thais wanted to hear.

In the 1980s, the military cooperation between China and Thailand was strengthened by Thai purchases of Chinese heavy weapons—including surface-

US President Richard Nixon (second right) conferring with Mao Zedong (center) as Prime Minister Zhou Enlai (left), National Security Adviser Henry Kissinger (right), and an interpreter look on during a historic meeting on 2 February 1972.

to-air missiles and naval vessels—at friendship prices.[8] Throughout the 1980s Southeast Asia remained split between the "Indochina bloc" of Vietnam, Laos and Cambodia, backed by the USSR, and the ASEAN countries supported by China and the US.

US Withdrawal Symptoms

Meanwhile, the OPEC oil shock of 1973, the withdrawal of US forces from the region and the fall of Saigon, Phnom Penh and Vientiane to Communist armies, as well as the subsequent intensification of the war in Indochina after 1979, together exercised a negative impact on the Thai economy. Having prospered in the 1960s by riding on US military-economic expansion during the Vietnam War boom, it was naturally hard-hit by the post-war withdrawal of American forces, US companies and drying up of US aid.

In the bleak economic landscape that unfolded in the aftermath of the Vietnam War, there were few Chinese success stories. The triumph of Communism in Laos, Cambodia and Vietnam stoked panic in Bangkok as rumors spread that Thailand could become the next domino to fall. Many affluent families sold their properties and emigrated to the US to escape Communism. Economic confidence was at an all-time low. Few people wanted to invest or start new businesses.

But one overseas-Chinese family stood out as an example that bucked the trend. This was the Chearavanont family who founded Charoen Pokphand Group (CP), one of Asia's largest conglomerates. Owned today by Dhanin Chearavanont and his family, the conglomerate started with Chia Tai, a modest seed store founded by Dhanin's father, Chia Ekchor, in the 1940s. Chia Tai was located in Bangkok's Chinatown and underwent rapid expansion during the 1960s and '70s. By the 1970s, CP had a virtual monopoly on the supply of chicken and eggs in Thailand.[9]

The economic situation continued to deteriorate further during the early '80s; the second OPEC oil price hike swelled Thailand's foreign debt and triggered inflation. Yet CP continued to expand remarkably well throughout this period. By the 1980s, the CP Group had over 60 companies in Thailand spread across poultry, pig-raising, feed-mills and other related agribusinesses. Not only did CP expand in Thailand but it also started similar ventures in Hong Kong, Indonesia, Malaysia, Taiwan and Singapore. Nevertheless, in Thailand, the overall situation was bleak—a banking crisis was compounded by a pyramid loan scandal; the baht was devalued and the commander-in-chief of the army threatened to launch a coup on primetime TV. By 1985, the country was slipping into recession, and in 1991 political disorder was culminating in yet another coup d'état.[10]

Thai Political Disunity

The political situation reflected severe disunity among social and political elites, embroiling national leaders in partisan rivalries and undermining their ability to deploy state power effectively. The seeds of Thailand's modern political divisions were sown at the turn of the century when King Chulalongkorn's reforms spawned "new" elites. These new elites consisted of state-centered bureaucrats and the modern standing army, which challenged both royalty and nobility and eventually toppled the absolute monarchy in 1932. The royalty and nobility, which comprised the traditional ruling class, were replaced by new bureaucratic and military elites, many of whom were ethnic Chinese involved in the Peoples' Party.

However, the royalist forces diminished by the military and bureaucratic elites in 1932 made a return during the post-war period. After the Pacific War, the 1949 constitution gave the monarchy back many of its powers that had been taken away by the 1932 revolution.[11] King Bhumibol Adulyadej returned from his education in Europe and, following his wedding, was formally crowned in 1950. Subsequently, following the coup d'état in 1957, a US-brokered alliance between the court and Field Marshal Sarit Thanarat led to a blossoming of royal power and influence in the country. Under the protective umbrella of the new royalty-military partnership, the old anti-royalist legacy of 1932 was suppressed. The military faction associated with Phibun and the Soi Rachakru clique was purged from its power base in the state apparatus.

Large state enterprises, which were the hallmark of the Phibun era and represented the economic base of the old military clique, were scaled back by Sarit. In sharp contrast to Phibun's National Socialist, public-sector-centered economic model, Sarit aggressively promoted the private sector. Sarit encouraged private business as the new engine of economic growth, enabling business to emerge as another new, elite social formation. In addition to the kingdom's pre-war elite

Soldiers patroling the streets of Bangkok to deter demonstrators and rioters after the election in 1957.

structure comprised of royalty, the bureaucracy and the military, a new member joined the kingdom's elite club—the predominantly Thai-Chinese business elite.

Under the Sarit-Thanom-Praphat military administration, the resurgent business sector became more institutionalized and complex. By the late 1960s, metropolitan business interests had become a powerful force in their own right, capable of challenging the powers that be. That challenge arrived in 1973. metropolitan conglomerates empowered by the economic growth of the late 1950s to early 1970s turned against the ruling military elite to rid their boards of rent-seeking generals and, in alliance with the student movement, toppled the military government of Thanom and Praphat, ushering in a period of democratic politics.[12]

Under the aegis of Thailand's new democracy, victorious metropolitan business interests formed political parties that competed directly for state power. The rise of political parties introduced yet another new social formation into the kingdom's elite matrix: party elites. After suffering a reactive setback in the counterrevolution of 1976, political parties and party elites gradually revived to become a dominant force in modern Thailand's political landscape.

The challenge posed by new party elites to the hegemony of traditional bureaucratic and military elites was captured in a poignant remark by General Suchinda Krayprayoon, who led the coup d'état in 1991: "A military officer has dignity ... and will not submit to politicians ... I am supposed to have breakfast with the prime minister (Chatichai Choonhavan) ... every Wednesday ... but I do not go. Why should I go? I do not bow to politicians. I cannot lower myself."[13] In fact, post-1973 Thai politics may be viewed, in the words of Bendict Anderson, as "the struggle of the bourgeoisie to develop and sustain its new political power against threats from the Left and Right."[14]

As electoral politics became institutionalized, new business interests from the provinces embodied in local established families and upstart *chao phor* (a term that means "godfather" and refers to organized crime groups) tended to penetrate nascent political parties and capture them from within.[15] Dissident military factions took the cue and jumped on the bandwagon, forming new parties of their own in alliance with provincial business interests. During the democratic and semi-democratic period of the 1980s, parties became new vehicles of elite mobilization driven by the political ambitions of provincial business elites and dissident generals. By the 1990s, Thailand's predominantly Chinese, bourgeois elite could no longer be labeled as "pariah entrepreneurs" playing second fiddle to their bureaucratic and military counterparts.[16]

The bourgeois elite, through the vehicle of political parties, had come into its own as a political force, capable of challenging and displacing traditional elites for dominance over Thai politics. In contrast to the Phibun era, Thai bureaucratic and military elites with pretensions of native superiority toned down anti-Chinese appeals to strike up new partnerships with business counterparts in Bangkok and the provinces. Unlike neighboring countries, business-cum-party elites encountered no obstacles in promoting their members to the highest political office of premiership—even those who were predominantly ethnic Chinese, including Banharn Silpa-archa and Chuan Leekpai. Such an opportunity for ethnic Chinese would be quite inconceivable in Indonesia and Malaysia.

The institutionalization of political parties further heightened squabbling, competition and rivalry, intensifying elite disunity. As provincial business interests increasingly dominated the Lower House, metropolitan conglomerates feared that they would be challenged in their own markets. Consequently, after aligning with democratic forces during the mid-1970s, metropolitan conglomerates abetted the conservative Class 5 military coup d'etat in 1991 against the Chartchai government, which largely represented provincial interests.[17]

The struggle among political parties to capture state power was reflected in their efforts to manipulate strategic processes in the coercive, judicial and bureaucratic arms of the state apparatus and in the regulatory agencies previously regarded as the traditional preserve of civil and military elites. Ruling parties infiltrated the Bank of Thailand, seeking insider information and regulatory favors; the independence of the National Economic and Social Development Board (NESDB) was compromised and its governing board purged.[18] Ministers transferred senior officials from key bureaucratic posts and state enterprise boards, replacing them with partisan appointments.[19] The most resented form of external intervention invariably concerned civilian attempts to cut the military budget and

From top, Field Marshal Sarit Thanarat, Field Marshal Thanom Kittikachorn, and Field Marshal Praphat Charusathien.

manipulate annual military promotions and personnel reshuffles. Cabinet attempts to influence military reshuffles and promotions sparked the 1991 coup d'état.

The resultant effect of external interference, intervention and regulatory capture was to reduce the effectiveness of state-centered actors who inevitably sided with competing party interests striving for control over state resources for the benefit of coalition partners and party bosses. Consequently, the Thai state became less able to assist the national leadership to address political, economic and financial crises. The state's limited capacity was reflected in the quality of economic planning, provincial administration and monetary management in the face of the 1997 Asian financial crisis.

Reinventing Leviathan

Back on the China front, Deng Xiaoping sought to end China's policy of isolation, which had been in place since the Cultural Revolution. The Moscow-Hanoi Axis established in November 1978 must have prompted Deng to hasten the normalization of relations with the US in December of the same year.[20] Ten days later, Vietnam invaded Cambodia. China's cross-border military engagement with Vietnam during the invasion of 1979 exposed the shortcomings of the Peoples' Liberation Army (PLA) in terms of equipment and modern military technology. Meanwhile, Soviet military doctrine, equipment and technology had undoubtedly improved the fighting capability of the Vietnamese army.

China had to make swift moves towards modernization. Deng began to seriously implement Mao Zedong's policy on the Four Modernizations. The First Modernization was in agriculture. Collective farming was phased out in favor of families producing for a free market in agricultural produce.[21] The Second Modernization was to make space for private industry in China's Communist economy. Private industry was to be allowed to compete with state-owned enterprises. The emphasis of this new private industry was on "improved technology," which comprised the essence of the Third Modernization. Finally, the Fourth Modernization was to modernize the military, whose weaknesses were exposed during the military engagement with Vietnam.

In tandem with the policy of the Four Modernizations, Deng moved to quickly lift the bamboo curtain, which had fallen on China after the Communist victory in 1949. Unless China opened its doors to the West to encourage foreign investment, technology transfer and tourism to bring in much-needed

A Chinese Army trooper stands guard outside the US Embassy in Beijing, opened on 1 March 1979 following the normalization of relations between China and the US.

foreign exchange, the policy of the Four Modernizations was bound to fail. China formally opened her doors to foreign investment in 1979.

The first official foreign investor to come in through China's open door was none other than the Thai-Chinese agribusiness company CP, which received Foreign Investment Certificate No: 0001 in the Shantou and Shenzen Special Economic Zones. By 1996, CP had operations in every single Chinese province and had become the largest foreign investor in the PRC. Known in China as the Zhengda Group, CP had more companies and more types of businesses than anyone else in China's newly opened Communist economy.[22]

Deng's convictions about the necessity for China to open herself up to the West in order to encourage progress was further confirmed 12 years later when the Gulf War shocked Beijing by demonstrating just how high-tech modern warfare had become. In the face of US weapons superiority, the PRC had little capacity for force projection beyond its shores. Meanwhile, throughout the 1980s and 1990s, the wealthier countries in Southeast Asia had significantly increased their own defense spending, most of it on the latest weapons systems.[23]

For the US, its de facto alliance with China enabled the country to extract itself from a losing war in Vietnam. After Nixon's visit to China, American withdrawal was just a matter of time, although it was unexpectedly hastened by the sudden collapse of the South Vietnamese regime, forcing the US to make an ignominious exit from Saigon in 1975.[24] On the other hand, extracting itself from a costly and unwinnable war in Vietnam enabled the US to make a fresh beginning in addressing its main adversary in the Cold War—the Soviet Union. For the USSR, attempts to fill the power vacuum left behind by the US after its withdrawal from Southeast Asia and increase its regional influence were not particularly successful.

Following Vietnam's invasion of Cambodia in 1978, the US and China pressured Vietnam economically and politically through trade embargoes and vetoes on multinational financial lending. Deng Xiaoping pursued a strategy of bleeding Vietnam into submission. Meanwhile, a US disengaged from Vietnam was able to focus its energies and resources on wearing out the Soviet Union in Afghanistan and undermining the Soviet economy by forcing it to keep up with the arms race. In the end it was the Soviet Union that proved to be the weak link in the chain of the Moscow-Hanoi Axis. The conflicts that developed between an overextended USSR bogged down in Afghanistan and an overextended Vietnam approaching economic collapse was more than the alliance could bear.

Under severe pressure, Vietnam agreed to withdraw from Cambodia by the end of 1989. Following a secret summit between China and Vietnam at Chengdu in 1990, the latter pledged to resolve the Cambodian problem in ways that China wanted. The turn of world events gave the Vietnamese little choice; faced with a

North-Vietnamese armored car crossing the railings in order to capture the presidential palace in Saigon on 30 April 1975.

Soviet Union on the verge of collapse, Vietnam had no other option but to rebuild relations with China.

With the end of the Third Indochina War, relative peace and social tranquility returned to the region, creating the foundation for renewed economic growth in the Asian region. Even the negative repercussions of the Tiananmen massacre in 1989 did not halt the momentum of China's accelerating economic growth.

Asia Rising

The economic boom that swept over China and Thailand came as a surprise. The World Bank and pundits had predicted a bleak economic outlook for Asia. But contrary to institutional predictions, the recession bottomed out quickly, followed by a strong economic upturn. Not only China and Thailand surged ahead in the late 1980s—Malaysia and Indonesia were also on the upswing. So were Vietnam, the Philippines and even Myanmar, though on a lesser scale.

The driving force was Japan. To overcome the second oil crisis, Japan had lowered and held down its exchange rate to export its way out of the oil crisis. In so doing, Japan built up huge trade surpluses with her trading partners, especially the US. Japan's trading partners cried foul and ganged up to force Japan to revalue the yen. In four years after the Plaza Accords of October 1985, the yen rose 89 percent against the US dollar.[25]

To escape the value of the yen, Japanese firms moved manufacturing out of Japan to the US, Europe and Asia. Between 1986 and 1993, Japanese firms invested US$47 billion in Asia to manufacture goods for export.[26] These investment flows spread export-oriented growth to Asian economies and gave rise to the Asian export model of development. China and Thailand were to become the leading exponents of export-led growth, flooding Western markets with cheap goods.

In Thailand the economic recession started bottoming out after the mid-1980s, although the effect was not immediately felt. By the late '80s the Thai economy was racing along at a double-digit pace. The resultant growth of the national economic pie suddenly created a win-win situation with enough surplus wealth and opportunities to share among rival elite groups. Elite disunity was temporarily swallowed up in a frenzied scramble to maximize opportunities to benefit from a rapidly expanding economy. Like the Tiananmen Square crackdown, the 1991 coup d'état and resultant loss of civilian lives created barely a splash in the swelling river of economic growth.

Thai entrepreneurs responded quickly. Within a few years they were exporting their way out of the recession by producing low-cost products, including garments, bags, canned fish, jewelry and plastic goods for the world's markets. Riding on the backs of Japanese investment, Thai companies were going global. Among the most spectacularly successful pioneers of globalization was a fourth-generation Hakka *lukchin* named Thaksin Shinawatra.

Thaksin represented the nouveau riche spawned by Bangkok's booming stock market, real estate revolution and expanding telecommunications sector. The economic base of this new breed of entrepreneur was quite different from the old moneyed class, including the royalty, old banking families, commodity traders and import substitution manufacturers of the Phibun and Sarit eras. The new capitalists disdained the conservatism of the old royalist-oriented establishment, while the latter despised the sharp, semi-legal business practices of the parvenu capitalists epitomized by Sia Song[27] and Thaksin Shinawatra.

In 1988, Thaksin ran a nascent company that sold computers to government departments. It performed better than most because of Thaksin's extensive kin, alumni and colleague networks in the bureaucracy, which had been built during his former career in the Royal Thai Police. From his computer company base, Thaksin expanded into technology-based businesses that thrived on growing urban demand for pay television, mobile phones, paging systems and data transfer facilities.[28]

In December 1993, Thaksin launched Thailand's first communications satellite and diversified into television broadcasting and telecommunications. Thaksin sourced his technology from all over the world: his cable TV service relied on US programming; the mobile phones were Scandinavian; the paging system was Japanese, and the Shinawatra satellite was made in the US, mounted on a French rocket and shot up from South America.[29]

Beginning in the late 1980s, Thaksin began to expand his

An early picture of Thaksin Shinawatra, the founder of IBC cable television company. He went on to become the prime minister of Thailand before being ousted by a military coup in 2006.

businesses into neighboring countries, including Vietnam, Laos, Cambodia, Burma and even further afield. Between 1985 and 1995 he had accumulated assets worth 70 billion baht.[30] Financially savvy, he used the stock exchange to expand his capital base. After 1988, he floated four companies, which by 1995 had a combined capitalization of over 200 billion baht. Thaksin's rapid rise to become one of the richest and high-profile success stories in the country has become something of a legend in Thailand.

Reflecting the pattern of symbiotic dependence between business and politics, Thaksin's dramatic accumulation of wealth translated into a formidable source of political financing. Initially supporting the Palang Dharma Party, led by Chamlong Sirmuang, Thaksin quickly displaced Chamlong as party leader. From the stepping stone of the Palang Dharma Party, Thaksin soon founded his own political party—the Thai Rak Thai (TRT) Party.

Thaksin deployed his new TRT Party to contest the 2001 general elections. After defeating the Democrat Party in a landslide victory, Thaksin capped his business success by becoming prime minister. The 2001 general elections ushered in the most politically divisive and controversial civilian administration in Thai history. Thaksin's legacy has left a heavy imprint on elite disunity in Thai politics and created a deep polarization between pro-democracy followers, who regard elections as the ultimate source of political legitimacy, and their challengers, who saw the Thaksin governments and its allies as corrupt and subsequently helped topple the elected government under the banner of "Defending the Monarchy."

In the ideological war of democracy versus monarchy, the battle line was drawn between two large camps. On the one hand, the TRT Party and the Northern-Northeastern Red Shirt Movement represented the upper half of the country. On the other, the Democrat Party, the Pro-Monarchy Yellow Shirt Movement, the middle class, and bureaucratic and military elites represented metropolitan business and southern provincial interests. The two opposing camps appeared to be equally matched. One side had the overwhelming electoral mandate of the people. The other enjoyed the support of the most powerful individuals and institutions in the country. Ironically, both sides traded accusations of dictatorship against each other. The opposition labeled the Thaksin-backed administration as a "parliamentary dictatorship" whilst the elected government alleged the opposition wanted to replace democracy with a military dictatorship.

Neither side could overcome the other despite the use of every political method in the book, including street protests, non-violent demonstrations, police crackdowns, court actions, judicial dissolution of government, political killings and counter-killings, and other forms of violence. Consequently, the political struggle resulted in a long stalemate, punctuated by the overthrow of three elected TRT governments and two coups d'états, in September 2006 and May

2014 respectively. The last one resulted in martial law and put a stop to the street protests that had paralyzed the capital city. Following the coup d'état in 2006, Thaksin was forced into exile. He now lives in Dubai but alledgedly remains constantly "connected" to TRT party executives in Bangkok, whom he directs via smart phone.

The People's Alliance for Democracy (PAD) or Yellow Shirts (left) and the United Front for Democracy against Dictatorship (UDD) or Red Shirts (right).

"The roaring nineties" also catapulted several new Thai overseas-Chinese business groups onto the global stage.[31] All of the top 10 richest Thais in the 2014 *Forbes 500 List* were families of Chinese descent, namely Chirathivat (Hailam); Chearavanont (Teochew); Sirivadhanabhakdi (Teochew), Yoovidhya (Hailam), Ratanarak (Teochew), Chaiyawan (Teochew), Bhirombhakdi (Hokkien), Prasarttong-Osoth, Maleenont (Teochew) and lastly, the Shinawatra (Hakka).

Less politically controversial than Thaksin Shinawatra but even more successful entrepreneurially was Dhanin Chearavanont, scion of the Teochew founding family of the Charoen Pokphand Group (CP). Avoiding political controversy, CP moved quietly but swiftly to position itself at the head of Asia's kitchen, insinuating itself into every step in the chain of food production from seed to servings of pre-cooked, ready-to-serve packaged food that feeds the on-the-go, growing, urban, Asian middle class. CP currently has production units in over a dozen countries in Asia, Europe and North America, as well as trading offices in most of the major cities of the world. By the mid-1990s, the overall group turnover was estimated at US$7 billion and growing at 10–15 percent annually.[32]

However, the mega-tycoon that captures headlines today is Charoen Sirivadhanabhakdi, the founder of a relatively new business group, ThaiBev. Charoen Sirivadhanabhakdi is a new face among the Thai-Chinese business elite. As the current chairman of Thai Beverage PLC (ThaiBev), Charoen has captured the public imagination through his glitteringly successful takeovers of numerous companies, not only in Thailand but also internationally, including Fraser and

Neave (F&N), hotels in the UK, Goldenland PLC, Sermsuk, Asia Books, Oishi Group, Univentures PLC, Southeast Insurance Group, Plaza Athénée Hotel and Berli Jucker PLC.

Charoen's strategy, based on American-style mergers and acquisitions (M&A), is to take over proven, successful companies. Today, ThaiBev is perhaps the fastest growing Thailand-based business group. Charoen's mastery of the use of M&A techniques have led pundits to dub him Thailand's "Takeover King."

Charoen's mission is to secure a leading position in the global beverage business. With the advent of the ASEAN Economic Community in 2015, Charoen is eyeing the opportunity to expand his customer base from 65 million consumers in Thailand to serve the potential demand of an estimated 600 million consumers and trading partners in the greater ASEAN market. The beverage industry is Charoen's core business; it is the industry in which he spent his formative years honing and perfecting his strong business instincts and acumen, both of which were to serve him well in the business rivalries and expansion of later years. Charoen's rise to become Thailand's most personable and charismatic mega-tycoon embodies the classic pattern of the overseas Chinese journey from scrabbling to riches. Charoen, whose Chinese name is Sou Hiogmeng (蘇旭明), is the sixth of 11 children born to a Chinese street vendor who sold fried mussels in the alley next to Peiying School. Growing up in the neighborhood, Charoen naturally attended the Peiying School next door to his home. However, he left school after only four years of primary education to pursue his passion for retail. Among his earliest efforts, he sold pencils and exercise books to students.

When he was still in his youth, a relative of his father found him a job at Sura-Mahakhun, a liquor distillery belonging to Sahas Mahakhun (Tia Langsing) and Udane Techapaibul. His apprenticeship at Sura-Mahakhun exposed him to the harsh realities of business rivalry. He soon learned about business politics and

Top: Chaoren and his wife, Khunying Wanna Sirivadhanabhakdi.

Bottom: A Thai Beverage PCL (ThaiBev) truck transporting Chang beer leaves the company's Beer Thip brewery in Ayudhya.

THE SIRIVADHANABHAKDI FAMILY

The family of Charoen and Khunying Wanna Sirivadhanabhakdi; (from left) Thapana and his wife, Paphatchya; Wallapa and her husband, Soammaphat Traisorat; Atinan and her husband, Chotiphat Bijananda; Thapanee and her husband, Aswin Techajareonvikul; and ML Trinuch and her husband, Panot.

Charoen finds his greatest support in wife, Wanna, whom he met at an evening accounting class and would play badminton with. Both of them were second-generation *lukchin* raised in the heart of Chinatown in the '50s and '60s. Growing up during the Cold War when China was a closed country, they shared a common outlook: they were proud of being Chinese but loyal to their adopted country, Thailand.

Khunying Wanna, Charoen's wife, is also a very capable executive who has worked alongside her husband in his rapid rise to fame and fortune. She is now the chairperson of the Imperial Hotels Group, as well as vice chairman of TCC Holding, the major investor in ThaiBev, Southeast Insurance, TCC Land and Berli Jucker. It was Khunying Wanna who has been responsible for human resource development and coordinating ThaiBev Group's corporate social responsibility (CSR) activities. She started the group's environmental program by replanting forests and establishing medical centers in far-away provinces where ThaiBev has facilities. For the 60th anniversary celebrations in 2007 for King Bhumibol Adulyadej accession to the throne, the Sirivadhanabhakdi Foundation donated over 2,400 million baht in construction and medical equipment for the Bhumirajanakarindra Kidney Institute Hospital founded by Khunying Wanna.

Charoen also finds corporate opportunities to do things together with his wife. Some of Charoen's and Khunying Wanna's most successful ventures are in real estate and hospitality. In a rare interview given to the press, Charoen denied that he was a real estate speculator; his investment strategy has always been long-term. Charoen has been buying real estate since 1967, when he was still a career executive. He found troubled assets challenging and took pride in turning them around. To help out friends and business partners, he often took over their problematic projects. Senanivet housing estate, Mae Ping Hotel in Chiang Mai, Pantip Plaza, Imperial Hotels Group, Plaza Athénée New York, Asiatique, Univentures and Goldenland are among his prime real estate deals. "I believe in the future of Thailand," was the simple explanation given to the press about his real estate acquisition.

In recognition of the contributions Charoen and Khunying Wanna have made to Thai society, King Bhumibol Adulyadej bestowed the surname of Sirivadhanabhakdi in 1982. The family has five children. Charoen's eldest daughter, Atinant, looks after Southeast Insurance and is supported by her husband Chotipat Bijananda. Wallapa Traisorat, his second daughter, looks after TCC Land with her husband Soammaphat Traisorat. His eldest son, Thapana, is now the chief executive officer (CEO) of ThaiBev. The youngest daughter, Thapanee, with her husband, Aswin Techajareonvikul, runs Berli Jucker PLC (BJC); and his youngest son Panot looks after the group's agriculture business and is the CEO of Univentures PLC and Frasers Centerpoint Limited.

ethics. During his apprenticeship, Charoen witnessed firsthand the shareholder battles that often spilled out of the confines of the boardroom and into the street. At Sura-Mahakhun, the conflicts between Sumet Techapaibul and Taleng Laochinda (Charoen's direct superior) that had been brewing since the 1970s eventually led to the violent whisky wars between the Mekhong and Hong Thong brands in the early 1980s before the rival groups merged in March 1986.

Like Sun Tzu, Charoen must have learned his lessons well in the art of (shareholder) war in the battleground of Sura-Mahakhun and the protracted whisky wars, which dragged on for years and caused heavy losses for both Mekhong and Hong Thong. It was Charoen's vision and management that convinced the conflicting parties that by merging they would be profitable and sustainable. The final outcome of the whisky wars was marked by the withdrawal of both Sumet and Taleng[33] from the liquor industry, leading Charoen to gain controlling interest after the government liberalized the alcohol industry in 2000. Charoen consolidated all the distilleries and its supporting operations to form Thai Beverage Company Ltd in 2003 and later listed on the Singapore Exchange in 2006.

Charoen's charming, bright and humble personality won him many friends among powerful bureaucratic, political, military and business elites. Among his most steadfast backers was Jiu Rungseng. Father of his wife, Khunying Wanna, he used to work for Kamron Techapaiboon, head of Maha Nakorn Bank. Jiu Rungseng assisted Charoen in arranging for finance at a critical juncture in the mega-boardroom battles. Jiu was also a personal friend of Chin Sophonpanich— Thailand's banker par excellence.

Charoen credits his father–in–law as one of two benign influences, in addition to his lessons in business hardball, that helped shape his life. (The other and perhaps most important was his own grandmother, to whom he was very attached.) Like the Chinese general of the Warring States, Sun Tzu, Jiu Rungseng was passionately fond of Chinese calligraphy, poetry and proverbs. The precious pearls of wisdom that Jiu imparted to Charoen were embodied in four traditional Chinese attributes: *ren* (忍), or patience and endurance; *rang* (讓), knowing how to bend; *jing* (靜), being calm; and *le* (樂), being content and enjoying life.

The 1997 Financial Crisis

Thailand's economic bust in 1997 came as a shock. With hindsight, pundits tended to argue that all booms naturally had to come to an end. However, before the crash, warning voices were few. The legacy of elite disunity had already taken its toll. Political interference and regulatory capture by special interests had reduced the effectiveness of government agencies. The financial crisis challenged the country's regulatory bodies and found them wanting. The professionalism of the Bank of Thailand, for example, in handling the hedge funds' attack on the Thai baht left much to be desired. In a misguided effort to prop up the baht, the BOT squandered nearly half of the country's foreign reserves.[34] Even when critics were not surprised by the occurrence of an economic downturn, they were completely unprepared for the severity of the 1997 Asian Financial Crisis.

In the wake of capital flight, liquidity crises and falling asset prices, there was no decisive, paramount national leader, like Prime Minister Mahathir of Malaysia, who could ramp up damage control of the externally driven, volatile capital flows. In the wake of the leadership vacuum, the IMF prescribed a remedy in the form of its standard stabilization plan, which proved to be worse than the disease it was intended to cure. Following the IMF-imposed deflation program, the Thai economy shrank at a frightful speed, the baht lost its value by half and foreign debt rose higher than total GNP.[35] Almost an entire generation of entrepreneurs— mostly Chinese who had created and accumulated wealth for the country—was wiped out almost overnight.

The 1997 bust that started out in Thailand was aptly dubbed the Tom Yum Kung crisis. The Thai bust rapidly spilled out into the region, causing the economies of Indonesia, Philippines and South Korea to collapse like dominoes. The economy of Malaysia escaped the worst effects of the crisis largely because the Malaysian government rejected the IMF-proposed stabilization program and acted unilaterally to close the country's capital account. Another country that weathered the 1997 crisis well was China.

China's resilience to the Asian economic crisis was due to the fact that the Chinese never surrendered the economy completely to market forces. Having seen how market forces had destroyed the Russian economy following the transition from communism to democracy, Deng Xiaoping had implemented economic liberalization gradually. Deng had always resisted pressures for democratic reform and cracked down brutally on pro-democracy protestors at Tiananmen in 1987.

China's economic reforms were achieved under the aegis of tight dictatorial control. Unlike the disastrous experience of Russia, economic liberalization and political liberalization were never allowed to occur together in China.

Similar to Southeast Asia, the 1990s were a decade of economic development for China as well. The Chinese economy grew at an average rate of 10 percent throughout the decade. This was comparatively higher than the growth rates in most Southeast Asian

Prime Minister Chavalit Yongchaiyudh calls in business leaders to discuss the crisis hitting the Thai economy. Charoen Sirivadhanabhakdi (seated, second left) and Dhanin Chearavanont (seated third left) are both in attendance.

countries, especially towards the end of the decade due to the impact of the 1997 economic crisis.

China's rapid economic development was fueled by massive foreign investment—much of it coming from Taiwan and the Chinese diaspora in Southeast Asia. In the 1990s, Southeast Asian investment in China rose absolutely and proportionately, with the fall-off of Western and Japanese investment following the Tiananmen massacre of pro-Democracy protestors. The principal increase occurred between 1991 and 1994 and increased steadily through 1998.[36]

The dominance of overseas-Chinese investment in China reflected the fact that overall, wealth and ownership of liquid assets by overseas Chinese were expanding greatly as Chinese business groups took advantage of globalization, as was the case in Thailand. In fact, overseas-Chinese capital within ASEAN countries became more important than combined foreign investment in driving the region's economic development. As the share of foreign ownership in the Southeast Asian economy fell, overseas-Chinese ownership increased in absolute terms in most ASEAN countries.

China again sought to attract overseas-Chinese capital and trade for the benefit of China's Four Modernizations, just as the Qing dynasty and the nationalists had done in the early 1900s. In fact, it was even easier for the PRC to do this in the 1990s because nationality was no longer a sensitive issue as it had been in the early 1900s. Ethnic Chinese in Southeast Asia were citizens of the host countries in which they resided with no longer any call on China. Overseas Chinese felt less insecure about their ethnicity, and at the same time, they felt naturally encouraged to invest in China, where they possessed advantages in speaking Chinese as well as access to clan and trading networks. By 1997, foreign direct investment (FDI) in China was almost double the figure for Southeast Asia.

For some overseas-Chinese business groups like CP, operations in China rapidly became more important than operations in Thailand. In addition to expanding its agribusiness throughout China, CP also diversified into motorcycle production, real estate, oil refining, distribution and retailing, telecommunication, construction materials, banking and other industries. CP even added basic capabilities in music, television and film production and sponsored the popular

Dhanin Chearavanont.

TV program in China in the early 1990s, *Zhengda Zongyi*, a variety show.[37]

As Southeast Asian business groups' operations in China became predominantly important, Southeast Asian governments naturally grew concerned, especially because ethnic Chinese controlled a disproportionate amount of national wealth in the host countries where they resided. The old specter of the divided loyalties of the overseas Chinese again reared its head, and the primary loyalties of the Chinese began to be questioned once again by their host governments.

Consequently, CP's endless fount of capital and its large influence on the Thai

CP Group's Super Brand Mall in Shanghai.

economy have generated suspicion of the company being a front organization of the PRC government.[38] Dhanin Chearavanont himself has not done much to dispel this image of CP and continues to sponsor visits by Chinese opera and other cultural troupes to Thailand, as well as acting as a diplomatic go-between to help resolve problems between Bangkok and Beijing. Perhaps to dilute its Chinese image, CP used the occasion of a press conference on an official project launch in China in August 1996 to declare itself a Thai conglomerate. Subsequently, it has arranged for the Thai monarch's popular daughter, HRH Princess Maha Chakri Sirindhorn, to go to China to inaugurate CP projects under the banner, "Wherever CP Group goes to invest we raise the Thai flag to display our pride of being Thai."[39]

As China becomes increasingly successful and powerful economically, the implications of Chinese dominance over the region become more obvious. The most current projection claims that China is on the verge of becoming the world's largest economy. The IMF estimated that by the end of 2014, China's economy would surpass the US in size: China will be valued at US$17.63 trillion versus America's US$17.42 trillion based on purchasing power parities.[40]

However one construes the IMF estimate, there can be no question of China's rise to superpower status. China's growth rate, at 7.4 percent in 2014, still far outpaces the rest of the advanced economies in the world. As China's economic power increases, so too does its military potential, provoking growing regional unease and stimulating increased military spending by ASEAN states, including Malaysia, Vietnam and the Philippines, whose relations with China have been soured by conflicting claims to the islands of the South China Sea. The fact that Thailand is among the ASEAN states with no outstanding contradictions with China over the South China Sea augurs well for the future of Thai-China relations.

HRH PRINCESS MAHA CHAKRI SIRINDHORN

Princess Maha Chakri Sirindhorn meets with Deng Xiaoping, Chinese Vice Chairman, during her visit to Beijing in May 1981.

In October 2009, China Radio International (CRI) organized a cyber-selection event for the "Top 10 International Friends of China." After 56 million votes had been collected, Henry Norman Bethune's (1890–1939) name was at the top of the list. Bethune, a Canadian physician, served in the Communist Eighth Route Army during the Second Sino-Japanese War and brought with him modern medicine to rural China. He often treated sick villagers as much as wounded soldiers. His selfless commitment to the Chinese people made a strong impression on Mao Zedong, prompting the Chairman to write Bethune a eulogy. Chinese students were required to memorize the eulogy for generations afterward, and statues in Bethune's honor can be found in cities throughout China. On the same top 10 list as Bethune was HRH Princess Maha Chakri Sirindhorn of Thailand.

The princess, who is the third child of King Bhumibol Adulyadej and Queen Sirikit, obtained a Bachelor of Arts in History from Chulalongkorn University in 1976, and a Master of Arts in Oriental Epigraphy (Sanskrit and Cambodian) from Silpakorn University in 1978. She also obtained a Master of Arts in Pali and Sanskrit from Chulalongkorn University in 1980, with a thesis entitled "Dasaparami in Theravada Buddhism." In an interview in Beijing, the princess told a Chinese Radio International reporter that it was her mother, Queen Sirikit, who suggested that she should study Chinese next.

Studying Chinese in a classroom with no opportunity to practice proved difficult. The opportunity to improve her studies came when she accepted Premier Zhao Ziyang's invitation to China. Thus, in 1981, the princess became the first high-ranking Thai royal from the House of Chakri to visit the Chinese mainland. Summing up her feelings before embarking on her first China visit, she said, "For us, China is mysterious and far away, which stimulates our curiosity." The trip was a resounding success for both countries. One of her hosts, the frail Deng Yingchao, Zhou Enlai's wife, got along so well with the young princess that she got up from her seat despite her doctor's warning, participating in toast after toast of the best spirits. To date, over 60,000 copies of the princess's memoir on this landmark visit have been sold to raise funds for over 23,000 scholarships in Thailand.

Over the years, the princess has become fluent in Chinese and has made over 43 visits to China. Counting both official and unofficial visits, she could claim that she had been to every province in China. But perhaps her more important legacy is her written works. Numerous travelogues and almost 10 translations of Chinese novels penned by Princess Sirindhorn are widely read in Thailand today. They help the Thai form a clear view of modern China. The princess observed, "Novels were a good way to learn more about a foreign country. Although a work of imagination, there is always an essence of reality perceivable in the background."

Voted by the Chinese public as one of China's "Top 10 International Friends" in 2009, HRH Princess Maha Chakri Sirindhorn delivered the following speech in Beijing—in fluent Chinese:

"A real friend is more valuable than any treasure in the world. Friendship is the driving force for the development of peace. I firmly believe that if only people from different countries live harmoniously, and treat each other as friends, can we realize our hope of creating a more peaceful, graceful and civilized world."

Her Royal Highness Princess Maha Chakri Sirindhorn at the Great Wall Museum during her nine-day China visit, in April 2011 in Qinhuangdao, Hebei Province of China.

GLOSSARY OF NAMES

Sino-Thai names in this book are those used in Siam, which may be Thai, Teochew, Hokkien, Hakka, Hainanese, Cantonese or Vietnamese.

NAME USED IN SIAM	PINYIN	CHINESE
CHAPTER 1		
Chao Krua Ngen (Tan [Ngeng])	Chen [Yin]	陳 [銀]
Chen Yizhong	Chen Yizhong	陳宜中
Jeen Chulee-Samutpakdi (Chen Zhaokua), luang	Chen Zhaokua	陳昭誇
Fei Xin	Fei Xin	費信
He Bahuan	He Bahuan	何八歡
He Yaba	He Yaba	何亞八
Li Dan	Li Dan	李旦
Lim Tohkiam	Lin Daoqian	林道乾
Lim Goniao	Lin Guniang	林姑娘
Ma Huan	Ma Huan	馬歡
Phraya of Tak (Pi Ia Tak/Pi Ia Sing)	Pi Ye Da/ Pi Ya Xin	披耶達 / 丕雅新
Srisombat (Ong Hengchuan), luang	Wang Xingquan	王興全
Xie Wenbin	Xie Wenbin	謝文彬
Zheng Chenggong (Koxinga)	Zheng Chenggong	鄭成功
Zhou Daguan	Zhou Daguan	周達觀
Zheng He	Zheng He	鄭和
Zheng Jing	Zheng Jing	鄭經
Zheng Zhilong	Zheng Zhilong	鄭芝龍
Zheng Zongxing	Zheng Zongxing	鄭宗興
CHAPTER 2		
Ng Kiam/Ng (Jeen Jiam)	Huang Qian	[黃謙]
Chao Krua Lian	See Rachasretthi Jeen (Tan Liang), phraya	
Jo Sue Gong (shrine)	Zu Shi Gong/Qing Shui Zu Shi	祖師公 / 清水祖師
Hien Su	[Xian Shi]	[賢士]
Hoac Nhiem	Huo Ran	霍然
Kraikosa (Lim Riksh Krairiksh), phraya	Lin [Le/Luo]	林 [勒/洛]
Lim Gongseng (Governer of Chantabun)	[Lin Gongsheng]	[林功盛]
Mac Cuu	Mo Jiu	鄭玖
Mac Khoan	Mo Kuan	鄭寬
Mac Sung	Mo Chong	鄭崇
Mac Thientu	Mo Tianci/ Mo Shilin	鄭天賜/鄭士麟
Mac Tuhoang	Mo Zihuang	鄭子潢
Phibulvanich (Lim Boonbing), luang	Lin Wenbing (Xixian)	林文炳 (希憲)
Phichaikosa (Na Lai), phraya	[Lan Lai]	[藍來]
Rachasretthi Jeen (Tan Liang), phraya	Chen Lian	陳聯
Ratanathibeth (Jeen Gun), chaophraya	[Jun]	[君]
So Siang Chatikavanij	Su Xiang	蘇祥
Sawasdiwari-Chim (Lim Im), phraya	Lin [Yin]	林 [蔭]
Sri Racha Arkorn (Tan Teckngeng), phraya	Chen Deyin	陳德銀
Tae Yong	Zheng Yong	鄭鏞
Tan Heng Banomyong	[Chen Xing]	[陳興]
Tan Seng Banomyong	[Chen Sheng]	[陳盛]
Tan Seng-U Banomyong	Chen Shengyu	陳盛于
Tran Thai	Chen Tai	陳太
Tu Dung	Xu Yong	徐湧
Hao Yiang Na Songkhla	Wu Rang	吳讓
CHAPTER 3		
Aphai-Vanich (So Jat Chatikavanij), luang	Su Zei	蘇賾
Anukulsiamkit (Tan Kimcheng), phraya	Chen Jinzhong	陳金鐘
Choduk-Rachasretthi (Chong, Ng Tienjong), phraya	[Huang Tianzhong]	[黃天鐘]
Choduk-Rachasretthi (Thongjeen Krairiksh), phraya	Lin [Tong Zhen]	林 [通真]
Gim Jeng (company)	Jin Zhong	金鐘

Gim Lohchae Posayananda	[Jin Luoxing]/Jin Dianqi	[金羅星] / 金典綺
Koh Guan (company)	Gao Yuan	高源
Phichaikhiri (Boon Hui Na Songkhla), chaophraya	Wu Wenhui	吳文褌
Pichai-Waree (Ng Mung Kanlayanamitra), luang	Huang Huan	黃緩
Prasert-Vanich (Tae Poh), phra	Zheng Bao	鄭寶
Prasert-Vanich (Tae Tiangseng), phra	Zheng Zhansheng	鄭展盛
Ratanasetthi (Kaw Sujiang Na Ranong), phraya	Xu Si Zhang	許泗璋
Raj- "Captain" (Lim Hoi), luang	Lin Hai	林海
Raj-Supawadee (Ng Daotoh, Chao Sua Toh Kanlayanamitra), phraya	Huang Dao	黃道
So Heng Tai (company)	Su Heng Tai	蘇恒泰
Tae Jiao	Zheng Zhao	鄭昭
Tae Hok	Zheng Fu	鄭福
Tae Hood	Zheng Fo	鄭佛
Tae Hua	Zheng Hua	鄭華
Tae Meng	Zheng Ming	鄭明
Tae TienBi	Zheng Tianbi	鄭天壁
Vichienkhiri (Hao Tienseng na Sonkhla), chaophraya	Wu Tiansheng	吳天生
Visetphakdi (Hao Tienjong na Sonkhla), phraya	Wu Tianzhong	吳天鐘
Wichit-Pakdi (Jeen Piew), khun	[Biao]	[標]
Kaw Simbee	Xu Xin Mei	許心美

CHAPTER 4

Amnartsingkhorn (Oh Keechuan), luang	Hu [Qiquan]	胡[其全]
Aramsakornket (Tan Tam, Tan Giaktam), luang	Chen [Tan]/Chen [Yutan]	陳 [談] / 陳[玉潭]
Chareon Rachaton (Theng, Lau Mahteck Laohasretthi), phra	Liu Made	劉媽德
Cheu (jeen)	Liu Chunzheng	劉淳正
Chinkananurak (Tan Julai), phra	Chen Zhulai	陳珠來
Chi Yi Gun	Xu Mei Zhang/Xu Erjun	徐美章 / 徐二君
Choduk-Rachasretthi (Huad, Li Guatchew Jotikabukkana), phraya	Li Fazhou	李發洲
Choduk-Rachasretthi (Min, Lau Chongmin Laohasretthi), phraya	Liu Congmin	劉聰敏
Choduk-Rachasretthi (Fak, Lim Fak), phraya	Lin [Fu]	林 [福]
Choduk-Rachasretthi (Thian, Liu Kianhin Jotikasthira), phraya	Liu Qian Xing	劉乾興
Choduk-Rachasretthi (Pook, Li Hok Jotikabukkana), phraya	Li Fu/Li Chengde	李福/李成德
Choduk-Rachasretthi (Phong, Li Taipong Jotikabukkana), phraya	Li Tai Peng/Li Dizhen	李泰鵬/李迪振
Jui Buay Niao	Shui Wei Niang	水尾娘
Chung Kengquee	Zheng Jinggui	鄭景貴
Ghee Hin (secret society) also known as Ghee Heng (Teochew pronunciation)	Yi Xing	義興
Ghee Hok (secret society)	Yi Fu	義福
Guan Tit Lee (mill)	Yuan De Li	源得利
Hai San (secret society)	Hai Shan	海山
Hon Wong Kong (shrine)	Han Wang Gong /Han Wang Miao	漢王宮 / 漢王廟
Huay Chung Long (steamship terminal)	Huo Chuan Lang	火船廊
Lau Beng Seng (mill)	Liu Ming Cheng	劉鳴成
Hoo Ahkay	Hu Yaji/Hu Xuanze	胡亞基 / 胡璇澤
Gim Seng Lee (company)	Jin Cheng Li	[金成利]
Gim Tung Hok Kee (trademark)	Jin Tang Fu Ji	錦堂福記
Gim Tung Huad Kee (trademark)	Jin Tang Fa Ji	錦堂發記
Kin Tye Lung (company)	Qian Tai Long	乾泰隆
Koh Hong Lee (mill)	Gao Feng Li	高豐利
Koh Nguanseng	Gao Yuan Sheng	高元盛
Koh Mahwah Kovattana	Gao Manhua/Gao Chuxiang	高滿華 / 高楚香
Koh Poh Gim	Gao Jin	高金

419

Khunying Sun (Huang Kunde) Yuktanandana	Huang Kunde	黃坤德
Leng Nei Yi (temple)	Long Lian Si	龍蓮寺
Lee Tit Guan (company)	Li De Yuan	李得源
Man Fat Cheung (company)	Wan Fa Chang	萬發昌
Nguan Seng, akorn	[Yuan Sheng]	[源盛]
Phasisombat (Jaosua Yim, Lau Poh	Liu [Ren]	劉 [仁]
Yim Bisalyaputra), phra later phraya		
Phisonsombatboribun		
Lau Boonkoei	Liu [Wen Qi]	劉 [文契]
Phisanpolpanich (Koh Chin Sóó, Sóó Bisalputra),	Gao Jinshi/Gao Yushu	高進仕 / 高玉樹
phraya		
Phisansupaphol (Koh Chun Bisalputra), phraya	Gao Cun/Gao Yingjie	高忖 / 高英傑
Prachimnakorn (Jia Bek-E), luang	Xie [Baiyi]	謝 [百意]
Praneejeenpracha (Tae Tianjin), phra	Zheng Tianzhen	鄭天振
Bo Ju Lee Gee (porcelain trademark)	Bao Zhu Li Ji	寶珠利記
Pun Tao Gong	Ben Tou Gong	本頭公
Ratanasretthi (Kaw Simgong Na Ranong), phraya	Xu Senguang	許森廣
Samretkitkorn (Tan Bui Kananurak), luang	Chen Zhongxin	陳忠信
Sathorn-Rachayut (Yom), luang	Liu [Yong]	劉 [永]
Sim Keung Pok	Shen Qin Pu	沈勤樸
Siew Li Gue (secret society)	[Shou Li Ju]	[收利居]
Sok Heng, venerable	Shi Xu Xing	釋續行
Tae Hor	Zheng [Hao]	鄭 [好]
Tae Sin also known as Phraya of Tak	Zheng Xin	鄭信 / 鄭新
Tan Jubeng	Chen Zhuming	陳珠明
Tan Cijong	Chen Cizong	陳慈宗
Tan Guangliang	Chen [Guangliang]	陳 [光亮]
Tan Seng Lee later Tan Guan Lee (company)	Chen Sheng Li	陳生利
	Chen Yuan Li	陳元利
Tan Tockseng	Chen Dusheng	陳篤生
Tan Tsuhuang Wanglee	Chen Cihong	陳慈黌
Tan Suang-E	Chen Xuanyi	陳宣衣
Tia U-Teng (Teng Sophanodon, akon Teng)	Zhang Youding/Zhang Zonghuang	張有丁 / 張宗煌
Tianhou Siaboh	Tianhou Shengmu	天后聖母
Toh Peh Gong	Da Bo Gong	大伯公
also known as Pun Tao Gong		
Wanglee (company)	Hong li	鼇利
Yap Ahloy	Ye Yalai	葉亞來
Yuan Fat Hong (company)	Yuan Fa Hang	源發行

CHAPTER 5

Anuwat-Rachaniyom (Tae Teeyong, Hong	Zheng Zhiyong	鄭智勇
Techavanit), phra also known as		
Yi Goh Hong		二哥豐
Buan An Tueng	Wan An Tang	萬安堂
Cheng-hua school	Cheng Hua Xuexiao	[成華學校]
Gong Hug	Gongfo	公佛
Gong Sha	Gongshan	公山
Hanjing Ribao	Hanjing Ribao	漢境日報
Hia Guang-iam lamsuree	Yi Guangyan	蟻光炎
Hoi (Tae Hoi Techakamput), khunphat	Chen Xie	鄭蟹
Xinmin School	Xin Min Xuexiao	新民學校
Hua Heng Bee	Hua Xing Mi	華興米
Huaxian Ribao also known as	Huaxianxinbao	華暹新報
Hua Siam Sinpo		華暹日報
Wun Tokkeng (Kosol Hoontrakul)	Yun Zhuting	雲竹亭 / 雲竹發
JitchamnongVanich (Lee Teckow), luang	Li Zhuyi	李竹漪
also known as sieow chik, chik sia		犭肖七 / 七舍 / 小七
Gim Seng Lee company	Jin Cheng Li	金成利
Koh Leechai	Gao Yifa/Gao Lichai	高懿發 / 高利財
Koh Behjiang Kovatana	Gao Borang	高伯勷

Koh Sengjue	Gao Shengzhi	高繩之
Kwang Hup Seng	Guang He Sheng	廣合盛
Kwong Kim Loong (Ng's sawmill)	Guang Jin Long Huoju Chang	廣金隆火鋸廠
Kwong Nguan Long (timber shop)	Guang Yuan Long	廣源隆
Lee Ben Bencharit	Li Bing	李秉
Lee Khun Seng (company)	Li Kun Sheng	李坤盛
Lee Teckkoi	Li [Zhuxi]	李 [竹溪]
Lee Taihua Nandabhiwat	Li Taihua	[李泰華]
Lee Tainguang	[Li Taiyuan]	[李泰源]
Leong Shaushan	Liang Shoushan	梁壽山
Low Banseng	Liu [Wan Cheng]	劉 [萬成]
Low Tiekchuang Bulasuk	Lu Diechuan	盧牒川
Mah Lapkun Bulakul	Ma Liqun	馬立群
Mah Tongcheng	Ma Tangzheng	馬棠政
Meinan Ribao	Meinan Ribao	美南日報
also known as Meinan Gongbao	Meinan Gongbao	湄南公報
Na Gimseng	Lan Jinsheng	藍金升
Ng Miaongian Lamsam	Wu Miaoyuan	伍淼源 / 藍衫
Ngo Hiepyu Hemachayut	Wu Xieyu	吳協裕
Ngou Hok (company)	Wu Fu	五福
Ng Yuklong Lamsam	Wu Yulang/Wu Zuonan	伍毓郎 / 伍佐南
Nipatjeennakorn (Jia Geesee), khun	Xie Shusi	謝樞泗
Peiying School	Peiying Xuexiao	培英學校
Phakdi-Puwanart (Koh Huijia), luang	Gao Huishi/Gao Xuexiu	高暉石 / 高學修
also known as Chik La	Qi Ye	七爺
Phakdi-Phattrakorn (Lao Gibing, Ow Jiew	Liu Jibin	劉繼賓
Utokaparch), phraya *also known as*	Hu Zhou Tou	湖州頭
Ow Jiew Tao		
Phibun-Pattanakon (Tan Giakueng), phraya	Chen Jiaqin	陳嘉勤
Phison (Toh, Tan Juegiag), phraya	Chen Zhijie	陳之傑
Poh Teck Tung Foundation	Huaqiaobaodeshantang	華僑報德善堂
Pradinun-Bhumirat (Liao Chiangsoon	Liao Baoshan	廖葆珊 / 廖昌順
Srethabhakdi), phraya		
Qinan Ribao *also known as*	Qinanribao	啟南日報
Kinan Sinpo	Qinanxinbao	啓南新報
Seng Sung Lee gold shop	Cheng Shun Li	成順利
Seow Hoodseng Sribunruang	Xiao Focheng	蕭佛成
Seow Nguangseng	Xiao [Yuansheng]	蕭 [源盛]
Sithithepkan (Ngou Gimliang, Leo Wangtan),	[Wu Jinliang]	[吳金良]
luang		
Sophonpetchrat (Tia Giangsam), phra	Zhang Jiansan	張見三
also known as Po Gee Sia		抱己舍
Srethabhakd (Liao Jingsong, Liao Gongpow), khun	Liao Gongpu	廖公圃
	Liao Zhensong	廖振松
Sung Hok Seng Bank	Shun Fu Cheng Yinhang	順福成銀行
Swamipak-Bhuwarat (Tae Taiching), phra	Zheng [Dachen]	鄭 [大臣]
Sze Hai Tong Banking Corporation	Si Hai Tong Yinhang	四海通銀行
Tae Juebing Techapaiboon	Zheng Zibin	鄭子彬
Tae Taihao	Zheng Daxiao	鄭大孝
Tai Hong Gong Shrine	Dafeng Zushi Miao	大峰祖師廟
Jittin Tautuvanit (Tan Jinggeng)	Chen Zhenjing	陳振敬
Tan Kahkee	Chen Jiageng	陳嘉庚
Tan Gengchuang Tanthana	Chen Jingchuan	陳景川
Tan Gimleng Kiangsiri	Chen [Jinlong]	陳 [金龍]
Tan Guangtee *also known as* Tan Lak-ia	[Chen Guangdi]	[陳光地]
Tan Lipbuay Wanglee	Chen Limei	陳立梅
	Chen Lunkui	陳掄魁
Tan U-seng Payakkaporn	Chen Yusheng	陳禹生
Tan Siang Gee Jang (company)	Chen [Xiang Ji Zhan]	陳 [祥記棧]
Tan Tengbo Wattanakul	Chen Chengbo	陳澄波
Tian Fah Hospital	Tianhua Yiyuan	天華醫院
Tongqiaobao	Tongqiao Bao	同橋報
Tung Wah Hospital	Donghua Yiyuan	東華醫院

U Chuliang Uahwatanasakul	Yu Ziliang	余子亮
Wong Hangchao	Wang Xingzhou	王杏洲
Wu Jiyue	Wu Jiyue	吳繼岳
Yang Shikee	Yang Shiqi	楊士琦
Yu Seng Heng Bank	Yu Cheng Xing Yinhang	裕成興銀行
Zhang Bishi	Zhang Bishi	張弼士
also known as Thio Thiau Siat		
Zhonghua Huiguan	Zhonghua Huiguan	中華會館
Zhongguoribao	Zhongguo Ribao	中國日報

CHAPTER 6

Cheng Yansheng	Cheng Yansheng	程演生
Chin Seng (Mill)		
Chu Tia-sua		
Dai Li	Dai Li	戴笠
Duan Xiwen	Duan Xiwen	段希文
Ekyu Chansue (Tan Ek-yu)	Chen Yiru	陳繹如
Feng Erhe	Feng Erhe	馮尔和
Feng Xiawei	Feng Xiawei	馮夏威
Gang Bingcai	Jiang Bingcai	[江炳財]
Guang Heng Lee (company)	Guang Xing Li	光興利
Guominribao	Guominribao	國民日報
Heng Bing	Wang Bin	王彬
Hia Muigao	Yi Meihou	蟻美厚
Huaqiaoribao	Huaqiaoribao	華僑日報
Huaxinghui	Huaxinghui	華興會
Huaxi Property Development Limited Company	Huaxi	華西
Kang Lian	Kang Lian	抗聯
Khu Gib Lekawat	Qiu Ji	丘及 / 邱及
Kwongsiew	Guangzhao	廣肇
Lan Yi She	Lan Yi She	藍衣社
Lao Yiek-eng	Liu Ruoying	劉若英
Lee Keehiong	Li Qixiong	李其雄
Lianqiaobao	Lianqiaobao	聯橋報
Li Cheksing	Li Yixin	李一新
Li Hua	Li Hua	李華
Lim Baegee	Lin Boqi	林伯岐
Lin Wenying	Lin Wenying	林文英
Lio Chia-hong		
Liqing shubaoshe	Liqing Shubaoshe	勵青書報社
Li Qixin	Li Qixin	李啓新
Liu Shushi	Liu Shushi	劉漱石
Li Wenhuan	Li Wenhuan	李文環
Longchu Teck (Lim Ngek-heng)	Lin Yuxing	林玉興
Sitsuropakorn (Nai Kuitai), luang	Lai Qudai	賴渠岱
Luan Vongvanij (Huang Youluan)	Huang Youluan	黃有鸞
Ma Xingshun	Ma Xingshun	馬興順
Nanqiao Zhongxue	Nanqiao Zhongxue	南僑中學
Pan Ziming (Prasit Rakpracha)	Pan Ziming	潘子明
Phinit-chonkhadi (Tan Yokseng), phra	Chen Yucheng	陳玉成
Qiaoshengbao	Qiaoshengbao	橋聲報
Sahat Mahakun (Tio Langcing)	Zhang Lanchen	張蘭臣
Sam Hingsi	Shen Xingsi	沈荇思
Shang Zhuan	Shangwu Zhuanyuan	商務專員
Siang Gee (factory)	Xiang Ji	祥記
Taihuashangbao	Taihuashangbao	泰華商報
Tan Genghua	Chen Jinghua	陳景華
Tan Kaihor/Tan Tengbo Wattanakul	Chen Kaihe	陳開河
	Chen Chengbo	陳澄波
Tan Lengsue	Chen Ningsi	陳寧思
Tan Lipping	Chen Libin	陳立濱
Tan Muitueng	Chen Meitang	陳美堂

Tan Hongngee	Chen Fengyi	陳鳳儀
Tan Peng Shun Bank	Chen Bing Chun	陳炳春
Tan Sialink	Chen Xilin	陳錫鄰
Tan Siewmeng	Chen Shouming	陳守明
Tan Siewting	Chen Shouzhen	陳守鎮
Tan Yongchiang	Chen Yongqiang	陳鏞鏘
Tie Xue Tuan	Tie Xue Tuan	鐵血團
Wu Chaoshu	Wu Chaoshu	伍朝樞
Xu Xia	Xu Xia	許俠
Yip Insoy	Ye Xiancai	葉賢才
Zhenhuabao	Zhenhuabao	真話報
Zhongguorenbao	Zhongguorenbao	中國人報
Zhongguoribao	Zhongguoribao	中國日報
Zhonghua Huiguan	Zhonghua Huiguan	中華會館
Zhonghua medical center	Zhonghua	中華
Zhonghua Minbao	Zhonghua Minbao	中華民報
Zhongyuanbao	Zhongyuanbao	中原報
Zhu Hexiang	Zhu Hexiang	朱鶴翔

CHAPTER 7

Amphan Charoensuklarp (Zhuang Meilong)	Zhuang Meilong	莊美隆
Chin Sophonpanich (Tan Biakcing)	Chen Bichen	陳弼臣
Dongnanribao	Dongnanribao	東南日報
Fu Biaowen	Fu Biaowen	符彪文
Fu Xuzhong	Fu Xuzhong	符繡忠
Fu Zhaoguang	Fu Zhaoguang	符照光
Hiap Seng Chiang	Xie Cheng Chang	協成昌
Huang Hongqiu	Huang Hongqiu	黃鴻秋
Li Hengtiam	Li Xingtian	李興添
Lim Juemeng	Lin Ziming	林 [子明]
Lin Baengnam	Lin Bingnan	林炳男
Lin Taishen	Lin Taishen	林太深
Li Tiezheng	Li Tiezheng	李鐵錚
Puey Ungpakorn (Ng Buaykiam)	Huang Peiqian	黃培謙
Quanminbao	Quanminbao	全民報
Ren Bishi	Ren Bishi	任弼時
Sou Gungkiam	Su Junqian	蘇君謙
Tan Hangsu	Chen Hanshi	陳漢士
Tan Gimliang (Vijit Vadhakan, luang)	Chen Jinliang	陳金良
Tan Tailong	Chen Dalong	陳大隆
Tan Tonghuad	Chen Tongfa	陳同發
Teck Heng Yoo	De Xingyu	德興裕
Udane Techapaiboon (Tae Ngoulao)	Zheng Wulou	鄭午樓
Xinzhongyuanbao	Xinzhongyuanbao	新中原報
Xingzhouribao	Xingzhouribao	星洲日報
Yan Fang Lou (restaurant)	Yan Fang Lou	宴芳樓

CHAPTER 8

Chia Ekchor	Xie Yichu	謝易初
Chia Tai	Zhengda	正大
Jiu Rungseng	Zhou [Runsheng]	周 [潤生]
Lee Intong		李引桐
Sou Hiogmeng	Su Xuming	蘇旭明
Zhengda Zongyi	Zhengda Zongyi	正大綜藝

GLOSSARY

Angyi – Chinese secret society.

Capitan China – A Portuguese title given to a Chinese person who is in charge of the Chinese enclave throughout Southeast Asia.

Chao Muang – Governor of each town.

Chaosua – A Thai word for a rich Chinese man.

Comprador – A native or Chinese manager who works as a middleman/supplier for Western companies.

Free Thai Movement – An underground movement formed by Thai political exiles, Thai students overseas and civil and military officials, to oppose the Japanese military presence in Thailand during the Pacific War.

Guomindang (GMD) – Chinese Nationalist Party, also known as the Kuomintang (KMT) founded after the Xinhai Revolution in 1911 with Sun Yatsen as one of the founders.

Hailam – Chinese dialect used by people from the island of Hainan.

Hakka – Also known as *keak;* Chinese dialect used by people from Eastern Guangdong and adjoining areas of Fujian and Jiangxi provinces.

Hokkien – Chinese dialect used by people from the southern part of Fujian province.

Huagong – Chinese laborers.

Huaqiao – Overseas Chinese.

Huashang – Chinese traders.

Huiguan – Chinese self-help organizations; branches in many big towns provide a gathering place where people from the same dialect group or locale could associate together when they were away from home. *Huiguan* sometimes provided temporary lodging and offered local food from the home province.

Jus Sanguinis – The citizenship right determined by the citizenship of one or both parents.

Jus Solis – A citizenship concept, which is opposite to *jus sangunis*. Under *jus solis* an individual's citizenship is determined by his place of birth.

Kalahom – A Thai ministry responsible for military affairs.

Khunnang – A Thai nobleman.

Klong Suan Plu – An important canal in Ayudhya with a large Chinese enclave during the late-Ayudhya period.

Kongsi (clan halls) – A Chinese social practice where people with common interests join together to form a self-help organization. The concept originated in China and was often adopted by the overseas Chinese.

Krom – A generic term for a governmental department.

Krom Tha Sai – A Siamese maritime department responsible for East Asian trade including China, Japan, Ryukyu and Vietnam. *Krom Tha Sai* also supervised VOC affairs because of the company's extensive trading interests in Japan and China.

Longchu – Manager of a shop or a factory.

Lukchin – Children of Chinese emigrants in Thailand.

Mahatthai – A ministry responsible for civilian affairs.

Mandala state – An ancient Hindu-Buddhist state where political power was decentralized to local fiefdoms. Some historians like Stanley J. Tambiah have coined the term "Galactic polity" to characterize such a state.

Muang – An old term used to call a town.

Nai Amphur Chin – A Chinese *khunnang* appointed by the authority to be in charge of the Chinese community in each district.

Okya – A title used to call nobles at the rank of Phraya. It is derived from the Khmer title, *okna*.

Palad Chin – A Chinese noble appointed by the authority to supervise *nai amphur chin* in a town that has more than one *nai amphur chin*.

People's Party – A group of civilians and military officers who overthrew Siam's absolute monarchy in 1932.

Phrai system – A part of the Siamese feudal system, where a corvée system determined the rights and obligations of Siamese commoners who could live and make a living freely but are obliged to work for the state six months of the year during the Ayudhya kingdom. *Phrai-luang* worked directly for the government and *phrai-som* worked for the *khunnang* (noblemen). During war time, *phrai* would have to go to war and during peacetime they were used to dig canals and clear waterways, build roads, palaces, *wats*, etc. They could also pay an exemption tax to avoid corvée obligations.

Phraklang – A ministry responsible for commerce and foreign affairs. Its responsibility was at some time extended to include the administration of port principalities.

Phraya Choduk – A royally granted title (shortened from Phraya Choduk-Rachasretthi), denoting a *khunnang* who controls the *Krom Tha Sai* and reports to Phraya Phraklang.

Phraya Phraklang – The position held by the head of the Phraklang ministry.

Poh Teck Tung Foundation – A foundation formed in 1909 by 12 prominent Chinese businessmen in Bangkok for the purpose of collecting kinless corpses in order to perform religious rites and burial.

Rajah – Sanskrit tem used in Southeast Asia to call the ruler/governor of towns or small states.

Teochew – Chinese dialect used by people from eastern Guangdong. The dialect also is used to define their ethnic origin. In Thailand, the majority of Teochew emigrants migrated to Bangkok and the southeastern part of Thailand. Teochew is the biggest dialect group in Thailand.

Three Seals Code – An old Siamese code of law.

Tongmenghui – An underground resistance movement with Sun Yatsen as one of the founders aimed "to expel the Manchu, revive the Nation, and found the Republic."

Triad – Chinese secret society.

Wang-na **(Front palace)** – A royal position second to the king, and considered to be the heir apparent to the throne. This position usually is granted to the king's son or brother. The last *wang-na*, Prince Wichaichan, was the son of King Pinklao. The position was abolished after Prince Wichaichan's death and was replaced by the position of a crown prince by King Chulalongkorn.

Wild Tiger Corps – The para-military group founded by King Vajiravudh in 1911.

Xinhai Revolution – Chinese revolution in 1911 that overthrew the Qing dynasty (the last Chinese imperial government) and established a republic.

Yaowarat – The main road in Bangkok's Chinatown. It sometimes is used to refer to the whole area.

Yellow Peril – The idea referred to the skin color of East Asians which posited that the immigration of Asians to Western countries, especially to the U.S., was a threat to Western civilization.

PICTURE CREDITS

In the event of errors or omissions, appropriate credit will be made in reprints of this work.

Agence France-Presse/Getty 151; 310
Andrew Taylor/Robert Harding World Imagery/Corbis 396
Arunee Sopitpongstorn 382; 383
Associated Press 360; 404
Athit Peerawongmetha 409(all)
Bangkok Post Cover (pic 8; 12; 13; 16; 22; 24), 365(top); 368; 375; 384; 403(top); 403(bottom); 410(top); 411; 413; 416
Chanchai Supanichvoraparch 18; 21
ChinaFotoPress/Getty 417
Christie's Images/Corbis 26; 180
Corbis 153
Dario Pignatelli/Bloomberg/Getty 410(bottom)
Dmitri Kessel/The LIFE Picture Collection/Getty 364
EDM Archive 69; 81; 120; 156
Francoise De Mulder/Roger Viollet/Getty 406
Genthe/Corbis 291
Haeckel collection/Ullstein Bild/Getty 227
Historical and Special Collections, Harvard Law School Library 272
Howard Sochurek/The LIFE Picture Collection/Getty 278; 358

IMAGESMORE Co, Ltd./Getty 20
John Dominis/The LIFE Picture Collection/Getty 402
John Nieuhoff/ Hong Kong Museum of Art Collection 31
Keystone-France/Gamma-Keystone/Getty 366
Kimimasa Mayama/Bloomberg/Getty 115(bottom)
Leemage/Getty 301
Luca Tettoni/Corbis 48; 63; 213
Margaret Talev/MCT/Getty 415
Mark Standen 250; 351
Martin Robinson/Getty 71
Mary Evans Picture Library 33; 35; 161; 163; 261; 264
Michael Freeman/Corbis 220
Mondadori Portfolio/Getty 345
National Archive of Thailand Cover (pic 9; 17; 18),87; 115(top); 124; 128(all); 134; 137(bottom); 159(bottom); 160; 176; 178; 179(top); 181; 194; 197; 203; 206; 207; 209(all); 214; 215; 216; 217; 243; 245; 251; 253; 256; 269; 273(top); 282; 289; 299; 304; 308; 314; 315; 318; 323; 317
National Library of Thailand 57
National Museum Bangkok 125(all)
National Palace Museum (The Republic of China) 112
Pairin Kankaew Cover (pic 1; 6); 12; 15; 23; 38; 43(all); 44; 46; 50; 54; 76; 79; 83; 91; 113; 114; 130; 144(top); 145; 147(all); 166; 169; 175(all); 189; 221; 287; 288; 387
Peter Charlesworth/LightRocket/Getty 407; 414
Popperfoto/Getty 238; 262
Pimpraphai Bisalputra Cover (pic 5; 10; 11; 15; 21; 23; 25; 26); 60; 74; 95; 98; 102; 117; 126; 127; 137(top); 170(top); 170(bottom); 177; 179(bottom); 183; 185; 186; 187(all); 188; 195; 199; 202; 205; 208; 210; 223; 224; 225(all); 234; 235; 236; 237; 241; 259(all); 266; 267; 273(bottom); 274; 275; 276; 277; 283; 290; 293(all); 302; 312; 313; 319; 324; 330(all); 333; 337; 338; 340; 342; 344; 347; 352; 354(all); 355; 356; 361; 362; 365(bottom); 370; 371; 376(all); 380; 381; 385; 386; 390; 391; 393; 395
RMN/Grand Palais/Jean-Manuel Salingue 53
RMN/Grand Palais (Musée du Louvre)/Theirry Le Mage 40
Roger Viollet Collection/Getty 37
Siam Society 16; 24; 58
Southeast Asian Visions, Cornell University Library Cover (pic 2; 3); 29; 39; 118; 123; 159 (top); 172; 184; 198; 201; 204; 281; 284; 286; 307(top)
Sovfoto/UIG/Getty 363
Steve Bartrick Antiques and Maps 149; 165
Steve Storey/Demotix/Corbis 348
Sunait Chutintaranond 90; 110
Thai Bank Museum 4
The Treasure of Pattani (Anake Nawigamune ed., 2014) 25; 27; 246
Time Life Pictures/National Archives/The LIFE Picture Collection/Getty 400
Underwood Archives/Getty 307(bottom)
Universal History Archive/Getty 138
Universal History Archive/UIG/Getty 141; 168; 169; 232; 240
Universal Images Group/Getty 22
Wolfgang Kaehler/Getty 19

ENDNOTES-CHAPTER 1

1 According to David K. Wyatt, U-Thong's wife was the daughter of the late king of Suphanburi, while his mother was the daughter of the ruler of Lopburi and his father was a Chinese merchant of Petchaburi.
2 China has always insisted that relations between foreign countries and China must be couched in terms of paying tribute to the Chinese emperor. Acceptance of Chinese suzerainty is a pre-condition for trade relations with China.
3 The term Annam denotes "The Pacified South."
4 Stuart Fox (Singapore, 2003), p. 46, 89.
5 Stuart Fox (Singapore, 2003), p. 45.
6 Miksic (Singapore, 2009), p. 71.
7 Manguin (Sydney, 2003).
8 Stuart Fox (Singapore, 2003), p. 30.
9 Stuart Fox(Singapore, 2003), p. 33.
10 Stuart Fox (Singapore, 2003), p. 33.
11 Stuart Fox (Singapore, 2003), p. 31.
12 Suzuki (2013), p. 7.
13 Lieberman (Cambridge, 2003), p. 106.
14 Lieberman (Cambridge, 2003), p. 222.
15 Skinner (New York, 1957), p. 1.
16 Stuart Fox (Singapore, 2003), p. 65
17 Stuart Fox (Singapore, 2003), p. 65.
18 Stuart Fox (Singapore, 2003), p. 65.
19 สืบแสง พรหมบุญ (๒๕๒๕) น.๖๐
20 According to Takashi Suzuki, ships coming back from the west had to wait about 7–8 months for the headwind to subside before crossing the Strait of Malacca, while overland travel lasted between 10–30 days depending on the route.
21 Skinner (New York, 1957), p. 2.
22 Skinner (New York, 1957), p. 2.
23 Stuart Fox (Singapore, 2003), p. 40.
24 Manguin (Sydney, 2003).
25 Skinner (New York, 1957) p. 2.
26 Skinner (New York, 1957), p. 3.
27 Ma Huan (Bangkok, 1977), p. 104.
28 สืบแสง พรหมบุญ (๒๕๒๕) น.๕๑
29 Skinner (New York, 1957), p. 4.
30 Chen (Bangkok, 1977), p. 1534.
31 Skinner (New York, 1957), p. 2.
32 Skinner (New York, 1957), p. 4.
33 Skinner (New York, 1957), p. 7.
34 Skinner (New York, 1957), p. 3.
35 Skinner (New York, 1957), p. 4.
36 Skinner (New York, 1957), p. 4.
37 Skinner (New York, 1957), p. 4.
38 Skinner (New York, 1957), p. 5.
39 Skinner (New York, 1957), p. 7.
40 Baker, Dhiravat and Wyatt van der Kraan, (Chiang Mai, 2005), p. 223.
41 สืบแสง พรหมบุญ (๒๕๒๕) น.๕๑
42 Skinner (New York, 1957), p. 8.
43 Lieberman (Cambridge, 2003), p. 287.
44 Lieberman (Cambridge, 2003), p. 288.
45 Charnvit and Wright (Bangkok, 2007), p. 148.
46 Lieberman (Cambridge, 2003), p. 298.
47 Lieberman (Cambridge, 2003), p. 290.
48 Skinner (New York, 1957), p. 8.
49 Charnvit and Wright (Bangkok, 2007), p. 148.
50 Skinner (New York, 1957), p. 8.
51 Skinner (New York, 1957), p. 8.
52 Skinner (New York, 1957), p. 9.
53 Jörg (London, 1993), p. 184–85.
54 Skinner (New York, 1957), p. 8.
55 Skinner, (New York, 1957), p. 9.
56 Bhawan Ruangsilp (2007), p. 20.
57 Bhawan Ruangsilp (2007), p. 20.
58 Skinner (New York, 1957), p. 10.
59 Jörg (London, 1993), p. 186.
60 Jörg (London, 1993), p. 188.
61 Ng (Singapore, 1983), p. 51.
62 Sarasin (1977), p. 45.
63 Medley (1993).
64 Sarasin (1997), p. 29.
65 The term *chaokrua* is an old Siamese phrase used to describe a wealthy patron or merchant. It should be noted that in those days all Chinese in Siam used their clan name together with only a one-syllable personal name—in this case, Ngeng.
66 Jörg (London, 1993), p. 192.
67 Lieberman (Cambridge, 2003), p. 287.
68 Raben and Dhiravat (Bangkok, 1997), p. 64, and Bhawan Ruangsilp (2007), p. 20.
69 Skinner (New York, 1957), p. 10, and Bhawan Ruangsilp (2007), p. 21.
70 Raben and Dhiravat (Bangkok, 1997), p. 64, and Bhawan Ruangsilp (2007), p. 21.
71 Bhawan Ruangsilp (2007), p. 21.
72 Skinner (New York, 1957), p. 10. There are other accounts of the years 1663–64 from Dutch primary sources, such G.V. Smith (1977), Ten Brummelhuis (1987) and Dhiravat (2003).
73 Skinner (New York, 1957), p. 11.
74 Sar Desai (Chiang Mai, 1997), p. 69.
75 Ibid, p. 69.
76 Ibid, p. 70
77 Ibid, p. 70.
78 See Farrington and Dhiravat, *The English Factory in Siam*, Introduction, Vol.1. "Country traders" were small, individual, private shipmasters as opposed to state trading or East India Companies.
79 Jörg (The Hague,1982), p. 19.
80 Gervaise (Bangkok, 1998), p. 49.
81 Skinner (New York, 1957), p. 11.
82 Skinner (New York, 1957), p. 11.
83 Lieberman (Cambridge, 2003), p. 288.
84 Kaempfer (Bangkok, 1998), p. 38.
85 สืบแสง พรหมบุญ (๒๕๒๕) น.๖๘
86 Jörg (1982), p. 18–19.
87 Dhiravat (1998), p. 111.
88 Dhiravat (1998), p. 111.
89 Dhiravat (1998), p. 111.
90 Dhiravat (1998), p. 111–12.
91 Caron and Schouten (1969), p. 131.
92 However, van Nijenrode, an earlier source than Schouten or van Vliet, suggests that the prime right of succession was the eldest son's, and Simon de la Loubère, a later source, also says that a king's son took priority. In other words, the question of royal succession is still unclear, prompting Dhiravat na Pombejra to suggest that it was left ambiguous so that the best (i.e., strongest) candidate would prevail.
93 Opponents of this view point out that Siamese were on both sides of those succession conflicts. Moreover, Prince Sorasak was also Phra Phetracha's son, although his mother was not a rightful queen. The ambiguity underlying the practice of royal succession lay at the root of Ayudhya's chronic royal succession struggles.
94 Dhiravat (1998), p. 104–14.
95 Dhiravat (1998), p. 117.
96 สืบแสง พรหมบุญ (๒๕๒๕) น.๖๘
97 Dhiravat (1998), p. 115–20.
98 สืบแสง พรหมบุญ (๒๕๒๕) น. ๖๙
99 Ng (1983), p. 191.
100 Sarasin (1997), p. 84–85.
101 Sarasin (1997), p. 86–87.
102 Dhiravat (1998), p. 118.
103 Dhiravat (1998), p. 119.
104 Dhiravat (1998), p. 116.
105 Dhiravat (1998), p. 118.
106 Dhiravat (1998), p. 118.
107 สารสิน วีระผล (๒๕๔๘) น. ๖๑
108 ก.ศ.ร. กุหลาบ น. ๒๘๐
109 Dhiravat (1998), p. 120–21.
110 Dhiravat (1998), p. 122.
111 Dhiravat (1998), p. 122.
112 The name Nai Kai is not Thai but Chinese. According to the 18th century dialect spoken in Zhangzhou Prefecture of Fujian, Nai Kai means "inner (city) road." The name of the market signifies the predominance of Zhangzhou Chinese in Ayudhya. Interestingly, a market named Nai Kai also exists in the next

largest Chinese bastion, in Ligor.
113 Kaempfer (1998), p. 44.
114 ก.ศ.ร. กุหลาบ
115 Dhiravat (1998), p. 122.
116 ก.ศ.ร. กุหลาบ
117 Dhiravat (1998), p. 122.
118 Dhiravat (1998), p. 122.
119 Skinner (New York, 1957), p. 18.
120 Wyatt (Chiang Mai, 2003), p. 114.

ENDNOTES-CHAPTER 2

1 Several Thai texts written during the early Bangkok period stated that Taksin's father was a *chin* Hai Yong referring to a Chinese from Hai Yang, the name of the Teochew area as it was known during the early Qing dynasty.
2 ณัฏฐภัทร (๒๕๒๓) น ๑๕.
3 Sakurai and Kitagawa (Bangkok, 1999), p. 154–55.
4 Chen (Bangkok, 1977).
5 It is interesting to note how legends and traditions have developed around King Taksin; both Wat Choeng Tha and Wat Samanakot, for instance, claim that Taksin was ordained or educated there. This reflects Taksin's place in the collective memory, or even the "national psyche" of Thailand.
6 อธิบายแผนที่พระนครศรีอยุธยา (๒๕๕๐) น ๑๒๕-๑๒๗
7 In his letter to the Qing court dated August 1771, King Taksin called himself Zheng Zhao (Masuda, 2007, p. 98), and his residence in the Thonburi Palace consisted of Chinese-style brick buildings.
8 In other other words, "Phraya of Tak named Sin."
9 *Khun phat* was the title of a gambling-den concessionaire.
10 อภินิหารบรรพบุรุษ (๒๕๔๕) น ๑-๗
11 Terwiel (Bangkok, 2005), p. 33.
12 Mergui was the seaport for Tenasserim, which was a river port as well as a provincial town.
13 Baker and Phongpaichit (Cambridge, 2005), p. 13.
14 Wyatt (Chiang Mai, 2003), p. 116.
15 Terwiel (Bangkok, 2005), p. 33.
16 The fatal cannon shot wound is mentioned in the Siamese chronicles. Lieberman says Alaungpaya died in a small town near Mottama on the way back to his capital, but makes no mention of any wound.
17 Terwiel (Bangkok, 2005), p. 36.
18 The royal chronicles of 1855 (Cushman, Bangkok, 2006, p. 506) described a later battle scene in 1676 between Phraya Phraklang and Namiao Thihapatei as follows: "At that time none of the inhabitants of the Holy Metropolis, either household heads or ascetics, had ever seen them fight each other and they persuaded each other to follow the brigades of the army out to watch them fight the Burmese in great numbers."
19 Terwiel (Bangkok, 2005), p. 36–37.
20 Terwiel (Bangkok, 2005), p. 38.
21 Wyatt (Chiang Mai, 2003), p. 111.
22 Wyatt (Chiang Mai, 2003), p. 111.
23 Wyatt (Chiang Mai, 2003), p. 111.
24 Wyatt (Chiang Mai, 2003), p. 111.
25 Baker and Phongpaichit (Cambridge, 2005), p. 19.
26 ขจร สุขพานิช (๒๕๕๖)
27 Lieberman (Cambridge, 2003), p. 300.
28 Lieberman (Cambridge, 2003), p. 300.
29 Wyatt (Chiang Mai, 2003), p. 117.
30 Wyatt (Chiang Mai, 2003), p. 117.
31 Wyatt (Chiang Mai, 2003), p. 118.
32 Wyatt (Chiang Mai, 2003), p. 118.
33 Taksin's regiment was listed among the list of troops. See คำให้การชาวกรุงเก่า น. ๕๖๙ และ ๕๘๙.
34 Terwiel (Bangkok, 2005), p. 33.
35 Wyatt (Chiang Mai, 2003), p. 117.
36 According to the royal chronicles, "The brigades of the Thai army failed to stand and fight. They were all simultaneously routed in defeat and fled to retreat down to Pho Sam Ton." A good secondary source is Professor Sunait Chutintaranond's work on the fall of Ayudhya based on the Konbaung chronicles, while the classic account is of course Prince Damrong's book, *Our Wars with the Burmese*.
37 Terwiel (Bangkok, 2005), p. 34.
38 Wyatt (Chiang Mai, 2003), p. 118.
39 Wyatt (Chiang Mai, 2003), p. 118.
40 Skinner (Cornell, 1958), p. 20.
41 Nidhi (Bangkok, 1993), p. 97.
42 คำให้การชาวกรุงเก่า น. ๕๖๙ และ ๕๘๙
43 Cushman, p. 506.
44 Cushman (Bangkok, 2006), p. 512.
45 List of *muang tho* include Sukhothai, Sawankhalok, Kamphaeng Phet, Nakorn Rachasima, Petchabun and Tenasserim.
46 ประชุมพงศาวดาร ภาคที่ ๓๙ (กรุงเทพ ๒๕๕๑) น.๒๗๐.
47 Terwiel (Bangkok, 2005), p. 40.
48 Terwiel (Bangkok, 2005), p. 40.
49 ณัฏฐภัทร (๒๕๒๓) น ๑๔.
50 ประชุมพงศาวดาร ภาคที่ ๓๙.
51 Launay (Paris, 1920), p. 230.
52 According to Nidhi, Phra Chiang Ngen was later appointed the *phraya* of Sukhothai, an important town in the defense against Burmese invasions.
53 Luang Phichai may have been either Phraya Phichai Chin, who was later in charge of the Phraklang ministry or Phraya Phichai Racha, a famous general who was appointed as the *chaophraya* of Sawankhalok.
54 Luang Phiphit was later appointed the governor of Ha Tien with the title Phraya Rachasretthi-Chin.
55 Central authority had broken down. French missionaries fleeing to Chantabun reported that the Gulf was infested with pirates. Chinese documents also confirmed the prevalence of piracy in the Gulf. According to Masuda, when Chen Wenbiao arrived in April/May 1766 at the mouth of the Gulf of Siam, he could not approach because of the large (number of) pirate ships.
56 According to the royal chronicles, there was a rainstorm early in the day that Taksin broke out of Wat Phichai. After the rain, there was a big fire. It was unclear whether Taksin used the cover of the rain or the fire, when Burmese attention was distracted, to get away.
57 Cushman, p. 512.
58 ประชุมพงศาวดาร ภาค ๓๙ (กรุงเทพ ๒๕๕๑) น. ๒๖๘.
59 Masuda (Taiwan, 2007), p. 86.
60 Wyatt (Chiang Mai, 2003), p. 118.
61 Baker and Phongpaichit (Cambridge, 2005), p. 23.
62 Masuda (Taiwan, 2007), p. 86.
63 Masuda (Taiwan, 2007), p. 86.
64 ประชุมพงศาวดาร ภาค ๓๙ (กรุงเทพ ๒๕๕๑) น. ๒๗๐
65 Wyatt (Chiang Mai, 2003), p. 118.
66 Masuda (Taiwan, 2007), p. 87.
67 Professor Dhiravat Na Pombejra affirms that the destruction of Ayudhya was a great catastrophe, although the Stone Age metaphor may be somewhat exaggerated. After Ayudhya's fall, the rapid mushrooming of power centers competing for dominance in 1767–69—including the *chao muang* of Ligor and the Ban Plu Luang's Prince Thepphiphit—demonstrated the resilience of Siamese culture and civilization. The fact that Taksin was able, subsequently, to rally forces rapidly from the remnants of Ayudhya's provincial bureaucracy through persuasion or coercion testified to the fact that the idea of Ayudhya continued to live on as an inspiration even after the capital city was obliterated in 1767.
68 Cushman (Bangkok, 2006), p. 514.
69 Cushman (Bangkok, 2006), p. 515.
70 Cushman (Bangkok, 2006), p. 515.
71 Cushman (Bangkok, 2006), p. 515.
72 Cushman (Bangkok, 2006), p. 528.
73 Baker and Phongpaichit (Cambridge, 2005), p. 17.
74 ขจร สุขพานิช (๒๕๕๖)
75 Cushman (Bangkok, 2006), p. 516.
76 พระราชพงศาวดารกรุงธนบุรี ฉบับหมอบรัดเล (กรุงเทพฯ: โฆษิต ๒๕๕๑) น ๑๒.
77 Cushman (Bangkok, 2006), p. 516.
78 Cushman (Bangkok, 2006), p. 517.
79 Terwiel (Bangkok, 2005), p. 41.
80 In the late 18th century, Ha Tien was an autonomous Cantonese tributary state of Nguyen Vietnam, which also acknowledged Siamese suzerainty.
81 Wyatt (Chiang Mai, 2003), p. 112.

82 Lieberman (Cambridge, 2003), p. 418.
83 Sakurai (2004), p. 45; Chen (Bangkok, 1977), p. 1552.
84 Chen (Bangkok, 1977), p. 1545.
85 Terwiel (Bangkok, 2005), p. 42.
86 Phra Ram Phichai was probably Phraya Phichai Racha,
    later appointed as *chaophraya* of Sawankhalok. Somdet
    Phra Panarat, the author of Bradley's version of the royal
    chronicles, distinguished him from the Chinese Phra Phichai
    who was later appointed Phraya Kosathibodi (See box
    "The Chinese Phraya Phichai [Na Lai 藍來, later Phraya
    Kosathibodi]"). In this incident, other royal chronicles simply
    called the commander Phra Phichai. Perhaps more evidence is
    needed to confirm which, among the several Phraya Phichai,
    this commander was.
87 พระราชพงศาวดารกรุงธนบุรี ฉบับหมอบรัดเล (กรุงเทพฯ: โฆษิต ๒๕๕๐)
    น.๒๓
88 Chen (Bangkok, 1977), p. 1545.
89 Wyatt (Chiang Mai, 2003), p. 122.
90 Phra Nai Khong พระนายกอง was the Mon General in command
    of Burmese forces guarding Ayudhya.
91 พระราชพงศาวดารกรุงธนบุรี ฉบับหมอบรัดเล (กรุงเทพฯ: ๒๕๕๐) น. ๓๑.
92 Terwiel (Bangkok, 2005), p. 43.
93 Son of King Borommakot.
94 Grandson of King Thaisa (see ธินวา น.๑๐).
95 Grandson of King Borommakot (see ธินวา น.๑๐).
96 พงศาวดารเมืองสงขลาและพัทลุง พระนคร ๒๕๐๕.
97 Wyatt (Chiang Mai, 1994), p. 137.
98 Wyatt (Chiang Mai, 1994), p. 137.
99 Wyatt (Chiang Mai, 2003), p. 122.
100 Wyatt (Chiang Mai, 2003), p. 125.
101 พระราชพงศาวดารกรุงธนบุรี ฉบับพันจันทนุมาศ (กรุงเทพฯ ๒๕๕๐) น.๗๐
102 Nithi (Bangkok, 2012), p. 254. พระราชพงศาวดารกรุงธนบุรี ฉบับ
    หมอบรัดเล (กรุงเทพฯ: โฆษิต ๒๕๕๐)
103 Nithi (Bangkok, 2012), p. 243–44.
104 According to Prince Damrong, Taksin apparently believed in
    an ancient prophecy that two attempts were required for the
    capture of Chiang Mai. (HRH Prince Damrong Rajanubhab
    [Bangkok, 1920], *Our Wars with the Burmese*.)
105 Damrong Rajanubhab (Bangkok ,1920), p. 444.
106 Wyatt (2003), p.125.
107 Wyatt (2003), p.125.
108 พระราชพงศาวดารกรุงธนบุรี ฉบับหมอบรัดเล (กรุงเทพฯ ๒๕๕๐)
109 พระราชพงศาวดารกรุงธนบุรี ฉบับพันทนุมาศ (กรุงเทพฯ ๒๕๕๐) น.๘๘
110 พระราชพงศาวดารกรุงธนบุรี ฉบับหมอบรัดเล (กรุงเทพฯ ๒๕๕๐)
111 Known in Thai texts as Azaewunky.
112 Wyatt (Chiang Mai, 1994), p. 137.
113 The southern Vietnamese kingdom ruled by the Nguyen
    dynasty in the 18th century went by the name of Quang Nam.
114 Puangthong (New York, 2004), p. 103.
115 Li Tana (New York, 2004), p. 9.
116 Li Tana (New York, 2004), p. 9.
117 Puangthong (New York, 2004), p. 103.
118 Li Tana (New York, 2004), p. 9.
119 Puangthong (New York, 2004), p. 102.
120 In April/May 1766, five Siamese ships fled to Ha Tien after
    being robbed of their merchandise. (See Masuda, 2007, p. 81.)
121 Sakurai and Kitakawa (Bangkok, 1999), p. 177.
122 Sakurai (1999), p. 176.
123 Chen (Bangkok, 1977), p. 1545.
124 Puangthong (New York, 2004), p. 104.
125 Chen (Bangkok, 1977), p. 1545.
126 The abundance of Teochew support for Taksin at this point
    was by no means a poor reflection upon the Hokkiens. The
    scanty presence of Hokkiens in Taksin's army was a grim
    testimony and reminder of the high death toll suffered by the
    Chinese in the defense of Ayudhya in 1767. Hokkiens who
    survived the destruction of Ayudhya tended to flee to the
    south where they had contacts.
127 Launay, 1920, Vol. II, Corre to M. le Fiscal de Malacca, 1 Nov.
    1769, p. 269.
128 Terwiel (Bangkok, 2005), p. 45.
129 Chen (Bangkok, 1977), p. 1547.
130 Chen (Bangkok, 1977), p. 1546–47, 1552. (The person charged
    with negotiating the extradition of Chao Chui with Mac
    Thientu was Phraya Phiphit, alias Tran Lien in Vietnamese and
    Chen Lian in Chinese.)
131 Chen (Bangkok, 1977), p. 1546.
132 Chen (Bangkok, 1977), p. 1548.
133 Chen (Bangkok, 1977), p. 1547.
134 Sakurai and Kitakawa (1999), p. 180.
135 Chen (Bangkok, 1977), p. 1547.
136 Puangthong (2004), p. 104.
137 Chen (Bangkok, 1977), p. 1552.
138 Chen (Bangkok, 1977), p. 1552.
139 Sakurai and Kitakawa (1999), p. 178.
140 Masuda (Taiwan, 2007), p. 81.
141 Li Tana (New York, 2004), p. 3.
142 Masuda (Taiwan, 2007), p. 79.
143 Chen (Bangkok, 1977), p. 1549.
144 Chen (Bangkok, 1977), p. 1549.
145 Forest products were commodities like eaglewood, cinnamon,
    ebony, ivory, sappanwood, birds' nests, wax and hides.
146 Chen (Bangkok, 1977), p. 1554.
147 Chen (Bangkok, 1977), p. 1554.
148 Chen (Bangkok, 1977), p. 1537.
149 Chen (Bangkok, 1977), p. 1537.
150 Chen (Bangkok, 1977), p. 1540.
151 Chen (Bangkok, 1977), p. 1545.
152 Sakurai and Kitakawa (1999), p. 173.
153 Chen (Bangkok, 1977), p.1545.
154 พระราชพงศาวดารกรุงธนบุรี ฉบับหมอบรัดเล (กรุงเทพฯ ๒๕๕๐)
155 พระราชพงศาวดารกรุงธนบุรี ฉบับหมอบรัดเล (กรุงเทพฯ ๒๕๕๐)
156 พระราชพงศาวดารกรุงธนบุรี ฉบับหมอบรัดเล (กรุงเทพฯ ๒๕๕๐) น. ๓๙
157 Masuda (Taipei, 2007), p. 88 and พระราชพงศาวดารกรุงธนบุรี ฉบับ
    หมอบรัดเล (กรุงเทพฯ: โฆษิต ๒๕๕๐) น. ๓๙
158 The Phraklang of Ayudhya was captured and taken hostage
    together with King Uthumporn to Burma. See Masuda (2007),
    p. 87.
159 จดหมายรายวันทัพสมัยกรุงธนบุรี คราวปราบเมืองพุทไธมาศและเขมร
    เมื่อ พ.ศ.๒๓๑๔ (กรุงเทพฯ : ศรีปัญญา ๒๕๕๐)
160 Terwiel (2011), p. 78.
161 Puangthong (New York, 2004), p. 102.
162 Chen (Bangkok, 1977), p. 1548.
163 พระราชพงศาวดารกรุงธนบุรี ฉบับหมอบรัดเล (กรุงเทพฯ ๒๕๕๐)
164 Chen (Bangkok, 1977), p. 1548.
165 Puangthong (New York, 2004), p. 105.
166 Chen (Bangkok, 1977), p. 1549.
167 Sakurai and Kitagawa (Bangkok, 1999), p. 181.
168 Chen (Bangkok, 1977), p. 1548.
169 Chen (Bangkok, 1977), p. 1549.
170 Chen Lai, whose official title was Phraya Phipit (called Tran
    Lai, Tran Lien, and Chieu-khoa Lien in Vietnamese) was
    probably Tan Liang in Teochew. At the time of the attack
    on Chantabun, Phraya Phipit was in Thonburi working in the
    Phraklang ministry while Phraya Phraklang, the Kosathibodi
    (Phraya Phichai chin—Na Lai, Lan Lai) was away in
    Battambang.
171 Chen (Bangkok, 1977), p. 1548.
172 Masuda (Taiwan, 2007), p. 97.
173 Sakurai and Kitagawa (Bangkok, 1999), p. 182.
174 Chen (Bangkok, 1977), p. 1548.
175 Chen (Bangkok, 1977), p. 1548.
176 Sakurai (New York, 2004), p. 45.
177 Chen (Bangkok, 1977), p. 1551.
178 Chen (Bangkok, 1977), p. 1551.
179 Puangthong (Bangkok, 2004), p. 101.
180 Chen (Bangkok, 1977), p. 1551.
181 Chen (Bangkok, 1977), p. 1550.
182 ประชุมพงศาวดารภาค ๓๙ (กรุงเทพฯ : ศรีปัญญา ๒๕๕๐) น. ๒๙๕-๒๙๖
183 Terwiel (2005), p. 49.
184 ธินวา (๒๕๕๕)
185 Masuda (Taiwan, 2007), p. 101.
186 Terwiel (2005), p. 49.
187 Chen (Bangkok, 1977), p. 1555.
188 Chen (Bangkok, 1977), p. 1550.
189 Puangthong (New York, 2004), p. 104.
190 Puangthong (New York, 2004), p. 105.
191 The abused daughter of Mac Thientu had been brought to
    Taksin by a servant of Phraya Phiphit.
192 In Chinese records, Tan Liang, which is in the Teochew dialect,
    appears as Chen Lai.
193 Chen (Bangkok, 1977), p. 1555.
194 Puangthong (New York, 2004), p. 104.
195 Chen (Bangkok, 1977), p. 1555.

196 Chen (Bangkok, 1977), p. 1555.
197 According to Sakurai, the Vietnamese record Gia Dinh Thong Chi called Phraya Phipit "Chieu Khoa Lian." The name was probably derived from *chao khua* Lian (เจ้าขรัวเหลียน-เจ้าขรัวเลี้ยง). *Chao khua* is an honorific name given to a wealthy man in Siam. ตั้งเลี้ยงตามสำเนียงแต้จิ๋ว
198 Chen (Bangkok, 1977), p. 1552–53.
199 Chen (Bangkok, 1977), p. 1548.
200 "จดหมายรายวันทัพสมัยกรุงธนบุรี คราวปราบเมืองพุทไธมาศและเขมร เมื่อ พ.ศ. ๒๓๑๔" (กรุงเทพฯ: ศรีปัญญา ๒๕๕๑)
201 พระราชพงศาวดารกรุงธนบุรี ฉบับพันจันทนุมาศ (กรุงเทพฯ: ศรีปัญญา ๒๕๕๑)
202 พระราชพงศาวดารกรุงธนบุรี ฉบับหมอบรัดเล (กรุงเทพฯ ๒๕๕๑)
203 พระราชพงศาวดารกรุงธนบุรี ฉบับหมอบรัดเล (กรุงเทพฯ ๒๕๕๑)
204 พระราชพงศาวดารกรุงธนบุรี ฉบับหมอบรัดเล (กรุงเทพฯ ๒๕๕๑)
205 Sakurai and Kitagawa (Bangkok, 1999), p. 196.
206 Chen (Bangkok, 1977), p. 1556.
207 Chen (Bangkok, 1977), p. 1556.
208 `Baker and Phongpaichit (Cambridge, 2005), p. 74.
209 Chen (Bangkok, 1977), p. 1556.
210 Sakurai (2004), p. 46.
211 Puangthong (New York, 2004), p. 105.
212 Chen (Bangkok, 1977), p. 1563.
213 Chen (Bangkok, 1977), p. 1558.
214 Chen (Bangkok, 1977), p. 1557.
215 Chen (Bangkok, 1977), p. 1558.
216 Chen (Bangkok, 1977), p. 1561.
217 Puangthong (2004), p. 105.
218 Overall Gulf trade declined due to the confused situation in Vietnam, Siam and Cambodia.
219 Chen (Bangkok, 1977), p. 1558.
220 Chen (Bangkok, 1977), p. 1561.
221 จดหมายเหตุความทรงจำฉบับ พ.ศ. ๒๔๕๙ (ศรีปัญญา ๒๕๕๑) น.๓๖๖
222 Terwiel (2005), p. 61.
223 Terwiel (2011), p. 78.
224 ปรีดี (๒๕๓๐) สกุลพนมยงค์
225 พิมพ์ประไพ (๒๕๕๕)
226 According to official records, the linguist, or *thongsu*, of this mission held the official title of Khun Photchana Phichit. See Masuda (2007), p. 108.
227 Phraya Sunthorn Aphai died on the way to Beijing in 1782.
228 ศุภการ (กรุงเทพฯ 2555) น. 105 - 106

ENDNOTES-CHAPTER 3

1 ประพฤทธิ์ ศุกลรัตนเมธี (กรุงเทพฯ ๒๕๔๒)
2 The Chakri kings later resumed King Taksin's (Tae Jiao's) clan name of Tae (Zheng); Rama I took on the name Tae Hua; Rama II, Tae Hood; Rama III, Tae Hok; and Rama IV, Tae Meng.
3 Crawfurd quoted in Purcell (1981), p. 95–96.
4 ทิพากรวงศ์ (กรุงเทพฯ ๒๕๓๙).
5 The word *chin* literally means "Chinese" in Thai. Thai records tend to preface references to ethnic Chinese with the word *chin* before the person's name. Thus Chin Kun means "the Chinese man named Kun."
6 ดำรงราชานุภาพ (๒๔๘๙).
7 Terwiel (Bangkok, 2005), p. 111–12.
8 Terwiel (Bangkok, 2005), p. 97.
9 Terwiel (Bangkok, 2005), p. 97.
10 ทิพากรวงศ์ (กรุงเทพฯ ๒๕๓๙).
11 Terwiel (Bangkok, 2005), p. 97.
12 Purcell (1981), p. 97.
13 Purcell (1981), p. 98.
14 Purcell (1981), p. 98–99.
15 Purcell (1981), p. 98.
16 The patriarch of the Chatikavanich family.
17 พิมพ์ประไพ (๒๕๕๕).
18 Baker, p. 35.
19 Landon, p. 12.
20 ศรีสมร ศรีเบญจพลางกูร (๒๕๓๙) น.๒๘๙
21 ศรีสมร ศรีเบญจพลางกูร (๒๕๓๙)
22 Noi was the illegitimate son of King Taksin. Noi's mother was Taksin's concubine who was given away to Phraya Nakhon (Phat). After Noi was born he was raised in Nakhon Si Thammarat as Phat's adopted son.
23 Somdet Phra Bawonratchao Maha Sakdiphonlasep (สมเด็จพระบวรราชเจ้ามหาศักดิพลเสพ1824–32) was the *uparat* appointed by Rama III as the titular heir to the throne. He was an uncle to the king.
24 Wyatt (Chiang Mai, 2003), p. 152–53.
25 Na Ranong (Bangkok, 1996).
26 Perhaps this lady was either Thao Thep Kasattri or Thao Sri Sunthorn. According to the history of the Andaman towns around that time, Thao Thep Kasattri and Thao Sri Sunthorn were the two sisters from the prestigious House of Na Thalang that defended Phuket against the Burmese in 1785. By the time Kaw Sujiang came to Takuapa in 1816–20, both of these ladies must have been very old if they were still alive.
27 Na Ranong (Bangkok, 1996).
28 Na Ranong (Bangkok, 1996).
29 สุธิวงศ์ (กรุงเทพฯ ๒๕๔๔) น. ๔๘-๔๙
30 Na Ranong (Bangkok, 1996).
31 Hobsbawm (1996), p. 1.
32 Hobsbawm (1996).
33 Hobsbawm (1996), p. 34.
34 Terwiel (Bangkok, 2005), p. 97.
35 Frankfurter (1914), p. 6, as quoted in Nidhi Eoseewong (1982), p. 60.
36 Terwiel (Bangkok, 2005), p. 110–11.
37 Terwiel (Bangkok, 2005), p. 110–11.
38 วุฒิชัย มูลศิลป์ (๒๕๔๒) น.๑๕๐
39 *Kongsi* means "a company"; or a small partnership of men in the same trade; or an organized secret society.
40 Lynn Pan described the *kongsi*, which appeared in Chinese settlements all over Southeast Asia, as "part government, part cooperative and part secret society."
41 A member of the well-known Sombatsiri Family.
42 ศุภรัตน์ เลิศพาณิชย์กุล (กรุงเทพฯ ๒๕๒๔) น. ๔๑
43 Bowring (1977), p. 87.
44 Bowring (1977, Vol. 2), p. 255.
45 ชาญ กัลยาณมิตร (กรุงเทพฯ ๒๕๓๖)
46 Son of Chaophraya Phraklang (Dit).
47 The term *hang punkang* mentioned in the royal chronicles meant "the Hong merchant in Canton who was the representative of the Siamese trade." Erika Matsuda's article mentioned Dr. Yoshizawa Seiichiro's opinion that the term *punkang* came from the Chinese term *benganghang*.
48 Suebsaeng Promboon (1971), p. 292.
49 Ye Mingchen, the governor of Guangzhou, starved to death as a British captive in Calcutta, two years after he lost Guangzhou.
50 Chaophraya Nikornbodin was a wealthy Hokkien *chaosua*, a personal friend of Rama III. His descendants were given the royal bestowed surname of Kalayanamitr.

ENDNOTES-CHAPTER 4

1 Bowring (1977), Vol. I, p. 85–86.
2 Dit Bunnag, Somdet Chaophraya Barommaha Prayurawongse (1788–1855).
3 Prince Wongsathiratsanit (1808–71).
4 Tad Bunnag, Somdet Chaophraya Barommaha Pichaiyat.
5 Chuang Bunnag, later Somdet Chaophraya Si Suriyawongse.
6 Bowring (1977), Vol. II, p. 288–89.
7 Chinese junk masters in the king's service were awarded official titles in the Krom Tha Sai under the Phraklang.
8 In 1913 when King Vajiravudh (1910–25) decreed that all Siamese citizens must have a surname, the palace-appointed surname for Phraya Phisan-Supaphol's descendants was Bisalputra.
9 *Bangkok Calendar* 1863, p. 111.
10 Cushman (1993), p. 18.
11 Cushman (1993).
12 Cushman (1993).
13 Westad (2012), p. 12.
14 Westad (2012), p. 18.
15 Westad (2012), p. 12.
16 Westad (2012), p. 12.

17 Cushman (1993).
18 พระอินทรมนตรี (แย้ม) (๒๕๑๗)
19 ดำรงราชานุภาพ, ตำนานเครื่องโต๊ะแลถ้วยปั้น
20 Wang Mianchang, http://yunnan.stis.cn/xnjw/dmkjjj/200410/t20041030_230196.htm.
21 Skinner, G.W. (1957).
22 Comber (1959).
23 Crawfurd (1830), II, p. 177.
24 Skinner (1957), p. 46.
25 Skinner (1957), p. 84.
26 Skinner (1957), p. 86–87.
27 The great-grandmother of Tarrin Nimmanahaeminda, who was Thailand's finance minister between 1997 and 2001.
28 Kichakorn "Tales of the Family" แพรว, บทสัมภาษณ์ คุณอุณณ์ (นิมมานเหมินท์) ชุติมา เรื่อง "สกุลนิมมานเหมินท์ หลีกราชภัยสู่คหบดีแห่งล้านนา".
29 Skinner (1957), p. 137.
30 Akira (1989), p. 80.
31 Skinner (1957), p. 47.
32 Skinner (1957), p. 50.
33 Skinner (1957), p. 50.
34 Comber (1959).
35 Skinner (1957), p. 47.
36 Skinner (1957), p. 44.
37 Skinner (1957), p. 86.
38 Skinner (1957), p. 84–86.
39 Skinner (1957), p. 44–49.
40 Skinner (1957), p. 83.
41 Skinner (1957), p. 47.
42 Skinner (1957), p. 47.
43 Skinner (1957), p. 47.
44 Skinner (1957), p. 84.
45 The Zheng (鄭) of the Sreshthaputra, Phosayachinda, Bhirombhakdi and Pranit; the Xu (許) of Xu Sizhang (許泗璋) of the Na Ranong; the Wu (吳) of the Na Songkhla; the Lim (林) of the Krairiksh; the Huang (黃) of the Kalayanamitra; the Su (蘇) of Chatikavanij; and the Liu (劉) of the Phisonyaputra.
46 The patriarch of the Kananurak family.
47 สุธิวงศ์ พงศ์ไพบูลย์และพวก (๒๕๔๔) น. ๑๘๗-๑๙๓
48 สุธิวงศ์ พงศ์ไพบูลย์และพวก (๒๕๔๔) น. ๑๘๗-๑๙๓
49 Skinner (1957), p. 51.
50 Skinner (1957), p. 47.
51 Skinner (1957), p. 48.
52 นวพร เรืองสกุล (๒๕๕๑) น.๑๖๒–๖๙.
53 Van Dyke (2012), p. 51.
54 Van Dyke (2012), p. 51.
55 Vajirayano's letter to Mr. Eddie as quoted in ณัฐวุฒิ สุทธิสงคราม (๒๕๒๕).
56 Tan Kimcheng had a Thai wife, Khunying Puen. Their descendants can be found among the prominent families of Bangkok, namely Vatcharapai, Virangkura, Oonhasiri and Tansakul.
57 Samuha Phra Kalahom (Von Bunnag)'s letter to King Chulalongkorn in 1882 as quoted in ณัฐวุฒิ สุทธิสงคราม (๒๕๒๕).
58 Comber, Leon (1959), p. 142.
59 W.H. Read was a prominent merchant based in Singapore.
60 Comber (1959), p.155–73.
61 จดหมายพระศรีสุนทรโวหาร ถึง ขุนศรีสยามกิจ ผู้ช่วยราชการกงสุลฝ่ายสยาม (๒๔๑๐) as quoted in ณัฐวุฒิ สุทธิสงคราม (๒๕๒๕).
62 The first survey of the Kra Canal was made in 1843 (see H.B. Smith, "Historic Proposals for a Kra Canal: Their Impact on International Relations in Southeast Asia with Emphasis on British Perspectives," *Asian Profile* 3, no.1 (February 1975), p. 43–58. According to the same report, in 1881 a British firm requested assistance from the British government in applying for a concession to construct the canal, and the discouraging response was, "Her Majesty's government could not recommend any particular applicants for the concession to the Siamese government."
63 สาส์นสมเด็จ สมเด็จกรมพระยาดำรงราชานุภาพ
64 ณัฐวุฒิ สุทธิสงคราม (๒๕๒๕).
65 Akira (1989), p. 74.
66 Akira (1989), p. 74.
67 ราชกิจจานุเบกษารัชกาลที่ ๔ แจ้งความมาที่ ๑๓, ฉบับพิมพ์ครั้งที่ ๕ (กรุงเทพฯ ๒๕๔๐).
68 Choi Chi-Cheung (1998), p. 37.
69 พิมพ์ประไพ พิศาลบุตร (๒๕๕๐) หน้า ๑๐๕.
70 According to the *Bangkok Calendar*, 1862, apart from numerous junks Phraya Phisan-Supaphon and his son Chin Sóó owned the followings rigs and steam boats:

English Name	Type	When Built/ Purchased	Tonnage	Owners
Castle	Barque	1851	400	P'aya P'isán
Paragon	Ship	1854	800	P'aya P'isán
Ocean Queen	Ship	1855	600	P'aya P'isán
Metropolis	Barque	1855 (Lost 1858)	400	P'aya P'isán
Bantek	Barque	1856	518	P'aya P'isán
Alexander	Brig	1856	200	Cheen Sóó
Shooting Star	Ship	1856	850	P'aya P'isán
Four Star	Barque	1857	280	Cheen Sóó
Lucky Star	Barque	1858	450	Cheen Sóó
Amy Douglas	Barque	1859		Cheen Sóó
Norfolk	Brig	-	120	Cheen Sóó
Kim Hong Sing	Barque	-	400	Cheen Sóó
Alligator	Serew	1859	200	P'aya P'isán
Viset Cunning	Serew	1861		P'aya P'isán

71 พระราชพงศาวดารกรุงรัตนโกสินทร์ รัชกาลที่ ๔ ฉบับเจ้าพระยาทิพากรวงศ์ (ขำ บุนนาค) (ต้นฉบับ ๒๕๔๗) น. ๓๔๖.
72 The family in Thailand used the Kovatana surname.
73 Choi Chi-Cheung (1998), p. 37.
74 ส. ศิวรักษ์, "ช่วงแห่งชีวิต"
75 Choi Chi-Cheung
76 Kim Lohchae arrived from Raoping in 1818 during the reign of Rama II. He married a local Thai from Angthong Province and settled down in one of the floating bazaars along the Bangkok shore. When his business grew, he purchased and built his shop on land and ventured into a successful junk trade. Kim Lohchae was the grandfather of Phraya Phipattanakorn (Chim Poshyananda).
77 Later, Yim was promoted to Phraya Phisonsombatboribun by King Chulalongkorn and his descendants were given the palace-appointed name of Phisonyabut.
78 Akira (1989), p. 46.
79 สงบ ส่งเมือง (๒๕๒๒) น. ๘๗
80 Akira (1989), p. 76.
81 Akira (1989), p. 77.
82 Prince Kitiyakara is the paternal grandfather of Queen Sirikit of Thailand.
83 Wright and Breakspear (1994), p. 146.
84 According to a survey compiled by Suehiro Akira, the production capacities of various rice milling groups in 1898 were Phisanpolpanich: 8,000 *piculs*/day; Koh Mahwah: 7,500 *piculs*/day; Phibun-Phattanakorn: 5,000 *piculs*/day; Iap Joo: 4,000 *piculs*/day; Tan Tsuhuang (Wanglee): 3,000 *piculs*/day; the European trading houses of Windsor & Co., A Markwald & Co., and the Arracan: 2,500 *piculs*/day each; other major Chinese rice mills, namely Akorn Teng, Phraya Phakdi, Luang Chareon, Lao Bang Seng and Lee Thye Hoa: 2,500 *piculs*/day each. Akira, Suehiro (1989), p. 51.
85 Akira (1989), p. 57.
86 Wang Gungwu (1997), p. 6.
87 Skinner (1957), p. 97.
88 Skinner (1957), p.114–15.
89 Skinner (1957), p. 114.
90 Skinner (1957), p.116,
91 Skinner (1957), p. 61.
92 ศุภรัตน์ (๒๕๒๔) หน้า 38.
93 Skinner (1957), p. 145–46.
95 ศุภรัตน์ (๒๕๒๔).
95 สุทธิวงศ์ พงศ์ไพบูลย์ (๒๕๔๔) น. ๕๒.
96 ศุภรัตน์ (๒๕๒๔).
97 Chinese district officer.
98 Chinese provincial officer.
99 ศุภรัตน์ (๒๕๒๔) น. ๒๗๙-๒๘๐.
100 Comber (1959), p. 33.
101 ศุภรัตน์ (๒๕๒๔) น. ๒๒๗.
102 กจช. ร.๕ กห. เล่ม ๖ เลขที่ ๕ จ.ศ.๑๒๓๓ ว่าด้วยให้ข้าหลวงคุมเรือรบไปอยู่รักษาเมืองภูเก็ต
103 ศุภรัตน์ (๒๕๒๔) น. ๑๔๘
104 Comber (1959), p.112
105 ศุภรัตน์ (๒๕๒๔) น. ๑๖๒-๑๖๙
106 ศุภรัตน์ (๒๕๒๔) น. ๑๖๙-๑๗๘
107 ศุภรัตน์ (๒๕๒๔) น. ๑๒๐-๑๓๔.
108 ศุภรัตน์ (๒๕๒๔) น. ๑๘๖.
109 Phra Artikorn-prakas (Luis Chatikavanij) was the chief of

police overseeing the Chinese in Bangkok. Luis himself was a Chinese from the Hokkien village in Talad Noi. His forefather had settled in Siam during the time of Thonburi Kingdom. The fact that he reported no Hokkien secret societies in Bangkok in 1906 suggests several things: 1) the Hokkien community in Bangkok had become numerically weaker after the Ayudhya period; 2) the current generation of Hokkiens had become so assimilated that they had lost their Chinese identity, unlike in the south where robust Hokkien secret societies were much in evidence.

110 ศุภรัตน์ (๒๕๒๔) หน้า ๕๘.
111 ศุภรัตน์ (๒๕๒๔) หน้า ๒๐๗.
112 Skinner (1957), p. 120.
113 Skinner (1957), p. 121.
114 Skinner (1957), p. 121–22.
115 Warren (2013), p. 586–87.
116 Warren (2013), p. 587.
117 Warren (2013), p. 587.
118 Warren (2013), p. 589–90.
119 Skinner (1957), p. 123.

ENDNOTES-CHAPTER 5

1 It was only in 1927 that the Siamese government could gain tariff autonomy, 20 years later than Japan. See Suehiro Akira (1989), p. 21.
2 Akira (1989), p. 21.
3 *Chao muang* is the Thai term that refers to local lords.
4 Steinberg (1971), p. 205.
5 Steinberg (1971), p. 205.
6 Steinberg (1971), p. 205.
7 Steinberg (1971), p. 206.
8 Steinberg (1971), p. 206.
9 ลักษมี จิระนคร "ขุนนิพัทธ์จีนนคร : วิถีชีวิต" (2544) น. 236–42.
10 ลักษมี จิระนคร "ขุนนิพัทธ์จีนนคร : วิถีชีวิต" (2544) น. 236–42.
11 Steinberg (1971), p. 208.
12 Tate (1979), p. 13.
13 Baker and Phongpaichit (2005), p. 82.
14 Baker and Phongpaichit (2005), p. 81.
15 Tate (1979), p. 509.
16 Baker and Phongpaichit (2005), p. 81.
17 Tate (1979), p. 508.
18 Akira (1989), p. 29.
19 Baker and Phongpaichit (2005), p. 83.
20 Steinberg (1971), p. 228.
21 Akira (1989), p. 27.
22 Steinberg (1971), p. 213.
23 Tate (1979), p. 51.
24 Gosling, L.A.P. (1983), p. 133.
25 Steinberg (1971), p. 228.
26 Choi Chi Cheung (1998), p. 38.
27 Choi Chi Cheung (1998), p. 42.
28 Choi Chi Cheung (1998), p. 38.
29 Several studies offered explanations on Yuan Fat Hong's failure, including the economic crisis, internal conflict among brothers and cousins, the overextention of business activities, and the nature of clan networking, including its dependence on maternal kin among others. See Choi Chi Cheung (1998) and พรรณี บัวเล็ก (2545).
30 Gosling, L.A.P. (1983), p. 133.
31 Akira (1989), p. 23.
32 Latham (1988), p. 91.
33 Skinner (1957), p. 105.
34 Baker and Phongpaichit (2005), p. 93.
35 Lee Tit Guan was set up by Phraya Choduk-Rachasretthi (Pook, Li Fu), a Teochew from Shantou.
36 The two sons of Phraya Phisan-Supaphol (Gao Chun), who was Siam's shipping magnate during the 1840–50s, reinforced their position in the rice trade by setting up several rice milling plants using Scottish machinery. Phraya Phisan-Pholpanich (Koh Chin Sóó, Gao Ji Shi), the eldest son, owned three rice mills under Koh Hong Lee while his younger brother (Koh Pho Kim) owned another mill, Guan Tit Lee.
37 The owner, Luiz Xavier, who was the father of Phraya Phipat-Kosa, was of Portuguese descent.
38 Luang Sophonpetcharat was the only son of Akon Tia Teng, the Teochew founder of Kim Seng Lee. Akon Tia Teng started his business in Tak, dealing mainly in teak, opium and spirit concessions in the northern territory. Later he moved to Bangkok and expanded into the rice trade.
39 Lau Chong Min was appointed the Choduk-Rachasretthi by King Vajiravudh.
40 Early in the reign of King Chulalongkorn, the proprietors of Siang Giee Jang, Phra Phibun-Pattanakon (Tan Gia Kueng) and his brother Tan Guang Tee, came to join their uncle, Phraya Phison (Toh, Tan Jue Giag), a famous tax farmer in Bangkok. The brothers later entered the rice trade and Tan Guang Tee was sent to Singapore to set up a branch office. The firm had three rice mills in Bangkok by 1907.
41 Akira (1989), p. 83.
42 Baker and Phongpaichit (2005), p. 94.
43 Baker and Phongpaichit (2005), p. 94.
44 Sze Hai Tong Banking and Insurance Company was established by Teochew businessmen in Singapore in 1906 to serve the overseas Teochew community. The bank was staffed by many Teochews, and provided a familiar, clan-like atmosphere for its customers. It opened a branch in Bangkok in 1909.
45 Gao Chuxiang.
46 Baker and Phongpaichit (2005), p. 94.
47 Choi Chi Cheung (1998), p. 26–27.
48 พรรณี บัวเล็ก (๒๕๔๑) น. ๑๒๑.
49 พรรณี บัวเล็ก (๒๔๔๑) น. ๑๒๘ และ ๑๑๐
50 พรรณี บัวเล็ก (๒๕๔๑).
51 Latham (1988), p. 94.
52 พรรณี บัวเล็ก (๒๕๔๕) น. ๕๘–๖๗; also Akira (1989), p. 76–77.
53 พรรณี บัวเล็ก (๒๕๔๕) น. ๕๘–๖๗.
54 วรวุฒิ จิราสมบัติ (๒๕๔๕) น. ๑๒๔–๓๔.
55 วรวุฒิ จิราสมบัติ (๒๕๔๗) น. ๑๒๔.
56 พรรณี บัวเล็ก (๒๕๔๕) น. ๑๒๔–๓๔.
57 พรรณี บัวเล็ก (๒๕๔๕) น. ๑๒๔–๓๔.
58 วรวุฒิ จิราสมบัติ (๒๕๔๗) น. ๑๒๔–๒๕.
59 พรรณี บัวเล็ก (๒๕๔๕) น. ๑๒๔–๓๔.
60 วรวุฒิ จิราสมบัติ (๒๕๔๗) น. ๑๒๔–๒๕.
61 Latham (1988), p. 99.
62 Akira (1989), p. 87.
63 Steinberg (1971), p. 246.
64 Wasana (2008), p. 166.
65 Steinberg (1971), p. 257.
66 Landon (1941), p. 18
67 Landon (1941), p. 17.
68 Coughlin (2012), p. 14.
69 Baker and Phongpaichit (2005), p. 48.
70 Son of Akon Tia Teng, the northern tycoon who owned numerous timber and spirits concessions in Tak and Chiang Mai.
71 Owner of Buan Ann Teung the licensed spirit distiller for Nakhon Rachasima. See *Siam from Ancient to Present Time* (Bangkok, 1927), p. XLI.
72 The bird's nest tycoon from Surat Thani.
73 Timber concessionaire for Suphanburi, Uthaithani, Kampengpetch, Lukon and Phrae.
74 Wang Gungwu (1992), p. 23.
75 Wang Gungwu (1992), p. 25.
76 Wang Gungwu (1992), p. 25.
77 Wang Gungwu (1992), p. 26.
78 Wang Gungwu (1992), p. 26.
79 Wang Gungwu (1992), p. 26.
80 Wasana Wongsurawat (November 2008), p. 164.
81 Wasana Wongsurawat (November 2008), p. 164.
82 Wasana Wongsurawat (November 2008), p. 165.
83 Wasana Wongsurawat (November 2008), p. 164.
84 Wasana Wongsurawat (November 2008), p. 165.
85 Wasana Wongsurawat (Singapore, 2011), p. 133.
86 Wang Gungwu (1992), p. 25.
87 Wasana Wongsurawat (Singapore 2011), p. 133.
88 Wright & Breakspear (1908), p. 169.
89 เอกสารโรงพยาบาลเทียนฟ้า.
90 Zhang Bishi was a prominent Indonesian-Chinese shipping tycoon.
91 Wasana Wongsurawat (Singapore, 2011), p. 134.
92 Wang Gungwu (1992), p. 27.

93 Wang Gungwu (1992), p. 25.
94 Landon (1941), p. 22.
95 Landon (1941), p. 22.
96 Steinberg (1971), p. 210.
97 Baker and Phongpaichit (2005), p. 50; quoted from a letter dated 18 May 1864, printed in Sinlapa Watthanatham 25, 3 (January 2004), p. 85.
98 Riggs (1967), p. 105.
99 Riggs (1967), p. 101.
100 Riggs (1967), p. 96, quoted from A. M. Hocart, Kingship (Oxford, 1927) p. 120–21. According to Hocart, "the Buddhist scriptures declare that both the Emperor and the Buddha to be the two beings that are born for the welfare of gods and men. He adds that the two are embodied in the Buddhist concept of the Great Man."
101 Riggs (1967), p. 97.
102 Riggs (1967), p. 97; quoted from H.G. Quaritch Wales, *Ancient Siamese Government and Administration* (London, 1934), p. 70.
Baker and Phongpaichit (2005), p. 50.
103 Baker and Phongpaichit (2005), p. 96.
104 Baker and Phongpaichit (2005), p. 108.
105 Batson (1984), p. 1.
106 Batson (1984), p. 2.
107 Riggs (1967), p. 94.
108 Patriarch of the Sopanodon family.
109 ศุภรัตน์ เลิศพาณิชย์กุล (๒๕๓๙) น, ๒๘๘–๘๙.
110 ศุภรัตน์ เลิศพาณิชย์กุล (๒๕๓๙) น, ๒๘๘–๙๑.
111 Taken from an interview with Charoen Tanmahabhram, who
112 wrote a biography on the Sophanodon family.
อู๋จี้เยียะ (๒๕๕๗) น. ๓๑๘–๑๙.
113 Patriarch of the Techakamput family.
114 ศุภรัตน์ เลิศพาณิชย์กุล(๒๕๓๙) น, ๒๙๓–๓๐๓.
115 Godley, Michael R. (1981), p. 9–10.
116 พรรณี บัวเล็ก (๒๕๔๕) น. ๕๑–๕๖.
117 Baker and Phongpaichit (2005), p. 91.
118 Baker and Phongpaichit (2005), p. 91.
119 Steinberg (1971), p. 200.
120 Tate (1979), p. 557.
121 Tate (1979), p. 557.
122 Tate (1979), p. 554.
123 Skinner (1957), p. 161.
124 Chaiyan Rajchagool, p. 149.
125 Skinner (1957), p. 160.
126 Edward W. Said, *Orientalism* (London, 1978). Although
127 Orientalism essentially describes phenomena in the Middle East, his later book *Culture and Imperialism* (1993) explains how Western racial prejudices inform the pattern of relationships between the modern metropolitan West and its overseas colonies.
Chaiyan Rajchagool (1994), p. 153.
128 Chaiyan Rajchagool (1994), p. 153.
129 Warrington Smyth, (1994), p. 320.
130 Warrington Smyth, (1994), p. 285–86.
131 Skinner (1957), p. 160, quoted from Campbell (1902), p.
132 272–74.
Skinner (1957), p. 161.
133 Skinner (1957), p. 161.
134 Wasana Wongsurawat has pointed out that the Siamese
135 court was well aware of the dangers of allowing the general public to be exposed to foreign political systems and ideas. The influence of political ideas from the West was tightly controlled in the local educational system. Only a select circle of high-ranking members of the royal family and young nobles destined to serve the court had been allowed to obtain higher education in Europe and America during the reign of Rama V. See Wasana Wongsurawat (2011), p. 131.
Skinner (1957), p. 161.
136 Skinner (1957), p. 155.
137 Skinner (1957), p. 163.
138 Skinner (1957), p. 163.
139 Wasana Wongsurawat (November 2008), p. 159.
140 Wasana Wongsurawat (November 2008), p. 166. The above
141 policy was often combined with the practice of trading honorary degree certificates for donations, which became a very effective means of fundraising during the last few decades of Manchu rule in China.
Wasana Wongsurawat (2011), p. 167.
142 Wasana Wongsurawat (2011), p. 163.
143 Landon (1941), p. 20.
144 Landon (1941), p. 21.
145 Landon (1941), p. 21.
146 Wasana Wongsurawat (2011), p. 131.
147 Vella (1978), p. 194.
148 Vella (1978), p. 189.
149 Wasana Wongsurawat, p. 131.
150 Skinner (1957), p. 164.
151 Landon (1941), p. 18.
152 Vella (1978), p. 192.
153 Vella (1978), p. 189.
154 Wasana Wongsurawat has wryly remarked, "For King
155 Vajiravudh, a Chinese is a Jew of the Orient only if he is not loyal to the crown. If he is clearly devoted to the Siamese court then he is not a Jew of the Orient."
156 Vella (1978), p. 60.
157 Chaiyan Rajchagool (1994), p. 150.
158 อนุสรณ์งานฌาปนกิจ คุณพ่อเล็ก เสรฐภักดี ๒ ธันวาคม ๒๕๔๕.
159 ดิลก วุฒิพาณิชย์ "ขุนเศรษฐภักดี : วิถีชีวิต" (๒๕๔๔), น. ๒๔๓–๔๘.
160 ดิลก วุฒิพาณิชย์ "ขุนเศรษฐภักดี : วิถีชีวิต" (๒๕๔๔), น. ๒๔๓–๔๘.
161 ดิลก วุฒิพาณิชย์ "ขุนเศรษฐภักดี : วิถีชีวิต" (๒๕๔๔), น. ๒๔๓–๔๘.
162 Charnvit Kasetsiri (2010).
163 ตระกูลวังตาล (๒๕๔๘).
164 ตระกูลวังตาล (๒๕๔๘).
165 ทำเนียบวัดคาทอลิกในประเทศไทย (๒๕๔๑).
166 'ย้อนอดีต...โดยคุณยายสุดจิตร สู้เสงี่ยม' เมล็ดพันธุ์ ๑๐๐ ปี ๑๐๐ ปีแห่งความเชื่อของกลุ่มคริสชน วัดนักบุญมาร์การิตา บางตาล ๒๕๕๖.
167 Interview with Praphaisith Tankeyura 2014.
168 ตระกูลวังตาล (๒๕๔๘).
169 พรรณี บัวเล็ก (๒๕๔๕) น.๑๘๓–๘๕.
170 พรรณี บัวเล็ก (๒๕๔๕) น.๑๘๓–๘๕. และ ทำเนียบวัดคาทอลิกในประเทศไทย (๒๕๔๑) น. ๓๙๙–๔๑๔.
171 Charnvit Kasetsiri, "Banpong Fire" (2010), p. 541–615.
172 ตระกูลวังตาล (๒๕๔๘).
173 พรรณี บัวเล็ก (๒๕๔๕) น.๑๘๓–๘๕.
174 หจช., ร.๗ รล.๑๙.๓/๓๗ นิวยอร์กไทม์ ลงข่าวเรื่องนายกิมเลี้ยง วังตาล
175 Charnvit Kasetsiri (2010).

ENDNOTES-CHAPTER 6

1 Wasana Wongsurawat (2011) p. 135.
2 The Manchu government had been pressing the Siamese government unsuccessfully to sign a treaty to establish diplomatic relations between the two countries.
3 Second Brother Hong's Chinese name was Tae Teeyong and his Thai name was Phra Anuwat-Rajniyom (Hong Techavanit).
4 สุวรรณา มาประเสริฐ (๒๕๔๗) น. ๗๐.
5 พรรณี บัวเล็ก (๒๕๔๕) น. ๒๗.
6 Murashima (2013), p. 154.
7 Bergere (1998), p. 115.
8 Bergere (1998), p. 91.
9 Bergere (1998), p. 86.
10 Murashima (2013), p. 155.
11 Murashima (2013), p. 155.
12 Murashima (2013), p. 160.
13 พรรณี บัวเล็ก (๒๕๔๕) น. ๒๗.
14 โรงพยาบาลเทียนฟ้ามูลนิธิ ครบรอบ ๑๐๐ ปี น.๑๑๘.
15 พรรณี บัวเล็ก (๒๕๔๕) น. ๒๗.
16 โรงพยาบาลเทียนฟ้ามูลนิธิ ครบรอบ ๑๐๐ ปี น. ๑๑๘.
17 โรงพยาบาลเทียนฟ้ามูลนิธิ ครบรอบ ๑๐๐ ปี น.๑๑๘.
18 พรรณี บัวเล็ก (๒๕๔๕) น. ๒๗.
19 โรงพยาบาลเทียนฟ้ามูลนิธิ ครบรอบ ๑๐๐ ปี น. ๑๑๙.
20 วรวุฒิ จิราสมบัติ ลูกจีนหลานมอญในกรุงสยาม (๒๕๔๗) น. ๑๑๑.
21 Wright and Breakspear (1908), p. 179.
22 วรวุฒิ จิราสมบัติ ลูกจีนหลานมอญในกรุงสยาม (๒๕๔๗) น. ๑๒๑.
23 โรงพยาบาลเทียนฟ้ามูลนิธิ ครบรอบ ๑๐๐ ปี น. ๑๑๙.
24 โรงพยาบาลเทียนฟ้ามูลนิธิ ครบรอบ ๑๐๐ ปี น. ๑๑๙.
25 โรงพยาบาลเทียนฟ้ามูลนิธิ ครบรอบ ๑๐๐ ปี น. ๑๒๓.
26 Murashima (2013), p. 150.
27 Murashima (2013), p. 161.
28 A Chinese term meaning "overseas Chinese."

29 Van Roy, (2006), p. 138.
30 Wasana Wongsurawat, (2011), p. 134.
31 Although several sources have mentioned Sun Yatsen's visit to Bangkok in 1906, Prof. Eiji Murashima suggests that the dating may be confused because the most detailed daily record of Sun Yatsen 孫中山年譜長編 which was published in 1991 in Beijing contained no reference to the 1906 visit to Siam.
32 เพ็ญพิสุทธิ์ อินทรภิรมย์ (๒๕๕๗).
33 เพ็ญพิสุทธิ์ อินทรภิรมย์ (๒๕๕๗). น. ๑–๕.
34 According to Thai records, in 1903 Sun visited Bangkok and stayed at Hotel De La Paix under a Japanese name, Takano. He came from Hanoi to meet three prominent Chinese merchants who were all French subjects with introductory letters from Mr. Hardouin.
35 Murashima (2013), p. 150.
36 Van Roy (2006), p. 138.
37 Van Ro (2006), p. 139.
38 Van Roy (2006), p. 139.
39 โรงพยาบาลเทียนฟ้ามูลนิธิ ครบรอบ ๑๐๐ ปี น.๑๐๘.
40 Murashima (2013), p. 152.
41 Murashima (2013), p. 152.
42 Murashima (2013), p. 161.
43 Son of Akon Teng, the northern tycoon who owned numerous timber and spirits concessions in Tak and Chiang Mai.
44 Tan KaiHor or Tan TengBo Vattanakul was the owner of Buan Ann Teung, the licensed spirit distiller for Nakorn Rachasima. See Siam from Ancient to Present Time (Bangkok, 1927), p. XLI, also สัมภาษณ์ วัย วรรธนะกุล ใน ร้อยคำบอกเล่าเรื่องมูลนิธิปอเต็กตึ๊ง (๒๕๕๑). น. ๑๗๓.
45 The bird's nest tycoon from Surat Thani.
46 Timber concessionaire for Suphanburi, Uthaithani, Kampengpetch, Lukon and Phrae.
47 Murashima (2013), p. 166.
48 Murashima (2013), p. 167.
49 Skinner (1957), p. 158.
50 The Chino-Siam Warasup alleged that the number of arrests in connection with the strike was only 400 and not 800 as recounted in the newspapers in China.
51 เพ็ญพิสุทธิ์ อินทรภิรมย์ (๒๕๕๗). น. ๑๕๘–๕๙.
52 The drying up of his sources of government concessions coupled with his overextended financial commitments in China eventually forced him into bankruptcy.
53 "ความเห็นของหนังสือพิมพ์เก็กเหมิง" จีโนสยามวารศัพท์ ฉบับวันศุกร์ที่ ๑๑ พฤศจิกยน ร.ศ.๑๒๙ น.๒
54 Grey (Chicago, 1986), p. 236.
55 Skinner (1957), p. 171.
56 Murashima (2002), p. 194.
57 Skinner (1957), p. 235.
58 เออิจิ มุราชิมา (๒๕๓๙), การเมืองจีนสยาม, น.๑.
59 Skinner (1957), p. 236.
60 Murashima (2002), p. 193.
61 Skinner (1957), p. 236.
62 Murashima (2002), p. 194.
63 Skinner (1957), p. 238.
64 เชาวน์ พงษ์พิชิต (2553) น. 68–78.
65 Murashima (2002), p. 194.
66 เชาวน์ พงษ์พิชิต (2553) น. 71.
67 Skinner (1957), p. 241.
68 Batson (1984), p. 2.
69 แถมสุข นุ่มนนท์ (2545) น. 26.
70 Chaiyan Rajchagool (1994), p. 16.
71 Chaiyan Rajchagool (1994), p. 160.
72 Landon (1941), p. 158.
73 Landon (1941), p. 158.
74 Landon (1941), p. 159.
75 Wilson (1962), p. 172.
76 Chaiyan Rajchagool (1994), p. 156.
77 Tate (1979), p. 557.
78 พอพันธ์ อุยยานนนท์ (๒๕๕๖) น. ๒๓.
79 Chaiyan Rajchagool (1994), p. 161.
80 Landon (1941), p. 20.
81 Skinner (1957), p. 240.
82 Skinner (1957), p. 259.
83 เออิจิ มุราชิมา (๒๕๓๙) น.๓๑
84 Murashima (2002), p. 195.
85 Skinner (1957), p. 242.
86 เออิจิ มุราชิมา (๒๕๓๙) น. ๑๘๗.

87 A picul is defined as the quantity that a man can carry across the shoulders. The official unit is equivalent to 60 kilograms.
88 พรรณี บัวเล็ก (๒๕๕๔) น.๑๒๘ น. ๒๗๒–๗๕ และ น. ๒๗๘.
89 Seow Hoodseng stayed in Canton until the death of Hu Hanmin, and the collapse of the southwest faction forced him to flee to Bangkok in July 1936 to escape arrest by Chiang Kai-shek.
90 เออิจิ มุราชิมา (๒๕๓๙), น.๕๑.
91 Liao Gongpow or Khun Srethabhakdi was also known as Liao Jingsong.
92 เออิจิ มุราชิมา (๒๕๓๙), น.๓๘.
93 เออิจิ มุราชิมา (๒๕๓๙), น.๔๐.
94 Also known as Ma Bulakul.
95 อัมพร เอี่ยมสุรีย์ (๒๕๓๗).
96 อัมพร เอี่ยมสุรีย์ (๒๕๓๗).
97 เออิจิ มุราชิมา (๒๕๓๙), น. ๔๐.
98 Khun Srethabhakdi has two Chinese names, Liao Gongpow and Liao Jingsong.
99 เออิจิ มุราชิมา (๒๕๓๙), น. ๔๒.
100 เออิจิ มุราชิมา (๒๕๓๙), น. ๔๒.
101 See ประสิทธิ์ รักประชา (๒๕๔๐).
102 เออิจิ มุราชิมา (๒๕๓๙), น.๔๘.
103 เออิจิ มุราชิมา (๒๕๓๙), น.๔๘.
104 Murashima (2002), p. 195.
105 เออิจิ มุราชิมา (๒๕๓๙), น. ๔๙.
106 เออิจิ มุราชิมา (๒๕๓๙),น. ๕๐.
107 เออิจิ มุราชิมา (๒๕๓๙), น. ๔๙.
108 เชาวน์ พงษ์พิชิต (๒๕๕๓) น. ๑๒๙–๓๐.
109 เออิจิ มุราชิมา (๒๕๓๙).
110 เชาร์ พงษ์พิชิต ลูกจีนรักชาติ (๒๕๕๓) น. ๑๐๘.
111 The fines collected were remitted to China to help the war effort.
112 เชาร์ พงษ์พิชิต ลูกจีนรักชาติ (๒๕๕๓).
113 ทักษ์ เฉลิมเตียรณ (๒๕๔๖)
114 สาฤชานานุสรณ์ นายล้วน ว่องวานิช (๒๕๐๘).
115 สาฤชานานุสรณ์ นายล้วน ว่องวานิช (๒๕๐๘).
116 เชาวน์ พงษ์พิชิต (๒๕๕๓) น. ๑๕๗.
117 Tate (1979), p. 552.
118 Murashima, (2002), p. 195.
119 Landon, (1940), p. 23.
120 Murashima (2002), p. 195.
121 Murashima (2002), p. 197.
122 Murashima (2002), p. 197.
123 Murashima (2002), p. 202.
124 Murashima (2002), p. 202.
125 Murashima (2002), p. 202.
126 Murashima (2002), p. 198.
127 Murashima (2002), p. 199.
128 Murashima (2002), p. 203.
129 Murashima (2002), p. 208.
130 Murashima (2002), p. 207.
131 Murashima (2002), p. 205.
132 คุณหญิงจำนงศรี รัตนิน (๒๕๓๗).
133 See เชาวน์ พงษ์พิชิต ๒๕๔๔.
134 Murashima (2002), p. 215.
135 Murashima (2002), p. 216.
136 คุณหญิงจำนงศรี รัตนิน (๒๕๓๗).
137 อัมพร เอี่ยมสุรีย์ (๒๕๓๗).

ENDNOTES-CHAPTER 7

1 อูฉี่เยียะ (๒๕๕๗), น. ๑๐๑–๓.
2 อูฉี่เยียะ (๒๕๕๗). น. ๙๕๒–๕๔.
3 Bangkok Post, 31 August 1946.
4 อูฉี่เยียะ (๒๕๕๗). น. ๙๕๒–๕๔.
5 During the post-war years, the foundation was under the chairmanship of Tan Chinkeng, known in Thailand as Jittin Tantuvanit. After Jittin retired in 1971, Udane Techapaiboon (see page 375) returned to head this prestigious huaqiao charitable institution.
6 อูฉี่เยียะ (๒๕๕๗), น. ๑๐๑–๓.
7 Bangkok Post, 9 July 1948.
8 Skinner (1957), p. 326.
9 Bangkok Post, 12 November 1953.

10 By the late 1930s, Chinese control over the economy was already weak after the first Phibun administration made the nationalization of Chinese-owned productive assets and the development of state enterprises the cornerstone of his National Socialist economic policy.

11 Akira (1989), p. 42.

12 อนุสรณ์งานพระราชทานเพลิงศพ นายชิน โสภณพนิช (๒๕๓๖) น. ๑๑๓–๑๔.

13 Yoshihara (1988), p. 48–49.

14 Mackie (2005), p. 83–85.

15 Mackie (2005), p. 83–85.

16 อู๋จี้เยี่ย (๒๕๕๗).

17 พอพันธ์ อุยยานนท์ (๒๕๕๖).

18 Akira (1989), p. 48.

19 Stifel (1981).

20 อนุสรณ์งานพระราชทานเพลิงศพ นายชิน โสภณพนิช (๒๕๓๑).

21 Seagrave (1995), p. 167–78.

22 Yoshihara (1988), p. 197.

23 According to Sterling Seagrave, "After the 1947 army coup, General Phin (Choonhavan) saw to it that Chin got the government monopoly on all gold trading, the monopoly on all foreign exchange transactions and the monopoly on all Chinese remittances to the Mainland."

24 Seagrave (1995), p. 167–78.

25 อนุสรณ์งานพระราชทานเพลิงศพ นายชินโสภณพนิช (๒๕๓๑).

26 Vatikiotis (2006), p. 223.

27 Vatikiotis (2006), p. 223.

28 Vatikiotis (2006), p. 223.

29 Saowarop Panyacheewin, Bangkok Post, 3 February 1989.

30 Saowarop Panyacheewin, Bangkok Post, 3 February 1989.

31 อู๋จี้เยี่ย (๒๕๕๗) น. ๑๒๖–๗.

32 อู๋จี้เยี่ย (๒๕๕๗) น. ๑๖๓.

33 Saowarop Panyacheewin, Bangkok Post, 3 February 1989.

34 กรรณิการ์ ตันประเสริฐ, (๒๕๕๓).

35 See Kiarti Srifuengfung on page 382

36 Yoshihara (1988), p.198–99.

37 บริษัท โอสถสภา (เต็กเฮงหยู) จำกัด อนุสรณ์ในงานพระราชทานเพลิงศพ นายสวัสดิ์ โอสถานุเคราะห์ ๒๕๒๘.

38 Yoshihara (1988), p. 195.

39 Fairbank and MacFarquhar (1987)

40 An interview with Fu Xuzhong (符緒忠) was conducted on 14 May 2014 in Bangkok.

41 Yoshihara (1988), p. 196.

42 อนุสรณ์ในงานพระราชทานดินและเครื่องขอฆมาในพิธีฮีบรรจุศพ นายถาวร พรประภา ๒๕๔๔.

43 Arunee Sopitpongstorn (1991), p. 7–17.

44 Arunee Sopitpongstorn (1991), p. 7–17.

45 Arunee Sopitpongstorn (1991), p. 7–17.

46 Arunee Sopitpongstorn (1991), p. 21–36.

47 Yoshihara (1988), p. 197–98.

48 Arunee Sopitpongstorn (1991), p. 21–36.

49 อนุสรณ์ในงานพระราชทานดินฝังศพ นางสายพิณ โชควัฒนา (๒๕๔๖).

50 อนุสรณ์ในงานพระราชทานดินฝังศพ นางสายพิณ โชควัฒนา (๒๕๔๖).

51 An interview with Lin Taishen (林太深) was conducted on 14 May 2014 in Bangkok.

52 Bao Gong, a famous magistrate in Chinese history, is often portrayed in black face and is known for his incorruptible honesty.

53 Amphan's father was from Puning (Powleng) in Chaozhou. He married a Hakka in Thailand. He was one of the founders of the Chueng Family Association and devoted himself to work in both the Teochew and Puning associations. The Puning association leader was Lee Chue Miang. Amphan's father was well respected by Chinese in the Saphanlueang and Samyan area.

54 An interview with Amphan Chareonsuklap was conducted on 30 June 2014.

55 Lao and Gering, Asiaweek, 24 December 1999.

2 Stuart-Fox (2003), p.196

3 Lee Intong was the son-in-law of the legendary overseas Chinese tycoon and philanthropist Tan Kahkee.

4 Bangkok Post, June 30th 1975

5 Stuart-Fox (2003), p. 194.

6 Stuart-Fox (2003), p. 200.

7 Stuart-Fox (2003), p. 204.

8 Stuart-Fox (2003), p. 205.

9 Baker (1996), p. 11.

10 Baker (1996), p. 2.

11 Handley (2006), p. 91–93.

12 Case (2002), p. 158.

13 Bangkok Post, 6 March 1990.

14 Anderson (1970), p. 40; quoted by Kevin Hewison in Southeast Asia in the 1990s in (1987), p. 170.

15 Case (2002), p. 160.

16 Fred Riggs argued that the Chinese in Thailand are dependent "pariah entrepreneurs" who could only survive by buying protection from the Thai bureaucratic and military elites (Riggs, 1966), p. 251.

17 Case (2002), p. 157.

18 Case (2002), p. 155.

19 Phongpaichit and Baker (2005), p. 241.

20 Stuart-Fox, (2003), p. 200.

21 Stuart-Fox (2003), p. 202.

22 Handley, (2006), p. 113.

23 Stuart-Fox (2003), p. 203.

24 Stuart-Fox (2003), p. 195.

25 Phongpaichit and Chris Baker (1996), p. 30.

26 Phongpaichit and Chris Baker (1996), p. 30.

27 A maverick stock market speculator, Sia Song's fabled success drew a huge following among ordinary investors who imitated his buy-and-sell orders in Thailand's heady stock market.

28 Phongpaichit and Chris Baker (1996), p. 30.

29 Phongpaichit and Chris Baker (1996), p. 30.

30 Phongpaichit and Chris Baker (1996), p. 29.

31 The phrase was taken from the title of Nobel Laureate Joseph Stiglitz's book, The Roaring Nineties (2003), to characterize the decade of Asian economic growth that came to grief in the financial crisis of 1997.

32 Handley, (2006), p. 113.

33 Talerng was originally Charoen's boss at Hong Thong and later his partner in the liquor industry.

34 Case (2002), p. 155.

35 Phongpaichit and Chris Baker (1996), p. 318.

36 Stuart-Fox (2003), p. 210.

37 Handley,(2006), p. 113.

38 Handley (2006), p. 113.

39 Handley (2006), p. 113.

40 "China's rise challenges IMF," The Nation, Monday 13 October 2014, p. 5B.

ENDNOTES-CHAPTER 8

1 The PRC played an important role on the world stage for the first time at the Geneva Conference in 1954. China's skillful mediation at the Geneva negotiations helped to end the First Indochina War in 1954.

BIBLIOGRAPHY

Akira, Suehiro. *Capital Accumulation in Thailand 1855-1985.* Tokyo: Silkworm Books, 1989.

Arunee Sopitpongstorn, *Kiarti Srifuengfung: The Boy from Suphanburi.* Bangkok: Sri Yarnie, 1991.

Baker, Chris et al. *Van Vliet's Siam.* Chiang Mai: Silkworm Books, 2005.

Baker, Chris and Pasuk Phongpaichit. *A History of Thailand.* Cambridge: Cambridge University Press, 2005.

Batson, Benjamin A. *The End of Absolute Monarchy in Siam.* Singapore: Oxford University Press, 1984

Bhawan Ruangsilp, *Dutch East India Company Merchants at the Court of Ayutthaya: Dutch Perceptions of the Thai Kingdom c.1604–1765.* Leiden: Brill, 2007.

Bowring, John, Sir. *The Kingdom and People of Siam: Volume One.* Kuala Lumpur: Oxford University Press, 1969.

Bowring, John, Sir. *The Kingdom and People of Siam: Volume Two.* Kuala Lumpur: Oxford University Press, 1969.

Breazeale, Kennon, eds. *From Japan to Arabia: Ayutthaya's Maritime Relations with Asia.* Bangkok: The Foundation for the Promotion of Social Sciences and Humanities Textbooks Project, 1999.

Chaiyan Rajchagool, *The Rise and Fall of the Thai Absolute Monarchy.* Bangkok: White Lotus, 1994.

Charnvit Kasetsiri and Michael Wright. *Discovering Ayutthaya.* Bangkok: Toyota Thailand Foundation and The Foundation for the Promotion of Social Science and Humanities Textbooks Projects, 2007.

Charnvit Kasetsiri, et al. *Mother: Back from Banpong to Paknam.* Bangkok: The Foundation for the Promotion of Social Science and Humanities Textbooks Projects, 2010

Chen, Chingho A. " Mac Thien Tu and Phraya Taksin: A Survey on Their Political Stand, Conflicts and Background." *Proceedings of the 7th IAHA Conference.* Bangkok, 1977. pp. 1534–1575.

Choi Chi-Cheung. "Competition among Brothers: The Kin Tye Lung Company and its Associate Companies." *Chinese Business Enterprise in Asia.* Rajeswary A. Brown, ed. London and New York: Routledge, 1995.

Choi Chi-Cheung. "Kinship and Business: Paternal and Maternal Kin in Chaozhou Chinese Family Firms." *Business History*, Vol 40, No.1 (1998)

Choi Chi-Cheung. "Stepping out? Women in the Chaoshan Emigrant Communities, 1850-1950." *Merchants' Daughters: Women, Commerce, and Regional Culture in South China,* Helen F. Siu, ed. Hong Kong: Hong Kong University Press, 2010.

Comber, Leon. *Chinese Secret Socitetes in Malaya: A Survey of the Triad Society from 1800 to 1900.* New York: J.J. Augustin, 1959.

Cooke, Nola and Li Tana, eds. *Water Frontier: Commerce and the Chinese in the Lower Mekong Region, 1750-1880.* Singapore: Singapore University Press, 2004.

Coughlin, Richard J. *Double Identity: The Chinese in Modern Thailand.* Bangkok: White Lotus, 2012.

Cushman, Richard D., *The Royal Chronicles of Ayutthaya; a Synoptic translation.* Bangkok: Siam Society, 2006.

Cushman, Jennifer Wayne. *Fields from the Sea: Chinese Junk Trade with Siam during the Late Eighteenth and Early Nineteenth Century.* New York: Cornell Southeast Asia Program, 1993.

Dhiravat na Pombejra. "Dutch and French Evidence Concerning Court Conflicts at the end of King Phetracha's Reign, c. 1699-1703." *Silpakorn University International Journal,* Volume 2 Number 1, January-June 2002. pp. 47-70

Dhiravat na Pombejra. "Prince, Pretenders, and the Chinese Phrakhlang: An Analysis of the Dutch Evidence Concerning Siamese Court Politics, 1699-1734.", *On the Eighteenth Century as a Category of Asian History Van Leur in Retrospect.* Leonard Blussé and Femme Gaastraedt, ed. Hampshire: Ashgate, 1998, pp. 107-130.

Dhiravat na Pombejra. "Western Evidence Concerning the Role of the Chinese at the Siamese Court, 1699-1734." *Paper Presented to the 13th IAHA Conference Sophia University, Tokyo 5-9 September 1994.*

Disaphol Chansiri. *The Chinese Émigrés of Thailand in the Twentieth Century.* New York: Cambria Press, 2008.

Elliott, David. *Thailand: Origins of Military Rule.* London: Zed Press, 1978.

Evans, Peter B., Dietrich Rueschemeyer and Theda Skocpol, eds. *Bringing the State Back In.* Cambridge: Cambridge University Press, 1985.

Fairbank, John K. and Roderick MacFarquhar. *The Cambridge History of Chinese.* Cambridge: Cambridge University Press. 1987.

Fitzgerald, C.P. *The Southern Expansion of the Chinese People.* Bangkok: White Lotus, 1972.

Frankfurter, "King Mongkut." *Journal of the Siam Society* Vol. 1, 1904.

Gervaise, Nicolas. *The Natural and Political History of the Kingdom of Siam.* Bangkok: White Lotus, 1998.

Godley, Michael R., *The Mandarin capitalists from Nanyang: Overseas Chinese enterprise in the modernization of China 1893-1911.* Cambridge: Cambridge University Press, 1981.

Gosling, L.A. Peter, "Chinese Crop Dealers in Malaysia and Thailand: The Myth of the Merciless Monopsonistic Middleman", *The Chinese in Southeast Asia, Vol. 1, Ethnicity and Economic Activity.* (Singapore, 1983)

Gray, Christine. *Thailand: The Soteriological State in the 1970s Volume Two.* PhD dissertation, University of Chicago, 1986. (Chicago, Illinois) the faculty of the division of social sciences, department of anthropology.

Grossman, Nicholas, ed. *Chronicle of Thailand: Headline News Since 1946,* Singapore: Editions Didier Millet and Bangkok Post, 2009.

Handley, Paul., "Chaoren Pokphand's Investment in China." *The Encyclopedia of the Chinese Overseas,* Lynn Pan, ed. Singapore: Editions Didier Millet, 2006.

Henley, David and Andrew Forbes, *The Haw: Traders of the Golden Triangle.* New Zealand: Asia Film House Pty Ltd, 1997.

Hobsbawm, Eric. *The Age of Capital 1848-1875.* New York: Vintage Books, 1996.

Kaempfer, Engelbert. *A Description of the Kingdom of Siam 1960.* Bangkok: Orchid Press, 1998.

Jörg, Christiaan J.A., *Porcelain and the Dutch China trade*. The Hague: Springer, 1982.

Jörg, Christiaan J.A. "Chinese Porcelain for the Dutch in the Seventeenth Century: Trading Networks and Private Enterprise." *The Porcelains of Jingdezhen, Colloquies on Art & Archaeology in Asia* No.16 (London, 1993)

Landon, Kenneth Perry. *The Chinese in Thailand*. New York: The Institute of Pacific Relations, 1941.

Lao, Jervina and Julian Gearing. "Bangkok's Biggest Catch: Why Thai Union Frozen Food Is Very Hot Stuff." *Asiaweek*. 24 December 1999.

Latham, A.J.H. "From Competition to Constraint: The International Rice Trade in the Nineteenth and Twentieth Centuries." *Business and Economic History: Journal of the Business History Conference*, Vol. 17.1988, p. 91-102.

Launay, Adrien, *Histoire de la Mission de Siam 1662-1811*. Paris: P. Téqui, 1920.

Lee Lai To and Lee Hock Guan, eds. *Sun Yat-Sen: Nanyang and the 1911 Revolution*. Singapore: ISEAS, 2011.

Lei Tong. *The Ex-KMT Refugees in Northern Thailand in the age of International-Political Transformation of Post Cold War Asia*. MA dissertation. Chulalongkorn University, 2011.

Lieberman, Victor. *Strange Parallels Southeast Asia in Global Context, c. 800-1830*, Volume 1. Cambridge: Cambridge University Press, 2003.

Li Tana. "The Water Frontier: An Introduction." *Water Frontier; Commerce and the Chinese in the Lower Mekong Region, 1750-1880*. Singapore: Singapore University Press, 2004.

Ma Huan. *Ying-yai Sheng-lan, The Overall Survey of the Ocean's Shore* [1433]. Bangkok: White Lotus, 1977.

Mackie, Jamie, *Bandung Conference 1955: Non-Alignment and Afro-Asian Solidarity*. Singapore: Editions Didier Millet, 2005.

Manguin, Pierre-Yves, "Trading Networks and Ships in the South China Sea", *Lost for 500 years: Sunken Treasures of Brunei Darussalam*. Sydney: Art Exhibitions Australia, 2003.

Masuda, Erika. "The Fall of Ayutthaya and Siam's Disrupted Order of Tribute to China (1767-1782), *Taiwan Journal of Southeast Asian Studies*, (Taipei, 2007) pp. 75-128.

Miksic, John, "Research on Ceramic Trade, within Southeast Asia and between Southeast Asia and China." *Southeast Asian Ceramics: New Light on Old Pottery*. Singapore: Editions Didier Millet, 2009.

Murashima, Eiji. "The Thai-Japanese Alliance and the Chinese of Thailand", *Southeast Asian Minorities in the Wartime Japanese Empire*. Paul Kratoska, ed. Oxon: RoutledgeCurzon, 2002.

Murashima, Eiji. "The Commemorative Character of Thai Historiography: The 1942-43 Thai Military Campaign in the Shan States Depicted as a Story of National Salvation and the Restoration of Thai Independence." *Modern Asian Studies*. Volume 40, Issue 4. United Kingdom: Cambridge University Press, 2006.

Murashima, Eiji. "The Origins of Chinese Nationalism in Thailand" *Journal of Asia-Pacific Studies* (Waseda University) No. 21 (August 2013)

F.W.Mote. "The Rural "Haw" (Yunnanese Chinese) of Northern Thailand." *Southeast Asian Tribes, Minorities, and Nations*. Peter Kunstadter, ed. New Jersey: Princeton University Press, 1970.

Na Ranong, Bonnie, "The Skin of the Tiger," *Writing from Asia: Treasures Myths and Traditions*. Bangkok: National Museum Volunteers, 1996.

Ng, Chin-keong. *Trade and Society: The Amoy Network on the China Coast 1683-1735*. Singapore: Singapore University Press, 1983.

Pan, Lynn, *Sons of the Yellow Emperor: The Story of the Overseas Chinese*. London: Mandarin, 1991

Puangthong Rungswasdisab. "Siam and the Contest for Control of the Trans-Mekong Trading Networks from the late Eighteenth to the Mid Nineteenth Century." *Water Frontier; Commerce and the Chinese in the Lower Mekong Region, 1750-1880*. Singapore: Singapore University Press, 2004.

Purcell Victor. *The Chinese in Southeast Asia*, Second Edition. Kuala Lumpur: Oxford University Press, 1981.

Raben, Remco and Dhiravat na Pombejra, "Tipping Balances: King Borommakot and the Dutch East India Company." *In the King's Trail, an 18th Century Dutch Journey to the Buddha's footprint, Theodorus Jacobus van den Heuvel's account of his voyage to Phra Phutthabat in 1737*. Bangkok: The Royal Netherlands Embassy, 1997.

Riggs, Fred W. *Thailand: The Modernization of a Bureaucratic Polity*. Honolulu: East-West Center Press, 1967.

Roth, Guenther and Claus Wittich, ed. *Max Weber Economy and Society: An Outline of Interpretive Sociology, Vol 2*. Berkeley: Univeristy of California Press, 1978.

Sakurai and Kitagawa. "Ha Tien or Banteay Meas in the Time of the Fall of Ayutthaya." *From Japan to Arabia: Ayutthaya's Maritime Relations with Asia*. Bangkok: The Foundation for the Promotion of Social Sciences and Humanities Textbooks Project, 1999.

Sakurai, Yumio. "Eighteenth-Century Chinese Pioneers on the Water Frontier of Indochina." *Water Frontier; Commerce and the Chinese in the Lower Mekong Region, 1750-1880*. Singapore: Singapore University Press, 2004.

Saowarop Panyacheewin. "An oversea Chinese now Thailand's oldest working journalist." *Bangkok Post*. 3 February 1989.

Sarasin Viraphol. *Tribute and Profit: Sino-Siamese Trade, 1652-1853*. Massachusetts: Harvard University Press, 1977.

Sardesai, D.R. *Southeast Asia Past and Present*. Chiangmai: Silkworm Books, 1997.

Seagrave, Sterling. *Lords of the Rim: The Invisible Empire of the Overseas Chinese*. London: Bantam Press,1996.

Skinner, G. William. *Chinese Society in Thailand: An Analytical History*. Ithaca, N.Y. : Cornell University Press, 1957.

Steinberg, David Joel, ed. *In Search of Southeast Asia: A Modern History*. Kuala Lumpur: Oxford University Press, 1971.

Stifel, Lawrence D. "Recollection of Puey Ungpakorn." *A Siamese for All Seasons*. Bangkok: Kamol Keemthong Foundation, 1981.

Stuart Fox, Martin, *A Short History of China and Southeast Asia: Tribute, Trade and Influence*. Crows Nest, N.S.W.: Allen & Unwin, 2003.

Suebsaeng Promboon. *Sino-Siamese Tributary Relations ,1282-1853*. PhD thesis, University of Wisconsin, Madison, 1971, 292.

Suthee Meanchainun, ed. *100th year Anniversary Thai-Chinese Chamber of Commerce*. Bangkok: Kyodo Nation, 2010.

Suzuki Takashi. *The Short History of Srivijaya*. Bangkok: Siam Society, 10 April 2013.

Tachard, Guy. *A Relation of the Voyage to Siam performed by six Jesuits sent by the French King, to the Indies and China, in the year 1685*. Bangkok: White Lotus, 1999.

Tate, D.J.M. *The Making of Modern South-east Asia: Volume 2 The Western Impact, Economic and Social Change*. Kuala Lumpur: Oxford University Press, 1979.

Terwiel, B.J., *Thailand's Political History From the Fall of Ayutthaya to Recent Times*. Bangkok: Riverbooks, 2005.

Terwiel, B. J. *Thailand's Political History: From the 13th Century to Recent Times*. Bangkok: River Books, 2005.

Van Dyke, Paul A., *The Canton Trade: Life and Enterprise on the China Coast, 1700-1845*. Hong Kong: Hong Kong University Press, 2012.

Van Roy, Edward. *Sampheng: Bangkok's Chinatown Inside Out*. Bangkok: Institute of Asian Studies Chulalongkorn University, 2007.

Vatikiotis, Michael R.J. "The Rise of the Bangkok Bank." *The Encyclopedia of the Chinese Overseas*. Singapore: Editions Didier Millet, 2006.

Vella, Walter F. *Siam Under Rama III 1824 −1831*. New York: Monograph of the Association of Asian Studies, 1957.

Vella, Walter F. *Chaiyo! King vajiravudh and the Development of Thai Nationalism*. Honolulu: University of Hawaii Press, 1978.

Wade, Geoff. "The Ming Shi-lu as a Source for Thai History 14th to 17th Century." *Fifth International Conference on Thai Studies*. SOAS, London, July 1993.

Wade, Geoff. "The Southern Chinese Borders in History." *Where China Meets Southeast Asia: Social & Cultural Change in the Border Regions*. Evans, Hutton and Kuah, eds. Bangkok: White Lotus, 2000.

Wang Gungwu. *Junzi: Scholar-Gentleman in Conversation with Asad-ul Iqbal Latif*. Singapore: ISEAS Publishing, 2010.

Wang Gungwu. *China and the Chinese Overseas*. Singapore: Times Academic Press, 1992.

Warrington Smyth. *Five Years in Siam from 1891-1896,* Bangkok: White Lotus, 1994.

Wasana Wongsurawat, "Contending for a Claim on Civilization: The Sino-Siamese Struggle to Control Overseas Chinese Education in Siam," *Journal of Chinese Overseas 4, 2* (November 2008).

Wasana Wongsurawat, "Thailand and the Xinhai Revolution: Expectation, Reality and Inspiration," *Sun Yat-sen: Nanyang and the 1911 Revolution*. Singapore : Chinese Heritage Centre: Institute of Southeast Asian Studies, 2011.

Warren, James A. *Gambling, the State and Society in Thailand, c.1800-1945*. Oxon: Routledge, 2013.

Warren, James A. "Troublesome spirits: alcohol, excise and extraterritoriality in nineteenth and early twentieth century Siam." *South East Asia Research*, 21, 4, pp. 575-599 (2013).

Wen-Chin Chang, "Ethnic Identity and the Thai Nation-State: The Complexities of Migration and Ethnic Identification of the KMT Yunnanese Chinese in Northern Thailand." *7th International Conference on Thai Studies Amsterdam*, 4-8 July 1999.

Westad, Odd Arne. *Restless Empire: China and the World Since 1750*. London: The Bodley Head, 2012.

Wilson, David A. *Politics in Thailand*. New York: Cornell University Press, 1966.

Wright, Arnold and Oliver T. Breakspear, eds. *Twentieth Century Impressions of Siam: Its History, People, Commerce, Industries and Resources*. Bangkok: White Lotus, 1994.

Wyatt, David K., *Studies in Thai History*. Chiang Mai: Silkworm Books 2008.

Wyatt, David K. *Thailand: A Short History*. Chiang Mai: Silkworm Books, 2003.

Wyatt, David K. "King Borommakot, his Court, and their World," In *the King's Trail, an 18th Century Dutch Journey to the Buddha's Footprint,Theodorus Jacobus van den Heuvel's account of his voyage to Phra Phutthabat in 1737*. Bangkok: The Royal Netherlands Embassy, 1997.

Yoshihara, Kunio *The Rise of Ersatz Capitalism in South-East Asia*. Singapore: Oxford University Press, 1988.

.............*The Chater Legacy: A Selection of Chater Collection*. Hong Kong: The Leisure and Cultural Service Department, 2007.

.............*From Beijing to Versailles: Artistic Relations between China and France*. Hong Kong: The Urban Council of Hong Kong, 1997.

Thai-language Sources:

............๗๙ ปี สุรัตน์ โอสถานุเคราะห์ อนุสรณ์ในงานพระราชทานเพลิงศพ นายสุรัตน์ โอสถานุเคราะห์ กรุงเทพฯ: สำนักพิมพ์อมรินทร์ ๒๕๕๑

............"คำให้การชาวกรุงเก่า" **พระราชพงศาวดารกรุงศรีอยุธยา ฉบับพันจันทนุมาศ (เจิม) และพระราชพงศาวดารกรุงศรีอยุธยาฉบับหลวงประเสริฐ คำให้การชาวกรุงเก่า คำให้การขุนหลวงหาวัด** กรุงเทพฯ : ศรีปัญญา ๒๕๕๓

............"จดหมายรายวันทัพสมัยกรุงธนบุรี คราวปราบเมืองพุทไธมาศและเขมร เมื่อ พ.ศ. ๒๓๑๔" **พระราชพงศาวดารกรุงธนบุรี ฉบับพันจันทนุมาศ (เจิม) จดหมายรายวันทัพ อภินิหารบรรพบุรุษและเอกสารอื่น** กรุงเทพฯ :ศรีปัญญา ๑๕๕๑

............"จดหมายเหตุของพวกคณะบาทหลวงฝรั่งเศสซึ่งเข้ามาตั้งครั้งกรุงศรีอยุธยาตอนแผ่นดินพระเจ้าเอกทัศกับครั้งกรุงธนบุรี และครั้งกรุงรัตนโกสินทรตอนต้น ภาค ๖" **พระราชพงศาวดารกรุงธนบุรี ฉบับพันจันทนุมาศ (เจิม) จดหมายรายวันทัพ อภินิหารบรรพบุรุษและเอกสารอื่น** กรุงเทพฯ: ศรีปัญญา ๒๕๕๑

............"จดหมายเหตุความทรงจำ ฉบับ พ.ศ. ๒๔๕๙" **พระราชพงศาวดารกรุงธนบุรี ฉบับพันจันทนุมาศ (เจิม) จดหมายรายวันทัพ อภินิหารบรรพบุรุษและเอกสารอื่น** กรุงเทพฯ: ศรีปัญญา ๒๕๕๑

............เชี่ยง ชุน เหล็ง หง ที่ระลึกในงานฌาปนกิจศพ นายเทียนส่าง จึงแย้ม

ปิ่น ณ วัดไชยชนะสงคราม (วัดตึก) วันที่ ๖ พฤษภาคม พ.ศ.๒๔๗๑ โรงพิมพ์
โสภณพิพรรฒนากร

...........โรงพยาบาลเทียนฟ้ามูลนิธิ ครบรอบ ๑๐๐ ปี กรุงเทพฯ: โรงพยาบาล
เทียนฟ้ามูลนิธิ

...........ปีระวัติตระกูลและสายเครือญาติ เนื่องในงานทำบุญครบรอบ
๑๒๐ ปี พระเจดีย์ทรงไทยในวัดมังกรกมลาวาส วันเสาร์ที่ ๑๕ กันยายน
๒๕๕๕

...........พระราชพงศาวดารกรุงธนบุรี ฉบับพันจันทนุมาศ (เจิม) กรุงเทพฯ:
ศรีปัญญา ๒๕๕๑

...........พระราชพงศาวดารกรุงธนบุรี ฉบับสมเด็จพระพนรัตน์ หรือฉบับ
หมอบรัดเล กรุงเทพฯ: โฆษิต ๒๕๕๑

...........พระราชพงศาวดารกรุงรัตนโกสินทร์ รัชกาลที่ ๑ ฉบับเจ้าพระยา
ทิพากรวงศ์ ฉบับตัวเขียน. ศ.ดร.นิธิ เอียวศรีวงศ์ บรรณาธิการ กรุงเทพฯ
๒๕๓๙

...........พระราชพงศาวดารกรุงรัตนโกสินทร์ รัชกาลที่ ๓ ฉบับเจ้าพระยา
ทิพากรวงศมหาโกษาธิบดี กรมศิลปากร ๒๕๓๘

...........พระราชพงศาวดารกรุงรัตนโกสินทร์ รัชกาลที่ ๔ ฉบับเจ้าพระยา
ทิพากรวงศ์ (ขำ บุนนาค) กรุงเทพฯ: ต้นฉบับ ๒๕๔๗

...........พระราชพงศาวดารกรุงศรีอยุธยา ฉบับพันจันทนุมาศ (เจิม)
กรุงเทพฯ: ศรีปัญญา ๒๕๕๓

...........พระราชพงศาวดาร ฉบับพระราชหัตถเลขา เล่ม ๒ กรุงเทพฯ :
กรมศิลปากร ๒๕๔๒

...........พงศาวดารเมืองสงขลาและพัทลุง พิมพ์เป็นอนุสรณ์ในงานฌาปนกิจ
ศพ คุณหญิงแข เพ็ชราภิบาล (แข ณ สงขลา) พระนคร ๒๕๐๕

...........ตระกูลวังตาล ธันวาคม ๒๕๔๘

...........สาธุชนานุสรณ์ พิมพ์เป็นธรรมบรรณาการ เนื่องในพิธีบรรจุศพ นาย
ล้วน ว่องวานิช กรุงเทพฯ: สว่างศิลป์ ๒๕๐๘

...........อธิบายแผนที่พระนครศรีอยุธยา กับคำวินิจฉัยของพระยาโบราณ
ราชธานินทร์ และภูมิสถานกรุงศรีอยุธยา กรุงเทพฯ : ต้นฉบับ ๒๕๕๐

...........อนุสรณ์งานฌาปนกิจ คุณพ่อเล็ก เสรฐภักดี (กรุงเทพฯ ๒๕๔๕)

กรรณิการ์ ตันประเสริฐ (บรรณาธิการ) ๙๐ ปี มูลนิธิป่อเต็กตึ๊งบนเส้นทาง
ประวัติศาสตร์สังคมไทย: ประวัติศาสตร์จากคำบอกเล่า กรุงเทพฯ: ด่าน
สุทธาการพิมพ์ ๒๕๓๓

ก.ศ.ร.กุหลาบ มหามุขมาตยานุกูลวงศ์ เล่ม ๑ ส่วนที่ ๒ (กรุงเทพฯ ร.ศ. ๑๒๔)

ขจร สุขพานิช ฐานันดรไพร่ กรุงเทพฯ: สมาคมประวัติศาสตร์ฯ ๒๕๕๖

ขวัญดี อัตวาวุฒิชัย, "ซินแสเขียวฮุดเส็ง นักหนังสือพิมพ์ไทย นักการเมืองจีน"
เส้นทางเศรษฐกิจฉบับพิเศษ เล่ม ๒

จำนงศรี รัตนิน ดุจนาวากลางมหาสมุทร กรุงเทพฯ: นานมีบุคส์ ๒๕๔๑

เจนจีนอักษร, พระ (สุดใจ ตัณฑากาศ) จดหมายเหตุเรื่องพระราชไมตรีระหว่าง
กรุงสยามกับกรุงจีน อนุสรณ์ในงานฌาปนกิจศพ นายโฉมิต เวชชาชีวะ
กรุงเทพฯ ๒๕๐๗

เจริญ ตันมหาพราน ๓ เจ้าสัวปางไม้ กรุงเทพฯ: ปราชญ์ ๒๕๕๔

เจริญ ตันมหาพราน ยี่กอฮง พระอนุวัตน์ราชนิยม กรุงเทพฯ: ปราชญ์ ๒๕๕๔

ชาญ กัลยาณมิตร สกุลกัลยาณมิตร กรุงเทพฯ: โรงพิมพ์ส่วนท้องถิ่น กรมการ
ปกครอง ๒๕๓๖

เชาวน์ พงษ์พิชิต ลูกจีนรักชาติ กรุงเทพฯ: มติชน ๒๕๕๓

ไชยยุทธ ปิ่นประดับ ประวัติความเป็นมาของอั้งยี่กับศาลเจ้าต้องย่องสู่
ภูเก็ต ภูเก็ต: ห้างหุ้นส่วนจำกัด วิเศษออฟเซ็ทคอมพิว ๒๕๔๐

เซี่ย กวง วิกรรมทางการเมืองของชาวจีนโพ้นทะเลในประเทศไทย (ค.ศ.๑๙๐๖-
๑๙๓๗) กรุงเทพฯ: สถาบันเอเชียศึกษา จุฬาลงกรณ์มหาวิทยาลัย ๒๕๔๖

เทพ บุญตานนท์ พระมงกุฎเกล้าเจ้าอยู่หัวกับการสร้างภาพลักษณ์ทางการ
ทหาร วิทยานิพนธ์ภาควิชาประวัติศาสตร์ จุฬาลงกรณ์มหาวิทยาลัย ๒๕๕๖

ณัฏฐภัทร จันทวิช "ข้อเท็จจริงบางประการเกี่ยวกับประวัติศาสตร์สมัยอยุธยา
ตอนปลายและกรุงธนบุรี จากจดหมายเหตุจีน" ศิลปากร ปีที่ ๒๔ เล่มที่ ๒
และ ๓ (๒๕๒๓)

ณัฐวุฒิ สุทธิสงคราม ชีวิตและงานกงสุลไทยของพระยาอนุกูลสยามกิจอุ
ปนิษิตสยามรัฐ (ตันกิมเจ๋ง) กงสุลเจเนอราลไทยคนแรก ณ เมือง
สิงคโปร์ กรุงเทพฯ: รุ่งเรืองสาส์นการพิมพ์ ๒๕๒๕

ดวงจิตร จิตรพงศ์, หม่อมเจ้าหญิง ป้าป้อนหลาน พิมพ์เป็นที่ระลึกในงานพระ
ชันษาครบ ๙๐ ปี ๒๖ กันยายน ๒๕๔๑

ติลก วุฒิพาณิชย์ "ขุนเศรษฐภักดี: วิถีชีวิต" จีนทักษิน: วิถีและพลัง กรุงเทพฯ:
สำนักงานกองทุนสนับสนุนการวิจัย ๒๕๔๔

ดำรงราชานุภาพ, สมเด็จพระเจ้าบรมวงศ์เธอกรมพระยา พระราชพงศาวดาร
กรุงรัตนโกสินทร์ รัชกาลที่ ๒ แจกในงานเผามณฑปหม่อมแก้ว ทินกร และ
นายฤทธิ์ลำแดง (เปลี่ยน ฐิตะรัต) ๒๔๗๘

ดำริห์ เรืองสุธรรม ขบวนการแรงงานไทยในการต่อต้านกองทัพญี่ปุ่นใน
สงครามโลกครั้งที่ ๒ กรุงเทพฯ: สุขภาพใจ ๒๕๔๔

ต้วน ลี เซิง พลิกต้นตระกูลไทย กรุงเทพฯ: พิราบสำนักพิมพ์ ๒๕๓๘

ถาวร พรประภา อนุสรณ์แห่งความทรงจำ อนุสรณ์งานพระราชทานดิน
และเครื่องขมา ในพิธีพระราชทานเพลิงศพ ดร.ถาวร พรประภา ป.ช.,ป.ม.,ท.จ. ณ ศาลา
กตัญญู สวนพฤกษชาติ ถาวร-อุษาธานี ตำบลโป่ง อำเภอบางละมุง (พัทยา)
จังหวัดชลบุรี ๑๓ ตุลาคม ๒๕๔๔

ถาวร สิกขโกศล แต้จิ๋ว: จีนกลุ่มน้อยที่ยิ่งใหญ่ กรุงเทพฯ: ศิลปวัฒนธรรม ๒๕๕๔

ถาวร สิกขโกศล ชื่อและแซ่ของคนจีน กรุงเทพฯ: สถาบันไทยคดีศึกษา
มหาวิทยาลัยธรรมศาสตร์ ๒๕๓๗

ถ่องแท้ รจนาสันต์ และ อุดม ประมวลวิทยา "ประวัติศาสตร์การทูตระหว่างไทย-
จีน" ประวัติการต่อสู้ของขุนศึกบุรุษไทย. พระนคร: คลังวิทยา ๒๕๐๖

แถมสุข นุ่มนนท์ ยังเติร์กรุ่นแรก (กบฏ ร.ศ. ๑๓๐ กรุงเทพฯ: สายธาร ๒๕๔๕

ทักษ์ เฉลิมเตียรณ "เราใช่เขา? ภาพเสนอคนจีนในวรรณกรรมไทย" ใน อ่าน ปีที่
๕ ฉบับที่ ๑ กรกฎาคม-ธันวาคม ๒๕๕๖

นวพร เรืองสกุล สีลม ย่าหยา และตำราอาหาร กรุงเทพฯ: นอร์เลจ พลัส
๒๕๕๑

นรนิติ เศรษฐบุตร สู่สยามนามขจร กรุงเทพฯ: ไม่บุระสำนักพิมพ์ ไม่ระบุปีที่
ตีพิมพ์

นากัส เศรษฐบุตร ล่องสำเภาเข้าสยาม สืบสายสกุลแห่งพระประเสริฐ
วานิช (โป๊) กรุงเทพฯ ๒๕๕๖

นิธิ เอียวศรีวงศ์ การเมืองไทยสมัยพระเจ้ากรุงธนบุรี กรุงเทพฯ: สำนักพิมพ์
มติชน ๒๕๕๕

เนื้ออ่อน วรเวทย์พิสิฐ ประมวลหลักฐานสมเด็จพระเจ้าตากสินมหาราช ภาค
๒ ที่ระลึกในงานพระราชทานเพลิงศพ พระยาเกษตรหิรัญรักษ์ (อุ่น ควานิ
เสน) ๒๔๘๒

บริษัท โอสถสภา (เต๊กเฮงหยู) จำกัด อนุสรณ์งานพระราชทานเพลิงศพนาย
สวัสดิ์ โอสถานุเคราะห์ ๒๕๒๔

ประพฤทธิ์ ศุกลรัตนเมธี แปล "พระราชสาส์นของสยามถึงข้าหลวงมณฑลกวางตุ้ง
กว่างซี" เอกสารประวัติศาสตร์จีนเกี่ยวกับความสัมพันธ์ไทย-จีน รัชสมัย
พระบาทสมเด็จพระพุทธยอดฟ้าจุฬาโลกฯ ใน ประวัติศาสตร์ปริทรรศน์
วินัย พงศ์ศรีเพียร บรรณาธิการ กรุงเทพฯ: กองทุนดำเนิร เลขะกูล เพื่อ
ประวัติศาสตร์ ๒๕๔๒

ประสิทธิ์ รักประชา ข้าพเจ้ากับเสรีไทยสายจีน กรุงเทพฯ: พี.วาทิน พับลิเคชั่น
๒๕๔๐

ปรีดี พนมยงค์ สกุลพนมยงค์ เนื่องในวันปรีดี พนมยงค์ ๑๑ พฤษภาคม ๒๕๓๐
(กรุงเทพฯ ๒๕๓๐)

ปาริชาต วิลาวรรณ **การค้าของป่าในประวัติศาสตร์อยุธยา พ.ศ.๑๘๙๓–๒๓๑๐** วิทยานิพนธ์ภาควิชาประวัติศาสตร์ จุฬาลงกรณ์มหาวิทยาลัย กรุงเทพฯ: ๒๕๒๘

พรรณี บัวเล็ก **ลักษณะของนายทุนไทย ในช่วงระหว่าง พ.ศ.๒๔๕๗-๒๔๘๒ บทเรียนจากความรุ่งโรจน์สู่โศกนาฏกรรม** กรุงเทพฯ: สำนักพิมพ์พันธกิจ ๒๕๔๕

พรรณี บัวเล็ก **สยามในกระแสธารแห่งการเปลี่ยนแปลง ประวัติศาสตร์ไทยตั้งแต่สมัย รัชกาลที่ ๕** กรุงเทพฯ เมืองโบราณ ๒๕๔๑

พอพันธ์ อุยยานนท์ "คณะราษฎรกับเศรษฐกิจไทย" ศิลปวัฒนธรรม ลำดับที่ ๔๐๐ ปีที่ ๓๔ ฉบับที่ ๔ เดือนกุมภาพันธ์ ๒๕๕๖

พิมพ์ประไพ พิศาลบุตร (บรรณาธิการ) **ลูกจีนหลานมอญในกรุงสยาม** กรุงเทพฯ: สารคดี ๒๕๔๗

พิมพ์ประไพ พิศาลบุตร **สำเภาสยาม ตำนานเจ๊กบางกอก** กรุงเทพฯ: นานมีบุ๊คส์, ๒๕๕๔

พิมพ์ประไพ พิศาลบุตร **นายแม่** กรุงเทพฯ: นานมีบุ๊คส์, ๒๕๕๕

พิมพ์ประไพ พิศาลบุตร **กระเบื้องถ้วยกะลาแตก** กรุงเทพฯ: นานมีบุ๊คส์, ๒๕๕๐

พิมพ์พัณธุ์ หาญสกุล **คนต้นแบบ ดร.บุญยง ว่องวานิช** กรุงเทพฯ: อมรินทร์ธรรมะ อมรินทร์พริ้นติ้งแอนด์พับลิชชิ่ง ๒๕๕๗

เพ็ญพิสุทธิ์ อินทรภิรมย์ **เซียวฮุดเสง สีบุญเรือง: ทัศนะและบทบาทของจีนสยามในสังคมไทย** กรุงเทพฯ: ศูนย์ประวัติศาสตร์ความสัมพันธ์ไทยกับประเทศในเอเชีย ภาควิชาประวัติศาสตร์ คณะอักษรศาสตร์ จุฬาลงกรณ์มหาวิทยาลัย ๒๕๔๗

วรวุฒิ จิราสมบัติ "ลูกสาวเจ้าสัวล่ำซำ" **ลูกจีนหลานมอญในกรุงสยาม** กรุงเทพฯ: สารคดี ๒๕๔๗

วรศักดิ์ มหัทธโนบล **"ฮากกา" คือ "จีนแคะ"** กรุงเทพฯ: มติชน ๒๕๕๑

วรางคณา นิพัทธ์สุขกิจ **กลุ่มคนที่สัมพันธ์กับการค้าในสังคมอยุธยา พ.ศ.๒๑๗๑–๒๓๑๐** วิทยานิพนธ์ภาควิชาประวัติศาสตร์ จุฬาลงกรณ์มหาวิทยาลัย กรุงเทพฯ ๒๕๔๘

วิทยา วิทยอำนวยคุณ **คนจีน ๒๐๐ ปี ภายใต้พระบรมโพธิสมภาร เนื่องในวโรกาสพระบาทสมเด็จพระเจ้าอยู่หัวทรงครองสิริราชสมบัติเป็นปีที่ ๕๐** กรุงทพฯ: เส้นทางเศรษฐกิจ

วินัย พงศ์ศรีเพียร บรรณาธิการ **ความยอกย้อนของอดีต: พิพิธนิพนธ์เชิดชูเกียรติ พลตรี หม่อมราชวงศ์ ศุภวัฒย์ เกษมศรี** กรุงเทพฯ: [ม.ป.พ.] ๒๕๓๗

วินัย พงศ์ศรีเพียร (บรรณาธิการ) **ปัญหาในประวัติศาสตร์ไทย จุลสารคณะกรรมการชำระประวัติศาสตร์ไทย** กรุงเทพฯ: สำนักเลขาธิการนายกรัฐมนตรี ปีที่ ๑ เล่มที่ ๒ กันยายน ๒๕๒๙ – สิงหาคม ๒๕๓๐

วุฒิชัย มูลศิลป์ "ปัญหาฝิ่นในเมืองไทยก่อนสนธิสัญญาบาวริง" **ประวัติศาสตร์ปริทรรศน์** วินัย พงศ์ศรีเพียร บรรณาธิการ กรุงเทพฯ: กองทุนดำเนิร เลขะกุลเพื่อประวัติศาสตร์ ๒๕๔๒

สงบ ส่งเมือง **การพัฒนาหัวเมืองสงขลา ในสมัยกรุงธนบุรีและสมัยรัตนโกสินทร์ตอนต้น (พ.ศ. ๒๓๑๐–๒๔๔๔)** รายงานการวิจัยภาควิชาประวัติศาสตร์ มหาวิทยาลัยศรีนครินทร์วิโรฒ สงขลา ๒๕๒๓

สรกล อดุลยานนท์ **จอมยุทธ์น้ำเมา เจริญ สิริวัฒนภักดี ผู้หาญกระตุกหนวดสิงห์** กรุงเทพฯ: มติชน ๒๕๔๑

สารสิน วีระผล **จิ้มก้องและกำไร : การค้าไทย-จีน ๒๑๙๕ – ๒๓๙๖** กรุงเทพฯ: มูลนิธิโครงการตำราสังคมศาสตร์และมนุษยศาสตร์ ๒๕๔๘

สื่อมวลชลคาทอลิกประเทศไทย ทำเนียบวัดคาทอลิกในประเทศไทย (กรุงเทพฯ ๒๕๔๑)

สืบแสง พรหมบุญ **ความสัมพันธ์ในระบบบรรณาการระหว่างจีนกับไทย ค.ศ. ๑๒๘๒–๑๘๕๓** กรุงเทพฯ: มูลนิธิโครงการตำราสังคมศาสตร์ และมนุษยศาสตร์ ๒๕๒๕

สืบแสง พรหมบุญ **รวมบทความทางประวัติศาสตร์ของผู้ช่วยศาสตราจารย์ ดร.สืบแสง พรหมบุญ** อนุสรณ์งานพระราชทานเพลิงศพ ผู้ช่วยศาสตราจารย์ ดร.สืบแสง พรหมบุญ ๒๒ กรกฎาคม ๒๕๕๕

สุดารา สุจฉายา (บรรณาธิการ) **ลูกจีนหลานมอญในกรุงสยาม** กรุงเทพฯ: สารคดี ๒๕๔๗

สุจิตต์ วงษ์เทศ (บรรณาธิการ) **อภินิหารบรรพบุรุษและปฐมวงศ์** กรุงเทพฯ: มติชน ๒๕๔๕

สุภาภรณ์ จรัลพัฒน์ **ภาษีฝิ่นกับนโยบายด้านการคลังของรัฐบาลไทย พ.ศ. ๒๓๖๗–๒๔๖๘** วิทยานิพนธ์ภาควิชาประวัติศาสตร์ จุฬาลงกรณ์มหาวิทยาลัย ๒๕๒๓

เสี่ยวจิว (นามแฝง) **ที่เรียกว่า 'แต้จิ๋ว'** กรุงเทพฯ: มติชน ๒๕๕๖

เสี่ยวจิว (นามแฝง) **ตัวตนคนแต้จิ๋ว** กรุงเทพฯ: ศิลปวัฒนธรรม ๒๕๕๔

สวน, มหาดเล็ก "โคลงยอพระเกียรติพระเจ้ากรุงธนบุรี" ฉบับพิมพ์โดยหอพระสมุดวชิรญาณ ๒๔๖๕

ศรีสมร ศรีเบญจพลางกูร **ประวัติศาสตร์เมืองสงขลา** (สงขลา ๒๕๓๙)

ศรีเสนา สมบัติศิริ **อนุสรณ์ในงานพระราชทานเพลิงศพนายศรีเสนา สมบัติศิริ** กรุงเทพฯ ๒๕๒๕

ศุภการ สิริไพศาล "นิราศกวางตุ้งของหลวงนายศักดิ์ พ.ศ. ๒๓๒๔ : วรรณกรรมประวัติศาสตร์ในบริบทความสัมพันธ์ไทย – จีนสมัยกรุงธนบุรี" ๑๐๐ เอกสารสำคัญ: **สรรพสาระประวัติศาสตร์ไทยลำดับที่ ๑๔** กรุงเทพฯ: สำนักงานกองทุนสนับสนุนการวิจัย ๒๕๕๕

ศุภรัตน์ เลิศพาณิชย์กุล "ขุนนางไทยเชื้อสายจีนบางตระกูลในสมัยรัตนโกสินทร์" **ชาวจีนแต้จิ๋วในประเทศไทย และในภูมิลำเนาเดิมที่เฉาซัน สมัยที่ ๒ ท่าเรือซ่านโถว ค.ศ.๑๘๖๐–๑๙๔๙** กรุงเทพฯ: สถาบันเอเชียศึกษา จุฬาลงกรณ์มหาวิทยาลัย ๒๕๓๙

ศุภรัตน์ เลิศพาณิชย์กุล **สมาคมลับอั้งยี่ในประเทศไทย พ.ศ. ๒๓๖๗ – ๒๔๕๓** วิทยานิพนธ์ภาควิชาประวัติศาสตร์ จุฬาลงกรณ์มหาวิทยาลัย ๒๕๒๔

ศุภวรรณ ชวรัตนวงศ์ **บทบาทของชาวจีนในไทยตั้งแต่สมัยอยุธยาตอนปลายถึงสมัยรัชกาลที่ ๓ แห่งกรุงรัตนโกสินทร์ พ.ศ.๒๑๗๒– ๒๓๙๔** วิทยานิพนธ์ภาควิชาประวัติศาสตร์ จุฬาลงกรณ์มหาวิทยาลัย ๒๔๕๐

ธิษณา วีรเกียรติสุนทร "จดหมายเหตุรายวันทัพรัชกาลสมเด็จพระเจ้ากรุงธนบุรีทรงตีเมืองพุทไธมาศและกัมพูชา" **๑๐๐ เอกสารสำคัญ: สรรพสาระประวัติศาสตร์ไทยลำดับที่ ๑๔** กรุงเทพฯ: สำนักงานกองทุนสนับสนุนการวิจัย ๒๕๕๕

อัมพร เอี่ยมสุรีย์ **รักชาติยิ่งชีพ** : **ชีวประวัติเหียกวงเอี่ยม** กรุงเทพฯ: มีเดียเพรส ๒๕๓๗

อินทรมนตรี (แย้ม) พระ "ระยะทางราชทูตไทยไปกรุงปักกิ่งประเทศจีน" **แถลงงานประวัติศาสตร์ เอกสารโบราณคดี** ปีที่ ๘ เล่ม ๑–๓ (มกราคม-ธันวาคม ๒๕๑๗)

เอนก นาวิกมูล บรรณาธิการ **สมบัติปัตตานี ๒๕๕๗** จังหวัดปัตตานี ๒๕๕๗

เออิจิ มูราชิมา **การเมืองจีนสยาม** : **การเคลื่อนไหวทางการเมืองของชาวจีนโพ้นทะเลในประเทศไทย ค.ศ. ๑๙๒๔–๑๙๔๑** กรุงเทพฯ: ศูนย์จีนศึกษา สถาบันเอเชียศึกษา จุฬาลงกรณ์มหาวิทยาลัย ๒๕๓๙

อู๋จี้เยียะ **จากบูรพาสู่อุษาคเนย์ ภาคแรก** ปนัดดา เลิศล้ำอำไพ บรรณาธิการแปล กรุงเทพฯ: โพสต์ ๒๕๕๗

暹羅中華總商會：追悼故主席陳守明先生特輯

INDEX

Thai and Chinese names are entered under the first name. Western names are inverted.

Principal coverage is entered in bold; illustrations are entered in italics.

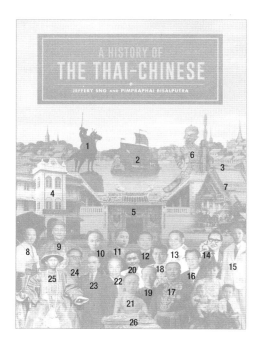

FRONT COVER

1 A statue of King Taksin on the Thonburi side of Bangkok **2** Chinese junk on the Chao Phraya River **3** Chao Phraya riverfront with Grand Palace in background **4** The original building of the Chinese Chamber of Commerce (CCC) on Sathorn Road, Bangkok **5** Wanglee Mansion in Bangkok's Thonburi **6** Chinese stone statue at Wat Pho (Bangkok) acts as guardian of the temple **7** Wat Kalayanamitra on the Thonburi side of Bangkok was built in honor of Rama III by Chaophraya Nikornbodin (Ng Taotoh) **8** U Chuliang, one of the prominent leaders of the Chinese community in Thailand **9** Phra Anuwat-Rajniyom (Tae Teeyong) or "Second Brother Hong" (Yi Goh Hong), one of the founders of the Peiying Chinese School **10** Phra Phisarn-Supaphol (Koh Guehong), the co-author's grandfather in traditional Chinese hairstyle **11** Tan Siewmeng, China's first commissioner of commerce in Bangkok **12** Charoen Sirivadhanabhakdi, chairman of Thai Beverage PLC (ThaiBev) **13** Banharn Silpa-archa, former head of Chat Thai Party and the 21st prime minister of Thailand **14** Chin Sophonpanich, the founder of Bangkok Bank **15** Tiam Chokwattana, the founder of Saha Group with his wife Saipin and two of his children **16** Chuan Leekpai, former head of the Democrat Party and the 20th prime minister of Thailand **17** Kaw Simbee, the most famous son of Kaw Sujiang, the founder of the Na Ranong family **18** Pridi Banomyong, one of the key members of the People's Party and the 7th prime minister of Thailand **19** Seow Hoodseng Sriboonruang, the co-founder of the *Meinan Ribao* and the founder of the *Chino-Siam Warasup* **20** Chung Yoonghoi, second generation Hakka in Thailand, later named himself Pasit Chungsiriwat **21** Koh Gueyin with his Manchu-style queue **22** Udane Techapaiboon (Tae Ngoulao), managing director of Bangkok Metropolitan Bank and main shareholder of Sura Maharas, whiskey company **23** Tan Libuay (Wanglee), one of the founders of the CCC **24** Dr Puey Ungpakorn, former dean and rector of Thammasat University **25** Phra Phisan-Pholpanich, the owner of Koh Hong Lee rice mills in Mandarin garb **26** Ayudhya Bencharong, Chinese export wares made to order for Siam